The Vicars Choral of York Minster:
The College at Bedern

By Julian D. Richards

Published for the York Archaeological Trust by the
Council for British Archaeology

2001

Contents

List of Figures

Figures 187–363 are included in the text and Figs.364–91 are presented on twelve unbound sheets in the folder. The figures on unbound sheets are distinguished in the text by s in bold type.

List of Tables

Volume 10 Fascicule 5

The Vicars Choral of York Minster: The College at Bedern

By Julian D. Richards

With contributions by R.M. Butler, A.R. Hall, J. Hamshaw-Thomas, J. Hillam, S. Jennings, H.K. Kenward, D. O'Connor, T.P. O'Connor, S. Rees Jones, A. Robertson, D.A. Stocker, J. Stopford, R. Tyson and L. Wong

Key words: architecture, building techniques, college, medieval, Minster, vicars choral, York

Introduction

The College of the Vicars Choral in York was a religious house of priest-vicars, who deputised for the canons at daily services in York Minster. They are best known from their extensive historical records, although the still-standing communal hall, chapel and later gatehouse indicate the position of a once extensive complex of college buildings in an area known as Bedern, bounded on three sides by present day Goodramgate, Aldwark and St Andrewgate. The college was located about 100m south-east of York Minster, being reached by way of Vicars' Lane, re-named College Street from about 1800 after the 15th century St William's College on its north-east side (RCHMY **5**, 117). The boundaries of the college precinct were still preserved on the 1852 Ordnance Survey map as they continued to define the extra-parochial area of Bedern which was part of the Liberty of St Peter (Fig.193, p.396). The name Bedern also came to be used to refer specifically to a cul-de-sac running into the college precinct, which originally formed the main courtyard of the college (see p.397, henceforth Bedern Close). The cul-de-sac was originally reached only from Goodramgate but in 1852 it was extended to form a street linking Goodramgate and St Andrewgate; its approximate position has been preserved in the urban housing development of the 1980s. It was

called Great Bedern (*Bederna Magna*) in around 1390 to distinguish it from Little Bedern which was on the northern side of Great Bedern, on the approximate site of 15–19 Goodramgate (see p.390). Back Bedern, also variously known as Bedern Back Yard, Bartle Garth or Bartle Yard, which originated as a second courtyard within the college precinct, was situated south-west of the hall from at least the 15th century. Further to the south-west a lane running east from Goodramgate towards St Andrewgate, on an alignment which would have taken it across the Bedern Foundry site, was formerly known as Baker's Lane (RCHMY **5**, 135).

The name Bedern is first recorded in, or shortly after, 1265 (*Charters*, 5–7, 106; see p.388). It is thought to have been derived from the Old English *gebed*, prayer, and *-aern*, house (Palliser 1978, 5); Harrison (1952, 29) believed that Bedern was the site of the residence of the early Norman chapter or even of a major Saxon ecclesiastical establishment. However, this has not been confirmed archaeologically, and it is more likely that Bedern was a new 13th century name for the college. Palliser (1978, 5) has argued that the use of the OE *gebed-aern* may have survived into the 13th century as the ME *bede-aern* to refer to a

Fig.187   *Bedern: general view of the excavation of Area 13.X around Bedern Hall, with York Minster in the background*

prayer-house (or religious college) as distinct from an almshouse. There was also a Bedern at Beverley, first recorded in 1280, and another at Ripon, first recorded in 1369; both were associated with colleges of vicars choral (ibid.).

An opportunity for excavation arose in 1971 when York City Council purchased a large block of land in this area, within which the college was located. The land had previously been owned by William Wright and Sons Ltd, whose buildings occupied the site. North-east of Bedern Close the area was partly occupied by a row of Victorian buildings used from 1953 for industrial purposes. A modern pre-fabricated building occupied the remaining area north-east of the close, replacing Victorian buildings demolished in the 1960s. To the south-west of Bedern Close

Wright's occupied the buildings of the Bedern National School, along with other more modern industrial buildings. These were all gradually demolished by the City Council with the exception of Bedern Hall and Chapel. Following the recommendations of the Esher Report (Esher and Pollen 1971) it was planned to convert the area into residential housing and the entire area was finally purchased for development by Simons of York in 1980.

With the permission of the City Council, York Archaeological Trust undertook excavations on a number of parts of the cleared site between 1973 and 1980 (Fig.193, p.396). Taken together, these constitute the largest area of medieval York ever to be investigated archaeologically. The results of the excavations are being published in several fascicules of *The Ar-*

chaeology of York. Work first commenced on the site of medieval industrial workshops, known as Bedern Foundry, on an area outside and to the south-west of the college (Fig.193, **12**). Work also started on a long trench (Fig.193, **11**) running almost the full width of the area, undertaken specifically to establish the depth and character of the archaeology, and to expose Roman deposits across the line of the legionary fortress defences. Smaller deep excavations exposing pre-medieval deposits also took place in 1976 in the bases of redundant cellars (Fig.193, **3, 7–8**). Further areas outside the college were excavated from 1975 onwards, namely an area adjacent to 1–5 Aldwark (Fig.193, **1**) and later, in 1979, at 2 Aldwark (Fig.193, **2**).

It was not until September 1976 that it was possible to investigate the succession of occupation within the college precinct itself. Work initially focused on an area south-west of Bedern Close, where trenches were opened on three sides of Bedern Hall (Bedern south-west) (Fig.187). From 1978 excavations were also conducted to the north-east of the close (Bedern north-east). Full-time excavation continued there until 1980, by which time almost 60% of the probable area of the college had been investigated. In 1978 it had been possible to make a basic record of the newly revealed south-east wall of Bedern Hall, but it was not possible to make any systematic record of the remainder of the building's fabric during its reconstruction between 1980 and 1984. The account below (pp.583–98) is derived from from photographs and notes made as circumstances permitted. In 1980, however, it was possible to excavate within the derelict chapel and to undertake a basic fabric survey.

In most trenches medieval deposits were encountered within the first half-metre, at a height of c.14·5–15·0m OD. The original development plans for Bedern indicated that new building foundations would not penetrate to a depth greater than 1·5m. Excavations within the area of the college were there-

fore restricted to this depth; it was hoped that earlier deposits beneath this level would be untouched in the forthcoming development, and they were left unexcavated. By a happy coincidence this 1·5m contained all the college archaeological deposits, beginning in the 13th century. It later transpired, however, that the highly destructive foundation technique adopted, comprising 'vibro-compaction', probably ruined much of the still-buried archaeology (Stockwell 1984).

The purpose of the present volume is to report on all the evidence for the College of the Vicars Choral, both medieval and post-medieval, comprising Bedern south-west (SE 60535209) and Bedern north-east (SE 60555212), as well as the college hall (SE 60525211) and chapel (SE 60505214), and evidence for medieval and post-medieval levels from the Bedern long trench (SE 60545207). The excavations of medieval tenements at 1–5 and 2 Aldwark have already been published in *AY* 10/2 and Bedern Foundry has been published in *AY* 10/3. Evidence from the part of the foundry site that may have been within the college precinct is recapitulated where it has a bearing on the interpretation of the college. Roman occupation in the Bedern area has been discussed in *AY* 3/3. Post-medieval occupation of the foundry site will be published in *AY* 13. The coins have been published in *AY* 18/1; other small finds will be published in *AY* 17/15, and the pottery will be published in *AY* 16/9. The considerable number of re-used architectural fragments recovered from the excavations have been published separately in *AY* 10/4. Historical research on the tenemental history of the Bedern and Aldwark area will be published in *AY* 20. All the finds and records for the sites discussed in this fascicule are deposited in the Yorkshire Museum under the site and accession numbers 1976–9.13.X (Bedern south-west), 1978–80.14.II/IV (Bedern north-east), 1973–6.13.I/II (Bedern Foundry), 1973–5.13.III/IV (Bedern south-west, long trench), 1980.20.I/II (Bedern Chapel) and 1980.13.XV (Bedern Hall).

A Short History of the College of the Vicars Choral

by S. Rees Jones

As part of post-excavation analysis of Bedern work has been undertaken on the documentary evidence for the site, concentrating on those aspects relevant for the interpretation of the archaeological evidence in the medieval period.

The archive

The surviving archive of the vicars choral is extensive and provides much scope for further research. Over 200 account rolls survive for the medieval period after 1300 alone, detailing the income and expenditure entailed in, firstly, running the college's estates, tileworks, brewery and appropriated churches, secondly, in its building and repair work and, thirdly, in the administration of the three major offices of the college. There is also a large collection of original deeds, a cartulary and copies of the vicars' statutes, as well as royal grants and records of various disputes and agreements. Most of these series are continued into the post-medieval period. Canon Frederick Harrison's *Life in a Medieval College* contains a summary of this archive, as he knew it between c.1925 and 1950, and is rich in anecdote (Harrison 1952). As a description of the records, however, it has now been superseded by the Minster Library's own catalogue, the production of which, mainly in the 1970s and 1980s, involved a significant degree of reorganisation, identification and renumbering of the different series of records (*York Minster Library, Vicars' Choral Archives, Catalogue*). In addition, Dr Nigel Tringham has published an edition of nearly 600 of the vicars' charters for the City of York and its suburbs to 1546, which also includes a useful summary of the medieval sections of the archive and its history up to 1936 (*Charters*, xx–xxiii).

Previous research

Since the rediscovery of a substantial part of its archives in 1925–6 (*Charters*, xxi), the college has been the subject of several studies. Canon Frederick Harrison's study of *Life in a Medieval College* was published in 1952 after some 30 years' work on the archives (see also Harrison 1927, 1936). Canon Harrison, himself a former vicar choral, described the book as 'a labour of love' (1952, xiv). The work focuses especially on the domestic life of the college and is filled with extensive though not always accurate quotations and summaries from the vicars' records, many of which he was the first to discover and bring to public attention (*Charters*, xixn, xxn, xliiin). The vicars still await, however, a more thorough history (Dobson 1977, 89, 163n). More recently the origins of the vicars choral and their early organisation have been discussed by Dr Nigel Tringham, who has also studied the charters revealing their acquisition of a large estate in York (Tringham 1978, 1993). The vicars' estate accounts have been used for a further study of their York estate, its management and fluctuating prosperity in the later medieval period (Rees Jones 1987, 117–27, 207–24, 238–70), and an edition of the surviving wills of vicars choral between 1520 and 1600 has been published (Cross 1984). Finally, mention must be made of Kathleen Edwards' study of the minor corporations which remains the first and only comparative scholarly study of vicars choral in England (Edwards 1967). All these studies provide a framework for the history of the college, but the identity, careers and daily life of the vicars themselves remain a relatively neglected, if well recorded, area for further research.

The following discussion does not attempt to fill the need for a new history of the vicars themselves but focuses upon the development of the college site, and its topography, in an effort to provide a brief historical context for the consideration of the excavated evidence from Bedern.

The origins of the Minster community

In order to understand more fully the nature of the collegiate institution in Bedern, however, it is necessary to trace its origins. The minster church at York was never a monastic (or regular) foundation, but was one of the nine English cathedrals served by secular clergy (Edwards 1967, 11). By the 11th century York was already served by canons, possibly seven in number, who by the 1060s were living some kind of common life (Brown 1984, 1). A famous passage opening the chronicle of Hugh the Chanter describes how when the first Norman archbishop, Thomas of Bayeux (1070–1100), first entered his archbishopric in 1072 he found only three canons remaining out of an original seven, and how, gradually, he increased their number and restored their common life (Hill and Brooke 1977, 25–6). After some years, but certainly by 1086, Thomas began establishing a secular chapter of a different style, more similar to that which he was accustomed to in Normandy, where he had previously been treasurer of Bayeux cathedral (ibid., 27; Brown 1980, 31–3). The new chapter was made up of a dean, treasurer, precentor, the *magister scholarum* (later to become the chancellor) and other canons (Brown 1984, 1). This community of canons no longer lived in common, but each canon was provided with a separate prebend (literally meaning provisions), and most were provided with separate residences near the Minster (Hill and Brooke 1977, 22; Rees Jones 1987, 97, 101–4, 108, 110–11). By the later 13th century a prebend usually took the form of land, the earliest such prebends being composed mainly of estates formerly belonging either to the chapter in common or to the archbishop (Brown 1980, 31–2). These estates provided an income from both spiritual and temporal properties (that is, from the profits of owning both parish churches and ordinary agricultural or residential land), and the prebends were mostly named after the more important groups of manors within those estates. In 1294 the final full complement of 36 canonries was reached with the creation of the prebend of Bilton in the Ainsty, now North Yorkshire (Hill and Brooke 1977, 29; Dobson 1977, 52–8).

The prebends of York Minster were exceptionally well endowed. This wealth made the position of canon very attractive to clerks serving in the royal and papal administrations, with the result that the majority of the canons were non-resident, and much of the chapter's wealth was diverted from the service of the Minster to form 'part of a vast spoils system operating in the interests of papal and governmental officials' (ibid., 57). The habit of absenteeism was widespread in all the cathedrals with secular chapters from a very early date, although the evidence is such that the practice is hard to quantify (Edwards 1967, 37–8; Hill and Brooke 1977, 23, 30–1). In 1222 the regulation of residence and non-residence among the canons at York was made considerably clearer, and from that time on there were no more than nine canons in residence at any one time, usu-

ally fewer, and even they were only formally required to spend half the year in York (Dobson 1977, 48–50, 60, 81). The absence of so many senior clergy meant that the onus of the daily running of the Minster and maintenance of worship there rested with the minor clergy of the cathedral church. Again this was true not just of York, but of the other secular cathedrals in England, all of which had an established hierarchy of minor clergy by the late medieval period (Edwards 1967, 251ff.; Orme 1981, 79). Of these, the largest and most senior group were usually the vicars choral, but there were also groups of chantry priests, clerks and choristers. By the early 15th century York Minster was staffed by three sacrists, over a dozen parsons or chantry priests as well as deacons, thurifers, vestry-clerks and choristers in addition to the 36 vicars choral (Dobson 1977, 86).

The vicars choral: their origins

It is impossible to know whether the vicars choral at York were ever founded in a formal sense, or whether their functions and position within the Minster community simply evolved as a response to the changing needs of worship and administration within the cathedral church and its community. In both St Paul's, London, and Exeter it was claimed, in the later 13th century, that the vicars there had been established at the same time as the canons soon after the Conquest, equalled them in number, and in Exeter at least were each assigned to one of the canons (Edwards 1967, 260; Orme 1981, 80). A similar date of origin may be suggested for the vicars at Salisbury (Edwards 1967, 263). Lack of evidence for the immediate post-Conquest period in York makes it impossible to verify these claims or to know whether a similar claim might have been made for the Minster.

The title vicar (*vicarius*) is first recorded in York in c.1138 x 43 as a description of a group of six men, three of whom are also individually described as priest (*presbiter*), who are listed after the precentor and canons as witnesses to a transaction of land (*York Minster Fasti* **1**, 53). Another charter of the early 1160s lists a group of sixteen vicars (*Early Yorkshire Charters* **2**, 92), and by the 1180s and 1190s groups of vicars, sometimes described as vicars of St Peter, are found in the witness lists of a number of charters (*York Minster Fasti* **2**, 106–8, 111, 114). From the end of this later period the vicars are often listed after their succentor, Alexander, a separate officer from the canons' succentor, and by the second decade of the 13th century the vicars were beginning to describe themselves as a community, to act corporately in the ownership of property and to use a common seal (*Charters*, xviii, 42–3, 46, 160).

There is very little direct evidence as to what the vicars did at this early date, or how they lived. It may be, as has so often been assumed and as the title 'vicar' suggests, that from the first they were appointed primarily as deputies for the canons in the singing of the daily offices in the Minster choir (Harrison 1952, 23). Orme has suggested that in Exeter vicars were not only the canons' deputies but were also their personal servants, each separately dependent on their canon for continued employment, and living and eating in the canons' households where they had menial domestic as well as spiritual duties (Orme 1981, 80–1). There is some evidence from York to support this view: among the sixteen vicars listed in 1160 x 65 two are separately identified as Robert the vicar of the dean (*vicarius decani*) and Richard the vicar of Gerald, possibly Gerald son of Serlo, a canon of York in the middle decades of the 12th century (*York Minster Fasti* **2**, 36; *Early Yorkshire Charters* **2**, 92), suggesting some form of personal dependency. It may then be the case that in this early period each York vicar lived with his canon in his prebendal residence, but as at Exeter and elsewhere this can only be inferred from later evidence. The statutes of the Dean and Chapter of 1290 addressed the issue of the status of the canons' households (*familiae*); they make no direct reference to vicars as members of those households, but do infer that the vicar of a deceased canon might have a special responsibility for administering his estate (*Statutes* 1900, 21). The statutes of 1291 made it clear that each canon should have a priest vicar to act for him in the Minster and that every prebendary, both resident and non-resident, should pay 40s a year for the maintenance of their vicar (ibid., 27). In 1317 statutes first recorded the right of the vicars to dine with the canons, although only in the morning when they had attended Matins, and also noted that when a canon died his vicar was to have his choir habit (ibid., 13). These dining rights were detailed further in a dispute between some of the resident canons and the vicars in 1344 and again in 1347: every day two vicars (and on double feasts four vicars) had the right to dine with the resident canons (Harrison 1952, 181, 189–90).

While the vicars undoubtedly did deputise for the canons, Edwards (1967, 264) has forcefully argued that the functions of the vicars and the intention behind their foundation can never have been restricted to this. Firstly, it is clear that by 1291 all the canons, both resident and non-resident, were to support vicars, and yet there were some residentiary canons' duties which could not be fulfilled by a vicar, and which in York might sometimes be fulfilled by a canon of the chapel of St Mary and the Holy Angels rather than by a vicar choral (Edwards 1967, 265). The small groups of vicars cited as witnesses to charters from c.1138 onwards (see p.381) also suggest that there were vicars within the Minster within a couple of generations of the establishment of the prebendal system and it is not impossible that the two bodies of senior and inferior clergy had even been established at the same time. By the mid 12th century the vicars were clearly recognised in these witness lists as a distinct group within the minster clergy and community, and by the end of the century there are signs of a degree of organisation which afforded some autonomy in the management of their affairs both temporal (in the acquisition of property) and spiritual under the leadership of their own succentor in the choir. Edwards emphasises the musical role of the vicars, referring to the regulations requiring them to be able to receive instruction and to be examined in reading and singing in 1252, and reiterated in 1291 as the requirement that a vicar should have a good voice (Edwards 1967, 265; *Statutes* 1900, 19, 22). The vicars may well have been seen as having an important role in cathedral worship quite distinct from any need to deputise for canons, whether resident or non-resident.

This was almost certainly true of one fundamental area of the vicars' work and that was the maintenance of the increasing number of prayers and masses for the dead founded at numerous altars within the Minster. Indeed so numerous were these services that by the 14th century they seem to dominate the life of the college as recorded in its various series of financial records; they almost certainly provided a more lucrative source of income for most vicars than the 40s they received each year from their canon. Their acquisition of a large estate, which financed their common life and underpinned their relative independence from the Dean and Chapter, was largely built up from the endowment of prayers and masses for the dead at altars within the Minster

(Rees Jones 1987, 117–27). Indeed the very earliest recorded *cantaria* in York Minster was endowed in 1201 for the support of an altar priest named Nicholas (*York Minster Fasti* **2**, 141, 143), who was probably also a vicar choral, for three contemporary charters name a vicar called Nicholas (ibid., 107; *Early Yorkshire Charters* **1**, 242n). Certainly, by 1276 and later this chantry's endowments were administered as part of the vicars' estates (YMA, L2/1 pt iv, fo.44; Rees Jones 1987, 118). The earliest recorded group of chantry and obit foundations date from the 1220s to the 1270s, and virtually all were made by senior clergy of the Minster and endowed with land in the city. Prominent among these were the various gifts of land bought by a small group of senior canons for the construction of the college itself, all of which were linked to the maintenance of prayers for the patrons' souls (see pp.385–91). Viewed from this perspective the foundation of Bedern was a pious enterprise, in effect the establishment of a chantry college for the Minster canons. This aspect of the vicars' work was, again, enforced by their earliest statutes. Legacies to the vicars were to be used for the purchase of rents and vicars were only to be paid for those obits which they attended (*Statutes* 1900, 19). The link between vicars choral and the support of prayers for the dead was found elsewhere (Edwards 1967, 266). At Lichfield cathedral the vicars choral were given the estate of the *martilogium* in the early 13th century (*Catalogue of the Muniments*, 159, 165–7, 171, 186).

In conclusion, it would seem that, although some of the vicars' early liturgical and spiritual responsibilities overlapped with those of the canons, from an early date, and certainly by 1200, some responsibilities were quite distinct and not determined solely by the habit of non-residence among the senior clergy. Similarly, although the canons bore some responsibility for the vicars' maintenance, by 1200 this was already being supplemented by other sources of income which suggests that the independent functions of the vicars would soon supersede any lingering sense of dependence on the canons.

In the 13th century the archbishop and chapter took a number of measures to address the financial and practical problems presented by the habit of non-residence among the senior clergy (Dobson 1977, 46–62). It is in the context of these reforms that the early evolution of the College of Vicars Choral should be viewed. On one hand its members served the spir-

itual needs of the cathedral church and of the souls of its departed canons. On the other, the endowment of the college also allowed the Minster community to re-acquire full possession of significant areas of its ancient estates in York, the full economic benefit of which had been lost, both because of the habit of non-residence among most of the prebendaries, and because many properties had been granted in perpetuity at rents which no longer reflected the real value of the property (Rees Jones 1987, 117–27, 132–3). Buying out such tenants was often an expensive and time-consuming business, but it was not a coincidence that most of the vicars' new estates, including the site of the college itself, were to a large extent bought from land within the ancient estates of either the archbishops or the Dean and Chapter (ibid.; p.389). God and Mammon could be served at the same time.

The college: prosperity and decline

The acquisition of the first college site and its early buildings are described in some detail below. The foundation of the college was clearly the work of senior clergy, such as the treasurer John Romeyn, who were closely associated with the work of the reforming archbishop, Walter de Gray. The physical foundation of the college was followed by the confirmation of the earliest surviving statutes for the vicars in 1252. These laid down the services which vicars were to attend in the Minster, including services for the dead. They confirmed that the vicars were to elect a warden (*custos*) to take overall care of their needs and also that the college had a chamberlain to look after financial affairs and to keep records of the attendance of individual vicars at services (*Statutes* 1900, 18–19). In time the number of offices within the college grew. The chamberlain was aided by a *custos domorum* by the 14th century, and by the 1360s it was the college bursar who had prime responsibility for keeping a record of vicars' attendance and paying their stipends accordingly. Other officials such as the maltster and the kitchener looked after particular aspects of the college's domestic life.

The college estates grew in size as the vicars continued to attract endowments, especially from the canons but occasionally from their own members or from laity (*Charters*, xxxii–xxxv). The peak of their prosperity was reached in the 1380s and 1390s. By 1399 they had an income of about £160 per annum from some 240 tenants in York plus income from three parish churches, from some independent chantries in the Minster and from various miscellaneous activities such as the sale of ale and building materials (Rees Jones 1987, 207–12). The college also owned two mills and two tile works outside the city walls, in Layerthorpe near the Foss and outside North Street Postern. These establishments made roofing tile and bricks for use on the college's own buildings and for sale; over 144,000 tiles were produced in 1427 (YMA, VC 6/7).

The college was already running into financial difficulties, however, because the costs of maintaining the obits and chantries to which they were committed were increasing faster than their ability to pay for them, a position which became far more serious as the value of rents began to decline after 1400 (Rees Jones 1987, 212–17, 220–2). By the winter of 1389–90 some services for the dead, including some ancient endowments made in perpetuity, were no longer being observed and the money saved was used initially to pay the vicars' basic stipends (YMA, VC 6/2/33 et seq.). Later the savings were simply absorbed into the chamberlains' nominal income, accounting for over one-quarter of it by the mid 15th century (YMA, VC 6/2/59). Such radical cuts did not compensate for the even more dramatic decline in their rental income (by 1500 they took less than £80 per annum from their York estates) and the equally disabling problem of a relative lack of new endowments in the 15th century (Rees Jones 1987, 222–7, 253–5; Charters, xxxvi). While the college's financial problems in the 15th century were, in part, a reflection of an ailing urban economy, they may also have reflected a shift in the fashion of religious endowments as their 'natural' patrons, the canons, were increasingly likely to endow chantries elsewhere, especially with independent parsons in the Minster, for whom a new college (St William's) was built and endowed in 1461. In 1425 one treasurer of the Minster, Thomas Haxey, even went so far as to make the mayor and commonality of the city trustees of his chantry in the Minster, bequeathing to them 600 marks plus an estate of city property worth over £10 per annum (YCA, C 82.4).

Such financial worries were not the only concern of the vicars and of the chapter. There was also a fairly constant preoccupation with the vicars' morals and a concern to reform the quality of their collegiate life.

In the final decade of the 14th century this resulted in an expensive programme of reform both to address the economic problems of the vicars and to upgrade the quality of their spiritual life. Documentary evidence suggests that the vicars were acquiring new land to accommodate an expansion of the college site at that time (p.391), as well as petitioning successfully for the church of St Sampson in York, which was given to them expressly for the support of their common life in dining together in hall (Cal. Pat. 1391–6, 712–25). The church remained in their hands until 1936. In 1396 the vicars bought a licence to enable them to build a bridge across Goodramgate, at first-floor level, to enable them to reach the Minster without hindrance (ibid., 712). Described as introitum sive perambulatorium, it was to be of sufficient height to enable vehicles to pass beneath. The reforms culminated in a new set of statutes for the college which again placed considerable emphasis on dining and the common life. The attempted reform of the vicars choral of York was not a purely local initiative. The 1380s and 1390s also saw attempts in Chichester, Exeter, Wells, Lichfield and Hereford either to instigate or revive the common life among their colleges of vicars, often through the provision of common halls or new residences (Orme 1981, 86–7; Cartulary of Chichester; Barrett 1980, 8; Tringham 1990, 62). The success of this reformation is, as yet, hard to judge, but it is important to point out that in York it coincided with the redesign of the college precinct during the final third of the 14th century, when a new common hall was provided (which survives today), along with a new kitchen revealed by excavation (pp.475–6). Probably most vicars continued to eat informally in their residences in addition to taking formal meals 'in hall'. In the end the practice of the common life, at least as symbolised in the provision of a daily dinner, proved remarkably resilient to both financial and political crisis and was not abandoned until 1574.

The end of the medieval period

Increasing financial difficulties meant that by 1449 it was no longer possible to maintain Bedern at its full strength of 36 vicars (YMA VC6/4/23 et seq.). Indeed by 1484 when the Dean and Chapter enlisted Richard III's support in a vain attempt to secure Cottingham church for the vicars, their numbers had fallen to fewer than 30 'because of the growing poverty of their rents and possessions' (BIHR, Reg. Rotherham, i. fo.100; quoted in Dobson 1977, 93).

By the 16th century the college was in decline. By 1502–3 the number of vicars had fallen to 28, and by 1534–5 to 21 (*Charters*, xviii). When the chantry commissioners came to York in 1546 there were only twenty vicars. The commissioners reported of Bedern that:

the fundacion of the same is observyed and kept in all poyntes, savyng ther lacketh xvi persons of the said nomber of xxxvi, whereof the said college is incorporate, th'occassion whereof is by reason of the decaye of landes and revenues of the cytie of York, beying sore in ruyne and decaye (Cert. Chantries 1546, 26).

In the *Valor Ecclesiasticus* of 1535 the net income of the vicars was assessed as £255 per annum (compared with Lincoln £358, Salisbury £272 and Wells £100). By 1547, as well as 169 houses within the city, the college still possessed farms and rents at Scarborough, North Grimston, Bubwith, Warthill, Huntington, Skirpenbeck, Skelton, Acaster Malbis and Selby. In 1548 Edward VI sold the college buildings and close to Thomas Golding and Walter Cely for £1,924 10s 1d (Whellan 1857, 485), but this sale was annulled and the vicars choral continued to exist, following rules made by Archbishop Holgate in 1552.

Nevertheless, the changing religious climate, in addition to financial inadequacies, made it impossible for the college to regain its former status. By 1558 there were only ten vicars (Cross 1977, 200). By this date the practice of employing lay singers to supplement the declining number of vicars in the Minster choir was well established. In 1552 Archbishop Holgate ordered that the singing-men who made up the number of men's voices to twenty should each be paid £8 per annum (Aston 1977, 398). The number of vicars stabilised at around nine or ten from 1575–86 (Harrison 1952, 246). However, the granting of permission to the clergy to marry by the convocations of York and Canterbury in 1549 really meant the end of corporate life of vicars choral everywhere. The vicars' cubicles were by no means large enough for a wife and family; the vicars took houses elsewhere in York. On 27 June 1574 the tradition of communal dining came to an end, when the vicars decided no longer to take dinner, the one remaining common meal, together (ibid., 245). As a result, the kitchen equipment was sold in 1581, mostly to the vicars themselves, and the table linen was divided amongst the vicars in 1592, although the hall was still used for feasts and meetings until 1628. The later history of Bedern appears on pp.627–41.

The vicars' acquisition of the Bedern site

The vicars' own account of the history of their college records that the site was given to them by William de Laneham (or *Lanum*), a canon of York Minster, and later historians have traditionally placed the date in the 1240s (Harrison 1952, 29, *Charters*, xix, both citing Dugdale 1846 edition, vi (3) 1193). William de Laneham was a canon of York and archdeacon of Durham between 1224 and his death, which Dr Nigel Tringham has dated to 17 April 1245 x 1249 (*York Minster Fasti* 2, 9; *Charters*, 97–8). The earliest record of his donation occurs in March 1276 as part of a survey conducted by inquest into the extent of the liberty of St Peter in York. It reads as follows:

Dicunt quod Bederna est de terra Beati Petri, et data fuit Deo et Beato Petro et vicariis Deo servientibus, in puram et perpetuam elemosinam, per Willelmum de Lanum, quondam canonicum eiusdem; et maior pars est de communa terra Ulf, et quedam pars est de feudo archiepiscopi et elemosinata per eundem.

They [the jurors at the inquest] *say that Bedern is of the land of the blessed Peter and was given to God and to the blessed Peter and to the vicars serving God, in pure and perpetual alms, by William de Laneham, formerly a canon there* [lit: of the same]; *and the greater part is of the common land of Ulf, and another part is of the fee of the archbishop and was given in alms by him.* (Fig.188, plots 5–11; for discussion see below.)

The survey continues with a description of two adjacent pieces of land owned by the vicars, as follows:

Item dicunt quod vicarii tenent totam terram inter Bedernam et domos Domine de Queneby de prebenda de Wetewang, et fuit illa terra de prebenda a tempore a quo non extat memoria.

Item, they say that the vicars hold all the land between the Bedern and the houses of the lady of Whenby from the prebend of Wetwang, and that land was of the prebend from a time beyond memory. (Fig.188, plot 9; for discussion see below.)

Item vicarii tenent totam terram inter Aldewerk et domos Magistri Willelmi de Pothow; et dantur eisdem vicariis, in puram et perpetuam elemosinam, per Dominum Walterum de Gray, Archiepiscopum, et est illa terra de feudo archiepiscopi de baronia.

Item, the vicars hold all the land between Aldwark and the houses of master William de Pothow, and it is [lit: they are] given to the vicars, in pure and perpetual alms, by dominus Walter de Gray, archbishop, and that land is of the fee of the archbishop of his barony (YMA, L2/1, pt iv, fo.44; YMA, L2/2a, fo.22). Fig.188, plots 1–3; for discussion see below.)

The survey immediately makes it clear that Bedern, although largely the gift of William de Laneham, was also partly given to the new college by the archbishop from land belonging to him. The vicars' acquisition of the site was clearly more complicated than the traditional story suggests and the charter evidence for the site bears this out. It will probably never prove possible to reconstruct the history of the foundation of Bedern in all its detail but it is clear that the site was not acquired all at once and that a number of donors, many of them canons of the Minster, were involved over perhaps as much as 50 years in helping the vicars piece together the site. There are several obstacles to reconstructing the vicars' acquisition of the site. Firstly, the records are not complete: the fact that Laneham's grant to the vicars is not recorded until between 27 and 52 years after it must have been made is only the most obvious of the missing pieces of evidence. Secondly, the records that do survive are mainly charters and while these do occasionally provide some clear descriptions of land they are usually rather vague in describing the location, size and appearance of property. Establishing the boundaries between properties must to a large extent depend upon educated guess work, often using those recorded on the 1852 Ordnance Survey map of York as a guide to their likely location in the medieval period. Finally, the 13th century customs of land ownership and conveyancing were quite different from those of today. Property granted to the vicars was not necessarily theirs to occupy straight away. Quite often all the vicars first acquired in a piece of land would be a right which, while making them the 'lords' of the land, entitled them to nothing more than a fixed rent from tenants who remained in full occupation of the property. Buying out these tenants could be a long and expensive process and in several cases

the vicars might well have to wait 30 years between first acquiring a title in a property and finally acquiring full use of the land so that they could occupy it and redevelop it in whichever way they chose.

Land belonging to the prebend of Wetwang: plots 6–11 (23–39 Goodramgate)

The oldest title deed in the vicars' surviving archives for Bedern records a transaction concerning the land on the site of 23–39 Goodramgate and extending backwards towards St Andrewgate (Fig.188, plots 6–11). In the late 11th century William Malpas, canon of York, granted to Hugh Puset his prebendal land in Goodramgate which Hugh's father had previously held, for an annual rent of 4s and 1lb of pepper (*Charters*, 70–1). Although not described in detail, its full extent is revealed in later grants made by Hugh Puset and others.

Hugh Puset subsequently divided this land into two parts. In 1194 x 1198 (ibid., 71–2) he retained for himself all the land next to the street (Fig.188, plots 6 and 8) except for a gateway 11ft wide (Fig.188, plot 7). He also retained an area described as *apud curiam* (perhaps, within the court) of 88ft in depth (Fig.188, plot 9). The land which Hugh Puset may be presumed to have reserved for himself is marked on Fig.188. Its later history, described below, suggests that this was never fully incorporated into the college site and so its location has been partly inferred from the course of the parish boundaries. There is a plot of land (Fig.188, plot 9) to the rear of 31–9 Goodramgate which lies outside the extra-parochial area of Bedern within the parish of St John-del-Pyke, and which occupies a site approximately 88ft in depth behind the houses fronting onto the street. The remainder of the site Puset sold to Ralph de Bolebec, including a toft in St Andrewgate (Fig.188, possibly plot 11 or part of it). Bolebec was to pay Puset the rent of 1lb pepper owed to the prebend plus 18d per annum for the land in St Andrewgate.

Bolebec, in turn, further divided his share of the holding into two parts (Fig.188, plots 10–11). In 1199 x 1217 (*Charters*, 73) Ralph Bolebec sold his share of the land in Goodramgate (Fig.188, plot 10) to William de Romeyn, nephew of John Romeyn canon of York, and William was to take over the responsibility for the payment of 1lb pepper to Puset for the prebend

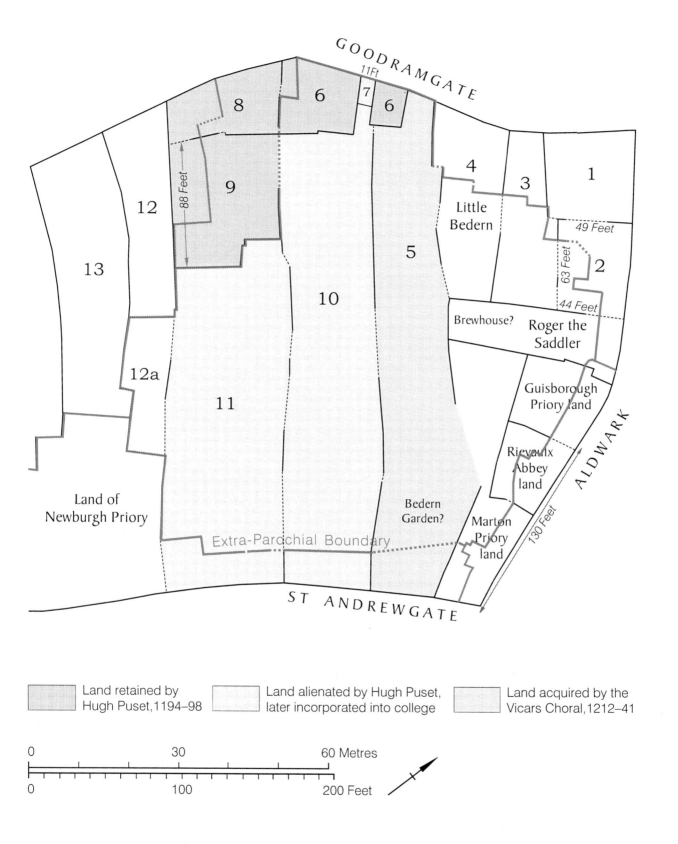

GOODRAMGATE

11Ft

8

6

7

6

4

3

1

Little
Bedern

49 Feet

9

12

5

63 Feet

2

88 Feet

13

10

44 Feet

Brewhouse?

Roger the
Saddler

12a

Guisborough
Priory land

11

Rievaulx
Abbey
land

ALDWARK

Land of
Newburgh Priory

Bedern
Garden?

130 Feet

Marton
Priory
land

Extra-Parochial Boundary

ST ANDREWGATE

Land retained by
Hugh Puset, 1194–98

Land alienated by Hugh Puset,
later incorporated into college

Land acquired by the
Vicars Choral, 1212–41

0   30   60 Metres

0   100   200 Feet

Fig.188 *Land acquired by the Vicars Choral in and next to Bedern in Goodramgate. The outline of parish boundaries (in green)*
defining the precinct of the College of the Vicars Choral is based on the 1852 Ordnance Survey map. Solid lines in black represent
property boundaries recorded on the 1852 map; dashed lines are conjectural. Scale 1:750

which is clearly identified for the first time in this charter as the prebend of Wetwang. This is almost certainly the same property which John Romeyn granted to the vicars in 1228 x 1241 (*Charters*, 82) and which he then described as a house with an orchard in Goodramgate which had belonged to his nephew Peter, and which owed 2s per annum to the prebend of Wetwang. This evidence therefore suggests that the major part of the original site of the vicars' college (made up of less than half the land which Hugh Puset had once held from the prebend of Wetwang) was given to the vicars by John Romeyn, while he was sub-dean of York between 1228 and 1241. That he was a principal patron of the new college is underlined by a further reference in a later deed of c.1273 when the whole site (Fig.188, plots 6–11) was confirmed to the vicars as the land which they had from John Romeyn (ibid., 73–4).

William de Laneham was, however, clearly involved too. In 1212 x 1224 Ralph Bolebec sold the rest of his land here (Fig.188, plot 11) to Laneham, describing it as a toft of land between the house of the prior of Newburgh and the house of William de Laneham, for a rent of 8d per annum (ibid., 251–2). A much later marginal note next to the cartulary copy of this deed notes that it was part of Bedern (*pars Bederne*). Another quitclaim, possibly dated before 1224, also refers to Laneham acquiring land in St Andrewgate on either the same or possibly an adjacent site (ibid., 253). No record survives of the transfer of land in St Andrewgate to the vicars, but they presumably acquired it at about the same time as they acquired plot 10. Together with land in plot 5, described below, these transactions are the strongest indications of Laneham's involvement in the purchase of a site for the new college preserved in the surviving charter evidence. It is possible therefore that the vicars had land on which to start building up to twenty years earlier than the traditional histories suggest, and that the site which was first available to them lay well behind the Goodramgate frontage but extended right back to St Andrewgate.

Within a generation of the foundation of the college, however, the vicars managed to acquire the rest of the land belonging to the prebend of Wetwang (Fig.188, plots 6–9). Between 1256 and 1281 the vicars gradually acquired possession of the plot marked 9 on Fig.188 (ibid., 101–3). Much of the negotiating was undertaken by the agents of John Maunsel, the

treasurer of York Minster, and the property was finally given to the vicars by his executors shortly after his death in 1265 (*Charters*, 102). Even then the vicars had to defend their title in a court case which was not resolved until 1281 (ibid., 103). In 1256 x 1263 the property was described as a messuage with garden and houses built on it, and in c.1265 as a house with garden and orchard. Its position was described in 1256 x 1263 as lying between the houses which the vicars had from John Romeyn (plot 10) and the messuage of William Hagent knight (plot 12), and it owed 4s per annum plus 1lb pepper to the prebend of Wetwang (ibid., 101–2). For a while after John Maunsel acquired it, the secular tenants were allowed to continue in occupation, and indeed it seems that this property may never have been incorporated into the college but continued to be rented out to tenants. In 1274 x 1277 the vicars assigned a rent from this property towards the celebration of an obit for a member of their college (ibid., 102, 106). The site was then described as lying between the land of the lady of Whenby (plot 12) and that which Thomas de Tollerton once held (possibly plot 8), and this description matches that of the land next to Bedern described as belonging to the vicars in the survey of 1276 (YMA, L2/1, pt iv, fo.44; see above).

The process by which the vicars acquired the area along the street frontage (Fig.188, plots 6 and 8) is less clear. Nevertheless a sale to the vicars, some time after 1265, of land with buildings described as lying between the vicars' Bedern and the land which was once of John Maunsel (plot 9) in length and in breadth in Goodramgate seems to describe this site (*Charters*, 106), and the only copy of this deed in the cartulary was copied onto the same folio as Bolebec's sale of plot 10 to William Romeyn (YMA, VC 3/1/1, fo.15r–v).

Finally, in c.1273, the vicars' title to the whole site which had been pieced together from the land of the prebend of Wetwang was confirmed to them by the current holder of the prebend, Thomas de Ludham (*Charters*, 73–4). In his grant the site was described as land with buildings in Goodramgate which the vicars had from John Romeyn, to be held of the prebend for the annual rent of 4s and the celebration of his obit.

The history of the major part of the Bedern site is therefore complicated because the original holding of the prebend of Wetwang had been divided between several owners and had to be pieced back together again for the vicars over a period of time perhaps extending over 50 years. During this process it would seem that the legal details might become confused. It is not always clear, for example, precisely which portion of the land was burdened with the 4s rent and 1lb pepper owed each year to the prebend, and in different documents John Romeyn, William Laneham and John Maunsel are all named as principal donors. The impression is certainly that the foundation of the college was an expensive and legally complex business in which a number of the senior canons of the Minster participated. It is significant that the canons chose to repurchase for the college land which was already within St Peter's fee, as part of the endowments of one of their prebends. The survey of 1276 makes it clear that the greater part of the site had originally come to the Minster from the land of Ulf, or Ulf son of Thorald, an Anglo-Saxon thegn, who made a substantial donation of lands throughout Yorkshire and in the city to the common holding of the chapter between 1066 and 1086 (Rees Jones 1987, 110–11). Ulf's horn, the symbol of his patronage of the Minster, can still be seen in the Minster treasury (Hill and Brooke 1977, 39). This is the only indication in the documentary evidence of the pre-Conquest history of the site.

Land belonging to the archbishop: plot 5 (21 Goodramgate and land behind)

The survey of 1276 refers to part of Bedern as being part of the fee of the archbishop and given by him (see above). This probably relates to land immediately to the east of the prebend of Wetwang's land which is described in a deed of 1224 x 1245–49 (Charters, 75). In this charter William de Laneham, then archdeacon of Durham, bought from Henry de Wistow two pieces of land adjoining property which was already in his possession (presumably a reference to the rest of the Bedern site, plots 10–11). The first piece was described as one part of Wistow's land in Goodramgate which was 20ft wide at the street frontage and 20ft wide at the northern head of Roger the saddler's brewhouse (which can be identified as part of a property which fronted on to Aldwark, see below), and extended in length between those two points, next to Laneham's land on one side. The second piece was described as land lying in length from the northern head of the same brewhouse and extending towards the south, and in width between

Roger the saddler's land and Laneham's own property. This would seem to indicate a plot set well back from the street front (which is not mentioned) and possibly extending as far as St Andrewgate. The whole area has changed so much with the redevelopment of the site by the college that it is impossible to be certain where the boundaries of these plots might have been. It is possible that the narrow plot fronting on to Goodramgate was on or near the site of 21 Goodramgate. However, both plots were clearly part of the fee of the archbishop, to whom husgable (the burgage rent) was due. Again, as with Laneham's role in the acquisition of plot 11, there is no record of when plot 5 was given to the college, except that the survey of 1276 clearly indicates that it was an integral part of the Bedern site by that date and presumably was given to the vicars at the time of the building of the first college, together with plots 10 and 11.

A later quitclaim of a rent owed from land once belonging to Laneham in Goodramgate may refer to this property (Charters, 76).

Plots 1–3, and property in Aldwark (approximately 9–13 Goodramgate and 2–12 Aldwark)

As the vicars were being provided with a site for their college so they were also building up a large estate within the city, including several properties near to the college site. Among these were a group of three tenements on the corner of Aldwark and Goodramgate which were also part of the archbishop's fee and were described in 1276 as having been given to the vicars by Archbishop Walter de Gray (see above). In the early 1220s these tenements were in the hands of lay tenants, when they were given to the Dominican friars of York, possibly with the intention of providing them with their first residence in the city (Charters, 83–6; pp.55, 62, AY 10/2). In 1227 the friars were given a permanent site in Toft Green and they then granted the land back to Archbishop Walter de Gray (Charters, 86). Gray granted the property briefly to John de Bulmer in 1254, who in turn granted it to the vicars in 1272–3 (ibid., 87–8). The vicars' title to this and a number of other properties fronting onto Aldwark was finally confirmed by the executors of canon William de Walesby as part of an endowment for his obit in 1274 (ibid., 8). The property is simply described as land, although in the early 1220s the dimensions of plot 2 were given and these are shown on Fig.188 (ibid., 85). By 1309 John de Pontebellum, another canon of the Minster, had financed the building of a row of four cottages on this site, fronting on to Aldwark, which were rented out to tenants (YMA, VC 4/1/1; Fig.20, *AY* 10/2).

The adjacent property in Aldwark to the southeast was described as the land of Roger the saddler in the 1220s and 1240s (*Charters*, 85, 87), as the land once of Walter de Aula in 1272–3 (ibid., 88) and as the house of William de Cawood in 1274 (ibid., 8). The history of this site is summarised in *AY* 10/2 (pp.59–60). It contained three small tenements, one of which was held from Guisborough priory, occupied first by Roger the saddler and then by his son-in-law William Cawood, a farrier, and finally, after 1286, by William's nephew, John. The title to Roger the saddler's house was acquired by the vicars by the 1230s but it continued to be occupied by lay tenants and was partly redeveloped with a row of cottages for letting in the 1330s (Ludham Rents; Fig.20, *AY* 10/2), although there was still a house known as 'Cawoodhall' there in 1352. Nearer the corner with St Andrewgate the vicars acquired two tenements: one in c.1268 from Rievaulx abbey, which had earlier been described as backing onto Bedern (*Charters*, 5–7), and next to that, in 1272–3, a piece of land in the parish of St Helen-on-the-Walls which had once belonged to Marton priory and which extended in length from St Andrewgate to the land of Rievaulx abbey and in width from Aldwark to the garden of Bedern (ibid., 7, 253–4, 289–90). This land was later extended by purchase of a narrow strip of land from the city corporation in 1335, which gave the length of the two plots together as 130ft (ibid., 12). By that date these two plots seem to have been included within the Bedern garden, but they were soon redeveloped, as was the St Andrewgate frontage of the Bedern garden, with rows of small cottages, the rents from which supported the obits of various clergy in the Minster after whom the rows were usually named (pp.56–8, *AY* 10/2; Rees Jones 1987, 207–10; *Charters*, xxxii, 11–13, 254–5, 289–90).

Plot 4: Little Bedern (approximately 15–19 Goodramgate)

The property to the north of plot 5 in Goodramgate, plot 4, is variously described as the land of Thomas of the Vestry in the 1220s (*Charters*, 84, 86), the house of magister Henry de Wiketofft in the 1240s

(ibid., 87), the land of William Croft in 1272–3 (ibid., 88) and the land of magister William de Pothow in 1274 (ibid., 8). The sale of the land by the executors of William de Croft, former rector of Sutton on Derwent, to magister William de Pothow is recorded in 1276, together with a quitclaim following a dispute over his title in 1278 (ibid., 105–6). It was then described as houses and a toft. The vicars probably did not acquire this property until c.1338. In 1331 a tenement in Goodramgate, described as lying in breadth between the tenements of the vicars on either side and in length extending from the street to the tenement of Guisborough priory, was granted to John Gower, and an endorsement on the deed links this to a property called 'Hugate' in Goodramgate (ibid., 117). In 1340 the vicars undertook to maintain an obit for Nicholas de Hugate, late canon of York, in return for certain tenements which his executors had given them (YMA, VC 3/3/49). The tenements were in Goodramgate and described as lying 'next to the Bedern, on the Bedern's north side, that is between the vicars' land to the north [plots 1–3] and the Bedern to the south [plot 5]' (ibid.). The property called 'Hugate' (sometimes Hugaterent) first appears on the vicars' rent rolls in 1342 (YMA, VC 4/1/7) as a group of ten houses in Goodramgate, but by 1378 it was also known as 'Little Bedern' and had by then been extended to a group of thirteen houses, probably by taking in some adjacent property; the rent roll describes the group as *infra parva Bederna et extra, quondam Nich[ola]i de Hugat* (YMA, VC 6/2/28). Although Little Bedern has sometimes been identified with Baker's Yard to the south of Bedern (Palliser 1978, 5; p.151, *AY* 10/3), this location, to the north of the main Bedern, seems to be clearly indicated in the documentary evidence.

Plot 12: Baker's Yard (41–5 Goodramgate)

In deeds concerning plot 9 this property was described in 1256 x 63 as the messuage of William Hagent knight, and in 1274 x 1277 as the land of the lady of Whenby (*Queneby*) (see p.385). In c.1300 Robert Haget of Whenby (*Queneby*) granted to Hamo de Allewardethorp, chaplain, his houses in the parish of Holy Trinity in Goodramgate (*Charters*, 111). By 1329 the property belonged to John de Beverley, a mercer, and was then described as a tenement with buildings lying in length from Goodramgate to the land of Newburgh priory and in width between the vicars' land on one side and more land belonging to John de Beverley on the other (Fig.188, possibly plot 13) (ibid., 112). These descriptions enable this property to be fairly securely identified with the site of Baker's Yard at and behind 41–5 Goodramgate. The vicars did not acquire plot 12 until 1390 (confirmed by licence in 1392) (ibid., 114–15). Their intention seems to have been to secure some extra land next to the courtyard of their new common hall (see below). In 1391 the vicars allowed the Beverley family to continue in occupation of a part of the new property, but seem to have kept the rear portion for incorporation into the college site (ibid., 124). This arrangement is at least indicated by the parish boundaries which show a small plot of the extra-parochial liberty of Bedern (which was attached for administrative purposes to the Minster Yard and, until 1836, came under the special jurisdiction of the Dean and Chapter; Leak 1990) extending over the rear end of plot 12. The portion which was granted to Henry de Beverley for his life in 1391 was described as 'a shop with a chamber built over it which Robert Ward held of John de Beverley' towards Goodramgate, and a portion of garden lying in width between a post of the vicars' brewhouse and the land of John de Beverley (possibly plot 13), and in length from the corner of a certain stable to the said post, between the vicars' land (possibly plot 9) and John de Beverley's land (possibly plot 13) (*Charters*, 124). Henry was to hold the buildings for life, but to rent the portion of garden only for up to twelve years after his father's death. This indenture is kept in the vicars' archive together with a separate agreement, made in 1392, by which John de Beverley granted his son, Henry, all that messuage in which Henry then lived in Goodramgate for the rest of his (John's) life, although John retained for his own use *le Warehus* for his things and utensils, giving Henry some shops elsewhere in the city (ibid., 124–5). This indenture may refer to property on the site of plot 13 (which is shown as Powell's Yard by 1852) and may perhaps infer that this property too was later acquired by the vicars; this seems to be borne out by excavation on the site (p.203, *AY* 10/3).

Colleges of vicars choral in England

Other than at York, eight medieval English cathedrals were served by colleges of vicars choral, although several of the larger secular colleges also had similar institutions, including the Archbishop's collegiate churches at Beverley, Ripon and Southwell. Although

there has been excavation at several of these other sites, none has been investigated as fully as the York Bedern.

Although the York Bedern was built at a time when the foundation of resident communities of secular priests was becoming increasingly popular, it is of particular interest because it is one of the earliest recorded common residences of its kind to be built in England. Virtually all other evidence for the development of collegiate architecture dates from the 14th and 15th centuries. In addition to the vicars choral of York, those of Beverley, Lincoln, London, and possibly Lichfield, are thought to have acquired common residences before the end of the 13th century (Leach 1897, li; Edwards 1967, 276; Kettle and Johnson 1970, 148). Almost nothing is known of the domestic arrangements of these early colleges.

Among the remaining buildings, the earliest are those of the vicars at Lincoln, dating from the early 14th century, and of Wells, dating from 1348 and later (Figs.190–1; Maddison 1878, 8; Jones, Major and Varley 1987; Rodwell 1982). The college at Lichfield was established on its present site in 1315 and the surviving buildings date from the later and post-medieval periods (Tringham 1990, 62–3). The vicars' close at Chichester (Fig.189) was built between 1394 and the early 15th century (VCH 1935; Tatton-Brown 1994) whilst that at Exeter, now largely demolished, was constructed over a similar period (Chanter 1933). At Hereford the vicars' first hall (of the late 14th century) survives enclosed in a later house (RCHME 1931, 141), although they were moved to a new purpose-built college closer to the cathedral in 1473 (Edwards 1967, 277; Barrett 1980, 8). At Salisbury the layout of the buildings granted to the vicars in 1409 has now been reconstructed from surviving remains (Edwards 1967, 278; RCHME 1993, 88–96). The architecture of these colleges has many similarities with early collegiate architecture in the universities of Oxford and Cambridge where several 14th and 15th century ranges survive: the Mob Quadrangle at Merton College in Oxford, for example, which dates from the early 14th century (RCHME 1939, 81; RCHME 1959, lxxvi).

These colleges are usually arranged according to one of two basic plans. The first consisted of ranges of single chambers or small suites of rooms on both ground and upper floors shared each by between one and four occupants and accesssed from a common staircase. This plan type became the norm at the two universities and was also adopted by some of the earliest colleges of vicars choral, for example, Lincoln. The second type was adopted only by the colleges of vicars choral after the mid 14th century, and consisted of terraces of individual houses each containing an upper and lower chamber.

In addition to ranges of bed chambers and studies, each college was provided with a common hall, a kitchen block and other service rooms. The earliest colleges contained no chapel or library, but contained only the domestic buildings needed for accommodation, since the religious duties of the college members lay outside their closes in the cathedral or university churches (Willis and Clark 1886, 248).

The buildings in the Mob Quadrangle at Merton and the southern range of the vicars' court in Lincoln are the earliest standing collegiate buildings with which Bedern can be compared. Both were of the 'staircase-and-chamber' pattern which was to become typical of collegiate architecture at Oxford and Cam-

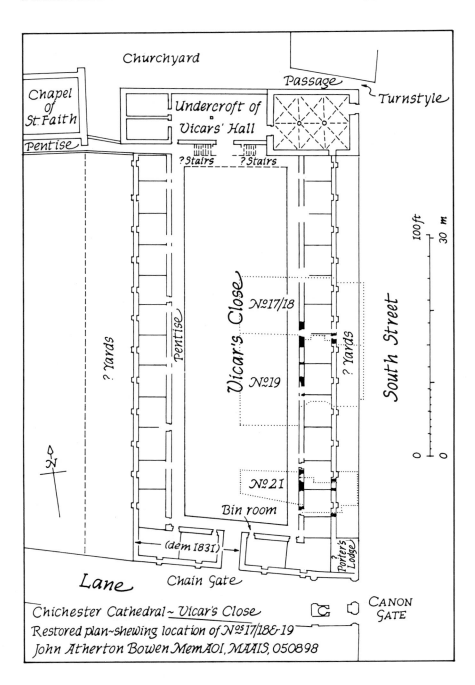

Fig.189 *Plan of Vicars' Close and Hall, Chichester (after Tatton-Brown 1990). Scale 1:500*

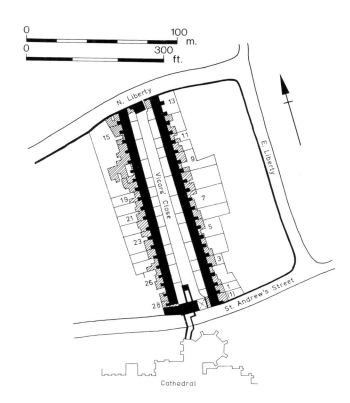

Fig.190 *Plan of Vicars' Close, Wells (after Rodwell 1982)*

bridge in the 14th century (Pantin 1959). The accommodation was arranged in two-storeyed ranges one room in depth, with two upper and two lower chambers serviced by each staircase. In both cases each chamber was probably shared by several college members, although at Lincoln there are almost enough chambers for each vicar to have a separate chamber, each with a private garderobe set in buttressing towers to the south. These chambers were quite large. At Merton they measured 22 × 17ft and at Lincoln 27–30 × 18ft. The layout typified at Lincoln was probably adopted by all those colleges of vicars choral which were built before the mid 14th century. Indeed, the college at Salisbury, given to the vicars in 1409, offered this type of accommodation, rather than separate houses, and the first college at

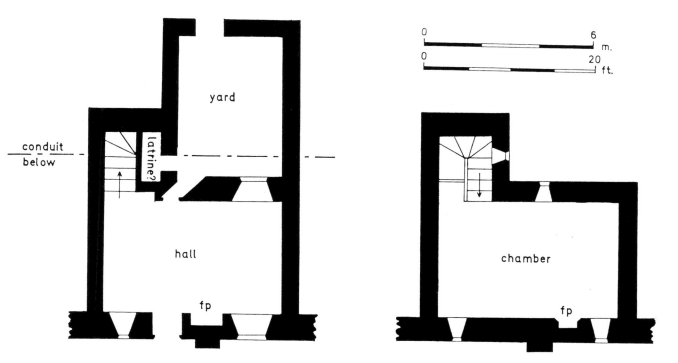

Fig.191 *Plan of the ground floor and first floor of vicars' houses, Wells (after Rodwell 1982)*

393

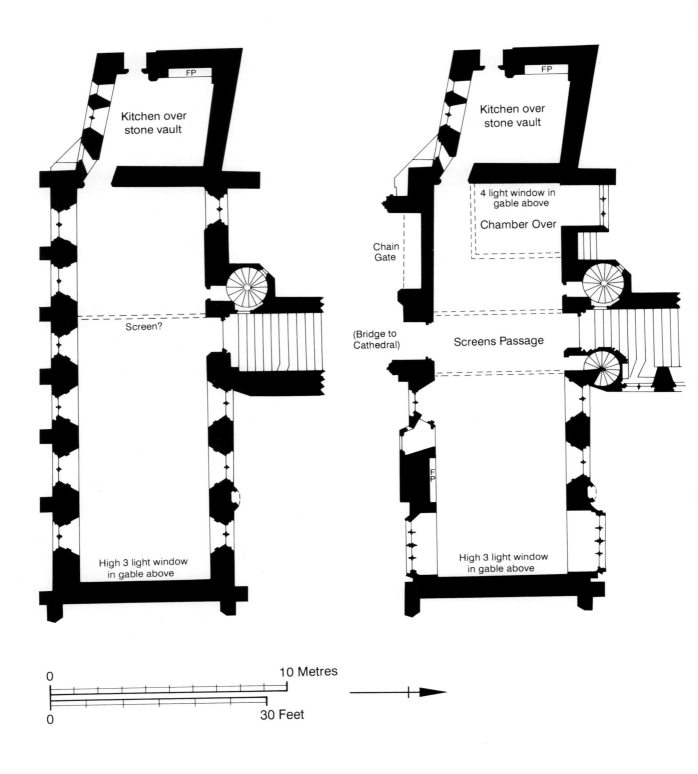

Labels in figure (a), left plan:

FP

Kitchen over
stone vault

Screen?

High 3 light window
in gable above

Labels in figure (b), right plan:

FP

Kitchen over
stone vault

4 light window in
gable above

Chamber Over

Chain
Gate

(Bridge to
Cathedral)

Screens Passage

FP

High 3 light window
in gable above

Scale bars:

0   10 Metres
0   30 Feet

Fig.192   Interpretative plans of the Vicars' Hall, Wells (based on plan of the ground floor in the Archaeological Journal *1930, 471, and a survey made by Warwick Rodwell in 1980; see also Rodwell 1982 and Colchester 1987): (a) Phase 1, mid 14th century; (b) Phase 3, 1440s–c.1510*

Hereford (in existence in the late 14th century) may have been similar.

Authorities on the history of college architecture have suggested that the model for this style of college development was not monastic but based on an adaptation of the elements of a typical contemporary secular hall-house (Willis and Clark 1886; Pantin 1959). Before the foundation of colleges many vicars would have lodged in such houses in the town (often those belonging to their masters, the canons) and such lodgings could have provided the model for the collegiate buildings which were intended to replace them. At Chichester the earliest part of the vicars' buildings to the north of the close, the vicars' hall, was reconstructed in 1394–7 (Fig.189). The new building was extended to provide a range of service rooms and chambers, which may have provided the vicars' accommodation before the remainder of the close to the south was built (Hannah 1914, 107; Tatton-Brown 1994).

While the influence of secular buildings on early college plans is clear, monastic influence should not be totally discounted. Improving standards of comfort and domestic privacy from the early 13th century led to modifications in the previously austere conditions of the medieval monastery. By the end of the 13th century the typical dorter, in which the monks slept, was divided by wainscott into individual cubicles down each side of a central corridor (Knowles 1948, 289). Such cubicles would have been smaller than the private chambers of the vicars of Lincoln, but would have afforded much the same level of privacy as a shared college room at Merton.

Given the comparatively early date of the foundation of the vicars' college in York, however, it is possible that the first dwellings were modelled not on those of the early colleges like Lincoln and Merton, but on those in the monastic tradition such as the dormitories at newly constructed friaries (which like Bedern often had to adapt the conventional plan to constricted sites). Rather than occupying discrete chambers, it is possible then that the York vicars were originally provided with accommodation in something like a dorter. Monastic dorters were typically between seven and fourteen bays long and by the 13th century were often subdivided into individual cubicles. The tradition in the York Bedern of describing the vicars' accommodation as 'cubicles', which persisted into the 16th century, further suggests that originally the design of the domestic buildings in Bedern may have owed more to the monastic than to the secular model.

However, both the documentary evidence and the archaeology suggest that by the mid 14th century the buildings in the vicars' close were evolving to provide greater privacy, with the original communal buildings being subdivided to form separate 'houses'. An indication of what these 14th century vicars' houses may have looked like is provided by the surviving contemporary vicars' close at Wells Cathedral (Fig.190; Rodwell 1982, 218). At Wells, each house was built to a common plan (Fig.191), comprising one substantial room (the hall) on the ground floor, measuring 20 × 13ft (6 × 4m), and a chamber of similar size above; both had fireplaces. At the rear of each house was a projecting staircase and an enclosed yard. In addition to the houses Wells retains the vicars' first-floor hall, supported on a vaulted undercroft and above the gateway, and also the two-storey chapel (Fig.192; Rodwell 1982, 221). The vicars' close at Wells was a new development of the later 14th century and this is reflected in the regularity of the college plan; it represents the ideal layout towards which the less tidy piecemeal buildings at York had been moving over the previous century.

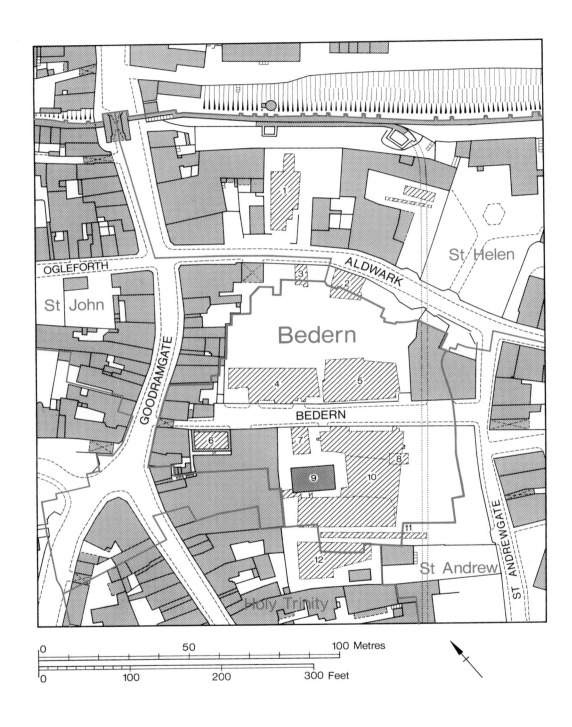

Fig.193 *Plan showing the location of excavations and building recording in the Bedern area. The outline of the parish boundaries (in green) defining the precinct of the College of the Vicars Choral is based on the 1852 Ordnance Survey map. (1) 1–5 Aldwark; (2) 2 Aldwark; (3) Cellar, 1976.14.I; (4) Bedern north-east, 1978–9.14.II; (5) Bedern north-east, 1979–80.14.IV; (6) Bedern Chapel, 1980.20.I/II; (7) Cellar, 1976.13.V; (8) Cellar 1976.13.VI; (9) Bedern Hall, 1980.13.XV; (10) Bedern south-west, 1976–9.13.X (11) Bedern Trench III/IV (long trench) 1973–5.13.III/IV; (12) Bedern Foundry. 1973–6.13.I/II. (Reproduced from the Ordnance Survey map with the permission of Her Majesty's Stationery Office, © Crown Copyright MC 100012225.) Scale 1:1250*

The Excavation and Building Recording

From the documentary records and from the position of college buildings which still survive, a plan of the probable layout of the college was produced. The excavation trenches were then positioned to expose what was hoped would be the main college buildings and associated land. Properties on the Aldwark and St Andrewgate street frontages were avoided as it was believed that these mostly lay outside the college precinct. Bedern was originally a cul-de-sac reached only from the college gatehouse on Goodramgate. The street lay within the college where it probably formed the main central courtyard, or college close, around which the buildings were arranged. However, with the opening up of Bedern to join St Andrewgate in 1852, it became a thoroughfare and remained in use as a public road during the excavation, effectively dividing the excavations in two.

Site code 13 was used to refer to trenches to the south-west of Bedern; site code 14 for trenches to the north-east. An open area excavation technique was used within each trench, with a series of section baulks running across the trenches (Fig.194). A large proportion of the post-medieval deposits was mechanically excavated down to the first identifiable medieval layers; thereafter all excavation was by hand. Contexts were allocated individual numbers, with each trench being allocated a block of numbers. Over 3,500 medieval and post-medieval contexts were recorded in total.

The Bedern long trench (Area 13.III/IV), c.35m × 2m, lay on a north-west/south-east line with its south-east end at a point c.20m to the north-west of St Andrewgate and c.35m south-west of the junction of St Andrewgate with the then course of Bedern (Fig.193, **11**). The trench was intended to establish the depth and state of preservation of Roman features, and to ascertain the feasibility of incorporating any of them in the Aldwark housing development. It was subdivided for recording purposes into two areas (13.III, north-west: contexts 1001–1253; 13.IV, south-east: contexts 1500–1740), excavated from 1973 to 1976. Some 3·6m of archaeological deposits were found, dating from the Roman to post-medieval periods.

The main Bedern south-west site (Area 13.X; Fig.193, **10**) comprised 1,400m² excavated on three sides of Bedern Hall from September 1976 to July 1979. The excavation was arbitrarily divided into three areas, with context numbers allocated in three blocks: 5000–5542, 6000–6374 and 7000–7638. As these areas were excavated at different times between 1976 and 1979, some difficulty with stratigraphic correlation has subsequently been encountered, although this report deals with the area as a whole.

Specific blocks of numbers were allocated to excavations into Roman deposits which followed the removal of modern cellars. A first cellar (1976.13.V: 3000–3098) was excavated on the south-west street frontage of Bedern, underneath school buildings erected in 1873 and demolished in 1975 (Fig.193, **7**). Excavations under the cellar floor in an area up to 8.8 × 5m took place in 1976. A second cellar (1976.13.VI: 3100–3119) was located c.10m south-west of Bedern (Fig.193, **8**). In both cases little post-Roman material was found as the cellars had been cut down into Roman levels.

Photographic records and notes were made of Bedern Hall (Fig.193, **9**) by RCHME in the 1960s and the south-east gable wall was recorded in outline in 1978 (Fig.234, p.474; Stocker and Wilson 1980a, 1980b). The remainder of the building, however, was not recorded, either during the excavations of 1973–80 or during the period between 1980 and 1984 when the building was partially reconstructed. David Stocker's report makes use of the 1978 YAT work and RCHME information, supplemented by notes he made during the reconstruction of the building between 1979 and 1981.

Information derived from the Bedern Foundry excavation relevant to the development of the College of the Vicars Choral is also included in this fascicule (and is discussed in full in *AY* 10/3). The Bedern Foundry site (Fig.193, **12**) was initially subdivided into two areas: Area I to the south-east and Area II to the north-west, but these were subsequently combined into one open area, c.215m², excavated from June 1973 to December 1976. A further 2,270 contexts were recorded for this site: 1–999,

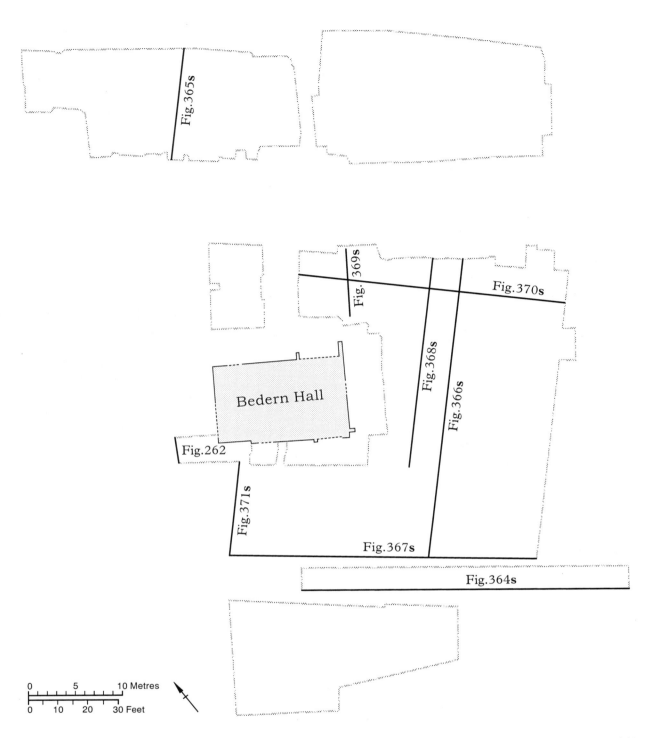

Fig.194 *Plan showing location of illustrated sections. Figure numbers ending with s denote a folded sheet in the separate folder*

2000–2999 and 4000–4270. As far as the medieval period is concerned, the north-eastern strip which fell within the college precinct is referred to in summary form below.

To the north-east of Bedern an area of c.825m² was excavated in the hope that the residential buildings of the college which fronted on to the close could be examined. The north-west part of this area had been occupied by a row of Victorian buildings, re-used by William Wright and Sons Ltd for industrial purposes from 1953, and demolished in 1975. A modern pre-fabricated building occupied the area to the south-east, replacing earlier Victorian buildings demolished in the 1960s. This building was removed in early 1979. The area available for excavation was divided into two trenches, Area 14.II to the north-west (Fig.193, 4), 25m × 12m, excavated from July 1978 to October 1979 (contexts 1000–1799), and Area 14.IV to the south-east (Fig.193, 5), 25m × 14m, excavated from March 1979 to April 1980 (contexts 4000–4493).

The interior of the standing Bedern Chapel (Fig.193, 6), c.12m × 6m, was excavated from April to June 1980 (contexts 9000–9099). Unfortunately, the stabilisation works carried out in 1925 had involved positioning three sunken tie-beams across the chapel. These were connected to upright steel joists which had the dual function of shoring the already outward-leaning north-east wall, and supporting the roof. The beams had disturbed all the levels of the chapel, effectively dividing it into four areas. In addition, a small trench, 1·70m (north-west/south-east) × 1·10m, was excavated in the gap between the chapel and the next building to the south-west. This trench ex-posed the chapel foundations, as well as providing a section through the external deposits (contexts 8000–8008). Prior to the excavation, stone which had been removed from the upper six or seven courses of all four walls in 1961 and stacked in the shell of the chapel was catalogued and removed, and representa-tive examples were stored by YAT. As part of that work a stone-by-stone record of the surviving eleva-tions (inside and out) was undertaken using a recti-fied photographic technique. The drawings generated by this survey (Figs.302–7, between pp.544–5) have since been found to contain some errors of interpreta-tion, but they provide valuable evidence, nonethe-less and are published here largely as drawn in 1980. No effort was made to identify phases within the fab-ric during work on site and, consequently, the changes in fabric proposed in this fascicule were not investigated and confirmed in the field. This has meant that the phasing of the fabric can only be ten-tative. In conjunction with this survey, records were made of both the in-situ architectural details and of the many fragments of architectural masonry which were found to have been re-used in the fabric of the chapel and which were visible in the wall faces and tops. These ex-situ architectural fragments are re-ported on separately (AY 10/4).

Post-Excavation Analysis

The Aldwark/Bedern project, conducted over seven years, represents the largest block of medieval and post-medieval York ever excavated. Given the scale of the excavations and the urban location, only relatively small areas of the site were open at any one time. This meant that the site could never be viewed as a whole during the excavation, and it is only subsequently that it has been possible to attempt to describe an overall picture. The methods of excavation and recording developed at a time when urban archaeology was itself evolving and Bedern has consequently been both pioneer and victim. The project was one of the first in York to employ a recording method based on a single series of context numbers, although this was initially applied in what by more recent standards appears an idiosyncratic fashion, with, for example, the cuts and fills of features not being separately numbered. The post-excavation project has retained the original context numbers and not introduced new ones. In addition, not all contexts were planned and it has proved impossible to identify the location of them all.

The continuing demands of rescue archaeology within the City of York have led to a considerable time lapse before the Bedern excavations could be brought to publication. In the intervening period most of those who originally worked on the excavations have moved on, although M. Stockwell and A. Clarke had undertaken the substantial task of checking the archive and producing Level III drafts. M. Stockwell, who directed the excavations of Bedern north-east and the chapel, had prepared archive reports for these sites, and some publication drafts; A. Clarke had written an archive report and publication drafts for Area 13.X. Unfortunately, this work was undertaken before final pottery dating was available and the initial phasing has subsequently been substantially revised. The present author was commissioned to write up the excavations within the precinct of the College of the Vicars Choral in Bedern in June 1990. He inherited substantial archive reports for Areas 13.X and 14.II/IV, and draft plans for Areas 14.II/IV.

The post-excavation project has involved detailed checking of phasing for Areas 13.X and 14.II/IV, using absolute dating evidence provided by coins, pot-

tery and re-used architectural fragments, and correlating this with the stratigraphic sequence presented in the site archive reports. In the case of Bedern Foundry and the long trench, the present author has also produced stratigraphic matrices for each site and undertaken primary phasing. Scientific dating methods have proved to be of limited value in assigning absolute dates to the Bedern deposits. With the exception of the rafters of Bedern Hall, timber was not sufficiently well preserved to allow any use to be made of dendrochronology. Samples were taken for archaeomagnetic dating from a number of hearths (Noel 1978), but revisions to the archaeomagnetic calibration curve mean that the published dates are unreliable and should now be disregarded, with the exception of the medieval dating published for Bedern Foundry (AY 10/3; C. Batt, pers. comm.).

Although this report presents the evidence for the successive phases of development of the college on a site-wide basis, it must be recognised that since these areas were excavated at different times and never physically joined, the inter-site phasing represents the best interpretation possible on the available evidence. In the period-by-period discussion which follows, a summary of developments across the site will be presented first (in normal type size), followed by a more detailed description on a trench-by-trench basis, working from the north-east to south-west (in a smaller type size).

In order to avoid prejudicing the interpretation of the function of buildings they have been referred to by numbers, except in the cases of the college hall and chapel, where there has been continuity of usage and the identification is secure. The kitchen is also identified by name as its function was apparent as a result of the archaeology. Other buildings have been allocated arbitrary numbers according to a rough chronological order, although where buildings have been rebuilt the original numbers have generally been retained. Compass directions have been used to refer to specific parts of the site. On all plans (except Fig.188, p.387) the top of the page (site north) is approximately magnetic north-east.

The published plans are primarily intended to show the location and character of structural remains and the principal cut features. For those periods (6–9) which have have been divided into more than one phase considerations of space have made it impossible to publish a plan for each. In the text those contexts which are shown on a plan are identified by means of an asterisk (*) in the description of the relevant period and phase, where applicable, but not in the description of earlier or later periods and phases. The numbers of contexts which are shown on section are usually followed by the relevant figure number. Figures on unbound sheets are distinguished in the text by s in bold type.

Where they add to an understanding of Bedern, a number of aspects of the finds evidence, including architectural fragments, pottery, small finds, animal bones and environmental evidence, have been incorporated into this report, although in some cases they will be described more fully elsewhere.

The pottery from the site has been analysed by **Sarah Jennings** who reports as follows:

A large quantity of pottery was recovered from this site, some 160 boxes, with a main date range of early 13th century to 17th century. Roman, Anglo-Scandinavian and late 11th–12th century pottery is represented but, with the exception of the material from the long trench, this is all residual. Pottery from the 18th to 20th centuries was also recovered but much of this was not retained.

Terminology and definitions of the wares and fabrics used are mainly those established by Brooks (AY 16/3), and also Holdsworth (AY 16/1) and Mainman (AY 16/5). Unfortunately not all the material recovered is now available for study, and all the examples of some of the minor wares are missing.

The pottery was initially sorted into fabrics and recorded by sherd count and weight by Miss C.M. Brooks; a number of vessels were reconstructed. When further work was done on the pottery assemblage by the author, it was decided not to extend the quantification to include estimated vessel equivalents (EVEs). This was largely because the individual contexts themselves were frequently not large enough and the sherd/vessel ratio was too small to make the results statistically viable. Additionally, the problems of dealing with reconstructed vessels that came from a number of different contexts would have further prejudiced the data.

Activity on the site in the mid 13th century which involved the commencement of the building of the College of the Vicars Choral is reflected in the pottery assemblage. At this time York glazed ware was declining and was being replaced by Brandsby-type ware. The earliest contexts also confirm that the production centres making red sandy wares were already established. Gritty ware jars and cooking vessels are not common as a contemporary element, but this is probably due in part to the fact that food preparation and storage vessels are not nearly as frequent on this site as they are on domestic sites; this is the case throughout the assemblage. Earlier occupation of the area is reflected in the range of redeposited residual material dating from the Roman period, but principally from the 11th and 12th centuries.

As is usual on intensively occupied urban sites covering several centuries, residual pottery is a common part of the assemblage. The percentages from the College of Vicars Choral are extremely variable and unfortunately tend to be higher for the contexts yielding larger groups. The total form range is standard for sites of this period in York, but the proportions of certain vessel forms are different from those found on domestic sites such as 16–22 Coppergate. There are far fewer vessels that could have been used for cooking than would normally be expected, particularly in the period from the mid 13th to the end of the 16th century. Conversely, there are larger numbers of urinals. This becomes particularly apparent when Humber wares become common in the early part of the 14th century as that industry produced purpose-made urinals that are easily identified even in a fragmentary form. Additionally, tests on residues have shown that the small unglazed Humber ware jug form, often called a drinking jug, was also frequently used for that same purpose as is shown in manuscript illustrations (Jennings 1992, 29).

Regional imports and wares from mainland Europe were both present on the site. In the 13th and 14th centuries European wares are represented by a few Rouen-type vessels and rather more Saintonge ware jugs, including several polychrome examples. Although the numbers are never very large, particularly when compared with the very high numbers found in Hull (Watkins 1987, 125), in percentage terms there are probably more than from most York sites. Towards the end of the 14th century and in the 15th century the emphasis of imported pottery moves from France to the Low Countries and the Rhineland. There are a few Low Countries red ware tripod cooking vessels and frying pans, but in smaller numbers than found at 16–22 Coppergate, and none of the dripping dishes found on that site have been identified in the Bedern assemblage. German stonewares are more common, particularly the larger jugs from the Siegburg and Langerwehe industries. Proportionally, there are fewer of the classic Raeren drinking jugs, compared with the larger Siegburg and Langerwehe jugs, than one might expect. Perhaps the main drinking vessels did not survive in the archaeological record.

There are two specific groups of pottery within the assemblage particularly worthy of note. The first was a large assemblage of sherds dating to the second half of the 13th century from two Period 5 contexts in Area 14.II (1544, 1588, p.439). The group comprises some 5,000 sherds and, with the exception of five sherds, all are from glazed jugs. Although many of the sherds are small, a number of vessels are nearly complete and others can be reconstructed. The vessels are from a number of sources but Brandsby-type wares are dominant. The dating of this pottery is earlier than the Period 5 (early 14th century) contexts in which it was deposited. Several of the reconstructed vessels have manufacturing or firing faults and may have been seconds or wasters. They may represent the unsaleable debris from a pottery seller which was subsequently re-used as hard core. This interpretation would explain the small size of many of the sherds, but not the completeness of the vessels. Unusually for Bedern, this assemblage contains very few, if any, residual sherds, and the only pieces not from jugs are fragments of a single bowl and a lamp.

The second significant group is defined by its function and not by its stratigraphic location, as it was distinctive enough to be identified from a number of fairly dispersed contexts. It is a group of pottery made specifically for industrial purposes and the fabrics, glazes and forms are all atypical. A short preliminary statement and examples of the forms were published in Interim (Jennings 1991, 30–4). Justine Bayley's preliminary examination of a few of the fragments identified the presence of metals on some of the sherds and further analysis has been undertaken by Catherine Mortimer which will be published in AY 17/15. The forms include industrial bases, sand baths, crucibles, lids and bowls; other forms, including vessels with exceptionally long tripods, were found and research into them is continuing. In addition to the ceramic elements it is clear that some of the other parts of the related apparatus would have been made of glass and/or metal. A few of the glass fragments were identified as having come from industrial vessels and certainly some of the high number of convex 'base' fragments were tentatively identified by Rachel Tyson as possibly being from alembic domes (p.616).

This group of pottery was made from an unusual and very distinctive fabric which has enabled even small pieces to be identified despite the fact they were widely distributed across the site. It is unclear from the stratigraphic evidence whether or not the fragments found in the earliest contexts represent primary deposition, but much of the group was subsequently redeposited. Unfortunately, there are no associated sherds in the earliest deposits to confirm the dating for this group, but it is likely to have originated in the 14th century, and most probably in the second half of that century.

Preliminary work has already shown that the ceramic assemblage from the College of Vicars Choral is typical of York in the range of sources of supply, but it seems to be significantly different in the proportions of vessel forms. The ceramics do not indicate either wealth or lack of it but do suggest a different lifestyle from that followed on other sites of the period. Full details of the pottery from Bedern will be published in AY 16/9.

As far as the small finds are concerned, this report has been prepared without the benefit of a full study of the material from the site. It is anticipated that full publication of the finds in *AY 17/15* may add considerably to our understanding of daily life in the college, although a decision was taken not to delay this publication until such time as that analysis might be completed. The present author has sought to extract some interpretative evidence from the finds, and cross-references have been added to indicate the context of the most significant objects.

J.F. Hamshaw-Thomas has examined the animal bones and has provided the following discussion. The information this provides for the vicars' diet is summarised by him on pp.618–26.

A substantial sample of animal bones (c.30,000 identified fragments) has been examined from medieval and post-medieval deposits relating to the College of the Vicars Choral. Unfortunately, the excavations were undertaken prior to the large-scale sieving of archaeological deposits, which is now standard practice at York Archaeological Trust. The contents of a number of pits were sieved, which with the exception of context 1505 (from Period 9 pit 1510) produced insignificant animal bone samples (Scott 1985). This sieved sample has been treated as a separate entity, and not integrated into the main body of quantitative data. While the diligence of the excavators is clearly visible, in the form of a larger than expected sample of small bird and fish bones, the total faunal (here defined as mammal, fish and bird bone) sample must be regarded as severely biased in favour of adult bones from large-boned taxa (Levitan 1982).

The analysis of the Bedern faunal material has been complicated by the fact that it has been undertaken in two quite distinct stages, firstly by S. Scott (1985) and secondly by J. Hamshaw-Thomas (1994). Considerable efforts were made to resolve this problem but there remains some disparity in many aspects of the methodology and the practical approach to the analysis of the material.

The considerable size of the archaeofauna excavated from Bedern presented a problem frequently faced by zooarchaeologists working with urban material. The detailed analysis of all the material would be neither cost effective nor especially rewarding. In these instances a series of priority decisions must be made such that a balance is achieved between archaeological questions, zooarchaeological questions and practical considerations (O'Connor 1989).

From the total area excavated within the Bedern precinct only faunal material from Bedern north-east (14.II and 14.IV) and Bedern south-west (13.X) was considered. The 1985 analysis made a detailed record of all faunal material excavated from Area 14.II and a detailed record was also made of the largest samples from the south-west part of Area 13.X. A cursory analysis, recording only presence or absence, was undertaken on the largest contexts from Area 14.IV and the north-east part of Area 13.X (Scott 1985). The 1994 analysis was concerned with these areas. Following a rapid assessment of this material, 14% of the bone-bearing contexts were selected for detailed analysis. For details of the analysis of the 1994 data and the rephased 1985 data the reader is referred to Hamshaw-Thomas 1994.

For the 1985 sample the detailed bone-by-bone recording followed the standard Environmental Archaeology Unit procedure in use at the time. The mechanics are detailed in Scott (1985) and AY 15/2 (pp.70–1). In the case of the 1994 sample a detailed account of the methodology is presented elsewhere (Hamshaw-Thomas 1994).

A number of problems have arisen from the fact that the research has been undertaken in two stages. The most significant problem is the disparity between the range of anatomical elements identified. This has the effect, when comparing the two data sets, of distorting the relative abun-

dance of the different taxa. Some differences also exist between the level of identification which has been made, most noticeably in the sample of wild birds. This is not a serious problem and simply reflects personal differences in the approach to difficult identifications.

In the course of the analysis data from a number of period groups were amalgamated in order to increase the sample size. In the case of summing data from Periods 2 to 5 this was on archaeological grounds and was considered quite acceptable in terms of the zooarchaeological interpretations. Certain aspects of the analysis are, however, based on samples drawn from all periods. This therefore introduces the possible problems of creating a time-averaged sample of little interpretative value. As is demonstrated below, there are a number of features of the sample which are quite clearly genuine reflections of past activities. This, together with the fairly consistent nature of the occupation of the site (87% of the sample is derived from the collegiate periods) and the requirement of large sample sizes, justifies the amalgamation of samples of differing periods.

Some understanding of the nature of the faunal sample is required to place any interpretations in context. In particular, it is necessary to be aware of the potential loss of material during excavation. In general one can expect the bones of small-sized taxa and the bones of young individuals to be grossly under-represented in hand-collected samples. Levitan (1982) has described how fragment size, distribution, abundance within the soil and the perception of the excavator are the determining factors in the recovery of bone fragments. In the case of Bedern it is worth pointing out that the proportion of bones of medium- and small-sized animals will be depressed in relation to larger animals. Therefore, as is demonstrated by the sieved sample from context 1505 (Scott 1985), the excavated sample is not a true reflection of the diversity and relative proportions of taxa in the deposited assemblage.

On the basis of a semi-quantitative assessment of the 1994 sample a number of points are worth making. In general the sample showed considerable homogeneity in both spatial and chronological terms. The principal variation appeared to be within, rather than between, contexts. This raises the thorny problem of the extent to which each context contained a residual or intrusive faunal element. Interestingly, there was no obvious correlation between pottery residuality and what are assumed to be indicators of faunal mixing, a point of some significance for zooarchaeologists. Some correlation was, however, noted between contexts defined as 'spreads', and variation in the angularity and colour of the faunal material. This implies that such contexts contain a greater proportion of mixed or residual material. However, the vast majority of the larger bone-bearing contexts contained a small fraction of material which appeared to be residual or intrusive, typically 5–10%. This is considered acceptable in view of the duration and intensity of the occupation in Bedern.

Elucidating the pre-depositional taphonomy in urban faunal assemblages is a particular problem. The role of scavengers, and in particular domestic dogs, in assemblage formation processes has been detailed by a number of researchers (Brain 1981; Stallibrass 1984). A considerable number of the bones examined from Bedern bore the distinctive patterns of damage, which can clearly be attributed to both dogs and cats. These agents will have influenced the composition of the sample through the destruction and redistribution of bone fragments. The high proportion of fragments gnawed by cats, dogs and indeed rats (Fig.340, p.612) demonstrates their ease of access to both butchery and table waste, implying, by modern standards, relatively poor refuse disposal practices.

Of considerable bearing on the interpretation of the faunal material is the question of what factors were involved in the deposition of the various bone samples. For example, the large undistinguished bone assemblages from medieval Coppergate, provide a 'general' picture (O'Connor 1986a; AY 15/5), while the assemblage from post-medieval Walmgate represents evidence of specialised activity (AY 15/1). In the context of Bedern, the problem of interpretation was investigated on the Period 2–8 samples by means of an examination of the relationship between context type and the relative proportion of the different species. In general terms this failed to indicate any substantial variation in the distribution of the different species. Minor variations in the relative abundance of cattle as opposed to sheep and poultry may be taken to indicate some differences in the blend of table versus kitchen versus butchery waste, but interpretations based on such variations must remain, at best, tentative. This general similarity could be taken as indicating a degree of uniformity in the function of the different contexts as repositories for waste. An alternative, and possibly more accurate, interpretation is that the lack of any identifiable pattern in the waste disposal strategy is a reflection of both the mixing of deposits, and the coarse level of analysis. A notable exception to the above is the relatively high incidence of cat bones in the 'garden soil' and 'external spread' contexts from the south-west part of Area 13.X examined

in 1985, which may point to the burial of dead pets in the garden areas of Bedern. While the argument is somewhat circular, the apparently non-specific disposal of bone waste supports the amalgamation of the period groups in the analysis.

Dr T.P. O'Connor examined the post-medieval (Period 9) animal bones and provides the following assessment of the evidence.

Discussion of the post-medieval animal bones is limited to two late 18th–19th century deposits from Bedern south-west (5027, a Period 9 Phase 2 layer, and 6014, a Period 9 Phase 1 pit fill). All the material was recovered by hand-collection during excavation, and will therefore have been biased towards the larger elements, and towards larger-boned taxa. Although this will have a material influence on the interpretation of the results, much of the information to be had from these assemblages lies in what was present in them, rather than in what was absent. In other words, although the biasing effect of the recovery method is acknowledged, its effect on the interpretation of the results and the reliability of the information thus obtained is thought to be acceptably minor. Certainly, recovery was consistent with the best standards of urban excavation in the mid-1970s. Specimens were identified to the level of part of element of species, with identification of every specimen at least attempted. The results of the analysis are referred to on pp.621–6.

The other biological remains were analysed by **Dr A.R. Hall, H.K. Kenward and A. Robertson** who note the following.

The sampling strategy for biological remains, although good by the standards of the time, was fairly selective. Only very limited bulk-sieving was carried out and no site riddling was undertaken (cf. Dobney et al. 1992). Samples for processing in the laboratory were prioritised by the post-excavation team and analyses undertaken sporadically through the period 1976–89. Laboratory processing methods varied through the period of practical work. In the early stages, separate subsamples were taken for insect and plant macrofossil analyses; latterly these remains were examined from the same subsamples. Initially, methods for extraction and recording of insect and plant remains followed those of Kenward et al. (1980). Later, the abbreviated 'test processing' method of Kenward et al. (1986) was employed for processing subsamples for both plant and insect analyses. Subsamples for analysis of the eggs of intestinal parasite worms were treated following the 'modified Stoll method' summarised by Dainton (1992, 59–60). The discussion of the biological evidence in this report is derived from the technical reports of Hall et al. (1993a–c), where the detailed results are presented. The methodology and a summary of the results are presented in this section; the interpretation of individual samples is discussed at the appropriate point in the archaeological report. Further discussion of how this evidence may illuminate the daily life and diet of the college is to be found on pp.618–20.

A total of more than 300 samples from 188 contexts were examined from medieval and post-medieval deposits, of which 128 samples from 107 contexts were analysed for insects and 134 samples from 95 contexts for plants. A large proportion of the contexts were also examined for parasite eggs. These samples represent some of the first post-Conquest to post-medieval material examined extensively for waterlogged biological remains in York. Their significance lies at least as much in their contribution to a broader synthesis as in their value in enhancing archaeological reconstruction and interpretation of the deposits. It should be remembered, though, that this work was begun before the methods currently adopted by the Environmental Archaeology Unit were fully developed and that it was carried out over a very long period of time and, necessarily, without full archaeological information.

As has frequently been observed for urban deposits of 13th century and later date in York (and elsewhere), many of the layers gave poor preservation of delicate organic materials or included only small numbers of fossils, often of the more durable kinds. This doubtless reflects standards of cleanliness and building construction considerably better than in earlier periods, such as the Anglo-Scandinavian, as revealed by deposits at 16–22 Coppergate (AY 14/7). In some cases there were reasonably large assemblages of invertebrate and plant remains indicating diverse ecological origins; these have proved to be of limited interpretative value, except in as much as they suggest the presence of small quantities of heterogeneous plant matter and invertebrates of 'background' origin. Deposits with such assemblages may often have incorporated redeposited earlier material, thrown up by building or horticultural activities, for example.

By contrast, some, largely 'primary', deposits, mainly fills of pits, gave good preservation of large quantities of plant and invertebrate remains. Much of this material was clearly faecal in origin (with a diversity of wild and cultivated fruits represented) and, to judge from the worm eggs recorded, probably human waste, though the presence of faeces of pigs cannot be ruled out and in some instances there appeared to be something like stable manure. Insect communities associated with these deposits included 'house fauna' of a kind quite likely to have occurred in stables, although a large proportion of the samples gave at least a few insects which would not be out of place in a relatively clean domestic building of the last few hundred years, and some assemblages consisted mainly of such species. Grain beetles were frequently recorded and may have originated in animal feed rather than in significant stores of grain for human consumption at or near the site. There was sometimes a component of insects associated with foul decomposing matter. Overall, however, the biota — or lack of it — indicates rather clean living conditions and well-organised waste disposal. In general, the decomposer insects seem to have entered the material dumped into pits at source rather than invading in situ, and it is probable that most pits containing foul matter were dug and filled in a short space of time. Others were probably long-lived latrines, placed within the buildings so that invasion by insects other than 'domestics' was limited. Records of ectoparasites from these deposits are few; for the fleas, this probably reflects rarity, but lice may not have been recognised when the material was examined.

As mentioned above, eggs of the two gut parasites commonly encountered in urban archaeological deposits, Trichuris and Ascaris, were frequently present in small numbers, but only occasionally abundant. Trichuris was, as is almost always the case, the more abundant of the two. Even in deposits identified on other evidence as including faeces, however, parasite eggs were by no means as abundant as recorded from some other sites, such as Anglo-Scandinavian levels at 16–22 Coppergate (AY 14/7). This may reflect smaller worm burdens at this later date, perhaps in turn reflecting improved sanitation and the relatively high social status of the inhabitants of Bedern.

The Structural Sequence

During initial post-excavation work the structural development of the site was divided into nine periods, which were distinguished on the basis of stratigraphic evidence for major construction activity. On integration of the absolute dating information provided by the pottery and coin evidence, it became apparent that the first five periods witnessed rapid development over a short space of time with little dating material to distinguish the specific periods whereas Periods 6–9 covered slower development over several centuries. Nevertheless, for the sake of the integrity of the extensive archive, it has been decided to retain the original period divisions in this report, although the opportunity presented by refine-

Table 11 Bedern buildings: period of first construction and function

Building No.	Location	Period	Function (if known)
–	SW	6.1?	Timber-framed hall
–	SW	7.1	Kitchen
–	SW	7.2a	Stone hall
3	NE	1	?
4	NE	1	?
5	NE	2	Residential block (rebuilt P7.2b)
6	NW	2	Residential?
7	NE	3	Addition to Building 5 block
8	NE	3	Addition to Building 5 block
9	SW	3	Residential block
10	SW	3	Residential?
11	SW	4	Residential — replaces Building 9
12	SW	4	?
13	SW	4	?
14	SW	5	Residential
15	SW	7.2b	Lavatory
16	NE	6.1	Residential — addition to Building 5 block (rebuilt P7.1)
17	SW	6.1	Residential — (rebuilt P7.2b)
18	SW	6.1	?
19	SW	6.1	?
20	SW	6.2	Buttery for early hall
21	NE	7.1	Addition to Building 5 block
22	NE	7.1	?
23	NE	7.2a	?
24	SW	7.2b	?
25	SW	7.1	Buttery
26	SW	7.2a	?
27	SW	7.2a	Evidence room
27A	SW	7.2b	
28	SW	7.2b	?
29	SW	7.3	?
30	SW	7.4	?
31	SW	7.4	?
32	SW	8.1	?
33	SW	8.1	?
34	NE	8.2	?
35	SW	8.2	Brewhouse
36	NE	8.3	House?
39	SW	9	House

ments of the dating evidence has been taken to allow a division of Periods 6–9 into two or more subphases.

Period 0 is a label used to cover all pre-Conquest activity. This evidence is described in detail in *AY* 3/3 and in *AY* 8, but is summarised below. Periods 1–8 span the 13th–early 17th centuries during which time the site was occupied by the College of the Vicars Choral. By Period 9, the post-medieval phase, the college property was mainly occupied by tenants of the vicars (see pp.627–41). See Table 11.

The medieval Bedern Foundry was fully published in *AY* 10/3. In this fascicule there are summaries at the end of the relevant college period descriptions of medieval developments in the northeast part of the foundry site (Areas P, U and V; see Fig.56, *AY* 10/3) which is thought to have been part of the property of the vicars choral (p.151, *AY* 10/3). Post-medieval developments on the foundry site after the mid 16th century when it was occupied by a bakery will be published in *AY* 13. The periods on the foundry site are numbered in a different sequence from the college site: medieval periods are numbered 1–5; the first post-foundry period is Period 6 which is equivalent to Bedern Period 8, Phase 3, and the post-medieval is Period 7, equivalent to Bedern Period 9. For an introduction to the archaeology of the foundry in Foundry Periods 6–7 see p.185, *AY* 10/3. In the summaries of the archaeology of the foundry in this fascicule, foundry phasing is given in the headings but the discussion uses the phasing sequence from the college site to allow comparisons to be made more easily.

Period 0: Roman and Anglo-Scandinavian

During the Roman period the area investigated by the Bedern excavations lay within the eastern corner of the Roman legionary fortress. However, since the excavations generally stopped at a depth of 1·5m below the modern ground surface, Roman deposits were rarely encountered. Traces of Roman structures were excavated in three areas (1976.14.I, 1976.13.V, 1976.13.VI; Fig.193, **3**, **7** and **8**, p.396) made available by the removal of post-medieval cellars. In addition, Roman stratigraphy, including the legionary fortress defences, was examined in Bedern long trench (1973.13.III/IV, Fig.193, **11**). Each of these sites is fully

described in *AY* 3/3. Roman levels were reached in two areas of the Bedern Foundry site (1973.13.I/II, Fig.193, **12**): an inspection trench to aid removal of a medieval barrel-lined well and a trial trench across the site (p.159, *AY* 10/3). In these trenches the natural clay was immediately overlain by c.0·5m of silty clay loams containing ash, charcoal, fragments of painted wall plaster, roof tile and large quantities of animal bone. These layers contained almost exclusively Roman pottery and were interpreted as material derived from the demolition and levelling of Roman buildings.

A clean slightly sandy clay was encountered at a depth of c.12m OD in the foundry excavation, and at 11·60m OD in the long trench (not at 12·50m as incorrectly given on p.165 in *AY* 3/3). This deposit is interpreted as natural, pre-Roman material. The difference in height suggests a natural slope down from south-west to north-east with its edge running along the line of a major north-west/south-east wall-line on the foundry site. This wall had some significance for the medieval development of the site as it appears to have marked the south-western limit of the precinct of the College of the Vicars Choral, dividing their property from the main building range of Bedern Foundry, further to the south-west (see Fig.219, p.447). The instability of the wall can be blamed, at least in part, upon the natural slope at this point, although the vicars must themselves bear some of the responsibility because of their habit of digging substantial rubbish pits in the thick silty clay deposits which had been dumped against it in the late 12th and early 13th century (p.167, *AY* 10/3).

Roman stratigraphy was not encountered in any of the main sites excavated within the precinct of the College of the Vicars Choral, although it may be assumed that structures of the Roman fortress lay below the medieval levels. Substantial quantities of residual Roman pottery were recovered as well as a number of Roman small finds.

A claim that the Roman emperor Constantine the Great was born in Bedern (*Peternae natum in Eboracensi civitate*) seems to have been first made by the English bishops at the Council of Basle in 1431 to support their claim for precedence over the French. It was known to Anthony Wright, sub-chanter, and to the antiquary Henry Keepe in about 1680, and was repeated by Drake (1736) and Hargrove (1818) in spite of the fact that the future emperor, though proclaimed at York following his father's death there in 306, was apparently born at Naissus, now Nis, in Serbia. The most likely explanation of this improbable claim is that impressive Roman remains had been found in Bedern during the early 15th century building work, suggesting to scholars that a structure of the importance of the imperial palace had stood on the site. Drake (1736) mentions mosaic pavements 'anciently' found there and a fragment was found at a depth of 12ft near the school in 1880 (Raine 1955). A 4th century mosaic with a female bust was revealed in a house excavated immediately outside the fortress under the now vanished church of St Helen-on-the-Walls in 1974 (AY 6/1, 40–2).

In the Bedern long trench the latest Roman deposits were succeeded at its north-west end by a row, 6·5m long, of roughly finished and unmortared limestone blocks on a line slightly oblique to that of the trench. The row of blocks returned to the north-east at its north-west end. The blocks may have formed the footings for the wall of a timber building. While pottery from layers overlying them was Anglo-Scandinavian, the blocks themselves may be earlier (AY 7/2, pp.191–2, 256).

The only Anglian find from the Bedern sites was a silver styca of Eanred (c.810–41; AY 18/1, 16) recovered from a Period 7 floor in Bedern Chapel. A pit in Bedern cellar I was radiocarbon dated to the 7th–8th century (AY 14/5, 272), but its fill was similar to that of three other features dated by pottery to the Anglo-Scandinavian period (AY 3/3, 150). A pit in Bedern cellar VI with a wattle lining was also dated by pottery to the Anglo-Scandinavian period (ibid., 164). In addition to the pits, Anglo-Scandinavian pottery and finds were recovered from many of the medieval contexts.

Period 1A: 11th–12th century (Fig.364s)

Clay loam deposits dating to the 11th and 12th centuries were excavated only in the long trench where they sealed late Roman strata and the possible Anglian or Anglo-Scandinavian structure. These deposits continued to accumulate after the Anglo-

Norman period; there was only limited building activity or occupation until the college was established.

Bedern long trench

Overlying Roman and post-Roman contexts in the long trench there was a series of clay loam deposits (1131, 1208, 1210, 1214, 1216, 1221–2, 1224, 1659; Fig.364s) containing pottery of 11th and early 12th century date, and a number of finds including an antler comb (8105, AY 17/12) and antler working debris (8089, 8091, 8098–9), and a mercury-gilded iron object, probably from horse harness (sf858).

In the north-western part of the trench (Area III) the loam deposits were cut by features probably dating to the 12th century: 1137 with fill 1138; 1219 with fill 1225 (Fig.364s) containing a fired clay crucible (sf932) and two post-holes 1133, 1213. Also overlying the loams were a series of hard-packed clay floors: 1125, 1142 (Fig.364s), 1143 associated with a collapsed rubble wall (1139) with clay footings (1140). These contexts had been cut by a pit (1134) with an organic fill (1135), and a post-hole 1130. Spreads of clay (1127–8) were associated.

One of the earliest medieval features encountered in the south-east part of the trench (Area IV) was the robbing trench (1656, Fig.364s) for the Roman legionary fortress wall; pottery from the backfilling (1649, 1655, Fig.364s) suggests that it dates to the 12th century. The backfill comprised waterlogged silts with inclusions of wood, twigs and other organic material such as bone, including a skate (8081, AY 17/12), and leather items clearly deriving from refuse. A wattle fence (1650), of which a few fragments survived (orientation not recorded), had been erected over the robber trench backfill.

A gully (1653, Fig.364s) running north-west/south-east had been cut into the fortress rampart and had been backfilled with organic silt (1652, Fig.364s) containing bone, oyster and mussel shells, and 11th century pottery. There was also a pit (1662*, Fig.364s) with 11th century pottery in the fill (1683, Fig.364s).

These features were sealed during the 12th/early 13th century by further deposits of clay loam (1099, 1100, 1113–14, 1118–19, 1123, 1126, 1200, 1203, 1599, 1611, 1641, 1644; Fig.364s). These layers contained evidence for industrial activity, including antler manufacturing debris (8094, 8097, 8101, 8103), glass manufacturing debris (sf847) and an iron auger bit with remains of a wooden handle (sf5253).

Period 1: early–mid 13th century (Fig.195)

The earliest medieval deposit encountered across the main excavation areas was a loamy soil, possibly the result of agricultural activity before the foundation of the college. It is possible that the patchy survival of pre-college occupation is a result of a deliberate attempt to clear the land prior to construction of the college, although it appears that occupation was never intensive.

The earliest features comprised various drainage ditches, gullies and pits (no plans survive). The presence of a 12th century barrel-lined well (no surviving plan) in Area 14.II may indicate nearby habitation, probably along Goodramgate street front. The surrounding soil deposits contained domestic refuse such as bone and charcoal, along with building rubble containing some of the earliest fragments of roof tile

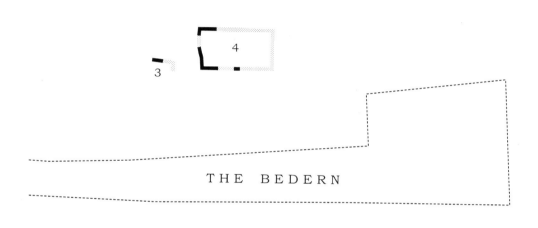

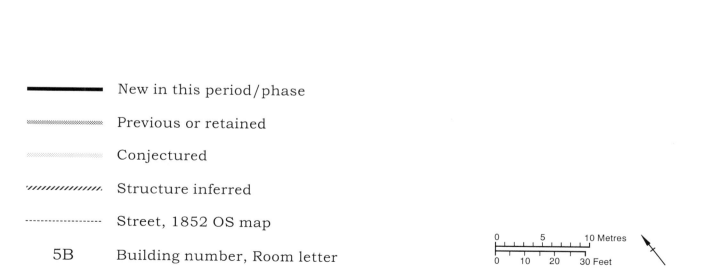

———————— New in this period/phase

▓▓▓▓▓▓▓▓ Previous or retained

░░░░░░░░ Conjectured

///////////. Structure inferred

----------------- Street, 1852 OS map

5B   Building number, Room letter

0   5   10 Metres
0 10 20 30 Feet

Fig.195 *Period 1: interpretative summary phase plan, showing building development (the key is for use with all the summary phase plans). Scale 1:400*

in Bedern. The features can be dated by associated pottery to the early part of the 13th century. If the land was open and used for agricultural purposes it probably also served as a dumping ground for waste from adjoining properties. The ditches themselves may have been used as property boundaries but insufficient survived for them to be assigned to particular street front plots.

At some time during the first half of the 13th century, construction of buildings began on this open land. One of the earliest of these, **Building 1** in the north-west part of area 14.II, was represented only by a deposit of ash covered by a heavily burnt clay. The latter is interpreted as a floor level, the heavy burning suggesting that this building had been destroyed by fire. The loam covering these floor levels is interpreted as a deposit relating to dereliction of the area, preceding the construction of a second building, **Building 2**. Again, no structural evidence for this second building remained, but the successive deposits which were seen to form straight edges on their north and west sides are interpreted as floor levels within a small structure. These levels consisted of clay floors interleaved with charcoal. There was also evidence of clay repairs to several of the floor levels, although no trace of a hearth was found in either building, which may indicate that they were not lived in.

The layers of charcoal and the heavily burnt nature of all the deposits interpreted as floor levels indicates that the associated structures were probably timber-built, and were either accidentally burnt down or deliberately fired for clearance purposes. As there was no other evidence of occupation on the site at this time, it is suggested that these structures had a non-residential use, perhaps for storage or agricultural purposes. The fragmentary nature of their remains means it is impossible to assign dimensions to them.

Towards the end of Period 1, in the north-west part of the site, two small buildings were constructed over Buildings 1 and 2. **Building 3** lay mainly outside (to the north-west of) the area of excavation, and was only represented by a north-east wall built of limestone rubble blocks and cobbles, and two floor deposits (Fig.372**s**).

To the south-east of Building 3, **Building 4** was represented by parts of three surviving foundation walls of limestone and cobble (Fig.372**s**). Later disturbance makes interpretation difficult but the presence of a padstone suggests that Building 4 was timber-framed. It went through at least two phases of use, both of which contained a hearth. Both Building 3 and 4 were of a more substantial construction than the earlier buildings on site, but their life spans were short. It is unlikely that they had any residential use, although there were several related cess pits. The walls of both buildings showed traces of reddening, presumably the evidence of the fire which destroyed them, possibly during the clearance prior to the building of the college.

A pitched tile hearth in Area 14.IV is seen as the only remaining evidence for a structure in this part of the site; the construction of the hearth was similar to that found elsewhere within later buildings. This hearth appeared to be associated with a cess pit and a retaining tile wall.

To the south-west of the site, in Area 13.X, the earliest deposit encountered consisted of an almost uniform loam extending over the entire excavation area, with little structural evidence for occupation. A major drainage gully or property boundary ditch (for the cut of which no plan survives, although later fill layers were planned) ran north-east/south-west across the site immediately to the north-west of where Building 10 would be erected in Period 3. In the long trench there was evidence for a timber building, but this was not observed in the adjacent excavations, possibly because it remained obscured by unexcavated later 13th century deposits there. In spite of post-Roman levelling, there still appears to have been a substantial slope down from the south-west to the north-east, the top of which ran parallel to the north-eastern edge of the foundry site. In later periods this change in slope was used to define a property boundary, and appears to have marked the division between the precinct of the vicars choral and the foundry buildings to the south-west.

The pottery from Period 1 is dominated by York glazed ware which is particularly characteristic of the first half of the 13th century, indicating a limited timespan for the events described above. Given that the documentary evidence shows that the land in Bedern was probably not acquired by the vicars until the mid 13th century, Period 1 is interpreted as a brief pre-college phase of activity. For much of this period the excavated area presumably formed part of the town estates of Laneham, Romeyn and Walter de Gray (see pp.385–91).

The end of Period 1 in areas 14.II and 14.IV is marked by the deposition of an extensive layer of silty loam. This levelled up the area before the next period of use, obliterating all traces of Buildings 3 and 4.

Bedern North-East (Fig.372s)

The earliest deposits encountered on the site were extensive layers of loam (1485). At the north-west end of the site a substantial ditch (1784) had cut through the upper part of a barrel well (1796), c.1m in diameter (no plan survives of either feature). The upper barrel was only observed in section, but it was clear that at least one other barrel lay beneath it.

The ditch (1784), running north-west/south-east, was excavated over a 4m length. Its width at the north-west end was approximately 1·6m and at the south-east 2m. No record of the depth survives. Two fills were identified: an upper fill (1784A) of thick clay, becoming increasingly organic towards its base; and a lower fill (1784B) of heavily compacted peat up to 0·2m thick in parts. The north side of the ditch and its upper fill were found to have been cut away by a large pit (1793) filled with black silt. A second pit (1783) was also cut into the ditch. These features were dated to the early part of the 13th century by the pottery evidence. Processing of samples of the lower ditch fills yielded a range of components, including bone, nutshell, snails, shellfish, charred grain, faecal concretions, pottery, brick or tile, coal, wood and charcoal. Amongst the plant remains it was noted that walnut and hempseed were both present (Hall et al. 1993c).

Building 1

The barrel well, and associated ditch and pits were superseded by three phases of building during Period 1. The first was represented by Building 1, in the north-west part of Area 14.II, surviving only as probable floor levels consisting of an irregular deposit of ash (1791), c.1·5 × 2m, covered by a spread of heavily burnt clay (1788). A small circular pit (1792) filled with brown clay and limestone rubble appears to have been contemporary with this building.

After the disuse of Building 1 a layer of sandy loam (1779) was dumped over this area. This was cut by a pit (1787) containing cobbles in a matrix of grey silty loam. The pit was itself sealed by a dump of clay loam and charcoal (1789).

Building 2

The next phase was represented by the construction of Building 2. No evidence for walling remained, but a series of at least four deposits of clay and charcoal with straight edges on the north and west sides defined an area of c.3·4 × 3·2m. The first of these was an irregular and uneven surface of clay with charcoal inclusions (1786), covered by a clay deposit (1776), in turn covered by a charcoal spread (1777) patchily overlain by clay (1781). This was subsequently overlain by occupation deposits of sandy loam (1780) intermixed with charcoal (1778). These deposits were then sealed by a clay floor (1766) upon which deposits of sandy loam (1765) and charcoal (1767) built up. The floor was cut by a pit (1775) containing water-worn cobbles. Pottery from these internal deposits provides a date in the first half of the 13th century.

Building 3 (Fig.372s)

Building 2 was replaced by two structures, Buildings 3 and 4. The surviving north-east wall of Building 3 (1752*) was at least 1·4m long and 0·4m wide; it survived to a maximum height of 0·12m. Its construction was of unmortared limestone rubble blocks and cobbles set upon a clay loam spread (1753). The entire wall had been reddened by intense heat. The south-east end of this wall and the south-east wall of Building 3 had apparently been removed by a later intrusion and some large limestone blocks further to the south-east may have come from these walls. Within the presumed interior was a clay floor (1750) overlain by an ashy occupation spread (1749*). The remainder of Building 3 was outside the excavated area.

Building 4 (Fig.372s)

Building 4 was located to the south-east of Building 3 and was represented by three foundation walls built on top of a series of small mixed clay spreads (1768–72). The south-west wall (1757*) was built of clay-bonded limestone rubble set in a clay-filled construction trench (1764). It survived for a length of c.1·6m and was 0·2m wide; like the wall of Building 3 it was reddened by heat. A single large, shattered padstone (1763*) 2·2m further to the south-east, and two post-holes (1797*), 0·9m and 1·1m from it, continued the line of the wall, giving a possible length of c.5m. The north-east wall (1773*) was only represented by a small linear scatter of cobbles and limestone rubble. The north-west wall (1547*) was similar to the south-west wall; it too was built in a clay-filled construction trench (1552) and it was also reddened by fire. It survived for a length of c.3·8m, with a gap towards the north-east end 1·2m wide, flanked by slightly larger limestone blocks. Its junction with the north-east wall did not survive. No remains of a south-east wall survived.

Within Building 4 a series of deposits consisting of clay, ash and loam (1688*, 1759–60) accumulated, sealing a shallow cobble-filled pit (1730). Two large faunal samples were recovered from these internal spreads. Of the farmyard animals, sheep were slightly more numerous than cattle, with pigs as common as poultry (here defined as chicken and geese). Other mammals represented include horse, fallow deer and cat (Hamshaw-Thomas 1994). Set into these deposits in the west corner of the building was a large rectangular hearth (1748*), 1·6 × 1·2m, formed of cobbles set into a shallow construction pit backfilled with clay. Associated with it, in the extreme west corner of Building 4, was a patchy cobble surface (1756*) bedded onto a small spread of burnt clay and ash (1762). The hearth was later covered by a deposit of clay (1755) into which was dug a replacement hearth (1746), represented only by a small area of burnt clay. This was finally covered by an extensive spread of ash and clay (1739).

To the south-west of Building 4 was a pit (1761*) with a primary fill of domestic rubbish, shell and fish bone in cess, sealed by a top fill of cobbles. A second pit (1391*), close to the east corner of Building 4, was filled with an organic silt with a small amount of weeds and parasites. It is suggested that this was a latrine pit later backfilled, as evidenced by the presence of much stone, tile and lumps of clay within the silt. To the north-west there was a clay and cobble spread (1677).

To the north-east of both Buildings 3 and 4 was a linear scatter of cobbles and small limestone rubble (1782*) 5·6m long north-west/south-east and about 0·4m wide.

In Area 14.IV, the earliest feature cut into a loam equivalent to 1485 was a pitched tile hearth (4486*) aligned north-east/south-west, narrowing towards the south-west end, its south-east side destroyed by a modern intrusion. The hearth was covered by a thick layer of wood ash which produced pottery dating to the first half of the 13th century. No evidence for any associated structure was found.

To the south-east was a large and deep pit (4493*) filled with bands of mortar, tile and loam (Fig.196). The fill included a variety of debris, including brick, bone, eggshell, charcoal, limestone, pottery and wood. The pit contained 86 grey gurnard bones, which, while being an unusual concentration, does not represent more than a couple of individuals (Hamshaw-Thomas 1994). Analysis of a sample of the pit fill yielded quite a large assemblage of identifiable plants, most of them weeds, although fig and elderberry may represent food remains (Hall et al. 1993c). The south-west edge of this pit was marked by a line of tiles running north-west/south-east, two abreast, forming a wall (4492*) varying from three to eight tiles high (Fig.196). The latest pit fill overlapped the tiles in places, especially at the south-east end where the tiles were at their lowest. It is not known what events these features

Fig.196 *Area 14.IV, Period 1: stacked tile wall 4492 and pit 4493, looking south. Scale unit 0·1m*

412

were contemporary with, but it is assumed that the hearth was associated with a structure standing at much the same time as those buildings in Area 14.II.

At the end of Period 1, Buildings 3 and 4, associated levels and the features to the south-east were all buried beneath a thick layer of loam (1740, Fig.365s, 1754, 4482) which effectively levelled what had been an irregular surface and covered two small pits (1741, 1751).

Bedern South-West

In Area 13.X a general layer of silty clay loam (5463, 5498, Fig.367s, 5505, 5518, 5522) contained inclusions of mortar, bone, charcoal, tile and domestic refuse, as well as patches of dark organic peaty loam, interrupted by tile spreads. Elsewhere it appeared to be more of a pure culti- vated soil (6337, 6343, 6362, 7631, 7633–8) cut into by at least one post-hole (6336) and a north-east/south-west gully (unnumbered), at least 4m in length and 0·4m deep. Pottery from these levels comprised a high degree of re- sidual material, including Roman sherds, but it suggests they were exposed until the mid 13th century.

Area 13.VI

In the north-western half of Area 13.VI (Fig.193, 8, p.396) two medieval pits (3101, 3104) were exposed in the base of the modern cellar cut, containing pottery of the late 12th to mid 13th century.

Bedern long trench

The Period 1A loam deposits had been cut by six clus- ters of piles (1109/1207: three stakes), (1117/1206: six stakes), (1623–5: three stakes), (1627–31: five stakes), (1633– 7: five stakes), (1606, 1620–22, 1626, 1638–9: seven stakes), as well as an individual stone-packed post (1122), all of which presumably represent the foundations of some early timber structure running diagonally across the trench.

The loam deposits had also been cut by pits with or- ganic fills: 1116 and 1120 with wattle lining 1129. 1132 (Fig.364s) was probably cut at this level, although the origi- nal section drawing appeared to show it overlain by 1114 (Period 1A). The lower fill of 1132 was 1136 which was overlain by a series of thin deposits: 1098, 1101, 1104, 1110, 1115 (all Fig.364s). 1110 was cut by a post-hole (1111) with a peaty fill (1098), packed with three tiles and the base of a cylindrical jug (1102) which appeared to have been used to provide a firm base for the point of the post.

In the south-east part of the trench were pits 1616 and 1640 (Fig.364s) with fill 1643 (Fig.364s) containing a cop- per alloy ring-headed pin (sf776) and a chalk mould (sf778) for casting pewter counters. 1640 was cut by pit 1645 (Fig.364s) with fill layers including 1651 and 1684 (Fig.364s).

Bedern Foundry

Towards the north-eastern limit of the foundry site a substantial natural slope running down from south-west to north-east (4245) was observed. Here the ground had been levelled up by over 0·8m with successive tips of silt and peaty deposits (4253–4, Fig.62, AY 10/3). The pottery recovered from this phase indicates that the levelling did not take place before the mid 13th century (p.162, AY 10/3).

Period 2: mid 13th century (Fig.197)

Documentary evidence indicates that by the mid 13th century the College of the Vicars Choral had acquired land in Bedern on which to construct their college buildings (see pp.385–6). This land had not previously been intensively occupied; any earlier structures were levelled before new building work took place. Traces of two major buildings have been identified as belonging to the first phase of college occupation, on opposite sides of a courtyard which became Bedern Close; there may have been others in the unexcavated portions of the precinct.

The most impressive of these buildings was a large structure, **Building 5**, parallel to the north-east side of Bedern. It was at least 40m in length and c.10·6m wide, with a wing projecting to the north- east at the south-east end.

The north-east limestone sill wall of the main range incorporated regularly spaced post-pads to carry the main posts, creating bays c.2·4m long. Be- neath these post-pads were cobble- and clay-filled foundation pits. A larger pit, at the corner of the junc-

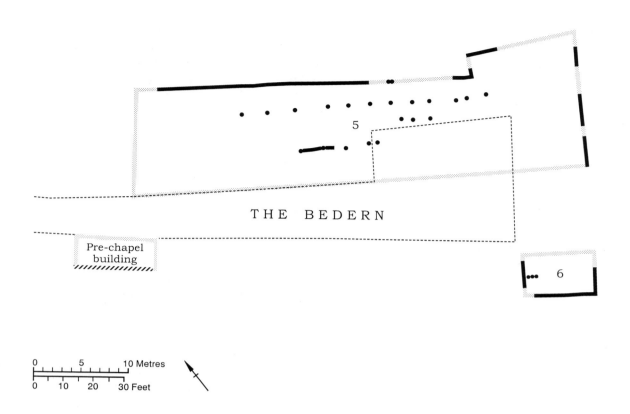

THE BEDERN

Pre-chapel
building

5

6

0   5   10 Metres

0   10   20   30 Feet

Fig.197 *Period 2: interpretative summary phase plan, showing building development. For the key, see Fig.195, p.409. Scale 1:400*

tion with the south-east wing, probably provided extra support for a substantial corner post. A gap between two of the padstones in the north-east wall may have been an original entrance which was blocked towards the end of Period 2. The south-east wall was also constructed on a sill with a series of pits filled with broken limestone, cobbles and loam, but differed from the north-east wall in having no surviving padstones within its length. As revealed in the excavation, the south-west wall survived only as a short length of clay while the north-west wall was outside the excavated area, the full length of the building, therefore, remaining unknown.

Within the building there were two parallel lines of pits and padstones, probably serving as supports for freestanding timber posts. From the spacing of the padstones which would have carried the timber framing posts, it is possible to estimate that there were at least seventeen bays within the building. A shorter line of three post-pads along the central axis towards

the south-east end suggests that some extra internal structure existed at this point, possibly a smoke hood.

Little evidence of occupation during this early period was found inside the building, presumably because the earth floor was kept clean, or because subsequent developments had obliterated it. Outside the north-east wall of Building 5, earlier features had been backfilled and levelled. This area was then occupied by a line of latrine pits. External deposits of clay and loam to the south-east of Building 5 seem to have been used to level up an uneven surface in preparation for later building activity.

This period saw the introduction of Brandsby ware pottery, usually attributed to the mid 13th century. This date ties in with documentary evidence for the construction of the first college buildings on land given to the vicars in 1248. Documentary sources for the college indicate that its original development was restricted by the nature of the available site and that

414

Bedern was initially laid out with a narrow rectangular close around which the college buildings were grouped. Building 5 is thought to correspond to one of those buildings mentioned in the sources as being situated to the north-east of the rectangular court. It may well be identified as the *magna aula* or great hall referred to in the documents, which also mention a garden area to the north-east of the college buildings. Little indication is given of use of the *magna aula*, but it presumably provided the main living accommodation for the vicars at this early date. The use of the term *cubiculum* in York to describe a vicar's accommodation may suggest that their rooms originally bore a greater resemblance to the cubicles of the monastic dormitory than to the fully fledged chambers of later colleges.

Below the earliest levels of the present chapel, after the foundation trenches had been excavated, the south-west and north-west walls of a **pre-chapel** building were identified on the basis of a large backfilled robbing trench (see Fig.202, p.418). The building is unlikely to have extended beyond the close to the north-east and so it may have measured c.8 × 5m. Associated pottery suggests a date in the mid to late 13th century, placing it in Period 2. The interpretation of this structure as an early chapel has been dismissed because of its small size and the absence of documentary evidence. This pre-chapel structure must be interpreted, therefore, as an an early college building of unknown function.

On the south-east side of the courtyard, in Area 13.X, a smaller timber-framed structure, **Building 6**, was constructed (Fig.374s). Three walls were within the area of excavation, but its north-east wall probably lay under Bedern Close. The building must have been c.8m long by at least 5m wide, with its longer axis parallel to the close, opposite the south-east end of Building 5. The walls rested on limestone foundation sills, with padstones set over cobble-filled pits marking the position of the upright timbers. There was a doorway, and an entrance vestibule, in the west corner. Inside there were a succession of clay and mortar floors, with a tiled hearth. The hearth and floor levels support the interpretation of Building 6 as college residential accommodation, but the lack of diagnostic finds hinders any more precise attribution.

Outside this building was a network of large ditches, presumably for drainage around the build-ings on this part of the site. Evidence for a cess pit was recovered from Area 13.V, c.20m to the north-west of Building 6. Further to the south-west there was little evidence of any activity in this period away from the courtyard area, although there were traces of a timber structure and associated occupation floors in the long trench.

Bedern North-East

Building 5 (Figs.198, 373s)

Building 5 was represented by its north-east, south-west and south-east walls and various internal features. The north-east wall (1262*, 1373*, Fig.365s) ran from the north-west edge of site for a distance of c.33m before turning 90° to the north-east for c.2·5m, forming a rectangular projection (4477*), and then turning a right-angle again for another c.11m, although only c.3m of this last stretch survived.

Prior to the construction of this wall, a series of shallow pits (1715–24*) had been excavated along its intended line. The pits were each backfilled with cobbles in clay, and each measured approximately 0·5–0·6m in diameter and 0·2m in depth (Figs.199–200). At least fourteen such pits were identified within the excavated length, positioned approximately 2·5m apart, with one larger pit (on Fig.373s, but unnumbered) being positioned at the south-west corner of the wall of the north-east projection.

The wall itself, surviving to a height of approximately 0·45m and having a maximum width of 0·4m, was constructed of mortar-bonded limestone rubble. At intervals, above the cobble-filled pits, there were larger limestone blocks (given the same numbers as the pits), probably post-pads, which were incorporated into the thickness of the wall and formed an integral part of it. The north-east projection was of a slightly different build with a course of tiles.

Initially a gap of 2·4m was left at the north-west end of 1373 between the limestone filled pits 1718 and 1719. At some later stage during Period 2 this gap was filled by a limestone rubble wall (1683*) set on cobble foundations.

The south-east wall (4441*), like the north-east wall, was also constructed on a series of pits filled with broken limestone and cobbles (Fig.201). It was set into a mortar-filled construction trench (4389) and built of limestone blocks with a course of flat-laid roof tiles. The north-east end of this wall, where it joined up with the north-east wall, had been destroyed by later intrusions. A copper alloy strap-end (sf873) was found in the construction trench fill.

Fig.198 *Area 14.II, Period 2: Building 5, general view looking north-west, showing the north-east wall 1373 and external pits. Scale unit 0·5m*

The south-west wall (4426A) survived as a line of clay with some limestone fragments in it; more substantial remains presumably lay to the south-west of the excavated area.

Within the main body of this building were two parallel rows of post-pads and pits, with a similar but shorter row between them towards the south-east end of the central aisle. Approximately 2·5–3·0m south-west of the north-east wall, the distance increasing from north-east to south-west, there were at least twelve pits (1581*, 1663*,

1684*, 1685*, 1698*, 1703*, 1704*, 1705*, 1707*, 4487*, 4488*, 4490*) corresponding in position, more or less, to the pits under the north-east wall. The six pits at the north-west end of the line were similar to one another in having a fill of limestone chippings, on top of which was set a single large post-pad. The six pits at the south-east end of the line were of a different construction. The three north-westernmost (1663*, 1698*, 1707*) contained decayed timber posts which had been driven through the base of the pit, while the remaining three pits (4487–8*, 4490*) to the south-east were filled with cobbles packed with loam, but

Fig.199 Area 14.II, Period 2: Building 5 cobbled post-pad 1716. Scale unit 0·1m

Fig.200 Area 14.II, Period 2: Building 5 cobbled post-pad 1718. Scale unit 0·1m

no posts survived. Of this second group of six pits, only three were topped with post-pads. Despite the differences in construction, stratigraphy confirms that there was no time lag between the digging of these pits; the variations may, therefore, be seen as the work of different construction gangs, rather than different sub-phases. The pit at the far south-east end (4487*) lay c.2·5m into the projecting bay. South-east of it was a shallow linear feature (4471*) containing clay and traces of wood, which continued the line of the pits. Further deposits to the south-east were destroyed by later intrusions.

Approximately 4m to the south-west of the line of post bases was a corresponding series of pits and post-pads. This line was traced only towards the north-west end of the building where five features (1727*, 1731–3*, 1736*) were found. Of these, the most north-westerly (1733*) was of a more massive construction than the others, consisting of a large stone set into the backfill of the underlying pit and supporting a smaller square limestone post-pad to which it was mortared (see Fig.365s). The two post-pads at the south-east end (1731*, 1736*) were slightly north-east of the alignment of the others. Further to the south-

Fig.201 Area 14.IV, Period 2: south-east wall of Building 5 (4441) at construction level, looking north-west. Scale unit 0·1m

east on a similar alignment was a linear spread of clay and cobbles (4483–4*).

Along the central axis of Building 5 there were at least four more pits containing cobbles. Three (1655*, 1710–11*) contained the remains of posts in the base and were similar to the three pits opposite them to the north-east, although less regularly spaced. There were several more cobble-filled pits (no plan survives) further to the south-east which may also have been part of this alignment.

Various small construction spreads of limestone rubble and cobbles were found in association with this building (1556, 1608, 1702, Fig.365s, 4392, 4445, 4468–70, 4476, 4479–80). Within the building a layer of loam (1466/1582) appears to represent a remnant of an initial floor level. This was overlain by a rubble and clay spread (1559), possibly a repair.

To the north-east of Building 5 the Period 1 pit (1391) was backfilled with a deposit of clay (1540) followed by a small layer of peat (1541). This pit was then sealed by a

clay deposit (1444) which spread over the edges of the pit. This immediate area, including the backfilled pit, was then levelled with the deposition of a layer of charcoal-flecked loam (1445*). In the area of backfilled pit 1391 was a post-hole (1557).

Several new pits were then dug in this area, the organic peaty nature of their fills pointing to their use as latrine pits. To the south-east was a pit (1501*), approximately 1·3m in diameter and 0·35m deep, which cut a small spread of mortar (1504*, Fig.365s). The pit had been filled with a layer of organic material, possibly cess, containing large fragments of mortar and tile.

At the north-west end of this area, immediately north-east of Building 5, was an extensive spread of clay (1530*) partly covered by a thin spread of ash and charcoal (1531*) and a small clay spread (1528). Two small pits (1537, 1572) were cut into the clay, and filled with charcoal and organic matter. A few of the pits had associated post-holes, possibly of wooden superstructures, and there was a circular area of posts (1532*) containing decayed wood in situ. A

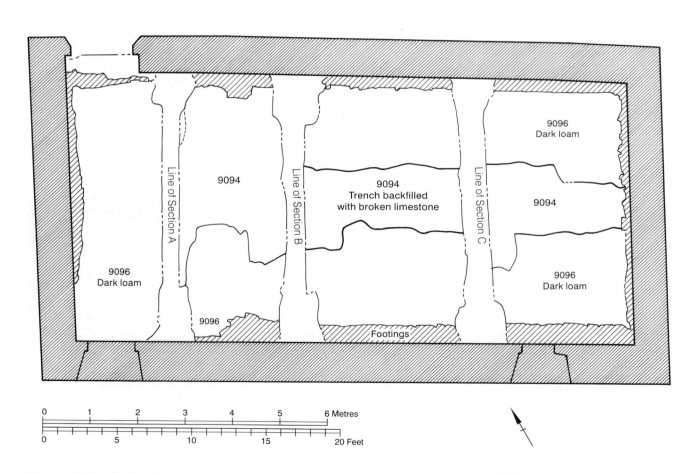

Fig.202 *Plan of Bedern Chapel in Period 2 showing robber trench 9094 for the pre-chapel building. The three lines of north-west facing sections relate to Fig.232a–c, facing p.472. Scale 1:80*

small circular cut (1529) filled with organic material was also excavated.

A further latrine pit (1774*) had a fill containing mammal and bird bones, pottery, brick/tile, charcoal, wood, nutshell fragments, fruitstones, seeds, numerous fly puparia and faecal material. It is also likely that there was some hay or other cut grassland vegetation present, to judge from the moderate numbers of buttercup and traces of cow parsley, hogweed, self-heal and yellow-rattle recorded. The trace of saw-sedge perhaps points to the presence of cut wetland vegetation too (Hall et al. 1993c). The faunal assemblage was dominated by large mammal fragments, cattle being the most abundant, with lesser quantities of sheep and small numbers of pig. Poultry, red deer, horse and hare bones were also present, as was a small quantity of fish (Hamshaw-Thomas 1994). This assemblage appears to represent the use of the pit as a general dump for rubbish following its discontinuation in use as a cess pit. Fragments of the rim and body of a glass flask or urinal (sf933) recovered from the fill may, however, relate to the pit's primary function.

Pre-chapel building (Figs.202–3)

The earliest deposits examined within the surviving chapel consisted of a dark loam 9096* (Fig.232c, facing p.472) and mortar spreads (9075, 9081). These had been cut by a trench, backfilled with broken limestone and mortar (9094*, Fig.232b–c), which defined the south-west and north-west walls of an earlier structure (Fig.203). The pottery from 9096 suggests a date no later than the mid–late 13th century.

Fig.203   *Bedern Chapel, Period 2, showing robbing trench for a wall of the pre-chapel building, looking north-west. The 1m scale in the foreground lies on the trench backfill 9094; stubs of the north-west wall of the Period 5 chapel lie to the left and right of the 1m scale in the background*

Bedern South-West

The earliest building encountered in Area 13.X was constructed on top of the Period 1 loams to the north-east of the site.

Building 6 (Fig.374s)

Limestone rubble and post-pad foundations defined three walls of Building 6. The south-west wall survived only as a line of cobbles (7600*, Figs.368s, 370s; 7617, Fig.370s) with a mortar spread at its south-east end, and two or three possible post-pad pits. Towards its north-west end there was a section of well-built unmortared limestone blocks, ending with a double padstone and a gap before its junction with the north-west wall. The north-west wall (7558*, Fig.370s) was constructed of limestone blocks bonded with mortar, and incorporated post-pads and one cobble-filled pit beneath its main build. The south-east wall (7584*, Fig.366s) was of a similar construction. A loam and mortar layer (7592, Fig.370s) was laid down immediately after the construction of wall 7558*, butting against the outside. There was a further patch of mortar and broken tile (7618, Fig.368s) and a small spread of mortar inside the building.

The earliest floor levels consisted of an extensive dark loam spread (7609*, Figs.368s, 370s) dated by the pottery to the first half of the 13th century. This layer also produced a moderate sized bone sample, with cattle, sheep, pig and poultry each in approximately equal proportions. These bones may reflect a high input of table waste into this deposit, a notion consistent with the proposed residential function of Building 6 (Hamshaw-Thomas 1994). A square limestone block (7619*) was set in a pit cutting the floor at the north-west end of the building. An extensive spread of ash and charcoal (7548*) partially overlay the floor. A small deposit of mixed mortar and clay (7547) spread over this and outside the building to the south-west. Inside, a patchy deposit of brown clay and sand (7567, Fig.368s) was cut by a rectangular pit (7523*, Fig.370s) lined with edge-set tiles. This pit had been filled with large limestone and sandstone blocks with an apparent centre division of edge-set tiles. Inside the entrance, running at 90° to the north-west wall, a short stretch of wall (7559*) was constructed over a sandy clay loam spread (7577). The wall survived as a 1·5m length of limestone blocks bonded with mortar, with a clay infill (7541) between the stones. Following the construction of this internal wall, a sequence of ash, clay and mortar spreads (7557, 7562, Fig.370s, 7571–3, 7576, 7578) was deposited. A shallow pit (7616) filled with a mixture of peaty ash and loam was also cut into 7609. Lying largely beyond the north-east edge of the trench was a tile hearth (7615) with a flat-laid brick-edging set into a clay-filled construction pit.

A gully (7603*) was dug outside the south-west wall, and parallel to it, apparently to provide a drainage channel. It was probably contemporary with a gully (7597*) running from the north around the north-west side of Building 6. To the south-west, clay loam (6343) was deposited in the north-east/south-west gully originally cut in Period 1.

Area 13.V

Little post-Roman material was found in Area 13.V (Fig.193, 7, p.396) as the modern cellar had been cut down into Roman levels. The only certain post-Roman feature found was the base of a wattle-lined pit (3005) at the south-east end of the trench; it was dated from pottery found in the backfill to the second half of the 13th century (location shown on fig.92, AY 3/3). The fill comprised very organic silty clay with bone, shell, and preserved wood and leather. It is interpreted as a cess fill.

Bedern long trench

There was further levelling up of the area of the long trench in the mid 13th century, with a series of loam and rubble dumps (1107, 1597–8, 1613, 1615, 1617, 1632).

In Area III these levelling dumps were cut by two square post-holes (1105, 1108). A wattle wall (1092) ran diagonally across the trench (no plan survives) and was dated by pottery to the mid 13th century. There was a possible clay floor (1095) north-west of the wall. A wattle-lined pit (1204) with an organic fill (1205), and a pit (1202) with a gritty fill (1201) may also have been associated.

Period 3: mid–late 13th century (Fig.204)

Towards the end of the 13th century internal modifications to the early buildings of the college began. Some buildings were demolished and a major new building was constructed south-west of the close. Over the next 50 years, spanning Periods 3–5, the college underwent an almost continual round of alterations and rebuilding along with the construction of many new buildings. Recognising distinct stages in this process is not helped by the dating evidence, especially the pottery — from the late 13th to the early 14th centuries there are few introductions. Much of the division of this activity into periods has been made with reference to the buildings themselves and the possible useful life of certain features. This

has its own difficulties as the relative speed of accumulation of the various deposits is sometimes impossible to judge.

This increase in building activity was probably a result of an increase in the number of vicars requiring accommodation in the college and the need for more service buildings. For the first time we see evidence for occupation of **Building 5** with the construction of a tiled hearth against the south-east end wall. The north-east and south-east aisles appear to have been used for some new purpose as connecting walls were built between the aisle posts, presumably separating off the central aisle of the building. The floors

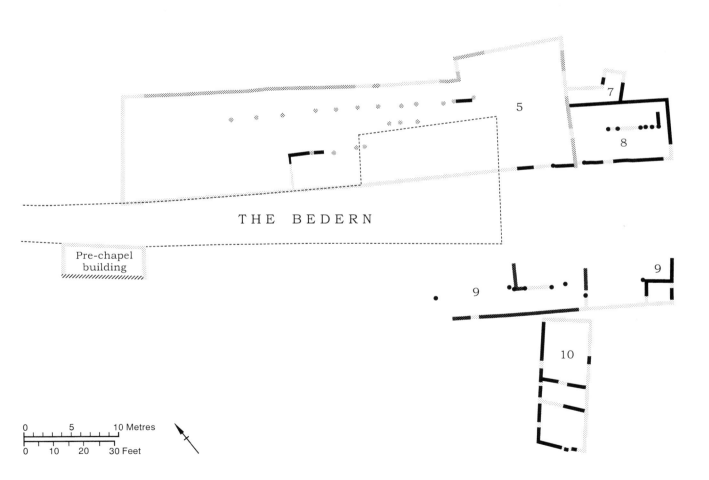

Fig.204 *Period 3: interpretative summary phase plan, showing building development. For the key, see Fig.195, p.409. Scale 1:400*

within the north-east and south-west aisles show that they were lived in, although the central aisle was still without occupation deposits.

An area of cobbling in the north-east aisle at the north-west end of the excavated building shows evidence of careful construction, with the insertion of tiles between the cobbles in an attempt to present a level surface. This cobbling may have served as a foundation for some structure rather than as a surface in its own right. The straight edge of the cobbling at its south-east limit may indicate the position of a timber partition wall.

The divisions within the building, although not continuous along its whole length, combined with evidence for an internal drain and the cobbling, suggest that more intensive use of the building than hitherto occurred in the latter half of the 13th century. At least some of this use was probably domestic, as indicated by the presence of the hearth, at least one floor deposit in the north-east aisle and some floor levels in the south-west aisle. The external cess pits to the north-east of Building 5 also remained open and in use during the course of this period.

The open area to the south-east of Building 5 was built over with the construction of two new buildings (Fig.373s). Both of these were built directly onto the hall, incorporating its south-east end wall. The first of these, **Building 7**, can only be considered as an outhouse due to its small size. Apparently set into a shallow depression, it was an L-shaped timber-framed structure. No indication was found of its use.

Shortly after the construction of Building 7 a much larger rectangular structure, **Building 8**, was added on to the end of Building 5, and against Building 7. The walls were apparently built in sections, which differed from one another in their constructional form, but all exhibited freestanding padstones connected with a sill wall. The centre of the building was divided with a line of post-pads which probably indicate the position of an internal partition, and may well indicate support for an upper storey. An internal wall at the south-east end may mark the position of the entrance passage. The remains of plaster rendering on the interior of the north-east and south-east walls suggests that this building was of a high quality internally and may have been lived in, despite the lack of a hearth.

On the south-west side of the close major building works were carried out during Period 3, with the construction of two large halls. The first, **Building 9**, appears to have been a timber-framed aisled hall, erected parallel to the close and to Building 5 (Fig.376s). It was constructed over demolished Building 6, but the north-east and south-west end walls of the earlier building appear to have been retained as internal partitions within the new building. The full extent of Building 9 is not known as both its north-west and north-east walls were beyond the edge of excavation. Nevertheless, it must have been at least 24m in length and 7–8m wide. A line of post-pads, parallel with the south-west wall, may represent the remains of aisle posts, with traces of a continuation at the north-west end of the trench. If so, then they indicate that the south-west aisle was c.2·5m wide. Only part of the south-east outer wall remained, as a single line of clay- and mortar-bonded limestone foundations set into a shallow construction trench. There were a variety of internal floor levels, mainly corresponding to the bay divisions, comprising clay and mortar floors in some areas, but rough limestone and cobble surfaces in others. Towards the south-east end of the building there was a square, tiled hearth, suggesting that part, at least, of Building 9 was used for residential purposes or was otherwise occupied.

To the south-west of Building 9 a second substantial timber-framed structure was constructed, with its long axis running at right-angles to Bedern Close. This was **Building 10**, at least 12m long and c.4·5m wide. Its north-west wall was the best preserved, but there were also traces of its south-west and south-east walls (Fig.376s). The presence of cobble-filled pits in the foundations of the north-west wall suggests that Building 10 was also timber-framed. The north-east wall, and any connection with Building 9, had been removed by later intrusions. The excavated area of Building 10 had been divided into three rooms by internal partitions, although the central area was fairly narrow and may represent a passage. The three areas contained floor levels of mortar, limestone and sandy clay, some of them burnt, as well as an extensive deposit of clay loam incorporating large quantities of fired clay moulds, extending over most of the central passageway and south-west room. This material may have been taken from the nearby foundry site (*AY* 10/3) for use as a suitable floor make-up. Placed within the north-east room was a tiled hearth, unusual in that some of its tiles were at right-angles to the rest. The discovery of two bone parchment prickers (*8036, 8049, AY 17/12*) in association with the well-defined floor levels, and the presence of a hearth, suggest that this building was both lived and worked in.

Ubiquitous garden loams surrounded all these buildings, and were cut by a variety of features, mostly pits and gullies, the latter perhaps associated with drainage. The pits extended to the south-west edge of the college precinct, where they were encountered along the edge of the foundry site. The Period 1 gully to the north-west of Building 10 was backfilled and levelled by a sequence of loams, mortar, clay moulds, ash and organic materials, as the use of this area was altered from agricultural to residential.

Bedern North-East (Fig.375s)

Building 5

On the south-west side of Building 5 the three post-pads (1727*, 1732*, 1733*) were connected by a low limestone rubble wall (1674*) which had been set in a construction trench and bonded with lime mortar. At the south-east end of this wall the construction levels were overlain by a loam spread (1725) and cut by a small pit (1713). A less substantial wall (1714*) of single unbonded limestone blocks ran south-west from the north-westernmost post-pad (1733*), possibly to join up with the main south-west wall of Building 5 which lay outside the excavated area. Within the right-angle formed by these two walls there were deposits of limestone rubble (1681*), tile fragments and sand (1680), and lime mortar (1728, Fig.365s). Sealing these deposits was a silty loam (1687) containing a number of snail shells. This sealing layer does not seem to be a typical internal floor deposit and may indicate a different use for this part of the building at this time, or simply that this area had become disused.

There were similar changes to those described above at the south-east end of the north-east aisle. Two Period 2 post-pads (4487–8*) were connected by a wall of limestone and clay (4459*) which may originally have connected all the padstones of the arcade. Layers of mortar and lime (4464), and, to the south-east, a loam spread (4447) were deposited.

Three small post-holes (1670–2) were located 0·5m south-east of one of the central post-pads in the north-east aisle. Each was about 0·1m in diameter and approximately 0·4m deep, and together they formed a rough north-west/ south-east line, 0·6m long. No associated timber survived.

Set against the south-east end wall (4441), and presumably situated in the corner where this wall would have formed a junction with the north-east wall (4477), there was a pitched tile hearth (4166*) on a bed of clay.

At the extreme north-west end of the north-east aisle a thick spread of cobbles and limestone rubble (1549*) was laid over the Period 2 clay loam, possibly as the foundation for an internal structure, as the surface was carefully levelled by the insertion of tiles between the cobbles. The cobbling contained a fragment of re-used roll moulding (266) of early to mid 13th century date (*AY* 10/4). The south-east limit of the cobbling was straight-edged, suggesting that this once finished against a partition.

Within the central aisle of Building 5 the Period 2 clay loam was cut by a shallow drain or gully (1747*, Fig.365s), approximately 1m in length, running parallel to the new connecting wall in the south-west aisle, and sealed by a clay spread 1743. A second shallow linear feature (1744) ran westwards, continuing the line of wall 1674, for some 4·2m. Both features were covered by a layer of mixed rubble (1708, Fig.365s). To the north of wall 1674 lay an extensive layer of clay loam and charcoal (1712) which produced a bone sample with a relatively high incidence of sheep, pig and poultry. Cattle remained the second most abundant animal (Hamshaw-Thomas 1994). To the south of 1674 there were a series of ashy spreads (1679).

The remaining walls of Building 5 and the external area to the north-east remained unchanged during this period. To the south-east of Building 5, a sequence of clay and loam dumps (4475, 4473, 4462, 4457) were deposited as levelling for Building 7. These dumps produced large faunal assemblages dominated by the bones of cattle and sheep, with considerably fewer pig and a small number of chicken and goose bones. The presence of red deer, cat, dog and hare was also noted (Hamshaw-Thomas 1994). A lead weight (sf904) was found here. The dumps had been cut by two small pits (4384, 4386).

Building 7

At much the same time as the developments within Building 5 described above, Building 7 was built against its south-east wall. The first operation in its construction appeared to be the excavation of a large L-shaped shallow pit or scoop cutting into the upward-sloping land to the north-east, although this depression may have been present originally and merely enlarged and backfilled in such a way as to provide the necessary foundations for a new building.

The south-west wall (4454*) of this structure was built of clay-bonded limestone set onto a foundation of packed clay overlying a layer of broken flat-laid roof tiles. This wall was packed tightly against the face of the L-shaped cut, with edge-set tiles inserted between the top of the cut and the newly constructed wall. The wall incorporated a single upright, wooden post, resting upon a section of rotted wooden sill beam packed against and protected by the protruding edge-set tiles (Fig.205).

The south-east wall (4449*) only partially survived as a 1·7m length of limestone wall with mortar bonding, incorporating a timber sill beam beneath part of it. A re-used stone shaft of late 12th or 13th century date was recovered from this wall (253), helping to date the construction of the building to sometime after the early 13th century (AY 10/4). The depression left in the centre of the L-shaped scoop was then filled with broken limestone and covered by loam (4455).

The wall forming the north-west side of the projection to the north-east (4453*) of this L-shaped structure did not survive in its entirety although it was represented by a 0·7m length consisting of three limestone blocks running north-east/south-west.

Building 8

It appears that the north-east wall (4421*/4438*) of Building 8 replaced the south-west wall of Building 7, the remaining walls of which still stood. This north-east wall was built in two different styles. The south-east part (4421*) employed a construction trench of which the north-east side was lined with edge-set tiles. A mortar-bonded limestone wall a single block thick with regularly placed padstones was set into this construction trench, which was then backfilled with a sandy loam (4465). The building style changed approximately 1·6m to the south-east of the wall's junction with the south-east wall of Building 7. The north-west part (4438*) consisted of tile-packed limestone rubble covered with clay, with the occasional limestone post-pad, some twinned, along its length (Fig.206). Much of the central portion of this north-west part did not survive. Despite alterations, the original layout of the wall is reflected in the regular spacing of post-pads throughout its entire length.

The south-east wall (4420*) was one limestone block thick with mortar bonding, incorporating padstones, set on a crushed limestone foundation spread. Remains of fine mortar-rendering survived on the inner faces of both this wall and the north-east wall. The corner junction between this wall and the south-west wall was outside the area of excavation.

The south-west wall (4426*) continued the line of the south-west wall of Building 5. It survived only partially, consisting of a line of small limestone blocks and clay between larger padstones set onto backfilled construction pits.

Internally, an irregularly spaced line of at least six small pits was located along the centre of the long axis of the building, forming the basis for a partition wall which divided the building into two halves, with access between them at each end. This partition continued the alignment of the south-west arcade of Building 5. These pits were filled with loam, mortar and broken tile, onto which were set padstones (4446*). The line of padstones stopped 3·2m short of the north-west wall and a 0·9m gap was left between the last padstone and the south-east wall.

A short length of limestone walling (4451*) at the south-east end, and at right-angles to this central line, may have formed the side wall of an enclosed passage leading from an outside doorway through to the south-west portion of the building where a deposit of clay and tiles formed a threshold.

Fig.205 Area 14.IV, Period 3: Building 7, south-west wall 4454, looking north-west. Scale unit 0·1m

Fig.206   Area 14.IV, Period 3: Building 8, wall 4438, looking north-west. Scale unit 0·1m

Bedern South-West

Before Building 9 could be constructed, the footings to the south-west wall (7600) of Building 6 had to be removed. The Period 2 drainage gully (7597/7603) was backfilled with mixed rubble and loam (7582, Figs.366s, 368s, 370s) and covered by a layer of sandy silt loam (7569, Fig.370s). A spread of broken tile and loam (7594, Figs.366s, 368s) partly slumped into the gully at the south-east end. This was covered by a deposit of loam (7585, Fig.368s) along the south-west edge of the gully, and a series of mixed clay fills (7544, 7537, 7535, 7532, 7524, Fig.370s) were deposited at the north-west end. Overlying the now-redundant portion of wall 7558 was an extensive spread of sandy clay loam (7499*) incorporating a spread of limestone and cobble blocks to the south-east, whilst a deposit of mortar (7518*) was laid down over the now-redundant south-west portion of wall 7584. The remaining length of the redundant south-west wall (7600) was finally covered by a linear deposit of clay (7519*, Figs.368s, 370s). A demo-

lition spread of brown ash with charcoal flecking (7529) was deposited across the interior of Building 6.

At the south-east end of the site there was a sequence of patchy spreads of crushed limestone (7627), mortar and rubble (7630, Fig.370s), and ash (7632), all sealed by an extensive silty clay spread (7620). An Edward I penny (*AY* 18/1, *104*) recovered from the spread, probably deposited c.1320–51, is seen as intrusive in this context as the pottery from the same layer gives a mid–late 13th century date. Given that this level was exposed for nearly twelve months before excavation, this contamination is perhaps not surprising.

Building 9 (Figs.207, 376s)

The south-west wall of Building 9 (7593*, Figs.368–9s) was built over construction spreads of mortar and loam (7625, Fig.368s, 7614). This wall comprised mortar-bonded limestone, two blocks wide, although only two courses

Fig.207 *Area 13.X, Period 3: Building 9 from the south-east. The south-west wall 7593 is upper left; in the foreground is wall 7628 running right to left and joined at right-angles by wall 7624. Scale unit 0·5m*

survived. A padstone (7623*) at the south-east end of this wall was set onto a cobble-filled pit, and two further padstones were incorporated along its length, one approximately 2m from the south-east end, also set above a cobble-filled pit, and one 4·5m north-west of 7623. A similar pit also existed at the north-west end of the wall, but did not carry a padstone. A spread of mortar (7565*) cut by a post-hole (7564*) against the north-east edge of the excavation might indicate that the north-east wall was only just outside the excavated area.

The south-east wall (7628*) was represented by a single line of mortar and clay-bonded limestone, set into a shal-

low construction trench. A similarly constructed internal wall (7624*) ran at right-angles to the outer wall. It survived for a distance of 2·4m, and incorporated a number of re-used worked stones including 226 and 254 (AY 10/4). A narrow slot (7129*) running south-west from wall 7624 may represent the position of another robbed-out internal division.

The south-west aisle was marked by six padstone settings (all numbered 7521* but not all shown on Fig.376s), set into a clay foundation deposit, although only four actual padstones survived. The two north-westernmost padstones had a section of limestone wall between them.

Both padstones had foundation pits (7516*, Fig.368s, 7566*, Fig.370s) filled with cobbles or with limestone and sandstone blocks packed with clay. The south-eastern pit (7516) also contained fragments of painted wall plaster (sf2783). There were a number of construction spreads (7542, 7546, 7580, Fig.370s) associated with the wall-line, possibly representing upcast from the foundation pits, but also partially backfilling them.

There was further structural evidence at the north-west end of the area, where further post-pads may represent the continuation of the aisle. At least one of the padstones rested on a foundation of three timber piles driven into a pit and packed with limestone. The stub ends of the posts were covered by a spread of broken tiles and clay (7605*) which left the top of the padstone exposed. Later than 7605 was a silty loam (7604*, Fig.370s) which extended to the edge of the trench and was overlain by a small deposit of limestone fragments (unnumbered, but visible on Fig.376s), probably the base for another post-pad. There was also an area of hard limestone standing (7601*) set into loam 7604.

Towards the north-west end internal layers included a sandy rubble and limestone spread (7496*, Fig.370s), and layers of sandy loam 7589 (Figs.368–9s), 7591* (Fig.369s) and 7608* (Fig.368s), against the south-west wall, containing a bone die (8075) and a tooth plate (8107) from a single-sided composite antler comb (AY 17/12). A deposit of cobbles, limestone and broken tiles in a clay silt (7575*) was laid down to form a threshold at the south-east end of wall 7593.

A loam spread (7534*) partly covered the construction spread for the aisle posts and was itself covered by clay (7533*). Contemporary with these deposits was another clay spread (7517*, Fig.368s) which ran up to the aisle posts. Against the internal partition wall (7558*) there was a succession of sandy clay floor deposits (7554–5*, 7563*). A square foundation pit for a pitched tile hearth (7526*) was cut into the clay floor. Spreading from this hearth was an ash deposit (7520*). A clay floor deposit (7514) was laid down to the south-east of the hearth; a sample yielded small amounts of fish and mammal bone, charcoal, and traces of shellfish and eggshell, as well as a little brick/tile, stone and a fragment of cinder (Hall et al. 1993a). This material was typical of trampled floor surfaces found on Bedern. To the south-east was another clay deposit (7495*) cut by a pit (7512*) which was later backfilled with limestone and sandstone blocks bonded with sand and clay. The pit was later covered by a deposit of burnt clay (7494), whilst further to the south-east was a spread of silty loam (7540).

Outside Building 9 to the south-west there was a build-up of loam (7612) and an extensive spread of silty loam, mortar and tile chips (7613, Fig.368s) butting against wall 7593 (Fig.368s) and covering its construction levels. Pottery from these levels suggests they were deposited in the mid–late 13th century. The bone assemblage from 7613 was unusual, having a relatively high incidence of the remains of poultry, which may represent an intrusive 'table waste' element (Hamshaw-Thomas 1994). A gold brooch (sf2847), comprising a circle of thin gold wire enclosed in a woven gold wire mesh, was also recovered from the external spread associated with Building 9. The deposits described above were cut by a shallow linear feature (7556) filled with a mixture of clay and loam, found in association with a shallow pit (7598) backfilled with a similar material. A small ash-filled pit (7626) was located to the south-east, with a large pit (7606*), filled with broken tiles and loam including a stone mortar (sf2856), to the south-west of this. At about the same time a silty loam (7621, Fig.370s) was deposited over most of the area south-east of Building 9.

In the northern corner of the site there were three pits (7539*, 7596*, 7599*) backfilled with a mixture of loam, mortar flecks, limestone and tile rubble. The backfill of 7596 included an unfinished carved limestone figurine (286, AY 10/4) depicting a figure with the head and hands lost kneeling on a crouching figure. A sample from the fill of pit 7539 yielded a modest list of plant remains, including moderate amounts of vegetation from marginal wetland or wet meadow (Hall et al. 1993a). It is unlikely that so many wetland plants would have been growing together on an occupation site. Traces of fig, and the presence of fish bone, brick/tile, charcoal, eggshell and mortar indicate that some occupation material was clearly finding its way into this pit. After pits 7596 and 7599 had been backfilled they were covered by a loam spread (7595) and a further pit (7581, Fig.369s) was then dug in this north-west portion of the site, later to be backfilled with a silty loam containing charcoal and limestone chips.

Building 10 (Figs.208, 376s)

The north-west wall of Building 10 (6345*) survived in the most complete form. This wall was later than external deposits which had already built up against Building 9, suggesting that Building 10 was constructed as a second stage of development. It was built on cobble and limestone rubble foundations bonded with clay, and set into a shallow construction trench with tile and limestone fragments packed against the outer face of the wall. The presence of irregular cobble-filled pits along the wall length indicates that this building was also timber-framed. The foundations did not survive for the entire length of the wall, however; to the south-west, they had been partially removed by a later (Period 5) robber trench (6327), whilst in the centre all that remained was 1·5m of a timber plank built onto the footings where they were abutted by an internal partition (6341*). A bone die (8076) was found associated with the wall (AY 17/12).

Remains of the south-west wall (6326*) survived at the base of a later (Period 5) robber and construction trench (6321). The south-east wall (7611*) survived only as two blocks of limestone set into a shallow foundation trench packed with tile and broken limestone. The south-west extent of this wall may have been removed by a shallow robber trench, but this area had been extensively disturbed by 19th century intrusions. The north-east wall did not survive, although Building 10 may once have butted up to, and made use of, the south-west wall of Building 9 (7593).

This long building was divided by two internal partitions running across its width, but only the north-eastern of these (6341*/6374*) survived as recognisable wall foundations of clay-bonded limestone, including re-used worked blocks (239–40, AY 10/4). The north-west end of wall 6341 had been reduced to an alignment of scattered stones, whilst to the south-east it had been extensively removed by the Period 5 robber trench (6320), its continuation only visible as a line of small stones in the base of this trench. A bone parchment pricker (9036) and pair of scissors (sf2483) were found associated with this internal wall.

The line of the south-western partition wall was visible only as a backfilled gully of Period 4 (6344*, Fig.366s) and a number of post-holes (only 6335* is shown on Fig.376s).

These internal partitions effectively divided Building 10 into three rooms, that to the north-east of division 6341/6374 containing spreads of mortar and limestone (7439*, Fig.368s) partially covered by sandy clays (7434*/7436*/7440*), which were overlain in turn by patches of burnt clay (7427, 7429). A second parchment pricker (8049) was found in these internal deposits. Immediately to the north-east of partition 6341*, the earlier (Period 1) deposit 6343 acted as a bedding for a patchily surviving mortar floor (6299*), contemporary with a tiled hearth (6302*, Fig.366s) set into a clay-filled construction trench.

To the south-west of the internal partition 6341 there was a 0·2m thick deposit of clay loam (6334*) containing large quantities of fired clay mould fragments, whilst to the south-west of the south-western internal partition there was a similar floor deposit containing moulds (6328*, Fig.366s) interleaved by a pure sand lens (6373, Fig.366s), extending across the full width of the building and occu-

Fig.208 *Area 13.X, Period 3: the north-west (6345) and south-west walls (6326) of Building 10, cut by the more substantial Building 27, looking south-east. Scale unit 0·5m*

pying its entire south-west bay. Pottery from these occupation deposits suggests that they may have built up during the second half of the 13th century.

Immediately after the construction of wall 6345, the Period 1 gully to the north-west of it (p.413) was partially backfilled, with a mixed sequence of fills of loams, clay moulds and organic materials (6358, 6361, 6363–4). A sample of a humic slightly clayey silt (6361) contained several predominantly small seeds, some fine, very pale, plant fragments, and a few assorted fly puparia and poorly preserved beetles (Hall et al. 1993a). There was evidence of some faecal contamination. The fill also included a fragment of a glass flask or urinal, or alembic dome (sf2561). Amongst the plants recorded were modest numbers of toad-rush seeds, consistent with deposition in a place with impeded drainage and perhaps some trampling or other disturbance. Layer 6358 contained a worked stone block (221) dated to before the 13th century on the basis of its tooling (AY 10/4). Deposit 6363 contained a cut halfpenny (AY 18/1, 81), probably deposited after c.1256. The latest pottery from these levels was of 13th century date.

Bedern Foundry (AY 10/3: Period 1, Phase 2)

In that part of the foundry site that was within the college precinct a succession of pits were cut into the Period 1 surface, although their plans were generally not recorded (4162 with fill 4161, 4163 with fills 4126–7/4255, 2624 with fills 2611–12, and pits 4194 and 4266, Fig.61, AY 10/3). The fills were characterised as compact silty amorphous peats, although they also contained several lenses of ash. Sometimes it was possible to identify a small proportion of yellow straw (in 4126) or fragments of leather and birch bark (in 2612). The animal bones from one fill (4127) were predominantly cattle rib fragments, plus cattle, sheep and horse mandibles. This may represent butchery debris, though the assemblage is rather small. The bone assemblage from a second pit (2624) was dominated by cattle and caprine (probably sheep) ribs, together with bird and fish bones. The bones were well preserved and show little abrasion; they can probably be attributed to in situ occupation debris.

Period 4: late 13th century (Fig.209)

During Period 4 there was continued expansion and development of the college buildings. Absolute dating for this activity is based only on the pottery, much of it falling within the same date range as the previous period. Clearly within a period of about 50 years there was a considerable amount of construction within the college.

In **Building 5** the process of subdivision continued, probably in an effort to create more living space, although the deposits resulting from occupation were not extensive. The south-east wing was divided by a long wall situated approximately 7m to the north-west of, and parallel to, the south-east end wall, creating a room at the south-east end of the building (Fig.377s). The area of the south-east room was partitioned by a number of insubstantial timber-framed walls. In that part of the room to the south-east of these walls there were deposits of loam more typical of accumulations found in an external environment, whilst to the north-west of the walls and running up to the new wall across the width of the building there

were floor deposits of ash and clay. One possible explanation for the difference in the nature of these deposits is that the south-east area of the room served as an earth-floored passageway with access to the outside at one end, although the disturbed nature of the walls and the many intrusions make it difficult to understand fully the arrangements at this end of the building.

Within the main body of Building 5 earlier walls linking the south-west arcade were replaced by more substantial ones, and a hard rubble surface floored the south-west aisle. The solid nature of these deposits is unlike those associated with living quarters and they may represent the floor of a storage or work area. In the central aisle a number of drains were constructed, but the lack of floor deposits again suggests that this area was not lived in. Indeed, most of the deposits within Building 5 at this time seem to be the result of only light occupation, except for more intensively used areas within the north-east aisle, where two new hearths were inserted, although the

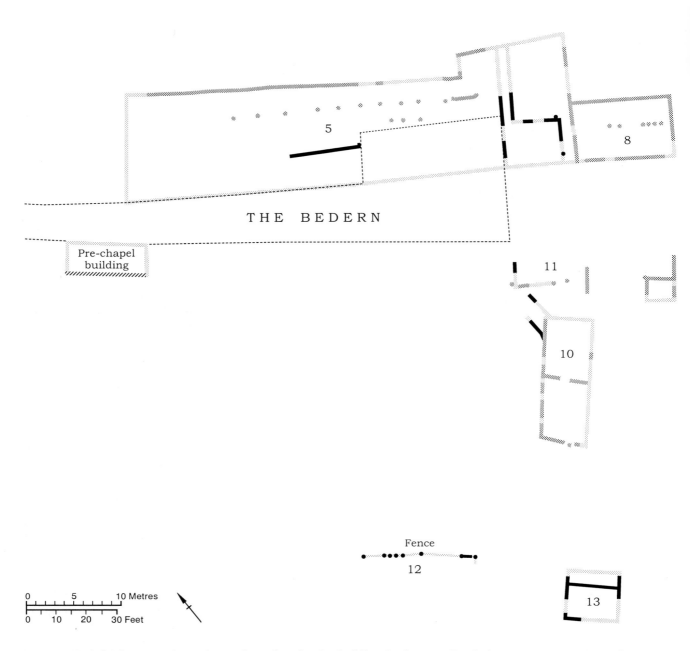

THE BEDERN

5

8

Pre-chapel
building

11

10

Fence

12

0   5   10 Metres

0   10   20   30 Feet

13

Fig.209 *Period 4: interpretative summary phase plan, showing building development. For the key, see Fig.195, p.409. Scale 1:400*

earlier hearth in the south-east wing was no longer used. As the new hearths were set into similar deposits they are thought to be contemporary, possibly separated into two different rooms by a light partition which did not survive in the archaeological record. The cess pits situated in the external yard north-east of Building 5 remained open and in use.

Once again, this period seems to show the trend towards domestic use, with the north-east aisle now being occupied. It appears that the remainder of the ground floor retained its storage function.

The small outhouse, Building 7, against the end of Building 5, was demolished, possibly to make way for a path which was now built against the north-east outside wall of **Building 8**. With use, this was gradually worn down and the worn areas were repaired with limestone gravel. A more complete re-surfacing of sandy loam and tile was added at a later date. Developments within Building 8 during Period 4 were confined to the insertion of a new clay floor, indicating continued occupation.

On the south-west side of Bedern Close there were a number of changes during Period 4. Building 9 was at least partially demolished, although the seven bays at the south-east end appear to have continued in use, as **Building 11** (Fig.380s). A new north-west wall was constructed, slightly offset to the north-west from the north-west internal partition wall of Building 9. Entry into this building was through an opening c.0·7m in width, situated towards the south-west end of this new wall and flanked on either side by a large padstone. A series of crushed limestone and clay deposits collected over the top of the demolished foundations of the earlier wall to create a threshold. A major drain now crossed the open area to the north-west of Building 11, and a pair of diagonal walls defined a passageway leading from the corner of the close to Building 10. Within **Building 10** the south-west partition wall was removed, effectively leaving the building divided into two equal halves in which new floor levels were laid.

That area of the site to the south-west of these buildings contained a depth of featureless clay loam, and was apparently a garden associated with the college, although it is possible that this area had not yet been acquired by the vicars (pp.390–1). At its south-westerly limit was an insubstantial structure, **Building 12**, possibly an agricultural building or enclosure, represented by a line of post-holes, some with the remains of posts, marking its north-east wall (Fig.378s).

Two parallel stone foundation sills crossing the long trench on a north-east/south-west line defined a timber-framed building, **Building 13**, 5m wide (north-west/south-east; Fig.378s). The west corner of this structure was excavated in the foundry site, with traces of internal floor levels. The north-east wall was beyond the north-east edge of the long trench, but since no trace of it was found in Area 13.X, Building 13 cannot have been more than 6m in length. An internal partition wall created two rooms.

The area along the north-east edge of the foundry site continued to be used for rubbish disposal and more pits were dug here during the late 13th century.

Bedern North-East (Fig.377s)

Building 5

The new internal wall (4020*) in the south-east wing of Building 5 divided it into two unequal parts. Four evenly spaced pits filled with cobbles and loam formed the foundations for this wall, the most south-westerly being the largest. Over these a mortar-bonded wall was built, two limestones in width, with padstones set along its length. The surviving section of this wall was approximately 7·5m in length, but 2·5m of the central portion had been removed by a modern intrusion. The north-east end appears to have terminated at the earlier (Period 2) linear feature (4471*), but could have continued to meet the north-east wall of Building 5.

Clay loam (4404, 4443) was deposited to the south-east, on top of which a new wall (4440*) was built. This new wall was constructed in three stretches. The first consisted of a 3m length of wall located 1m to the south-east of the partition (4020), running north-east/south-west from the projected line of the north-east aisle division. It was set in a shallow construction trench, and built of limestones bonded with mortar. At its south-west end it made a right-angled turn and the second stretch of wall ran in a north-west/south-east direction to a large padstone (4452*) sunk into pre-college deposits. Shortly after the construction of this wall, its south-east end was removed by a large pit (4439*), aligned north-east/south-west, measuring approximately 3 × 1m. This pit was later backfilled with a reddish clay, and over it was constructed a new south-east section (4442*). The wall continued south-west, incorporating two more padstones set into foundation pits (4435*, 4450*) before presumably joining up with the main south-west wall of Building 5. Associated with this entire wall was a complex sequence of internal ash and clay floors and external clay loams (4402, 4410, 4412–15, 4417–18, 4424–5, 4427, 4433, 4437, 4460) which, because of later intrusions, had been much disturbed, as had the wall itself. With the construction of these new walls, the Period 3 hearth (4166) presumably went out of use.

A number of spreads were laid down within Building 5. A dark loam (4434) butted against the south-east wall (4441). This was partially covered by mortar (4432) and then by a loam spread (4428). A small square feature of flat-laid tiles (4431) was built to the west of the Period 2 wall (4477) in the north.

Within the main body of Building 5, the Period 3 wall dividing off the south-west aisle (1674) was replaced by a more substantial 7m length of wall (1542*, 1571*, Fig.365s), disturbed by a later (Period 6) robber trench (1667*) and subsequent intrusion. The new wall was set onto a construction spread of mortar and limestone chippings which was deposited on top of the Period 2 wall (1674), completely sealing the upper surfaces of the padstones. The new wall was built from small, mortar-bonded, roughly squared limestone blocks. The area to the south-west of this new wall was covered by an extensive rubble spread (1619), which in turn was overlain by a clay spread (1605). An area to the south-east of this latter deposit, although totally isolated stratigraphically by later intrusions, appears to have consisted of similar deposits, the first of these being a spread of clay loam (1650). This was cut by a shallow linear feature edged with tiles on its north-east side (1651*) running north-west to south-east, at least 3·6m long and 0·5m wide, filled with limestone, mortar and tile chippings.

In the centre of Building 5, to the north-east of the new wall (1542/1571), an extensive clay loam (1668, Fig.365s) was deposited, into which was cut a shallow pit (1673) with a backfill of ashy clay. A cut farthing from a long cross penny, dated 1247–72 (AY 18/1, 84), was found in the pit fill, which confirms the general late 13th century date obtained from the pottery for this period. Also cut into the loam, parallel to and 1·2m north-east of the wall, was a drain (1664*), 4·4m long and 0·3m wide, consisting of an irregular double line of small limestones set in a shallow clay-packed construction trench. Fragments of roof tile surrounding and overlying portions of the drain were probably all that remained of a capping. Silty deposits containing snail shells filled the gully and spread over the backfill of the construction trench. This drain was possibly a replacement for the Period 3 drain (1747) situated further to the north-west.

Associated with this feature, and running east from a point 1·8m from the north-west end of it, was a soakaway (1665*), approximately 3m in length. This comprised a trench with a V-shaped cross-section, its sides lined at one point with several roof tile fragments. A single course of large unbonded limestones and cobbles covered by a second course of smaller unbonded limestones and cobbles had been placed into this trench. At the east end, the stones were replaced by a single, curved ridge tile resting on its edges. Beneath this tile was a sandy clay silt fill containing snail shells, eggshell, and traces of fig, weld and dyers' rocket seeds (Hall et al. 1993c). The soakaway terminated in a shallow circular pit at its east end (1709*), 0·3m in diameter and 0·1m deep, containing a fill of tile and limestone rubble in a clay loam.

In the vicinity of these features was a burnt clay loam (1638), several tile and limestone rubble dumps (1648, 1653, 1666*), and a deposit of crushed limestone (1652).

At the south-east end of Area 14.II there was a rectangular stone-lined pit (1691*), 1·8 × 0·8m, constructed from clay-bonded limestone blocks, and excavated to a depth of 0·15m. The only fills comprised lensed ash and white lime mortar. This pit appears to have been built against the interior of the north-east wall of Building 5, but modern intrusions had disturbed the exact relationship.

Towards the north-west end of Building 5 there were two extensive spreads of silty loam flecked with charcoal (1550–1) overlying the Period 3 cobbling (1549). Two hearths composed of pitched tiles were set into shallow construction trenches backfilled with clay. One of the hearths (1539) lay partly under the north-west edge of the excavation; the other (1548*) was set approximately 3m further south-east, but had been largely destroyed by a later pit. Each was sealed by a thick layer of ash and charcoal. Layers of silty clay (1678, 1682, 1745, Fig.365s) appear to represent associated occupation levels, although they did not define clear room divisions. The exterior area to the north-east of Building 5, containing several pits, remained unchanged in this period.

With the demolition of Building 7 an external pathway was laid north-east of Building 8. Initially a layer of sandy loam (4458) was spread as a foundation level; it was then covered by a tile and limestone spread (4423*). During Period 4 the path was resurfaced with a limestone spread (4419). Overlying this was another deposit of sandy loam and tile (4411). Meanwhile, within Building 8, a mixed clay loam (4416) was deposited, butting against the plaster face of the south-east wall (4420), and filling a shallow depression in front of the wall. This was overlain by a layer of clay with crushed brick (4409) and a layer of clay and mortar (4405). Finally, an extensive floor deposit of clay (4401) was laid down, apparently contemporary with the exterior loam and tile (4411) to the north-east.

Bedern South-West

Building 11 (Fig.378s)

During Period 4, clay (7486, Fig.368s) was deposited within Building 9, the Period 3 forerunner of Building 11, covering deposits 7494 and 7495, sealing the edges of hearth 7526 and covering the line of the internal wall 7558, signalling its disuse. In its place wall (7337*) was constructed as a new north-west external wall (only a short length is shown on Fig.378s) and Building 11 was created. This wall was offset to the north-west of the earlier wall 7558, and was composed of limestone blocks bonded with clay and mortar. A gap of c.0·7m was left to the south-west, probably as an entrance, with a large padstone flanking either side (not illustrated).

The ridge left covering the now-demolished wall 7558 formed a threshold to the entrance into Building 11, and against its inner face were a series of deposits, starting with a spread of mortar and crushed limestone (7483). This was overlain by finely crushed limestone (7482) which in turn was covered by clay (7480).

The position of the new south-west wall is unclear, although it may have followed the line of the south-west aisle, represented by the row of Period 3 post-pads (7521).

An external deposit of mixed rubble and loam (7588*, Figs.369–70s) now covered the earlier levels outside the new north-west wall. A bone thread-reel (8021, AY 17/12) was found in this dump. This deposit was cut by a partially tile-lined drain (7511*, Fig.370s) running north-east/south-west. The north-east end of the drain led off from an elongated pit (7506*) whilst the south-east end ran into the edge of excavation. Its top edges were defined by linear bands of clay, perhaps packing for the upper edges of the lining tiles. The drain incorporated a re-used limestone shaft fragment (255), dated to the 13th century (AY 10/4). It cut through the south-west wall of Building 9 (Period 3), further indicating its disuse.

To the south-west there was an ash layer (7500) with two post-holes cut into it, covered by silty and ashy clays (7497, Fig.368s; 7498, Figs.368s, 370s). A loam spread (7287), in which a crucible (sf2909) was found, levelled the Period 3 pit 7606.

A pair of north–south walls were constructed across the area north of Building 10, cutting across the Building 9 foundations and forming a passageway to Building 10. The first wall (7538*) was built from a large padstone in Building 10's north-west wall (6345) in a northerly direction, the north end being apparently destroyed by later activity. This wall was set onto the Period 2 mortar (7547), and was constructed from limestone blocks and broken tiles packed with clay. Post-dating its construction were a series of mixed clay spreads and pits filled with broken tiles and clay (7366, 7369, 7488, 7503, 7528, 7530, 7543, 7553). A second wall, forming the east side of the passage (7489*), ran southwards from Building 11, although not actually joining it; its southern extent was masked by a modern intrusion. A spread of limestones with cobbles bonded with the earlier clay (7499, Fig.370s) butted against the west face of this wall, and was covered by deposits of sandy clay (7441, 7502, Fig.370s). Patches of mortar (7437) spread either side of the wall, over these deposits, were in turn overlain by silty clays (7400, 7438, Fig.370s, 7416, Fig.370s). In the angle between wall 7489 and Building 11 was a sequence of deposits: silty loam (7493, Fig.368s), clay (7490), charcoal spread (7433) and clay (7430, Fig.368s).

Building 10

As noted above, the removal of the south-west partition inside Building 10 left a small gully (6344*, Fig.366s) which was immediately backfilled with sand (6333, Fig.366s). The north-east partition (6341) was retained, however, and so Building 10 was now apparently divided into two halves. In the south-western half a clay floor (6339, Fig.366s) overlay the gully; it was later covered by a patch

of mortar (6332*), itself overlain by a mixed level of clay and occupation debris (6329, Fig.366s) and finally sealed by a burnt clay loam (6318, Fig.366s). The north-western half of the Period 3 floor make-up containing clay moulds (6328, Fig.366s) was now overlain by an extensive deposit of clay (63148, Fig.366s). These earlier floor levels were cut by a clay-filled depression (6313*), a stake-hole (6316*), a shallow post-hole (6312*) and a shallow pit with a fill of limestone rubble in loam (6315*). Those flooring deposits to the north-east of the central partition continued in use. The mortar floor (6299) was now covered by an ashy floor deposit (6301*, Fig.366s), derived from continued use of the Period 3 hearth (6302, Fig.366s). Pottery from these layers is consistent with their deposition during the late 13th century.

The external area north-west of Building 10 was cut by several intercutting pits (6346, 6348, 6350–5) and a shallow gully (6349). These were rapidly backfilled with a uniform clay loam, mortar and tile, and then sealed by a loam spread (6342) containing a stone mould (sf2628), a fragment of a yellow, high-lead, glass jug (sf2632), a glass hanging lamp base (sf2537) and glass slag (sf2630).

Building 12 (Fig.378s)

In the south-west part of the site the garden soil was cut by a series of post-holes (5509–15* and 5516–17), most of which survived only as rectangular post stains, but at least two of which had fragmentary post remains and some remaining fill. It is thought that these post-holes were part of a structure, also represented by a fragment of walling to the south-east on the same alignment (not numbered), which may mark the position of a stone threshold. These features defined a structure at least 12m in length, although its interior was mostly outside the excavation and there were no discernible internal deposits surviving. The lack of any substantial wall footings or floor levels suggests that Building 12 may simply represent some fenced enclosure within the open ground to the south-west of the college, possibly for keeping pigs, or for some other undefined agricultural purpose.

Bedern long trench

Building 13 (Fig.378s) was built over the earlier (Period 1–2) deposits. A substantial mortared stone ashlar wall (1572*, Fig.364s), up to 0·45m wide and up to 0·4m deep, ran north-east/south-west across the trench. There was a parallel wall (1603*, Fig.364s) of mortared limestone, tile and brick, c.5m to the south-east. Joining these two walls and running north-west/south-east along the axis of the trench was an internal partition wall which had been heavily robbed. For most of its length the robber trench (1602*) was the only trace, but at the north-west end there was a stub of mortared limestone wall (1574*) butting against 1572. The earlier loam dumps were also cut by a pit (1619).

Bedern Foundry (pp.163–6, Fig.61, *AY* 10/3: Period 2)

In the east corner of the foundry site the west corner of Building 13 was excavated, defined by a stretch of mortared and tile-coursed wall footing (2943, Fig.61, *AY* 10/3), approximately 1·5m long × 0·2m wide. There were traces of timber uprights (4152) set into the top of this foundation. The wall had been built in a construction trench (2958, 4074), 0·1m wider than the wall, and 0·1m in depth, with a 45° slope. The return wall was presumably on the same line as the Period 5 rebuild (2956, p.447) which had destroyed all traces of it. A clay floor surface (2941) was revealed to the north-east of this wall, generally 0·1m thick, and with mortar and charcoal flecks. It was overlain by an occupation deposit of grey silt (2940).

To the north-west a large pit (4112, Fig.62, *AY* 10/3) had been cut into the extensive silt and peat backfilling within the earlier downslope (4245, p.413). During Period 4 it was filled with a succession of silty structured peats (4112A–K). Towards the end of this period it was fully backfilled and levelled with dark grey silts containing wood, leather and tile, and mortar and cobble rubble (4072, Fig.62, *AY* 10/3).

A second large pit (2661) extending to the edge of the excavation, may also have been filled in Period 4, although the pottery suggests that its basal fill (2702), at least, was deposited during Period 2 or 3. It was backfilled with successive layers of compacted peats and silts (2666–8, 2701) including, within the upper fill, a fragment of worked stone capital (*152*), probably of the first half of the 12th century (*AY* 10/4). The fills also contained a number of textile fragments (sf1380, sf1381, sf1395).

During Period 4 this pit was cut by two further pits. Firstly, the Period 3 pit (4266, p.429) was recut by a second pit (2671) with peaty fills (2658, 2670, 2680, 2688). Analysis of a sample taken from one of the fills (2658) revealed the presence of human faecal material. This pit was subsequently cut by another large pit (2693), with clay fills (2685–7, 2689–90, 2699, 2724) containing further mould fragments, many large fragments of limestone and tile, and decayed timbers, including small branches. The pit had been capped with a rubbly clay seal (2690). A group of post-holes (2722, 2739, 2747, 2953–4) may represent the remains of a related superstructure.

Period 5: early 14th century (Fig.210)

Period 5 is marked by further internal alterations within existing buildings, and the construction of new buildings on the south-west side of Bedern Close. Many of the buildings were refloored; many of the floor layers identified resulted from the slow accumulation of deposits, either the debris from continual sweeping or the repair and patching of worn surfaces.

Building 5 was shortened by 7m with the demolition of the south-east part of the south-east wing down to foundation level, the nature of the timber framing apparently allowing this rather drastic change to take place without much effect on the rest of the structure. An internal wall constructed during Period 4 became the new south-east end wall. Mention in the documents of the payment of 8s made in

1328–9 for the 'stopping up of the wall of the great hall with stone' may refer to the construction of this wall.

Previous occupation in Building 5 had mostly been confined to areas within the north-east and south-west aisles; these early divisions were now all removed and new rooms laid out. Clear remains of three new rooms (5A, 5B and 5C) were found, one with a hearth, another with a possible latrine pit. Although modern intrusions had removed most traces of possible further rooms in the south-west aisle, the presence of hearths and floors suggests that the central aisle was occupied for the first time during this period. Connecting the two side aisles was an internal diagonal passageway, confirming that the central space was now occupied.

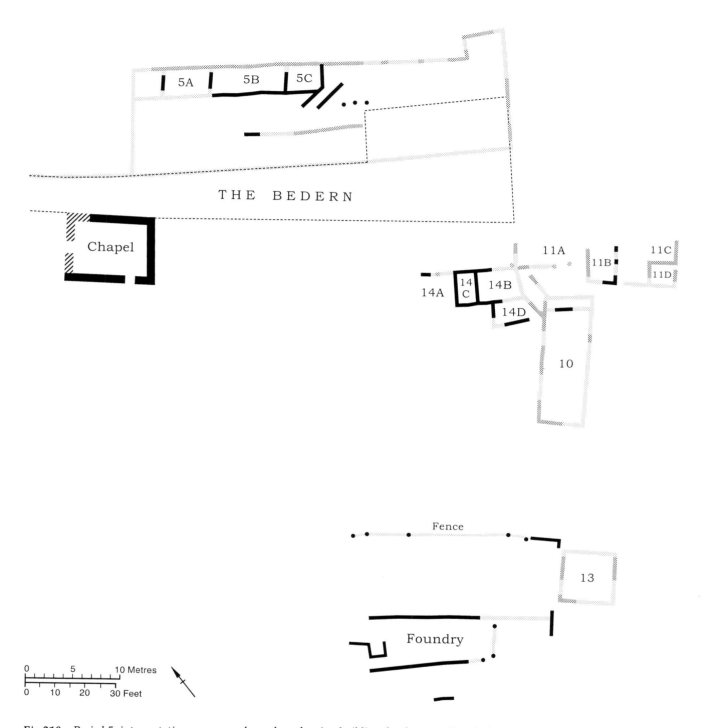

Fig.210   Period 5: interpretative summary phase plan, showing building development. For the key, see Fig.195, p.409. Scale 1:400

At the same time Building 8, attached to the south-east end of the south-east wing, was demolished as part of the same process. Shortly after the demolition of Building 8, a drain was constructed through the area, passing through the south-east end wall of

Building 5 before turning 90° internally and heading for the south-west wall. The drain was formed from a trench, the sides of which were lined with lime-stone blocks. A sand bedding was placed in the channel between these blocks and covered with a lining

435

of broken roof tiles, the whole structure being capped with large limestones spanning the entire width of the construction. At the south-east end of the drain there was a soakaway. The drain's course through the building may have been dictated by the need for internal inlets.

After the demolition of the pre-chapel building, a larger structure, c.9m (north-west/south-east) × 6m was erected. This is interpreted as the first **chapel** (pp.441–2).

To the south-west of Bedern Close Building 11 continued in use but there was a new complex of buildings to the south-west, following the disuse of the external drain. In **Building 11** (Fig.380s) the internal threshold floor levels were cut by the construction trench for a new hearth of unusual design in that bricks had been set on edge around its perimeter, with the centre being formed of pitched tiles in clay. The most common type of flooring material in this building was an extensive silty loam. Evidence was found for a second internal Room, 11B, with a mortar floor, defined by a beam trench for a possible north-west/south-east partition on the south-west side, and some roughly aligned limestone blocks at right-angles to this. At a later stage Room 11B underwent small-scale structural alterations in the form of a rebuild of the south corner. There were also at least two rooms, 11C and 11D, at the south-east end of the building. At the end of Period 5 Building 11 was disused, as indicated by the deposition of a spread of clay which covered many of the wall foundations and the floors.

Building 14 was a small timber-framed building of a length greater than 9·5m and a width of c.4m (Fig.380s). It was set back from the line of Bedern as it was by the post-medieval period suggesting that the close must have been wider in the 14th century. Building 14 was initially divided into two rooms, 14A and 14B, by a limestone-founded wall of the usual padstone construction. Its south-west and north-east walls contained padstones located directly opposite each other in at least the south-east room (Room B), and there was evidence for an entrance in the north-east wall, flanked by two padstones, with an associated tiled threshold. A slightly later subdivision of Room B at a point one bay to the south-east of the internal wall may have formed an entrance vestibule, Room 14C, which had a hearth set against the south-west wall of the building.

Rooms 14B and 14C underwent several small alterations, one of which saw the eventual removal of the partition wall by a shallow trench subsequently filled with a patchy mortar spread forming a floor level for this part of the building. The history of Room 14A is much simpler, or so it would seem from the evidence, in that a patchy mortar spread was all that survived of the internal layers.

The function of this building can only be guessed at, given the paucity of diagnostic finds. However, once more, the presence of a hearth and floor levels points to a residential use. The fragment of a stone quern found in one of the floor levels may also be evidence for the building's function.

At the southern corner of Building 14 was a fourth room, 14D, of unusual shape, being constrained by the need to maintain the diagonal passageway from the corner of the close to Building 10, which formed its south-east wall. The south-west wall was built first, with foundations of clay-bonded cobbles and limestone. The north-west wall was built next and the north-east wall was the south-west wall of Room 14B. Although oddly shaped and small in size, measuring only c.5 × 2m at its widest points, Room 14D contained a well-defined mortar floor cut by the clay-packed construction trench for a substantial pitched tile hearth.

There was an open ditch outside Building 14 to the south-west, presumably associated with the drainage of the area surrounding the buildings.

Building 10 underwent structural alterations during Period 5, probably necessitated by the subsidence of the padstone situated at its west corner which apparently rolled south-west pulling part of the walls with it. To rectify this situation the length of wall running south-west from the probable doorway in the north-west wall, and the entire south-west wall, were dismantled, and replacement walls were built in a new construction trench. These walls were set on similar foundations of limestone and cobbles, with evidence for the timber-framing in the form of limestone block settings.

These changes to the exterior walls of the building were matched by internal alterations which involved the dismantling of the remaining partition and its replacement with a more substantial dividing wall founded on limestone blocks further to the north-east. This resulted in the creation of a narrow passage on the north-east side of the building and a large open room to the south-west (Fig.380s). The floor levels of this building consisted largely of spreads of mortar, clay and loam, as well as several laminated occupation deposits.

The earlier hearth was replaced by a new hearth situated further to the north-east, of the usual pitched tile construction. This coincided with the removal of levels in the south-west part of Building 10 to create a depression which was then filled with clay to bring the floor surface up to that further to the north-east. Contemporary with these alterations was a circular spread of clay interpreted as a standing place for a brazier, and a light screens passage against the south-west wall of the building. A small semi-circular area of cobbles ringed by pitched tiles, interpreted as a standing for a barrel, was located against the north-west wall. Various spreads of limestone rubble and disturbed burnt deposits within Building 10 indicate intermittent building work throughout Period 5.

The loam deposits outside Building 10 were now once more cut by pits and gullies, perhaps for the continuing drainage of these external areas. The picture is one of the fairly rapid backfilling and then redigging of these features throughout this period, with the backfills containing a mixture of window and vessel glass.

During Period 5 Building 12 was replaced by a **fence line** on the same alignment, but apparently extending further to the south-east, with an overall length of c.22m (Fig.380s). This fence line was represented by a series of components including a linear spread of clay, limestone post-pads set over clay-filled pits, post-holes, some of which contained the remains of wooden posts, and post-settings. This fence is presumed to be that described as being behind the latrine and between Bedern and the land of the priory of Newburgh in documents of the early 14th century (pp.576–7). The documentary sources suggest that the upright posts supported boarding daubed with clay. There was archaeological evidence for a well-built wall with a foundation of cobbles, broken tiles and limestone blocks packed with clay joining the fence to the north-west wall of Building 13. The fact that the post-holes were dug from apparently different levels points to a certain amount of replacement

of the timber posts, well testified in the documentary sources which suggest it needed repair at least once every ten years (p.577). To the south-west of the fence line rubbish disposal and pit-digging continued to take place in the open yard area north-east of the foundry.

To the north-east of the south-east end of this fence was a small outhouse, **Building 15**, its outer walls represented only by two post-pads. The interior levels consisted of a hearth and an associated clay floor. The hearth was apparently short-lived, being quickly covered by clay loam deposits which were subsequently cut by several cess pits, all containing a similar fill of clay loam and peat, some with pieces of timber. All these pits intercut one another and this points to a fairly long period of redigging and re-use. It is possible to estimate that there were at least three pits in use at any one time. It is likely that Building 15 was constructed specifically to house cess pits and it is presumably to be identified as the latrine described as being in front of the garden fence in records of the early 14th century (p.577).

Also in the garden area north-east of the fence line there were more intercutting cess pits with fills of peat, loam and rotted straw, containing a quantity of shoe leather. These pits appear to have been sited in the open air.

Further to the south-west, the area along the north-east edge of the foundry site continued to be occupied by rubbish pits. **Building 13** was partially rebuilt in the same position, although there was no evidence for this in the long trench to match the new wall defined in the east corner of the foundry site. The internal partition, however, does appear to have been removed in this period (Fig.380s).

A substantial building was erected in approximately the centre of the foundry site (p.166, Fig.68, AY 10/3). Its north-east wall appears to have marked the boundary of the college precinct in this and subsequent periods. The wall was built from mortared ashlar blocks, with an outer face of two or three courses with larger facing stones set at the base. The care taken with the external appearance of this wall presumably reflects the fact that it faced onto the college property. Despite its elaborate foundations, however, it suffered from major structural instability (p.167, AY 10/3) and toppled over to the north-east along its whole length (see Fig.219, p.447). This instability appears to have been principally caused by the fact that it was built over a slope in the underlying ground surface (p.413).

Bedern North-East (Fig.379s)

Building 5

At the far south-east end of Building 5, the original (Period 2) south-east wall (4441) was demolished down to foundation level and a spread of limestone rubble (4430*) scattered on either side, overlain by loam (4429). The Period 4 L-shaped wall (4440) inserted between the end wall (4441) and the internal wall (4020) was also demolished; deposits of ash and clay were placed over the remaining foundations in an attempt to level the area. A pit cutting these deposits (4397*) was filled with limestone and cobble and could have served as a soakaway. The former internal wall (4020) became the south-east end wall of the new building. The north-east and south-west outer walls, and the south-west aisle wall, seem to have survived unchanged.

At the same time as the shortening of Building 5, the interior was also undergoing alteration. An extensive

Fig.211   Area 14.II, Period 5: Building 5, looking south-east. Scale unit 0·5m

spread of clay loam (1560, Fig.365s, 1586, 1595–6, 4200) covered and levelled the previous internal surfaces, forming a raised construction level for a variety of new features within the building. One of the first of these was an internal passage formed by two parallel walls running diagonally across the central aisle. The north-east ends of these two walls rested on Period 2 padstones (1704, 1685) of the north-east aisle. The north-western passage wall (unnumbered, but shown on Fig.379s) survived as a linear scatter of stones some 3m in length; the south-eastern wall (1625*) consisted of small unbonded limestone blocks. A limestone spread (1626*) abutted the south-east side of the wall. Limestone chippings and loam (1584*) between these two walls formed a hard surface. This passageway appears to have linked the north-east and south-west aisles, although its south-western continuation did not survive. At its north-east end was a possible wooden structure represented by several post-holes (1567–8).

A new line of post-pads (1587*) was built within the central aisle and formed a further internal division to the north-west of, and continuing the line of, the earlier arrangement of post-pads there. This new line comprised three evenly spaced post-pads and ran for a length of 3·8m. Each post-pad had been set in a shallow construction pit cutting the deposits within the building, and in all three cases the pits had been packed with tile and limestone set in clay. Other new features included a shallow circular pit (1645) filled with loose tile and rubble, a clay-filled gully (1628, Fig.365s) and a post-hole (1607).

Later alterations inside Building 5 involved the construction of a rough limestone wall (1465*/1484*) connecting some of the post-pads along the north-east aisle, leading to the creation of at least three rooms (Fig.211). Although the central portion of the wall had been removed by modern intrusions it was clear that it had been set in a shallow construction trench (1516*) packed with clay. At the north-west end of this trench there were two large circular post-holes (1513*, 1514*). At the south-east end of the construction trench, a new post-pad (1689) was inserted between the two Period 2 aisle post-pads and the wall (1484) turned through 90° to form a return running towards the north-east outer wall of Building 5. The new wall-line cut the internal deposits, but appears to have been constructed over a clay levelling deposit (1546, 1606) which became a floor level and was cut by a square pit (1639).

The space between the outer and internal walls was then divided into the three rooms, 5A, 5B and 5C, by two partition walls. Between Rooms 5A and 5B the partition survived as a 2·2m length of limestone cobbles (1458*) within a shallow clay-packed construction trench. Between Rooms 5B and 5C it was represented by a slot (1483*) surviving to a length of 2·1m, its junction with the north-east wall having been removed by modern intrusions. It joined the south-west wall at a post-pad, with a possible continuation to the south-west represented by a scatter of loose edge-set tiles and limestones (1517*). There was a post-hole (1512*) at the north-east end of 1483.

Within Room 5A, a light brown clay (1471) abutted the outer wall. The earlier hearth (1539) was sealed beneath a thick deposit of ash and charcoal (1457). The remaining area of Room 5A was covered by a sandy clay (1453*) flecked with mortar and charcoal. This sandy clay was cut by a linear slot (1400*), aligned north-east/south-west, which may have represented the remains of a wall which partitioned Room 5A from another room to the north-west.

Within Room 5B a series of internal layers were deposited: a loam (1472), covered by a clay layer (1473*) which was in turn sealed by a layer of limestone chippings (1474*, 1475*). Cut into the south-east part of the limestone deposit was a rectangular pit (1459*), 1·2 × 0·8m. The original fill did not survive, but this pit may have served as a cess pit, later to be backfilled with limestones and cobbles. The limestone chippings were then sealed by a clay loam occupation level (1480).

Within Room 5C there was an extensive charcoal-flecked clay floor (1486*, Fig.365s) but there were no associated internal structures.

A similar division into internal rooms cannot be traced at the south-east end of Building 5. A spread of sandy loam, cobbles and broken tile (4200*) was laid down in the vicinity of what remained of the south-east wing of the building. On the surface of this were large areas of ash. There were associated clay spreads (4199), as well as later deposits of cobble, tile and loam.

Within the south-west aisle of Building 5, similar room divisions may have been made, using the upstanding (Period 4) aisle wall (1542/1571). This wall may have been extended to the north-west at this time as shown by a linear clay-filled foundation slot (1495*) on a similar alignment.

The south-west aisle lay largely outside the area of excavation, but a few clay and loam floor deposits were recorded in the south-eastern part. In a small area at least three phases of use were discerned, the earliest represented by various occupation deposits (1630, 1635–6, 1640–4, 1647, 1649), some spreading beyond the projected line of the south-west aisle, indicating that at least some of these chambers must have been open on this side. The isolated nature of these deposits makes it impossible to assign them to specific rooms within the south-west aisle.

The next event in this part of the building, in the south-east corner of Area 14.II, was the digging of a pit (1629*),

c.1m in diameter, which was later filled with limestone chippings and some sandstone blocks, but may have originally functioned as a latrine pit. It was sealed by a mortary loam (1627*) which is interpreted as an occupation level, covered by a clay loam floor (1624*). At the north-west end of this stratigraphic island the corresponding layers are a dark loam (1623) and an ashy loam (1622*) on which a pitched tile hearth (1489) was constructed. Associated with this hearth was a burnt clay layer (1490) and a thick spread of wood ash (1491). At a slightly later date, another pit (1634*) measuring 0·9m in diameter and 0·6m in depth, later filled with clay and tile rubble, was cut through the loam floor (1624). Towards the end of Period 5 this floor fell into disuse and a padstone (1618*) was placed on a line with the south-west aisle wall further to the north-west.

Alterations within the central aisle had been extensively disturbed by modern intrusions, although there were traces of a possible floor level (1493*) at the north-west end. A drain ran down the centre of the building, represented by a disturbed line of tile and stone (1494*) running parallel to the outer walls for a distance of approximately 3m. A knife with a pattern-welded blade (sf492) was found in the drain. An extensive floor (1580*, 1389) was deposited north-east of the drain, containing a possible post void (1579*).

South-west of the diagonal passageway in the centre of Building 5 was a hearth (1611*) consisting of a shallow scoop filled with pitched tiles bonded with clay, and measuring 0·8 × 0·6m overall. Surrounding it was a thin spread of clay (1612*), and worn into its upper surface was a slight hollow filled with ash (1613*).

To the south-east of this hearth was a spread of clay loam and charcoal (1610) covered by a clay spread (1588). This in turn was overlain by a compact deposit of limestone chippings (1544*), 3m × 1m, laid down parallel to and abutting the south-west side of the central padstones (1587*). The clay spread and limestone deposit laid over it each contained a very large number of pottery sherds, over 5,000 in total (see p.402). These apparently represented a large group of jugs, including many seconds, which had been smashed, but many of which could be reconstructed. Although the jugs can be closely dated to the mid–late 13th century, their deposition in the early 14th century is not considered problematic, as they are interpreted as a group which was dumped in a single operation. Context 1544 also contained an inlaid knife blade.

After the demolition of the southern diagonal passageway wall (1625), a clay loam flecked with mortar (1583) was deposited north-east of the wall padstones, covering the passageway foundations. This in turn was covered by a similar deposit consisting of clay (1543*) containing patches of mortar (1570).

Fig.212 *(left) Area 14.IV, Period 5: drain 4016 with capstones removed, looking north-west. Scale unit 0·1m*

Fig.213 *(above) Area 14.IV, Period 5: drain 4396, looking south with blocking stone in situ. Scale unit 0·1m*

In the external area to the north-east of Building 5 the earlier deposits were partly covered by a spread of loam with tile (4383) as well as by loam and mortar (4379).

A stone-built, capped drain (4016*) was built through the south-east wall (4020) of Building 5 and cut silt (4400), silty clay (4399*), and various ash spreads (4403, 4406*, 4408*). 4406 was cut by a small pit (4407*) filled with limestone and cobble. The drain was set into a trench, lined with limestone blocks (Fig.212). Sand bedding was then placed in the channel between these blocks, onto which was set a base lining of broken roof tiles. The whole was then capped with large limestones which spanned the entire width of the structure. This stone-built drain ran north-east for c.3m from the south-west edge of the excavation, before making a right-angled turn to the south-east through the end wall of Building 5 and continuing for approximately 10m parallel to the edge of the excavation. Analysis of the moist, slightly clayey, sand fill revealed traces of a wide range of materials, including eggshell,

fish bone and scale, mammal and bird bone, mussel shell and ostrocods, indicating the presence of standing water cr of the incorporation of fresh water into the fill (Hall et al. 1993c). A pit (4377*), later backfilled with clay and ash, marked the south-east extent of this drain, and may have served as a soakaway. A small external side drain (4396), consisting of a short trench lined on its sides with roof tiles and flat limestones (Fig.213), led into the main drain from a small pit. At some later stage this trench was blocked with a limestone block, and the side drain was backfilled with clay.

Immediately after the construction of the drain, a spread of ashy clay (4344) was deposited over its construction spread, and various clay spreads were laid down in its vicinity, including rubble (4367), sandy silt (4376), ash (4333) and clay (4331, 4356–8, 4364, 4366, 4368, 4378). A number of other clay and sandy clay spreads (4380–1, 4385, 4387, 4390–1, 4394, 4398*) were also deposited within Building 5 during this period.

Bedern Chapel (Figs.214–16; see also Fig.232, facing p.472)

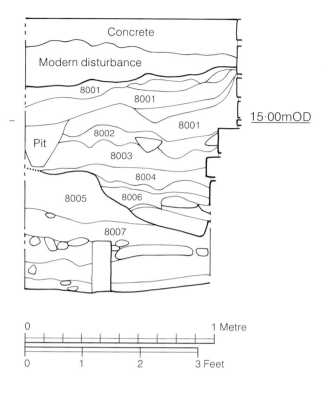

Fig.214 Bedern Chapel: section along sides of external trench showing foundation deposits. Scale 1:20

As the present chapel building was to be left standing undisturbed, only the backfill of the foundation trenches on the inside of the standing walls was excavated.

In the case of the north-east wall layers of cobbles (9098, Fig.232b) and sandy clay (9087, Fig.232b–c) were laid in the bottom of the construction trench for the north-east wall. The north-east wall was then built using rough unfaced masonry (on the inside), its lower courses bonded with a mixture of clay and mortar. The construction trench was backfilled with a mixture of mortar (9089, Fig.232b), loam (9067, Fig.232b) and clay (9078, Fig.232b). This covered the foundation courses of the wall and some spread beyond the trench into the interior of the building.

The construction trench for the north-west wall was cut through the Period 2 mortar layers (9075, 9081). The first layer within the trench was a deposit of cobbles (9099, Figs.216, 232a); a gap in the centre probably indicates the location of a doorway (see Fig.313, p.551). 9099 was overlain by limestone chips and rubble (9091, Fig.232a), and mortar (9095, Fig.232a), in turn covered by mixed clay and loam (9088, 9090, both on Fig.232a). The stone wall itself (9083), of which stubs had been left at each side of the chapel after the extension to the north-west in Period 7 (see p.471), was then built over these packing layers. Ma-

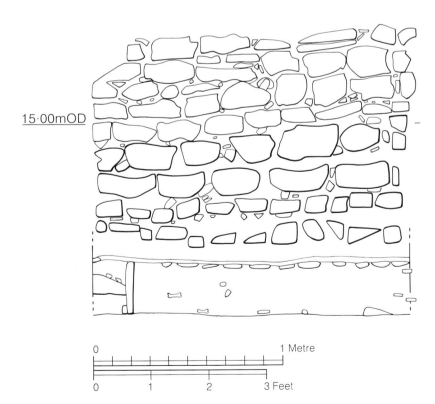

Fig.215 Bedern Chapel: elevation of the foundations of the south-west wall. Scale 1:20

Fig.216 *Bedern Chapel: north-west end, looking north-east, showing the Period 5 foundation of the north-west wall of the first chapel (9099). Scale unit 0.1m*

sonry from the south-west stub is shown on the right side of Fig.232a and mortar bedding on the left side.

Pottery from the construction trenches suggests the chapel was erected in the early 14th century.

In the trench excavated south-west of the chapel a dark organic loam (8005, Fig.214) overlying 8007 associated with the pre-chapel building may be contemporary with the chapel.

Bedern South-West

Building 11 (Fig.380s)

A deposit of clay (7477) covered the threshold area at the north-west end of Building 11 (see p.432) and spread further north-east on its inside. It was cut by a construction trench containing a hearth with a brick-on-edge perimeter (7474*), only three sides of which survived, with some evidence of pitched tiles in clay in the centre. Covering 7477 at the threshold, but also spreading across Room 11A, was an extensive deposit of silty loam (7465, Fig.368s).

To the south-east a second room, 11B, at least 3m × 4m, was constructed within Building 11. The Period 3 surface (7575) was covered by a loam (7561, Fig.370s) which produced a sizeable faunal sample, including a worked fallow deer bone. The nearby presence of rats is attested by the find of a single rat incisor (Hamshaw-Thomas 1994). This loam spread was then cut by a post-pit (7549*), later backfilled with clay containing mortar inclusions, and by a feature comprising two large limestone blocks (7570*) set into a shallow depression packed with clay. A short section of an internal wall (7560*) remained, consisting of small, irregular limestone blocks with tiles set onto the loam deposit 7561. Evidence for this wall-line also survived to the north-east as a small trench containing three limestone blocks packed with clay (7545*), one of which was a re-used shaft fragment (*163, AY* 10/4). Between these two surviving lengths of wall was a single remaining padstone (shown but not numbered on Fig.380s). The actual south corner, the junction between the south-east and south-west walls, was not present in its earliest build, but survived as an intrusive later rebuild. The south-west wall to Room 11B was represented only by two limestone blocks (7568*, Fig.370s) set into the earlier loam, whilst the north-east wall did not survive within the excavated area.

Inside Room 11B a deposit of mortar (7536*) on the north-east side was overlain by a series of very thin mortar deposits (7531*) which were also found further to the south-east. Within these deposits were a few limestone blocks forming an internal construction roughly aligned north-east/south-west. A lead pilgrim badge (sf2791) was also found in the mortar. A linear feature, possibly a beam slot, was then dug into 7531*, meeting wall trench 7560* at its south-east end.

Later in Period 5 Room 11B underwent small-scale rebuilding represented only by a later build of the south corner junction, consisting of three limestone blocks (7233*) set onto a rubble layer (7230*) which was dumped against a line of edge-set tiles resting against the face of wall 7568.

At the south-eastern end of Building 11 the latest phase of use was represented by a floor level (7130, Fig.370s) confined to the south-easternmost bay, into which was cut a single post-hole (7132*). A copper alloy jetton from 7130 (*AY* 18/1, *145*) dated to Edward II's reign (1307–27) confirms the pottery dating of this later usage. A seal matrix (sf2805) was also recovered from this layer.

The internal wall (7624), constructed in Period 3, now divided this bay into two rooms, 11C and 11D. Internal deposits to the south-west of wall 7624 consisted of contemporary clay spreads (7126*, 7131*) overlain by a series of thin and patchy ash, clay and loam layers (7116–17*, 7120, 7122*, 7123–4, 7125*, 7128). A jet bead (sf2542) was recovered from these levels. The pottery evidence for these internal deposits also gives a late 13th–early 14th century date. A similar sequence of internal deposits occurred to the north-east of wall 7624, made up of clay loams, ash and mortar (7134/7231, 7224*, 7258–60, 7266*–7, 7269–70, 7273). A sample from one of these floor levels (7224) yielded a few plant remains, most of them weeds of waste ground and cultivated soils; coal and cinder were quite common, together with moderate amounts of charcoal and mammal, bird and fish bone, fish scale, and traces of shellfish and eggshell (Hall et al. 1993a). A parchment pricker (*8037*) and a bone die (*8077*) were found in these deposits (*AY* 17/12).

Between Rooms 11B and 11C/D there was an L-shaped area which does not appear to have been lived in but may have served as an access passageway. To the south-east of Building 11 there were external loam deposits (7216).

At the end of Period 5 Building 11 was disused, as indicated by a spread of clay (7525) which covered Room 11B and backfilled the foundation trenches of its partition walls. This was then covered by ashy loams (7338–9). Subsequently, new buildings were erected across Rooms 11A and 11B, although the plan of Rooms 11C and 11D may have been incorporated into Building 18 in Period 6.

Building 14 (Figs.217, 380s)

The north-east wall (7551*, Fig.369s) of Building 14 was built from limestone blocks and contained regularly spaced padstones, except at the north-west end of the south-east part where the padstone at the corner with wall 7487* was only separated from the next to the south-east by two limestone blocks. These two padstones were set onto pits (as were most of the others) filled with limestone blocks and supported by wooden piles. Only two limestone blocks

Fig.217 *Area 13.X, Period 5, looking north-west, with Building 11 on the right and Building 14 upper centre. Scale unit 0·5m*

remained of the far north-west part of this wall, although the spread of limestone blocks (7601) from Period 3 appeared to have been left exposed and re-used in this new building.

The south-west wall (7374*) survived as a foundation of limestone and cobbles above which were three equally spaced padstones set in clay, matching those on the north-east wall. The north-west wall of Building 14 lay outside the area of excavation, and no evidence survived for a south-east wall.

An internal partition (7487) appears to have divided Building 14 into two rooms, 14A and 14B, the evidence suggesting that it consisted of a limestone wall bonded with clay, containing one central padstone. Clay construction deposits (7509, 7574) from the main building walls spread throughout Room 14B to the south-east. At some stage a further internal wall was built across the building, forming a central vestibule, 14C. This division removed a padstone in the north-east wall 7551, and left a depression (shown on Fig.380s, but not numbered) cut through 7509; no other evidence for its construction survived.

A silty ash (7478, Fig.369s) in this vestibule was overlain by a spread of broken roof tiles (7476*) in the north corner, covered by a spread of sand mixed with a gravelly mixture of mortar and limestone chippings (7472), probably comprising a threshold deposit for an entrance defined by a pair of padstones in the north-east wall (designated E on Fig.380s). Cutting the earliest internal deposits in the opposite side of this vestibule was a pitched tile hearth (7504*) bonded with clay.

During the life of Building 14 the clay loam backfill of the Period 4 drain cut 7511 slumped. Spreads of crushed clay moulds (7479*, 7468, 7470*) were employed to level up this clay and other depressions within Building 14. A small spread of clay (7467*) was deposited over 7468 and 7476 in the north-west bay of Room 14B, i.e. Room 14C, on top of which, and at the side of the original padstone in the centre of wall 7487, another padstone was placed.

The history of this building was one of several small, short-term changes to its interior. The next replanning involved the removal of the internal wall between Rooms 14B and 14C and the deposition of a patchy mortar spread (7459, Fig.369s) over a large portion of the interior of Rooms 14B and 14C, filling the robber trench left by the demolition of the wall. This mortar also covered the disused hearth 7504, and was eventually obscured by a thick spread of limestone rubble (7446, Figs.366s, 369s), confined to the north-west end.

In Room 14A, the construction deposit for the internal wall 7487 was covered by a thin spread of sand overlain by a mortar spread (7508), possibly equivalent to mortar 7459 in the south-east room.

Room 14D comprised a smaller outbuilding attached to the south-east corner of Building 14. Its south-west wall comprised a clay-bonded cobble and limestone wall (7501*) containing one group of two stacked padstones. The southeast end of this wall did not appear to survive in its initial build. A limestone and cobble wall (7461*), set onto a clay (7409) which was laid down immediately after the construction of wall 7374, was taken to be the north-west wall.

The first internal deposit in Room 14D was a spread of mortar (7453*) cut by the construction trench for a pitched tile hearth (7450*) packed with clay. A spread of charcoal (7448) partially covered the construction trench fill and was apparently one of the last use deposits associated with the hearth, which was then cut by a pit (7382*) with a clay fill. A heavily gnawed chicken bone from the pit fill demonstrates that domestic food refuse was readily accessible to rodent pests (Hamshaw-Thomas 1994).

Outside Room 14D, the diagonal passageway constructed in Period 4 was floored with cobbles and limestone fragments (7396*) partially covered by a spread of sandy clay (7385).

Building 10 (Fig.380s)

During Period 5 Building 10 underwent fairly extensive alterations, apparently caused by the subsidence of its western corner. At the same time as Building 14 was being constructed, a north-east/south-west ditch (7344*) was dug in order to improve drainage alongside the north-west wall (6345) of Building 10. A robber trench (6321*/6327) then removed much of the south-west wall and the south-west end of wall 6345. This robber trench was backfilled with clay, and fresh walls immediately set into a new construction trench (6321*), from which a variety of domestic refuse was recovered, including a parchment pricker (8050), a stone disc (sf2469) and a bone gaming counter (sf2487). The south-west end of the new north-west wall (6297*) survived as a double row of water-worn cobbles and small limestone blocks, although a Period 7 robber trench (6308) had removed its north-east end. A substantial limestone padstone was inserted c.1·9m from the corner, set into a deep foundation pit (6371*) packed with cobbles, tile fragments and clay loam. Three fragments of a yellow, high-lead glass jug (sf2617) were also excavated from this pit. Very little survived of the new south-west wall (6326*) which appeared to have been rebuilt around and over the original subsided padstone at the west corner of the building; here a few disturbed limestone cobbles were all that remained of this rebuild.

All Building 10 deposits had been cut through by the walls of a later (Period 7) structure (Building 27) resulting in an artificial division of the internal layers. At the north-east end of Building 10 a new internal wall (7419*) was set over a thin clay layer (7420), creating a narrow passageway. Both ends of this wall had been destroyed by later intrusions, but it was clear from the surviving length that its construction was of limestone blocks bonded with clay, set onto a spread of mortar the width of the wall. It is suggested that this strip of mortar was all that survived of the contemporary floor levels which had been removed from either side of the wall by later intrusions.

In the main room to the south-west there was a spread of loam associated with a newly constructed square hearth (7234*) of pitched tiles set in a construction pit and covered by spreads of mortar (7244) and charcoal (7250). An extensive clay deposit (7418, Fig.368s) with inclusions of ash, charcoal, tile, mortar and clay, spread down the north-west side of Building 10. This was partially overlain by a small spread of mortar (7262), itself covered by a spread of clay (7261).

At this same time a robber trench (6320*, Fig.366s) removed the Period 3 internal partition 6341, and was then filled with clay in preparation for the next sequence of internal levels, beginning with a series of thin, sandy clay silt layers (6300, Fig.366s), the uppermost of which showed evidence of burning. Two rush species were recorded in samples from these floors, along with moderate amounts of charcoal, fish bone and sand, and traces of other occupation debris, including mammal bone, eggshell, coal and mortar (Hall et al. 1993a). These layers were themselves covered by yet another patchy floor deposit of mortar (6288*, Fig.366s). A patchy spread of mortar (6319*, Fig.366s) sealed the robber trench fill 6320, and was then covered by a series of thin laminated layers (6296*, Fig.366s), the first of which was made up entirely of vegetable matter, which also covered the surface of the mortar floor (6288). A sample of this deposit contained modest amounts of unidentified faecal concretions, fish bone, mortar and sand, with a range of other occupation debris (including crab, mussel and oyster shell, charcoal and coal), suggesting that there had been dumping of rubbish. The three plants identified were all essentially weeds (Hall et al. 1993a). The south-west edge of the earlier deposit 6318 was cut away at this time to create a depression into which was placed an extensive clay deposit with limestone and brick rubble inclusions (6290*, Fig.366s, and 6147), cut by a small pit (6282) containing a fill of compacted ash and charcoal. The clay contained an Edward I penny (AY 18/1, 95), probably deposited by c.1300. Layer 6290 spread over the entire south-west part of Building 10 and was overlain by a circular deposit of clay (6307*) showing traces of light burning, surrounded by a scatter of charcoal. Four post-settings or pads (6311A–D*) were set in this clay, probably creating a screens passage. There was an area of cobbles (6303*) arranged in a rough semi-circle, associated with

the north-west wall (6297) and sited over the construction trench backfill.

To the north-west of Building 10 the Period 4 loam (6342) was cut by another sequence of pits (6368–70) shown on Fig.380s as an incomplete cut (6368*) since a complete record does not survive.

Garden fence (Fig.380s)

During Period 5 Building 12 (Period 4) was replaced and its north-east wall, represented by a line of post-holes, was extended on the same line over a series of intermixed clay loams (5488, Fig.367s, 5521, 5500, Fig.367s, 5538) to form a long fence line. The loams contained a dark red, opaque glass droplet (sf2579) and an iron auger bit (sf2544). The evidence for this fence comprised a linear spread of clay (5496*) with associated limestone blocks set over clay-filled pits (5529*/201, AY 10/4, Fig.366s, 5532*); post-holes (5480*–81, 5489–93*); and pits capped with tiles (5528*, 5530*). Earlier deposits were covered by a loam (5477, Fig.367s) containing limestone blocks and post-settings in a rough north-west/south-east alignment, including a post-hole (5483*) containing the remains of two wooden posts set at angles, edged by large tile fragments and limestone blocks. All these elements together formed a rough north-west/south-east line, at least 23m in length. There were no interior levels on either side of this fence line, confirming that it functioned as a property boundary. Adjoining the fence there was a wall (5541*, Fig.367s) forming a return to the south-west which survived as a rough build of cobbles, broken tiles and limestone blocks packed with clay.

Building 15

A limestone block (5533*), possibly a post-pad, and a post-pit (5531*) containing the remnants of a post packed with clay and loam, may be all that survived of a small structure adjoining the north-east side of the garden fence. A hearth (5537*) consisting of a base spread of clay into which were set several pitched tiles, was positioned inside this small structure, overlying a spread of charcoal loam (5539) and one of clay (5540). The hearth was covered by burnt clay and ash (5536). Towards the end of Period 5 the hearth was disused and covered by clay deposits mixed with loam (5524–5).

Bedern long trench

During Period 5 a series of clay and clay loam layers were deposited (1093–4, 1096–7, 1106, 1592). Two layers of decayed wood (1066, 1088) formed external surfaces between the foundry and the garden fence at the south-western extent of the college.

A clay loam spread (1600/1609, Fig.364s) was deposited within Building 13.

Bedern Foundry (pp.166–71, Fig.68, AY 10/3: Period 3, Phases 1 and 2)

A substantial stone wall was erected parallel with the north-eastern edge of the foundry site, forming the north-east wall of the central foundry building (Fig.68, AY 10/3; Fig.218). The south-eastern stretch of the wall had been erected in a construction trench (2843) some 0·15m deep and 0·5m wide, with concave sides and a flat base, filled with layers of limestone, tile and mortar fragments, and topped with mortared flat-laid tiles. The mortared wall (962–3: shown on Fig.68, AY 10/3, but unnumbered; elevation is on Fig.71) was built from large ashlar blocks, with the outer, or north-eastern, face of three courses having generally deeper facing stones at the base. The blocks

were roughly faced and had been cross-jointed; there was some use of tile levelling wedges. The inner face consisted of six courses of smaller cobbles and limestone blocks.

The north-western stretch of wall (130/607) had a construction trench (2865) filled with tightly packed cobble and limestone fragments (2771, 2894–5). Up to 0·2m of clay (2904) had been deposited on this, followed by rubble packing (2922). The wall itself incorporated large re-used ashlars on the north-east face, and small squared limestone blocks on the south-west (Figs.69–70, AY 10/3). It had toppled over to the north-east along its length, with slippage of the upper courses away from the lower at the east end (Fig.219). It was generally 0·46m wide × 0·5m high on an offset footing (2886). On the north-east face two courses of ashlars survived; on the south-west five courses. Many of the re-used stones in the wall were of 12th century date (152, 154, 175–7, 209–11, 238, AY 10/4). Along the south-western edge the construction trench had been backfilled

Fig.218 *Area 13.I/II: general view of the foundry site looking south-east, showing foundry Periods 3 and 4. The property of the vicars choral lies to the left of the wall on the left side of the picture. Scale unit 0·5m*

Fig.219 *Area 13.I/II: faced ashlar blocks of foundry wall 607, showing the collapse of the wall north-eastwards (towards the college precinct). Scale unit 0·1m*

with silt and clay (2863–4) from which a parchment pricker was recovered (*7971, AY* 17/12), probably derived from the college precinct. There were at least four sets of piles under this north-east wall.

In the east corner of the foundry site, there was evidence that the south-west end of the north-west wall of Building 13 was rebuilt, destroying all trace of the Period 4 wall. The new wall (2956) was 0·42m wide, with cobble facings which had been heavily mortared. There was clear evidence for a construction trench (2942) on the south-west side, and a mortar construction level (2957) to the south-east, 0·07m deep. In addition there was a small stone-packed post-hole (2974) against the side of the construction trench. In the west corner of Building 13 a patchy cobble and sandy clay floor (2881) was probably in use during Period 5.

Along the north-east edge of the site there was an extensive ground surface make-up of compact sandy clay (2697, 2770, 2777, 935, 944, 975). The Period 4 make-up (4072, p.434) was covered by a more rubbly deposit (2623, 2629, 2664, Fig.62, *AY* 10/3) with angular limestone, cobble and tile fragments, probably builders' rubble from the construction of a major foundry building to the south-west.

This area was principally used for a series of rubbish pits during Period 5. The initial group comprised two pits (2544, Figs.62, 79, *AY* 10/3; 2653) extending to the north-east beyond the limit of excavation. The former was backfilled with compact silty clay with mortar, limestone and tile rubble; the latter with amorphous peat (2652) covered by grey silt (2648). A general layer of dark brown peaty clay (2628) was also deposited over the rubble.

A spread of laminated organic peat (936, 968, 2005, 2269) was laid over the clay surface. Analysis of a sample taken from one of these layers (2269) revealed the presence of human faeces.

Along the north-east edge of the excavation, there were a number of peat-filled pits (2475, 2665, and 2780 with fills 2754–7, 4034). Some of these pits may in fact have originated in earlier periods; indeed the five potsherds from one (2475) were of the late 12th–early 13th century, while none of the more substantial pottery from a second (2780) need date as late as the 14th century. A sample taken of 2780 contained chaff and charred grain, including oats, possibly representing hearth sweepings.

Period 6: mid 14th century (Fig.220)

From the middle of the 14th century there was extensive remodelling of earlier buildings and the construction of several new ones. Continued expansion of the college along with the apparent need constantly to upgrade the accommodation probably led to this move. It was towards the end of this period that the vicars reached the peak of their prosperity (pp.383–4). The intensity of activity requires the division of these changes into two phases.

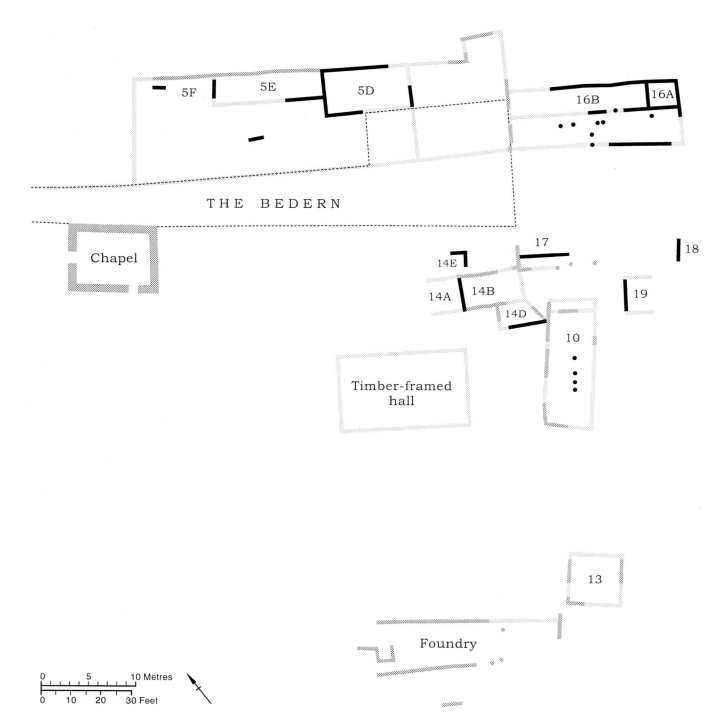

Fig.220 *Period 6.1: interpretative summary phase plan, showing building development. For the key, see Fig.195, p.409. Scale 1:400*

Period 6, Phase 1

Along the north-east side of the close **Building 5** underwent a major rebuild; in fact it is unclear whether it survived in its previous form at all (Fig.381s). The wall dividing the central aisle from the south-west aisle was demolished and the arcade padstones covered with rubble, the posts they carried having been removed. A gold and sapphire ring, presumably lost by one of the previous inhabitants of Building 5, became incorporated in this demolition debris (see p.450). Features in the central aisle of the building were also levelled and covered. This may indicate an alteration in the building form with the original roof replaced by one with an alternative means of support, probably employing a single tie-beam leaving an internal space unencumbered by aisle posts. It is documented that in the 14th century gradual improvements in roof construction dispensed with aisles by raising the whole system of roof support on tie-beams (Smith 1955). This change to Building 5 probably involved the extensive dismantling and rebuilding of the basic structure whilst retaining the outer sill walls. During this period the cess pits to the north-east of Building 5 were also backfilled and sealed with clay.

At the same time as demolition cleared the south-west aisle there were new internal developments, beginning with the construction of at least one new room, 5D, and the modification and rebuilding of the rest of the rooms in the north-east aisle. Room 5D was created to the south-east of what had been Room 5C and was at least 8m in length (north-west/south-east). The south-west wall was a wooden partition. The internal levels included a hearth with a small stone-lined cess pit and a series of floor deposits suggesting that it was used as living quarters.

To the north-west of Room 5D another new room, Room 5E, was built against the outer wall of Building 5, amalgamating the earlier Rooms 5B and 5C. A sequence of hearths and floor levels were found within this room, their construction separated by what appears to be only a fairly short span of time. To the north-west of Room 5E, Room 5F was created in the same position as the earlier Room 5A, against the north-east outer wall of Building 5.

The initial demolition of the wall between the central aisle and south-west aisle and the structures within the central aisle of Building 5 may mark a change in function of this portion of the building. This is implied by the deposition of loamy soils of a type more typically found externally. There was also renewed occupation in the south-west aisle, within a new room which extended beyond the limit of the excavation. Only part of a north-east wall of this room was found in the excavated area.

At the south-east end of Building 5 it is possible that there was a similar system of room divisions to that found within the rest of the building, although intrusions have removed much of the evidence. A pitched tile hearth was constructed against the south-west face of the north-east outer wall of the building; this must have entailed the dismantling or narrowing of a portion of the framing to insert a fireproof hearth-back, surviving only as a line of small limestones on the sill wall.

After 1328–9 the great hall or *magna aula* is not mentioned again in the documentary sources, and the alterations in the early 14th century suggested by both the documentary and the archaeological evidence, seem to have been caused by, or initiated, a change in the use of the building.

Building 16 was built onto the end of Building 5 in the mid 14th, a date suggested by an Edward III penny sealed in its construction dump (see p.452). It was built in the position of the earlier Building 8 and due to its similar form may be considered as a replacement, incorporating the Period 5 drain within its interior. Building 16 was divided into two portions by a central wall. To the north-east were two rooms, 16A and 16B, neither of which contained hearths. In the centre and running the length of the building was an open timber arcade set on padstones, close to the south-western room walls. The area between this arcade and the south-west outer wall was used as one room, but again with no hearth.

To the south-west of the close Building 11 had fallen into disuse by the end of Period 5, with the deposition of several clay, mortar and limestone spreads. In Period 6 it was replaced by several separate structures (Fig.382s). The main building, **Building 17**, initially had a long corridor on its south-west side, and a room containing a hearth facing onto the close. The corridor was entered from its north-west end, where a spread of crushed limestone representing a small courtyard led directly off Bedern.

The south-eastern bay of Building 11 was extensively rebuilt as **Building 18**. Only some of the foundations of the rebuild survive, although new floors were inserted. Once again, there was no evidence for a hearth or other internal fitments.

Even less can be said of **Building 19**, represented only by a short length of limestone wall foundation, with the suggestion of an associated brick floor. The original extent of Building 19 was difficult to trace due to modern intrusions, but the surviving walls appear to have made up the north-west wall of the building and there were internal levels to its south-east. It is suggested that this building may once have been attached to the south-west side of Building 18, but this can only be speculation.

Building 14 underwent further alterations, this time of a structural kind involving the dismantling of the central division between what had been Rooms 14A and 14B/C in Period 5 and its immediate replacement by a similar partition on a slightly different alignment, contemporary with and butting up to a short length of wall set against the inside of the south-west wall. The reasons for these alterations can only be guessed at, as can the function of this building, given the paucity of diagnostic finds. Once more, however, the presence of a hearth and floor levels points to a residential use. Period 6 also witnessed the addition of a small outbuilding, Room 14E, at least 4m in length and up to 2·5m wide, against the north-east side of Building 14, by the entrance. In addition, the south-west wall of Room 14D was rebuilt, but there were no corresponding internal changes.

Building 10 was further altered with the addition of a short length of partition walling keyed into the north-west wall (Fig.382s). Further occupation deposits built up in the interior, and a new hearth was constructed. Drainage gullies to the north-west of Building 10 were completely backfilled at this time. The area to the south-west of Building 10 was covered and levelled by yet another series of extensive clay loams and was increasingly encroached upon by large rubbish and cess pits. Further cess pits were found along the north-east edge of the foundry excavations, where a substantial north-west/south-east wall continued to mark the limit of the college

precinct. Evidence for timber-planked floors and waterlogged rushes was recovered both from the long trench and the foundry site.

An early timber-framed common hall may have been constructed during Period 6 on the site of the present standing building (see p.475).

Bedern North-East (Fig.381s)

Building 5

At the beginning of Period 6 the Period 4 south-west aisle connecting wall (1542/1571) was demolished; some of the stone was completely robbed away with the digging of a trench (1667) along its footings. Several demolition spreads (1574, Fig.365s, 1593) accumulated and the remaining foundations were covered by a clay spread (1561) extending across the surrounding area. In this layer were found a Henry III cut halfpenny dated c.1251–6 (*AY* 18/1, 79) and a gold and sapphire ring (sf390). A layer of compacted limestone chippings (1524, Fig.365s) was then deposited over the clay. It appears that the diagonal passageway in the central aisle was also demolished, along with any other internal structures. This demolition resulted in the accumulation of deposits of rubble (1515) in the north-west part of the building, over the limestone chippings (1524). This rubble was sealed by a layer of broken tiles set in clay (1502) which also covered the three central padstones (1587).

During the creation of Room 5D, the stretch of the north-east outer wall of Building 5 corresponding to the north-east wall of Room 5D was rebuilt from foundation level, possibly altering the entrance which once led into the earlier diagonal passageway. This new stretch of wall (1257*) was a direct replacement of the original wall (1373), on the same line. It was built with clay-bonded roughly dressed limestone and cobbles, containing at least two padstones along its length. The north-west wall of Room 5D (1289*) was also new, the earlier demolition debris being covered by a clay layer on which the wall was built. The wall consisted of squared limestones surviving as an irregular line. The south-east wall (1525*) survived as a short but wide and well-built wall-line, 2·2m in length, sealing the earlier aisle padstone pits. Later intrusions had removed any evidence of its original length. It was constructed of clay-bonded limestone blocks, some of them worked.

An internal partition wall was built to the south-west of the earlier padstones (1587). A clay spread (1526) was first laid down, and a linear slot full of clay (1477*) marks the position of the wall division.

Although most of the south-west portion of Room 5D had been removed by modern intrusions, internal deposits survived in the north-east part where spreads of clay (1313, 1448*, 1478) were also used to bond the north-east wall. The clay had been cut by a circular feature (1535) and an associated post-hole (1536). Covering these clay layers was an extensive layer of compacted limestone chippings (1230*), cut by a pitched tile hearth (1312*). The limestone floor (1230) contained an Edward II jetton (*AY* 18/1, *154*) of 1307–27, which had been used as a brooch with a clip attached to the obverse. The floor had been covered by a fragmentary clay deposit (1267), itself overlain by a small spread of charcoal (1222). A scale-tang knife with inlaid cutler's mark was found in 1267. In the north corner of the room, against the walls, was a small square stone-lined pit (1336*) set into a construction trench (1442) packed with clay. This pit had an initial fill of silty clay containing gravel and limestone, which was found to contain some faecal contamination. Analysis also revealed fig and elderberry seeds as well as four specimens of a type of spider beetle particularly associated with fairly old, somewhat damp buildings (Hall et al. 1993b). The upper fill appears to be a later backfill. Pottery dates the use of Room 5D to the late 13th or early 14th century.

At its creation, Room 5E was much larger than any of the original north-east aisle rooms as it amalgamated Rooms 5B and 5C of Period 5, which were now covered by a layer of clay (1424, Fig.365s) forming a floor. The south-west wall (1423*) replaced and overlay the earlier wall (1465), consisting in parts of one remaining course of roughly squared limestones. Most of this wall, however, survived only as fragmentary rubble disturbed by later intrusions. The north-west wall only survived as a ridge of clay (1407*), probably representing a slot, later backfilled, which once contained a timber partition. The south-east wall (1289*) separated Room 5E from Room 5D.

Room 5E appears to have had several periods of use, as indicated by a succession of hearths. The first of these was represented by a thick deposit of burnt clay and charcoal (1461) set onto the clay floor (1424), and covered by a thick layer of ashy loam derived from its usage (1425, Fig.365s).

Two clay spreads (1615–16) were laid and the Period 5 hearth (1489) was replaced by another (1614) consisting of a shallow pit partially lined with tile and filled with clay, sand, loam and tile rubble, and then sealed by a layer of pitched tiles in burnt clay.

The next period of use is represented by a thick deposit of charcoal and loam (1420), which covered almost the entire area of the room. Set into this were several flat-laid bricks (1422) forming a further hearth (Fig.221), the south-eastern side of which had been removed by a modern intrusion. These bricks were covered by a spread of crushed coal (1460).

Room 5F was formed when the Period 5 north-west wall of Room 5A (1400) was removed and the slot backfilled with fragmented limestone (1402). This spread over the entire area of Room 5F. Set into it against the south-east wall was a hearth (1398*), of which only the south-east edging remained, consisting of a line of clay-bonded tile and limestone, with evidence of possible returns to the north-west at both ends. Within this edging, there were alternate layers of ash or burnt clay separated by layers of unburnt clay. The floor was later covered by a spread of charcoal-flecked clay loam (1387), into which was cut a linear north-west/south-east slot (1385*) which divided the room into two portions, possibly with a timber partition. It appears that this partition did not extend the full length of the room, thereby allowing the hearth to be used at one end.

At the same time as the creation and development of these new north-east aisle rooms, a charcoal loam (1447*) was deposited in the south-west part of Area 14.II upon which a new wall (1452*) was constructed in the area of the earlier south-west aisle, possibly denoting the position of a further room. This new wall consisted of clay-bonded limestones, of which only a short section survived, approximately 2m in length. To the south-west a clay floor (1446*) extended to the trench edge.

The charcoal loam (1447) contained two adjoining fragments from the base of a glass hanging lamp (sf338), and appears to be stratigraphically equivalent to clay loam deposits (1215/1245*, Fig.365s) in the centre of Building 5, and rubble spreads (1280, 1388) further to the south-east. These deposits appear to have spread to the south-east as far as a possible continuation to the south-west of the wall (1289) of Room 5D.

At the south-east end of Building 5 a deposit of red loamy clay (4192) was placed against the inner face of the north-eastern external wall (4477), into which a tile hearth

Fig.221 Area 14.II, Period 6: hearth 1422, looking east. Scale unit 0·1m

(4186*) was set. The north-east edge of this hearth was marked by a line of limestone blocks, including a single padstone, which were set on top of the inner half of the external wall, presumably after the dismantling of the timber framing at this point. The area to the south-west of this hearth was much disturbed by intrusions; this made it difficul to relate events here to those in the rest of the building. At a similar date to the construction of hearth 4186 a clay loam (4059*) was deposited. The faunal assemblage from this layer was dominated by the remains of pigs and sheep, cattle being present in relatively small numbers. Cat, dog, chicken and rat were also recorded, the latter indicating the continued presence of vermin (Hamshaw-Thomas 1994). Overlying the clay loam was a deposit of burnt clay (4014*), possibly a further hearth, abutted by a patchy deposit of clay (4058*) containing a small amount of mortar and crushed rubble. The next deposit to cover these layers was a spread of tile, mortar and limestone rubble (4096) which was then cut by a limestone-filled pit (4087). The area was later sealed by a layer of rubble and loam (4077), which in turn was covered by an extensive limestone spread (4010/4150).

To the north-east of Building 5 in Area 14.II a linear trench was filled with peat (1503*). The cess pits which had served Building 5 in previous periods were, in the main, backfilled and levelled during the course of Period 6. One pit (1510*) contained layered deposits of organic peat (1438, 1505) which were extensively sampled. Analysis confirmed the presence of human faecal material with a substantial number of parasite eggs, and breeding communities of insect fauna, indicating moderately foul deposits which were not left exposed for too long. Food components identified included traces of fig, blackberry, strawberry, apple, plum and hazel nut. There were also substantial amounts of corncockle seed fragments (presumably from milled grain-based food) and moderate amounts of cornflower, another grain contaminant (Hall et al. 1993b). This was one of the few contexts that was sieved, and demonstrates the value of such an exercise (Scott 1985, 37). The sieved material was dominated by the bones of squirrel of which distal limb elements, metapodials and phalanges made up over 97% of the 267 bones. Such a specific range of skeletal elements is best interpreted as the waste from the later stages of the preparation of squirrel pelts, the feet being brought onto Bedern on semi-prepared pelts, rather than as food residue (ibid.). The large number of fish bones which were recovered represent the principal food residue. Herring was by far the most abundant species, followed by common eel, haddock and cod. A number of other species were also represented: elasmabrachii, whiting, ray sp., conger eel, salmonidae, cyprinidae, roach, gurnard, plaice/flounder, witch and sole. The pit functioned as a trap for a number of unsuspecting small animals, thus giving some idea of the micropalaeoecology of the area. The presence of significant numbers of amphibian (mainly frog but some toad) bones

accords well with the botanical data illustrating the dank nature of the area north-east of Building 5. The relatively high numbers of black rat bones is a good indication of this animal's prevalence on the site. The remains of bank vole, house and wood mouse indicate the presence of nearby overgrown vegetation (Hamshaw-Thomas 1994). Towards the end of Period 6 the pit was levelled with a mixture of clay and tiles, and then an extensive deposit of clay (1555) placed over this. The clay was itself partly covered by a spread of loam (1578) and a silty clay (1554) containing charcoal inclusions.

South-east of Building 5 in Area 14.IV tile and cobble rubble demolition debris (4205), a sandy loam spread (4201), broken tiles in clay (4197) and two further demolition spreads (4184, 4196) were deposited at the beginning of Period 6. A mixed loam with mortar and tiles (4203*) was deposited north-east of Building 5, abutting the outside wall (4477). Within the area that had been inside Building 8 a rubble deposit of tile and limestone (4375) was overlapped by a peaty clay (4456) to the east. The rubble contained a fragment of stone moulding (297, AY 10/4) and a faunal assemblage dominated by cattle (and large mammal material), with lesser quantities of sheep and pig. Red and fallow deer, dog, hare and food birds were also recorded (Hamshaw-Thomas 1994).

Building 16 (Fig.222)

The Building 8 foundations were covered by a series of rubble and clay spreads (4210, 4213, 4219, 4244, 4262, 4277, 4284, 4303, 4314, 4323), including a loam (4395) which partly overlay the foundations of Period 3 wall 4421. These spreads were then covered by an extensive layer of clay loam (4374*), covering most of this south-east part of the site, in association with several other clay, mortar and tile layers (4336, 4343). This was then succeeded by a further extensive loam spread (4382*). An Edward I penny, deposited probably before c.1300 (AY 18/1, 86), and a reused corbel of late 12th century date (137, AY 10/4) were both found in these deposits. The loam (4382) was then cut by a north-east/south-west shallow trench (4393*), backfilled with clay and loam. A linear depression (4388*) immediately to the north-west was filled with mixed rubble, mortar and loam. A steep-sided, oval pit (4088), c.0·6m in depth, was packed with smooth, water-worn cobbles which formed an irregular spread (4095).

Before the construction of Building 16, clay (4360) and loam spreads (4369–70) were deposited near the Period 5 drain (4016). A copper alloy jetton of Edward II (AY 18/1, 149) was found in one of these spreads. The construction of this building can be dated to the mid 14th century by an Edward III penny (AY 18/1, 132) found in the clay (4277) deposited immediately prior to its construction.

Fig.222   Area 14.IV, Period 6: Building 16, looking north-west. Scale unit 0·5m

All four exterior walls to Building 16 survived. The Period 4 south-east end wall (4020) of Building 5 appears to have been used as the north-west end wall, although a group of four large limestone blocks (4273*) packed together with clay, and resting upon on a base of smaller limestones packed with clay and some rubble, appears to have been placed at the south-west end of 4020 where it probably met the south-west wall of Building 16 beyond the trench edge to the south-west. The south-west wall (4355*), recorded at the south-east end of the trench, consisted of well-built limestone blocks bonded with mortar and set into a construction trench packed with limestone chips and mortar. The south-east wall (4311*) consisted of

a lower course of limestone blocks covered by bricks and cobbles. A re-used piece of roll moulding (262, *AY* 10/4) of early or mid 13th century date was recovered from this wall. The north-east wall was of several different builds, at least partly corresponding to the room divisions within, but also perhaps the result of later rebuilds. The stretch at the south-east end (4308*) comprised large mortar-bonded limestone blocks, covered with mortared brick. The north-west continuation had been removed by a Period 7 repair but was represented by a clay construction level (4351). Further along, the wall consisted of a build of cobbles set in clay (4324*). The next stretch to the north-west (4330*) survived only as a ridge of clay and crushed limestone.

This section ran from a limestone padstone north-west to a point where it was cut by a modern intrusion. The north-westernmost stretch (4021*) was built from limestone blocks set into a construction trench, in the base of which was a layer of cobbles covered by sand and clay. Larger cobbles occurred in the construction trench to the north-west. A re-used, recut shaft base (251, AY 10/4) of mid 13th century date had been incorporated in this fill. Building 16 had been patched up in subsequent periods and a 16th century German jetton of Hans Schultes (AY 18/1, 278), recovered from the south-east wall (4311), must come from these later repairs.

Building 16 was divided into two areas by a series of at least six unevenly spaced post-pads (4373A–F*), four of which were set onto backfilled foundation pits.

To the north-east of this line of post-pads, the area was divided into two rooms which were separated from the post-pad division by an inner wall, leaving a gap of c.1m. These rooms originally consisted of a small room, 16A, at the south-east end and a larger room, 16B, before being further subdivided into up to five rooms at a later date.

Room 16A was built at the south-east end of Building 16, and made use of the north-east and south-east outer walls (4308, 4311), with new south-west and north-west walls. The south-west wall (4318*) was built on the line of an earlier (Period 3) post-pad wall (4446), and was itself constructed of limestone padstones associated with a short length of connecting wall of cobbles and small limestones set in clay. The spacing between the south-easternmost padstone and the south-east end wall was slightly greater than between the rest of the padstones. The north-west wall (4361*) consisted of cobbles and limestones packed with clay. The room created was c.3 x 2·5m. The internal deposits within Room 16A consisted of a sequence of layers of sandy clay, loam, ash, clay and mortar. The earliest of these was a sandy clay deposit (4288) covered by a clay (4289), overlain by a loam and ash deposit (4281). This was then covered by a spread of mortar and clay (4280), which was itself overlain by a deposit of mortar (4268) containing an Edward I jetton (AY 18/1, 142) and a builder's trowel (sf740). The final deposit in this room in this period was a spread of compacted mortar (4276).

Room 16B was situated to the north-west of Room 16A, separated from it by the partition wall 4361. Its north-west and north-east walls were provided by the outer walls of Building 16. On its south-west side a new wall was constructed which, like the north-east outer wall, comprised several different builds. The south-east stretch (4329*) was constructed of cobbles set into clay on a tile footing, its north-west end consisting largely of clay with only a few cobbles and tiles. To the north-west the wall build changed, and survived as a linear feature of crushed limestone and

mortar (4322*). The north-westernmost length of this wall, which should have connected with the end wall (4020), did not survive.

Deposits within Room 16B consist of a series of patchy spreads of clay, charcoal and ash with various inclusions (4245–6, 4267, 4274, 4285, 4305–6, 4335). There were also traces of a tile and cobble feature (4349) thought to represent a hearth.

Contemporary with the construction of these early rooms, and a little to the south-west of the line of post-pads (4373), was a linear clay ridge (4362*) and a small spread of broken tiles in a clay loam (4363*).

Outside Building 16, to the north-east, spreads of clay (4271–2) butted against the external wall.

Bedern Chapel

At the south-east end of Bedern Chapel a dark loam (9086, see Fig.232c, facing p.472) was deposited. The pottery within this layer shows that it cannot be earlier than the 14th century, and was probably deposited towards the middle of the 14th century.

Bedern South-West

Building 17 (Fig.382s)

A new short length of wall (7452*) was built to infill the 0·7m entrance gap left in wall 7337, the north-west wall of Building 11 (Period 5) and was bonded with clay. This wall was constructed from small limestone blocks, perhaps blocking the entrance or providing a new threshold step. Contemporary with the insertion of this infill wall, an internal division (7353*) was constructed running off wall 7337 to the north-east of the entrance in a north-west/south-east direction, creating a passageway, c.1m wide, to the south-west, and living quarters to the north-east. This wall was set onto a sandy clay loam construction deposit (7356) at the south-east, and a clay layer (7359) to the north-west; it was constructed from limestone blocks with some bricks, all packed with clay.

The south-west wall of Building 11 remained in use, but a small addition or repair was made at its south-east end, consisting of a small tile and clay linear feature (7454*).

With the blocking of the entrance in 7337 and the insertion of internal wall 7353, the old (Period 2) south-east wall (7584) of Building 11 was disused and its foundations covered by clay spreads (7457, 7485). A pit (7484*, Fig.366s), later filled with clay, cobbles, some limestone blocks and broken tiles, was dug through the line of the foundations of wall 7584. There was no evidence for a new wall on the line of 7584 forming a south-east wall to Building 17, and it is possible that remnants of the Period 5 south-east wall of Room 11B were made use of here.

Internal deposits to the north-east of the corridor in Building 17 consisted of clay deposits (7458*, 7392*) associated with a clay-bonded pitched tile hearth (7379*) set in a rectangular construction trench. Contemporary with the construction of this hearth was the deposition of silty clay (7384) to the south-east, covered by a sandy silt (7375). The hearth was later partially covered by clay deposit (7377) which spread to the north-west, and was itself covered by a spread of charcoal (7376) partially covering the hearth, as did a sand and charcoal layer (7371). Other deposits in this area included a spread of clay and ash (7333) as well as a deposit of silty clay loam (7469, Fig.366s) sloping away to the north-east.

At the south-east end of the corridor at this time was a sandy loam (7444), covered by a silty clay (7442). A number of silty clays (7432, 7425, 7417, 7397, 7394, Fig.366s) built up against the south-east face of wall 7452. There was a deposit of silty clay (7368, Fig.366s) covered by patchy clays (7350, 7342, Fig.366s) with inclusions of charcoal and mortar in the south-west part of the corridor, and a small deposit of silty clay (7340) in the north-east part of the corridor. Covering both 7340 and 7342 was a thin layer of sandy silt loam (7336, Fig.366s) with inclusions of tile, limestone, mortar and charcoal. Outside Building 17 a new courtyard surface of limestone rubble (7283*) was laid to the north-west.

Building 18 (Fig.382s; see Fig.271, p.516)

The south-west part of Building 11's south-east wall (7628) was demolished, from its junction with the now disused (originally Period 3) internal division 7624, and Building 18 was built. The coal, ash and limestone blocks filling a pit (7119*) appeared to cover the south-west part of 7628, and on top of this fill was a deposit of sandy loam (7115) and a mixed layer of silt and ash (7114). Both 7115 and 7119 were covered by an extensive layer of sandy clay and loam (7111) also running over the now demolished wall 7624, as did clay and brick dump (7101). Inside what had been Building 11 was a deposit of mixed mortar and brick chips (7137) covered by a fine loamy sand with large brick fragments and broken tile inclusions (7135). These were overlain by a compacted sand (7103) cut by a linear feature (7102*) running parallel to the foundations of wall 7628. The fill of this feature contained three jet beads (sfs2412–14). A small pit (7146*) was dug up against the north-west side of this wall, and later filled with broken brick, tile and limestone fragments, many of which showed evidence of burning on half their surface as if once partly set into the ground. This pit may be all that remained of a large post-hole set into the bottom of the foundation cut prior to the construction of the new wall.

A large deposit of limestone fragments mixed with mortar (7147) covering the foundations of the earlier south-east wall (7628) of Building 11 is interpreted as the foundations for a new wall built in approximately the same position. No evidence remained for a south-west wall to Building 18; it was probably on the line of the modern intrusion here. Covering 7103 was a deposit of ash and charcoal (7098) which contained an amber bead (sf2409), and a small nondescript faunal assemblage which produced the tip of a claw of an edible crab (Hamshaw-Thomas 1994). 7098 was partially covered to the south-west by a compacted mortar surface (7052), and to the north-east by a deposit of mortar (7097). A clay loam (7104) was also covered by the mortar 7052.

Outside Building 18 to the south-west was a surface of limestone blocks set into a compacted loam (7051*, Fig.370s) from which a bone tuning peg (8064, AY 17/12) was recovered. This spread was cut by a pit (7236*, Fig.370s) which was later filled with cobbles and limestones. Inside Building 18 was a layer of loam and mortar (7205) covered by a sandy clay (7203*) cut by an ash-filled pit (7202*).

Building 19 (Fig.382s)

Building 19 was constructed south-west of Building 18, although only sections of the north-west outer wall (7622*, Fig.370s, 7629*) survived, consisting of two builds of limestone. Pottery incorporated within the wall indicates that it cannot have been built before the 14th century. The interior of Building 19 apparently lay to the south-east, where the patchy spread of clay and bricks set in mortar (also 7629) may be all that remained of a clay-bedded brick floor.

Building 14 (Fig.382s)

A clay loam (7435) ran over the foundations of the Period 5 internal partition between Rooms 14A and 14B/C, leaving only the south-east padstone uncovered and projecting into Room 14B. The partition was then rebuilt on a slightly different line as a limestone wall (7423*) bonded with clay, incorporating the south-east padstone of the earlier line. Contemporary with the new partition, a similar wall (7415*) was built against the south-west wall of Room 14B, running for a distance of 2m.

Little survived of the north-east wall of Room 14E apart from a padstone (7590) set onto a foundation pit filled and levelled by sand, and a possible structural pit (7586*) filled with limestone blocks. Further to the north-west the line of the north-east wall can be traced as a concentration of tiles within the later destruction layer 7583 (Fig.370s; Period 7.1) which partially covered a mortar spread (7587, Fig.370s) containing a fired clay crucible (sf2825). To the south-east the wall survived as a line of limestone blocks

(7527*) ending with a limestone padstone at the east corner. Running south-west from this padstone the wall continued to another padstone, and was itself constructed on a slight ridge of soil. This last padstone stopped short of a connection with the main north-east wall of Building 14, although, if continued, the line would have connected to the north-west side of the surmised entrance to this building.

Inside Room 14E the first deposit was a spread of clay (7515*, Fig.370s) separated from wall 7527 by a line of edge-set tiles running against the inner side of this wall and containing several limestone blocks. This was overlain by a deposit of mortar topped with ash (7513, Fig.370s), covered by a thin charcoal layer (7510). A deposit of clay (7507) was placed adjacent to wall 7527.

At the same time, a deposit of loam (7550, Fig.369s) was laid against the exterior of the Period 5 north-east wall of Room 14B (7551) and then covered by an extensive spread of loam (7522, Figs.369–70s) containing mortar flecking and domestic refuse which included a bone parchment pricker (8056, AY 17/12) and a gaming counter chipped from a tile (sf2789). Pottery from this spread suggests it may have been deposited during the first half of the 14th century. In addition, Period 5 ditch 7344 was backfilled with loam (7463) which was then cut by a secondary pit (7403) which, once it was filled, was sealed by a deposit of clay loam (7401). A secondary ditch cut was then made into the earlier fills.

Room 14D was altered with the replacement of its north-west wall by a wall (7408*) founded on a double line of clay-bonded cobbles. At the same time its south-west wall was replaced by a limestone block wall-line (7481*) bonded with clay and small chunks of limestone, which extended the length of the earlier build and ran south-east to a padstone in the north-west wall of Building 10. The south-east wall probably remained the Period 4 passage wall (7538).

Between the edge of the excavation and Building 14 the earlier levels were covered by a silty clay (7406) which butted up against the south-west wall of Building 14. This was then covered by a layer of clay (7372), itself covered by crushed coal (7367).

To the south-west of Room 14D a large pit (7329*) was dug. The basal fill comprised a brown peaty deposit with clay mottling. It is possible that some faecal material or food waste was present in this deposit, to judge by the presence of traces of fig seeds and moderate amounts of corncockle seed fragments (Hall et al. 1993a). There were also traces of hazel nutshell, sloe fruitstone fragments and elderberry seeds. Most of the plants were weeds, however, apart from moderate numbers of toad-rush — per-

haps an indicator of wet, trampled places nearby. Hemp was also present — one of only two records for this important oil/fibre crop in the medieval deposits examined from Area 13.X. This basal fill was overlain by a silty loam with mortar inclusions (7327). A deposit of clay moulds and ash (7324) was then dumped into the pit and also spread around the surrounding area covering the backfill of the earlier ditch (7344). A large rubbish pit (7280) was found against the south-west edge of the excavation. It contained a mixture of loam and ash with inclusions of mortar, limestone chunks and oyster shells in this area.

Building 10 (Fig.382s)

A small L-shaped limestone wall repair (7443*) was added to the middle portion of the north-west wall of Building 10, with three blocks built over the wall and the Period 5 ditch fill, and a short line of walling running in a south-easterly direction into the building interior for about 2m. An extensive loam (7183, Fig.368s) was found spreading to either side of the internal partition (7419) at the north-east end, perhaps through a doorway, and was thought to be contemporary with a small spread of sand (7422) against the south-east wall. The loam contained a mixed charcoal and loam lens (7197). South-west of the partition was a rectangular hearth (7185*) comprising three large cobbles set into a construction pit, edged with tiles. This may have replaced the Period 5 hearth (7234), as this was now partially covered by the patchy remains of a mortar spread (7172). A mixed mortar layer (7200) was also situated in this general area. A small standing of edge-set bricks (7157*) was set into a construction trench packed with clay, against the south-west side of the partition.

North-east of the partition wall there was a steady build-up of layers, including mortar containing some crushed tile and charcoal flecking (7201*). This was almost immediately covered by a mixed charcoal deposit (7198) containing tile, brick and bones, which once spread over the entire area of this north-east room. Several loamy spreads (7426, 7421, 7247) were located throughout this room, cut by a pit (7148, Fig.368s) containing a fill of limestones, cobbles and broken tile. Towards its base were larger limestone and cobble blocks, and butting up against it was a small spread of charcoal (7241) overlain by a sandy clay loam (7238). A second pit (7153) contained a padstone, as well as domestic refuse including a clay gaming counter (sf2571).

At the south-west end of Building 10 there were traces of a mortar floor (6323*) bedded onto the earlier (Period 5) clay (6290), which had apparently once covered this entire south-west area. There was a shallow linear scoop (6322) in the floor. An ashy spread (6309) was covered by rubble and disturbed burnt material (6306) and sealed by a clay spread (6304).

The gully cut in Period 1 to the north-west of where Building 10 was later sited was completely backfilled at this time. First, a large pit (6365*) cut through the earlier gully fills and was backfilled with clay. A number of mixed fills were then dumped in the gully, starting with a thick layer of mortar (6357) containing pottery dated to the first half of the 14th century. This was followed by a succession of fills (6356, 6359–60), including sandy loams and clay mould fragments. A fragment of stone hone (sf2574) and several fragments of a yellow, high-lead, glass jug (sfs2615, 2619) were also recovered from these fills. The north-east section of the gully was backfilled with a comparable sequence of deposits (6372A–H) commencing with silty clay loam, and progressing through peat, ash and clay mould fragment deposits. A sample of one of the fills (6372F) included a very large number of stinging nettle achenes with moderate numbers of sedge nutlets; all the remaining plants pointed to weedy vegetation with perhaps some slight indication of wetland (Hall et al. 1993a). The abundant nettles perhaps point to an area of neglect in the vicinity as the gully fill formed. This fill also contained a fragment of wool clothing woven in a 2/1 twill (sf2677) in a good-quality, medium-weight fabric. Other fills included eight body fragments from a glass vessel (sf2664 in 6372D) and the kicked base of a glass flask (sf2683 in 6372H). The Period 5 pits (6368–70, Fig.380s) were now backfilled with clay loam with charcoal inclusions (6367) which included another kicked base from a glass flask (sf2606). The area was then levelled by sandy clay loam (6330, 6347) with inclusions of charcoal, tile and mortar, and a convex base from a glass flask or urinal, or alembic dome (sf2555). This layer spread to the north-west edge of the excavation.

Garden fence (Fig.382s)

To the south-west, a series of clay loams (5422, 5423, 5431, Fig.367s, 5465, Fig.367s, 5472, Figs. 366–7s, 5504) were deposited over the Period 5 remains of Building 15. Inside the line of where the wall of Building 15 had stood there was a mixed mortar spread (5484) into which four cess pits (5306*, 5382*, 5387*, 5391*, all Fig.367s) were cut. One pit contained pointed wooden stakes set fast into its base, whilst another held a wooden post down one side and a flat plank at the bottom. A number of samples were taken of the pit fills (Hall et al. 1993a). Food remains included fig, strawberry, blackberry, elderberry, apple, sloe, wheat, barley and oats. The cereals were charred, indicating that they probably arrived with ash. The other food remains perhaps originated in faeces; there were modest numbers of parasite eggs in most of the fills. The presence of abundant corncockle seed fragments suggest that flour-based food contaminated with this arable weed was incorporated into the deposit. The weeds also included other cornfield species, but there were other species likely to have been weeds of cultivated soil (but perhaps not cornfields) or waste places. There were also woodworm beetles, presum-

ably from timber nearby, and various other insects which may have originated within structures. A sample from pit 5382 yielded several grain weevils. Phytophages included a few species offering a hint that hay-like cut vegetation was incorporated, so that this may have been stable manure. A fairly small group of beetles from pit 5391 included grain pests and may also have originated indoors, in a stable or a dirty human dwelling.

In the centre of the trench at its south-west end, there was a spread of clay loam (5486, Fig.366s) and broken tile and mortar (5474). A number of pits were dug (5428*, 5461, 5497*, Fig.366s, 5501*, Fig.366s, 5502–3*, 5506–7*, 5519, 5520*, Fig.366s, 5523*, 5526*) containing similar fills of clay loam and peat, with some pieces of wood. Lying horizontally within pit 5506 was a rectangular piece of timber (5508*/timber 8190) with two smaller cross planks at each end.

Samples were analysed from two of the pits (5497, 5501) (Hall et al. 1993a). A mixture of communities can be discerned amongst the beetle fauna, but most of the assemblage may have originated within a stable-like building. The 'house fauna' element was also strongly represented. Overall, the similarity between this group and material from dwellings or workshops of Anglo-Scandinavian date at 16–22 Coppergate is remarkable. A large assemblage of plant remains was also recovered. That the material was largely faecal in origin is attested by the abundance of faecal concretions recorded, supported by quantities of fig seeds, corncockle seed fragments, and 'bran', as well as mineralised cotyledons of a *Brassica* or *Sinapis* species — perhaps some kind of mustard. Parasite eggs were also present in quite large amounts. The range of foodplants represented was similar to that from other Bedern samples, with blackberry, strawberry, apple, sloe, fennel, but also summer savory. Again, there was a wide spectrum of weeds and wetland plants, but only *Sphagnum* to represent possible peatland exploitation.

These pits also contained a range of domestic refuse. One pit (5523) contained a bird bone, cut obliquely across the lower end, in order that it could be used as a stylus (*8059, AY 17/12*); a second pit (5503) contained bone manufacturing debris (*7991*); in a third (5497) a jet handle (sf2566) was found.

Towards the north-west end of the garden area there were several more large intercutting pits (5466–8*, 5470*, 5473*, 5475–6*, 5495) filled with peat and loam, and in one case, rotted straw. Samples were analysed from two of these pits (5466, 5468; Hall et al. 1993a). The beetle assemblages had an underlying character like many from Bedern, with 'house fauna' and some grain pests. It is possible that some of the these, including the saw-toothed grain beetle, may have originated in animal feed rather than directly from stored grain. There were several species likely to have invaded somewhat foul organic remains, either in the pit or prior to dumping of the fill. Human fleas were also recovered. Plant remains included moderate amounts of sheep's sorrel, turnip seeds and leaves of *Sphagnum* moss. The latter, with cotton-grass and heather, perhaps points to the exploitation of peatland. There were weeds of cultivated or neglected land with a few plants of wetland habitats. Food plants included fig, strawberry, blackberry, sloe, apple, grapes, opium poppy, hazel nut, oats, barley and wheat/rye 'bran'. The presence of a few remains preserved by mineralisation rather than waterlogging or charring perhaps points to the presence of a high concentration of salts as in a cess pit. A range of occupation debris was also present in the samples, notably coke, with some coal, charcoal, burnt and unburnt bone, metallic slag, eggshell and mortar. The finds retrieved from the pits also included a number of leather fragments, a stone gaming counter (sf2505) and an iron jew's harp (sf3380).

This may have been post-use infill incorporating a small amount of primary faecal material. Overall, the numbers of parasite eggs were rather low, although another sample included a small component of moss, including forms typically associated with latrine pits. A substantial component of the assemblage, however, is likely to have originated in stable manure. All the evidence, therefore, suggests this area was an open yard functioning as some form of animal enclosure.

Bedern long trench

At the north-west end of the trench there were several spreads of waterlogged rushes (1085–7) which appear to have been placed in shallow depressions. A fragment of enamelled beaker (sf757) was found in the rushes. Further to the south-east there was an irregular limestone spread (1075), a clay spread (1069) and a patch of mortar and tiles (1074) against the south-west side of the trench. There were two areas of decayed wood (1080–1) at the other side. In some cases it was possible to distinguish individual flat planks and these may represent parts of a decayed timber platform. A group of three posts set around a limestone block (1079) may have been associated.

At the south-east end of the trench there was a layer of compressed wood fragments (1585) which had been sealed by a series of dark organic spreads (1590, 1594, 1596). These were cut by a shallow pit (1614) and overlain by a spread of mortared cobbles (1595, Fig.364s).

Bedern Foundry (p.172, Fig.68, AY 10/3: Period 3, Phase 3)

During Period 6 the Period 5 pits along the north-eastern edge of the foundry site were replaced by a massive pit (2558), 4 × 1·5m, which was cut through the earlier fills. There was evidence that this had been lined with wooden planks as a large number of stakes, planks and laths were recovered from the fills. The basal fill (2574) consisted of a compacted peat with wood fragments and mineralised undulating peaty plates containing oak fragments and fly puparia. This was covered by a succession of peaty fills (2482, 2571, 2573), some mineralised, some with compacted straw and more fly puparia, and some with woody concentrations. Analysis of a sample of one of the fills (2573) revealed that the primary constituent was human faeces, mixed with some straw. The rich insect assemblage suggested that it had been left standing open for some time. The fills also contained a number of textile fragments, comprising two groups of silk yarn (sfs1379, 1382) and a fragment of patterned wool textile of a tabby weave with coloured bands (sf1384), known as 'ray'. P. Walton Rogers comments that rays seem to have been worn by both sexes, and especially by the servants in wealthy households, as part of their livery. By the second half of the 14th century they had also become the mark of 'bawds and strumpettes', although this example is probably more likely to have come from the clothing of a servant at the college, rather than from some local strumpette's headgear (AY 17/15 in prep.).

Beyond the north-western edge of this pit there was a second smaller pit (2625) with similar fills (2627, 2630, 2632) of compact laminated peats with clear stalks of grass, and more amorphous peats and silts. North-west again was a third round pit (2672) with laminated peaty fills (2696, 2715) interleaved with silts, and including quantities of grasses, possibly rushes. A fourth pit (2714) had been dug through the third. Again it was filled with interleaved peats and silts (2663, 2712–13) containing well-preserved grasses, rushes, fern and moss with fly puparia, and in it another textile fragment (sf1401) was found. The last two pits had each been sealed by a layer of grey silt (2695).

The Period 5 pits had also been sealed by a compact mortar-flecked surface (2548, 2769) which ran up against the precinct wall. Clay loam (2547) and silt (2542) were packed against the wall. Silty clay (967, 2268) and a compact limestone and clay surface (2461) with tile and mortar fragments were also deposited. It was cut by a substantial post-hole (2471) with stone packing and a clay fill (2459).

Period 6, Phase 2 (Fig.223)

During the later part of the period there were further internal alterations to the room organisation within **Building 5** (Fig.381s). The division of Room 5D into two was made more permanent, with the replacement of the timber partition by a narrow limestone wall. Room 5E may have been divided into two separate rooms, each with a hearth.

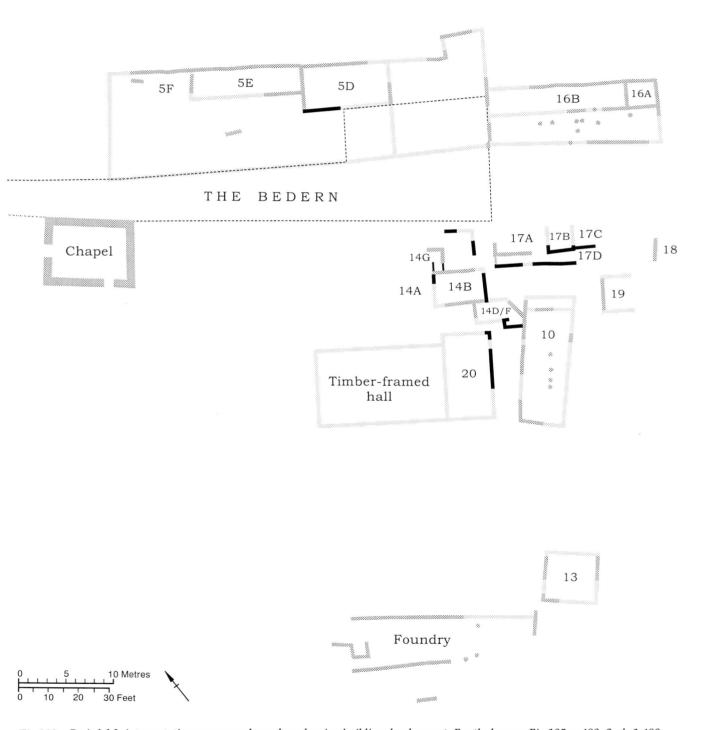

0   5   10 Metres
0   10   20   30 Feet

Fig.223   *Period 6.2: interpretative summary phase plan, showing building development. For the key, see Fig.195, p.409. Scale 1:400*

To the south-west of the close, the south-west wall of **Building 17** was rebuilt, still apparently with timber framing, but this time using brick rather than limestone to build the sill wall (Fig.223). The single room on the north-east side was eventually divided into three areas, Rooms A, B and C, with partition walls, although none contained hearths. A cobble-filled pit and a brick-standing in one of the areas seems to suggest that it was not used as living quarters.

Further alterations to **Building 14** during this phase involved the removal of the infill wall used to block the original (Period 5) entrance in the north-east wall, followed by the insertion of another entrance further to the south-east. This north-east wall now had two openings, therefore, although it was apparently not long before another short length of infill wall was used to block the original (north-west) entrance. Inside the building there was a sequence of clay floors and occupation deposits, associated with a pitched tile hearth, its construction apparently coinciding with the removal of the infill wall in the original entranceway. Once more, it appears that the interior of this building was now accessible by two entrances in the north-east wall. A new entrance was also built between Rooms 14A and 14B. To the north-east, Room 14E was rebuilt with a hearth, as Room 14G (Fig.223).

At this time Room 14D was disused, and a tile-lined pit was sunk through its foundations. Room 14F was then constructed in what had been the approximate area of Room 14D. This new room (14F) utilised the south-east wall of Room 14D, resulting in a room smaller than 14D, but of the same unusual shape. Once again the surviving wall foundations incorporated padstones which suggests that it had a timber-framed construction. The new room had a clay floor, but there was no evidence of a hearth. By the end of Period 6 Room 14F had fallen into disuse and was demolished. The immediate area was then levelled.

A line of limestone wall foundations aligned north-west/south-east, associated with a cobble surface on the north-east side of Area 13.X, may indicate the presence of further buildings fronting onto Bedern Close at this time.

In the area between Buildings 14 and 17, a narrow alleyway c.1·5m wide was formed, its south-east limits demarcated by the north-west wall of Building 17, and its north-west edge by a new wall-line. This passageway probably provided access from the close to the rear of the buildings fronting onto it.

Following the backfilling of the earlier drainage ditches, another substantial timber-framed building was then constructed in the area north-west of Building 10, with its long axis also at right-angles to Bedern Close. This was **Building 20**, most of which was beyond the north-west edge of excavation, although the south-east wall and a fragment of the north-east wall were identified (Fig.223). Building 20 was of similar construction to Building 10, judging from the surviving limestone rubble foundations set into a construction trench of its south-east wall. This wall had been of typical timber-framed construction with a sill beam and dwarf wall constructed between the upright wall-posts. Within the c.4·3m length was evidence for settings for upright timbers, but, with only a small part of the south-east end of this building surviving, little more can be said about its construction as a whole. It appears that the interior of Building 20 was to the north-west, and that it only had one floor level, a lime mortar. A trench inside Building 20, parallel with its south-east wall, may have been associated with industrial activity; slag and casting moulds were recovered from its backfill.

At the south-western limit of the college precinct the area of extensive pits was levelled towards the end of Period 6 and **Building 13** was demolished.

Bedern North-East

Building 5 (Fig.381s)

During Phase 2 of Period 6 the south-west wall of Room 5D was replaced and moved slightly to the south-west. The original slot (1477) was backfilled with clay, and was replaced by a wall (1286*) consisting of clay-bonded limestone, surviving as a narrow irregular line. In the area south-west of Room 5D was a linear spread of tiles and cobbles (1511*). This spread was later covered by a deposit of limestone chippings (1464).

At the end of Period 6, an extensive demolition spread of clay loam (1274, 1285), containing tile fragments and flecks of mortar, was deposited over the limestone chippings (1464) in the south-east part of Room 5D. This was cut by a number of small and short-lived features including three post-holes (1288, 1296, 1310), and a linear slot (1281) with a fourth post-hole (1327) within it.

Fig.224 *Area 14.II, Period 6: hearth 1301, looking south-east, showing a re-used half-millstone under the scale. Scale unit 0·1m*

Room 5E was apparently subdivided into two in a manner appearing to correspond to the earlier room layout of Rooms 5B and 5C. Although no new partition survived, the existence of two contemporary hearths, each with its own associated floor and use spread, implies this subdivision. The north-west half of the room contained a rectangular clay-bonded hearth (1412, 1414) built into the earlier floor deposit (1420), and overlain by a charcoal spread (1395), covered in turn by a spread of burnt sandy mortar (1426). A small, steep-sided pit (1409) sealed by a thick layer of clay (1396) was associated with these layers. Contemporary with the hearth, and at the south-east end of Room 5E, there was a second pitched tile hearth (1205) constructed on an earlier floor deposit (1425, Fig.365s) in a similar position to the earlier spread of charcoal (1461).

During the final period of use, when the subdivsion had presumably been abandoned, a deposit of clay and charcoal with mortar and tile inclusions was laid down. Set into this were the remains of a semi-circular hearth (1301*) of pitched tiles radiating from a broken half-millstone in its centre (Fig.224). To the south-east of this, and separated from it by a modern intrusion, there was another small remnant of the same hearth, consisting of cobbles and a few pitched tiles set into burnt clay (1417*). To the south-west there was a small irregular spread of flat limestone slabs (1406*) within a shallow scoop which may be all that remains of a small oven. A limestone spread (1371) con-

taining a fragment of stone four-lobed flower was also deposited in this area (242, AY 10/4).

Within Room 5F the internal partition (1385) was removed, returning the room to its original arrangement. Following this a new clay floor (1295) was laid down in association with two hearths. One of these, 1234, consisting of pitched tiles, was set to the south-east of the room, presumably against the south-east wall separating this room from Room 5E. The other, 1380, was towards the north-west of the room, and only survived as several small flat tiles. Associated with hearth 1234 was a spread of charcoal (1236). There was a further hearth, 1455, consisting of pitched tiles bonded with clay, partly lying beneath the north-west edge of the excavation.

Bedern South-West

Building 17 (Fig.383s)

The corridor within Building 17 was altered during the latter part of Period 6 by the creation of two new wall-lines. The south-west wall (7521*, Fig.382s) was disused and its foundations were covered by a thick clay (7229, Fig.370s) which also overlay an exterior deposit of mixed sand and limestone chips (7219). This clay contained an Edward I penny deposited c.1320–51 (AY 18/1, 101). A new south-west wall (7302*) was built on the same alignment, in a construction trench bedded in sandy clay (7325*) and backfilled with more clay (7320, Fig.368s) containing fragments of painted wall plaster (sf2701–2). This new wall was brick-built with evenly spaced limestone post-pads. It was later partially robbed by means of a shallow cut (7323) filled with charcoal and clay. A nearby padstone (7175*) may have been associated.

Wall 7353 was also altered at this stage, being replaced at several points along its length, resulting in a wall of four different builds. The first 3m running south-east from the north-west wall (7337) remained unchanged, but the next 2m section was removed and the trench backfilled with clay (7326*, Fig.368s), forming a slight sandy clay ridge. The wall-line was then continued by a new stretch of wall (7322*, Fig.366s), approximately 2m in length. This consisted of a single line of limestones with brick footings and post-pads, set in a construction trench. The construction cut was backfilled with a sandy clay (7319, Fig.366s) which spread along the corridor to the south-west and with a similar construction spread (7162, Fig.366s) to the north-east inside a newly created room. The final length of wall (7332*) consisted of a single line of limestone blocks with some brick and cobble set into clay, and it appeared to have been built slanting to the north-east, making the corridor wider at its south-east end.

The corridor contained a series of very mixed spreads, mostly consisting of silty loams with crushed tile and limestone, ash and mortar. These do not appear to represent deliberate flooring, but rather a gradual build-up over time.

A layer of sandy silt and crushed brick (7314) spread down the corridor and ran up to the threshold at the north-west. This was covered by a deposit of silty loam containing crushed tile and limestone (7306, Fig.366s) which ran the full length of the corridor as a thin layer, thickening at the north-west end with inclusions of ash where it ran against the south-west wall. This was overlain by a thin patchy spread of clay (7303, Fig.366s), and a deposit of sand (7311, Fig.368s) against the south-west wall, spreading into the corridor, but also set into a shallow trench. Several deposits of mixed sandy clay loams, some with ash, mortar and broken tile (7077–9, 7178), were also found in this area. In the extreme south-east of the corridor, butting up against its north-east side, was a clay and charcoal layer (7217) overlain by a dark ashy loam (7180).

The contrast with the area to the north-east of the corridor wall was by now very great, as this was divided into at least three rooms by the construction of two partitions running north-east from the main internal division. The evidence surviving for the nature of these walls was slight, but they employed foundation blocks of limestone bonded with clay.

The first internal wall was inserted from the junction of walls 7326 and 7322, and ran beyond the edge of the excavation. This wall was constructed of thin limestone blocks packed with clay. Another similar, slight internal wall was apparently built further to the south-east, at the junction of walls 7322 and 7332, although only one limestone block survived. These two divisions partitioned the interior of Building 17 into three rooms, which explains the differing builds of the corridor wall. The rooms are designated from the north-west as A, B and C.

Room 17A was c.6m long; within it was a small pit (7373) backfilled with cobbles and limestone rubble. Amongst the first internal deposits were clays (7387, 7391) and ash and charcoal (7156). The latter was cut by the construction pit for a post-pad, backfilled with sand (7383) and clay (7378). Several sandy clay deposits (7363–5) were next laid down, covered by a mortar deposit (7357, Fig.368s). Also in this area were a series of clay loams, some with charcoal and ash (7173*, Fig.368s, 7221, 7227, 7286, 7288, 7290, 7294–5, 7328, 7330, Fig.368s, 7334, 7341, 7348, 7351). The finds evidence provides no real clue as to function of this room; a bone tuning peg (8063, AY 17/12) and a fired clay gaming counter (sf2722) chipped from a tile were all that were recovered. Cutting clay 7173 was a brick standing (7188*) and a re-used limestone block (7174*), now functioning as a possible post-pad. This clay was also cut by two small pits (7165*, Fig.368s, 7171*) with fills of clay loam, bricks and mortar.

Room 17B was smaller, being c.3m in length. The first internal deposit was a sandy clay loam (7162) spreading from the construction of the corridor wall (7322). Spreads of sandy clay loams (7345, Fig.368s, 7346) were then deposited, covered by a mortar deposit (7152*) with inclusions of limestone fragments, which ran under a limestone post-pad to the south-east, packed with a greasy clay. This post-pad was possibly associated with the partition between Rooms 17B and 17C. It is likely that 7152 and 7173 were contemporary.

As for Room 17C, all internal levels were beyond the edge of the excavation.

Building 14 (Fig.383s)

Building 14 was also altered during Period 6, Phase 2, beginning with the infilling of the gap between the two 'entrance' padstones of wall 7551 (E on Fig.383s). Traces of the infill wall had been removed by a later robber trench (7343) but it was indicated by two coterminous layers: a charcoal spread (7411, Figs.369–70s) which ran north-east, and a layer of crushed limestone (7402, Fig.369s) which ran south-west, up to the Phase 1 internal wall (7423, Fig.382s), and covered the Phase 1 south-west buttress wall (7515). A large upstanding lump of mortar (7413) was found butting against the padstone at the south-east end of the south-west wall (7374, Fig.380s), surrounded by an extensive spread of clay loam (7395). At the same time a new entrance was created in the north-east wall, further to the south-east. Here, a length of wall was dismantled to its foundations, and then a series of ash, charcoal and clay layers (7386, 7389–90) built up against them, overlying 7395. Finally a clay layer with flecks of mortar (7381), overlain by a mortar spread with one small limestone block (7380), covered the foundations entirely and spread northeast over the Phase 1 courtyard spread (7283). A later intrusion made it impossible to estimate the original width of this entrance.

To the south-west, inside Building 14, a peaty clay (7370, Fig.369s) covered the earlier limestone 7402 and the internal wall 7423, as well as extending in a south-easterly direction. All internal deposits were covered by an extensive clay (7347, Fig.369s) which merged with clay (7354) to the south-west. This clay contained fragments of painted wall plaster (sfs2732, 2737, 2744; see p.606) and quantities of fish bone (Hall et al. 1993a).

It then appears that once again the original opening in the north-east wall was reinstated, this time by the removal of the small length of infill wall by a robber trench which cut down through clay 7347 and was then immediately filled with clay (7343) to form a small ridge. After this, a deposit of crushed limestone (7335, Fig.369s) was placed in the centre of the building, covered by an ashy loam (7331, Fig.369s). These deposits also contained further fragments of painted wall plaster (sfs2718, 2724). In the south-east of the building was a spread of ash and charcoal (7355). The first hearth (7248*, Fig.369s) to be built cut ash 7331 and was of the usual pitched tile construction. There is no evidence that the second entrance to this building was blocked up at this point.

The south-east wall of Building 14 (i.e. of Room B) comprised a line of limestones (7243*) with clay packing. The internal partition wall between Rooms 14A and 14B was replaced by a wall with a limestone threshold (7410*) with a post-pad at its south-west side. A thin deposit of mortar (7431*) in Room 14A may represent a new floor level.

At the same time Room 14E was replaced by the more elaborate Room 14G, represented by several lengths of walling and two hearths. The original entrance to Room 14E was blocked by a north-east/south-west line of worked limestone blocks (7460*, Fig.370s), including a moulded voussoir (180, AY 10/4) of the late 12th century. Approximately 1m to the north-west, and extending north-east from the division between Rooms 14A and 14B, was a second short length of limestone block and padstone wall (7362*). This wall was built in a shallow foundation trench filled with limestone and rubble bonded with clay, and also contained some fragments of painted wall plaster (sf2747).

The remainder of Room 14G was presumably to the north-west, where a substantial hearth (7064*, Fig.370s) consisted of an edging of limestone blocks with a wall of stacked tile (Fig.225). It was set onto layers of sandy clay loam and mortar (7414, 7424), with a clay foundation deposit set into a construction trench, delimited by a north-west/south-east limestone block wall with a broken limestone top build. On the north-west and south-east sides of this hearth was an edging of limestone blocks.

Fig.225   Area 13.X, Period 6: Building 14 hearth 7064, looking south-east. Scale unit 0·1m

Inside the south-east side of this edging and to the inside of the wall to the north-east was a horizontally stacked roof tile wall bonded with mortar and built over part of the north-east wall. The floor of the hearth was of clay-bonded limestone and broken tile, all subsequently burnt through continued use. A layer of ash and charcoal (7118*) was the last use deposit spread around the hearth.

A spread of clay (7110) covered ash 7118, and a second south-east stacked tile wall was built against the earlier one (7064), slightly realigning the hearth.

In the north corner of the trench at this time was a pitched tile feature (7405*) edged on the south-east and south-west sides with limestone blocks. Although there was no evidence of burning this was probably another hearth.

Hearth 7064 went out of use with the deposition of a large spread of clay loam (7050) at the north-east end of the site, which covered its north-east wall as well as fully covering 7405. A pitched tile feature (7028), another possible hearth, was built over the area of hearth 7064, after its disuse.

Outside Building 14 to the north-east was an area of crushed limestone, with one large limestone block on its surface (7412, Fig.369s). In the south-east this was overlain by a clay spread with limestone and charcoal inclusions (7407) which partially extended over the Phase 1 courtyard spread 7283, as well as by sandy clays (7304, 7307), mortar and crushed limestone (7305), and charcoal and clay (7298). A mortared limestone wall (7293*) at the north edge of the trench was set into a mixed clay loam (7285) just to the north-east of a small area of limestone (7292*), the possible remnants of a cobbled stone surface.

To the east of Building 14 there was a line of cobbles (7276*) set onto clay packing. Although the junction of this wall with Building 14 had been removed by a later cess pit (7039, Fig.370s), it appears to have formed the north-west side of an alleyway to which Building 17 formed part of the south-east side. Where this alleyway enclosed the earlier courtyard surface (7283) this was repaired with a spread of crushed tile (7491*) and continued in use. The alleyway also enclosed a dark sand which had later been consolidated with some cobbles (7133*, Fig.370s).

The disuse of Room 14D was marked by the digging of a lined pit (7275*) cutting deposit 7354, which backed onto part of wall 7374 (Fig.226). The north-east wall of the pit was of stacked tile, and both the south-west and south-east walls were of tile, limestone and brick, the south-east wall being backed by a new and substantial limestone wall. With the disuse of this building, ditch 7344 (Period 5, Fig.380s) was backfilled with a clay which merged with a

Fig.226   Area 13.X, Period 6: stacked tile-lined pit 7275, looking north-west. Scale unit 0·1m

deposit of rubble and mortar (7404). This deposit also partly covered the foundations of the Phase 1 wall 7481 after its disuse. A small pit (7388*) cut both 7404 and wall 7481; it was backfilled with clay and included much of the articulated skeleton of a dog.

Room 14D was superseded by new Room 14F with the construction of a wall (7398*) which formed the north-west and south-west sides of an extension to the original room. This wall was L-shaped and roughly built from large limestone blocks packed with mortar and clay, with padstones situated at both ends. Where its south-east end joined Building 10 a new padstone was inserted, while the west corner was marked by a double padstone (7317*), both being positioned in a pit packed with clay and cobbles. A circular pattern of post voids found beneath the double padstone suggests that this was set upon timber piling, presumably to combat subsidence into the soft ditch fills at this point. The new north-east wall (7473*) of limestone and cobble was built on clay (7471) which also bonded this new wall. The only surviving interior deposit was a small patch of clay (7399*) covering 7404.

The south-east wall still appears to have been formed by the north–south alleyway wall 7538, although towards the end of Period 6 the Period 4 clay deposit 7430 was covered by an ash spread (7428) which contained much broken pottery, as well as some tumble from Period 4 wall 7489, indicating that this wall fell into disuse shortly after the deposition of the ash, and that Room 14F must have been short-lived.

Building 20 (Fig.383s)

The north-east wall (7105*) of Building 20 comprised small limestone blocks infilled with tile fragments, resting on limestone and brick footings (7255). The tops of the blocks were bonded with mortar, the rest with loam. The continuation to the south-west was marked by a line of bricks (7106*), although this had been interrupted by a later intrusion. The main stretch of south-east wall (6294*) was set into a construction trench (6331) which cut into the earlier silty loams. It was constructed of limestone rubble foundations surviving only to a maximum height of 0·2m. The excavated length was 4·3m, its greatest width 0·2m. Included in the fabric of the wall were a few re-used stone blocks, including a section with angled faces (*208, AY* 10/4), dated to before the 13th century on the basis of the tooling, and a fragment from a large 'waterleaf' type capital (*3*). The stylistic similarity between capital fragment *3* and capitals from Archbishop Roger's 12th century Minster choir has led to the suggestion of a possible Minster origin (ibid., p.243). However, since the choir was not demolished until 1394 and Building 20 must pre-date the major 14th century construction phase of the vicars choral another origin must be preferred. In fact similar pieces are also known from other York churches, such as St Michael Spurriergate.

At a distance of 0·35m from the north-east end of the wall there was a large limestone post-pad, 0·4m square and 0·25m thick. A further 2·65m to the south-west there was a socket for a timber post, comprising a c.0·2m square aperture, 0·06m deep, framed by laid tiles on the north-east side and by a single limestone on the south-west side, with a single limestone in its base. The interior levels to Building 20 lay to the north-west and survived only as a very small deposit of white lime mortar (6325*). Evidence for an irregular linear feature (6324), at least 4m long, was recovered along the north-west edge of the excavation, inside Building 20. This was filled with clay and clay loam, producing evidence for industrial activity in the form of slag and casting moulds, as well as the kicked base from a glass flask (sf2458) and pottery on which there were industrial residues.

Bedern long trench

A small pit with a sandy fill (1089) had been cut through the Phase 1 deposits, but was mostly beyond the north-western end of the trench. There was a small pit with an organic fill (1090) and a small rubble-filled pit (1091) further to the south-east. Towards the end of Period 6 a small dump of mortar (1063) was also placed in this area.

Building 13 went out of use and 1566 and 1571 (Fig.364s), both containing pottery of the mid 14th century, were deposited over wall 1572. 1566 was cut by a pit

1601 (Fig.364s) with several organic fills (1604–5, Fig.364s). Clay spreads (1573, 1575, Fig.364s) then sealed Building 13 and pit 1601, and were in turn covered by a further clay layer (1570, Fig.364s). Spread 1575 was cut by a pit (1612) on the north-east side of the trench. The Period 5 loam spread (1609) was overlain by clay with mortar and tile rubble (1608, 1610), and then cut by a pit (1607, Fig.364s).

Bedern Foundry (pp.172–3, Fig.68, AY 10/3:
Period 3, Phases 4–6)

During Period 6.2 the north-eastern area continued to be utilised for pits and the Phase 1 surface was cut by a further pit with interleaved peaty and silty fills (2478–80) with remains of yellowish grass or reeds. A new surface make-up of sandy clay and rubble (2472) was also deposited at about this time. A thin layer of mortar fragments (966) was deposited, and this was cut by a small pit or post-hole (2654).

Towards the end of Period 6 this heavily pitted area was levelled with dumps of grey silts (2570, 2572, 2631, 2662) up to 0·37m deep over the earlier pits. The silt contained part of a possible money box in an orange sandy ware (*AY* 16/9 in prep., B431). A number of horizontal planks (2618) from the side of the Phase 1 wood-lined pit (2558, see p.458) may represent the demolition of the remains of its lining.

One earlier pit (2654) was capped with a rubble surface of pitched tiles and limestone fragments (2647). Traces of a wooden beam (971) may represent the lower part of a toppled post. The rubble was sealed by a layer of clay (965) with tile and mortar fragments. Clay and tile rubble (2023, 2939) was deposited over the wall footings of Building 13.

465

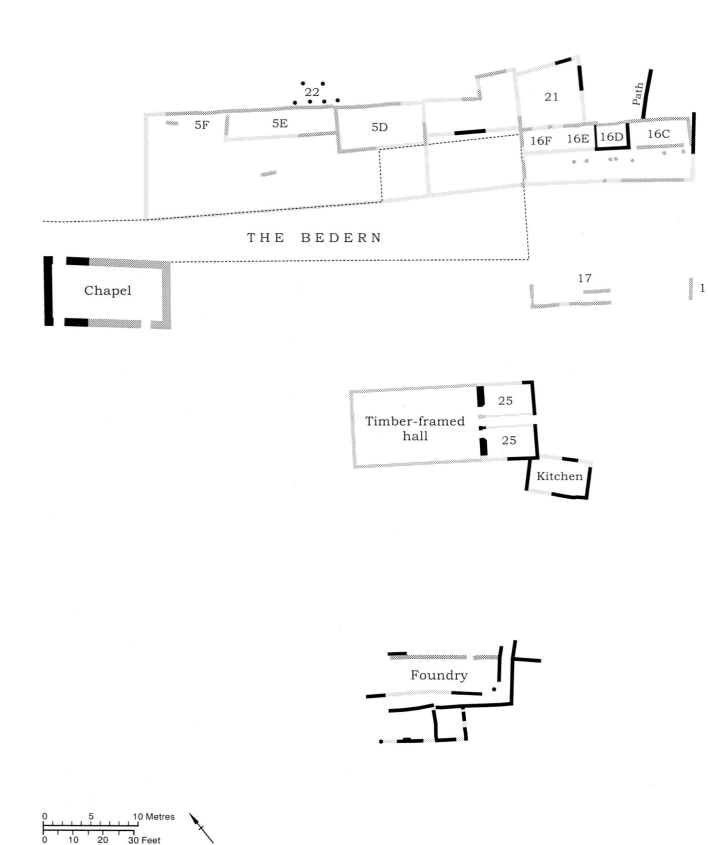

THE BEDERN

5F   5E   5D   22   21   Path

16F 16E 16D 16C

Chapel

17   1

Timber-framed hall   25   25   Kitchen

Foundry

0   5   10 Metres
0   10   20   30 Feet

Fig.227   Period 7.1: interpretative summary phase plan, showing building development. For the key, see Fig.195, p.409. Scale 1:400

466

Period 7: mid 14th–early 15th century (Fig.227)

During Period 7 there was a major transformation of Bedern, coinciding with renewed attempts to revive communal life in the college. This was concentrated on newly acquired land south-west of the close and involved the reconstruction of the common hall, the building of a service wing, including a kitchen block, and the development of a second courtyard to the south-west of it. From the last quarter of the 14th century until the early 15th century it appears, from both documentary and archaeological evidence, that there was almost continuous building activity throughout Bedern, including the alteration of existing buildings and the erection of new ones, and the expansion of the chapel. It was during this period also that the vicars obtained a licence to construct a bridge over Goodramgate.

Period 7, Phase 1

The interior of **Building 16** underwent a series of alterations. The original south-east end wall was thickened and strengthened, possibly to allow an extension to the south-east. Within the building, four new rooms, 16C–16F, were created in the area originally divided into the two rooms 16A and 16B. All but one contained a hearth, and one contained a stone-lined latrine pit. Unfortunately, however, few of the partitions between these rooms survived. The area within Building 16 to the south-west of the central post-pads remained as in the previous period, with its extensive earthen floor apparently undisturbed, perhaps indicating that this was not used as living quarters.

To the north-east of Building 16 **Building 21** was constructed. Although poorly preserved, its plan can be reconstructed from its north-east and south-east limestone walls. The other walls and most of the internal levels had been removed by modern intrusions, but there was at least one mortar floor deposit. There was an external limestone path, parallel with its south-east wall, which ran to an entrance in the north-east wall of Building 16. South-east of the path and parallel with it, was a limestone and cobble wall running up to and abutting Building 16. As no other building walls appear to be associated with this wall, it probably served as a boundary in open land.

The external area north-east of Building 5 now contained a small timber-framed outbuilding, **Building 22**. This may have been used in association with the cess pits dug further to the south-east at this time, although it does not appear to have enclosed them. A linear tiled drain running north-east/south-west associated with these pits was also perhaps used in connection with the outbuilding.

In Period 7 the north-west wall of **Bedern Chapel** was demolished and the building was extended to the north-west to produce a rectangular structure, c.14m (north-west/south-east) × 8m, the present chapel. Earth was piled against the crude stonework at the base of the new walls and at the same time was presumably piled around the other walls thus giving the impression that the chapel was built on a slight mound.

Replanning of the alleyway (originally established in Period 6) north-west of Building 17 is assigned to Phase 2b with the construction of three new lengths of wall. Building 14 is therefore thought to have been demolished in Phase 1. A pitched tile hearth located to the north-west of this alleyway indicated the presence of further buildings in this area, but the structural evidence for these was inconclusive.

In the east corner of Area 13.X it appears that **Building 18** may have continued in use throughout Period 7.

Building 10 was demolished to make way for major construction operations. The focus of this activity was the reconstruction of the college **hall**, as well as the creation of a kitchen block; an open courtyard lay to the south-west and a garden area to the south-east. Although all archaeological traces of any earlier hall had been removed by the massive stone foundations of its replacement, the position of the former can be inferred from the adjacent service wing, Building 25, which can be shown to pre-date the surviving hall. It is assumed that the first hall was timber-framed, and probably of the same size as its replacement, c.14m (north-west/south-east) × 8·5m externally.

Building 25 was constructed in a similar position to that of Building 20. There was little evidence for Building 25 within the excavation, apart from the foundations of three of its walls. It measured c.9m in length (north-east/south-west) and is assumed to have been c.6·2m wide, from its relationship with Bedern Hall. The south-east wall contained a central entrance, c.1·1m wide. The construction trenches for the wall foundations were c.0·8m wide by 0·5m deep. They were solidly packed with limestone chippings, onto which the wall footings had been directly placed. The foundations were of mortar-bonded limestone, with some re-used ashlar work, containing occasional tile-bonding courses. Each side wall contained a plinth course. A brick feature, possibly for an exterior post, butted onto the south-east end of the south-east wall. Only one floor level was identified within Building 25, consisting of an extensive spread of clay, apparently well worn and repaired at least once. Building 25 was obviously of some importance, to judge from its substantial construction. The massive foundations suggest that its lower storey was built in stone, although timber-framing from the upper part of its north-west wall was preserved below the eaves of Bedern Hall (see Fig.234, p.474), demonstrating that the upper storey must have been timber-framed, and that the building was c.9m high, to the apex of the roof. Its position in relation to the college hall suggests that this was the service wing, comprising the pantry and buttery, with access to the kitchen block beyond. It would not be unusual for the importance of the security of this wing to warrant at least partial construction in stone, even though the hall itself was initially timber-framed in its entirety.

Immediately to the south-east was an open area where extensive dumps of clay and other material accumulated. The **kitchen** itself was situated south-west of this, beyond a timber-framed partition. The south-west wall of the kitchen only survived in part, its north-west portion having been removed by a later building. It is suggested also that the north-west kitchen wall had been removed by a later robber trench. Four stages of use were traced within the kitchen, each stage involving a reorganisation of the facilities. During the first phase, a central hearth and a tile-lined drain were constructed.

To the south-west it appears that the area beyond the fence may have served as a stable area, although a number of rubbish pits were still in use.

Bedern North-East (Fig.384s)

Building 16

The rooms in the north-east half of Building 16 appear to have been altered, and at least some of its outer walls were repaired. A new section (4315*) was inserted into the north-east wall, comprising clay-bonded cobbles and small limestone blocks set on to a tile footing. Pottery sherds from the clay bonding date this rebuild to the late 14th or 15th century. To the south-east of the building, a new line of limestones (4319*) was constructed parallel and adjacent to the Period 6 wall (4311), with three stake-holes to the south-east. Butting against the new wall was a spread of silt (4325) which also filled the stake-holes. Another line of limestone and brick (4312*) was then constructed over this silt, against the new wall.

An extensive clay spread (4206) was deposited over the earlier (Period 6) north-west partition wall (4361) to Room 16A, spreading to either side of it. At the same time a new limestone and cobble wall, packed with clay (4307*), was inserted approximately 3m to the north-west of the earlier partition, resulting in the creation of a larger room, 16C. This wall contained two limestone padstones, one in the centre and one at its south-west end. Internal floors consisted of a series of sandy clay and loam deposits (4227, 4225, 4212, 4211). There was no evidence of a hearth.

The area to the north-west of Room 16C was then sub-divided into three rooms. The first of these rooms, 16D, was probably created with the insertion of a north-west division. Although this did not survive, it may have run from a large limestone post-pad (4371*) to another padstone in the north-east wall, and may be represented by a rubble deposit (4234*). During the creation of Room 16D the north-west end of its south-west wall (i.e. formerly the south-west wall of Room 16B, 4322) was replaced by a length of faced limestone and brick wall set into a construction trench filled with clay and ash (4146*). This terminated at the post-pad (4371) which was set into the fill of a pit (4372).

Within Room 16D a large hearth (4207; replaced in Phase 2a by 4204*, see p.479) was built against the north-east wall, a stacked roof-tile fire-proof back (4237*) probably replacing the sill wall and any timber framing here. The opportunity was also taken at this stage partly to rebuild this north-east wall in brick, set on a sandy clay bedding (4241). Other internal levels consisted of mixed ash and clay (4309), a loam spread (4209), a small clay and broken tile feature (4224*) set into a spread of clay loam (4261), against the south-east wall, and a dark loam (4236) butted against the stacked tile wall. A thin spread of ash and charcoal (4214) was associated with the hearth.

Fig.228 Area 14.IV, Period 7: rectangular tile-lined feature 4131, looking south. Scale unit 0·1m

Adjoining 16D was 16E, a room of similar size created by the probable insertion of a division wall to the north-west, which unfortunately did not survive. Internally, several clay spreads (4259, 4263, 4282) were deposited, overlain by a small spread of mortar and crushed lime-stone (4256) and a clay loam (4253). This was covered by a thin ash deposit (4279), onto which was set a hearth of pitched tiles (4242*) with a stacked tile wall to the north-west (4250) and a row of small limestones packed in clay to the south-east. There were several associated clay, ash and charcoal spreads (4223, 4231, 4240, 4295, 4304). A rec-tangular, stone-lined pit (4345*) was dug into deposits within Room 16E; re-used stone consisting of a mullion moulding patch (247) and a mullion section (249), both of late 13th–early 14th century date, were found within the lining (*AY* 10/4). The pit fill comprised sandy clay silt with patches of yellow and black ash, and burnt soil. A sample contained a few plant remains, including greater celandine and elderberry, as well as charcoal, bone, fish scale and eggshell (Hall et al. 1993c).

At the north-west end of this building was Room 16F, which contained a hearth (4027*) with a limestone and cobble kerbing on its south-east and south-west sides, con-structed not only of pitched tiles but also, more unusually, of broken edge-set pottery. Contemporary with this was a floor of sandy loam (4194), covering a deposit of loam with mortar flecks (4202).

Within the south-west portion of Building 16, a number of pits had been cut through the earlier levels at the begin-ning of Period 7. These comprised a large circular cobble-and limestone-filled pit (4359*), a shallow pit (4208), a small pit with mixed rubble fills (4352), and a fourth pit (4348) which contained a fragment of glass tubing (sf836). The pits seem to bear no relation to one another, but are as-sumed to be contemporary because they were all sealed by a sandy loam spread (4198*).

North-east of Building 16 a path of limestone rubble and crushed limestone (4162*) was laid down over a loam spread (4180*). A limestone and cobble wall (4178*) was then built parallel to this, to the south-east. A long cross penny of 1256–60 (*AY* 18/1, *82*) was found within this wall. Cut into these external deposits there was a rectangular tile-lined feature (4131; Fig.228) containing sandy silty fills, set into four 'compartments' formed with tiles. It incorpor-ated a small fragment of roll moulding (*232, AY* 10/4) in its construction. The small flot from the sampled fill in-cluded much plant material, with a trace of elderberry in the residue (Hall et al. 1993c). From the nature of the fills it would appear that this feature once contained water.

Building 21

The south-east wall of Building 21 (4141*), cutting the loam deposit (4180), was built from limestone blocks bonded with mortar. At its south-west end the wall pack-ing was of coarse mortar and clay (4167/4159) which ex-tended to the north-west as a construction spread, whilst at the north-east end the wall was set directly over the Period 3 pitched tile hearth (4166), with its construction trench cutting through it. The north-east wall (4190*) only survived for a length of approximately 1m, and consisted of a limestone wall set into a construction trench cutting the clay loam (4116) in this area.

The deposits within this building are difficult to correl-ate due to the amount of modern disturbance, but associ-ated with the south-east wall (4141*) were sandy silt layers (4152) overlain by a mortar floor (4153). To the north-west of these deposits, and entirely isolated by modern intru-sions, was a small area of highly compacted ash (4123*).

Building 22

In the external area to the north-east of Building 5, little can be traced in the south-eastern part of Area 14.II be-cause of modern intrusions. However, to the north-west of these intrusions was a pit (1456) filled with organic de-posits, cutting another similar pit (1469/70) filled with peat, ashy soil and charcoal. The beetle fauna suggested that the first pit was a cess pit, probably well-sealed. The plants included traces of deadly nightshade, as well as fig, *Sphagnum* leaves and several weeds of waste ground or damp areas. The sample also yielded traces of occupation debris including bark, bone, stone and wood (Hall et al. 1993b). The bone assemblage was dominated by the remains of sheep, with lesser numbers of cattle bones, a relatively low incidence of pig, and a high incidence of poultry. Cat was also present. Interestingly, a relatively large sample of haddock and gadid bones were recovered; given the recovery problems they may be all that survived of a diverse fish bone assemblage (Hamshaw-Thomas 1994). An attempt had been made to level the pits with dumped deposits (1344, 1378). Towards the centre of this area, an extensive layer of charcoal-flecked clay loam (1418, Fig.365s/1256) was deposited. A fragment of an enamelled beaker (sf323) was excavated from this layer. Set into it and forming a rectangular structure were at least five postpads (1432–4*, 1435*, Fig.365s, 1476* and one unnumbered on Fig.384s), each consisting of a rectangular limestone block surrounded by and set on top of a foundation of small limestones and tiles.

To the east of Building 22, also cut into the clay loam (1418/1256), was a large pit (1479*) filled with a deposit of organic peat. A sample of the fill yielded a modest list of identifiable plants (Hall et al. 1993b). For the most part, the plants were weeds of one kind or another, with some evidence for grassland or weed vegetation on damper soils. Evidence for faeces was present in the form of traces of faecal concretions but the only probable food remains were fig seeds and elderberry. Fish and mammal bone, and fish scale and oyster shell, all present in trace amounts, may also represent food waste, but there were other components such as coal, mortar, chalk, brick/tile and rather large amounts of sand too. The insects included spider beetles and woodworm which may have come from a building, perhaps in sweepings. This pit was cut in turn by another (1500) filled with peat, tile and rubble in clay. Associated with these pits was an irregular clay spread containing tile (1450*), representing the remains of a drain running north-east/south-west. A sample of the slightly sandy silty clay fill contained brick/tile, limestone, charcoal, pottery, eggshell, bone and shellfish (Hall et al. 1993b). The identifiable plant remains included greater celandine and traces of two aquatic plants — duckweed and pond-

Fig.229   Area 14.II, Period 7: Building 5, wall 1262 in the foreground with cobble surface 1427 beyond, looking north-east. Scale unit 0·5m

weed. It seems unlikely that the drain carried floating and floating-leaved aquatic plants, so perhaps these remains arrived in river or pond water which was disposed of into the drain.

To the north-west an extensive spread of silty clay mixed with organic material (1386*) sealed all the Period 6 pits and deposits. This was itself cut by a pit (1384*) containing an organic peaty fill (1394) with evidence for an abundance of faecal material (Hall et al. 1993b). Faecal concretions, corncockle seed fragments and fig seeds were all recorded in large amounts and there was a considerable component of cereal 'bran'. Apart from traces of strawberry, blackberry, fennel, sloe and grape, most of the plants were probably weeds of some kind, though the presence of *Sphagnum* leaves and cotton-grass suggests some peatland materials, possibly peat itself, were present in this fill. There were also traces of occupation debris such as brick/tile, charcoal, bone and mortar. The faunal assemblage produced a large sample of gadid bones, dominated by cod and ling (Hamshaw-Thomas 1994).

To the north-west of this pit there was an extensive spread of large rounded cobbles (1427*), containing some tiles and limestones (Fig.229), and overlain by a spread of sandy mortar (1265). A fragment of a ceramic louver was recovered from the cobbles which joined a second piece found in the clay loam (1418, see p.608) beneath Building 22. Further pieces of a similar type were recovered from the area of Room 5H and Building 23 (see below). The faunal assemblage from the external spread was dominated by cattle, with significantly fewer numbers of sheep and pig. The number of horse bones was unusual. Deer, dog and cat were also present (Hamshaw-Thomas 1994).

Bedern Chapel (Fig.232, facing p.472)

In order to extend the chapel to the north-west the north-west wall (9083) of the Period 5 chapel was demolished, leaving only small projecting stubs at the north-east and south-west ends (the latter visible on Fig.232a).

A construction trench was dug for the extension to the south-west wall, cutting the earlier loams (9074, 9086). The trench was first lined with mortar (9082) and then loam (9079). At the north-western end of the south-west wall the trench was shallower, the first fill recognised being a sandy loam.

From the evidence of the trench dug to the south-west of the chapel (Fig.214, p.441), it appears that only a shallow construction trench (8006) was used (cut from 15.58m OD), as seen on the interior. The cut had been backfilled with loam mixed with mortar (8004), and loam dumps (8001, 8003) with some limestone blocks (8002) had then been piled against the wall. Above the cut the rough na-

Fig.230 *Trench south-west of Bedern Chapel, showing the foundations of the chapel south-west wall. Scale unit 0·1m*

ture of the stone work appears to indicate that it was still not meant to be seen (Fig.230). It is possible, therefore, that earth was originally banked up against these foundation courses, as high as the good coursed masonry, giving the appearance that the chapel was built upon a slight mound.

The new north-west wall was built in a construction cut over a mortar lining (9084), and the cut was then backfilled with a dark loam (9080). The first layer (9072) deposited after the construction runs up to each of the walls, covering their foundations. After the completion of building work a series of deposits were put down to level the interior before a usable floor surface was laid. The area where the old north-west wall had stood was covered by a mixed mortar layer (9077, Fig.232a) filling the robber trench. A dark loam (9071), containing some large limestone blocks (in which there was a chalk spindle whorl, sf148), was dumped to one side. The south-east end of the interior was then levelled with a loam dump (9068, Fig.232c), but this was immediately cut by a pit (9066) before a layer of crushed limestone (9064) was placed on top. At the same time it appears that a deposit of burnt sand (9057, Fig.232b) built up, perhaps as a result of a small fire or brazier used in the building works. A thick mixed mortar (9076) filled a depression in the south-west.

A general layer of dark loam (9059, Fig.232b) may have been used to level the centre of the building. It contained a 17th century German jetton (AY 18/1, 303), but since the pottery is mainly 15th century, with possibly two 16th century sherds, this coin may be intrusive. A copper alloy buckle pin (sf137), an antler tine (8121, AY 17/12), and some silver wire (sf138) were found in the same layer. If the floor were boarded then each of these items may have fallen through gaps between the floorboards. At the south-

471

east end a deposit of mortar (9073, Fig.232c) was used to level the area.

Spreads of crushed mortar and limestone (9061, 9069, Fig.232a) were then deposited across the interior, except in the north-east corner where a small platform of limestone blocks (9070) was created above the construction trench.

The first apparent floor level comprised a layer of thin mortar and sand (9056, Fig.232b). A similar but heavily subsided layer (9058) was recorded at the south-east end of the chapel. At the north-west end of the chapel this floor level consisted of a series of interleaved lenses of sandy silts and sand (9062), containing a silver styca of Eanred, c.810–41, (AY 18/1, 16). These layers may represent the bedding for floor tiles, or they may have been floor surfaces in their own right, without any covering. A small pit was cut into the floor at the south-east end, and filled with a mixture of mortar and sand (9060), with large limestone blocks at its base. Pottery from these floor levels suggests they were deposited in the late 14th or 15th century.

Bedern South-West

Building 25 (Figs.234, 386s)

At the beginning of Period 7, Building 10 was demolished with the removal of a portion of the north-west wall by a robber trench (6308). A pit (7445), subsequently filled with cobbles, limestone and tiles, was cut through the internal wall 7419.

These changes coincided with the levelling up of the area immediately to the north-west of Building 10 by a series of garden loams (6338, 6340*, Fig.368s, 6305*, 6285), followed by the deposition of a large dump of domestic rubbish and clay loam (6310*). Pottery from these deposits suggests that this occurred during the late 14th or early 15th century. Some of this material spread into the building through the gap created by the removal of wall 6297, before a layer of clean brown clay (6174*, Fig.368s) with inclusions of brick, tile and limestone rubble filled the robber trench 6308 and spread south-east and north-west over the rubbish dump 6310. There were a variety of artefacts within clay layer 6174, including two bone parchment prickers (8052, 8054, AY 17/12), an ivory handle (8116), a stone hone (sf2447) and an iron rowel spur (sf2446). Set into the surface of 6174 was a small pit (6163). It was at this time that the south-east wall foundations of Building 20 were sealed throughout their length by clay (6293), which also filled the robber trench 6308 and covered deposit 6310. By this time, therefore, Building 20 was disused. The entire area north-west of Building 10, including the interior of Building 20, was then covered by an extensive clay deposit (6271, Fig.368s, 6284) with a heavy ash content which contained a variety of domestic refuse, in-

cluding bone manufacturing debris (7997), two stone hones (sfs2390, 2394), white-painted plaster (sf2410), and a copper alloy jetton of Edward I, 1272–1307 (AY 18/1, 140). Examination of the faunal assemblage from context 6271 (AY 15/5) revealed considerable numbers of cattle bones, a smaller proportion of sheep, and some pig. The cattle bones included several fragments from the skull of a young calf, though other elements were mostly from mature individuals. There were also a number of bones from domestic fowl and geese, plus duck, woodcock and dove.

A levelling deposit of loam (6280) sealed the clay and ash (6271 = 6284), and set into this were the construction

Fig.231 Area 13.X, Period 7: Building 25, looking south-west, showing (left) the south-east wall 6061/6145. Scale unit 0·1m

South-West

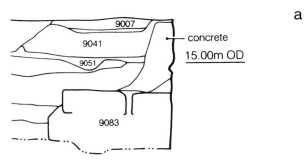

a

9007
9041
9051
concrete
15.00m OD
9083

South-West

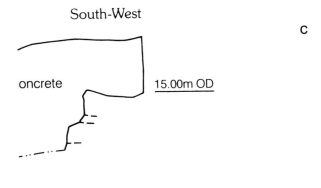

b

)029
9018
9014
9020
9031
9047
9049
51
9059
15.00m OD

South-West

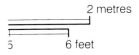

c

oncrete
15.00m OD

2 metres

5
6 feet

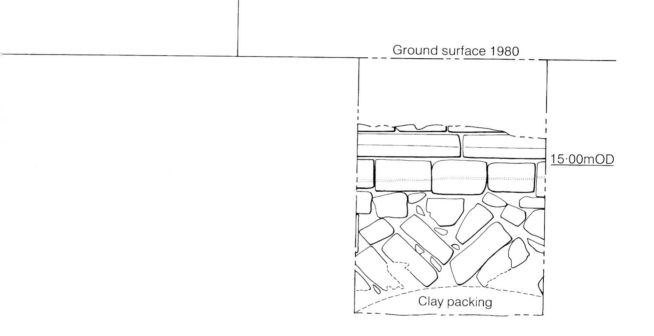

Ground surface 1980

15·00mOD

Clay packing

1   2 Metres

4   6 Feet

trenches for Building 25. The north-west wall of this building was outside the area of excavation, as were much of the north-east and south-west walls, but the south-east wall (6061*/6145*) survived almost in full. The construction trenches were filled with densely packed limestone chippings, with the walls directly constructed onto these footings. The foundations of each wall were of mortar-bonded limestone, with plentiful re-used moulded work involving a large number of ashlar blocks (e.g. *115, 145*). It has been suggested (*AY 10/4*) that several of these pieces originated in Archbishop Roger's Minster choir, which was demolished in the late 14th century, in which case they are likely to have been brought to Bedern in the very late 14th or early 15th century. One wall also incorporated a fragment of a stone mortar (sf2707). Occasional tile bonding courses were visible. Each of the walls was approximately 0·8m thick, and beneath the north-east and south-west walls a plinth course increased the thickness at that point to c.0·9m. The maximum surviving height of the demolished structure was c.1m above the top of the foundation packing. No plinth was visible beneath the south-east wall (6061*/6145*, Fig.231), the construction of which was otherwise identical to that of both the north-east wall (6224*) and the south-west wall (6146*). However, a 19th century construction trench had destroyed much of the south-east wall's north-east end. At the centre point of the south-east wall was an opening 1·1m in width across which the construction trench had not been carried. Overlying a mixed clay loam (6254, Fig.368s) was a brick feature (6255*) butting onto the south-east end of wall 6145*, possibly to support an exterior post. Situated nearby was a small patch of clay (6253). The pottery recovered from the construction trenches and associated levels of this building is very late in date in some cases; it is possible that we are dealing with contamination from the 19th century construction trench, or that there was a later rebuild of this end of Building 25 which entirely removed all evidence for the original build. Nonetheless, the large pottery assemblage from the major levelling layer under Building 25 (6271 = 6284) is consistent with construction in the late 14th century. The earliest levels identified within Building 25 were a clay floor (6292*, Fig.366s) which had been repaired in the east corner, and a crushed limestone surface (6080*) of which a small part appears on Fig.386s.

Building 25: Architectural discussion

By D.A. Stocker

The unequivocal evidence that the south-east wall of the surviving hall incorporated the remains of an earlier building, located to the south-east (i.e. Building 25), is laid out below (p.587). We can say, then, that Building 25 was of rectangular plan, measuring 9 × 6·25m internally. It was constructed on stone foundations and, although these foundations were slight when compared with those of the later hall to the

north-west, they are not inconsistent with a half-timbered building. What survives of this building's north-west wall (i.e. the present hall's south-east wall) is in two parts: an upper timber-framed part and a lower stone-built portion (Fig.234). Although there may be some doubt about the date of the present stone wall (see below), there can be little doubt that the timber framing belonged to a half-timbered building as there is no accommodation for any framing below it. The present lower rail is, therefore, a sill beam.

The timber framing of the upper part of the wall is featureless; it contains no windows or other openings. The bay division of the studs, however, suggests not only that the walls which adjoined it to the south-east were of timber-framed construction but also, if Building 25 was connected to a building to the north-west, on the site of the present hall, then that building too must have had thinner walls than the present stone walls. The alternative, that a predecessor of the present hall was stone built but with walls placed outside the line of the present ones, is not compatible with the excavation results, at the points where the foundations of the present hall were investigated (p.481). The key evidence, however, as to whether or not the pre-existing half-timbered building (Building 25) was connected to a building to the north-west, on the site of the present hall, is contained within the lower, stone-built, part of the wall.

Only crude measurements were possible when this area was reconstructed in 1980 but it is clear that there were originally a trio of doors here (see Fig.325, p.588). Trios of doors are characteristic of the service ends of halls, the three doors leading, by custom, to the buttery, the pantry (usually the two side doors) and the kitchen (often via the central doorway). The arrangement of doors in this fashion is so common as to be a standard arrangement and, where three doors are found with this layout, it would be necessary to find arguments against its being a hall service rather than to make arguments for such a function.

In this case, however, the key question is, are these service doorways (and the contemporary stone wall in which they were set) contemporary with the timber framing above it, or had the timber frame been under-built with a new stone wall (including doorways) when the present hall was built? This would

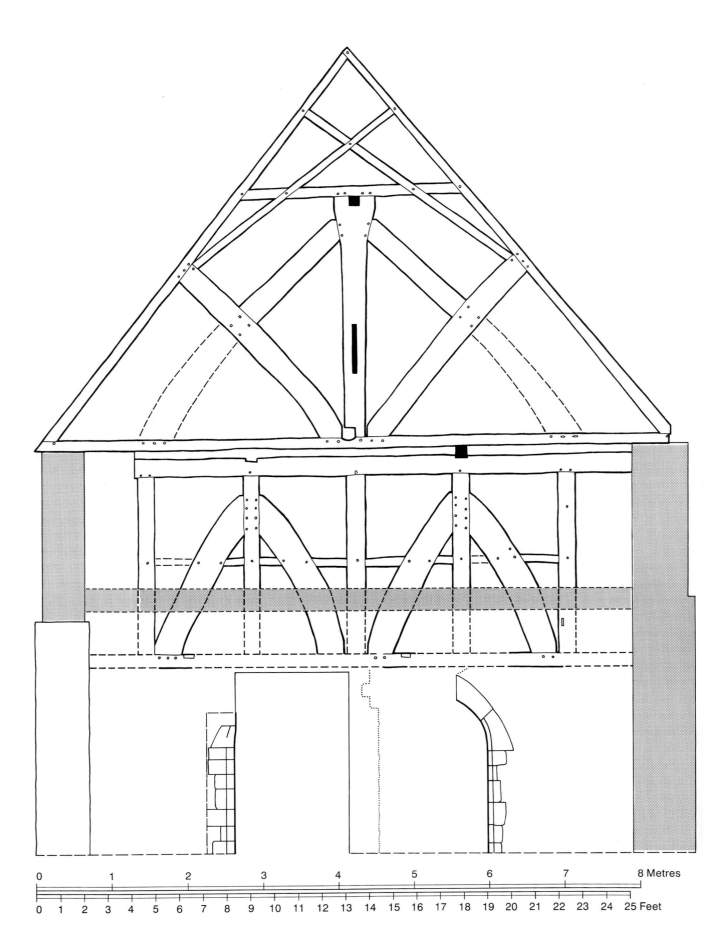

have been a difficult stratigraphic question to answer had a recording opportunity been available, but it was not and so certainty on the point is not possible. The critical evidence, at the point where the stone wall (i.e. north-west wall of Building 25) joined the north-east and south-west walls of the hall, had, anyway, been obscured by the reconstruction of the south-east end of the hall in the 19th century. The simplest explanation would be, however, not to interpose the additional complexity of a rebuilding of the lower part of the south-east wall when the present hall was built and this leaves us with the conclusion that the north-west wall of Building 25 was equipped with a trio of doors from its original construction.

As has been indicated, it is almost inconceivable that a trio of doorways of this sort would have been built in any other location except at the low end of a hall and, therefore, if the doors are contemporary with the early timber-framing, Building 25 must have been the service block for an earlier hall on the site of the present one. What is more, the bay division of the timber-framed part of the wall would suggest that this hall was on more or less the same lines as the later one but was of timber-framed construction.

Building 25, then, was perhaps a half-timbered, two-storeyed, service block serving a timber-framed hall on the site of the present one. The surviving sawn-off rafters show that it was roofed in three bays north-east to south-west and this would suggest that it was a cross-range viz-a-viz the hypothetical hall to the north-west. The excavation of Building 25 suggests that it was indeed divided into three internally, two chambers (the buttery and pantry?) to the north-east and south-west of a central passageway, which led right through the building and out to a detached kitchen via an open yard.

The dating of Building 25, and the earlier hall which may have gone with it, is reliant on the excavated sequence in the south-eastern part of Building 25. The timber-framing of the upper part of the wall is not sufficiently distinctive to permit accurate dating and, even if we are correct in presuming that the

Fig.234 (facing page) Elevation of the south-east wall of Bedern Hall showing the timber-framing, below the gable, surviving from the north-west wall of Building 25. The dotted lines represent the extent of the post-medieval rebuild; the toned areas represent post-medieval structural elements. Scale 1:50

trio of doors go with this earlier building, they are far too simple in form to date with any accuracy. For both the framing and the doorways, however, a 14th century date is probable.

Kitchen (Fig.386s)

To the south-east of Building 25 there was an open yard which contained an extensive layer of clay with a high proportion of ash (6270). The north-east wall of the kitchen (6127*) comprised a lower course of limestone rubble bonded with lime mortar concrete, set in a rectangular construction trench. This supported a limestone post-pad (6177*) measuring 0·35m square. The whole structure had subsided into the underlying Period 4 gully (6344), the west corner sinking the most. The subsidence was sealed in places by occupation deposits, suggesting that movement took place soon after construction. A broad circular depression in the upper fills of the gully, lying immediately to the west of the post-pad, had been levelled with limestone chippings before the construction of the wall, an action which may have been necessitated by subsidence. The wall had been built against the post-pad (6177) with a cut (6240) being made for its tile footing (6176*) set on to rubble (6243, 6154), over a rubble construction spread (6160). A stone tile (*336, AY 10/4*) with a nail hole near one of the short sides, had been incorporated into the wall. The remains of a brick wall (or pier) on cobble footings (6244*) may have formed a stub wall edging the entrance into the kitchen.

Another new wall (5016*, Fig.366s) formed part of the south-west side of the kitchen, its north-west extent destroyed by a later cellar. Its construction was similar to that of the Phase 2 garden wall (see pp.482–4), as shown by the surviving foundations, although a greater proportion of limestone rubble was used, set into yellow clay, and it was constructed in a trench (6273, Fig.366s). The north-west kitchen wall had been removed by a later robber trench (6247*) which had been cut between a point on the south-west wall of Building 25, 1·2m north-west of the south quoin, and a point on the line of wall 5016*. It measured between 0·9 and 1·0m wide, and up to 0·3m deep, and had been backfilled with loam and limestone chippings. The original south-east wall had presumably been removed by the garden wall (see below).

Within the kitchen several small dumps of material were initially laid onto the ashy surface (6200*, Fig.366s, 6230*), for the most part consisting of sandy clay loams, sometimes incorporating small quantities of burnt clay. These deposits were mixed, containing rubble spreads and small pits (6210, 6217, 6225*, 6234–9, 6256–61, 6265–6). Sandy clay loam 6235 produced a French jetton (*AY 18/1, 210*) dated to c.1226–1325; 6265 yielded a bone die (*8078, AY 17/12*). The latest pottery from these levels is dated to the 14th and early 15th century.

The earliest kitchen hearth was represented by a central shallow scoop filled with burnt clay and limestone chips (6198*/6204*). Contemporary with this was a drain (6175*) set in a shallow trench against the north-west face of the garden wall. The drain was c.0·30m wide and c.0·10–0·15m deep, and floored with tiles. A low wall had been inserted against the north-west side of the construction trench to form the other side of the drain. This consisted of a lower course of tile rubble and limestone, a second course of whole tiles, and a third of limestone cobbles. Both drain and wall had then been capped with whole tiles. The south-east edge of those tiles capping the drain rested on a rebate on the inside of the garden wall. The drain survived only as a c.2·4m length since both ends had been removed by modern intrusions but it is fairly certain that it did not extend beyond the partition wall. There was evidence for a very slight fill from the north-east to the south-west.

Bedern long trench

At the beginning of Period 7 a layer of clay loam (1055, Fig.364s) was deposited throughout the north-west part of the trench (Area III). Equivalent material (1578, 1588) had been deposited in the south-east part of the trench (Area IV), and there was a spread of sand (1567) overlain by loam with tile and mortar (1568, Fig.364s). Pottery from these levels dates this activity to the late 14th or early 15th century.

Bedern Foundry (pp.173–7, Fig.73, AY 10/3:
Period 4, Phases 1–2)

Most of the north-east area of the foundry site continued to be open ground, occupied principally by rubbish pits. In the north-western part there were a number of deposits of grey clay loam (295, 986, 2047, 2302, 2543, 2569) which have the appearance of garden soils. A bone parchment pricker (7974, AY 17/12) was recovered from these levels.

A deposit of black clay mould fragments (2108, Fig.79, AY 10/3) and sandy clays (987, 2014, Fig.79, AY 10/3, and 2110) had been dumped on the garden soils. At the south-

eastern extent of these layers there was a band of clay (970), with nails both within and around it. This may have decayed from a wooden beam which could have formed the foundation for a partition wall dividing the garden soils from more floor-like deposits to the south-east. A shallow trench (984) filled with limestone chippings and tile fragments may have been another structural feature, or possibly a drainage channel; it was sealed by more clay and tile rubble (985, 2277).

One of the first deposits to the south-east was a brown sandy gravel (983) which appears to have served as a foundation for a clay floor (855, Fig.79, AY 10/3). The floor had been heavily worn and cut by a rectangular pit, c.0·8 × 1m, with rubbly fills (854, 964) including a bone parchment pricker (7973, AY 17/12).

Further south-east a brown clay loam (2295) was cut by three pits. The first (2442) was filled with rubbly clay loams (2240–1, 2435); the second (2319) had a basal compact peaty fill and was then backfilled with a succession of silts and clays (2300–1, 2316–18) which also contained charcoal, clinker and clay mould fragments. Both were sealed by clay loam (870) containing nearly 2kg of mould fragments, and silt (2304), clay (891), and a spread of limestone fragments (892). The third pit had further clay fills (2112, 2340, 2342) but was not sealed until later.

To the south-east an amorphous peaty loam (2170, 2173) was dumped, and clay with numerous flat-laid tiles (2172) was packed against the outside of the foundry buildings to the south-west. A substantial pit (2441) with vertical sides was then cut through these layers. The basal fill (2440) was an organic silt containing numerous blackened animal bones, twigs and wood chips, with some larger hard timbers (2463) suggesting the possible presence of tannin. This had been covered by a compacted fibrous peat (2439) with compressed grasses and more animal bones, and possibly leather. Analysis of a sample revealed the presence of some human faeces but the primary constituent was possibly stable manure. The pit had been sealed by various clay layers (739, 2169, 2429), containing a worked 12th century chamfered stone fragment (217, AY 10/4).

Period 7, Phase 2

Analysis of re-used architectural fragments suggests that Phase 2 can be divided into two parts, a and b, based on groups of stone from different sources (pp.233–4, *AY* 10/4). In Phase 2a, dated c.1365, construction work in Buildings 16, 26 and 27 made use of stone from an unknown church, possibly St Mary-ad-Valvas (Group 1C), and from some part of the 13th century Minster (Group 2B). In Phase 2b, dated c.1370–1400, Buildings 5, 17, 24 and the garden wall incorporated stone from the demolished 12th century Minster choir (Group 1A).

Phase 2a (Fig.235)

In Room 16D of **Building 16** the hearth was enlarged. In Room 16E the hearth was disused and a new south-west room wall was constructed, presumably replacing an earlier wall for which no evidence was found. In this later stage, Room 16E appears to have had no hearth. North-east of Building 16 an irregular wall, running north-east/south-west, of single unmortared limestone blocks was built north-west of the path, possibly replacing the earlier boundary wall.

The timber-framed college hall was now replaced by a grander stone building, the surviving **Bedern Hall**, built onto the north-west end of Building 25, c.1370 (Fig.234). It should be noted that the hall pre-dates Building 26, a relationship which was not taken account of in the discussion of the architectural fragments where the hall was assigned to Period 7.2b (pp.232–4, *AY* 10/4). The hall was a single-storeyed structure of four bays, 14m (north-west/south-east) × 8·5m overall. It was built of coursed limestone walls, but retained the timber-framing of the original hall as its south-east wall where it butted onto Building 25 (see Fig.234, p.474). At the south-east end there was a screens passage, dividing the hall from Building 25 (see Fig.325, p.588). There was probably an open hearth, with a wooden louver above, in the second bay from the north-west. At the north-west end there was a raised dais, covered by a canopy, with a vaulted bay window in the south-west wall providing extra light for a high table on the dais. In addition, there were three two-light windows in both the north-east and south-west walls. The hall foundations were set onto relieving arches (see Figs.238–9, pp.480–1), and soil was then dumped against the foundations.

Excavations in the trial trench outside the south-west corner of the hall revealed a substantial structure, **Building 26** (Fig.386s). The majority of the building lay outside the excavated area and only the foundations of the south-west wall were found. They consisted of clay-bonded limestone and cobbles, with the large stones at its south-east end resting on the plinth of the north-west wall of the hall. Outside these two buildings to the south-west there was evidence of a drain.

At the same time as the hall was rebuilt **Building 25** was refloored, and the **kitchen** was extended to the north-west and equipped with two new hearths. To the south-east of the hall and kitchen, a major **garden wall** was built, running north-east/south-west, forming the south-east end wall of the kitchen and extending to the south-west as far as the foundry, thereby enclosing an area to the south-west of the hall. In all its phases it formed an important building line for the remaining period of the college's existence, and it is known that the wall's north-east end remained in use until at least 1852, despite undergoing considerable modification in the early modern period.

South-west of the kitchen the garden wall is thought to have been a freestanding boundary separating a cobbled yard and garden to the south-east from a courtyard area crossed by a limestone and gravel path to the north-west. In 1401 documentary sources indicate that a barrel-lined well was constructed in the courtyard south-west of the hall, presumably for use by the kitchen block (p.579). However, all trace of it was probably removed by a brick-lined replacement in Period 8 (5008, p.532). The cobbled yard south-east of the garden wall may be seen as a service yard entered from St Andrewgate. The garden wall was identified crossing the long trench and also in the eastern corner of the foundry site where it abutted the east corner of the foundry buildings. Throughout the occupation of the foundry site this line defined the boundary between the foundry buildings and an open area to the south-east. Apart from two post-settings parallel to this garden wall there was no evidence of associated structures or floor levels. Running perpendicular to, and under, the wall was a substantial brick and tile-built drain which appears to have been designed to re-

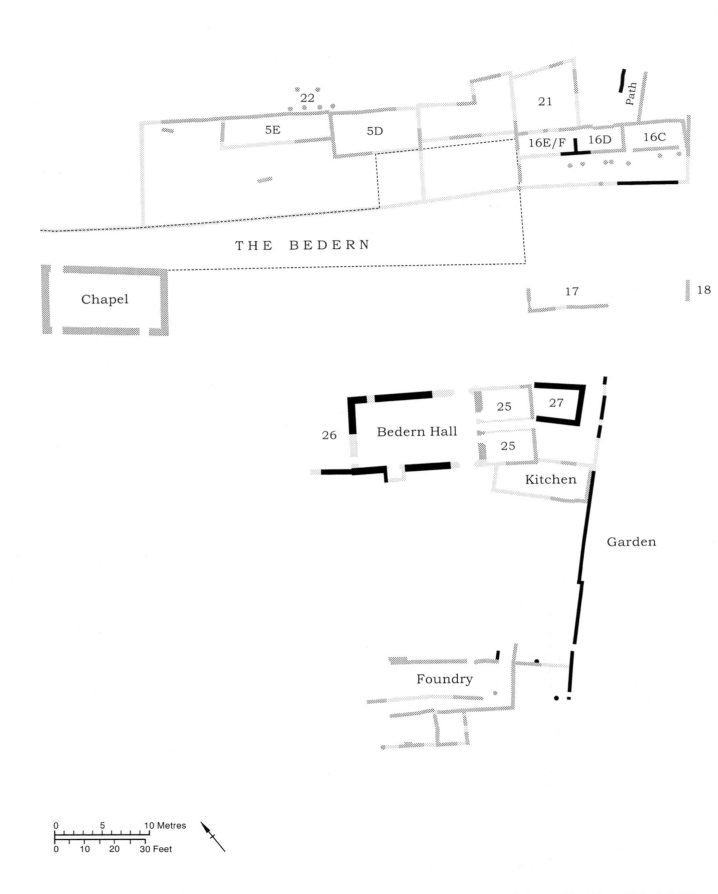

Fig.235 *Period 7.2a: interpretative summary phase plan, showing building development. For the key, see Fig.195, p.409. Scale 1:400*

478

move domestic waste from the now enclosed college precinct (Figs.245, 386s). At the south-west end of Area 13.X there were traces of a possible entrance into the open area to the south-west of the fence.

The construction of the garden wall, and the demarcation of the limits of the college precinct south-west of Bedern Close, led to a significant change in alignment of the college buildings on this part of the site. Whilst the hall and its service wing followed the initial alignment of the close, all new buildings south-west of the close were now spatially limited to the south-east by this new boundary wall. The first of these was **Building 27**, butted onto the east corner of Building 25 (Fig.386s). The long axis of this building lay north-west/south-east, and its exterior length was 5·48m by 4·64m wide at the south-east end, narrowing to 4·22m wide at the north-west end. The north-east and south-west walls were not parallel, with the building's axis being inclined slightly towards the long axis of Building 25, so as to form an angle of approximately 80° with it. All three walls of Building 27 were structurally similar with variations in detail, consisting generally of facing stones of either rubble or ashlar, interior and exterior plinth courses, and a concrete core (Fig.244, facing p.484).

The inside of these walls was plastered as indicated by the remnants of white lime plaster recovered. There is no evidence that this building was timber-framed, and it may have been the first completely stone-built structure in the college.

Also unusual was the sunken interior to Building 27, floored by white mortar containing brick chips and tile rubble. At the north-west end of the building was evidence for a post-built construction, perhaps a stair base, surviving only as four stake-holes forming a square. A consistent feature of later floors within this building (see Period 8, p.511) were signs that some slight structure, perhaps shelving, may have stood around the walls. If this was indeed the case, then it may be that this small building was used as a library, a function that may also help to explain its substantial build. It may also be this structure that is referred to as the 'counting house' in the early 15th century and as the evidence room or archives room in the 17th century (p.576).

Bedern North-East

Building 16

The second phase of Room 16D is marked by the construction of another tile hearth (4204*), consisting of mostly complete tiles steeply slanted and packed with clay, partially destroying the earlier (Phase 1) hearth (4207), and extending the size of the hearth area (Fig.236). A series of overlapping ash spreads (4168, 4170, 4172, 4176–7, 4179, 4182, 4187, 4193, 4226) partially covered the area of both hearths.

In Room 16E a new south-west room wall (4218*) was cut through the last use spreads of the hearth (4242), presumably replacing an earlier wall of which no trace remained. The new wall was of a single-width mortar-bonded limestone and cobble construction, joining wall (4146) at a padstone (4371). It contained re-used stone from a simple string course of 12th–early 13th century date (*193*, *AY* 10/4). A shallow linear feature filled with mortar and limestone rubble (4217*) abutted the new wall, and ran north-east from it, possibly representing an internal partition within Room 16E.

Overlying the backfill of the Phase 1 tile-lined feature north-east of Building 16, there was an irregular wall of single unmortared limestone blocks (4156*) with deposits of clay loam to either side. This was of a character which suggested that it probably served as an external boundary wall. It is possible that wall 4178 had gone out of use by this time.

Fig.236   Area 14.IV, Period 7: Room 16D hearth 4204, looking west. Scale unit 0·1m

Fig.237 *Area 13.X: general view from the south, showing the position of Bedern Hall in relation to the excavated area. In the foreground is the Period 7 cobbled surface 5349. Scale unit 0·5m*

Fig.238 *Area 13.X: Bedern Hall foundations at the south-west corner, showing the relieving arch and offset plinth course, looking north-east. Scale unit 0·1m*

Bedern South-West

Bedern Hall

Bedern Hall was built onto the north-west end of Building 25. Excavations in the eastern trial trench, on its south-west side, revealed information about the hall's construction. A construction trench (5368/5454) was cut into the Period 1 silty loams (5463) into the base of which timber piles (5534–5), circular in section, were driven. A series of relieving arches for the foundations were then set into the trench (Figs.238–9; see also Fig.233, facing p.473). A thick clay (5469, Fig.371s) was used as the initial infilling of the trench and for packing under the arches. The trench was then backfilled with mortar and clay covered by a limestone rubble and mortar (5364). The south-west wall of the hall was built over the relieving arches and subsequently a series of dumps of clay, sand and loam (5451, Fig.371s, 5455–60) were deposited against it. A mor-

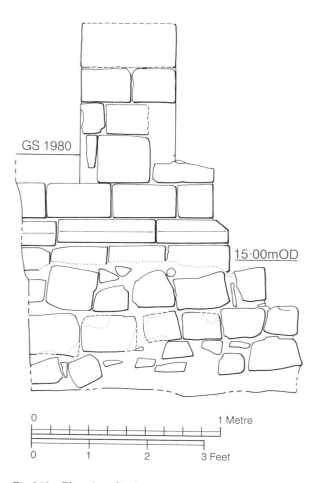

Fig.240 Elevation of Bedern Hall at its north-west end, looking south-east (GS = ground surface). Scale 1:20

Fig.239 (above) Area 13.X: eastern trial trench, showing Bedern Hall foundations with the relieving arch in the south-west wall, looking north-east. Scale unit 0·1m

Fig.241 (right) Area 13.X: western trial trench, showing the foundation wall (5527) of the external bay of Bedern Hall with the later brick wall constructed over. Scale unit 0·1m

481

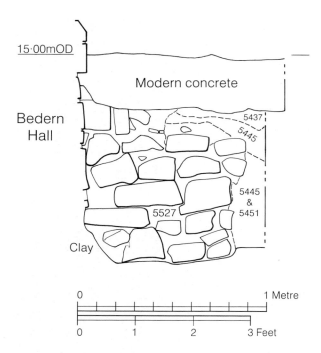

15·00mOD

Modern concrete

Bedern
Hall

5437

5445

5445
&
5451

5527

Clay

| 0 | | | | | | | | | | 1 Metre |

| 0 | 1 | 2 | 3 Feet |

Fig.242 *Bedern Hall, Period 7: elevation of wall 5527, looking south-east at the south-east end of the western trial trench. Scale 1:20*

tar spread (5453) may also be associated with the hall's construction.

Cutting the clay dumps, in the western trial trench south-west of the hall, there was a construction trench for a well-built limestone wall (5527*) running south-west from the main hall wall (Figs.241–2). These footings appear to represent the foundations of the north-west wall of a projecting bay, further evidence of which was found during the investigation of the standing structure (p.583).

Kitchen

Towards the end of Phase 1 a robber trench (6247*) removed part of the north-west wall of the kitchen, marking the onset of the second phase of use of this area. The location of the new north-west wall is unknown. The robbing trench was filled and levelled by a mortar spread (6218), and brick and tile rubble (6214). Within the trench there was also a small pit (6263) with a loose fill of heavy clay loam and some domestic refuse (6215), including bone, chalk, coal, eggshell, pot and shellfish (Hall et al. 1993a), dark clay loams (6211, 6213) including a fragment of a decorative roof finial (see p.608), a tile, brick rubble and mortar (6212), a mortar spread (6190), clay spread and rubble (6193), a rubble-filled pit (6189), and a thin spread of mortar (6209). Two contemporary hearths were set into these layers. The north-easterly one (6232*) was situated

near the south corner of Building 25, and consisted of an area of burnt clay edged with half bricks. This hearth was sampled for archaeomagnetic determination by Dr Mark Noel and given a date of 1290–1350 which would have made it too early for this phase (Noel 1978). However, a revision to the archaeomagnetic calibration curve (Clark et al. 1988) means that there is now no intersection with the curve and so the hearth is undatable (C. Batt, pers. comm.). Approximately 1·4m to its south-east, and in association, was an almost circular pit (6199*, Fig.368s) floored with stiff clay and broken roof tile and filled mainly with ash.

The more southerly hearth also comprised an area of burnt clay (6205*) edged with bricks and flanked by a clay spread (6222*). These deposits were cut by a rubble-filled pit (6166*) and a second shallow pit (6231) was dug through the floor and backfilled with brick rubble (6245, Fig.368s) as a preliminary to the sealing of the immediate area by a layer of loam and burnt material (6229) which also covered a mortar spread with tile fragments in loam (6233).

Building 26 (Fig.386s)

In the western trial trench Building 26 was represented by a substantial wall (5438*, Fig.262, facing p.504) built over the hall construction dumps. This wall was of clay-bonded limestone and cobbles, including a number of re-used worked stones (*116, 118, 138, 147–8*); the large stones at its south-east end rested on the plinth of the hall wall, clearly making it a later construction. An extensive layer of mixed clay loam (5445, Figs.262, 371s) was deposited over the construction levels. The loam included a fragment of a glass table vessel of the 15th century (sf2404).

A curving gully (5450, Fig.371s) was dug to the south-east through 5445 and 5451 (although this was not clearly recorded on the section Fig.371s) and lined with limestone chips and mortar. Finally spreads of ashy loam (5447–8, Fig.371s) were deposited. Pottery from these levels suggests these activities took place during the late 14th or early 15th century.

Building 25 (Fig.386s)

A new floor of clay loam (6077) was laid down in Building 25, from which were recovered a copper alloy jetton dated to the reign of Edward II, 1307–27 (*AY* 18/1, *148*), and pottery deposited up to the 14th or early 15th century. A small pit located in the south corner of the building, filled with limestone chippings (6141), may have been intended as a way of combating rising damp.

Garden wall (Figs.243, 386s)

Initially, extensive clay and sandy loams (5301–2, 5303, Fig.366s, 5410, Fig.366s, 5418–19, 6262, Fig.366s, 6264, 6267,

Fig.243 *Area 13.X: general view of the south-west of the site, looking north-east, showing the garden wall with water-filled latrine pits in the foreground, the kitchen, and Buildings 25 and 27 in the background. Scale unit 0·5m*

6279, Fig.368s, 6286, Fig.368s, 6295, 6298, Fig.366s) were laid down as levelling deposits. They contained a variety of artefacts (AY 17), including an iron wedge (sf2269), an iron knife with an inlaid cutler's mark (sf2365), a possible bone pen (8061) and a dark green glass bead (sf2277). These deposits were then cut by a series of small ash-, tile- and rubble-filled pits (5299*, 5424, 5440, 5452, 6159, 6278), as well as by some filled with clay loam, tiles, mortar and limestone (5378, 5381, 5411, 5413, 5420, 5425). Pit 5411 contained an Edward II penny (AY 18/1, 116) probably deposited c.1325–50 or later, and deposit 6279 contained a continental coin (ibid., 202) minted c.1344–6. Loam 6262 contained a copper alloy jetton dated to Edward II's reign, 1307–27 (ibid., 147). 6262 was cut by a square feature (5479) lined with clay and filled with sand, showing evidence of subsidence and subsequent repair at one corner. There was one limestone post-pad (5429) in a pit filled with tile, loam and charcoal. A slot-shaped feature (6287) was dug through these levelling deposits, as was a south-east/north-west ditch (6274) running from the south corner of Building 25 into the area of garden loams. A pit and associated rubble spread (6272, Fig.366s) was also located here.

It was then that a substantial north-east/south-west garden wall (5300*/6103*/6104*/6136*/6276*) was constructed, running for a distance greater than 20m, from a point south-west of Building 17 to a point near the south-west edge of Area 13.X. The north-east stretch of this wall formed one side of the kitchen complex. This part of the wall was clay-bonded (6283), the clay filling slot 6287. Its foundation courses consisted of limestone rubble and cobbles set into clay, with small amounts of tile, and included some re-used worked blocks (204, 214, AY 10/4). The wall was approximately 0·45m thick with a maximum surviving height of c.1·25m, although in places it had subsided so that it was inclined at an angle of 20° to the vertical. This may have been the result of slumping of the wall foundations into the soft fills of the underlying pits and ditches. To a certain extent this appears to have been anticipated by the builders. Where the wall crossed the earlier series of pits, a shallow construction trench (6275) had been dug and backfilled with a lime mortar into which substantial cobbles had been set while the mortar was still wet, with the garden wall being constructed directly over this foundation. Where the garden wall crossed the earlier ditch (6274, Fig.366s), a different solution was adopted and the ditch was apparently left open during building operations, since the wall was found to be sealing only the bottom fill of this feature. The foundations of the wall were made wider at this point, reaching 0·6m, in order to provide the extra stability required. Considerable dumping of clay and limestone rubble was found in this ditch, all of it abutting the north-west face of the garden wall and presumably backfilling and consolidating it (6241, 6242, Fig.366s, 6246, 6248, Fig.366s, 6249–52, 6268–9). One dump deposit (6241) contained a French jetton (AY 18/1, 232) of possible 15th century date. Limited subsidence neverthe-

less took place. There was no evidence of an original opening in the garden wall, although lengths totalling 5·2m had been destroyed by 19th and 20th century intrusions.

Building 27 (Figs.244, 246–7, 386s; see also Fig.208, p.428)

Before Building 27 was built a series of rubble layers were deposited over the remains of Building 10, including limestone and brick rubble (7253). The south-west half of Building 10 was sealed by extensive dumps of rubble and mortar in a clay matrix (6161–2, 6170–3), including a number of worked stones from the demolition of Building 10 (30, 268, AY 10/4).

All three walls of Building 27 (6058, Fig.368s, 6059*, 6060*, Fig.368s) were constructed in mortar-bonded limestone, and included large quantities of tile and brick rubble used for packing and levelling purposes. Although all appeared to have been built at the same time, there were minor differences between them. The north-east and south-east walls (6058–9) were built of coursed rubble; both possessed interior and exterior plinth courses, that below the north-east wall being broader on the outside, whilst that beneath the south-east wall was broader on the inside. By contrast, the south-west wall (6060) was made of well-coursed ashlar, showing evidence for the use of a claw chisel, and including re-used blocks (122–3) which may have originated from York Minster in 1394 (AY 10/4). It too possessed a plinth course which, like that of the south-east wall, was wider on the inside, although the narrow exterior plinth was constructed in brick, and set into a clay-filled construction trench (6289). Each of the walls was faced with ashlar and rubble. The presence of small areas of interior white lime plaster was also common to all three walls.

Building 27 was slightly sunken beneath the contemporary ground surface, and the first interior level was a dark clay loam with heavy inclusions of tile rubble, mortar and charcoal (6223, Fig.368s). Three adjoining rim fragments of a colourless glass bowl with an applied blue trail (sf2274) were found in this floor deposit. On top of this was a white mortar (6220*, Fig.368s) containing brick chips and tile rubble. This deposit produced a pair of small bells (sf2286) in one of which was a textile fragment. At the north-west end of the room, four post-holes (6221*) represented some square feature (Fig.247), possibly the footings of a staircase to an upper storey. Each was rectangular in plan and narrowed to a point at the bottom. The north-west post-hole contained a much-decayed timber stump; the other three held soft organic material.

The construction of Building 27 resulted in the general disuse of the area surrounding it, which now contained small spreads of charcoal (7254), a clay dump (7108), and mortar and broken tile (7155). These were all covered by

4·50mOD

d

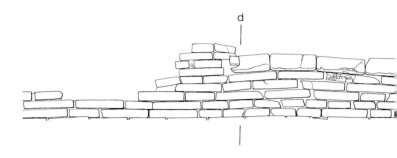

f

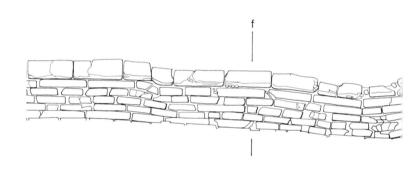

D

| 1 | 2 Metres |
| 2 | 4 | 6 Feet |

n 5318: (A) north-east facing; (B) south-west facing. Also shown is cross-secti

e

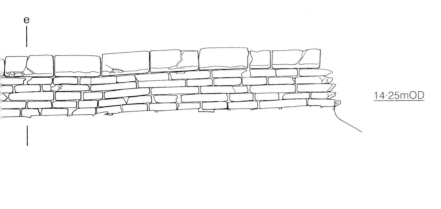

14·25mOD

c

14·25mOD

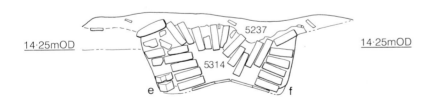

14·25mOD   14·25mOD

5237

5314

e   f

n e–f through the drain. Cross-section c–d appears on Fig.366s. Scale 1:20

Fig.246 Area 13.X, Period 7: Buildings 25 and 27, looking south-west. Scale unit 0·5m

Fig.247 Area 13.X, Period 7: Building 27, looking south-east, showing the group of four post-holes 6221. Scale unit 0·1m

485

an extensive layer of clay loam (7075, Fig.368s) with inclusions of mortar, charcoal, broken tile and brick, also containing an ash and charcoal lens (7082) with plenty of bone and antler manufacturing debris, including a disc or counter (8112, *AY* 17/12), and an iron saw blade (sf2456). Some limestone blocks, including part of moulded doorway jamb (*134*), possibly from York Minster, were set into the north-west and north-east edges of layer 7075 (*AY* 10/4).

Cutting 7075 and immediately north-east of 6058 was a post-hole (7076*), packed with brick and cobbles, and covered by a spread of loamy clay and tiles (7067), and a pit filled with clay, sand and mortar (7083*). A charcoal spread (7142) overlay 7075. Subsequently this area was occupied by Building 28.

Phase 2b (Fig.248)

Building 5 underwent what appear to have been major structural alterations. Part of the north-east outer wall was demolished, the foundations being covered and levelled by a layer of clay. A substantial new wall was constructed in its place exhibiting three different types of construction, apparently corresponding to the internal room divisions. This wall was of a greater width and different construction to the original one which had served as a sill wall to carry timber-framing. It is suggested that this new wall was of stone throughout. It was also set on a slightly different alignment to the earlier wall, although the reason for this is unclear. It would seem, therefore, that most of Building 5 was rebuilt in stone, although the original timber-framed south-east wing continued in use. The rooms themselves underwent some further alteration and modification.

Room 5D was modified by the removal of its internal partition and the replacement of some of its walls to form one large room, 5G. Within this room a central tiled hearth and a possible latrine pit were set into a clay floor.

Room 5H, formed within the earlier Room 5E, now followed the pattern set by Room 5G, in that it was a narrow room extending almost the full width of the building. Towards the south-west end of this room the insertion of a mortar-bonded limestone wall incorporating two post-pads, and a new south-west side wall, created Room 5H and a narrow room or passageway in which a sand floor was set at a lower level than the rest of the building. The deposits within Room 5H survived only patchily but suggest it was used as living quarters; these deposits included a clay floor cut by a hearth constructed of flat-laid limestone blocks rather than of the more usual pitched tiles. A stone-lined latrine pit was set in the east corner of this room; it appears that there was now a trend for latrines to be located within living quarters.

To the north-west of Room 5H was Room 5I (also created out of Room 5E) extending across much of Building 5. Two short stretches of wall built at the north-west side of this room were possibly the remains of a small internal partition. The substantial Period 6 hearth continued in use during this period, in association with a new clay floor.

Room 5J was a new room situated to the north-west of Room 5I with a rubble floor surface cut by a pit which contained an unusual collection of horse skulls and sheep bones, some of which had apparently been boiled. Further occupation of Room 5J created a new floor surface into which was set a pitched tile hearth.

Within the south-east end of Building 5, to the south-east of Room 5G, a similar series of floor levels and hearths to those in the north-west rooms is evident, but modern intrusions have confused the evidence in this area and it has not been possible to distinguish actual rooms. In the centre of this part of the building, however, a new length of wall was built in a north-west/south-east direction. The presence of two hearths in close proximity to each other, and apparently in contemporary use at the beginning of the period, suggests that other room divisions may once have existed. The whole area to the north-east of Building 5 was covered and levelled and one new cess pit was dug, surrounded by a cobbled surface or yard.

Building 23 was built to the north-west of Building 22 and attached to the north-eastern outer wall of Building 5 (Fig.384s). Only the fairly insubstantial south-east wall of unfaced limestone and tile was within the excavated area. Two phases of use have been identified, the first seeing the division of the building into at least two portions. Within the north-east portion of the building was a clay loam floor cut by two contemporary tile-built hearths. The floors with associated hearths indicate that the building may have had a domestic function, perhaps as an annexe to Building 5.

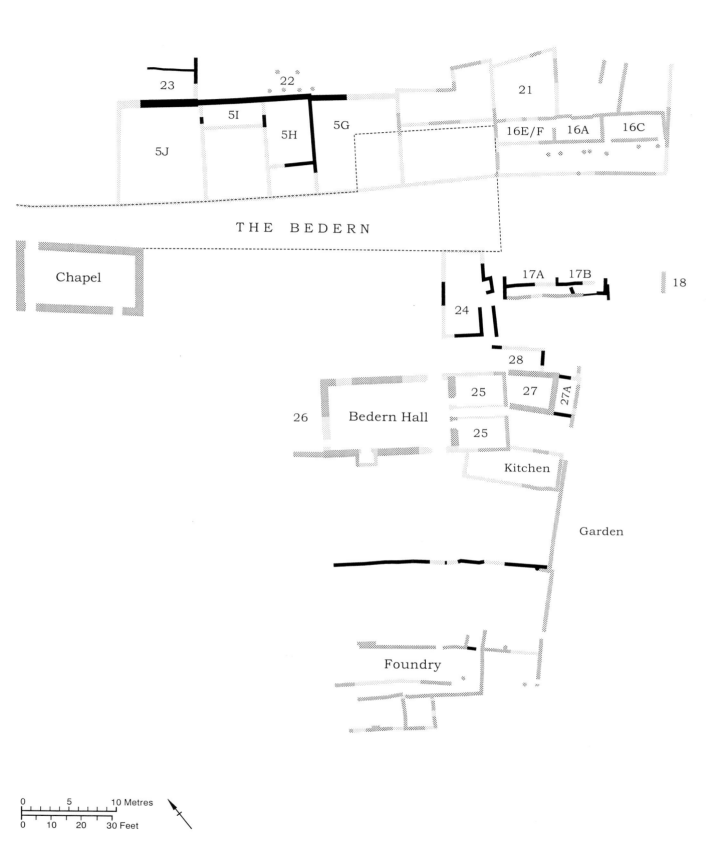

THE BEDERN

23 22 21
5I 16E/F 16A 16C
5J 5H 5G
Chapel
17A 17B 18
24
28
26 Bedern Hall 25 27 27A
25
Kitchen
Garden
Foundry

0   5   10 Metres
0   10   20   30 Feet

Fig.248   *Period 7.2b: interpretative summary phase plan, showing building development. For the key, see Fig.195, p.409. Scale 1:400*

The main building fronting onto the south-west side of the close, **Building 17**, was rebuilt. The new building was c.10·5m in length, and at least 4m wide. The original south-west wall was retained but the north-west and south-east walls were new constructions; the north-east wall was still beyond the edge of excavation. The internal arrangements for this building differed considerably from those of the earlier building, in that there was no longer a central division along the long axis of the building defining a narrow corridor to the south-west. Instead there was a short length of limestone walling, running from the north-west end wall on the same line as the earlier division. The building was also divided by a diagonal wall running north from the south-west wall. A slight partition wall now divided the north-east section into two rooms, 17A and 17B. A brick cess pit was built in the open area against the back wall of Building 17, inside a small outhouse.

Building 14 was replaced by **Building 24**, built end-on to the close, with its frontage on the line of the later street. New north-west and south-west walls were constructed on the same line as the Building 14 walls. No evidence survived for a north-east wall, but the size of this building can be estimated as at least c.5·5m (north-east/south-west) × 3·5m. Within Building 24 was a clay floor, a paved area of tiles and a hearth of clay-bonded pitched tiles surrounded by an edging of bricks. Subsequently this hearth was replaced by a brick-built version made up of a base of flat-laid mortar-bonded bricks bedded in sand and edged on three sides by edge-set bricks which showed evidence of burning.

The construction of Building 27 was followed by the addition of a small **annexe (27A)** onto its south-east end, created by the erection of partition walls between the garden wall and Building 27. The area enclosed measured c.3·8 × 2m, and although that portion of it to the north-east was floored with clay spreads, the south-west area contained deposits that resembled demolition dumps cut by small pits and a slot running parallel to the garden wall. There are no clues as to the use this small pentice was put to, or even the nature of its construction. In the area formerly occupied by Room 14F, to the north-east of Building 27, there was evidence for a brick-built structure, **Building 28**, with a tiled hearth and a brick floor.

Bedern North-East (Fig.384s)

Building 5

Three new lengths of walling (1029/1157, Fig.365s/1158*) replaced part of the earlier north-east wall of Building 5, on a slightly different alignment (Fig.249), with the Period 2 wall (4477) still surviving to the south-east. These new lengths of wall were not of a continuous build and formed butt joints with each other. They were of a different construction to the earlier wall and nearly twice the width, consisting of construction trenches (1233, 1319*, Fig.365s) into which limestone rubble and mortar foundations had been set. An iron wedge (sf244), probably used during the building work, was recovered from the trench backfill. The construction trench cut a thick dump of clay (1132) containing inclusions of tile, mortar and wall plaster which had been placed over the Period 2 demolished wall (1262/1373). These foundations supported walls of a mortar-bonded limestone skin with a rubble core, surviving to a height of two to three courses. Re-used stones (1–2, 28, 37, 155) incorporated into the build of the new wall date from the 12th century on stylistic grounds, but may have come to Bedern from the demolition of the Minster choir in c.1390–4 (*AY* 10/4).

The construction of the new north-eastern outer wall to Building 5 coincided with changes to the rooms within. Room 5D was modified by the removal of the Period 6 internal partition (1286) to form Room 5G, c.8·8m square, which consisted of the south-east wall (1525), and a north-west wall incorporating the Period 6 part to the north-east (1289*) and a new south-west part (1197*). The new addition to the north-west wall (1197) was constructed over a clay layer (1268) and a limestone rubble spread (1269). It comprised small re-used and dressed limestones bonded with mortar, and survived to a height of two courses. A post-hole (1467) was located at the north-east end.

Internal levels of Room 5G consisted initially of an extensive layer of clay (1200*) which was laid down over the remaining foundations of the internal partition wall, spreading into the areas on either side. A pitched tile hearth (1154*) was cut into this layer, with an associated fragmentary tile retaining wall. Also cut into clay 1200 was a possible cess pit (1226*) against the north-west wall, containing several stake-holes and some wood in situ. The hearth was then cut by a later hearth (1184) and the cess pit was backfilled with mortar. To the north-east of the hearth there was a spread of charcoal-stained clay (1247).

To the north-west of Room 5G a new room was created, 4·8 × 6·8m (Fig.250). Room 5H was defined by the north-east outer wall, a south-east wall (1140/1289) dividing it from Room 5G, a new south-west wall (1084*, Fig.365s), and a north-west wall largely removed by mod-

ern intrusions (1399*/1401*). The new south-west wall was built from mortar-bonded limestone. It contained two post-pads, one of which had been cut into the partition wall with Room 5G. This wall also divided Room 5H from another room to the south-west. There were associated construction levels (1534) which contained a fragment of undercut roll moulding of 13th century date (*263, AY 10/4*).

The internal levels to Room 5H survive only patchily. A clay deposit mixed with rubble (1219) covered the foundations of the Period 6 wall 1423. In its earliest stages, the room contained a pitched tile hearth (1187, Fig.365s), set into clay (1259), with an associated stacked tile-built and clay-bonded fireback wall (1188). This hearth was associated with a clay deposit (1212, Fig.365s) which abutted the south-west wall (1084). Set over this clay was a spread of charcoal and sand (1214), and several loam layers (1213, Fig.365s, 1216, 1220). Cutting the Period 6 levels in the east of this room was a square latrine pit edged with limestone blocks (1292*). This latrine had a brick floor and contained two backfills, the lower one of sand and the upper one of loam with inclusions of mortar and brick. After what was apparently a short period of use, the hearth in Room 5H was demolished, and covered by a spread of tile in mortar-flecked clay (1217), and then the entire room floor was covered by a spread of ashy clay with patches of crushed limestone (1193, Fig.365s), which contained a fragment of elaborate moulding of early 13th century date (*257, AY 10/4*). This layer was then cut by several pits (1176, Fig.365s, 1179, 1202) and overlain by clay and ashy mortar spreads (1169, 1174–5, 1186, Fig.365s, 1192, Fig.365s). In the north-east of Room 5H a second hearth (1287*), composed of flat, burnt limestones, was then set into a bed of clay (1309).

The internal area to the south-west of the south-west wall of Room 5H (1084) appeared to be lower than contemporary levels in the rest of the building. The first deposit in this room consisted of a thick layer of sand (1196*, Fig.365s).

To the north-west of Room 5H, another room was created, 2·4 × 6·4m. Room 5I consisted in its earliest stages of the north-east outer wall, a south-east wall in common with Room 5H (1399/1401) and largely removed by modern intrusions. The internal deposits were patchy, and the extent of the walls and their associated surfaces is unclear, but the Period 6 hearth (1301) continued in use in this room, and a new clay spread (1372) was laid down. This produced a cut halfpenny of 1248 (*AY 18/1, 78*).

Fig.249 Area 14.II, Period 7: Building 5 wall 1029, looking south-east. Scale unit 0·1m

Fig.250 *Area 14.II, Period 7: Room 5H, looking south-west, showing the north-east wall (1157) in the foreground, the south-east wall (1140) to the left and the south-west wall (1084) at the top, with hearths 1287/1205. Scale unit 0·1m*

The area to the south-west of Room 5I had been extensively disturbed by modern intrusions, making the remaining archaeological levels very difficult to correlate with the rest of the building sequence. This area contained several structural elements: a clay ridge (1381), a post-hole (1374), a circular cut (1379), two limestone blocks bonded with clay (1370), and three post-holes (1334, 1346–7). Associated with these structural elements were spreads of clay loam (1382), mortar (1376), loam (1375), peat (1368), clay (1348, 1349/1360, 1362, 1366), silty clay (1337) and sand (1363).

To the south-west of Room 5I the Period 6 wall (1452) was apparently still in use, with internal room deposits on its south-west side.

Room 5J was the north-westernmost room examined, consisting of the north-eastern exterior wall (1029), a probable south-east wall which did not survive, and south-west and north-west walls outside the excavation. A wall was noticed in the edge of trench section, however, which may

have been the north-west wall. Shortly after the construction of the north-east wall (1029), a clay, tile and limestone rubble deposit (1101, 1131) was laid down and then cut by a pit (1105) containing horse and sheep skulls and bones. A new floor in Room 5J then sealed the Phase 1 pit. A spread of tile in mortar with some clay (1143*) abutted the north-east wall. Set into this was a pitched tile hearth (1070*) bedded in clay (Fig.251). That this hearth was used while the outer wall stood is shown by the signs of burning on the south-west face of the wall. The hearth, like the wall, also incorporated worked stone fragments (*10–11, AY 10/4*).

At the south-east end of Building 5, south-east of Room 5G, a deposit of clay loam (4149) filled a shallow depression (4150) in the Period 6 levels. This loam formed the construction level for a new internal wall (4104*) running in a north-west/south-east direction. This wall was constructed from cobbles and limestones with at least two limestone padstones situated along its length. The wall did not connect with the south-east end wall (4020) of

Fig.251 Area 14.II, Period 7: Room 5J hearth 1070. Scale unit 0·1m

Building 5, but may have once joined the partition wall (1525) to the north-west, although this continuation did not survive. Set against the north-east side of wall 4104 was a pitched tile hearth (4130*), both the tiles and the wall itself being bonded by clay (4129). Associated with this hearth was an ash spread (4126*) and several contemporary floor levels, consisting of a slightly sandy clay silt (4102*) situated to the north-east of the wall, a deposit of sand (4093), and limestone and mortar (4101*) which spread around the south-east end of the wall. A sample from 4102 was unusual in yielding rather large numbers of greater celandine seeds, a species typically found growing under walls, and represented in another three samples analysed from Areas II/IV in Period 7. The other plants represented included fig, cotton-grass and four weed plants (Hall et al. 1993c). Small amounts of bone, stone, pot and shell made up the residue.

It is presumed that the Period 6 hearth (4186*) continued in use during Period 7, and a spread of clay loam (4185) was deposited around it, containing a substantial faunal assemblage with roughly equal proportions of cattle, sheep, pig and poultry. Cat, hare and dog were also present (Hamshaw-Thomas 1994).

After a period of time, the Phase 1 wall (4104) appears to have gone out of use, with the deposition of a small

spread of mortar and limestone (4094) over its south-east end, as well as another spread of mortar (4099) over part of its north-west end. The latter was then covered by a deposit of compacted rubble and mortar (4085). The deposition of these layers preceded the construction of a new wall (4061). This was a much-disturbed wall of small limestones and cobbles; its south-east extent was never fully determined. Running parallel to this wall, approximately 2·2m to the south-west, was another wall indicated only by a later robber trench (4071) filled with clay containing inclusions of tile rubble and mortar (4069). Within the area limited by these two walls were a series of patchily surviving floor levels. The lowest was a mixed clay (4092), covered by light brown sandy silt with a small amount of mortar (4082). A sample contained charcoal, small seeds and a very few plant fragments, including a freshwater green alga, most likely to have arrived in water brought to the site (Hall et al. 1993c). This was covered by a compacted grey-brown sandy silt with moderate amounts of mortar (4073). Only two identifiable plants were recorded from a subsample of this material, one of which was greater celandine (Hall et al. 1993c). This layer also incorporated moderate amounts of coal and a small range of other occupation debris such as bone, charcoal and shellfish. It was overlain by an ashy surface (4063), itself covered by a patchy deposit of mortar (4062) and a further layer of sand (4056).

Building 23

The south-east wall of Building 23 was fairly insub-stantial and made up of unfaced limestones and some tile (1208*). Its presumed junction with the north-east wall of Building 5 had been removed by a later intrusion. An in-ternal division represented by a linear cut (1278*) ran in a north-west/south-east direction across the structure, c.3m from the south-west wall (1029*, i.e. the north-east wall of Building 5). At one point, near the south-east end, several large blocks of limestone (1304*) were situated to either side of the cut (1278*), and at the south-west end of these blocks was a small circular pit (1383*).

During the first phase of use in the south-west portion of Building 23 no new internal layers were deposited, the pre-building mortar surface (1265) surviving instead. To the north-east of the division, the earliest internal spread was one of mortar-flecked loam (1305). Overlying this was a deposit of charcoal-stained clay loam (1306*), set into which were two contemporary tile-built hearths (1299–1300*) at the edge of the excavation.

Bedern South-West

Building 17 (Fig.386s)

Building 17 was demolished down to its foundations, and a series of sandy clay loams were deposited in the area before it was rebuilt. Wall 7302* was retained as the south-west wall to this building, but it had the addition at its south-east end of a brick infill (7209*) consisting of five stacked and broken clay-bonded bricks and one moulded sandstone block (197, AY 10/4). A new north-west wall (7049*) of brick and limestone was built, the bricks being clay-bonded and the limestone mortar-bonded. The south-east foundation was built of brick (7181*) with a tile cap-ping, contained within a construction trench. To the south-east was another wall (7191*) within a construction trench (7196), which may be the north-west end of another building, lost to intrusions, or may have been an external wall associated with the Building 17 latrine.

Within Building 17 a new north-west/south-east par-tition wall (7032*) was set into a construction trench (7034) and joined with the Period 6 wall 7162 to form a corridor to the south-west. A short length of limestone and brick wall (7068*, Fig.366s) bonded with clay, set onto a series of clay loam and mortar spreads (7043, 7066, Fig.366s, 7069, 7080–1, 7145, Fig.366s, 7161, 7169), formed a diagonal di-vision in the south-west half of Building 17. To the north-west of this partition a coarse surface of limestone chip-pings (7277, Fig.368s), including a fragment of an elabor-ate 13th century moulding (256, AY 10/4), was deposited in the corridor as resurfacing or consolidation. This was overlain by a thick deposit of clay (7192, Fig.368s) and a

thin compacted mortar (7190*) covered by a sandy loam (7179, Fig.366s).

A slight north-east/south-west tile wall (7164*), set onto an ash and clay spread (7170), was located just to the north-west of the Period 6 wall 7174 and recreated the di-vision between Rooms 17A and 17B. Internal levels in Room B consisted of a series of mixed clay loams, sub-sequently overlain by an uneven mortar floor surface (7159*) at the south-east end. There was a large pit (7579*) dug into the north-west end of Room B which was filled with rubbish spreads, including fired clay and slag (sf2911).

Outside and to the south-west of Building 17 there was an extensive patchy clay (7349, Figs.368s, 370s) covering the Period 6 deposit 7428, and partly covered by an ash spread (7352).

During Period 7 a small latrine was constructed to the south-west of Building 17, represented by two limestone walls and centred on cess pit 7020*. A single line of lime-stone blocks (7360*), including a re-used section of pier shaft (6), set into a clay-packed construction trench, ran from a large post-pad to the north-west to the edge of the cess pit. The pier shaft is thought to have originated in Archbishop Roger's Minster choir, demolished in 1394, and so would have been available for re-use on Bedern from the very late 14th century (AY 10/4). A second wall (7361*), comprising gritstone and limestone blocks with the stones' partially faced on their south-east face, ran south from wall 7360. Inside, the cess pit consisted of four brick walls which sloped slightly outwards (Fig.252). To the south-east of it a number of layers built up, the earliest being a spread of crushed limestone and mortar (7358), overlain by a char-coal spread (7251) and clay deposits (7246, 7296) which butted against the latrine. Further deposits built up on top of the charcoal, beginning with a layer of fine mortar (7249), which was covered by a thin ash deposit (7239) overlain by clay (7237). The cess pit had later been backfilled with rubble dumps of clay loam with mortar, broken tile, brick and charcoal. The top fill sealed the pit and ran over the top of the brick wall. Immediately to the south-west of the cess pit a small pit (7030*, Fig.370s) was cut into a rough limestone and mortar spread (7044). The pit contained a copper alloy jetton (AY 18/1, 155) of Edward II.

The alleyway to the north-west was replanned (Fig.253), with the demolition of Period 6 wall-lines 7243 and 7293, and their covering by a mixed clay deposit with inclusions of brick and mortar (7070, 7087, Figs.369–70s). This deposit, marking the demolition of Building 14, con-tained a parchment pricker (8057, AY 17/12) and a frag-ment of wall plaster decorated with red flecks on a buff background. Spreading over 7087 were layers of ash from the use of hearth 7064. These were overlain by a sand path-way (7072*), probably the top alleyway level. The new

Fig.252 *Area 13.X, Period 7: brick-lined pit 7020, showing a jug in situ in the fill, looking north-west. Scale unit 0·1m*

north-west wall (7049*) to Building 17 was set in a construction trench cut through 7072 and formed part of the south-east wall to the replanned alleyway. The north-west alleyway wall was made up of three lengths of wall, the differing foundations perhaps reflecting the surfaces on which they were built. The north-eastern stretch (7055*) was set into a construction trench and consisted of four mortar-bonded limestones edged to their north-west by three limestone blocks filling the construction trench. To the south-west was a wall-line of limestone ashlar blocks (7053*) set on top of a cobble foundation (7265). This wall consisted of an outer facing of limestone ashlar to the south-east, with cobble and small limestone infill to the north-west, which may have been its centre infill. There was the possibility of a slight construction trench. This wall was separated from its continuation to the south-west (7071*) by a Period 8 cess pit. The continuation was constructed of irregular limestones and cobbles, bonded with clay. At the south-west end there was a limestone postpad (7207*), set in a pit filled with loam, broken bricks and tile, and a cobble and limestone spread (7208*).

Fig.253 *Area 13.X: north side of the excavation area, Period 7 alleyway, looking north-east. Upper left is wall 7053. Scale unit 0·1m*

Building 24 (Fig.386s)

At the beginning of Period 7 Building 14 was demolished and an irregular tumble of limestone rubble (7456) from the collapse of Room 14F spread across the fill of Period 5 ditch 7344. The rubble incorporated a rim and three body fragments of a colourless glass bowl with an applied blue trail round the rim (sf2765). A loamy clay (7313/7316) was deposited over Room 14F, finally filling the Period 6 pit (7329) as well as spreading over the surrounding area. 7329 contained a number of finds, including two parchment prickers (8040–1) and a stone mortar (sf2700). A small deep pit (7315) was cut into the top of the clay and later backfilled with clay, broken tiles and some cobbles.

A deposit of loamy clay (7297) containing some wall plaster and incorporating a lens of peaty loam (7312) covered the walls and interior levels of Room 14F, as well as spreading outside. This was covered by a mixed mortar and rubble deposit (7284). Tile and limestone rubble (7583, Fig.370s) spread over the north-west area of Building 14, and the demolition surface was then levelled with deposits of silty clay loam (7475, 7285, Figs.369–70s) which covered the old courtyard surface (7283), indicating its disuse. The footings of the north-east wall (7551) were covered by clay dumps (7321, 7447, 7505), a thin spread of sandy loam (7466), and a mortar and limestone spread (7464, Fig.370s). To the north-east a silty clay layer (7451) covered this spread, while a clay loam (7393) was deposited over remaining parts of 7475. Period 6 hearths (7028, 7064) were covered by sandy clay, mortar and tile (7029, Fig.370s). The disuse of the south-west wall of Building 14 was followed by the cutting of a pit (7300) through its line (no plan survives of the feature). The sandy silt fill was sampled and yielded a typical insect 'house fauna' and large amounts of faecal concretions. Apart from fig seeds, there was a trace of coriander and possibly some fennel and elderberry seeds, but otherwise food remains were limited to mammal and fish bone and a trace of charred cereal grain. The presence of *Daphnia* and water-crowfoot perhaps points to the incorporation of fresh water from a pond or river edge into the pit (Hall et al. 1993a). A fragment of wall plaster decorated with a red line and a black line on a buff background was also recovered from the pit. It was sealed by a sandy clay lens (7289) and the north-west area was then levelled by a series of clay deposits (7215) upon which Building 24 was constructed.

The new wall-lines survived very patchily, so it is difficult to ascertain the exact nature of Building 24. However, it appears that it was shorter than Building 14, both to the south-east and the north-west. A new north-west wall was constructed on the same line as the annexe wall 7410/7362 (Period 6, Building 14), surviving as a double row of cobbles (7318*, Fig.370s). A line of limestones and sandstones (7299*) formed the new south-east wall. These joined the new south-west wall (7310*), a rebuild of 7374 (Period 5, Building 14), which survived as clay-bonded limestone blocks set onto a construction spread of mortar and limestone mixed with clay (7309), overlying a mixed clay loam deposit (7308*).

Within Building 24 the Period 6 hearth (7248) was superseded by a new hearth (7121*, Fig.369s) which was constructed in a shallow pit partially filled with a mixture of clay, limestone fragments and broken tiles, onto which were placed the clay-bonded pitched tiles with their edging of edge-set bricks (Fig.254). An extensive clay floor (7127*, Figs.369–70s) was laid, running over the clay ridge 7343. A French jetton (*AY* 18/1, 244) had been lost in this room and trampled into the floor surface. A small cobble-filled pit (7301*) was later cut through this floor. To the north-east was a paved area (7107*, Fig.369s) comprising small tile fragments irregularly laid on edge and bonded with clay. The north-east face was edged with flat-laid tiles. A spread of mortar (7149) north-west of the hearth was covered by thin layers of charcoal (7143), clay (7141) and ash (7136, Fig.369s). The paved area was later cut by the construction pit for a limestone post-pad (7140*), backfilled with clay loam, on the line of the earlier (Period 5) wall 7551.

During Phase 2 hearth 7121 was replaced by a new hearth (7058; Figs.255, 369s), constructed from flat-laid mortar-bonded bricks set on top of a sand-bedding and edged on three sides with edge-set bricks set into a shallow construction trench packed with mortar. These bricks showed evidence of burning on their upper surface. This hearth was sampled for dating by archaeomagnetic determination and a date of c.1350 was published (Noel 1978) for its last use, which would have been too early for this phase. However, recent revision of the archaeomagnetic calibration curve suggests that a more cautious dating would place the hearth between 1290 and 1420 (C. Batt, pers. comm.) which is archaeologically acceptable.

Building 27 annexe

The construction deposit (6283) of the garden wall spread throughout the area between it and Building 27, forming a surface which sealed the earlier extensive rubble spread. The area was then enclosed by a pair of brick-founded walls running from the east and south corners of Building 27, and perpendicular to the garden wall. The south-east end of the north-east wall (6107*) had been lost to a drain cut and a 19th century pit; the remaining section was two bricks wide (about 0·28m) and bonded with a white lime mortar. It survived to a maximum height of 0·12m, and at this height had been bonded into the south-east wall of Building 27. Its construction trench cut the spread from the construction of the garden wall and it was constructed over a dump of clay (6277, Fig.366s) which contained a number of worked blocks (126–8, *AY* 10/4)

Fig.254 *Area 13.X, Period 7: hearth 7121, looking south. Scale unit 0·1m*

Fig.255 *Area 13.X, Period 7: Building 24, hearth 7058 (bottom right) and alley (top right). Scale unit 0·1m*

and fragments of wall plaster painted with a pinkish wash over a buff background. The south-west wall (6155*) had been damaged by intrusions; only a portion c.0·45m long remained, but in character and construction it was identical to 6107* to the north-east, comprising clay-bonded brick with limestone rubble.

There was an ashy dump of domestic rubbish (6158) nearby and clay spreads (6156*, 6283) floored the north-east part of this area, while the south-west end was covered with demolition material (6148, Fig.366s) from the earlier buildings, including worked blocks (124–5). 6148 was cut by a pit (6153) with a fill of mortar, tile, and brick rubble in clay. The three deposits referred to were cut by a linear feature (6281*), 0·5m long and 0·2m deep, which abutted the garden wall and ran alongside it for a surviving distance of 2·6m, being interrupted at its north-east end, like the garden wall, by a 19th century drain trench.

Building 28 (Fig.386s)

Alongside the north-east wall of Building 27 there was a brick structure, Building 28, which may have originally extended across the area that had been Room 14F. To the south-west of the south corner of Building 24, the Period 6 pit (7275) was backfilled with clay (7263, 7274); the south-west part of the pit was then covered by a mixed clay loam (7213). The north-east wall of Building 28 (7204*), surviving two bricks wide and one brick high, was laid onto this clay bedding. A pitched tile hearth (7279*) was constructed abutting this wall to the south-west.

Against the north-east wall of Building 27 there were traces of a brick floor (7099*) laid onto a clay layer (7092, Fig.368s) which was cut by the construction trench (7095) for a limestone and cobble wall (7100*), built onto and over two sides of the brick floor. Two short stretches of wall running north-east from Building 27 appear to have formed the south-east wall of Building 28. There was c.1m of a wall-line (7139*) of clay-bonded limestone blocks and two limestone blocks (7109*). Covering these blocks was an ashy loam with broken tile fragments (7084) which butted against Building 27. A mixed mortar deposit (7086) butted against the south-east side of the blocks and against Building 27. This was overlain by a mixed rubble spread of mortar, tile and plaster (7093), and a clay loam (7085).

The south-western courtyard and the garden (Fig.386s)

The garden fence rebuild was represented by a north-east wall (5325*) over 10m in length, consisting of a row of limestone cobbles, with some faced stone, possibly re-used, on the south-west side. No construction trench was visible for this wall and it is possible that it was built on uneven ground, which would account for the irregular nature of its footings. A deposit of clay (5326) had been placed

against the north-east external face. At the north-west end of the wall, and on the same alignment, was a clay and loam deposit (5390*), apparently a continuation of the wall-line and possibly representing packing to its footings.

Running south-east, and cutting the earlier clay loams, there was a tile-lined trench (5471, Fig.366s), apparently representing a further continuation of the wall. Along the south-west side of this feature there was a line of stacked tiles, some limestone slabs and small limestone blocks (5494*). In its centre was a single line of tiles (5478*) placed

Fig.256 Area 13.X: brick drain 5318 after removal of the arching, looking north-west. Scale unit 0·1m

on edge, supported on the north-east face by a small stacked tile buttress (5487*), and by a stack of flat-laid tiles (5482) on the south-west face. The rest of the width of the trench to the north-east was then filled with clay (5485*, Fig.366s) set against a second line of edge-set tiles along the north-east edge. The south-east extent of Building 15 was defined by the north-west wall of Building 13 (in the long trench).

In the south-west part of the site the garden wall (5300) is thought to have functioned as a property division. Sandstone and cobbles were used in the construction of the wall in this area; its construction levels were set in the clay loam spread (5410), its north-east end covering the earlier pit 5299. The clay-bonded stone and brick foundations of a stub wall (5412*) set into a shallow construction trench formed a butt joint against the north-west face of the garden wall at its south-west end, and may be part of an entrance into the open area to the south-east. Also marking this entrance were three limestone blocks (5417*), one large and two small, in a clay-filled construction trench, the edges of which were defined by broken tiles set vertically, and a post setting (5394*) consisting of a few large vertically set roof tiles, located within the adjacent loam spread (5292*, Fig.371s).

Associated with the garden wall, and parallel to it, were two post-settings (5388–9*), one with a worked limestone block (*190, AY* 10/4) set in a small pit filled with loam, broken tiles and mortar.

A brick and tile-built covered drain (5318*, Fig.366s) had been constructed at the same time as the garden wall and ran perpendicular to it (Fig.245, facing p.485; Fig.256). This drain was built with two stacked brick walls, clay-bonded, set into a construction trench backfilled with clay. Its base was built of flat-laid roof tiles packed in clay, and it was roofed with a brick arching resting on the side walls. The drain survived for a length of c.4m. The north-west end had been cut away by a later cellar, but at the south-east end the garden wall had been built around the outlet. A linear cobble and limestone spread (5305*), possibly part of a side drain, was located adjacent to the garden wall.

To the north-west, a rubble spread (5376) was laid down, covered by a limestone and gravel path (5271*; Fig.257). At the south-east end a second layer of limestone chippings and small fragments of limestone had been laid, separated from the first by a thin loam spread. A contemporary pit (5343*) with a fill containing clay mould fragments was located adjacent to the path.

During Period 7, therefore, this south-west courtyard area was defined by a garden wall to the south-east, with an associated drain, and a path running at right-angles to it. South-east of the wall, in the garden, an area of re-

Fig.257   *Area 13.X: pathway 5271, looking north-west across the garden area. Scale unit 0·1m*

deposited natural clay (5373) contaminated with some occupation debris was covered by a spread of mould fragments overlain by sand packing (5372). An extensive irregular cobble surface (5349*, Fig.367s) was bedded onto this (Fig.237, p.480; Fig.258), much disturbed by later intrusions, and later repaired (5363*) where it had slumped into a large pit. A small pit or post-hole (5369) cut through these cobbles. South-east of the garden wall also a pit (5371*) was cut into the loam spread and later filled with a sandy loam and mortar.

Fig.258 *Area 13.X: general view, looking north-west across the south-west part of the site, showing the Period 7 cobbled surface (5349) in the foreground, cut by later intrusions. Scale unit 0·5m*

In the far south-west of the site there was a spread of broken roof tile in clay (5393), as well as a garden soil (5403, Fig.367s), both covered by an extensive silty loam (5292*, Fig.371s, 5392, Fig.367s) of some depth, which probably spread over the entire width of the site. A variety of domestic refuse was incorporated into this layer, including an iron wedge (sf2213), bone manufacturing debris (7987, AY 17/12), and a fragment of an antler comb (8109). There were also three clumps of raw animal fibre (sfs2003–4, 2118) from this layer, each identified by H.M. Appleyard as goat hair. It is easy to imagine loose tufts of fibre from work animals being trodden into the ground surface. Examination of the animal bones from this extensive layer revealed roughly equal proportions of cattle and sheep bones, with few particularly young individuals. All parts of the cattle skeleton seemed to be about equally represented. Pig bones were mostly sub-adult, and included most of the skeleton. Other taxa included parts of at least two cats, and small proportions of dog, hare, rabbit, roe deer and horse. The bird bones included domestic fowl and geese, plus duck, grouse, partridge, woodcock and thrush. The fish included cod, haddock and halibut.

The loam had been cut by a tile-lined pit (5462*), south of the south-east end of path 5271, containing a slightly sandy, amorphous organic fill. This was sampled and yielded many fly fragments, several mites, one scale insect, a human flea and a beetle assemblage consistent with a mud-like pit fill, although examples of a 'house fauna' were also recognised. Despite a high proportion of faecal concretions the sample was barren of parasite eggs, and food remains were rather sparse, with only traces of fig and cereal 'bran'. The most abundant plants represented were weeds likely to have been growing around a midden or dung-heap. Other weeds, such as corn marigold and shepherd's needle, are more likely to be grain contaminants, along with corncockle (which was present as seed fragments). Ostrocods were also recognised; these freshwater invertebrates are perhaps most likely to have arrived with water discarded into the pit rather than living in a pit fill rich in waste matter such as faeces (Hall et al. 1993a). The pit had itself been cut by a second pit (5433*) filled with sandy silt with abundant bone and small quantities of limestone and brick/tile. A sample included charcoal, eggshell and fish bone along with both burnt and unburnt bone, suggesting the presence of domestic waste, much of it from fire ash (Hall et al. 1993a).

Bedern long trench

The garden wall (1500*, Figs.259, 364s, 386s) was identified in the long trench, where it was constructed over clay and mortar footings (1543, 1571, Fig.364s) set in a construction trench (1569, Fig.364s) cut through 1572, the Period 4 wall of Building 13. After the wall had been built the construction trench had been backfilled with clay (1049,

Fig.259   Bedern long trench (Area 13.III/IV): garden wall 1500, looking north-west. Scale unit 0·1m

499

Fig.364s). Two post-holes (1050–1) were cut into the trench against the wall. The trench was then sealed by a band of mortar (1026).

A patch of mortar (1060) had been dumped on the Phase 1 surface, followed by a lens of cess (1062), sealed by a second mortar spread (1059) and clay (1061). In the south-east part of the trench (Area IV) the earlier deposits had been sealed by a number of cobble spreads (1582*, Fig.364s, 1586, 1587*, Fig.364s) presumably equivalent to the cobble spread (5349) recovered in Area 13.X. An area of baked clay and mortar (1580/1589) had also been set onto the Phase 1 surface. There was a spread of burnt wattle and daub (1564*, Fig.364s) containing quantities of slag and some fragments of a clay mould (sf2881), which was cut by a shallow ditch (1579* with fill 1584) and sealed by clay loam (1551).

A pit (unnumbered) was cut into Phase 1 loam deposit 1055 (Fig.364s). In its base were layers of mortar (1064) and loam (1076), sealed by tile, mortar and domestic refuse (1068). There was a second small pit (1078) filled with mortar and tile debris on the north-eastern edge of the trench.

Bedern Foundry (pp.175–8, Fig.73, AY 10/3:

Period 4, Phases 2–3)

In the east corner a wall (2019) was found to the north-east of, and on the same alignment as, the south-east wall of the foundry buildings. It also ran on the same line as the north-west wall of Building 13 (2956, see p.447). The new limestone ashlar wall (2019) was more substantial than the south-east wall of the foundry building, and appears to have been the continuation of the garden wall extending south-west from Bedern Area X and the long trench (pp.497, 499) to form a junction with the foundry buildings. It incorporated a late 12th century re-used corbel (136) once more identified as being derived from the 1390–4 demolition at York Minster (AY 10/4). The wall rested on footings (2880) of brick, tile and mortar rubble, 0·05m deep.

The earlier floors and pits against the north-east edge of the foundry site were sealed by a layer of mortar and limestone rubble with tile fragments (869, 887, 909, 2223), including a 12th century ashlar block (212, AY 10/4). The bone assemblage from 887 was a little unusual in containing much fragmented cattle skull. The bones also showed a lot of gnawing damage, many of the bird bones having been gnawed by cats.

Further to the south-east there were limestone and mortar rubble deposits (2004, 2007) which were apparently contemporaneous with the mortar and limestone surfaces to the south-east. They also included clay loams with a high proportion of mortar flecking (636, 639, 972–3) which contained part of a Humber ware urinal (AY 16/9 in prep., B421).

A patch of mortar (2171), 0·06m thick, and dumps of clay (2163, 2168) were also deposited in this area. A layer of over 5kg of clay mould fragments (2175) was used to level up the surface of the earlier pit (2441, p.476), although its south-eastern third had later collapsed. The area was then divided in two by a north-east/south-west fence (2177) which followed the line of slope in the mould fragment layer 2175 and appeared to join the north-east building wall (829) at the point where a padstone projected from its footings. Over ten stake-holes were observed (2212–19, 2367–8), each c.0·05m in diameter, and two collapsed stakes (2210–11).

Period 7, Phase 3

During Phase 3 several buildings underwent internal modification and some new structures were erected. In the northern corner of the site, in **Building 23**, a new pitched tile hearth replaced the earlier hearths, and was associated with a sequence of clay floors. On the south-west side of the courtyard, **Building 28** was at least partially rebuilt.

A small structure, **Building 29**, was built against the south-east side of the north-east end of the garden wall (Fig.386s). Evidence for this building was very slight, consisting only of a partially surviving section of its north-east wall associated with several post-pads and a pitched tile hearth which suggests that this building was occupied.

The next stage of **kitchen** use commenced with the sealing of the Phase 2 hearth by a brick floor, subsequently heavily burnt. The remaining earlier kitchen elements were dismantled before a substantial oven was built in the east corner. In the **south-western courtyard** the path was now disused and cut by several rubbish pits, some lined with peat and containing ash, and others containing pieces of wood, perhaps from wooden superstructures.

Bedern North-East (Fig.384s)

Building 23

A spread of clay (1365) was deposited over the earlier mortar surface (1265) in Building 23. This was covered by a layer of sandy silt and cobbles (1339*) which spread on both sides of the earlier internal division. In the north-east of this structure, a small clay spread (1351) was deposited; associated with this was a pitched tile hearth (1354), surviving only in a fragmentary form, and situated in a similar position to the Phase 2 hearth (1299*). This hearth was overlain by a patch of heavily burnt clay (1345), and all these deposits were later covered by clay and charcoal demolition spreads (1207, 1211, 1224–5, 1242–4, 1253–4, 1261, 1276*, 1277).

Bedern South-West

Building 28

Building 28 was modified by the construction of a clay-bonded brick wall set on to a clay footing (7090), on the same alignment as the Phase 2 wall (7139) to the north-east. A north-west/south-east stacked tile wall (7094), with a tile capping, was built over the foundations of the now-demolished Phase 2 wall 7100, and the brick feature was now enclosed on at least three sides.

Building 29 (Fig.386s)

Building 29 was represented only by the partially surviving section of what was probably its north-east wall (7264*). This consisted of a sandy loam with inclusions of clay and broken tile rubble, into which was set a large limestone block, probably a post-pad (7610*). A line of limestone blocks (7281*), 0·4m wide, set with cobbles into a shallow trench, with some larger limestone blocks to the north-east, may also have been part of this wall. The south-east end had been cut away by a pit (7268*), later filled with loam containing limestone fragments, bricks and tiles. There was a pitched tile hearth (7282*) inside Building 29.

Kitchen (Fig.386s)

Within the kitchen the Phase 2 hearth (6232) and pit (6199) were sealed by a brick floor (6196*) which formed a quarter circle with a heavily burnt surface. A stone oven (6197*) bonded with rubble (6203) was constructed in the east corner of the room sealing all previous features here, and representing a replanning of the earliest cooking and heating arrangements. The north-east end of the Phase 2 drain (6175) was deliberately filled with brown clay in order to allow it to sustain the weight of the oven; the remainder was allowed to become choked up with ash and domestic rubbish. On excavation, the oven was shown to comprise a wall of limestone cobbles set in a bonding clay. It was probably originally circular in plan, but later intrusions had reduced its area by about a third. The thickness of this wall as built appears to have been about 0·45m, giving an internal diameter of 1·75m. It survived to a maximum of three courses, c.0·3m high. The interior was thinly floored with a clean brown clay and tile rubble, and neither this floor nor the walls showed more than minimal signs of burning. A layer of tile rubble (6186, Fig.366s) was deposited against the oven, and covered by a thin layer of wood ash (6185). These were covered by a deposit of mortar (6182, Fig.366s), overlain by further layers of ash and burning (6179–80, Fig.366s).

To the west of and abutting the oven there was an extensive clay spread containing a quantity of brick and tile rubble. Although this material may have originated from the oven construction, the bonding of which it closely resembled, this deposit showed signs of having been subsequently used as a floor surface. It completely covered those areas of the central hearth which had not already been obliterated by the oven.

At the end of this third stage of kitchen development, the demolition of these features was marked by the steady build-up of spreads sealing them. A thin layer of sandy clay (6227), followed by layers of wood ash, mortar and burnt material (6228, Fig.366s), accumulated over the oven. Similarly the brick-floor of hearth 6196 was covered by rubble, dug from a tile- and mortar-filled pit (6187/8) which was cut through it. Sealing this were further spreads of ash and brick rubble (6191, 6219) covered by the very extensive spread from a second large pit backfilled with tile rubble and mortar. Finally, a large dump of clay loam (6226) incorporating rubble, charcoal and mortar was laid over virtually the whole extent of the kitchen as a preliminary to major replanning of the cooking facilities in Phase 4.

The south-western courtyard (Fig.386s)

The courtyard area north-west of the garden wall was cut by a large number of pits, marking the disuse of the Phase 2 pathway (5271) which was also overlain by a clay loam (5270). The pits (5190*, Fig.367s, 5195*, Fig.367s, 5206–9, 5309*, 5311, 5315, 5339–42*, 5346*–7, 5366*, 5367*) were largely filled with rubble or ash and peat. A pair of smith's tongs (sf2070) was found in 5339. Another pit (5348*) contained some wood, and was lined with peat. Several other pits were sealed by clay deposits.

These pits were extensively sampled (Hall et al. 1993a). Faecal material was a major component of the fill of one (5309). It contained large amounts of cereal 'bran', corncockle seed fragments and faecal concretions. Other food remains included fig, blackberry, apple, field bean, grape, coriander, fennel and possibly leek. There was also eggshell membrane, and fish and mammal bone. The remainder of the plant assemblage comprised a range of weeds, some perhaps grain contaminants like the corncockle, others probably growing near the pit. However, a second sample from the same pit revealed that litter from within a building had also been dumped here. The pit also contained a clump of horse hair (sf2081), which may have been used as a latrine wipe. Other pit fills (5340, 5342, 5346–8, 5367) also suggested that these were mainly rubbish pits. Fill 5340 contained an iron trowel (sf2042).

Parasite eggs and food plants were absent or rare. The samples yielded mainly occupation debris, including brick/tile, mortar, charcoal, coal, metallic slag and cinders, wool textile fragments (sf2030, sf2038, sf2917), fish and mammal bone, eggshell, and mussel and oyster shell. Remains of a wooden beam, possibly from a tapestry loom or embroidery frame (9237, *AY* 17/13), and a leather shoe (sf2037) were also found in pit 5342. The plant remains of one sample (5346C) included weeds of waste and cultivated ground, such as fat-hen, although hempseed was also recorded. Another sample (5347E) contained a distinctive component of probable grassland plants, some from the wetter pastures or meadows, others from drier ground. The plants included marsh marigold, yellow-rattle and sedges, which might all have originated in hay or other cut vegetation (or in dung from animals grazing on such vegetation). There were traces, too, of plants such as ragged robin, red clover, cow parsley, and some grasses and rushes, all perhaps from hay-like material. The presence of uncharred oat grains is further evidence that we may be dealing with stable manure. One pit (5367) contained clumps of cattle hair (sf2179). Traces of charred field bean were also found in two samples.

Towards the centre of this part of the site there was a large pit (5198*) containing a succession of silty clay fills with ash, mortar, peat, tiles, charcoal and animal bones (5162, 5168–70, 5186–7, 5198–9, 5200, 5203–5, 5222, 5249–50, 5263). Samples of the fills yielded seeds, charcoal, cinders, slag and coal, mammal and fish bone, eggshell, shellfish, brick/tile and wood. The few plant remains were mainly weeds. There were no traces of parasite eggs. A sample of one fill (5222) also yielded several fly puparia and mites, an ant head and a dog flea. The beetles consisted predominantly of decomposers likely to have lived together in fairly foul organic matter, which was perhaps open-textured (such as stable manure trampled into a clay floor) (Hall et al. 1993a). A bone pen (8062, *AY* 17/12) and a gaming counter chipped from a tile (sf2105) were also recovered from the pit fills.

This central pit had itself been cut by two smaller features (5273, 5310). The first contained dark purplish-brown silt with grey sandy clay lumps and a small quantity of wood. A sample of this deposit included coal, charcoal and slag, eggshell, limestone, mammal bone, mortar, oyster shell, several seeds, a few fly puparia, wasps and mites, two fleas and a scale insect. The beetle assemblage seems likely to have originated within a structure, in material taken from a litter-covered floor. There was also a large assemblage of plant remains, representing a wide range of habitats, with weeds of waste and cultivated ground predominating. A trace of bracken stem material may also indicate litter of some kind (Hall et al. 1993a).

Patchy spreads of silty clay (5138, 5155–6, 5158–9) cut by a shallow linear depression (5149) and patches of ashy clay and mortar (5171–3) were located in this general area, cut by a shallow linear depression (5149). A sample from one of the clay spreads (5159) yielded a few beetles consistent with stable manure and moderate quantities of oyster shell and other occupation debris (Hall et al. 1993a). An iron chisel (sf1861) was recovered from 5155.

Bedern long trench

The cobbled surface (1582, 1587, 1591) to the southeast of the garden wall (1500) was partially covered by sandy clay (1577, 1583, Fig.364s, 1593). Context 1583 contained a crucible fragment (sf2882) with a layer of turquoise glass or glazing on the exterior.

Bedern Foundry (pp.178–9, Fig.73, AY 10/3:

Period 4, Phase 4)

A number of mixed loams (771, 881, 900, 917, 955–6, 2049, 2111, 2113) were deposited over the Phase 2 mortar and limestone rubble. These layers were frequently rich in bone debris and other finds including a bone toggle (7978). The bird bones from one of these layers (955) again showed traces of gnawing, this time attributable to rodents.

A number of other features may also belong to this phase. These include a tile-lined gully (992, Fig.79, *AY* 10/3) with a shallow V-shaped cross-section, which may have been a land drain, and a pair of tile post-pads, in the north. The south-westernmost one of the pair (918, 989) comprised vertically set tiles, packed in a depression 0·08m deep. Its partner (993) was 1m to the north-east, and the tiles were more randomly arranged in a shallower depression. They appeared to be joined by a shallow trench (2303) cutting a spread of compact clay (2109, 2331) and filled with loose material containing many iron fragments. Perhaps this was a partition or other flimsy wooden structure, with vertical posts resting upon the tile post-pads.

A dark grey clay loam (2255) was deposited over the southern corner of the mortar surface (2007, p.500). A posthole (701), containing a French jetton (*AY* 18/1, *215*) of c.1328–64, was also cut into the earlier surfaces.

To the south-east there were dumps of organic material (2166, 2179) which had been covered by further deposits of clay mould fragments (2350), possibly in an attempt to level the area. A sample of the organic material (2166) revealed it was an amorphous peat, containing an insect fauna typical of floor refuse.

Period 7, Phase 4

Within Building 5 the end of Period 7 is marked by the deposition of rubble in most of the rooms, along with the digging of various small pits through what had once been floor levels, suggesting that the building was temporarily unoccupied.

A walled area, 1 × 3m, was built against the south-west wall of **Bedern Hall**, alongside the projecting bay, possibly as a fuel store. On the south-west side of Bedern Hall a cobbled path now ran alongside the building. A new building, **Building 30**, was constructed. The only evidence for this was a substantial limestone ashlar wall which clearly continued to the south-west, beyond the excavated area (Figs.260, 386s). This must have formed the south-east side of a major building beyond the college precinct to the north-west which created an enclosed courtyard in this part of the college. This was cut by a substantial cess pit.

At the end of Period 7 Building 29 was apparently demolished and replaced fairly quickly by another construction, **Building 31** (Fig.386s). Once again the survival of this building is poor, but the

garden wall appears to have formed its north-west wall, and it had a newly constructed south-west wall. The interior of this building was to the north-east, and the floor was of clay with a pitched tiled hearth cut into its west corner.

Within the **kitchen** the demolition of the earlier features was marked by the steady build up of rubble spreads sealing them, capped by a large dump of clay loam which spread over virtually the whole extent of the kitchen. The previous arrangement of individual large hearths was abandoned in favour of four smaller clay hearths set around the walls of the kitchen, one on each of the north-east and south-west walls, and two against the south-east wall.

Towards the end of Period 7, there was further accumulation of garden loam and a succession of pits in the south-western courtyard. Building 15 and the fence which ran across the south-west of the site both appear to have been demolished at the end of Period 7, clearing the way for new more substantial buildings in this area in Period 8.

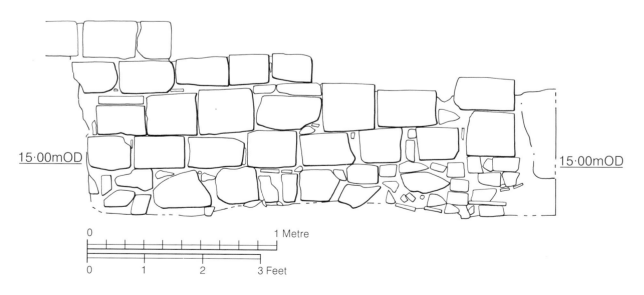

15·00mOD

15·00mOD

0   1 Metre

0   1   2   3 Feet

Fig.260 *Building 30, elevation of wall 5405. Scale 1:20*

Bedern North-East

Building 5 (Fig.384s)

In Room 5G hearth (1154) was cut by a pit with a mortar and clay fill (1249) and the surrounding areas were covered by a clay loam and rubble deposit (1195). In Room 5H, disuse is indicated by spreads of mortar and limestone rubble (1223/9), loam (1416), small limestones and tile (1252), and pits 1275 and 1308* (Fig.365s), the latter being large, rectangular, and containing mixed clays and several flat tiles. The presence of a black rat femur in the fill indicates the continued infestation of Building 5 (Scott 1985). Pit 1308 cut through hearth 1287 destroying its east corner. The demise of room 5J is marked by a spread of sandy clay (1321/2) containing inclusions of stone, charcoal and tile fragments, as well as a large quantity of small bone.

Bedern South-West

Building 30 (Fig.386s)

Before Building 30 was constructed a clay loam (5444, Fig.262) and an ashy loam (5443) were deposited, the latter running up to the walls of the hall. A new construction trench (5446) was dug to take a solid mortar-bonded ashlar limestone wall (5405*) and backfilled with tile and clay packing (Figs.260–1). This wall represents the south-east wall of Building 30, the interior of which lay to the north-west, outside the excavation. A mixed rubble and sandy clay deposit (5441, Fig.262) covered the construction trench and ran up against the north-west side of the wall of Building 30. This deposit extended as far as the remains of Building 26 but not over them, although wall 5438 was disused by now and covered at its north-west end by a deposit of clay (5434, Fig.262, 5439).

Outside Building 30 there were various clay loams and rubble spreads, covered by a clay and mortar deposit (5432, Fig.262) in the north-west corner of the trench. A sandy clay loam (5442) built up against the north-west face of the hall external store, possibly representing support for the foundation. Overlying 5441 was a sandy loam with rubble inclusions (5407, Fig.262). This was covered by a loam and mortar with tile and limestone (5409, Fig.262), in turn overlain by a sandy clay silt with charcoal, limestone, clinker and coal (5408, Fig.262). A sample of this clay spread yielded occupation debris, including shellfish, eggshell, fish bone and scale (Hall et al. 1993a). A pit (5406*) was cut into these levels, with a woody organic lining. It contained a sequence of backfills varying from soft material to well-preserved lengths of horizontal timbers, and wattle or interwoven twigs. The fills were sampled, revealing a range of occupation debris, including wood fragments, brick/tile, limestone, bone, eggshell and shellfish (Hall et al. 1993a). The beetle assemblage included sub-

Fig.261 *Area 13.X, Period 7: Building 30, wall 5405, looking north-west. Scale unit 0·1m*

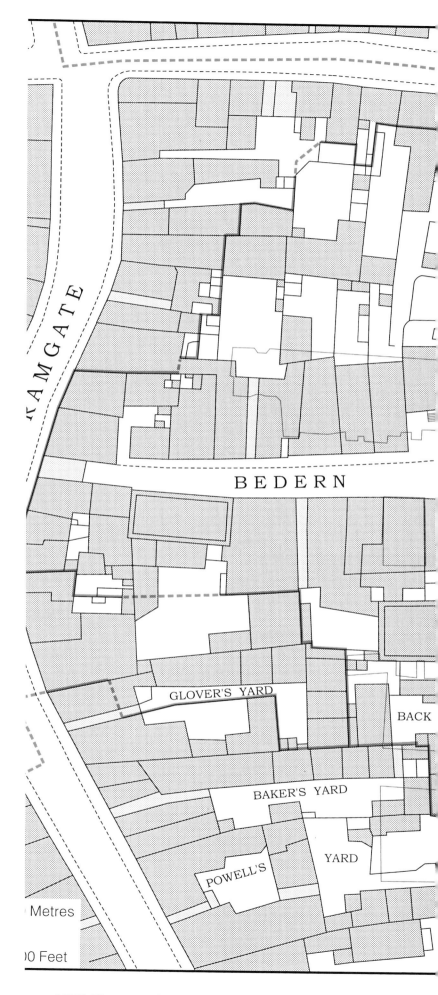

map of 1852. The excavated areas are outlined in red, the parish boundaries in green.

ALDWARK

ST ANDREWGATE

BEDERN

Scale 1:500

terranean burrowers and other decomposers, including 'house fauna'. Substantial numbers of parasite eggs were detected in the lowest fill; a small amount of food waste was evidently present to judge from the abundant fig seeds and frequent strawberry seeds and corncockle seed fragments. Most of the other plants were weeds, though there were traces of elderberry, raspberry and sloe fruitstones. After it had been completely backfilled the pit was covered by a spread of rubble and sandy loam (5404).

Building 28

At the end of Period 7 the disuse of Building 28 was marked by the deposition of a spread of clay loam and tile (7096, Fig.368s) within it. A stone spindle whorl (sf2406) was found in this deposit.

Building 31 (Fig.386s)

Only two of the outer walls of Building 31 survived and in a partial condition: the north-west wall which was formed from the old Period 3 south-east wall 7611 (Fig.376s) to Building 10, and a poorly surviving south-west wall (7223*) consisting of limestone blocks and bricks with smaller fragments of tile, brick and limestone set into a construction trench backfilled with mortar and clay. This wall covered Phase 3 hearth 7282 from Building 29, and was just to the south-west of Building 29's north-east wall (7281). The interior of Building 31 was to the north-east, and covering the south-east part of 7281 was a clay and tile feature (7278) with traces of ash and mortar. This feature was overlain to the north-east by a sandy loam (7271) cut by a small pit (7272) filled with loam and broken tiles. This was itself covered by a spread of ashy loam (7257) containing some pitched tiles, possibly the remains of a hearth, cut by a small patch of burnt clay (7256) covered by yet more clay spreads (7252, 7235).

A new hearth (7214*) was then constructed against the north-west wall from pitched tiles, with a stacked tile wall (7186*) bounding its north-west and south-west sides. Covering the hearth was a deposit of ash (7189*), probably representing the latest use. A small spread of burnt clay (7187) then covered the stacked tile wall (7186) as well as the edge of the ash (7189). The hearth was then altered with the construction of an additional stacked tile wall (7186a) built over the earlier wall (7186) and covering the clay (7187). The ash covering the first hearth was itself covered with a small lens of limestone chips covered with a mixed mortar and ash layer (7166), representing the use surface associated with the second stage of the hearth. At a similar time to these alterations a layer of sandy ash and charcoal (7112) was deposited to the south-east.

Kitchen (Fig.386s)

Four clay hearths were now set around the kitchen walls: one on each of the north-east (6150*) and south-

west (6142*, Fig.368s) sides, and two on the south-east side (6144, 6082). That on the north-east side, 6150, was set into a fireplace of generous proportions. The exact width of this feature is not known since the presumed position of the south-east wall was subsequently cut by a 19th century pit, but it was certainly in excess of 2·4m and may have extended 3·25m to the garden wall itself, giving added significance to the existence of a brick capping there. It is suggested that this hearth was set against the north-east wall (6127*), and that a new north-east wall (6151*), including a large square limestone post-pad set in a pit (6152), was built to enclose it partially. A fragment of a high-lead glass jug or pouring flask rim (sf2214) was excavated from the pit fill. The north-west wall abutted the earlier stone post-pad (6177), but was further offset to the north-west. It was constructed of brick bonded with white lime mortar and measured c.0·3m thick, surviving to a height of c.0·15m. It was deeply founded on packed cobbles, perhaps in response to subsidence in the post-pad. Both walls (6127 and 6151) showed signs of intense heat. There was evidence for a contemporary brick floor (6149*) to the west.

The four hearth surfaces (6082, 6142, 6144, 6150) were very similar in character, with only minor differences in detail. That in the large fireplace (6150) consisted of a spread of clay, heavily burnt, not extending beyond the south-west limit of the north-west wall of the fireplace, and occupying a shallow scoop to a depth of c.0·07m. The clay was sampled for archaeomagnetic determination. The date obtained was 1440 ± 50 (Noel 1978). This is consistent with a final usage towards the end of Period 7, although the large associated error range could in fact allow it to be placed anywhere within Period 7 or the first phase of Period 8. A modified calibration curve places the date anywhere between 1290 and 1500 (Batt 1997).

On the south-west edge of this hearth, a small circular pit (6183*) had been dug through the hearth and a broad bowl-shaped pot placed in it. The resulting hole was later filled with sand. The base of the pot had a perforation c.0·07m in diameter cut through it, plugged with clay. The pot itself contained several fills consisting of a lowermost layer of fine wood and charcoal, a coarse burnt sand, and an uppermost layer of sandy clay with mortar flecking and small tile fragments.

The arrangements of the remaining hearths were comparatively uncomplicated. All three were set against walls, demanding some kind of hood. Each consisted of a clay-filled scoop in the underlying dump, and two (6142, 6144) revealed evidence for light ancillary structures. In each case this took the form of a row of half bricks laid onto the clay, lying close alongside the surface of the back wall, forming firebacks. This sort of arrangement may also have existed for 6082, but an intrusion had destroyed some of this surface.

Connected with the use of these hearths were a large number of small shallow depressions filled with fine black ash (6085, 6090, Fig.366s, 6093–5) set into the underlying clay (6084, Fig.368s) which formed the surface throughout this final stage in the development of the kitchen area. A parchment pricker (8051) was found in this clay.

The garden and south-western courtyard
(Fig.386s)

Within the garden the period of disuse and pit digging was followed by the deposition of an extensive layer of dark sandy loam (5146, Fig.371s, 5283–4) filling all the pits and depressions, and marking a new horizon of development. The faunal assemblage from loam 5146 was unusual in having a high incidence of cat (c.16% of the total number of fragments); this may be a reflection of the discrete burial of pets, rather than disposing of them with the bulk of the bone refuse (Hamshaw-Thomas 1994). Layer 5146 also contained a knife with an inlaid cutler's mark (AY 17/15 in prep., sf1951). A new pit and gully system (5147) was dug into this loam, with a distinctive fill of ash and clay. There were many other associated pits (5153–4, 5180, 5185, 5230*, 5231*, 5280, 5316), overlain by various spreads of broken tile (5319). The pits were generally filled with dark loam and ash and, with the gully system, are surmised to have had a horticultural function, although some also contained domestic rubbish which could have been added as fertiliser. Pit 5180 contained a parchment pricker (8039) and a pair of shears with an inlaid cutler's mark (sf1969); pit 5230 contained a continental coin (AY 18/1, 197) struck for William I of Namur, c.1337–91. A sample of the silty sand fill contained charcoal with vegetative plant remains and a few seeds; there were no insect remains or parasite eggs (Hall et al. 1993a). Pit 5231 contained charcoal and slag, and supported a breeding community of beetles consistent with open-textured rotting matter. There was a modest assemblage of identifiable plant remains, together with a variety of occupation debris including coal, cinders, fish bone and scale, mortar and mussel shell. Possible foodplants present included linseed, fig, elderberry and charred bread/club wheat. This was perhaps food waste rather than faecal material. Only background numbers of parasite eggs were recovered (Hall et al. 1993a).

In the courtyard overlying 5292 in the south-west area of the site was a mixed loam (5383, Fig.367s) containing limestone, mortar and broken tile. A concentration of iron nails, mostly bent, was found in this deposit. There was a post-hole (5356*) cutting 5292, overlain by a small spread of clay (5345). In the far south-west there was an ashy loam (5293, Figs.367s, 371s), into which was set a linear tile feature (5295). This ashy soil produced a copper alloy jetton (AY 18/1, 138) dated to Edward I's reign, 1272–1307. The ashy loam was cut by a linear spread of clay (5395) with a concentration of mortar and a few small set stones and

tile at its north-west end. Overlying 5383 was a clay (5375) cut by five post-holes which formed no discernible pattern. This in its turn was covered by a mixed clay (5320, Fig.367s) also cut by a series of post-holes and settings (5321–3) of coarse limestone rubble, all sharing the same alignment. Related to these was a possible post-pad of limestone cobbles (5324) and a rubble-packed pit (5275*).

The cess pits on the south-west edge of the trench were backfilled with a mixture of clay loam, tile, mortar and rubble, and then levelled over. Cess pit 5391 (Fig.367s) was sealed by charcoal and tiles (5291, Fig.367s) which had slumped into the pit, and a rubble spread (5290, Fig.367s) overlay pits 5306 and 5382. Pottery suggests that the area was levelled in the early 15th century. The north-east wall of Building 15 (5325, Fig.386s) was partly covered by various clay and rubble layers (5287, 5298, both Fig.367s) containing bone manufacturing debris (AY 17/12, 7996) and a chalk spindle whorl (sf1964).

Bedern Hall (Fig.386s)

During Phase 4 Building 26 appears to have fallen into disuse and to the north-east it was abutted by clay rubble (5449, Fig.262, facing p.504), possibly later tumble. The levels associated with the disused Building 26 were then cut by a construction trench packed with clay (5437, Fig.371s), containing the limestone walls (5351*, Fig.371s) of a structure built against Bedern Hall (Figs.264–5). Some 3m of the south-west wall and 1m of the north-west wall survived, enclosing a rectangular area built alongside the projecting bay, extending the outer line of this bay as far as the west corner of the hall. This may have formed an extension to the bay, although there was no evidence for such an extension in the standing stonework and, in this position, it would have blocked the light to the end window in the hall's south-west wall. It is more likely, therefore, that the footings represent a low lean-to structure built against the hall, possibly functioning as a fuel store to judge from the deposits of coal laid in its interior in Period 8. Outside this structure, a cobble and limestone surface (5304*, Fig.371s) was laid over a sand bedding (5358, Fig.371s) and a silty clay loam (5359, Fig.371s), and over layer 5146 (see above). These cobbles formed a hard path to the south-west of the lean-to, and appear to be slightly later than the first internal levels. The cobbles had an angled surface which allowed them to act as a small surface drain running parallel to the hall wall. The cobbles were also found in the eastern trial trench where they ran up to the south-west wall of the hall (Fig.266).

There was a small build up of loam over the foundations of the hall and the external store against the south-west side of Bedern Hall was then rebuilt (no plan survives). The new walls (unnumbered) consisted of rounded limestone blocks set into a large mass of mortar with some tile coursing, topped with large mortar-bonded

Fig.264 (right) Area 13.X, Period 7.4: western trial trench, external store with exterior cobble surface (5304), Building 26 wall (5438) at top centre, and the lowest courses of the wall of Bedern Hall, looking north-west. Scale unit 0·1m

Fig.265 (below) Area 13.X, Period 7.4: western trial trench, detail of external store wall 5351, right of scale, abutting Bedern Hall at its south-west corner, looking north-east. Scale unit 0·1m

Fig.266 (right) Area 13.X, Period 7.4: cobble surface running up to Bedern Hall in the eastern trial trench, looking north-east. Scale unit 0·1m

limestone blocks. The external cobble path was cut by this rebuild and the irregular edge created made good with a packing of small pebbles. A deposit of mortar covered the join between the cobbles and the wall.

New deposits within the store building consisted of a dark loamy soil with many inclusions of coal chips, tile, limestone and small bones. A dark grey sandy clay silt (5336, Fig.371s) was deposited outside, containing a high proportion of brick/tile, coal and limestone rubble. A thin deposit of coal (5335, Fig.371s) was dumped to the south-west and north-east.

Bedern long trench

At the end of Period 7 a clay levelling layer (1565, Fig.364s), c.0·2m thick, was deposited in the south-eastern part of the trench (Area IV).

Bedern Foundry (pp.178–9, AY 10/3: Period 4, Phase 4)

The Period 7.3 land-drain (992, p.502) and some of the pits were sealed by rubble-strewn deposits (893, 908, 957, 961, 991, Fig.79, AY 10/3) containing much tile and mortar.

To the south-east, a surface of limestone chippings (2174) with some reddish-brown sand (2176) was laid. More deposits of mould fragments (740, 2096, 2178) had been dumped on this, and there was a small mortar patch (2165). A sample of one of these layers (740) revealed that it contained lumps of peat, such as might be left in the residue of a peat stack.

Period 8: mid 15th–early 17th century (Fig.267)

No major new buildings were erected within the college precinct during Period 8, although there was continued modification of existing structures. By the mid 15th century the college's income had begun to drop and from the end of the century this was accompanied by a steady fall in the number of vicars. It is known that in 1574 the vicars gave up dining in common, and so presumably after this date the college buildings fell increasingly into disuse or were sold off or leased to private individuals. By the end of Period 8 many of those buildings fronting onto Bedern Close were pulled down, and the area was given over to rubble dumps, cess pits and rubbish pits. Bedern Hall survived as the communal meeting and refectory building for the college until the mid 17th century, when it passed into private hands. The building additions made to the hall in this period can perhaps be dated to the late 16th century. Buildings 25 and 27 apparently continued in use, with some internal alterations, and there was no indication that the kitchen fell into disuse at this time, although the area south-east of these buildings was increasingly used as gardens. The courtyard to the south-west now contained at least two fairly substantial structures, one of which may have been a brewhouse, as well as what may have been a small outbuilding containing a cess pit.

Period 8, Phase 1: mid 15th–early 16th century

At the beginning of Period 8 **Building 5** was shortened once again, with the demolition of the south-east wing and the use of a former internal wall as the new south-east end of the building (Fig.385s). A portion of the north-east outer wall was also demolished, leaving only two courses upstanding. Onto this a new length of limestone wall was built, while internally the rooms were altered.

The area which had been Room 5G in Period 7 was now divided into two new rooms by the addition of a north-east/south-west wall, although modern intrusions removed any evidence for the room to the south-east. To the north-west of this partition was Room 5K. The north-west wall of this room was also partially new, replacing the Period 7 wall. Room 5K was itself divided by a partition which created a 2m wide area to the north-east in which there was a

pitched tile hearth with a brick retaining wall, set into a clay floor. The south-west area also contained a hearth, surviving as a small area of burnt clay edged with bricks and at least two floor levels of clay and mortar. It seems likely that both areas were used as living quarters.

Room 5L developed out of Room 5H, with new internal deposits and a new south-east wall in common with Room 5K. Two phases of use within this room have been identified, separated by a period of apparent disuse. In the first phase, there was a pitched tile hearth set into a clay floor. Following an apparently short period of use, this hearth was demolished and the entire room was then covered by mixed deposits and cut by several pits.

At the north-west end of Building 5 the earlier layout was changed. Two new rooms were created, 5M and 5N. Room 5N ran across the width of the building, replacing in part Room 5I. Two new limestone walls were constructed at right-angles to each other, near the north-east wall of Building 5, that on a north-east/south-west alignment defining the north-west wall of Room 5N. These two walls were associated with a spread of cobbles to the north-east, and a deposit of clay laid down inside the angle between them. It is not clear which deposits or features continued in use from Room 5I or whether this part of the building continued to be used as living quarters. Room 5M, to the north-west of 5N, was created out of Room 5J. A mortar floor and a pitched tile hearth suggest that Room 5M was also used as living quarters.

While these alterations were being made within Building 5, **Building 22** and the associated drain to the north-east of Building 5 were demolished, the resulting debris of tile and limestone rubble being spread across the area. To the north-west of Building 22, **Building 23** was also demolished and replaced by an extensive cobble yard adjacent to a large cess pit.

With the shortening of Building 5, **Building 16** (in Area 14.IV) was demolished and the area levelled. A cobble wall was then constructed in this area, but, as no other walls were associated with it, its purpose remains unclear. Modern clearance has removed any further evidence in this part of the site.

509

34

36

5M

5N   5L   5K

THE BEDERN

Chapel

17

24

31

25   27

Bedern Hall

26

25

Kitchen

Bartle Garth
or
Back Bedern

30

Garden

35

33

32

13

Foundry

0   5   10 Metres

0   10   20   30 Feet

Fig.267 *Period 8, phases 1–3: interpretative summary phase plan, showing building development. Development in Periods 7.3 and 7.4 is not shown as 'new' on any of the summary phase plans. For the key, see Fig.195, p.409. Scale 1:400*

North-east of Building 16, **Building 21** appears to show no further developments during this period, and may also have been demolished at an early stage as shown by the accumulation of typical demolition debris in the area. The boundary wall south-east of Building 21 was also disused at this time.

Documentary evidence suggests that minor alterations to the college buildings in the 15th century were largely connected with the increasing tendency of the vicars to establish independent households; some vicars began renting portions of the Bedern gardens for private use, and there is evidence to suggest that they built private kitchens and garderobes onto their houses. It is possible that the shortening of Building 5 was to allow this sort of activity. The pre-demolition deposits within all the buildings described above appear to be the last identifiable remains of occupation belonging to the college. Subsequent rebuilding on the site after their demolition was mostly removed by modern clearance.

During the first part of Period 8 the internal organisation of the **chapel** was unchanged although new floor levels were laid.

South-west of the close, there was some construction on the site of Building 18 during the late 15th–early 16th century possibly in the form of a building to the north-west of the line of its north-west wall. Outside this building to the south-east was a brick and cobble drain.

Building 17 continued in use with some minor internal alterations, and the insertion of a second brick-lined latrine pit in its south-west wall. **Building 24** also continued in use and new floor levels built up around the Period 7 hearth. A brick-lined pit was inserted into the south-east wall, and solid brick and limestone floors were laid in the centre of the building (Figs.274, 370s, 387s).

Buildings 26 and **30**, built against the south-western corner of Bedern Hall, continued in use during Period 8, as did the hall itself. **Building 25** also remained standing, with **Building 27**, the kitchen and associated areas undergoing alterations (Fig.387s). Within Building 27 the internal staircase was removed, and the interior levelled up with a clay surface, followed by the construction of a new staircase replacing the earlier one. This was then followed by

the deposition of a sequence of floor levels — sand, mortar and clay — which never spread to the edges of the room, suggesting the existence of internal fittings, perhaps shelving, inside the walls. All these floor levels produced evidence of burning, and were successively repaired and patched, before the deposition of a substantial sand surface. At a later stage the staircase was removed and the resulting cavity backfilled, before the deposition of more internal layers. In the centre of this building was a patch of heat-reddened clay, presumably a hearth. Other internal structures were represented by a series of rectangular post-holes and pads of roof tiles in small pits, set around the north-east, south-west and south-east sides of the room, at a distance of c.0·4m from the walls. The nature of the fittings excavated within Building 27 suggest that it had a sustained use of a particular kind over a long period of time. It is known that the college possessed an 'evidence room' in this general area (which was burgled during the Civil War; see p.576). The surprising and disproportionate thickness of the walls, the single and somewhat awkward access, the shelving or benches around the sides of the room, and the presumed use of braziers, all suggest that this building was used for the storage of college records.

There was a brick standing, perhaps for a water butt, against the north-east wall of Building 27; the area between it and Building 17 appears to have been open, with the demolition of Building 28, and the deposition of a tile, cobble and limestone courtyard surface.

Within **Building 31** two pitched tile hearths, one with an edging, were constructed (Fig.387s). The hearths in the **kitchen** area were now disused, and a new period of use initiated by the construction of a large brick-built hearth with a limestone sill. The kitchen floor revealed a piecemeal build up on its surface of laminated fine ash and charcoal intermixed with kitchen and domestic debris.

At this time a considerable alteration to the **garden wall** was undertaken, beginning with the demolition of the south-west wall of the small annexe attached to the end of Building 27, followed by the construction of three equidistant limestone buttresses on the garden wall to allow for the insertion of two brick-lined latrine pits against its south-east side (Fig.387s). Subsequently a new wall, founded on limestone rubble and brick, replaced the demolished south-west wall of the annexe. This was displaced to the north-east of the original one, reducing the annexe in size to c.3 × 2m.

The construction of the buttresses coincided with the build up of mixed rubble spreads cut by rubble-filled pits in the area between Building 27 and the kitchen. Once the alterations to the garden wall had been completed, this part of the college precinct was floored, and provided access from Building 25 into the kitchen through a doorway in its north-east wall.

The south-west area of the site was given over to a courtyard and garden both cut by numerous pits, some of them probably for cess, with the garden wall still dividing this area into two. South-east of this wall a small structure, c.2 × 2m, was built against the garden wall to contain a cess pit, and beyond this was a flat-laid brick and tile path which had been repeatedly repaired (Fig.387s). North-west of the garden wall, the Period 7 drain was allowed to silt up. The history of this part of the site is somewhat unclear due to the disruption caused by the siting of a large brick building here in the 17th century (p.650). Nevertheless, it is apparent that there was considerable demolition in the 16th century, defined by spreads of rubble, and tile- and rubble-filled pits. It is tempting to see the whole episode as dating from the Reformation when it is known that the college suffered considerably.

Two new buildings were erected at the south-west edge of the site (Figs.371s, 387s). **Building 32** was represented only by part of its north-east and south-east walls founded on construction spreads of clay, tile, mortar and limestone. The rest of the building was outside the excavation, but it did appear to have had a mortar floor. A rectangular structure, **Building 33**, 7m (north-east/south-west) × 4m, was set onto the south-east end of Building 32, abutting its south-east wall. The north-eastern half of Building 33 was revealed in Area 13.X; the southern corner was excavated in the north-west corner of the long trench (Area 13.III), whilst the western corner was exposed beyond the edge of the long trench after the removal of the modern concrete. Associated with this small building complex were rubbish dumps and pits, and a cobbled surface abutting the south-east side of Building 33.

The area now enclosed on its north-east side by Bedern Hall, on its south-east side by the kitchen range and on its south-west side by Buildings 32 and 33 appears to have been an open courtyard. On the 1852 Ordnance Survey map it is identifiable as Back Bedern Court (see Fig.263, facing p.505).

Along the north-east edge of the foundry site there were further pits but the area was also encroached on by foundry-related activity and to the north-east of the main furnace building a working platform was constructed, providing access to the foundry, possibly for fuel supply to the furnace. A surface of limestone chippings and mortar was laid in the threshold of the alleyway providing access to the south-west end of the college precinct from the foundry site.

Bedern North-East

Building 5 (Fig.385s)

The shortening of Building 5 involved the demolition of Period 2 wall 4477 down to its foundation sill, part of which was then covered by a deposit of loam (4188*). Deposits of clay, mortar and tile rubble (4060, 4055, 4051), presumably resulting from the demolition, covered earlier internal deposits at the south-east end of the original building. A French imitation of an English penny, struck c.1292–8 (*AY* 18/1, *195*), was found in one of these layers (4055). A large pit (4091*) was dug through the north-east end of the old outer wall (Fig.268). This pit was lined on three

Fig.268   Area 14.IV, Period 8: pit 4091, looking north-east, with cross-section of backfill. Scale unit 0·1m

sides with a well-laid mixture of brick and limestone rubble set into construction trenches dug into the base of the pit cut, while the north-east side used the remaining foundations of the Building 5 wall (4477) as a partial facing. The base of the pit was covered with mortar, tile and limestone rubble (4103), which was then overlain by a deposit of finely textured, sandy silty clay (4100). Of the four plant taxa recorded from a sample of this deposit, three are likely to have been weeds growing in the area, with the fourth, fig, representing food waste, although no faecal material was noted and the other components of the residue comprised a narrow range of materials like charcoal, eggshell, fish bone and oyster shell, as well as plaster, mortar and brick or tile. A second sample yielded two wetland taxa: water-plantain and toad-rush (Hall et al. 1993c).

Building 5 seems to have then used the Period 6 internal wall (1525) as its new south-east end wall. After shortening, Building 5 underwent further alterations involving the demolition of a section of the north-east outer wall (1157), leaving only two courses upstanding. A new length of limestone wall (1077*, Fig.365s) was then built on these footings.

At the same time, the rooms within Building 5 were altered. Two new rooms were created out of Room 5G, but the entire area of the south-east room up to the end wall (1525) had been removed by modern intrusions. The room north-west of what had been 5G, i.e. Room 5K, was represented, firstly, by a south-east wall consisting of two new lengths of walling (1201*/1203*), the north-east part (1201) being made up of two large cobblestones set in a mortar-filled construction trench, and the south-west part (1203) being made up of limestones and cobbles. Secondly, there was a partially new north-west wall (1140/1204*), replacing the Period 7 structure (1289). The south-west wall of Room 5K is presumed to have been outside the area of excavation. On its north-east side Room 5K extended to the outer wall of Building 5 (1158).

Internal events in this room began with the deposition of a sandy mortar spread (1232) possibly relating to the alteration to the room. The now disused hearths from Room 5G were sealed by an extensive floor of mixed clay (1155) with evidence of later repair (1090, 1178). A line of mortared cobble foundations were set into this clay, representing a north-west/south-east partition wall (1150*) dividing Room 5K into two unequal portions. The south-west portion of Room 5K was the larger of the two, and contained a hearth (1107*), consisting of a small area of burnt clay in a shallow construction scoop and edged on the north-west and south-west sides with the fragmentary remains of heat-shattered brick walls. The clay floor (1155) was overlain by a mortar spread (1185). The north-east portion of Room 5K contained a clay deposit (1159*) and a small pitched tile hearth (1165*) set into and bonded

with clay. On the north-east side of this hearth were the remains of a brick retaining wall surviving to a height of one course. The clay (1159) had been cut by various small pits (1160, 1163, 1170, 1190, 1199).

At a later stage, the internal partition (1150) may have been repaired or had an entrance through it blocked by the insertion of a deposit of sand and rubble (1142), and a length of wall consisting of sand-bonded cobbles (1089) was inserted into the north-west wall (1140).

To the north-west, Room 5I was replaced by a different layout. It is unclear if its south-east wall (1401) survived in this period. At its north-west end a small structure was built, surviving only as two walls (1353*/1355*) which formed a corner. Built of sand-bonded limestone blocks, these walls were associated with a spread of cobbles (1342*) to the north-east. A deposit of clay (1096*) was laid down within the angle of walls 1353 and 1355.

In the area to the south-west of this structure, the Period 6 wall 1452 and its associated floor 1446 were covered by an extensive spread of sandy mortar (1441). This in turn was covered by a fairly thick deposit of loam (1439), which itself was overlain by a spread of limestone chippings (1431). A sequence of clay deposits (1436, 1429–30) represent both the demolition of the room and a levelling up of the surrounding area for other uses. They incorporated fragments from the vessel rim and body of a glass hanging lamp (sf329) which may once have been in use in the room. On top of these deposits was a spread of clay loam containing much mortar and tile (1428*) which in turn underlay a demolition or garden spread (1293).

Room 5M was created to the north-west of this area out of Room 5J. It appears to have been built against the north-east outer wall (1029*), and comprised a possible north-west wall visible in the section, a south-east wall removed by modern intrusions, and a south-west wall outside the area of excavation. The earliest internal deposits in this room consisted of mortar spread (1086) onto which was set a pitched tile hearth (1072) in a construction scoop backfilled with clay (Fig.269).

Outside Building 5 to the north-east further fills (1456B) were deposited in the pit (1456) originally cut in Period 7. A sample from the fill yielded a somewhat unusual mixture of plant remains, including figwort and a wetland moss, perhaps both from aquatic marginal habitats (Hall et al. 1993b). The only other indicators of wetland were *Chara*, a plant of standing water in ponds and pools, and a rush. The other plants were mostly weeds of arable land or otherwise disturbed habitats. Towards the centre of the north-east area, an extensive spread of tile and limestone rubble (1156*, Fig.365s) was deposited in the area of the earlier drain (1450) and outbuilding, Building 22. It con-

Fig.269   Area 14.II, Period 8: hearth 1072, looking east. Scale unit 0·1m

tained a fragment of a ceramic louver of similar fabric to those pieces found in Period 7 deposits in this area but had a flaring rim and a light green glaze (see p.608). It also contained an iron holdfast (sf265). Further to the north-west was a large circular pit (1326*) with six layers of an organic peaty fill (1359) which was extensively sampled and found to contain much faecal contamination (Hall et al. 1993b). There were abundant beetle remains, representing a breeding community in fairly foul conditions. Other insects, including spider beetles and woodworm, came from outside the pit, and an origin in dumped rubbish, such as floor sweepings, seems possible. There were substantial numbers of parasite eggs and traces of food remains, including fig seeds, sloe and grape, hazel nut and possibly raspberry, blackberry and pea. The presence of moderate amounts of corncockle seed fragments probably points to the incorporation of milled grain-based foods in the deposit. Other plants represented included sedge, spike-rush, stinging nettle, sheep's sorrel and buttercup. The uppermost fill had been exposed for some time to allow the beetle populations to build up to modest levels — weeks perhaps. The small assemblage of plant remains consisted entirely of weeds and wet grassland taxa, perhaps not surprising for an uppermost fill.

There were also two slightly later pits in this area (1328, 1331) and associated with them were a mortar spread (1338), a clay loam (1341) and a garden soil (1340). At the north-west end of this external area, the earlier building and associated demolition spreads were covered by a fairly extensive cobble spread (1209).

At the south-east end of Area II there were a number of pits, including a large rectangular pit (1600) used for domestic refuse (1602), backfilled with rubble (1601) and levelled with clay (1598–9). This pit produced an unusual bone assemblage of roughly equal proportions of cattle and poultry, with a high number of cod and gadid bones (Hamshaw-Thomas 1994).

Building 16

The evidence for the disuse of Building 16 (originally established in Period 6) was clearest in the south-eastern part of Area 14.IV. Overlying the Period 7 deposit 4198 were limestone cobbles, rubble and loam (4165/4157*). The rubble included a section of arch head from a traceried window (278) of 13th or early 14th century date which may have come from the original fenestration of Building 16 (*AY* 10/4). An unusual inlaid knife blade (sf5133) was found in 4165. This layer was covered in turn by loam (4171), and a deposit of clay loam and rubble (4169/4135*) which was contemporary with a crushed limestone spread (4189), in turn covered by a sandy loam (4181). An extensive layer of limestone and cobble rubble (4164*) mixed with a sandy loam and particles of clay was then deposited across most of this area. All these deposits were overlain by post-medieval clearance levels. The disuse of the north-east part of Building 16 is represented by a series of demolition deposits and pits: a shallow pit (4221) containing a fill of loam and lime; a shallow pit (4222) containing a fill of loam; a large, roughly circular spread of tile and limestone rubble (4251) set in a clay loam with inclusions of mortar and some ash and charcoal. The Period 7 stone-lined pit in Room 16E (4345) was backfilled with clay containing ash, shell and charcoal.

The north-west wall (4020) of Building 16 was demolished. To its south-east there was a shallow trench (4220*) filled with crushed limestone. Rubble and clay spreads (4243, 4239) partly overlay a limestone padstone in the wall. An iron spade blade (sf1800) was found in 4239. Several clay loams (4084) accumulated, and were overlain by a deposit of tile rubble (4086) spreading from the now-disused hearth (4027). Also covering this hearth was a deposit of brown clay (4080) containing an Edward I penny of c.1300–10 originally deposited before 1351 (*AY* 18/1, *107*). This clay was cut by a small pit (4081) with an upper fill of compacted ashy material, and a lower fill of lime mortar and crushed limestone. Overlying both clay (4080) and backfilled trench (4220) was a disturbed wall (4139*) consisting of a linear arrangement of water-worn cobbles containing limestone padstones and its associated construction spread (4142). Another clay and rubble spread (4112*) in this general area contained a jetton of Edward II (*AY* 18/1, *153*). A fragment of roll moulding (*259, AY* 10/4) in the rubble is of a form dated to the early to mid 13th century. To the north-west of the demolished wall (4020) there was a rubble spread (4076) and several rubble-filled pits (4074–5), probably representing demolition in this area.

Building 21

During Period 8, Building 21 (constructed in Period 7) was also disused, as indicated by the extensive spread of brick and mortar rubble (4113) covering the floor. Disuse of the 'boundary' wall (4178) to the south-east probably took place during this period, although modern clearance has removed the evidence.

Bedern Chapel

At the beginning of Period 8 a new series of floor deposits was placed over the earlier floor levels. A series of very thin sandy lenses (9055) built up at the north-west end. These lenses appear to have wear patterns in them, suggesting excessive wear near the doorway, with a central raised hump, perhaps where more sand was deposited to fill the hollow. At the same time, layers of mortar (9054, 9063, Fig.232a, facing p.472) were laid down across the rest of the interior.

Subsequently, a new floor deposit (9051, Fig.232a–c) built up across much of the interior (Fig.270). This comprised a series of very thin sandy lenses which must represent the gradual accumulation of material over some time. The layer can be divided into two parts (9051A and 9051B), separated by an almost continuous charcoal layer,

Fig.270 *Bedern Chapel, looking north-west, showing Period 8 floor levels (9051). Scale unit 0.1m*

Fig.271 *Area 13.X: general view across the north-east end of the site, looking north-west, with Building 18 in the foreground, Building 17 towards the centre and Building 27 at top left. Scale unit 0·5m*

perhaps the result of an interior fire. At the south-east end this material filled a linear north-east/south-west feature, cut into the earlier mortar. A pit (9039, Fig.232a) was also dug into the earlier levels at the north-west end, and filled with a mixture of floor tiles and sand.

Bedern South-West

A possible building to the north-west of what had been the north-west wall of Building 18 was represented by a 1m length of robber trench (7091*). 7089* was probably an internal clay layer. To the south-east a mortar and loam deposit (7177) covered the Period 6 wall-line 7147. A drain (7163) was constructed, running north-east/south-west, although it had also been robbed by a later (Phase 3) trench (7013). The drain had been laid onto a sand packing layer (7194); it was constructed from flat-laid bricks with cobbles sloping down gently on either side. The south-east edge of these cobbles was marked by an edge-set tile line and covered by broken tiles (7176*). Two small pits (7022*, 7031*) were dug south-west of the area just described.

Building 17 (Figs.271, 387s)

Building 17 appears to have continued in use during Period 8, although the Period 7 internal wall (7068) became redundant and was overlain by a hard-packed fine mortar (7035, Fig.366s). A second brick-lined sump or cess pit (7027*, Figs.272, 370s) was constructed against the outside of the south-west wall, set into a sandy mortar construction spread (7199) which overlay the ashy clay loams and mortar spreads in this area. An ash and charcoal layer

Fig.273   Area 13.X, Period 8: brick-lined pit 7039. Scale unit 0·1m

(7168) butted up against the south-west edge of the pit. There was a build up of loamy soil (7019) against the south-east wall of Building 17.

Building 24 (Figs.273–4, 387s)

The Period 7 floor was covered by a new floor level (7074*), although the hearth (7058*) may have continued in use, with associated spreads of mortar (7056*), and charcoal and ash (7057*). A small copper alloy object (sf2675) to which three layers of silk had been riveted was found incorporated in the floor deposit. Towards the centre of Building 24 there was a limestone and cobble spread (7048*) and a large limestone ashlar spread (7047*, Fig.370s) containing some irregularly shaped cobbles. At

Fig.272   Area 13.X, Period 8: brick-lined pit 7027. Scale unit 0·1m

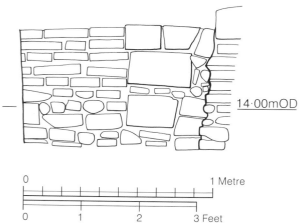

Fig.274   Elevation of the north-west wall of brick-lined pit 7039. Scale 1:20

the same time a brick-lined pit (7039*, Figs.273–4, 370s) was inserted into the south-east wall (7053). A single springer from a blind arcade, probably from Archbishop Roger's Minster choir, had been re-used in its construction (46, AY 10/4). Adjacent to the pit and abutting it was a surface of bricks (7046*, Fig.370s) set on edge in some mortar, laid onto a dump of mixed brown clay (7026) at its north-west end. The clay dump produced a continental coin (AY 18/1, 198) initially deposited before 1351. A limestone block packed with clay and tile was set into the clay, and covered by clay and clay loam (7011, Fig.370s, 7015) spreading to the north-east.

Bedern Hall

Deposits continued to accumulate within the structure against the south-west side of Bedern Hall, including a layer of hard-packed pure coal (5353, Fig.371s). It was overlain by a dark ashy loam (5337, Fig.371s), a sample of which contained fish and mammal bone, shellfish, mortar, brick/tile, coal, charcoal and sand. Traces of fig and elderberry seeds were also identified (Hall et al. 1993a). The animal bone assemblage from loam 5337 is dominated by the bones of sheep; cattle are second in frequency, followed by pig and a little cat, dog and rabbit. There were also domestic fowl and geese, as well as some duck, plus salmon, gadidae, cod and ling (AY 15).

An extensive layer of clay loam (5354) was found in the western trial trench covering the hall construction level (5364), equivalent to the extensive clay loams (5131–2) encountered in the main excavation trench (Area 13.X, see p.523). This was cut by two pits; the first (5362) was backfilled with clay loam, broken tile and limestone, and later with ash (5361), and then sealed and levelled by dumps of clay loam (5355, 5360). A sample of the primary fill (i.e. deposit 5362) contained cinders, coal, slag, charcoal, brick/tile, limestone and bone, with traces of elderberry seeds (Hall et al. 1993a). The second pit (5370) contained a mixture of clay and organic fills. Cereal 'bran' and faecal concretions were quite common in a sample of the fill, suggesting that faeces formed a major part of this deposit, although there was little indication of parasite eggs and no other evidence of plant foods. The identifiable plants consisted mostly of weeds of both cultivated and neglected soils, including moderate amounts of toadrush and sheep's sorrel. Two plants recorded in a second sample were of some interest, however. The first (*Montia fontana* ssp. *chondrosperma*) is typical of short wet turf and shallow ditches, whilst the second (*Reseda lutea*) favours dry, typically calcareous, habitats (Hall et al. 1993a).

Building 25

A number of floor deposits were laid down during Period 8, including a clay spread (6079*) and several sandy spreads (6075–6*, 6078*).

Building 27 (Fig.387s)

The staircase posts (6221) were removed, and a new level comprising a deposit of clay (6208*, Fig.368s) was laid down, filling the post-holes and raising the floor level across the interior of Building 27 to the top of the plinth course. Cut through this was a small pit filled with loose clay loam and limestone chips (6202). A new staircase structure was constructed slightly to the north-east of the original one. Its outline was identifiable from the robber trench fills, with evidence for successive levels accumulating against it before it was removed. This staircase was rectangular, measuring 1·68 × 1m, and occupied the north corner of Building 27. The lower cavity contained rubbish deposits (6143) comprising sandy silt with limestone, charcoal, bone, brick/tile and pot. A sample yielded further occupation debris, including considerable amounts of cinders, eggshell and shellfish (Hall et al. 1993a). These deposits also produced an Edward I penny (AY 18/1, 102) minted between 1300 and 1310. In the centre of the room at this time was a small area of clay reddened by heat, and an extensive scatter of charcoal. The presence of other substantial structures was indicated by a series of small rectangular post-holes, interspersed with pads of roof tile in small pits filled with dirty sand, set around the north-east, south-west and south-east sides of the room, at a distance of about 0·4m from the walls.

These features were overlain by a thin spread of sand (6207) covering the entire building area and presenting a worn and patchy surface. A band of cleaner material around the north-east, south-west and south-east walls extended some 0·4m into the room, covering the sand deposit in these areas.

This sand surface was sealed by a deposit of clay (6195, Fig.368s) which showed signs of burning in the same area as the earlier clay deposit, with an accompanying charcoal scatter. Near the centre of the room this surface was covered by 6207 (Fig.368s) and 6194 (Fig.368s), a thin layer of mortar which sealed the irregularities in the underlying surface. This mortar and the succeeding sand deposit (6184, Fig.368s) all spread to within 0·4m of the room walls indicating that there were still fittings around the edge of the room. The four succeeding levels also respected these fittings. The first of these was of coarse sand (6181, Fig.368s), patched as before by a mortar and clay spread preceding the deposition of another sand surface (6178, Fig.368s). This in turn was patched with a mortar deposit containing limestone chippings. A new material, ash, was used for the next extensive repair. At the same time some re-used bricks were placed in the eastern corner, replacing the fittings here, and forming a wider surface. All these repairs and alterations were then sealed beneath an extensive new sand surface (6164/5, Fig.368s). This deposit underwent considerable patching as evidenced by the numerous small spreads of clean sand occupying shallow depressions in the overall layer.

Covering the Period 7 deposits to the north-east of Building 27 was a mixed spread of clay loam (7063), a dump of clay (7061) and a rubble spread (7059*). The loam was overlain by a brick feature (7062*) set against the north-east wall of Building 27. This had been chiselled into a curve on the outer south-east side, perhaps for a barrel stand. Also in this area between Buildings 27 and 17 were a mixture of clays (7042, 7144, 7211, Figs.368s, 370s, 7220, Fig.370s, 7222, 7232), sands and ashes (7154, 7218, 7225, 7245), brick and tile (7160), and mortars (7195, 7226, Fig.370s, 7242) cut by various pits (7151*, 7158*, 7193*).

Building 31 (Fig.387s)

Two new hearths (6110*, 6111*) were constructed over the Period 7 hearth (7214). The smaller (6110) comprised pitched tiles packed with clay loam; the larger (6111; Fig.275) consisted of a pitched tile centre packed with burnt clay, bounded by stacked tile and limestone edging (6097*), and an ash and charcoal spread (6099). Contemporary with the hearths was a loosely built clay-bonded wall (6098*) of limestone blocks at the north-west end and brick at the south-east, surviving to two courses high. Its slight construction suggests that it may have provided the base for an internal timber-framed partition.

Kitchen (Fig.387s)

Major modifications took place with the demolition and sealing of the hearth against the south-west wall by a clay loam, and of the two hearths against the garden wall, the south-west one by an ash-pit (6081*), the upper mortar fill of which spread across the burning surface, and the north-east one by the sand bedding for a brick platform (6131*). This brick platform may have formed the base for some additional support for the span of the large fireplace to the north-west, since it is possible that this was already being affected by the south-east subsidence of the garden wall. Identical sand bedding was used for a new large brick-built hearth (6083*; Figs.276, 366s), set into a shallow scoop cutting the Period 7.4, clay surface (6150) within the earlier hearth. In this scoop was a coarse yellow sand into which thin, re-used bricks had been set on edge, all aligned north-east/south-west apart from the north corner where there was evidence for repair work. Along the south-west edge of this brickwork was a shallow linear cut holding a row of six limestones set in a thin bedding layer of mortar. These were lightly polished by wear, and can be interpreted as the sill of the hearth. Large areas of the hearth surface and the north-westernmost limestone had been damaged by intense heat. There was a small intrusion (6087, Fig.366s) into the surface of the hearth.

Up to this time the area between Building 27 and the kitchen had remained an open yard in which there were clay spreads (6088*, Fig.368s, 6089*) and ash (6092) apparently deposited during the late 15th and 16th centuries. The area now becomes a room within the building complex and well-defined floor levels (6073*) were deposited, although much was lost to modern intrusions. The area defined by these floors measured c.6 × 4m, no intermediate roof support being necessary in so small a room. The room was reached by way of a doorway in the south-east

Fig.275 Area 13.X, Period 8: Building 31, hearth 6111. Scale unit 0·1m

Fig.276 Area 13.X, Period 8: kitchen, showing brick hearth 6083, looking north-east. Scale unit 0·1m

Fig.277 Area 13.X: Period 7.2 garden wall (6103–4, 6276) and Period 8.1 piers (6100–2), looking north-west. Scale unit 0·1m

wall of Building 25 and there was probably also a doorway in the north-east wall of the kitchen, as indicated by the spread of the floor deposits here.

South-west of the kitchen there were deposits composed of demolition material (6064, Fig.366s, 6119–20*, 6128*), and rubble-filled pits (6071–2, 6123*). Deposit 6064 contained a French jetton (AY 18/1, 240) minted c.1550–74. The Period 7 pit (6166, Fig.386s) was cut by a rubbish pit (6168) and a linear feature (6169) was covered by a clay spread (6167).

Garden wall (Fig.387s)

A considerable alteration to the garden wall was executed to accommodate two external latrine pits. As a preliminary, the brick south-west wall of the Building 27 annexe was demolished and three large cuts were made through the garden wall to receive three approximately equidistant stone piers (6100*, 6101*, 6102*, Fig.277). The central, and largest, of these (6101) lay 2·4m to the south-east of the south quoin of Building 27. The north-east pier (6100) and the south-west pier (6102) were separated from the central pier by c.1·9 and 2m respectively.

The construction of all three piers was very similar: at the bottom of the construction pits a course of small limestones and river cobbles was laid before the limestones of the piers were set in place. In every case, each of the surviving courses of stone was offset behind the course below, giving a profile of a series of shallow steps. The average depth of each offset was about 0·03–0·05m, although in all three cases the lowermost course alone projected c.0.1m. Virtually all the stone showed signs of previous use, and was mostly of damaged ashlar (132–3, 205, AY 10/4). The lowest course of the central pier was formed by a single plinth stone with a simple chamfer, while two courses above it a high-quality double-splay window sill had been incorporated into the masonry. The bonding was a yellow lime mortar of a type also used to backfill the construction trenches. The piers survived to a height of approximately 0·3–0·4m above the contemporary ground level, the construction pits (6115, 6117–18) being cut to a depth of c.0·5m below ground. A copper alloy tablet, possibly a weight (AY 18/1, 397), was recovered from the south-west pier (6102).

The construction pits had cut a number of earlier features, including a post-hole (6116), a deposit of mixed clay, mortar, stone, tile and brick rubble (6069, Fig.366s) containing a post-hole (6074), and a mortar-filled pit (6066) containing some wall plaster. A linear depression was located in the surface of 6069, filled with mortar and rubble (6091).

A pair of large, rectangular, brick-lined latrine pits was then constructed against the outside, south-east, face of the garden wall (Figs.278–9). The larger and earlier of the two (6013*) measured 1·7 × 1·3m, and survived to a depth of c.1m. The brickwork, in double thickness for the short walls, and treble thickness for the south-east wall, was laid in irregular stretcher-bond with a light brown, sandy mortar, and appeared to have been built hard up against the sides of its construction trench. On the north-west side where the brickwork was only two bricks deep, it was returned against the face of the garden wall. All four walls were founded on pitched brick (Fig.279), and in the south corner of the feature one surviving flat-laid brick may have been the remains of a floor, later removed.

Subsequently, a second latrine pit (6012*), 1·9 × 1·1m, was sunk immediately to the south-west of the first. There was no north-west lining, and the south-east and south-west walls made butt joints with the south-west wall of the earlier pit and the face of the garden wall respectively. In construction this feature was a slighter affair than its neighbour, being of double brick thickness throughout, in stretcher-bond, with cream lime mortar. The south-east wall of this pit was slightly offset to the south-east from that of the earlier structure. The lower fill of these pits comprised a grey silty clay with mortar flecks, fragments of tile and charcoal (6019).

Immediately after the construction of the latrines at least two courses of brick (6105*, 6106*) were added to the top of the garden wall foundations, sealing and adhering to the mortar of the pier construction trenches, and providing entrance thresholds to the latrines from the courtyard.

The final work of this rebuild was the construction of a wall (6062*, Fig.366s) of limestone rubble with some brick, between the central pier and the south quoin of Building 27. This wall included some re-used worked blocks (105, 275), the second of which may have originally been part of a doorway of a 14th century Bedern building (AY 10/4). Measuring 0·4m in thickness, bonded in lime mortar, and surviving as two courses to a height of c.0·2m, this wall is probably best interpreted as the replacement for the demolished south-west wall to the Building 27 annexe. It was slightly displaced to the north-east of the original alignment, giving a shorter room measuring 2 × 3·1m. Within the room thus created a clay floor (6065*, Fig.366s) was deposited.

A third latrine was built to the south-west, against the south-east side of the garden wall, with the construction of two new walls (5217*) which consisted of mortar and clay-bonded wall footings, river cobbles, some small limestones and some tiles (Fig.280). At the east corner the wall junction was supported by two overlaid corner stones. Inside the latrine was a floor level of clay (5233*) cut by a large pit (5332*) which was partially filled with a series of

Fig.278 Area 13.X: brick-lined latrine pits 6012 (left) and 6013 (right), looking north-west. Scale unit 0·1m

Fig.279 Area 13.X, Period 8: pitched brick footings for latrine 6013. Scale unit 0·1m

Fig.280 Area 13.X: latrine pit 5332 within enclosing walls 5217, looking north-east, with the garden wall on the left. Scale unit 0·1m

deposits, mostly of clay (5338). Samples from these fills indicated the presence of food remains, including fig, strawberry, elderberry, apple, hazel nutshell, grape, coriander and fennel; there was also a trace of charred cereal grain. There were substantial numbers of parasite eggs, representing faecal contamination. The beetle assemblage clearly originated in a building, probably one with stable manure on the floor (Hall et al. 1993a).

The garden (Fig.387s)

To the south-east of Building 27 and the kitchen range was a layer of garden soil (6009). Found in it were a French jetton (*AY* 18/1, *225*) of the late 14th or early 15th century and a Spanish coin of James II of Aragon (*207*) probably deposited late in the 14th century. This layer also contained a brass coin weight for an English gold ryal of Edward IV (*165*), deposited at some time between 1465 and c.1600. Dug into 6009 were a linear feature (6038/6068) and a rubbish pit (6048). These features were overlain by another layer of garden soil (6008*) containing domestic refuse including two bone tuning pegs (*8068–9, AY* 17/12), a bone pin (*8013*) and an auger bit (sf3395). Cut into this were several rubbish pits and linear features (6010, 6015, 6017–18*, 6028–9, 6031–2, 6035–6*, 6040–1, 6050*, 6055, 6126).

Against the south-west edge of the trench, to the south-east of the garden wall, several garden loams (5430, 5268, Fig.367s, 5329, Fig.367s) and a clay and rubble spread (5330, Fig.367s) built up. A sample from 5268 contained a range of occupation materials, including bone, chalk, charcoal, eggshell, shellfish and a trace of elderberry seeds (Hall et al. 1993a). A gaming counter (sf2076) was also found in this layer. A half-groat from Edward III's reign (*AY* 18/1, *121*), deposited 1360–80 or later, was also recovered. The animal bone assemblage from loam 5268 included roughly equal proportions of cattle and sheep, with considerably lower numbers of pig, horse, both fallow and red deer, several cats and some dog. The birds included domestic fowl and geese, plus shelduck, teal and peacock. The fish included cod and ling (*AY* 15). Immediately south-east of the garden wall and to the south-west of the external latrine building (incorporating walls 5217*) a rubble and mortar spread (5374*, Fig.367s) with a surface capping of tile rubble was deposited over the Period 7.2b cobbles 5349. 5330 and 5374 were cut by a tile- and loam-filled pit (5352*, Fig.367s).

Subsequently, in the south corner of the site a mortar spread (5329*, Fig.367s) was covered by a series of rubble spreads (5331, Fig.367s, 5236, 5220*) and a charcoal-flecked soil (5243). An Edward I penny (*AY* 18/1, *94*) estimated to have been deposited c.1351–75, and a gaming counter (sf2021) chipped from a Roman tile, were recovered from the rubble spread. In the south corner 5331 was overlain by an ash spread (5245*, Fig.367s), itself overlain by an area of six flat-laid bricks (5235*), continued to the south-

east by a cobble and tile deposit (5234*, Fig.367s), possibly representing a garden path. 5245 was cut by a pit (5269*). This had been backfilled with slightly sandy silty clay, a sample of which yielded remains of buttercups, sedges and other flora likely to have originated on grassy waste ground (Hall et al. 1993a). It had been sealed by a layer of charcoal and bone (5278). Two other pits (5276, 5265) were cut through this deposit, filled with a mixture of loam, wood ash, mortar and tile, and later sealed by clay (5264). A sample from one of these pits (5265) comprised concreted sandy clay silt with small stones, charcoal, bone, mortar, brick/tile and shellfish. The plant remains were probably mainly weeds (Hall et al. 1993a). The area as a whole contained patchy spreads of clay and loam (5246–8, 5254, 5261–2) in which a bone tuning peg (*8066*) and a slate tablet (sf1992) were found. These were cut by a pit sealed with rubble (5277*) with two small possible post-holes (5244, 5252) to the north-east.

The south-western courtyard

To the north-west of the garden wall, following the deposition of an extensive clay loam (5237, Fig.366s) containing some brick and tile rubble, the Period 7.2 wall (5412) was disused. The Period 7.2 drain (5318) silted up with a series of sandy clays and silty loams (5386) which reached two-thirds of the way up the drain sides at the north-west end. The arching was removed at the southeast end, and the drain channel filled with a demolition deposit (5314, Fig.366s) consisting of silty clay loam with brick rubble and clay lumps, from which was recovered an Edward III penny (*AY* 18/1, *125*) estimated to have been deposited c.1370–1400. A sample of this deposit provided traces of elderberry seed and charred wheat, as well as traces of bone, mortar, shellfish, coal and stone (Hall et al. 1993a). A later intrusion into the covered part of the drain destroyed a portion of arching, and a large sandstone block later placed over the still-intact arching caused its collapse, probably because of excessive weight over an only partially silt-filled area. The drain was covered by ashy loam (5312, Fig.366s) which was then cut by an ash-filled pit (5267*) and a shallow scoop (5313) with a fill of mortary clay, tile and limestones, and covered by tile rubble and small limestones (5240).

To the north-east of the courtyard, a succession of clay loams (5131–2) were deposited. These contained a number of finds including a copper alloy buckle (sf1808), a silvered copper alloy strap-end (sf1809), a stone lamp (sf1967) and an iron wedge (sf1807). The loams were cut by various pits (5201–2) and covered by an extensive but patchy sandy layer (5128) containing a high proportion of brick, tile and limestone rubble.

The demolition debris across the south-west edge of the site was cut by several shallow ash-filled features (5285–6, Fig.367s, 5294) containing animal and fish bones, and covered by a clay spread with tile rubble (5288). The final use of this area, probably during the late 15th or early 16th century, was when a deposit of sand (5142) was laid down over the area of pits. This in turn was covered by another rubble-filled deposit (5139–40) and a clay loam (5183, Fig.367s) containing tile rubble, mortar and charcoal.

Building 32 (Figs.281, 387s)

In the south-western part of the site a levelling deposit of clay and charcoal (5136) was covered by a rubble spread (5123). This layer was cut by a pit (5133) with a fill of burnt clay and charcoal. In the same area a clayey deposit (5189, Fig.367s) was succeeded by a charcoal-flecked silt (5181, Fig.367s). Equivalent deposits to the south-east were 5113, Fig.367s, 5144, Fig.367s, 5192, 5272 and 5317. They were covered by two layers containing oyster shells, the earlier one (5114) separated from the later (5112) by a mortar spread (5115).

Deposits 5144 and 5181 were cut by the construction trenches for Building 32 (5161, Fig.371s, 5174, Fig.367s), most of the interior of which was beyond the south-west edge of the excavation. The footings for the north-east and south-east walls (both numbered 5023*, Figs.367s, 371s), the latter being also the south-west part of the north-west wall of Building 33, comprised a lower layer of limestone blocks including a worked stone (187, AY 10/4) and tile rubble, and an upper layer of broken bricks and mortar. A deposit of clay (5119) with tile, mortar and limestone inclusions was found here as part of the construction spread, in association with its mortar construction packing (5118).

Inside the building a mortar floor (5178, Fig.367s) was itself covered by an extensive rubble deposit (5107, Fig.367s) with a high proportion of tiles, mortar, brick and sand.

Building 33 (Figs.281, 387s)

Layer 5112 was cut by the north-eastern part of the north-west wall of Building 33 (5116*), butting the eastern corner of Building 32. This wall had two builds, the earlier of which was sealed by a thin layer of charcoal on top of which one course of the later build rested. There was a

Fig.281 *Area 13.X: general view looking south-east, showing Period 8 Buildings 32 and 33 in right foreground with post-medieval house (Building 39) foundations in the background. Scale unit 0·5m*

524

possible offset course to the interior, although this may have been later demolition tumble.

Deposit 5144 was cut by the south-east wall (5021*, Fig.367s) of Building 33 which was constructed of brick and limestone, including at least one re-used medieval block (35, AY 10/4). There was only a shallow foundation trench, packed with soil. The north-east wall (5020*) was set in a construction trench (5121) filled with mortar and brick. Rectangular pits (5134–5) at each corner, filled with clay, charcoal, tile and mortar fragments (5117) may have formed foundation pits for the corner junctions. This wall comprised rough limestones surviving one or two courses high and incorporating re-used medieval masonry (49, 51, AY 10/4). In some places a brick capping was present.

Butting against the outside of Building 33 was a clay layer (5122) with some broken tile, overlying the construction trench fill. The external levels were cut by a linear feature (5145) filled with broken tile and mortar, overlain by a spread of broken tiles and limestone rubble (5130), itself cut by a shallow pit (5193) filled with tile rubble and mortar.

Bedern long trench

The south-west end of Building 33 was found at the north-west end of the long trench and in an area investi-gated immediately outside it. The south-west wall, and north-west and south-east returns (1001*) were composed of brick and re-used limestone blocks (Fig.282). In the angle enclosed by the wall there was a loam with charcoal flecks (1067).

A layer of clay loam (1040) containing a bone pin (sf728), followed by a yellow clay (1058) and a spread of charcoal and ash (1003, Fig.364s), was deposited outside Building 33. These were later covered by a layer of sandy clay and rubble (1037, Fig.364s) and a clay spread (1038, Fig.364s). Pottery from 1040 indicates that these deposits built up from the late 15th century onwards.

Bedern Foundry (pp.179–80, Fig.73, AY 10/3: Period 4, Phases 5–9)

Further pits were dug along the north-east edge of the foundry site, including a shallow intrusion with clay fills (901, 925, 937) containing two 14th century coins of John the Blind of Luxembourg (AY 18/1, 200, 205), two cuts with rubble fills (899, 953) containing secondarily deposited occupation refuse, a rectangular pit with much tile and mortar rubble (2048, Fig.66, AY 10/3) and a fifth pit containing many wood fragments (2022, 2050). Analysis of samples taken from the fills revealed the presence of

Fig.282 Bedern long trench (Area 13.III/IV), north-west end: Building 33, wall 1001, looking south-west in Period 8.1. Scale unit 0·1m

525

well-rotted human faeces. The small proportions of insect remains were suggestive of rapid dumping and sealing.

To the north-east of the main foundry building there was a timber platform with a central pit (2046) which had a basal peaty fill (2006), and two upper fills separated by a vertical edge, perhaps suggesting the position of some planked partition. On one side was a compacted silt (2008) with clinker, coal, charcoal and some clay mould fragments; on the other side the fill (2045) consisted almost entirely of over 1kg of burnt clay mould fragments.

There were trenches on two sides of this pit, each with almost identical depositional sequences, which may represent the foundations of the working platform. To the north-east the trench (943) was almost 3m long by 0·2m wide. It had a basal fill (978) of compacted sandy clay with clinker, coal and tile fragments. This was overlain by a compacted peat (976) with numerous fly puparia, in turn covered by a sandy silt (942) containing much tile, charcoal and coal. The south-western trench (959) was of similar width but only c.2m in length. At the south-eastern end traces of packing (2673) survived. This was covered by a clay loam (981), and then by a layer of clinker (977), paralleling the basal fill in the northern trench (978). It was overlain by a deep brown peaty fill (974), itself covered by a brown loam (940) containing much charcoal and coal, as well as animal bones. This trench was finally sealed by an upper make-up layer of sandy clay (705). This con-

tained a penny of Henry V (*AY* 18/1, *161*), probably deposited c.1430.

Later in this phase a fresh ground surface make-up of clay loam (894, 947) with numerous animal bones sealed some of the earlier pits. To the south-east there was a general layer of clay loam (652, 709, 711, 880, Fig.79, *AY* 10/3, 941). A fence line (788–90, 856) defined a strip of land 2m wide, north-east of the foundry buildings, enclosing the pits.

To the south-east, clay and mortar with many flat-laid tiles (741–4, 2104, 2161, 2167) and limestone chippings (2090) may have been dumped at this time. These layers appear to have been intended to provide a working surface. Areas of tile rubble (708, 882) also extended to the north-west. Dumps of rubble and clay (2091, 2162, 2164) had been cut by a small pit (2089), also backfilled with clay.

Deposits of limestone chippings (549–50) were laid in the threshold at the north-east end of alleyway J, sealing a layer of charcoal (948) and the other earlier levels. A similar solid deposit of limestone chippings and mortar (2016, 2088) was also laid nearby. A number of silty clay occupation levels (745, 996, 2074–5, 2082, 2084) built up on this surface. Towards the end of Phase 1 there were a number of deposits which may represent a final phase of industrial usage, or may simply be demolition dumps. These included layers of tile and mortar (753–4, 980, 994), sandy clay (979, 982, 997) and charcoal (746, 954).

Period 8, Phase 2: mid–late 16th century

Within **Building 5** Room 5L was now divided by a partition wall, on approximately the same line as the Phase 1 division in Room 5K. This partition created a very small area to the north-east with a larger one to the south-west. Neither of these rooms contained hearths, suggesting a possible change from the earlier use of Room 5L, although the ashy spreads would seem to represent floors. In Room 5M two pits, including a brick-lined latrine, were cut through the hearth, indicating its disuse. A brick floor may once have covered the entire room.

After the disuse of the cess pit to the north-east of Building 5 the adjacent cobble yard was replaced by **Building 34**, in the same position as the earlier Building 23. This new building had a south-east wall of flat-laid roof tiles bonded with clay and a south-west wall represented by a robber trench; the other walls lay outside the excavated area. The building was

probably divided by a wooden partition. A mortar floor with a pitched tile hearth was found within Building 34; outside was a contemporary cess pit.

To the south-east an area of mortar-bonded limestone rubble may have formed the foundation for a chimney stack built against the new length of outer wall of Building 5, although modern intrusions inside the building have removed any evidence for an internal hearth.

At the end of Phase 2, Building 5 fell into disuse, and was demolished down to its foundations. Various rubble deposits were the result of this process. Modern clearance has removed all later developments after the demolition of Building 5. Building 34 underwent a similar process of demolition followed by the accumulation of debris.

During Phase 2 the internal layout of the **chapel** was altered. The stalls were arranged in a U-shape, the screen wall to the north-west forming the rear part of the stalls.

Building 26 was rebuilt against the hall during this phase. Only its south-west wall survived within the excavation, founded on mortared limestone blocks bonded with clay (Fig.387s) and probably timber-framed.

Building 27 was replanned, beginning with the demolition of the Phase 1 fittings. First the staircase base was removed and backfilled with clay spreading over the domestic refuse which had built up in the lower cavity. All previous floors and features were then sealed by a thick deposit of ash, into which was sunk a linear feature against the interior of the north-east wall, overlain by a hearth. It would appear that the fittings which had respected the internal walls had by now been dismantled. A brick wall was constructed north-east/south-west across the room, dividing Building 27 into two approximately equal parts, with a doorway between them against the north-east wall. The building interior was now wholly or partially floored in brick laid onto mortar and sand bedding, preceding the construction of a further wall enclosing a drainage pit in the southern corner.

To the north-east, **Building 31** was demolished and the immediate area was cut by five parallel and similarly shaped elongated pits, all containing fills of tile and loam.

Building 35, 4 × 6m, was constructed in the open area against the north-west side of the garden wall (Fig.387s), now known as Bartle Yard (see p.638). The building appears to have been a timber-framed structure erected on clay and brick sills, with a passage-way running down its south-east side. Building 35 is interpreted as a brewhouse, from the evidence found for a brick standing for a large barrel or vat. The brewhouse is believed to have already been in Bartle Yard, but may originally have been further to the north-west (p.389). It was served by a brick-lined well which was sunk between Buildings 33 and 35 at this time. This may be identified as the well near the dung-heap south-west of the hall which, it is recorded, replaced a barrel-lined well constructed here in 1401, of which no trace remained (p.579). To the

north-west the courtyard area was given over to the digging of rubbish pits. The latrine building south-east of and at the south-west end of the garden wall was disused and the area sealed by an extensive clay loam cut by several rubbish pits.

To the south-east of Building 33 there may have been a new structure between it and the foundry, possibly built against the garden wall, although insufficient lay within the excavated areas to define a coherent building. Nevertheless, there were at least two walls, and several ovens, one on the south-west edge of the long trench, and another two on the north-east edge of the foundry site.

There was considerable activity along the north-east edge of the foundry site during this phase, including the construction of three parallel walls running north-east/south-west. These walls may have been external buttresses, although the presence of associated floor levels suggests that they may have defined outbuildings constructed against the main foundry range. The entrance from the foundry alley-way was initially provided with a door, but later appears to have been at least partially blocked. To the south-east there was a massive curving wall which may have been associated with the building in the eastern corner of the site.

Bedern North-East

Building 5 (Fig.385s)

Room 5L was altered with the insertion of a partition wall (1173*), surviving as a much-damaged wall of mortared, rough limestone blocks set in a single row, which may be the foundation for a timber partition. This wall divided the room into two unequal portions, the south-west portion containing an extensive deposit of ash (1137*) and that to the north-east retaining the floor surfaces from the earlier phase of use.

Later events in Room 5M involve the disuse of the Phase 1 hearth when a pit (1082) was cut through it. The pit was then backfilled with the latest fill consisting of large amounts of bone set into a matrix of slightly sandy silty clay, which spread beyond the pit, sealing the hearth. Immediately overlying the pit was an insubstantial wall of cobbles (1083*). Also cutting hearth 1072 was a brick-lined pit (1042*; Figs.283–4), partly damaged by modern intrusions. The construction of this pit was of unmortared brick on limestone footings. A series of eight stakes had been driven into its base. The original fill did not survive, and it is suggested that this pit was re-used in Period 9. To the south-east of the pit there was an associated brick floor set in sand.

To the north-west of Building 5 an extensive clay loam (1117, Fig.365s) was deposited over the tile and limestone rubble (1156, Fig.365s) sealing the last use-fill of pit 1326, and several mortar- and rubble-filled pits (1141, 1151) were then cut into this clay loam. The bone assemblage from the capping layer included a mandible fragment from a butchered grey seal, a most unusual addition to the diet (Scott 1985, 11). A remarkable fragment of blue glass (sf227), with black painted decoration consisting of a circular, zig-zag border, with a six-pointed Star of David within that, and feathery foliate decoration around the star, was also recovered from the same layer. A construction layer (1127, Fig.365s) overlying clay loam (1117) contained mortar-bonded limestone rubble including a small highly decorated waterleaf capital (4) possibly derived from the crypt of York Minster (AY 10/4); this feature may have been the remains a chimney stack against the north-east wall of Building 5.

By the end of Phase 2 Building 5 had fallen into disuse, as indicated by various internal deposits. Within Room 5K, however, no disuse deposits survived as modern clearance and intrusions had removed all evidence of them.

Covering the final use deposits within Room 5L was a layer of brick rubble in sand (1130, Fig.365s, 1136), which was in turn covered by an ashy spread (1129) cut by a linear feature (1135). Overlying this was a mortar deposit (1119) and a layer of mortar, brick and tile in sand (1085, Fig.365s). These deposits lay directly under modern deposits. In the area between Room 5L and Room 5M the latest use surfaces were covered by a sandy clay deposit (1357) with inclusions of limestone, tile and mortar. This deposit is similar to an extensive spread of mixed clays with mortar, tile and brick (1293) which was deposited to the south-west of this area. Although Room 5M was also disused, it is thought that pit (1042) was re-used after the demolition of Building 5.

Outside Building 5 to the north-east was an extensive dump of clay loam and tile (1449, 1454), while further to the north-west was an extensive rubble layer (1060) directly under material removed in mechanical clearance.

Building 34 (Fig.385s)

This new building was represented by a south-east wall (1139*) with an associated padstone (1138*), and a robber trench (1260*) which may have removed the south-west wall. The north-east and north-west walls were outside

Fig.283 *Area 14.II, Periods 8–9: cess pit 1042, looking south-east. Scale unit 0·1m*

Fig.284 *Area 14.II, Periods 8–9: cess pit 1042, looking north-west. Scale unit 0·1m*

the area of excavation. There were traces of a possible internal division represented by padstone (1153*) set into a construction pit (1180). The south-east wall (1139) consisted of a line of flat-laid re-used roofing tiles bonded with clay (1177), with the padstone (1138) situated at its south-west end. Internally, deposits of clay and tile (1152*, 1172) abutted the padstones. Overlying these deposits was a spread of mortar (1147) into which was dug a pitched tile hearth (1133*) bonded with clay, and two loam-filled pits (1146, 1149). An ashy spread (1148) overlay the hearth, which was at a later stage sealed by a deposit of clay loam (1134).

Outside Building 34 a pit (1183*) had been dug into the loam spread (1108*). Its fill was extensively sampled and found to contain much faecal material and parasite eggs (Hall et al. 1993b). The plant remains were dominated by foodplants, notably fig, strawberry, blackberry, raspberry, fennel, dill, plum, cherry, linseed and coriander. Rather rarer were apple and opium poppy. There were

modest components of weeds (mainly arable plants likely to have arrived with grain or grain-based foods) and some wetland or peatland plants, including *Sphagnum* leaves. There were a number of other ephemeral features cut in this area (1164, 1182, 1189, 1358), including a linear cut (1078) which contained a 15th century French copper alloy jetton (*AY* 18/1, 231). The humerus of a barn owl was found in feature 1358; this is the first archaeological record of this species from York (Scott 1985, 34). Rim and body fragments of a second glass hanging lamp (sf853) were also recovered from a small pit (1161).

Bedern Chapel

The north-western half of the chapel was altered with the construction of a small brick and limestone wall (9023; see Fig.358, p.646). It is assumed that this was the foundation for a wooden screen across the chapel. An ivory figurine (sf125) had become incorporated into the wall build.

Fig.285 Bedern Chapel in Period 8, looking north-west, showing the brick foundations of the pew stalls. Scale unit 0·1m

At the same time two parallel walls (9043, 9052, Fig.232a–b, facing p.472), each consisting of a single line of bricks, were constructed running down either side of the building (Fig.285). These may have been foundations for pew stalls down the sides of the chapel. The earlier floor (9051) continued in use during this period.

Bedern South-West

Building 26 (Figs.262, 387s)

The new south-west wall (5397*) consisted of mortared limestone blocks including a re-used chamfered block (146, AY 10/4) with a tile infill, bonded with a deposit of clay (5416) which spread to the south-west. A drain hole was set into the centre of the wall, bridged with two capstones. It was partially filled with a deposit of clay loam similar to the clay bonding, which was later covered by a silt fill (5421). Two 'post-voids' (5435–6*) were incorporated within the wall and appeared to have taken upright posts built into it. These voids were later capped with poorly bonded limestone when a wall (5426*) was built onto Building 26.

Building 27 (Figs.286–7, 387s)

The removal of the Phase 1 staircase left a backfilling of clay spread over part of the surrounding area of sand (6122, Fig.368s), which in turn overlay an extensive ash spread (6157, Fig.368s). The clay also sealed a small posthole in the surface of 6122. The sand was overlain by a patchy clay spread (6130) in which there was a shallow depression (6134) with a fill of clay loam incorporating four bricks arranged in two pairs, one brick upon another. A small pit (6138) was cut into the clay fill and filled with quantities of shell and bone in sand. Occupying a shallow depression against the south-west wall was a spread of limestone rubble (6135, Fig.368s) topped by a thin spread of sand. Occupying a small depression in 6122 was a shallow dump of sand containing a high proportion of charcoal (6129), and a small pit (6133) with a fill of ashy clay and limestone rubble. There was a limestone spread (6140) including a worked stone (140, AY 10/4) in the east corner of the building, and a dump of domestic rubbish (6137). Overall these levelling deposits raised the floor level by 0·5m.

All previous floors and features were then sealed by a thick deposit of ash (6049, Fig.368s) containing a lens of limestone rubble and mortar (6121). A linear feature (6044), measuring 0·45 × 3·56m, and in places reaching a depth of 0·17m, was cut into this against the north-east wall. In the limestone rubble backfill of this feature were found fragments of painted glass, as well as a 15th century French jetton (AY 18/1, 227). It is possible that a small hearth was situated over the backfill of this feature because a scatter of burnt bricks and limestone fragments (6054) were found here. Covering most of this area was a sandy spread with charcoal inclusions, partially overlain by another sandy clay deposit (6045), probably a floor level, which contained a number of worked stones (111–14, 139, AY 10/4).

A brick wall (6020*) was constructed across the room from north-east to south-west, dividing Building 27 into two approximately equal parts. This partition wall was founded on pitched brick at the south-west end and coursed limestone rubble at the other, and was bonded throughout in coarse white lime mortar. A doorway 1m wide was left at its north-east end, marked by a single limestone block of substantial proportions, which appears to have carried the weight of the door frame, the lintel being inserted into the north-east wall at the appropriate height.

An extensive mortar spread (6047*, 6052) overlay the ash layer (6049) in the north-west room, acting either as a floor in its own right, or as make-up for the brick floor (6025*) located here (Fig.287). A circular feature (6053*) was cut through the mortar, which was overlain by a spread of ash (6046) with a high proportion of wood charcoal. In the south-east room was a thin sand layer which may have served as a bedding for a brick floor, the fragmentary remains of which (6030) were found beneath the wall (6021*) which was now constructed in order to enclose a small area, 0·8 × 1·2m, in the south corner of Building 27. The sand floor (6033*) occupying the south-eastern portion of Building 27 did not extend beyond this 'room' but petered out beneath its walls and may have formed its floor.

In the south corner was a shallow brick-lined and brick-floored pit (6022*), its south-west and south-east sides being formed by the external walls of Building 27, and the north-east side being composed of bricks set on edge into a shallow construction trench backfilled with sand. The brick floor of the pit was likewise bedded in a very shallow layer of coarse sand and brown clay.

Building 35 (Fig.387s)

The south-west and south-east walls of Building 35 (both numbered 5266*; the south-west wall is on Fig.366s) were represented by shallow trenches containing clay bedded on coarse sand; they contained occasional bricks, which may represent the footings for corner- or wall-posts, and were in places edged with tiles.

The south-east wall lay c.0·2m from the garden wall and ran parallel to it. An insubstantial wall of limestone and cobbles (5377*), c.2m in length, represented the remains of the north-west wall. At the western corner a small section of tile and brick (5196*), bonded with clay, had been used to strengthen the junction. A row of limestone blocks and bricks (5241*) formed the north-east wall, although the general build of this stretch was not of the same dense

Fig.286 (right) Area 13.X, Period 8: Building 27, showing rubble (6044), ash (6049) and clay floor (6130), looking north-west. Scale unit 0·1m

Fig.287 (below) Area 13.X, Periods 8–9: Building 27, looking south-east, showing brick floor 6025 and internal walls. Scale unit 0·1m

clay packing, and this may represent an entrance threshold. Foundation pits (5239* and 5289*, Fig.366s) for postpads in the north-east and south-west walls, and a small pit (5255*) midway between them may represent a 1m wide bay against the south-east wall providing an entrance passage. Pit 5289 had a fill of sandy clay loam with inclusions of limestone and brick rubble, and brick packing.

Internal levels consisted of a dark ashy sand (5259), possibly part of the construction spread. A brick-floored feature (5256*) was cut against the south-west wall; this was an almost circular pit c.0·1m deep to the brickwork, containing a well-laid brick floor set in sand (Fig.288). It was filled with an ash/clay mixture with small fragments of stone, masonry, tile, brick and burnt sand (5257–8). An ashy loam (5194) contained a number of finds including a parchment pricker (8043, AY 17/12) and a copper alloy and white enamel pendant (sf1883). It was contemporary with a sandy clay (5188).

Butting against the outside of Building 33 was a deposit of domestic rubbish (5127) containing tile rubble, shell, bone and bronze slag. A small rubbish pit (5129) containing shell, bone and charcoal was dug into this. Two other pits (5281, 5126) contained later fills of clay loam with inclusions of tile, and mortar flecks, and were contemporary with a cobbled surface (5022), butting against the north-west wall of Building 33. Cutting through all

these deposits was the construction pit (5125*) of a brick-lined well (5008*).

The garden (Figs.289, 387s)

To the south-east of the garden wall the remains of Building 31 were overlain by mixed spreads (6109) which were then cut by pits (6112–13*, 7060*, 7065*, 7073*) filled with tile and loam. A pit-like feature (7113*, Fig.366s) with a fill of sandy loam, ash, charcoal, bricks and stacked tiles may represent the north-east end of pit 7065, but was separated from it by the later intrusion which split the other pits in two.

The latrine (5332) in the south-west of the site also went out of use when a shallow backfill deposit of clay with mortar inclusions and tile fragments (5334) covered not only the earlier fills but also the external walls. This was covered by clay loam (5218, 5327) which had been levelled by a deposit of broken tiles (5328).

The south-east part of the garden area was then covered by an extensive deposit of sandy loam (5210, Fig.367s, 5296–7). This was cut by a number of slight features, comprising a grouping of stones (5212*) containing a limestone moulded column base (151, AY 10/4), a tile-edged feature (5224*), and several shallow pits (5211*, 5213–16*, 5221*,

Fig.288 *Area 13.X, Period 8.2: brick base of oven or hearth 5256. Scale unit 0·1m*

Fig.289 Area 13.X: general view looking north-west, showing garden levels in the southern corner of the site. The garden wall runs across the top of the photograph. Scale unit 0·5m

5307) filled with a mixture of clay loam, tiles and mortar, and post-holes (5228*, 5232*) packed with clay, broken tiles and stones. A sample from pit 5221 yielded a beetle assemblage which probably originated in a building with litter on its floor. The concentration of insects (estimated at nearly 300 per kg) was remarkably high bearing in mind that this deposit was dry, concreted silty clay. A number of foodplants were also identified, including fig and strawberry seeds and plum. Traces of parasite eggs indicated some faecal contamination (Hall et al. 1993a). Other features (5225–7*) contained fills of dark charcoal-flecked soil, wood ash, mortar and shell. A large pit (5219*) had a fill of clay loam (5260) containing a small amount of bronze slag, a bone spindle whorl (*8017, AY 17/12*) and wool (sf1905) with traces of red dye. Two blocks of clay (5218*, 5229*) were also set upon the loam, although none of these features appears to have been structural.

Bedern long trench

A line of limestone blocks (1028, Figs.364s and 387s) on clay footings (1053/1057, Fig.364s) set in a construction trench made a right-angled junction with the garden wall 1500. These blocks apparently represented the foundation sill for a wattle and daub superstructure, of which some fragments (1041, 1083) survived, along with a post-hole (1082, Fig.364s) set into the wall.

The construction and alignment of this wall suggests it may have been the south-west wall of a structure associated with Building 35 to the north-east. A layer of loam and rubble (1048, Fig.364s) was deposited north-west of garden wall (1500) and overlying the footing material (1057) of wall 1028. Pottery dates 1048 to the early 16th century. There were also traces of a cobble spread (1027,

Fig.290 *Bedern long trench (Area 13.III/IV), Period 8.2: cobbles 1027, wall 1028 and garden wall 1500 (left), looking south-west. Scale unit 0·1m*

Fig.364s) overlying wall 1028, and a layer of mortar (1052) and a layer of clay (1070) ran up aginst its south-west side (Fig.290).

In Building 33, at the north-west end of the trench, a new clay floor (1036) was laid, containing pottery of as late as the 16th century.

A number of features were cut during Period 8 which should probably be assigned to Phase 2. These included a pit (1071) filled with tiles and mortar (1077), followed by a layer of oyster shells (1035) and then by more tile rubble. There was also a clay spread (1072) cut by a small pit with an organic fill (1073) against the north-east edge of the trench.

To the south-east of wall 1500 a spread of burnt sand (1561, Fig.364s) and clay (1581) was laid over the Period 7 levelling layer (1565) as bedding for a rebuild of Building 13. This bedding layer ran up to the clay footings (1560) for a limestone, cobble and tile wall (1554), built on the same line as the Period 4 wall of Building 13 (1603). To the north-west of this wall were traces of an external mortar surface (1553, Fig.364s), cut by several post-holes (1555–7). Further to the south-east there was a clay surface (1525/1545, Fig.364s) overlain by 1546 (Fig.364s), 1548–9 and then mortar (1544, Fig.364s), much disturbed by later features. These deposits had been cut by a number of pits (1532–3, 1547–8) and were overlain by mortar (1530, 1550), cobbles (1576) and ash (1549).

Within Building 13 there were several construction dumps (1558–9) sealed by a clay floor spread (1552) containing pottery which indicates an early 16th century date.

Bedern Foundry (pp.180–4, Fig.78, *AY* 10/3: Period 5, Phases 1–4)

At least three substantial north-east/south-west buttress walls were erected during Phase 2. In the north corner, c.1m from the edge of excavation, the first wall (5/648, Fig.79, *AY* 10/3) was erected using very roughly trimmed limestone blocks with little evidence of tooling, held together by clay and a little mortar. The limestone blocks were clearly re-used as many still had mortar adhering to their surfaces, and there was a re-used worked stone (*184, AY* 10/4) of the 12th century or earlier. The wall appeared to have been constructed in a trench (647) containing roughly six courses of tile and brick rubble, packed with clay. The trench had been backfilled with compact clay loam and mortar (646).

There was a second wall, c.5m to the south-east, which survived only as a construction trench with footings (850) of small limestone and sandstone blocks with cobbles and bricks, apparently randomly arranged. The trench was packed with clay. There was a straight edge where this wall abutted the main foundry building wall footings (888). Towards the end of Phase 2 the wall (850) was robbed. The trench fill (860, Fig.79, *AY* 10/3) contained over 50%

clay lumps derived from the bonding of the wall; it was capped by a spread of mortar fragments.

Approximately 5m to the south-east a trench appears to represent the position of a third partition wall, possibly robbed out at some later date. It had a lower fill of brown loam (889) and tile rubble (707), and an upper fill of sandy clay with patches of mortar, sand and small limestone blocks (706).

The western edge of the threshold to the alleyway was overlain by a layer of clay (939) which formed the base for a post-pad (609), possibly for a door post or entrance structure. This was later removed and the entrance was at least partially blocked by a section of walling (608) with clay bonding (755).

Just within the north-east edge of the excavation, cobble and brick footings (810) for a possible circular oven were detected. To the north-west a number of clay loam layers (297–9) were deposited. There were also the remains of a drain (2056, Fig.79, *AY* 10/3) comprising rough limestone blocks set on edge with fragments of flat-laid tile for a base, and a large post-hole or pit (635). A further pit (593, Fig.79, *AY* 10/3) had a number of yellow-green stained fills (358, 868, 876–7) later capped with mixed cess and rubble (385–7); a third contained fills (328–32) of charcoal, ash and mortar.

This oven was later demolished leaving a saucer-shaped depression filled with compact sandy clay (590, 637, 757) with much mortar and tile rubble. It was cut by a feature (638) packed with cobble and brick. This was itself overlain by a tile and charcoal filled feature (585), and then cut by an oval pit (589) with fills of charcoal and ash (588, 768–9, Fig.79, *AY* 10/3).

Towards the south-east end of the foundry area, mortar construction levels (747, 865, 906, 952) underlay a massive wall (750/824), butting the north-east wall of the foundry buildings. This wall appeared to curve slightly as if enclosing a structure or area to the south-east, and may have continued to form a circular structure, although all trace of this had been removed by a later intrusion. The wall was at least 0·5m in width, with large mortared ashlar footings, but also utilised much brick. It had been set in a construction trench (867), backfilled with layers of charcoal (864), clay (748, 752) and sand (751). Nearby there were splashes of white mortar (749, 884) from the construction.

A clay floor (863, 879, 895) with specks of burnt red clay and charcoal was laid against this wall. An antler tuning peg (*AY* 17/12, 7984) was found in this layer. An oven was built on this floor, against the side of the curving wall (824). It was constructed on a brick foundation (905) and had walls with light cobble footings (825–6) which had been bonded with a clay (878) which was almost identical to that which had been laid as a floor. A bed of fine clean sand (828) had been laid upon the brick foundation. This had been covered with an oven floor surface of flat tiles (827) laid in three or four layers. There was a shallow indentation (832) caused by an upright post set into the sand base.

In the eastern corner of the site a massive wall (81) butted the garden wall (2019) and must represent a rebuilding of Building 13 (see p.534) It comprised roughly shaped limestone blocks, cobbles and bricks set in mortar, in a shallow construction trench (2358) packed with clay (2359–60) and mortar fragments. Where wall 81 joined the garden wall it had been thickened with further limestone blocks (4265). The rebuild included a re-used voussoir from a window arch (*40*), thought to have been removed from York Minster in the 1390–4 demolition (*AY* 10/4). The clay used to pack the construction trench (2360) included a concentration of 101 sheep metapodials out of 155 fragments, with only seven sheep phalanges. The upper courses of wall 81 were of brick (61, 65).

Period 8, Phase 3: late 16th–early 17th century

By the end of the 16th century many of the college buildings had been demolished, but some evidence of post-college construction has survived as limited areas of 16th century deposits in those parts of the site not disturbed by more modern developments.

In the north-east part of Area 14.IV, which was not as badly disturbed by modern development as the rest of the site, a building of the late 16th century did survive. **Building 36** was constructed on limestone footings; inside there was a clay floor and a pitched tile hearth against the south-east wall. Building 36 was apparently only used in the 16th century, its final demolition being indicated by a thick layer of rubble. Within the area once occupied by Building 16 a limestone, cobble and brick-lined pit was constructed, but there was little evidence for any other new activity on the north-east side of Bedern Close.

On the south-west side of the close **Building 18** was demolished when a robber trench removed part of its south-east wall, and at the south-west end of the site **Building 35** was demolished. There was activity around the hall, where **Building 26** was rebuilt once again when a new wall was built against the internal face of its south-west wall. It is suggested that the original wall supported a timber-framed construction, but that the wall was now rebuilt in stone, necessitating the widening of its base.

Within the north-east edge of the foundry site two brick-lined soakaways or cess pits were constructed, and the Phase 2 oven was demolished. **Building 13**, in the eastern corner of the foundry site, was rebuilt.

Bedern North-East

A limestone, cobble and brick-lined pit (4154) was constructed in Area IV; its north-east side was sloping and no stone lining survived. Some post-holes were cut into this slope. The backfill comprised sandy loam with inclusions of mortar and limestone blocks (4158) and contained some glass.

At the beginning of Phase 3, the Phase 1 pit (4091) was backfilled by a clay sealing layer (4097) which contained a limestone decorative finial of 14th or 15th century date, possibly from a statue destroyed during the Reformation (*285, AY* 10/4). This was covered by an ashy deposit (4090) containing a complete pottery vessel surrounded by charcoal (4098), capped by brick and tile rubble (4089). The pit was finally sealed by a clay loam (4137). Analysis of a sample from the ashy layer yielded a trace of fig seed and abundant faecal concretions with considerable amounts of sand and mammal bone. There was also a fragment of what may have been a dog coprolite. Samples from the charcoal yielded abundant faecal concretions and human parasite eggs, and there were large amounts of coal and coke, some fig seeds, and some mineralised seeds perhaps from sloe or plum stones (Hall et al. 1993c).

Building 36 (Fig.291)

A rectangular structure with walls 4001*, 4002*, 4004*, 4005* was constructed partly over pit 4091*. The walls were all of limestone; the north-west wall (4001) had a stakehole (4046) situated to the north of it. Within Building 36, a clay deposit (4079*) formed an internal surface, as well as covering the construction spread of the south-east wall (4004). To the north-east a garden soil (4008) butted against the outside wall.

To the north-west of Building 36 was a cess pit (4047*) with a sandy clay lower fill (4043) topped with rubble

(4042). Slumping down over the backfill were two thick clay spreads (4033, 4173). Analysis of samples from this pit yielded substantial plant and beetle assemblages (Hall et al. 1993c). In one sample it was estimated that there were 95 individuals, representing 53 taxa, with a moderate outdoor component. Woodworm was also abundant, presumably from nearby structural timbers. In the same sample there were 43 plant taxa, one of the largest assemblages from the medieval deposits from Bedern. There was clear evidence for faecal material in these deposits in the form of faecal concretions and parasite eggs, but more particularly from the moderate amounts of cereal (wheat/rye) 'bran' and corncockle seed fragments. Other foodplants were limited to fig, blackberry, strawberry, elderberry, and possibly celery seed, as well as a few charred barley and possibly oat grains. The most abundant component of the assemblage, however, was the weed group, representing a wide variety of habitats, including wetland and perhaps peatland as well. The faunal assemblage from this pit was dominated by the bones of several cats, mostly from the forelimb. Of special note is the presence of a complete adult cat mandible (Fig.341, p.617), with a series of parallel knife cuts which must have resulted from skinning (Hamshaw-Thomas 1994).

Fig.291 Area 14.IV, Period 8.3: Building 36, looking south-west. Scale unit 0·1m

Associated with Building 36 was a clay-bonded pitched tile hearth (4048*) set in a shallow cut against the outside of its south-east wall (4004). No other walls survived for the structure which presumably once contained this hearth. A clay spread (4108), resting upon a sand make-up layer (4109), surrounded the hearth, and may represent an associated floor level. The clay had later been covered by a limestone spread (4107), itself overlain by an ashy soil (4106), cut by a second hearth (4007) of pitched tiles with a brick sill along its south-east edge.

When Building 36 went out of use in the 16th century, its final demolition was indicated by a 0·1m thick layer of rubble (4037) containing broken bricks, tiles and limestone blocks, overlying the last internal use spreads of the building.

Bedern South-West (Fig.387s)

Building 18

The area of Building 18 was given over to pits. A robber trench (7088*) removed part of the south-east wall, and was backfilled with fragments of tile, loose mortar, mortar lumps, and fragments of limestone in a loamy soil. This backfill contained two coins, the first a half-groat of Elizabeth I (AY 18/1, 172) dated to c.1583–1603, and the second a German jetton of Hans Krauwinckel (287) of c.1580–1610. The south-west wall had also been removed by a robber trench (7091*) backfilled with clay, mortar, tile and brick. A further trench (7013*) removed the external drain (7163), which was then covered by a mixed clay loam (7167). The first demolition layer to be deposited in the east corner of the site was one of mortar and loam (7006) containing a stone mortar (sf2862) and a fragment of a limestone roof tile with a circular nail hole (see p.608). This layer covered the earlier (Period 6) deposit 7052 and was cut by various pits (7003*, 7025*), including a large one with several fills and recuts (7054*), and a smaller one (7008*) in which a limestone block was set. Samples from the larger pit (7054) yielded a range of occupation debris, including charcoal, ash, bone, shellfish, eggshell, brick/tile, mortar, slag with a few wood and plant fragments (Hall et al. 1993a). The faunal assemblage from pit 7003 was dominated by cattle, with a high relative abundance of poultry and a low occurrence of pig bones. It also included the claw of an edible crab (Hamshaw-Thomas 1994). A limestone rubble and mortar layer (7037, Fig.370s) covered the earlier deposit 7051. These levels were covered by a dark loamy soil (7010) with inclusions of charcoal, tile fragments, shell and some plaster, which contained a well-preserved 14th century seal stamp (sf2327). This soil was then cut by a mortar- and rubble-filled linear feature (7007, Fig.370s).

Building 26 (Fig.387s)

A construction trench (5427, Fig.262, facing p.504) was cut into the Phase 2 levels to take a new wall (5426*) built onto the north-east face of the Phase 2 outside wall (5397). This wall was of a mortar-bonded limestone and cobble build; its construction trench was packed with tile. To the north-east of wall 5426 a tile, mortar and rubble deposit (5415) was laid against the hall, abutted by a loam (5414, Fig.262).

Later, a rubble and loam spread (5399, Fig.262) was deposited against the outside of Building 26. The faunal assemblage has approximately equal numbers of cattle and sheep, with considerably less pig, and a relatively high number of cat bones (Hamshaw-Thomas 1994). A series of clay spreads (5396, Fig.262, 5400–2) were then laid, preceding the rebuild of Building 26 undertaken in Period 9. These deposits contained a fragment of roll moulding (279) similar to that used in the new choir of York Minster after 1361, and possibly damaged and discarded during construction (AY 10/4).

Building 35

Within Building 35 the floor was partially covered by a demolition spread of clay with small limestone blocks, and broken tile and brick rubble (5238, 5242, Fig.366s). Ash and charcoal (5182) covered these deposits and was contemporary with demolition layers of rubble and mortar (5157, 5163, 5165, 5179).

Bedern long trench

A circular brick structure (1013, Fig.364s) backfilled with rubble (1033) was cut through cobble surface 1027.

Late in the 16th century it appears that the rebuilt Building 13 was demolished and its south-east wall (1554) and the clay floor (1552) were both sealed by loam (1534, Fig.364s, 1535) and clay (1536, Fig.364s) deposits which were cut by a number of rubble-filled pits (1537–9, 1542). The demolition deposits contained 16th century pottery, as well as a Henry V penny (AY 18/1, 159) probably deposited c.1450 which must therefore be considered residual in this context. At the north-east edge of the excavation there was evidence of a north-west/south-east brick drain (1528) set in clay (1531) overlying the demolition deposits, running perpendicular to the garden wall.

In the early 17th century a number of rubble spreads (1516, Fig.364s, 1522–3, 1529) were deposited at the south-east end of the trench. These were cut by a large drainage sump (1514, Fig.364s) containing fragments of the bowl of a stone mortar (sf650) and a second soakaway (1562), itself recut by a further pit (1541, Fig.364s).

Discussion

edited by J.D. Richards

The partial examination of the medieval and early post-medieval college precinct makes it dangerous to assume that all buildings named in documentary sources must have been encountered within the excavated area. If it is assumed that, at its maximum extent, the college precinct was defined by the boundaries of the extra-parochial area of St Peter, as marked on the 1852 Ordnance Survey map (Fig.193, p.396, and see p.377) then it occupied some 8,750m² in total. Of this only c.2,500m², or 30%, was investigated through excavation, although it is assumed that the area under the modern street, Bedern, was an open close, and much of the area to the south-east was probably gardens. Therefore, the proportion of built land excavated is probably somewhat greater, perhaps in the region of 50% or more.

The 1852 Ordnance Survey map indicates that, apart from a 30m strip fronting onto Goodramgate on either side of the gatehouse, the boundaries of the college precinct were set back from the street frontages of Goodramgate, Aldwark and St Andrewgate which were occupied by private residences (Fig.263, facing p.505). These street frontage locations would have been more valuable for commercial properties, but would also probably have been less suitable for the enclosed precinct considered appropriate for the vicars choral. In some places the rear of the modern street frontage properties still follows the 1852 precinct boundary. In at least one place, adjacent to what was excavated as Building 30 (Period 7.4; see p.503), the back walls of present-day buildings to the north-west of the site can be seen to back up to a medieval wall, and in several other cases the 1852 boundary is represented by walls uncovered during the excavation. These include the north-east wall of Building 32 (Period 8), and the north-east wall of the main foundry building. The medieval layout of the college therefore influenced all subsequent developments, until at least the 19th century. Post-medieval and Victorian buildings were constructed on the same alignment as the college hall. The main garden wall, established at the beginning of Period 7, survived into the post-medieval period when it formed the

south-east wall of Building 39 (Period 9), and its alignment is still respected by property boundaries designated on 19th century plans of the precinct.

It has already been noted that the college was originally laid out on either side of a narrow close or courtyard extending back from the gatehouse on Goodramgate, with the chapel to the south-west immediately inside the gatehouse, and the major residential halls beyond that. A new stone-built hall was constructed c.1370 on the north-east side of a second courtyard built on open land now acquired to the south-west of the original precinct (Period 7; Fig.227, p.466). One passageway ran from the probable southern corner of the close to an open yard behind Building 17, following a 13th century route (established in Period 4) to Building 10 (demolished in Period 7). It is likely that a second passageway ran directly south-west from the close to the new hall. This route is still preserved on a plan of 1851 (Fig.349, p.636) where it is shown running through the former screens passage of the hall and into Bartle Yard. Its entrance is also shown on a Henry Cave view of the south-west side of the close, drawn in 1804 (see Fig.351, p.638).

The Plan of Bedern

by S. Rees Jones and J.D. Richards

The 13th and early 14th centuries

The original development of the college would have been restricted by the nature of the site, which was initially composed of perhaps three tenements forming a long narrow L-shaped block between Goodramgate and St Andrewgate. The site would thus have measured some 100–110m (330–360ft) in length between the two streets, with a width at Goodramgate of about 30m (100ft), and at St Andrewgate of about 52m (170ft). The street frontage tenements (including Plot 8, Fig.188, p.387) remained in private hands, those behind 31–37 Goodramgate (Plot 9, Fig.188) running back some 27m (88ft). Excavation has suggested that Bedern Close was laid out as a narrow rectangular courtyard, around which the college buildings were erected in the earliest phase of construction. Until 1852 the close extended only some two-thirds of its later length and had remained substantially unchanged since the 13th century. Behind the college buildings the college gardens extended to the rear of properties in Aldwark and to St Andrewgate.

On either side of Bedern Close two long narrow ranges of buildings, dating from the late 13th century, lay parallel to the courtyard. The exact function of the individual buildings is not clear, although it is possible that the vicars' personal accommodation lay towards the south-east end of the close. On the south-west side of the close, inside the gatehouse, lay the college chapel. Excavation of the buildings south-east and south-west of the chapel was not possible because of the intrusion of modern cellars and buildings.

The range excavated to the north-east of Bedern Close, nearest the gateway, appears to have been a hall (Building 5), over 42m long. The Chamberlains' accounts for 1319 and 1328–9 mention a great hall (*magna aula*), which appears to have been distinct from the common hall (*communa aula*), which is mentioned separately in the same accounts (YMA, VC 6/2/4 and 10). If this *magna aula* does correspond with Building 5, then the payment of 8s in 1328–9 may refer to alterations to the building represented by the division or shortening of Building 5 in Period 5 (p.434). The Chamberlains' rolls record: 'And to dominus Will. de Ampelford 8s for the wall of the great hall to be closed with stone' (*Et domino Willelmo de Ampleford 8s. pro eo quod clausit(ur) murum magne aule cum petra*). Harrison's version (1952, 37) is problematical because he places it in a paragraph on the orchard amid other expenses and this is not where it is found in the original. He also omits the term *dominus* which indicates that William was a priest and not a workman. Presumably William supervised the job, although an alternative interpretation might be that the 8s was a gift from him to pay for the work.

After 1328–9 the great hall is not mentioned again and the alterations in the 14th century suggested by both the documentary and archaeological evidence seem to mark a change in the use of the building.

The later 14th and 15th centuries

Although the earliest buildings of the college were grouped around a single close or courtyard, by the 1270s and 1280s the vicars had already substantially increased the area of the college precinct by acquiring neighbouring properties in Aldwark and Goodramgate (see pp.389–90). Most of these later acquisitions do not appear to have been incorporated into the Bedern site with the exception of some land in Aldwark, which may, initially, have allowed some further extension of the college gardens.

Redevelopment of the college precinct appears to have been prompted by a brief upturn in the local economy in the 1320s and 1330s (Rees Jones 1987, 208, 241–2). Between 1330 and 1340 the whole of the Aldwark and St Andrewgate street frontages behind the college were redeveloped with rows of small cottages for renting to lay tenants. The construction of these cottages accounted for the narrow strip of land along Aldwark and St Andrewgate which lies outside the extra-parochial area of Bedern and within the parishes of St Helen and St Andrew (Fig.263, facing p.505). Indeed the parish boundaries of the 1852 Ordnance Survey map, which define the extra-parochial area of Bedern, probably correspond closely with the limits of the college precinct as extended by the early 15th century.

Only one new addition was made to the area of the college in the late medieval period. In 1390 the rear half of a tenement on the south-west side of Bedern Close was bought and incorporated into the precinct (Plot 12, Fig.188, p.387). Archaeological excavation suggests an enlargement of Bedern at this time to include a second courtyard containing a more substantial common hall and a range of service buildings.

For the 13th and most of the 14th century, therefore, the plan of the college buildings was more contracted than it subsequently became, with all the major buildings, including the hall and kitchens, around the main Bedern courtyard. By the mid 14th century, although the vicars' accommodation was still known as *cubiculi*, there is both documentary and archaeological evidence to suggest that the college court had been redeveloped to allow each vicar individual chambers, resembling the later form of collegiate architecture developed especially in colleges of chantry priests and vicars choral at Wells Cathedral and Windsor Chapel.

By the end of the 14th century a second courtyard (which appears on 19th century maps as Back

Bedern) had been created, around which the new hall and service range were constructed. A bridge may have been built to facilitate access to the Minster Close, although detailed examination of documentary evidence and the standing structures on either side of Goodramgate failed to find any evidence for it (report by M.J. Jones, with P. Chitwood, C. Fraser, M. Prescott, J. Smith and R.L. Smith in the YAT archive). In addition the chapel was enlarged (p.471). At about the same time a group of houses to the north of Bedern began to be known as Little Bedern and provided housing for some of the vicars. It appears, therefore, that during the last two decades of the 14th century there was major construction and reorganisation in Bedern. There are numerous references in the Chamberlains' rolls for the 1380s (YMA, VC 6/

2/32) to payments for odd jobs, mainly cleaning up of builders' rubble and carpenters' waste, being done 'at the time of building' (*tempore edific'*). Unfortunately they don't specify what was being built, but it is an unusual phrase which suggests that a major project was in progress. This building programme coincided with attempts to reform the quality of college life, and to encourage the vicars to follow a communal life (p.384).

In addition to the main buildings the college site also now encompassed several gardens, including a kitchen garden and an orchard (towards St Andrewgate), as well as various outbuildings. These included a granary, garden sheds, latrines and a workhouse for the storage of building materials. A garden, with

Fig.292   Bedern gateway, view from the exterior (Goodramgate), showing the Tudor lintel with the chapel beyond

wood-shed and pigeon house or dovecote, lay towards Aldwark (RCHMY 5, 57). There were two common wells: the original one, later fitted with a pump, to the north, and a second, constructed in 1401, in the garden south-west of the hall (p.579). Further minor modifications in the 15th century were largely connected with the increasing tendency of the vicars to establish independent households. From the 15th century certain vicars began renting portions of the Bedern gardens for their private use, and there is evidence to suggest that vicars also began to build private kitchens and garderobes onto their houses.

Bedern Chapel (Figs.292–314)

by D.A. Stocker

The Chapel of the Holy Trinity, the Blessed Virgin and St Katherine, better known as Bedern Chapel, is a small, simple rectangular building of stone rubble, ashlar and brick standing on the south-west side of Bedern, just inside the gateway to Goodramgate (Fig.292). It was the only building which remained in the hands of the college from its erection until the college was dissolved in 1936, when it reverted to the Dean and Chapter.

It was roofed and in occasional use for ecclesiastical purposes until 1961 (Figs.294, 308), at which time the roof was removed and all four walls taken down to a height of 3m as a safety measure, by order of the Dean and Chapter (*Friends of York Minster Annual Report* 1962). At that time the architectural masonry from the window heads and one or two other features were stacked in the interior of the chapel (Fig.293); the roof timbers are also said to have been put into store. This masonry was removed from the chapel and recorded in 1980, prior to excavation, and representative sections were stored in the YAT stone store. Following excavation the chapel was re-edified; a new wall plate was placed on top of the lowered walls and a new, pitched roof was constructed (Fig.295). The building is now used as a store.

Unlike the hall, the chapel at Bedern has been the subject of several studies in the past. The earliest full account is in the manuscript *Antiquities of York Minster*

Fig.293 Bedern Chapel interior before clearance of rubble, looking west. Scale unit 0·1m

Fig.294 Bedern Chapel from the north-east, before partial demolition (© Crown copyright. National Monuments Record)

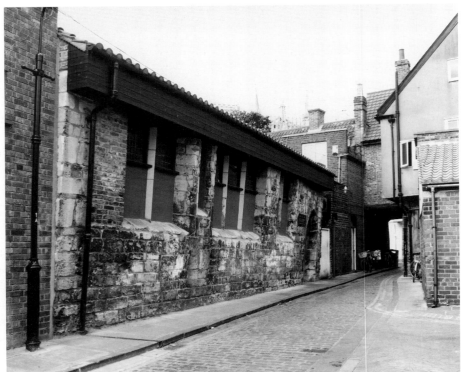

Fig.295 Bedern Chapel from the north-east, after truncation and restoration in 1994

542

written by the York antiquary James Torre in 1690–1 (YMA, published in part in Harrison 1924). Particularly valuable amongst later accounts, however, is the thorough architectural survey undertaken by A. Newton Thorpe in 1922 (working for the architectural practice of Walter Brierley) and also reported on by Harrison (1924) (Figs.296–301). The most recent report is by the Royal Commission on Historical Monuments (RCHMY **5**, 58–60). This report, which was based on observations made before the building was disassembled, proposes a complex structural history on the strength of the dates of several architectural details which the 1980 survey suggested were, in fact, re-used (Figs.302–7).

Description

The chapel is a small, cheap, unsophisticated building, in both its plan and its detailing. It has also been the subject of many episodes of small-scale patching, repair and, on occasion, of comprehensive rebuilding. For a long period it has been subject to differential settlement which has caused the north-east wall to lean outwards alarmingly. In plan, in its final form, it is a simple rectangle with internal dimensions of approximately 11·8 × 5·7m, although it is slightly wider at the north-west end than at the south-east (see Fig.313, p.551). It is, then, nearly a double square in plan. It still has three principal windows in each of the north-east and south-west walls (Figs.302–5); formerly it had a small but elaborate lancet in the south-east wall. Entry was latterly by means of a door at the north-west end of the north-east wall (Fig.302), though at various times previously there had been doorways in the south-east and north-west walls and at either end of the south-west wall also.

The north-east wall is faced with Magnesian Limestone ashlar on the north-east side where it faces Bedern (Fig.302) but, like the other three walls, its interior face is of coursed rubble (also of Magnesian Limestone). The external, ashlar, north-east face shows two major straight joints, towards the north-west end. The first, below the pillar between the central and the north-western windows and the second alongside the south-eastern jamb of the doorway at the north-western end. The south-easternmost straight joint is associated with a partly curved stone which might indicate that it once related to a doorway at this point. It is hard to see, however, where

such a doorway might have fitted into the proposed phasing of the chapel fabric and, as the stone was not investigated in 1980, it is best to regard this straight joint as evidence for a phase of reconstruction and nothing more. The area between the two straight joints is filled with a panel of uniform ashlar masonry of quite different grade and character from the remainder. The area of masonry in which the north-western door is set does not course through with the ashlar to the south-east, and the north quoin appears to have been rebuilt starting c.1m above the present ground level. Without investigation having occurred on site it is not easy to place these phases of activity in sequential order. Clearly, however, the south-eastern two-thirds of the wall has survived well with only minor patching but there have been at least two phases of reconstruction at the north-western end.

The interior face of the wall tells a similar story (Fig.303). The south-eastern 9m appears to be of a single build, disrupted only at the north-western end. On the interior face, however, there is only clear evidence for a single break in construction (marked by a discontinuity in the coursing) and the joint between the south-eastern and north-western sections falls not below the pier between the north-western and the central windows but about half way along the sill of the north-western window. The area over the door arch on the inside, however, is also greatly disturbed and here some brick is used in the facing as well as stone.

The north-east wall sits above a slight chamfered plinth (now in a poor state of survival) and, until 1966, had three windows with arched, cusped lights under square heads. The south-eastern and central windows are of three lights, the north-western window of only two. All three windows have tall lights divided by thin mullions of simple chamfered section, which rose to simple, ogee heads over the main lights and formed small, cusped, triangular panels below the square window frame. There was no hoodmoulding. The south-eastern light in the south-eastern window was blocked with brick before the remainder of the lights were themselves built up with brick (rendered to simulate mortar). The central and north-western windows share the same oddity; they do not have a moulded reveal to the north-westernmost light. Consequently the 1922 survey shows, in both cases, the simple chamfer mouldings in the tracery colliding with the jambs in a most uncomfortable way

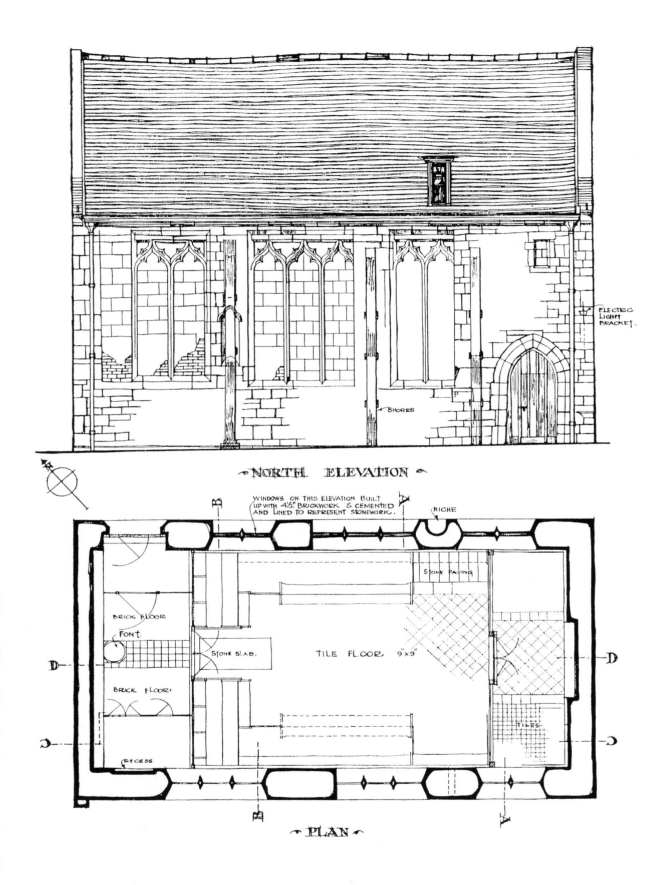

~ NORTH ELEVATION ~

ELECTRIC LIGHT BRACKET.

SHORES

P

WINDOWS ON THIS ELEVATION BUILT UP WITH 4½" BRICKWORK & CEMENTED AND LINED TO REPRESENT STONEWORK.

NICHE

STONE PAVING

BRICK FLOOR

FONT.

STONE SLAB.

TILE FLOOR 9"x9"

BRICK FLOOR.

TILES

RECESS.

~ PLAN ~

Figs.296–301 (above and facing) Bedern Chapel. Six 1922 survey drawings. Figs.296–300 are reproduced by kind permission of the Yorkshire Architectural and York Archaeological Society. These five figures were reproduced in an article on Bedern Chapel in YAJ **106**, 197–209. Fig.301 did not appear in that article and this illustration has been produced from a reversed copy which has been enhanced by hand. **Fig.296** (above, top) North-east wall, exterior; **Fig.297** (above) Plan of the chapel

1922 survey drawing:

Fig.302 *Bedern Chapel, 1980 survey ele*

1922 survey drawing:

<:

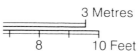

3 Metres

8   10 Feet

Fig.303 *Bedern Chapel, 1980 survey ele*

tion: north-east wall, exterior. Scale 1:40

on: north-east wall, interior. Scale 1:40

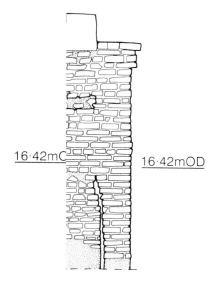

16·42mC 16·42mOD

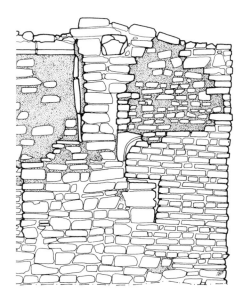

Metres

0 Feet

all, interior. Scale 1:40

Fig.307   *Bedern Chapel, 1980 survey elevation: north-west wall, interior. Scale 1:40*

(Fig.296). The 1922 survey also shows a small rectangular opening high up at the north-western end of the wall above the doorway; it had been blocked by then (Fig.296), though it is shown as glazed in a drawing of 1827 by G. Nicholson (Fig.308).

The north-west door is a simple, two-centred, arched opening with a broad hollow-chamfer moulding which runs continuously from the jamb into the head. Inside, the doorway has a simple segmental rear-arch. The door leaf, of pine with a wicket, is dated 1831 (RCHMY 5, 60). Between the south-eastern and central windows is a small, contemporary niche with a simple arched and cusped head (Fig.302). Into the inner face of the north-east wall, close to the east corner, is set a rectangular aumbry within an undecorated frame (Fig.303).

Above the doorway and to the south-east, on the inside, the 1922 survey recorded a large corbel with a simple semi-circular nose projecting into the chapel. It was answered by a similar one placed opposite in the south-west wall (Fig.299).

The south-east wall has never been fully recorded. The interior was surveyed in 1922 (Fig.298) and recorded in 1980 (Fig.306), but the exterior face has been obscured by adjacent buildings more or less continuously since the earliest views. The south-east wall was photographed by the Royal Commission in 1961, after the adjacent building had been demolished but before it was replaced. From these records it can be said that the east quoin continued the ashlar facing of the north-east wall onto the south-east wall for some 2m, where it gave way to a facing of coursed rubble. The whole gable, supported on a surviving ogival kneeler in the east corner, was of brickwork. Near the centre of the gable the 1922 survey records the location of a large rectangular blocked opening, probably representing a large, post-medieval, window (Fig.298). Within the wall, offset to the north-east (centred 1·25m from the east corner), was a single lancet window with a traceried head. The lancet was an unusual feature in that its traceried head was formed from a single monolith pierced to provide a cusped trefoil (with rounded lobes) over the single cusped light. It was the subject of a detailed drawing

Fig.308   Bedern Chapel, by George Nicholson, 1827 (reproduced by kind permission of York City Art Gallery)

by Ridsdale Tate in 1874 (YCA, Acc.28: 38–9). The stone itself was said to have been stored in 1961 but was not present in 1980.

On the inside the surviving (lower) parts of the south-east wall are of coursed rubble, though it was of brick in the gable. The southern corner of the building, including a substantial section of the south-western part of the south-eastern wall, has been rebuilt in brick (Fig.306), but, otherwise, it appears to be of a single period of construction and there is certainly no evidence to support the proposal that the distinction between the ashlar in the eastern corner and the coursed rubble to the south-west marks a distinction in building phase. In the centre of the wall there are the remains of two features superimposed upon each other. One is a large rectangular recess placed horizontally in the centre of the wall. It is about 0·4m deep, and originally some 2·5m wide and 1m high. The recess has a poorly constructed frame of stone with a mortared rubble sill, slabbed sides (narrowed to the north-east in brickwork) and a chamfered stone lintel. Above the recess are three projecting stones (*88, 90, 91, AY* 10/4). The centrally placed stone (*90*) is a re-used scallop capital with three simple scallops separated by fillets of triangular section. It originally came from a blind arcade or a similar feature and has had its astragal trimmed off to fit its new position here. The capital was set below a simple chamfered abacus, also of 12th century form. To the left and right of the niche are two symmetrically placed socles of a simple faceted form. Both stones, however, are also recuttings of earlier architectural details, the evidence for their earlier form being preserved on their back-plates. The stone to the north-east (*91*) was originally a scallop capital of similar size and form to that already described, whereas the stone to the south-west (*88*) was originally a delicate base of attic sequence and, like the capitals, of a distinctive mid 12th century type. By 1922, the recess was incorporated into the reredos behind the altar and was occupied by a painting of the sacred monogram set against clouds (Fig.298).

Superimposed on the recess (though the stratigraphic relationship was not investigated in 1980) a blocked opening c.1m wide appears to represent a small undecorated doorway. It would have needed a wooden frame to hold any door leaf. To the south-west of the recess and the doorway, and only some 1m above the contemporary ground level, were the remains of an arch-headed recess decorated with a chamfer and small broach stops. Although the south-western part of this the large feature had been obscured by the rebuilding of the quoin in brick, it seems likely that a stone three courses below it is the basin for a small piscina of which the arched stone formed part of the head (Fig.306).

There is no evidence at all in the fabric of the south-east wall for the large window of five lights with perpendicular tracery which is shown in a drawing — perhaps by Henry Cave — dated 1807 (York City Art Gallery, R3377) and, as the Royal Commission was the first to point out, it is very likely that this drawing is incorrectly labelled (RCHMY **5**, 58).

The chapel south-west wall is more fragmentary than the north-east and, unlike the north-east wall, it is faced with coursed rubble on both sides. The exterior face was recorded in 1980 (Fig.304) and, by then, was in very poor condition. Even so, several phases of patching and reconstruction were evident — much of it in brickwork. As has been mentioned the south quoin had been completely replaced in brickwork, and this replacement was of a similar character to several of the other areas of brickwork repair in the south-eastern and central parts of the wall. It was also evident, however, that there had been localised patching in stone as well and only the area of masonry in the lower parts, near the centre of the wall, seemed undisturbed. With the exception of the rebuilding of the south quoin, all of the confusion recorded in the central and south-eastern parts of the wall appears to represent patching and repair, whereas there is a clear building break towards the north-western end. This is marked by a discontinuity in the masonry coursing below the north-western part of the north-western window (approximately 9m from the south corner) and by a change of character in the masonry between this point and the west quoin.

On the interior face this discontinuity was also visible in the 1980 survey (Fig.305), at approximately the same point in the south-west wall, and so was the rebuilding of the south quoin in brick, but otherwise this face survived in a good condition. The doorway at the south-east end of the wall was blocked with a mixture of rubble and brick, but its original form was clear. It was a narrow opening with a two-centred arched head, less than 1m wide and decorated towards the chapel with an angle roll moulding of 'keeled' profile. The roll runs uninterrupted into the arch but has been crudely cut back to form its apex. The roll runs down the jambs and simply terminates against the rubble of the threshold. Several observations point to this doorway being constructed of re-used moulding fragments. First, the uncomfortable way in which the arch head has been formed, along with the way it simply dies against the rubble threshold, strongly suggest that it cannot have been cut for this position. Secondly, the moulding might be more at home in a large window rather than in a doorway, and further evidence that the stone is re-used was provided by the discovery of at least one other section of moulding from the same original feature or features elsewhere on the site (p.277, 93–4, AY 10/4). Finally, this moulding form is characteristic of the later 12th century in Yorkshire, that is, it should be dated earlier than the foundation of the college itself. Although the doorway seems to have been inserted into the chapel when the south-west wall was built, it was constructed from re-used stones which had formerly belonged to a different class of architectural feature.

The crude rear-arch of the door at the south-east end of the south-west wall, which was formed of mortared rubble, opens outwards and indicates that, when in use, this doorway was an internal communicating doorway, connecting the chapel with an interior space to the south-west. The same is true of the south-west facing reveal of the more simple blocked doorway towards the north-western end of the south-west wall; this doorway also communicated with an interior space. Its archway into the chapel was two-centred and it still retains a simple rebate for the door within a jamb decorated only with a simple rounded arris. By 1980 the doorway had been blocked with brick externally (Fig.304).

By 1980 the three windows in the south-west wall had lost their mullions and much of their jamb detail. In 1922, however, the windows were intact, though in poor condition. They were of the same type as those in the north-east wall, with tall lights under cusped, ogival heads with cusped, triangular panels below the square label. The pattern of lights, however, was somewhat different in that the south-easternmost window was of only two lights whereas the remaining two were of three lights (Figs.297 and 300). Just as on the

north-east side, the north-western jambs of the central and north-western windows were composed of straight ashlars, with the corresponding difficulties for the tracery profiles.

The north-west face of the north-west wall of the chapel had been entirely re-skinned in brick and was not recorded in 1980. The interior was recorded in 1980 when it was faced with coursed rubble below and brick above (Fig.307). The wall had several ledges in it, a lower one, close to what must have been medieval ground level, and a second, some 2·5m above it. Above the second ledge, the wall was entirely of brick and contained two heavy relieving arches. Between the two ledges the wall was basically of a single build, though it was clear that there were several periods of work around the north-western jamb of the door in the north-east wall. The centre of the north-west wall was occupied by a large rectangular disturbance representing a doorway which had been subsequently blocked with brick, rubble and timber. It would have been of similar proportions to the door in the south-east wall and would have required a door frame in timber in which to hang the leaf. To the south-west the remains of a second filled-in rectangular aumbry were recorded in 1980. It was represented by its intact undecorated stone frame, which was rebated for external doors.

The chapel roof was recorded by Royal Commission before it was removed and also by Newton-Thorpe in 1922. It was of five very unevenly spaced bays with collars to each rafter and additional scissor bracing to each truss. The 1922 survey clearly records purlins (apparently trapped by the trusses), tie beams associated with three of the four trusses, and what look like crude windbraces, evidently added later. The south-east gable panel had an additional cross-framed support and an upright post (Fig.298), whilst the north-west gable panel had an arrangement of two struts and a post as well as a second collar supporting the purlin (Fig.299). The roof was supported on sole-pieces and ashlar pieces and by 1922 had a covering of tile.

In the second bay from the north-west there was a small, flat-roofed bell cote projecting from the roof on the north-east side (Figs.299, 301). In it hung a single bell on a rocker which was rung by pulling a rope hanging down inside, to the south-east of the north-west door. The bell was that donated in 1782,

Fig.309 *(left) Bedern Chapel interior, looking north-west, photographed by W. Watson c.1925, after the installation of steel reinforcing girders, showing the font. Yorkshire Philosophical Society Collection, reproduced by kind permission of York City Library*

Fig.310 *(below) Bedern Chapel interior, looking south-east, photographed by W. Watson c.1920, showing the altar. York Library, Local Studies Collection, reproduced by kind permission of North Yorkshire County Library*

according to the inscription it carried, perhaps replacing the one referred to in the Chamberlains' roll of 1389–90. It is now in the Minster stonemasons' store (RCHMY **5**, xliv).

Although the building was, apparently, completely empty by the time of the Royal Commission recording in 1961, there are many records of the internal fittings, not least in the survey of 1922. At that date all four walls of the chapel were lined with simple wainscotting up to a height of c.1·5m and the chapel was divided into two parts by a timber screen: an antechapel (c.2·5m wide) across the width of the building at the north-west end and the chapel proper which occupied the remainder of the space. The screen itself (Fig.309) was a simple planked partition with a central archway allowing access from the antechapel to the chapel. Within the archway were two simple gates. Within the body of the chapel the vicars' stalls were arranged in collegiate fashion with a single bench and reading desk along the north-east and south-west walls which returned along the south-eastern face of the screen at the north-western end. The Chamberlains' rolls record that a desk was bought for books in the chapel in 1358–9 (YMA, VC 6/2/18). There is a measured drawing of the stalls dated 1879 in the Vicars' Red Scrapbook (BIHR, B8,

1336/1977). These benches were simply decorated with large ball-finials (Fig.310), although several records show fragments of medieval tracery in the screenwork to the south-west of the central entrance and other fragments of earlier carving elsewhere. The altar rail had heavy turned balusters supported by tall posts with ball finials and ran across the whole width of the south-east end of the chapel in front of the slight step in the floor marking the altar dais.

The altar itself, said to be made of 'marble' in the later 17th century (Torre, trans. Harrison 1924, 201), had disappeared by 1922 (Harrison 1924, 199) but the reredos was drawn and photographs also survive (Fig.310). The form of the reredos looks essentially 18th century, but it clearly re-used late medieval details. Both the 1922 survey and the surviving photographs show a number of cusped arched panels and, also, brattishing along the sides of the large rectangular recess. This recess is also shown in one early photograph to be filled with elaborate tracery elements in wood, obviously from a late medieval screen of very high quality (Fig.310). In 1922, however, this recess was still occupied by the large painting of the sacred monogram (Fig.298). The three reset capitals above the reredos were, by this date, used to support delicate crocketed spires (Fig.310), which must

Fig.311   Bedern Chapel altar area looking south-west, showing altar tiles and stones (9003, 9005 and 9006). Scale unit 0·1m

Fig.312   Bedern Chapel quarry tile floor 9002, looking south-west. Scale unit 0·1m

also represent some very elaborate late medieval furnishings. An earlier reredos was described by Torre before it was rebuilt in the Georgian period:

at the east end thereof an holy water pott [presumably the damaged piscina in the south-east wall] *and by it a marble altar-table covered with a green carpett. On the back is an old suit of tapestry hangings embroydered with caterfoyles and letters T. In the midst is wrought a little image of Our Lord, crowned and incircled with glory with hand[s] conjoyned on his brest and long rays of glory streaming from all parts of his body. Likewise in an ovall circle, encompassing his body are five angells wrought in gold, kneeling about him in postures of adoration* ... (trans. Harrison, 1924, 201; see also below, p.563).

The floor was also recorded in detail in 1922. The sanctuary was tiled in three parts with small tiles placed square with the building to north-east and south-west of the altar, and an area of diagonally placed tiles below the altar itself. The main body of the chapel was tiled with large tiles placed diagonally, though the stalls against the walls stood on strips of stone flagging (Figs.310–12). Immediately inside the arch through the screen was a large stone slab, which looks very much like a ledger stone and, beyond that, in the antechapel, a strip of tiling from the archway to the north-west wall provided an apron for the font. The remainder of the antechapel is said to have been floored in brick.

The font itself was a simple octagonal bowl on a circular pier with a moulded base (Fig.309). The wooden font cover had scrolled openwork set on its octagonal base supporting a central turned baluster surmounted by a dove. In 1941 both font and font cover were removed to the Minster crypt (*VCHY*, 356; Harrison 1952, 34; RCHMY 5).

The manuscript description by James Torre also includes a detailed account of the subjects depicted in the stained glass windows in the late 17th century (see pp.563–5; Harrison 1924, 201–6). Most of the triangular panels above the main lights were occupied by heraldry, which Harrison presumed related to benefactors, whilst the subjects in the main lights were clearly identified (Table 12).

Table 12 Bedern Chapel: subjects of stained glass in the chapel windows, late 17th century (see Fig.315, p.559, for window numbering)

North-east wall			
	north-western window (nV)	**central window (nIV)**	**south-eastern window (nIII)**
Light 1	Nativity	Betrayal	Ascension
Light 2	Magi and donor	Crucifixion	Pentecost
Light 3	–	Resurrection	Last Judgement
South-west wall			
	north-western window (sIV)	**central window (sIII)**	**south-eastern window (sII)**
Light 1	blank	Virgin enthroned	St Katherine
Light 2	heraldry	Miracle at Nain	St Katherine
Light 3	Descent from the cross	Annunciation	St Katherine

Analysis

Fortunately, repairs and alterations to the chapel have been recorded in some detail in the past, especially since the early 18th century. Consequently, we are able to identify the more modern alterations with more than usual accuracy. In doing so it is possible to see that much of the complexity recorded in 1980 was the result of relatively modern refurbishment. This combination of survey and surviving documentation has allowed us to suggest six main phases of the chapel's life up to 1961. Each phase starts with an event, or series of events, and is followed by a period of relative stability before the next major event marks the start of another phase. The first two phases represent the original construction of the chapel during Period 5 (pp.441–2), and its extension in Period 7 (pp.471–2). They are discussed in detail below. On archaeological grounds it is apparent that the chapel was also refurbished during Period 8, although there is neither documentary nor architectural evidence to date this change (see pp.529–30). The four subsequent phases, all within Period 9, correspond to the chapel's appropriation during the Interregnum, its reconversion at the Restoration (1660), its extensive reconstruction in 1757, and its re-use in the mid 19th century. They are also described below.

Construction and extension (Fig.313)

The great majority of the alterations recorded in the fabric in 1980 can be accounted for by two episodes of alteration, one in the 1640s and 1650s and the other in the mid 18th century (Period 9). However, the major structural event indicated by the break in the masonry towards the north-western ends of the north-east and south-west walls cannot be accounted for by either of these episodes. It is unlikely to be co-incidental that the breaks in the fabric in the north-east and south-west wall occur approximately

opposite each other and, even if the wall stub footings had not been found in excavation in 1980 (see Fig.203, p.419), this would probably have led to the conclusion that the chapel had been lengthened at some date, quite early on in its history. The excavations discovered the robber trench for the original north-west wall connecting the two building breaks identified in the north-east and south-west walls, and associated its construction with Period 5 (p.441). This original north-west wall was demolished and replaced with the present north-west wall in Period 7 (p.471).

Clearly then, the chapel had been lengthened to the north-west, but the lengthening was not entirely straightforward. The location of the presumed original north-western wall conflicts with the location of the north-westernmost windows in the south-west and north-east walls. Neither could have existed in the first phase of the chapel and they must have been introduced into the building once it was lengthened. However, if the two north-western windows are not

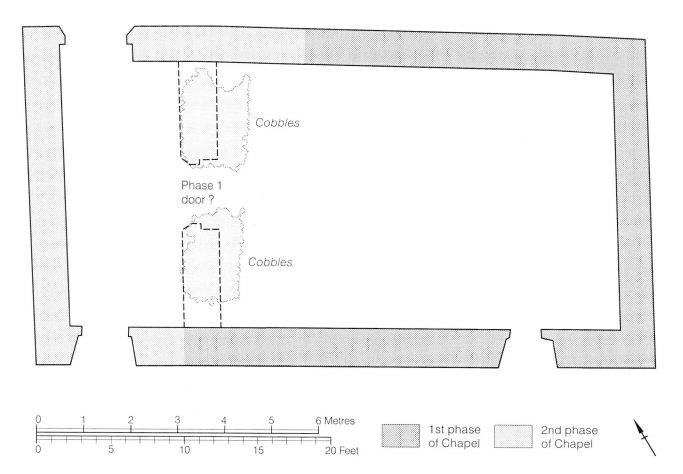

Fig.313 Bedern Chapel: ground plan. The dashed lines represent the conjectured first phase north-west wall. Scale 1:80

551

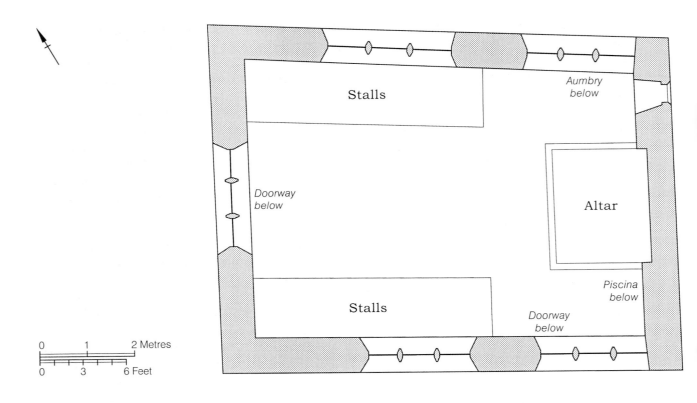

Fig.314 *Reconstructed plans of Bedern Chapel at window level: above, in Period 5; below, in Period 7. Scale 1:80*

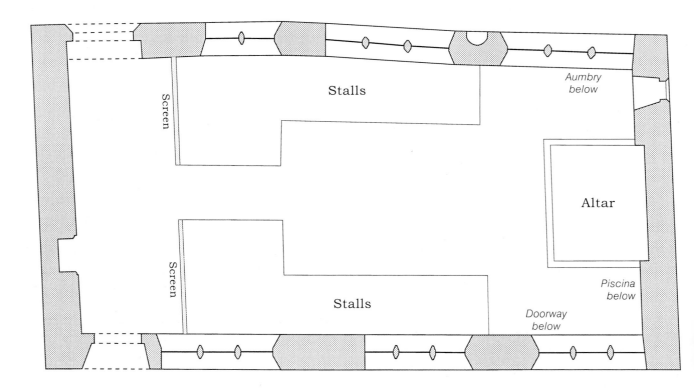

of the same date as those further south-east, why are they more or less identical? One answer may be that, when the chapel was extended, the two new north-westernmost windows were built re-using window fragments from a window from the Period 5 chapel which was now redundant and had been disassembled. Such a window might have existed, for example, in the old north-west wall and would, one could argue, have been similar to the original windows in the north-east and south-west walls. The need to re-use stone in this way might explain why several windows now have straight ashlar jambs, despite their moulded tracery. It may be that the masons extending the chapel were trying to eke out the masonry which originally made up five windows to produce six, even if that meant that several windows had to have ashlar jambs instead of moulded ones. Such an explanation would, of course, suggest that the central windows in the north-east and south-west walls were also dismantled and rebuilt when the chapel was extended, but this does not seem unlikely. Indeed the central window in the north-east wall does appear to have a levelling course below its sill which is absent in the south-eastern window.

If fragments from the original windows were being reset in the extended, Period 7, building, what about the doors? The present north-east door could also re-use masonry from an earlier opening; the arch stones are not well proportioned and the apex has been crudely packed to make it fit its present position. This could represent later repair, of course, and the possibility that the arch as a whole had been reset from elsewhere was not investigated in 1980. It is possible, however, that the door frame came from the north-west wall of the Period 5 building as there was probably a doorway of this type located here (see below). The masonry of the south-west doorway, however, was probably newly cut for its present position in the extended, Period 7, building.

If this analysis is correct, then, the original, Period 5, chapel was a smaller rectangular building than the present one with, perhaps, a door in the north-west wall and a second door (itself made of re-used masonry) in the south-eastern end of the south-west wall. It was probably lit by two main windows, each of three lights, in its north-east and south-west walls and by the small lancet towards the north-eastern end of the south-east wall. It is possible that there was another window in the building of the same type as

those in the north-east and south-west walls, which was to provide the masonry for the north-western windows in Period 7. This fifth window is perhaps most likely to have been in the north-west wall (Fig.314).

It is likely that some of the irregularity in the roof truss spacing recorded in 1922 is also due to its having being extended to cover the larger building. If the irregularity is due to its extension then the roof was not redesigned in Period 7 and, consequently, the design of the roof recorded in 1922 is likely to have originated in Period 5.

When the chapel was extended to achieve its present ground plan in Period 7 the whole of the north-west wall and parts of the north-east and south-west walls were probably taken down, before a new north-west wall was built some 2·5m north-west of the old one. The north-east and south-west walls were built up again, incorporating new windows. The masonry from the original north-east door may have simply been moved from the north-west wall and re-erected to make a new doorway in the new north corner. The two large corbels recorded in 1922 set in the north-east and south-west walls (Fig.299) suggest that there was a gallery over the antechapel and its existence is confirmed by the small rectangular window over the north-east door, by means of which it must have been lit (see Fig.308, p.545). The floor would presumably have been supported on the beam between the two corbels and on a ledge in the upper part of the north-west wall, evidence for which disappeared in 1757.

Date of construction

The construction of Bedern Chapel is thought to be dated by the account in the rent roll of John de Middleton for 1344–5 (YMA,VC 4/1/7 — transcribed, though incorrectly dated, in Harrison 1952, 33). Although it clearly relates to building at the chapel, this account does not record a major piece of work (Table 13). Thirty-two and a half man-days were spent by perhaps a total of eight workmen over a period of somewhat more than two weeks. They were paid a total of 7s 1½d in wages and consumed 8s 2d worth of materials which cost 9½d in carriage, although these costs do not include the value of the 20 stones (presumably good-quality Magnesian Limestones) which were used in the work. As striking the scaffolding seems to have been paid for in this account we may presume that this project was com-

Table 13 Building costs at Bedern Chapel, 1344–5

Wages

	Time spent (days)	Cost
Mason 1	?	?
Mason 2	14	3s 7d
Carpenter	1½	5½d
Tiler (with boy)	2	12d
Labourer 1	7½	15d
Labourer 2	1½	3d
Labourer 3	½	1d
Boys	5½	6d
Total	**32½**	**7s 1½d**

Materials

	Cost	Carriage
A thick plank	5d	–
20 stones (imported by river)	no charge	8d
1 gross spikes (two sizes)	3½d	–
60 lathes	3½d	–
21st of lead	7s	1½d
Drinks for workmen	2d	–
Total	**8s 2d**	**9½d**

pleted within this accounting period, but we cannot be sure that it was not started before this account begins. The account does not describe, consistently, the work done. However, the following tasks are indicated:

a) The payment for 'closing the window towards the east' most probably means 'closing' (that is, blocking up) a window in the south-east wall, or (perhaps less likely) a window to the east of the area of the work then being undertaken.

b) Since most of the wages are spent on a skilled mason and his assistant we may presume that some construction in stone is being undertaken. This mason seems to be a separate individual from the man engaged to deal with the window.

c) The 'spikes' (nails) and laths and the small quantity of lead, perhaps the employment of a carpenter, and later on the tiling, all indicate that roofing work is underway. It is not a large area of roofing, however — certainly not the whole of the chapel roof.

Taken on its own, this account could be seen as evidence not for the construction of the Period 5 chapel but for its extension in Period 7. It describes, after all, about the same scale of work which we know

was undertaken at that point — the demolition of the old north-west wall, the construction of the new north-west wall, the extension of the roof to cover the enlarged floor area and the skilled masonry work reconstructing the windows that this made necessary. We cannot be sure, however, that this roll represents the whole of the building work on the chapel project. It may only represent the final payments in a sequence of larger-scale works in the years immediately prior to 1344.

A second reason for doubting that the surviving account deals with the extension of the chapel in Period 7 is provided by the finds made during the chapel's excavation, which suggest that the extension took place towards the end of the 14th century (p.472).

Unfortunately, unlike those in the hall, the architectural details incorporated into the chapel are not of sufficient distinctiveness to be very closely dated. The major windows, with their square heads and ogival-headed lights, are a very common form throughout the central and later parts of the 14th century and would not be out of place in a building of any date between about 1320 and 1400. The simple moulding on the north door, similarly, cannot be placed much more accurately. The roof, likewise, was a simplified version of that over the hall (p.547) and, though it is comfortably placed in the 14th century, it is not distinctive enough to permit a more precise dating.

The small lancet window in the south-east wall is somewhat more closely datable, but its date presents us with further problems. Single lancets with tracery are not common, but there are a number of examples, almost all with tracery trefoils like that at Bedern. The early 14th century examples at Hailes parish church (Gloucestershire) are well known because of their association with the contemporary wall painting for which that church is so famous, but others of a similar date exist in church contexts, for example at Ripple (Worcestershire). There are domestic examples at a number of sites also, most notably in the early 14th century building erected on the south side of the College of Vicars Choral at Lincoln (Jones, Major and Varley 1987, 53–60). These traceried lancets are usually dated by reference to similar tracery patterns in windows of more than one light, and at Bedern this would indicate a date at the very end of the 13th century. The trefoil has not yet become pointed in this example, a characteristic which is usually associated with the last decade or so of the 13th century and which is seen, for example, in the dado arcade in York Minster nave, begun in 1291 (Gee 1977; Stocker 1986, 113–15). This window head, therefore, is two generations too early for the other architectural details in the chapel. However, we have already seen that late 12th century mouldings were re-used in the south-west wall (which appears to be of the same build as the south-east wall) and that 12th century capitals were re-used as socles in the south-east wall. These instances of re-use, furthermore, are in addition to the twenty or more fragments of worked stone dating from the 12th and 13th centuries which were re-used in the wall cores of the chapel (*AY* 10/4). Consequently the most satisfactory explanation of this window head is probably that it, like many other features in the chapel, has been re-used in its present position and, therefore, cannot help us date the Period 5 chapel. It is even possible that the payment to the mason in 1344 for 'closing' the window to the south-east was a payment for the installation of this notable item of architectural salvage.

It has been argued (e.g. RCHMY **5**, 58) that parts of the south-east wall with the window represent an in situ fragment of an earlier building which has been subsequently incorporated into the Period 5 chapel. Such arguments are based on the assumption that both the window's eccentric site in the wall and its location at the junction between an area of ashlar facing and an area of rubble facing suggest that a fragment of the south-east wall is older than that which surrounds it. There is no evidence in the fabric around the window on the inside that it has survived from an earlier building; on the contrary, it is bonded into the ashlar of the north-east wall, which is associated with the 14th century main fenestration. Furthermore, both the change in masonry from ashlar to rubble and the window's eccentric position in the wall can be explained much more easily by the proposition that there was a pre-existing building to the south-east of the chapel which obscured all but the north-eastern quarter of the south-east wall.

All this is surprisingly inconclusive. The surviving documentation for the building work at the chapel could relate either to the initial construction of the chapel (Period 5) or to its extension (Period 7), and the architectural details do not help us refine the dates for the two phases at all, beyond pointing to a mid 14th century date for Period 5 (on the strength of the windows). If we are correct in presuming the re-use of architectural features from Period 5 in Period 7 then it may be that the two phases are not separated by a great length of time, as such re-use would depend on the stonework surviving in a good state. In such an analysis, of course, the account for 1344–5 would presumably represent the last in a series of documents recording construction work in the preceding months or years, documents which are now lost.

Support for dating the chapel extension to Period 7 is found in the Chamberlains' rolls for 1390–1400, which suggest that there was a major refurbishment of the chapel during this period (YMA, VC 6/2/35). They record work on and around the chapel, commensurate with the completion of a major project, including the carriage of stones from outside the chapel and cleaning the house 'behind the chapel'. A carpenter and boy worked in the chapel for one week, and a tiler and boy for five days. A plumber was paid 3s 7d for casting 43 stone of lead; the rolls also record various small payments for ale for the workmen. In 1392 or 1398 there were further payments for 'waynscots' and tiling and another 21s 6d was spent on the chapel (YMA, VC 6/2/40). A late 14th century date for the extension of the chapel (p.472) is supported by the finds evidence from the robbing of the earlier wall foundations.

Cautiously then we may suggest that the first chapel was built in the early 1340s, work starting perhaps around 1340 and being completed in 1344. Thomas Sampson, canon of York, celebrated a solemn mass of the Trinity in the chapel of the Holy Trinity in Bedern on St Katherine's Day 1346 (YMA, VC 1/3/8). As it took place on the patronal feast day this could well have been the inaugural service. In 1348 the chantry of two vicars, Thomas of Otley and William of Cottingham, was founded within the chapel (YMA, VC 3/1/1, fo.22v). Work, however, was still being paid for (though it may already have been completed) because Archbishop de la Zouche issued an indulgence in favour of those contributing to the costs in 1348/9 (YMA, VC 3/1/1, fo.151v). The extension of the chapel is probably to be dated to the late 14th century. Given this it may be that the recorded reconsecration of an altar in the chapel by Archbishop Arundel in 1393 marked the completion of works on the chapel's reconstruction (Raine 1886, 425).

Function

It is a reasonable question to ask why the vicars, who were supposed to spend their 'working hours' performing the round of service in the Minster, should need a chapel at all. Indeed, there is no evidence that they had one for the whole period between 1252 and the early 1340s. The answer is probably to be found in the rising confidence and status of the college in the 14th century. All medieval institutions of a certain standing had their own chapel, where members of the institution could hear mass 'in common', and the construction of the chapel in the early 1340s probably marks the vicars' own perception that they had reached that status.

Whatever the original intentions for the use of the chapel, it very soon acquired the Otley/Cottingham chantry and so was given a substantial raison d'être. It may even be that Otley and Cottingham had intended founding a chantry from the first and used their position as vicars choral to encourage the college to construct a chapel in which to establish it. In any event, Torre's transcription of the original foundation deed (trans. Harrison 1924, 206–7) makes it clear that the two chantry founders had contributed 'liberally' to the initial construction of the chapel, before the chantry was established. The same deed explains that the chantry chaplain was to say prayers for the founders' souls once a day in the chapel 'before the tolling of the bell' and was then to 'remain by the Holy Water in the s[ai]d Chappell fulfilling there the offices of the Dead'. It seems, then, that each day the Otley/Cottingham chantry priest attended the chapel before the main service (almost certainly a mass) and then stayed behind, once it was finished, to perform a round of obsequies. It may be that the water consecrated during the mass itself was used in these subsequent rites, water which would, no doubt, have been contained in the piscina in the south-east wall.

It is clear, then, that both a full mass and a round of lesser services for the dead were being performed each day in the chapel. This would have necessitated, right from the start, a layout of stalls in the same arrangement as that which survived to be recorded in 1922, that is, a collegiate layout in which the stalls face each other across the central aisle as opposed to facing the east end as in a parish church. Presumably, however, there would not have been room in

the Period 5 chapel for an antechapel at the north-west end — indeed it would have been difficult to fit 36 vicars into either phase of chapel at any one time. If there was a collegiate layout of stalls, it is unlikely that there would have been a doorway in the north-east wall in Period 5 as this would have interfered with such an arrangement. The door in this phase, therefore, was presumably in the north-west wall and this, in turn, suggests that there was an open space to the north-west of the chapel at this date.

At the other end of the building, the altar was clearly quite a grand affair. The large rectangular recess in the south-east wall, which appears to belong to Period 5, would have been designed to hold either tapestry panels of the type described in this location by Torre in the late 17th century (p.550) or, perhaps, a large stone or alabaster relief, such as that (by coincidence also dedicated to St Katherine) discovered in Lincoln in 1796 (*Gentleman's Magazine*, 67/II, 1797, 650–1). The three socles above the altar (formed of re-used stones) will have been intended to support statues. It may be coincidence but there are three socles and three known dedicatees (Torre, trans. Harrison 1924, 207), which may suggest that the statues were of the Virgin and St Katherine (presumably to either side) and either a crucifix or a statue of the Trinity (perhaps like that at Holy Trinity, Micklegate).

The chantry priest had various ornaments and vestments (Harrison 1924, 206–7) which, along with those used in the college mass, would need to be stored in the correct conditions nearby — almost certainly in a sacristy. This is the most likely explanation of the south-east door in the south-west wall, which we know led to another internal space conveniently close to the chapel altar. This internal space was, however, a single-storeyed building as it had to fit in below the sills of the south-eastern and central windows in the south-west wall, which were raised higher than those on the north-east side for this reason.

The work which took place at the start of Period 7, to extend the chapel to the north-west, seems to have been undertaken primarily to provide an antechapel. The use of the main chapel space may not have changed greatly following the alterations, but it is likely that a new screen was built to divide the new antechapel space from the chapel and it may be that the fragments of high-quality woodwork tracery panels which have been recorded incorporated into the Georgian fittings came originally from a set of elaborate stalls provided at this date. From what can be seen of them in various records they appear to be in a Perpendicular style and are likely to date from the later 14th century, rather than any earlier. Consequently they should belong to the Period 7 chapel rather than Period 5 even if they were not installed immediately following the chapel's reconstruction. It is even possible that they were provided by the same craftsmen who produced those in the Minster itself, around 1400 (Harvey 1977, 181).

Given what has been said above about the probable reconstruction of the original Period 5 windows during Period 7, it is, perhaps, also more likely that the glass recorded by Torre would have been installed during Period 7. Certainly it cannot have been arranged in the way reported by Torre until the chapel had been extended. The iconography of the glass associates the chapel with its three known dedicatees. The Holy Trinity is represented by the cycle of windows in the north-east side which lead from the Nativity at the north-west end to the Last Judgment at the south-east, whilst the Virgin and St Katherine have a window each in the south-west wall (Table 12, p.550).

The use to which the antechapel was put can only be guessed at, but it must have formed an informal space between the outside and the liturgical choir, which may have been used for such things as the forming-up of processions. One use seems to have been for the storage of certain valuable items, such as service books; at least this is the implication of the aumbry in the north-west wall. It is unlikely that the chapel held baptismal rights during the medieval period, so the antechapel's use as a baptistry must be secondary. The 15th century font, first recorded in 1682 (Harrison 1924, 199), was probably brought here after the Reformation. Presumably access to the gallery over the antechapel would have been gained via a small staircase or a ladder from within the antechapel itself.

The gallery is an interesting, grandiose, feature to find in a chapel of this size. It was presumably intended to serve much the same purpose as the lofts over the screens at the entrance to many much grander late medieval chapels and choirs which were furnished in collegiate fashion, that is, as a platform for organs, musicians and sometimes for the clerics providing sung responses during the services, as reported, for example, in *The Rites of Durham* (Fowler 1903, 16).

The 1980 survey showed that the north-west door in the south-west wall of the chapel also led to another internal space. It is unlikely to have been a second entry to the sacristy, though its function remains a matter for speculation. The equivalent doorway at the vicars' chapel at Wells, for example, gave access to the vicars' library (Rodwell 1982, 223–5).

Architectural context

Unlike the hall, Bedern Chapel is not an outstanding building in architectural terms. It is a simple rectangular ground-floor chapel with a few simple architectural details. In this respect it is similar to many other chapels of the later medieval period, those attached to larger churches as well as isolated chapels and those within secular complexes. It is a near contemporary, for example, of the Zouche chapel at the Minster (built about 1350; Harvey 1977, 160–3). Although this is a much more sophisticated, vaulted, building, it also has three bays and is only slightly larger in overall dimensions. It was not, however, a college, but merely a chantry, and so it was not furnished in collegiate fashion and would have been devoted more or less exclusively to Archbishop Zouche's obsequies. The chapel of the Holy Sepulchre (now demolished), adjacent to the west end of the Minster nave (see Fig.87, AY 10/4), was collegiate and, although a much grander building, would have had some similarities of layout with Bedern Chapel. Unfortunately we know very little of its appearance.

The pattern for collegiate chapels nationally must have been provided by the layout of the monastic choirs, which were laid out in this fashion from very early on. This layout was adopted by the royal chapel of St Stephen attached to the Palace of Westminster in the first half of the 14th century. Like a number of later college chapels, St Stephen's was a rectangular building of four bays with a three-bay chapel furnished in collegiate fashion and a fourth bay, at the western end, used as an antechapel (Brown, Colvin and Taylor 1963, 520ff.). The plan was convenient and was adopted by several later medieval foundations at the ancient universities (Merton, New, Magdalen and All Souls Colleges at Oxford for example) and by lesser foundations such as the St Mary Magdalen's College chapel at Kingston, Surrey (Cook 1959, 166–9). Bedern Chapel is merely a small-scale example of this quite common building type.

Several of the other colleges of vicars choral attached to cathedrals acquired chapels also, though that at Bedern, like the hall, is one of the earliest to have been built. At Chichester the vicars shared the use of the chapel of St Faith to the north-west of their close, but the way this worked has not been investigated (VCH 1935). At Hereford no chapel is known at the college's first location, but once the vicars moved to their new premises to the south-east of the cathedral in the 1470s a chapel was provided. It is smaller than that at Bedern but it shares a similar layout. At Lincoln nothing is known of the layout of the chapel, although it was probably sited to the west of the gatehouse, on the north side of the vicars' court and may therefore have been of later 14th century date (Jones, Major and Varley 1987, 42–3). At Salisbury the chapel within the vicars' college is thought to be a small upstairs chamber and can have had few similarities with Bedern Chapel (RCHME 1993, 88–96). There seems little known about any chapel of the vicars at Lichfield, or even if it had a chapel at all. At Exeter the vicars had no dedicated chapel (Chanter 1933).

At Wells, on the other hand, a fine chapel was built for the vicars, perhaps between 1423 and 1430 (Rodwell 1982, 225). This is somewhat smaller in size than that at Bedern (c.11 × 7m), but it is a two-storeyed building with a contemporary library on the upper floor. The chapel itself, like that at Bedern during Period 7, is entered through a doorway at the western end of a long side (the south side in this case). It retains parts of its original woodwork, including the screen dividing the chapel from the antechapel and it is clear that its original layout was collegiate, exactly similar to that proposed at Bedern. Even more clearly than at Bedern, however, there could have been no question of all the vicars choral getting into the chapel stalls at one sitting.

Although we know relatively little about some of the other sites, it is easy to get the impression that Bedern Chapel, small though it is, was the expression of a relatively confident institution and at a relatively early date, when compared with its fellow colleges of vicars choral.

Conclusion

The survey and excavation work at Bedern Chapel did not reveal a medieval building of unsuspected quality, as was the case with the work at the hall. It was always a relatively modest building, provided with simple architectural detailing in its initial phase which probably dates from the early 1340s. The architectural detailing was not upgraded when the chapel was extended in Period 7, towards the end of the 14th century. Internally, however, its decoration may have been more lavish than the shell of the building implied. The elaboration of the altar, the stained glass windows, the provision of the gallery and, particularly, the woodwork, all speak of a well-appointed collegiate chapel. To maintain this show the chapel must have relied heavily on the moderate income from the Otley/Cottingham chantry (it was worth 5 marks per year to the chaplain — a very average figure for the mid 14th century in York; Dobson 1967, 30–2), but it would, no doubt, also have received a part of the surplus of the vicars' estates (a very considerable sum on occasion).

If the chapel proves to be an indicator of the status and income of the medieval college, its fabric provides us with an equally sensitive barometer indicating the course of the vicars' fortunes in the post-Reformation period. The chapel fabric provides us with valuable information to suggest that the vicars' property was simply appropriated by its neighbours in the aftermath of the Civil War, but at the Restoration the chapel, also, was restored. Once again this would have been a symbolic act by the vicars who, by now, had few other public expressions of their corporate identity. It will have been for similar reasons of pride in their public identity that the vicars kept the chapel in good order in the 18th century and reconstructed it in 1757. But the fortunes of the college were in terminal decline by the mid 19th century; this, combined with the decline of Bedern at this time, prevented any further restoration. Indeed, had it not been for a rising interest in conservation in the city it is likely that the chapel would not have long outlived the college (which was dissolved in 1936) and would have been demolished completely, rather than dismantled, in 1961.

The Bedern Stained Glass (Figs.315–20)

by D. O'Connor

Glass from Bedern Chapel (Group 1)

In the following account the Bedern Chapel windows are described according to their liturgical rather than their geographical location within the building, and following the window and panel numbering system used by the Corpus Vitrearum Medii Aevi, the international body responsible for recording and conserving medieval stained glass. The application of this system to a building like York Minster demands complex ground plans and diagrams (French and O'Connor 1987, xxi–xxii and figs.1 and 5), but exactly the same thinking applies in a more basic structure like the Bedern Chapel (Fig.315). Here too the windows are numbered from the liturgical east end (nII), now blocked, to the no longer extant west

window (W): on the north side (nIII–nV) and on the south (sII–sIV). An unusual feature of the fenestration is that there does not appear to be any evidence for there ever having been an east window (I) near the altar. A longitudinal section of the chapel looking south by A. Newton Thorpe (Fig.300, facing p.544), first published by Harrison (1924, 204), shows the forms of the now demolished square-headed windows (sII, sIII and sIV) very clearly. Each window is divided into two or three lights (a, b and, for three-light windows, c). Main-light panels are numbered from the bottom upwards in rows (1, 2, 3 and, at the head of the lights, 4). Tracery lights, which in Bedern Chapel consisted of a single row of trefoils and eyelets, are numbered from left to right (A1, A2, A3 and, for three-light windows, A4).

Measurements obtained from the exterior of the northern windows show that the two three-light windows (nIII and nIV) had panels approximately 0·80m

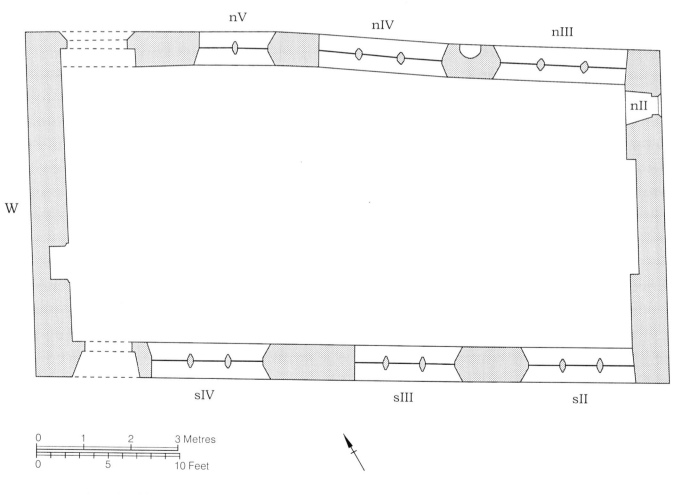

Fig.315 *Bedern Chapel (Period 7) showing window numbering. Scale 1:80*

wide, and that in the two-light window (nV) the panels were about 0·68m wide.

History of the chapel windows

Of the 210 fragments of window glass excavated from the Bedern Chapel in 1980 only nineteen have been included in the descriptive catalogue which follows (pp.568–70). Many of the uncatalogued pieces were also painted, but they were simply too fragmentary to be deciphered. All this material dates from the late medieval period but, whenever there was evidence to allow a narrower dating, everything pointed to the second quarter of the 14th century and probably to the period around 1340. Given the documentary evidence for the site there can be little doubt that the excavated fragments formed part of the original glazing of the first, Period 5, chapel, a building under construction in 1344–5 and consecrated in 1348/9. A completion date of c.1348 for the glazing would be entirely consistent with any independent evidence provided by the glass itself.

The original chapel appears to have been extended westwards in Period 7, probably towards the end of the 14th century (p.555). From what follows it seems likely that the builders not only re-used earlier stonework at this point, but also earlier glass, salvaged from the former west window (W). No late 14th century glass was identified among the finds from the site and there is no evidence from lost glass to suggest glazing work at this time. A very detailed description of the Bedern windows, written by the York antiquary James Torre in 1690–1 (pp.563–5), reads, for the most part, like an account of a mid 14th century scheme. There clearly were, however, some changes, repairs and additions. The Statute Book of the Vicars Choral records repairs to the chapel glazing and to other windows in the period 1419/22 (p.611). It may be purely coincidental that Johnston (Fig.316) and Torre record a Neville armorial in one window (sIV 2b), in a form which refers to a marriage that took place in 1420/1 (p.574, n.3).

Early heralds and antiquaries like Robert Glover, who carried out a visitation of Yorkshire in 1584–5, and Roger Dodsworth, who made extensive church notes in Yorkshire between 1619 and 1631, do not mention Bedern glazing. Sir William Dugdale, who recorded a great deal of heraldic glass on a visit to York in 1665, does not mention the chapel either. It

looks as if the windows survived the Reformation and the Civil War largely intact.

The earliest antiquarian record is the series of tricked heraldic drawings, eleven of stained glass and three of an early 16th century embroidered tapestry, produced by Henry Johnston in 1669–70 (pp.562–3 and Fig.316). By far the most important source for the chapel glazing is the account written only a few years later by Torre. His manuscripts provide a crucial record of the glass in the Minster and the parish churches at this time, but his description of the Bedern windows is especially valuable given the subsequent disappearance of the glass. Because of their importance, Torre's notes have been reproduced in full below (pp.563–5). Some glass had already vanished by the late 17th century, as he simply records white glass in the first light of sIV.

In Thomas Gent's brief account of 1730 (p.565) the windows were 'well preserv'd and entire'. Six years later, according to Francis Drake (1736, 573), the chapel 'still remains in good repair and its painted glass windows are pretty entire'. While it is possible that the glass was gradually falling into disrepair during the remainder of the century, nothing explains the disaster which befell in 1816, when the glazing was removed and transferred to the Minster, where it promptly disappeared. Writing two years later William Hargrove (1818, 2, 150–1) lamented its loss:

The building is yet nearly entire, and till within the last two years, it was very remarkable for its rich windows of painted glass, which were six in number — three in front, and three behind. It is, however, with some regret we observe the beautiful glass in the former, has lately been substituted by common small squares, by which much of the antique appearance of the chapel has been destroyed. The glass was removed with intent to enrich a newly-erected church in the country, but the dean having heard of the affair, very properly prevented its leaving York; and it is now deposited in one of the vestries in the cathedral.

In a note Hargrove (ibid., 64) suggests that it is probably the 'painted glass, in a small room or closet, near the chapel where morning prayers are performed'. The removal of the glass, presumably on the north side first, followed later by that on the south, is documented. In February 1819 the Minster paid 6s 4d to Clark, a whitesmith, 'for work done on removing some painted Glass from the windows in Beddern Chapel' (YMA, Fabric Accounts 1662–1826, fo.107v).

According to the Revd Powell (Harrison 1924, 206) Dean Markham was intending to re-use the Bedern panels in the Minster, but despite attempts to identify the glass in, for example, Holy Trinity Goodramgate (York City Reference Library, MS Y748 23113, J.W. Knowles, 'The Stained Glass of York Churches' 1, fo.66r) or in Minster nXXIX (*Friends of York Minster Annual Report* 1954, 23; Milner-White 1959, 6) and windows in the chapter house (*Friends of York Minster Annual Report*, 1959, 39), nothing remotely resembling the glass described by Torre has so far been positively identified. Very probably the Bedern panels were broken up and utilised as replacement pieces and stop-gaps for Minster windows. Some pieces may be identified as the Corpus Vitrearum catalogue of the Minster glass progresses or panels may turn up elsewhere. Perhaps greater attempts would have been made to preserve Bedern Chapel in 1961 had its stained glass windows still been in place.

The glazing

At the end of the 17th century, when Torre described Bedern Chapel, six windows contained stained glass: the three in the north wall (nIII–nV) and the three in the south wall (sII–sIV). None of the lights in these windows was blocked at the time so all are described as three-light windows, with the exception of the two-light window by the door (nV). Presumably the lancet in the east wall (nII) and anything to the west (W) were blocked in Torre's day.

The antiquarian sources provide crucial evidence for the subject matter, iconography, heraldry and colours of the Bedern glass. The recently excavated material, although far from extensive, provides valuable evidence which is particularly helpful in such areas as overall design of windows, colour and technique, ornament, style and dating. On the basis of all the evidence it is possible to get a reasonably clear picture of what the lateral windows looked like and what they contained.

Torre's evidence suggests that the chapel glazing presented a consistent and coherent scheme, with each window following much the same format. A single band of coloured figure panels ran the length

of the building to north and south in row 2. The one figure panel in row 1 (nV 1b) was probably a donor. Torre was not interested in decorative elements and does not mention architectural canopies. While nothing like this could be positively identified in the excavated material, a few tiny fragments amongst the uncatalogued material were probably architectural. All the evidence from surviving windows in York suggests that the Bedern figure panels would have been surmounted by canopies in row 3, possibly extending upwards into the heads of the lights in row 4.

Archaeological evidence shows that, as might be expected in the middle of the 14th century, naturalistic foliage grisaille formed an important element in the glazing. The bottom and top rows of the main lights of the windows (rows 1 and 4) are likely to have been mainly glazed in white glass. Around the main lights, within an outer white margin, were border designs including foliage ornament and heraldic devices, and some of the windows had inscriptions running across their base.

Although figural glazing appeared in one set of tracery lights (sIII) these were mainly given over to armorials. While it is possible to identify most of the shields, one or two remain problematic. Harrison (1924, 206), despite his familiarity with the vicars choral archives, found the heraldry difficult to interpret. Some shields, like those for King Arthur/St Edmund or Vavasour, may have commemorated Minster benefactors or represented a chantry served by one of the vicars. Others doubtless refer to families who donated funds. The shield bearing the Arma Christi acted as a devotional image.

Small scale and unsophisticated in its architecture Bedern Chapel may have been, but the evidence of its glazing and the recent finds present a different picture. The subject matter of the windows, whether religious or heraldic, supports both the status and the devotional interests of the establishment. Given the nature of the institution and its geographical location it is hardly surprising that the Bedern windows constantly reflect the design, the heraldry and the imagery of the great cathedral. Nor is this merely a pale reflection. Evidence presented here suggests that the Bedern stained glass was of very high artistic quality and that much of it was probably made by glaziers who worked on the most prestigious mid 14th century windows in the city.

The evidence of the antiquarian sources

In order to present the antiquarian evidence reasonably clearly transcripts are given of the most important written records, followed by an interpretation of this evidence for each window following the order in which they are described by Torre. While it is obvious that Torre moves from west to east on the north side of the chapel, on the south, where all the windows contain three lights, the orientation is less secure. That he describes the south windows from east to west is confirmed by Gent. Footnote references appear on pp.574–5.

Henry Johnston:

'Church Notes and Drawings 1669–70', Oxford, Bodleian Library, MS Top. Yorks C.14, fo.131r (Fig.316). This contains tricked drawings of eleven armorials in Bedern Chapel, eight in stained glass and three embroidered on a cloth above the high altar.

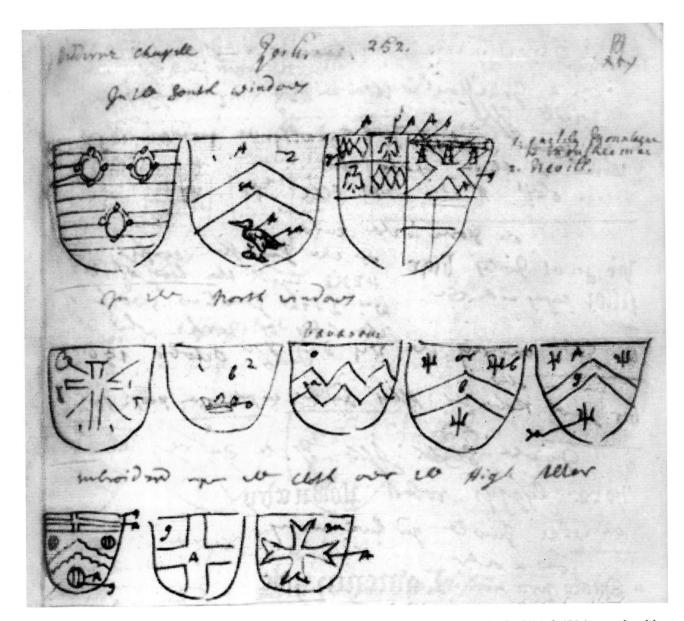

Fig.316 *Henry Johnston's sketch of eleven armorials in Bedern Chapel windows (MS Top. Yorks C.14, fo.131r), reproduced by permission of The Bodleian Library, University of Oxford, and York Minster Archive*

562

In the south windows [drawings of three armorials.

1. Barry of 9 argent and azure over all 3 chaplets gules (GREYSTOCK).[1]

2. Argent a chevron between 3 crows sable (ROKEBY).[2]

3. 1 and 4 quarterly 1 and 4 on a fess sable 3 besantes (MONTAGUE)

    2 and 3 argent an eagle displayed vert (MONTHERMER)

    2 and 3 gules a saltire argent with a label of 3 points azure (NEVILLE).[3] Johnston annotates the shield as] 1. qu*ar*terly Mountague & Monthermer 2. Nevill.

In the north windows [drawings of five armorials.

1. Untricked shield with a cross, vinegar rod and spear in saltire and, possibly, either nails or wounds (ARMA CHRISTI).[4]

2. Azure 3 ducal crowns or (KING ARTHUR or ST EDMUND).[5]

3. Or a fess dancetty sable (VAVASOUR).

4. Or a chevron between 3 fleurs de lis azure (UNIDENTI-FIED).[6]

5. Argent a chevron gules between 3 fleurs de lis sable (DIREWELL/DIXWELL).[7]]

Embroidered upon the cloth over the high altar [drawings of three armorials.

1. Sable a chevron engrailed argent between 3 plates each charged with a pallet or on a chief gules a cross argent (Sir Thomas DOCKWRA, Lord Prior of the Knights of St John of Jerusalem, 1502–19).[8]

2. Gules a cross argent (Order of the Knights of St John of Jerusalem).

3. Sable a cross ?fourchy argent (WEMME?) or possibly a Cross of Malta (Order of the Knights of St John).[9]

James Torre:

'Antiquities Ecclesiastical of the City of York' (1690–1), YMA, MS L1/7, fos.540–541v, published in Harrison 1924, 201–6. The present edition corrects a few omissions and errors with Torre's abbreviations expanded in italics.

[fo.540] The Chappell in the Bederne is next to be observed wh*ich* About A.D. mcccxlviii was founded by Thomas de Otteley & William de Colyngham [sic] & still remains in good Repairs for the use of divine service & sometimes for Christnings, for wh*ich* purpose there is on the left hand the door an old Font. And at the East-End thereof an Holy Water pott. And by it a marble Altar table, covered w*ith* a green carpett. On the back is an old suit of Tapestry hangings Embroydered w*ith* Caterfoils & Letters T.[10] In the midst is wrought a Little Image of our Lord, crowned &

incircled with glory, with his hand conjoined on his brest, & long Rays of glory streaming from all parts of his body. Likewise in an ovall circle encompassing his body are 5 Angells wrought in gold kneeling about him in postures of Adoration, with an Escroule on either side him bearing these words viz. DNS SCIT. And at Either end of the s*ai*d Hangings is Embroydered a Coat of Arms thus, viz. [sketches of two shields] Sab*le* a chevron Argent inter 3 plates, each charged with a pallet Or on a chief Or a cross of Argent [and] Sab*le* a cross furche Argent.

It is Enlightened by 6 Windows the Glass therein being adorned w*ith* these Coats of Arms & Imagry a discription whereof is as followes viz.

Bedernne Chapell *North* Side 1st Window [Sketch of window nV numbered to show position of panels].

The first Window on the North Side contains onely two Lights And at top of all [panel A2] is this Coat viz. [Sketch of shield] Pixwell, Argent a chevron gu*les* inter 3 *fleurs* de Lyz sab*le*./

Our Lords Nativity/

1. [panel 2a]/ In the 1st Light is our Lords Nativity thus Represented viz. Lyes an Asse (Or) & Oxe (Argent) under a Manger (B*lue*) And in the same sitts our Lady in golden hair & silver glory Robed Or breast gu*les*, holding on her lap her babe crined Or glory Or & Argent & wrapped in a golden mantle. At the Other End of the manger sitts in a chair a Reverend old man (probably for Joseph) habited Or & Ar*gent*, cap on his head gu*les* & leaning upon a golden staff./

3 Kings their Offering/

2. [panel 2b]/ In the 2*nd* Light is represented the 3 Kings offering their presents to our Lord, who being in a spotted garment Argent & Or (glory Or) born in the Arms of his mother standing in a golden & Azure Garment crowned Or, glory ver*t*. The postures & Robes of the s*ai*d Kings being thus viz. 1/ The 1st King kneels robed Or & vert offering a Golden cup covered. 2/ The 2*nd* King stands Robed Or & vert bearing in his hands a chest [(or Tabernacle) crossed out] Argent & Or. 3/ The 3rd King stands likewise robed vert & Or, bearing in his left hand a box, full of gold, & poynting to the virgin with the other hand.

3. [panel 1b]/ At bottom of this light is a little Image of a monk in the midst of flaming Fire/ wh*ich* perhapps may signifye Purgatory./

2nd Window [sketch of window nIV numbered to show position of panels]

his Betraying./

The 2nd Window contains 3 Lights & hath at top these 2 Coats viz. [Sketches of two shields] [panel A2] Or a chev*ron* inter 3 *fleurs* de Lyz Blue [and panel A3] Vavasour, Or a fess dauncette sab*le*/

his Betraying.

1./ [panel 2a] The first light represents our Lords betraying viz. In the midst stands our Lord robed & glory Argent, crined & mantled Or touching Malcus his ear (with his right hand) he being like a youth, habited *gules*, standing beneath him/ And Judas habited Or & Argent is standing to kiss our Lord And 3 souldiers standing by to apprehend him, two with Lanthorns in their hands, habited Or & Argent. And beyond them appears the head of Peter, or some other of the Apostles.

his Crucifixion.

2./ [panel 2b] In 2nd Light is our Lords Crucifixion viz His Naked body (with a golden garment about his Loynes) hands nayled to a cross *vert* on one side whereof stands our Lady Robed *vert* & Argent, Crined Or glory Argent And on the other, stands (St John) robed *vert* & Or, both with books closed in their hands./

his Resurrection.

3./ [panel 2c] The 3rd Light represents our Lords Resurrection, viz/

Att either End of an Arched sepulcre (raised upon 6 Round pillars (*vert* & *purpure*) leans a Souldier as asleep, Armed Argent & Or, with spears in their hands And over the sepulcre (between two little Angels kneeling in white, winged Or) sits our Lord with breast bare, Robed Or glory Argent & Or, his Right hand somewhat Elevated, & his left bearing a Cross-Staff with banner displayed Argent & Or, And one of his feet bare poynted downwards & pierced (with a Nayl).

[fo.541] Bederne Chappel 3rd Window [sketch of window nIII numbered to show position of panels]/.

The 3rd Window Contains also 3 Lights & hath at top these 2 Escocheons viz. [Sketches of two shields]

[panel A2] *Blue* 3 ducall Crowns Or [and panel A3, with only the outline of the shield drawn in] Severall Instruments of our Lords Crucifixion/

his Ascension/

1. [panel 2a]/ The 1st Light represents our Lords Ascension, where appears above (as hanging down out of a Cloud) the skirts of his white garment & his bare feet pierced. And beneath, stands our Lady in the midst of the 11 Apostles, all looking upwards, habited Or & Argent, she being robed *vert*, bosom & Arms Or, glory Argent & Or, with hands conjoyned on her breast/.

Holy Ghosts Descent/

2. [panel 2b]/ The 2nd Light contains the descent of the Holy Ghost/viz/ Above flies from a Cloud 3 long Rays of Golden Light & Cloven Tongues And a white dove descending with wings displayed. Beneath sitts our Lady robed Or Glory Argent & Or Arms *vert* & hands closed on her brest/ And on one side her kneel 6 of the Apostles habited Or & *gules*, And on the other side kneel 5 more of them habited Or & Argent./

Judgment/

3. [panel 2c]/ The 3rd Light represents the Last Judgement viz. In the midst sitts our Lord Inthroned Robed Argent &

Blue, Crined Or, glory *vert* his hands & feet pierced. On either side him stands an Angell the 1st robed Argent, Crined Or bearing a white Cross-staff in his hand, the other robed Argent winged Or bearing a Golden garland in one hand & a palme branch in the other. On either side beneath our Lord are severall as well kings, as others, rising out of their graves.

The other 3 Windows are on the *South* side.

South Side 1st Window [sketch of window sII numbered to show position of panels]

The 1st Window on the *South* side contains also 3 Lights And hath at top [panel A2] an Escocheon thus charged viz/ [tricked sketch of an argent shield with an indeterminate device of cross, heart and lozenge shapes in azure and or.][11]

St Katherine/.

1. [panel 2a]/ In the 1st Light kneels St Katherine habited *Blue*, crined Or, glory Argent, with hands conjoyned at prayer. Below her a little Angell.

2. [panel 2b]/ In 2nd Light kneels St Katherine again robed Or in the midst between two wheels over which hover 2 Angells in white, & golden Wings, with Naked swords in their hands, breaking the said wheels/ And beneath her stand two soldiers habited Or & Argent.

3. [panel 2c]/ The 3rd Light contains St Katherines Assumption viz. She is Represented in an azure habit sitting upon a prison below which kneel a King, robed Or & *gules*, crowned Or, & an other old father habited *Blue* and Or. Over the prison on either side her, stands an Angell in white, winged Or.

The 2nd window consists also of 3 Lights. [Sketch of window sIII numbered to show position of panels]

1. [panel A2]/ On top of all sitts our Lady Inthroned robed *vert* crowned Or, glory Argent.

2. [panel A3]/ And on the other side her sitts our Lord likewise Inthroned robed & crowned Or glory Argent, poynting with one hand & holding a book in the other/.

our Ladys Assumption/

1. [panel 2a] In the 1st light is represented Our Ladyes Assumption viz.

She standing (in an ovall Circle) robed *Blue*, glory Argent, with 2 Cherubims on Either side her head & 2 Angells, at her feet, robed Argent winged *gules*./

[fo.541v]

dead raised/

2. [panel 2b]/ In the 2nd Light is our Lord (robed *Blue*, breast & glory Argent) raising to Life the dead man (at Nain) from the bier, which is born on the Shoulders of severall men in white habitts.

3. [panel 2c]/ The 3rd Light showes our Ladyes Salutation, she being in Azure & golden Robes, crined Or, glory Argent & kneeling with a prayer book open before her, & looking backwards to the Angell which stands behind her robed Vert & Argent winged Or, bearing a palme branch in his hand And opposite to him issues a hand out of a Cloud.

3rd Window/ [Sketch of window sIV numbered to show position of panels]

The 3rd Window hath also 3 Lights And the top thereof is adorned with these 2 Coats viz. [Sketches of two shields] [panel A2] Greystock, Barry of 8 Argent & Blue over all 3 Chapletts gules. [panel A3] Argent a Chevron inter 3 Crowes vel magpies sable.

1. [panel 2a]/ The first Light is all of white glass.

2. [panel 2b]/ The 2nd Light hath onely this Coat in it viz/ [Sketch of shield] 1st & last/ Quarterly 1st/ Argent on a fess sable 3 bezantes. 2/ Or an Eagle displayed vert. 3rd as 2nd 4th as 1st. 2nd & 3rd/ gules a saltire Argent./

3. [panel 2c]/ In 3rd Light is the representation of Joseph of Arimathea taking down the body of our Lord from the Cross. He being habited gules glory vert & Or.

Thomas Gent:

The Antient and Modern History of the Famous City of York, York, 1730, 190–1.

The painted Glass-Windows are well preserv'd and entire. The first Window North contains the Birth of our Saviour, and the Adoration of the Eastern Kings. The 2d, His being betray'd, Crucifixion, and Resurrection. The 3d, His Ascent to Heaven, Virgin Mary and Apostles, Descent of the Holy Ghost, Christ's descent into Hell, and loosing the Spirits from Prison. The first Window South of the Altar contains the Martyrdom of St. Katherine, etc. The 2nd S.W. the Salutation of the Virgin, Death and Ascension etc. In this Chapel are the Arms of the Nevils, Vavasours etc.

The north wall

Torre's account shows that the windows in the north wall presented a coherent iconographic programme based, for the most part, around the life of Christ. A row of figure panels ran from west to east commencing with the Nativity (nV 2a) and ending with the Last Judgement (nIII 2c). The first window (nV) contained two Infancy scenes, the Nativity and the Adoration of the Magi; the middle window (nIV) three Passion or post-Passion scenes, the Arrest of Christ, the Crucifixion and the Resurrection, while the last window (nIII) completed the cycle with the Ascension, Pentecost and Last Judgement. Mention of an isolated panel of the Deposition, on the other side of the chapel (sII 2c) presents a problem as this would be more logical if placed in the correct chrono-

logical order in nIV 3c. Such a placement would force the Resurrection into window nIII, with the Ascension and Pentecost, forming a perfectly coherent grouping, but this would force the Last Judgement into another window (sII or W).

Torre's description provides a good account of the contents of each window, with sufficient detail on both iconography and colour to allow comparisons with extant glass from the area to be made and, sometimes, to suggest possible evidence for dating.

Window nV

Although this window belongs to the Period 7 extension of the chapel, the glass, consisting of the Nativity (2a) and the Adoration of the Magi (2b), appears to belong to a scheme dating from the first phase of the chapel, around 1348.

The iconography of the Nativity, with the Christ-child held on Mary's lap, is reminiscent of several Nativity images in York from the second quarter of the 14th century (Davidson and O'Connor 1978, 46–70): the Minster west window of 1338/9 (French and O'Connor 1987, 52 and pl.5b), window nII in All Saints North Street of c.1330–40 (Gee 1969, 158 and pl.XI; RCHMY 3, 8) and a contemporary panel in the east window (I) of St Michael-le-Belfrey (Knowles 1962, 155–6; RCHMY 5, 38 and pl.49) in which, as at Bedern, the ox and the ass are placed under the crib. Comparisons with other representations of the Adoration (Davidson and O'Connor 1978, 54–6) suggest that it is another panel in the All Saints North Street window (Gee 1969, 157 and pl.XXIIa; RCHMY 3, 8) that comes closest to the glass at Bedern.

A donor probably appeared at the bottom centre of the window (1b), possibly a member of the Pixwell family whose arms appeared in the tracery (A2). Torre, who describes him as 'a monk in the midst of flaming Fire', frequently used the word 'monk' to describe any tonsured ecclesiastic. Such a donor figure is likely to have been a vicar choral or other Minster cleric. Representations of Purgatory are extremely rare in medieval stained glass and, although it is highly unlikely that a donor would wish to be depicted in a perpetual state of torment, for chantry priests such an image would have had a special appeal.

Torre describes a richly coloured window with blue, green and red draperies, as well as much white and yellow glass, some of the latter presumably pot-metal and some, like the Virgin's hair or Christ's robe, using yellow stain. The combination of yellows and greens and the use of green glass, rather than white and yellow stain, for one of the Virgin's haloes, confirms that the window was 14th century in date.

Window nIV

This window contained the Arrest of Christ (2a), the Crucifixion (2b) and the Resurrection (2c). While there is little to distinguish the Arrest panel from other 13th and 15th century versions of the theme in York (Davidson and O'Connor 1978, 72–3), two details of the Crucifixion, the green cross and the closed books held by both the Virgin and St John, are elements commonly found in windows of c.1335–40, many of them associated with Master Robert and the Minster west end style: sII in St Martin-cum-Gregory (RCHMY **3**, 25 and pl.116), window sXXXVI in the Minster (French and O'Connor 1987, 78–81 and pls.16a, b and c), the west window of St Helen's (French and O'Connor 1987, 20 and pl.17a) and related glass in Beverley Minster (O'Connor 1989, 69, 79 and pl.XVe). The Resurrection, with its kneeling angels, sounds very similar to panels in nII at All Saints North Street (Gee 1969, 158 and pl.XXI; RCHMY **3**, 8) and the east window of St Michael-le-Belfrey (Knowles 1962, 155–6; RCHMY **5**, 38 and pl.49).

In the tracery lights were an unidentified shield (A2), possibly Mennys or Orannge, and the arms of the Vavasours of Hazlewood Castle (A3), great benefactors of the Minster and the founders of a perpetual chantry there. Some vicars choral also served as chantry priests and there may be a very specific reason for including the Vavasour arms here.

In its colour this window was similar to nV. Purple, which is likely to have been used for some flesh tones, is specifically mentioned in connection with the sepulchre. While the figures in the Arrest panel were predominantly in white and yellow glass, the colours in the Resurrection are not markedly different from those used in the Resurrection panel at All Saints North Street.

Window nIII

This window contained the Ascension (2a), Pentecost (2b) and Last Judgement (2c), all the scenes taking conventional iconographic forms. The Ascen-

sion, like most examples from York, included the Virgin Mary (Davidson and O'Connor 1978, 99–102) and was clearly closer in appearance to a damaged Master Robert panel at Lockington, North Yorkshire (French and O'Connor 1987, 21, 56 and pl.28d), than to the highly unusual composition, spread over two lights, in the west window of the Minster (French and O'Connor 1987, 56 and pl.6b). Pentecost was similar to a panel of c.1340 now in the choir clerestory of the Minster (SIV) (Davidson and O'Connor 1978, 101; French 1971, pl.xv b). In the Bedern Last Judgement, as kings and other representatives of society rose from their graves, the wounded Christ was shown flanked by angels holding passion emblems: the cross, the crown of thorns and, possibly, a whip. Although elements in this iconography can be found elsewhere in York from the 13th century onwards (Davidson and O'Connor 1987, 113–16), they occur in monumental form in the tracery lights of the east window of Selby Abbey, the original a York work of c.1340, attributed to Master Robert, but replaced by a Ward and Hughes copy following fire damage in 1906 (O'Connor and Reddish 1995).

There were two shields in the tracery of the window. On the left (A2) were the arms attributed to King Arthur or St Edmund, both important figures in the Minster (p.574, n.5). To the right (A3) was an Arma Christi, drawn by Johnston, depicting various instruments of the Passion (Davidson and O'Connor 1978, 77–9). This popular devotional image would have served to reinforce the passion imagery in the Last Judgement panel below.

While there is nothing in the iconography or the heraldry to preclude a date of c.1348 for this window there is nothing either to point exclusively to that period. Colour appears to be used in much the same way as elsewhere. Another green nimbus, for the Christ in Judgement, is again suggestive of a 14th century date.

The south wall

At first sight the windows on the south side of the chapel appear to present a less unified scheme than those on the north, although some of this has to do with the damage sustained by window sIV. Torre identified the solitary figure panel in the window in his time as the Deposition, although there is some doubt as to whether it belongs here. There is no doubt, however, about the contents of the other two windows which honoured two of the chapel's dedicatory saints, the Virgin Mary (sIII) and St Katherine (sII). Given the dedication of the chapel to the Holy Trinity, the Blessed Virgin and St Katherine, a window (sIV) containing specific Trinity imagery, not recorded elsewhere in the building, would make good sense. In such a scheme the south wall would have presented each of the three elements in the chapel's dedication, in the correct order, once again from west to east.

Window sII

This window contained three figure panels from the life of St Katherine although they were out of order when Torre saw them. In the first light (2a) he saw the kneeling saint at prayer and an angel. Although there is no mention of an executioner or a sword, the saint's martyrdom would almost certainly have been included and is probably what was represented here. In another window dedicated to St Katherine, the Heraldic Window in the Minster (nXXIII) of c.1307–10 (O'Connor and Haselock 1977, 349; Alexander and Binski 1987, no.5), the six main-light scenes culminate in the martyrdom of the saint who is beheaded, while kneeling at prayer, in the presence of angels. The central panel in the Bedern window (2b) depicted St Katherine delivered from the wheels in a form which followed the Heraldic Window panel (Harrison 1937, pl.V) pretty closely. Torre mistook the third panel (3c) for the Assumption of St Katherine, an error further compounded by Harrison (1924, 205) who transcribed Torre's 'prison' as 'prism'. The panel, which should have appeared at the beginning of the sequence, depicted St Katherine in Prison and again followed the format presented in the Heraldic Window in the Minster (O'Connor and Haselock 1977, pl.107). Torre's 'King' can be identified as the Empress Faustina, and his 'other old father' as the Emperor Maxentius's general, Porphyry, who, following their conversion, kneel on either side of the imprisoned saint in the Minster window. One angel attends the saint in the Minster panel, unlike the Bedern window where there were two.

Only one shield was recorded in the tracery by Torre, an indeterminate device in azure and or. The use of colour is consistent with the windows of the north wall. While there is nothing in the iconography to preclude a later date, its position in the building

and close parallels with the early 14th century glass of the Minster suggest that the glass formed part of the original c.1348 scheme.

Window sIII

The main lights and tracery of this window contained four scenes from the very end of the life of the Virgin. Once again they were out of sequence by Torre's time. The first panel in the series, now in the third light (2c) and described by Torre as 'our Ladyes Salutation', was the Annunciation of the Death of the Virgin, as the presence of the palm branch in the angel's hand makes clear (Davidson and O'Connor 1978, 103). Although very different in colour, the lost Bedern glass was remarkably like a Master Robert panel of c.1340 now in the choir clerestory of the Minster (SIV) (Knowles 1956, pl.II). Here too the hand of God issues from a cloud and Gabriel approaches the reading Virgin from behind, an example of the very innovative Italianate iconography which is such a feature of York glass of c.1340 (O'Connor and Haselock 1977, 378–9; French and O'Connor 1987, 18).

The central panel (2b), described by Torre as the miracle at Nain (Luke 7: 11–15), is the Funeral of the Virgin Mary in which the apostles, including St John with the palm given to Mary by the angel, were shown in procession, carrying the Virgin's coffin (Davidson and O'Connor 1978, 103–4). Another of the Marian panels of c.1340 in the Minster (SIV) provides an interesting comparison (O'Connor and Haselock 1987, 357 and pl.129). By analogy with this and other representations of the theme, Torre's resurrected young man must have been the Jew whose hands miraculously stuck to the Virgin's coffin when he attempted to upset it.

The third panel (now 2a) was the Assumption of the Virgin who was placed centrally in an oval mandorla and shown being taken up to heaven by four angels. This was another popular theme in York (Davidson and O'Connor 1978, 105–7) but no panel of this type has survived in the Marian cycle of c.1340 in the Minster. The Bedern panel must have looked something like the Assumption of c.1310–20 in window sIV at Beckley, Oxfordshire (Alexander and Binski 1987, no.30) but with fewer angels.

As was usual with windows on this theme, the series culminated in the Coronation of the Virgin, appropriately placed in two tracery openings (A2, A3). Unlike the example in the c.1340 series in the Minster (Knowles 1956, pl.II), in which the Virgin is shown being crowned by Christ and an angel, the Bedern panels took the more common form with the Virgin already crowned and Christ blessing (Davidson and O'Connor 1987, 107–11). This is the type used in the west window of the Minster in 1338/9 (French and O'Connor 1987, 61–2 and pl.3), window nII at All Saints North Street (Gee 1969, 158 and pl.XXIIb; RCHMY **3**, 8 and pl.102), St Mary Castlegate (RCHMY **5**, 34; French and O'Connor 1987, 19 and pl.23c), the east window of St Michael-le-Belfrey (Knowles 1962, 157; RCHMY **5**, 38) and two tracery-lights dated c.1340 at Nether Poppleton, near York (French and O'Connor 1987, 20 and pls.28 a and b). Usually though Christ holds an orb rather than a book.

The many links with other York windows confirm that the Bedern window was glazed c.1348. There is nothing particularly distinctive about the colours used, except that the angels in the Assumption panel had red, rather than the more usual golden, wings.

Window sIV

The stonework of this window belonged to the Period 7 extension of the chapel and there is evidence to confirm that some of its glass dated from the 15th century. The glazing was incomplete when Torre described it but, like the other windows in the lateral walls, it is likely to have contained figure panels and canopies in rows 2 and 3. In 1690 the first light contained white glass and the second, a post 1420–1 Neville armorial recorded by Johnston and Torre (pp.563, 565 and Fig.316). The latter described the only figural glass in the window (2c) as 'Joseph of Arimathea taking down the body of our Lord from the Cross', a subject which, as pointed out above, would have been more appropriate in the passion window (nIV). While there is no particular reason to question Torre and Gent's identification, the former only describes two figures in what is usually a more crowded scene. Two other Deposition panels from York (Davidson and O'Connor 1978, 83), a copy of a late 13th century medallion formerly in the Minster chapter house (now in SXXII) and a panel of c.1380–90 in the east window of All Saints Pavement (RCHMY **5**, 3 and pl.48), also include figures of the

Virgin, St John the Evangelist and Nicodemus. The presence of 15th century glass in the window suggests another possibility. Perhaps what Torre saw was a Corpus Christi Trinity image with a standing God the Father supporting the dead body of Christ, with the Holy Spirit as a dove. The cult of Corpus Christi, with its processions, plays and prestigious religious guild, made this a popular type of image in 15th century York and several examples survive in alabaster carving and glass (Davidson and O'Connor 1987, 85–7). As the other windows in this wall reflect the chapel's dedication, a Trinity image would be highly appropriate at this point.

In the tracery lights were the arms of Greystoke (A2), also represented in the late 13th century windows of the Minster chapter house (C/H nIV and sIII), and Rokeby (A3). John Rokeby was active as precentor at the Minster in 1545–74 (Aylmer and Cant 1977, 204 and 218) but the glass may well have been pre-Reformation in date.

Catalogue of window glass from Bedern Chapel (site code 1980.20; Period 9)

The catalogue numbers follow consecutively those in *AY* 10/4. Each entry ends with the context number, followed by small find number, prefixed sf.

This glass, which can be dated c.1340–50 on stylistic grounds, formed part of the original glazing of the Period 5 chapel, consecrated in 1348.

340   Fragment of white rectangular border piece with top of covered cup painted in reserve; 35 x 54 x 4mm, grozed edges confirming original width. 9000 sf2 (*Fig.317*)

341   Fragment of virtually opaque white and yellow stained naturalistic leaf grisaille with border of parallel lines; 3–5mm. 9000 sf2 (*Fig.317*)

342   Small white fragment of naturalistic leaf grisaille; 3mm. 9000 sf2. Not illustrated

343   Small fragment of white inscription with part of letter D, M or N; 3mm. 9000 sf8. Not illustrated

344   Fragment of opaque Lombardic inscription: /e̲./; 3mm. 9008 sf20 (*Fig.317*)

345   Fragment of virtually opaque white maple leaf with light exterior pitting. Probably from a border rather than grisaille; 40 x 48 x 3–4mm, grozed edges confirming original width. 9008 sf22 (*Fig.317*)

346   Small fragment of opaque background with delicately scratched out frond design within border; 3mm. 9008 sf44 (*Fig.317*)

347   Complete, very uneven piece of pale blue drapery with washes of smear shading and back painting. Good condition apart from some paint loss; 3–4mm. 9008 sf47 (*Fig.317*)

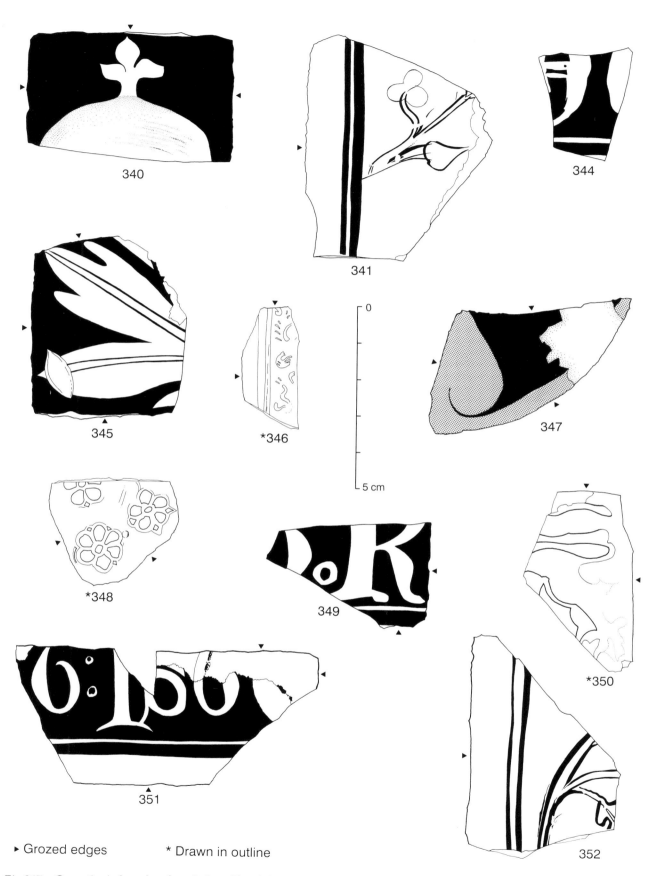

340

341

344

345

*346

0

5 cm

347

*348

349

*350

351

352

▸ Grozed edges   * Drawn in outline

Fig.317   Group 1 window glass from Bedern Chapel: 340–1, 344–52. Scale 1:1

348 Small opaque fragment, probably drapery, decorated with cinquefoil and sexfoil flowers in reserve; 2mm. 9008 sf47 (*Fig.317*)

349 Fragment of virtually opaque white inscription with parts of two letters from two words separated by punctuation: / .:R/; 3–4mm. 9008 sf54 (*Fig.317*)

350 Fragment of rectangular yellow stained border piece with part of an heraldic <u>lion passant guardant or</u> (England) painted in reserve; 2mm. 9014 sf53 (*Fig.317*)

351 Broken and uneven white fragment with yellow stained inscription, partially obscured by mortar. A tentative reading is: /t:P./; 3mm. 9014 sf98 (*Fig.317*)

352 Fragment of naturalistic oak leaf grisaille with yellow stained border; 2–4mm. 9014 sf98 (*Fig.317*)

353 Small fragment of oak leaf grisaille; 2mm. 9014 sf98. Not illustrated

354 Fragment of stem from naturalistic leaf grisaille; 3mm. 9014 sf98. Not illustrated

355 Broken, but almost complete rectangular border piece with yellow stained triple-towered castle and portcullis painted in reserve; 82 x 51 x 3–4mm, grozed edges confirming original width. 9014 sf98 (*Fig.318*)

356 White and yellow stained fragment of naturalistic stem and leaf border painted in reserve and reinforced with back-painted washes. Not enough survives to identify the leaf type; 52 x 51 x 2–3mm, grozed edges confirming original width. 9018 sf104 (*Fig.318*)

357 Virtually opaque fragment of naturalistic leaf grisaille with part of stem and subsidiary trefoil leaf; 2–3mm. 9018 sf104 (*Fig.318*)

358 Small fragment of pot-metal green maple-rinceau background. Good condition but some paint loss; 2mm. 9025 sf141 (*Fig.318*)

Condition

Although 89 of the 210 pieces excavated were completely opaque and one of the two pieces of flashed-ruby found on the site had disintegrated very badly into layers, probably because of its more complex method of manufacture (French and O'Connor 1987, 12–13), much of the rest of the glass is in rather better condition than is probably usual for material of this kind. The potash-rich glass of the medieval period tends to be an unstable material, frequently heavily pitted and corroded when still remaining in situ, let alone after being subjected to long periods of burial in damp conditions under ground (Newton and Davison 1988). How long the Bedern pieces lay buried is not known, but perhaps they remained in place until as late as 1816, when what survived of the medieval glazing of the chapel was transferred to the Minster, or even beyond. In any case the good physical condition of much York glass of the second quarter of the 14th century has been noted previously,

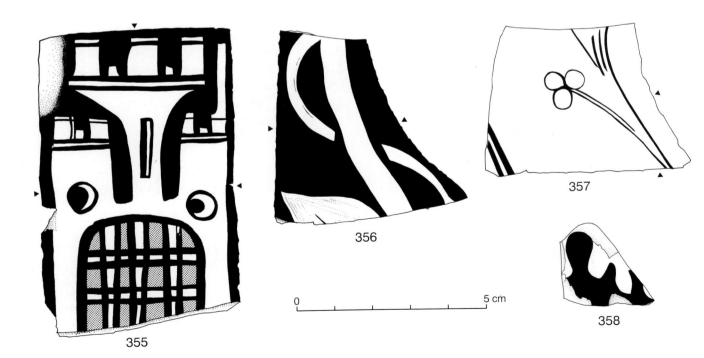

355   356   5 cm   357   358

Fig.318   *Group 1 window glass from Bedern Chapel: 355–8. Scale 1:1*

particularly with regard to material associated with Master Robert, possibly Robert Kettlebarn, who was responsible for the west window of York Minster (wI) in 1338/9 (French and O'Connor 1987, 8).

Several Bedern chapel pieces (including *347, 350* and *358*) show very little trace of corrosion and remain remarkably transparent and stable. Many fragments exhibit a very light pitting on what was originally their exterior surface, a type of corrosion which is likely to have commenced around 1348 when the panels were fixed in the stonework and were first exposed to the elements. Although no chemical analysis has been carried out on window glass from Bedern, many of the white pieces look like and feel similar to a lightly pitted mid 14th century white fragment from York Minster, part of a castle from a border, similar in type to *355*. This was analysed by Dr Kate Gillies in 1975 and found to have a chemical composition consistent with similarly preserved material in York Minster (French and O'Connor 1987, 92, Appendix 4).

Colour and technique

Eighty-nine of the fragments were so corroded as to have turned completely opaque, making it impossible to determine their original colour under normal conditions. In the Minster west window of 1338/9 only the pot-metal pink, used mainly for flesh tones and drapery, and some areas of dark blue in the borders, show pretty consistent decay of this kind (French and O'Connor 1987, 8).

It is significant that 126 pieces, well over half the number found on the site, are white. Band-window schemes with coloured medallions, figures and canopies set on backgrounds of foliage grisaille, as in the Minster chapter house and vestibule of c.1285–95 and the nave of c.1307–40 (O'Connor and Haselock 1977, 334–64), were a standard feature of English Decorated glass. White glass was used extensively in Bedern Chapel for naturalistic foliage grisaille of various types (*341–2, 352–4* and *357*), for border pieces (*340, 345, 350, 355–6*) and for inscriptions (*343, 349* and *351*).

One of the most obvious innovations to be found at the west end of York Minster in 1338/9 and in similar schemes is the increased emphasis on white glass, which is used extensively for figures, canopies and leaf ornament, often exploiting the relatively newly

invented technique of yellow stain (French and O'Connor 1987, 13–14; Alexander and Binski 1987, no.563, in colour). This method of turning white glass yellow or blue glass green made an early appearance at York in the Heraldic Window in the Minster (nXXIII) of c.1307–10 (ibid., no.5). Yellow stain occurs on 24 of the Bedern Chapel pieces to decorate foliage grisaille, border pieces and inscriptions. From Torre's account it is very clear that the technique was used extensively for patterned robes, hair and haloes.

The excavated pieces provide an additional source of information to add to Torre's more prosaic comments on colour. There were three pieces of pot-metal yellow and five pieces of green, one of which (*358*) was used for a rinceau background. Five pieces of blue were found, one of them (*347*) a very pale colour used for drapery. Only two pieces of flashed-ruby were recognised, one of them from a rinceau background.

The finds also provide some information on the techniques used by the 14th century glaziers (French and O'Connor 1987, 12–14). The standard reddish-brown iron-oxide pigments were used, sometimes as a thick black matt to paint border motifs or inscriptions in reserve, sometimes as a delicate transparent wash when used to shade drapery (*347*). The latter has back-painting, a feature of the Minster west windows, to reinforce shading on the drapery folds, as does a leaf-design from a border (*356*) and one of the uncatalogued pieces that may be drapery. Delicate stickwork and scratched out ornament (*346, 348* and *358*) attest to the technical skill of the craftsmen. There were further tiny examples of this technique in the uncatalogued material.

Also excluded from the catalogue are three edge-pieces from cylinder-blown or muff glass; two are white and the third opaque.

Glazing types: design and style

Although figure panels formed an important part of the chapel glazing no heads or hands were identified among the finds. Several tiny pieces may have come from drapery, but only two were firmly identified, a complete piece of finely painted blue drapery (*347*) and a fragment with a delicately scratched out pattern of cinquefoil and sexfoil flowers (*348*). Nothing architectural was positively identified.

Two background designs were found, one (346) with scratched out frond rinceau and the other (358) of maple-leaf rinceau. Such designs were commonly used behind figures, but they are also found on or behind shields and as backgrounds to borders. Frond rinceaux are used extensively in the west windows of the Minster and related glass (French and O'Connor 1987, 7 and pls.19i and ii) and maple is used by the same glaziers at Selby (O'Connor and Reddish 1995, 124 and 127).

Most of the fragments of naturalistic foliage grisaille included in the catalogue (341–2, 352–4 and 357) were too small to identify firmly, but two (352–3) are of oak leaf and in one case (357) a subsidiary trefoil leaf sprouts from the base of the stem. The white and yellow-stained quarries would have formed balanced designs of tightly curving foliage, the painted borders on the quarries reinforcing the trellis effect of the leadwork. The thin and delicate curling stems and leaves of Bedern are found elsewhere in the region at this time, for example, in the east window at Acaster Malbis, Yorkshire (French and O'Connor 1987, 5, 20 and pl.26d), a work of c.1340 in the Master Robert style. There is no evidence at Bedern, however, for the coloured trellis and more ornate arrangement of the Acaster grisaille.

Five border pieces have been identified. Three have heraldic designs: a yellow lion of England (350) and two devices which often appear together in the borders of windows, a white covered cup (340), possibly derived from the arms of Galicia, and a yellow castle (355), usually associated with Eleanor of Castile. These three designs were again used in the west wall of the Minster (French and O'Connor 1987, 7–8 and pl.20) and at Selby (O'Connor and Reddish 1995, 124 and 127), and in several of the parish churches, including All Saints North Street, St Michael-le-Belfrey and St Denys (Gee 1969, 176–7 and pl.16). In a three-light window in Bedern Chapel the outer lights are likely to have been given alternating cups and castles with precedence given to the royal lion which was probably positioned in a centre light, possibly with the fleur-de-lys of France. Two fragments (345 and 356) suggest that there were also borders of maple leaf and possibly other foliage designs.

Four pieces of inscription were found (343–4, 349 and 351), mostly on white glass and, in one case, with evidence of yellow stain. These pieces look like texts from the bottom of a window or from beneath figure panels, rather than scrolls held by figures. The letter forms are consistent with the mixed Lombardic and black-letter scripts used c.1340 in York (French and O'Connor 1987, 50), but only a tentative reading of a few letters can be given.

It would be foolish on the basis of so few fragments to try to identify the glaziers responsible for the Bedern windows. On the eve of the Black Death York glass-painters no doubt worked in similar ways and with shared materials and techniques. In colour, technique, design, iconography and even style, the many connections with the Minster windows suggest that the designers and makers of the Bedern windows were either direct associates of those, like Master Robert and Thomas de Bouesden, responsible for the west windows in the Minster nave or, like the so-called All Saints workshop (French and O'Connor 1987, 20; O'Connor and Reddish 1995, 124), were very heavily influenced by that prestigious scheme.

Group 2: Glass from other sites within the area of the College of the Vicars Choral

Some 200 fragments of window glass were found on other locations within the college precincts. Contexts suggest that a few of these (like 360) are Roman in date, but most were of modern glass. Only seventeen were thought to be significant enough to warrant cataloguing here. Some of the late medieval pieces probably wandered from the chapel, or formed part of the glazing of subsidiary buildings. The Statute Book, cited above, mentions repairs to windows in the counting house and in the common hall in 1419/22 (p.560).

A number of pieces are coeval with the chapel glazing and are likely to have originated there. They include a red fragment with a scratched out rinceau design of flowers on stalks (359) and two white pieces with frond designs (365 and 366). Also likely to have come from the chapel are a group of badly preserved 14th century drapery fragments (361) and some small fragments of 14th and 15th century inscriptions (364, 370 and 372). What appears to be part of a late medieval roundel with tree trunk and leaves (367) might make better sense in a domestic setting like the hall. Another fragment of cylinder-blown glass (362) was found among this material. Two unusually well-preserved blue pieces (*368* and *373*) may be of soda rather than potash glass. A group of very thin white pieces with yellow stain and variously coloured enamels (*371* and *375*) probably date from some time between 1580 and 1795 and may represent the work of the York glass-painters Bernard Dininckhof, Henry Gyles or William Peckitt (O'Connor and Haselock 1977, 385–9).

Catalogue of glass from other sites within the area of the College of Vicars Choral (site code given in parentheses)

359 Poorly preserved and very uneven flashed ruby fragment of scratched out rinceau background with simple circular flowers on stalks; 3–4mm; c.1325–50 (1976.13.X) 5030 sf1668 (P9) (*Fig.319*)

360 Well-preserved greenish-tinted white fragment; 3mm (1976.13.V) 3020 sf3077 (Roman). Not illustrated

361 Group of seven poorly preserved, partially grozed, opaque drapery fragments obscured by accretions. The vertical folds have smear-shaded washes on both surfaces, and one piece has a narrow band of scratched out beaded ornament; 3–4mm. Medieval, probably c.1300–50 (1977.13.X) 6044 sf2175 (P8). Not illustrated

362 Broken fragment of opaque, originally coloured, glass from the edge of a cylinder; 3–4mm. Late medieval (1978.13.X) 7349 sf2730 (P7). Not illustrated

363 Poorly preserved broken white fragment painted with thick and thin parallel lines; 1–2mm. Probably the borders of a grisaille quarry. Late medieval, probably 15th century (1978.14.II) 1116 sf186 (P8). Not illustrated

364 Virtually opaque white fragment of black-letter inscription; 2mm; 15th century (1978.14.II) 1108 sf207 (P8) (*Fig.319*)

365 Poorly preserved broken white fragment with remnants of scratched out curling frond rinceau background; 3–4mm. c.1325–50 (1978.14) 1135 sf193 (P8) (*Fig.319*)

366 Poorly preserved almost opaque white fragment with delicately scratched out frond ornament; 3mm. Probably c.1325–50 (1978.14.II) 1193 sf241 (P7) (*Fig.319*)

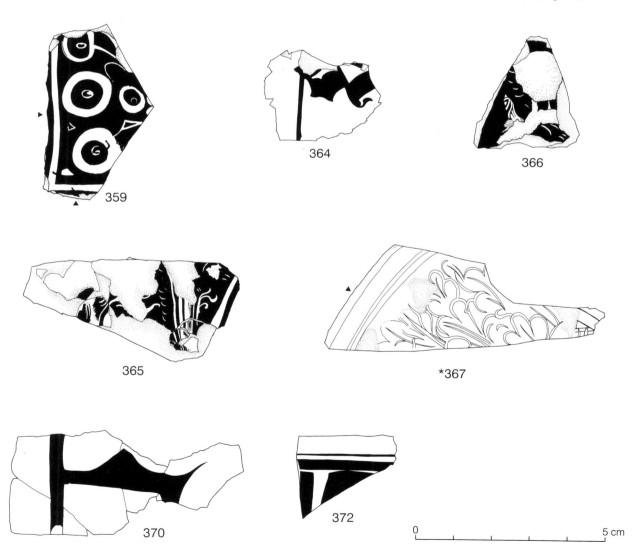

Fig.319 *Group 2 window glass: 359, 364–7, 370, 372. Scale 1:1*

367 Thin, flat, white fragment with curving grozed edge, delicately painted with leaves and part of a tree trunk; 1–2mm. Possibly from the top of a roundel, late 15th or early 16th century (1979.14.II) 1116 sf190 (P8) (*Fig.319*)

368 Well-preserved plain blue fragment with traces of grozed edge; 3–4mm. The unusual condition suggests it may be soda glass (1979.14.II) 1402 sf314 (P6). Not illustrated

369 Part of a broken plain white quarry with grozed edges; original measurements approximately 100 x 80 x 3mm. Late medieval (1979.14.II) 1428 sf320 (P8). Not illustrated

370 Broken opaque fragment with what appears to be part of a letter from an inscription; 3mm. Late medieval (1979.14.II) 1215 sf369 (P6) (*Fig.319*)

371 Group of seven related small thin white fragments with traces of what appears to be yellow stain and purple enamel; 1mm. Post-medieval, late 16th century or later (1979.14.IV) 4078 sf495 (P9). Not illustrated

372 Almost opaque white fragment of inscription in Lombardic capitals. Top of one letter, possibly an I, followed by a serif from another; 2mm. Probably c.1300–50 (1979.14.IV) 4154 sf532 (P8) (*Fig.319*)

373 Well-preserved plain blue fragment with two grozed edges, possibly rectangular originally; 2mm. The unusually good condition, similar to 372, suggests it may be soda glass (1979.14.II) 1588 sf584 (P5). Not illustrated

374 Small virtually opaque blue fragment with severe paint loss; 2mm. Within the one surviving grozed edge are traces of a background design within a plain border. Probably 14th century (1979.14.IV) 4177 sf616 (P7). Not illustrated

375 Two small thin white fragments with traces of blue, green and purple enamels; 1mm. Post-medieval, late 16th century or later (1979.14.IV) 4180 sf638 (P7). Not illustrated

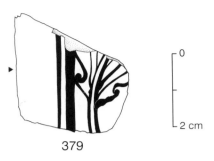

379

Fig.320   *Group 3 window glass: 379. Scale 1:1*

377 Virtually opaque pot-metal green fragment with traces of paint; 2–3mm. Medieval, probably 13th century (1976.13.II) 2380 sf1341 (P3). Not illustrated

378 Small poorly preserved fragment of flashed ruby with traces of paint; 1mm. Late medieval (1973.13.I/II) 63 sf163 (P7). Not illustrated

379 Small white fragment of oak leaf grisaille; 2mm. Probably c.1325–50 (1973.13.I/II) 223 sf352 (P6) (*Fig.320*)

Group 3: Glass from outside the area of the College of the Vicars Choral

Not surprisingly, fewer pieces of window glass turned up in the area outside the college precincts. Whilst it is possible that a few of these might be Roman in date, most were of modern glass. Of the 32 pieces found here only four are described in the catalogue below.

One of these pieces, a fragment of 14th century oak leaf grisaille (379), is similar to material already identified at the chapel. Traces of paint survive on only two other pieces, one of them (377) possibly 13th century in date, the other (378) dating from the later medieval period. A fourth medieval fragment (376) formed part of a plain blue rectangle.

Catalogue of glass from outside the area of the College of Vicars Choral (site code given in parentheses)

376 Poorly preserved plain pot-metal blue fragment with three grozed edges, probably rectangular originally; 3mm. Medieval (1973.13.I/II) 63 sf162 (P7). Not illustrated

References

1. The arms should be Barry of 8, as recorded by Torre; see Papworth and Morant 1874, 1125.

2. Woodcock, Grant and Graham 1996, 304–5. Johnston indicates some of the feathers as argent, although Torre (see p.565), unable to distinguish between crows and magpies, blazons the birds sable.

3. Richard Neville, Earl of Salisbury, married Alice, sole daughter and heiress of Thomas Montague, in 1420/1, thus becoming entitled to quarter the Montague arms.

4. For examples of Arma Christi images in York see Davidson and O'Connor 1978, 77–8 and the supplement, *Index to York Art*, 232–3.

5. Papworth and Morant 1874, 593. Either identification would make sense within the confines of York Minster. King Arthur, regarded as one of the founders of the cathedral, is almost certainly one of the 24 elders represented at the bottom of the great east window (I 1b) of 1405–8 and in the series of legendary and historic figures representing Northern Christianity in the western choir clerestory of c.1410–20 (SX 3d–4d); see French 1995, 138. The clerestory figure is wrongly identified as King Arigurus in Harrison 1922, 367. St Edmund, the 9th century king of the East Angles, was the focus of much devotion in York. The Minster owned relics of the saint and an altar was dedicated to him in the cathedral. For representations of him in York see Davidson and O'Connor 1978, 152–3.

6. The blazon is confirmed by Torre (see p.563). The nearest approximation to this shield recorded in the medieval period is Or a chevron between 3 fleurs de lis gules (MENYS and ORANNGE); Woodcock, Grant and Graham 1996, 340.

7. Ibid., 339. Torre (see p.563) attributes this shield to what sounds like a related family, Pixwell. A variant coat, Argent a

chevron between 3 fleurs de lys sable, is used by both Dixwell and Pixwell (Papworth and Morant 1874, 420).

8. Woodcock, Grant and Graham (1996), 398 and 410. For Dockwra himself see Gayre 1956, 30–1.

9. Torre (see p.563) describes the cross as fourchy but, as Harrison points out (1924, 201) draws what looks like a cross moline (WEMME); Papworth and Morant 1874, 620. Given the other two shields represented, it is possible that the device is related to the cross of Malta or the cross of eight points used by the Knights of St John; Berry c.1830, Vol.I (unpaginated) and Vol.III, pl.XXXII, fig.21.

10. The Ts were presumably for Thomas Dockwra whose arms adorned the hanging.

11. The fact that Torre did not blazon the shield suggests that it was probably not a proper heraldic device. Despite some of the shapes it does not appear to be connected with the Arma Christi. Perhaps it was a merchant's mark or some similar device.

Other college buildings

By S. Rees Jones and J.D. Richards

Apart from the standing buildings of hall, chapel and gatehouse it is difficult to ascribe particular functions to the various excavated structures. In most cases only the foundation sills of the timber-framed buildings have survived; floor levels have frequently been disturbed by later activity and ground plans are often incomplete. The movement of deposits across the site means that the distribution of particular classes of finds are of little help. Similarly, the presence of stable manure does not guarantee that the associated structure was a stable. Positioning in relation to known buildings, as well as internal fittings, helps identify the college kitchen and brewhouse, and various latrines. In one case (Building 27) the evidence for a stone superstructure and internal shelving suggests an identification of this building with the college evidence room or library. In most cases, however, all that can be said is that the presence of internal hearths suggests that a building was intended to be occupied.

Nevertheless, from the early 14th century many new sources of documentary evidence in the surviving account rolls of the college make it possible to discuss the maintenance and daily use of each part of the college in some detail. The account rolls record the administrative duties of the chief officials of the college who had particular responsibility for maintaining those parts of the college which were used in common by all the vicars. The common hall, kitchens, chapel, gardens and workshops are therefore the best recorded. In the 15th century these miscellaneous repairs to Bedern buildings are generally less well recorded, partly because of internal changes in the system of accounting. Much less can be gleaned about the nature of the vicars' houses. These were the responsibility of their occupants and, although referred to in some vicars' wills, are scarcely ever mentioned in the common accounts of the college.

The kitchen block

The first college kitchen was presumably that described in 1360 as lying next to the chapel, when 500 stavebrodd (a type of nail) were bought for the *coquina iuxta capellam* (YMA, VC 6/2/19). Although there is no earlier reference, it can be assumed that the kitchen was probably one of the first college buildings, contemporary with the hall. However, since there has never been the opportunity to excavate the area around the chapel, the precise location and nature of the first kitchen has never been ascertained. Documentary sources indicate that it was maintained into the second half of the 14th century. In 1363 two painters were paid for eight days' work in the kitchen of Bedern (Harrison 1952, 118).

In the late 14th century, when the hall was relocated in the second courtyard to the south-west, the kitchen was moved at the same time (Period 7, pp.475–6). Both kitchen and buttery were now located to the south-east of the hall, with access to them being provided by a screens passage. As far as the kitchen was concerned access also involved a short journey through an open yard. It is perhaps the new kitchen that was being completed when, c.1381–9, Richard Pert was paid 8d for working on one *silour* (possibly a ceiling, panelling, canopy or carving) within the Bedern kitchen (YMA, VC 6/2/32). At the same time 28d was spent on seven days' work on the 'gutter' in the Bedern kitchen, possibly the excavated tile-lined drain (6175) identified in the first phase of construction of the new kitchen (Period 7 Phase 1, p.476). During the same period 100 *walltiles* were bought for a gutter in Bedern, at a cost of 6d, plus 1d for carriage. In 1392 or 1397–8, 2s 3d was spent on making one *synk* in the Bedern kitchen (YMA, VC 6/2/40).

It is likely that the kitchen block also included the college bakehouse, which is separately referred to in the Chamberlains' accounts for 1392 or 1397–8. In 1403–4, Robert Plumer (a plumber) was paid 3s 10d for 6½ stone of lead for covering two pot cauldrons in the kitchen of the common hall (YMA, VC 6/2/42). The excavation revealed that the kitchen facilities were frequently reorganised during the late 14th and early 15th century, with a gradual expansion of the number of ovens. In 1471–2, 15d was paid to Blayklok and his servant for 1½ days (work) *super clibaun in Bederna* (YMA, VC 6/6/3). This is probably from *clebanus* meaning oven or furnace, although the source does not say where the oven was. There is a later reference to the kitchen block south-east of the screens passage being leased from before 1650, when it was described as 'consisting of two rooms below — a kitchen and a buttery called the College Kitchen and Buttery and another low room with three chambers over the same'. This is not the excavated kitchen, but Buildings 25 and 27 which remained standing until the late 19th century, by which time they had become a notorious slum (see p.655).

By the late 14th century the college brewhouse was somewhere in Bartle Yard, since it is mentioned as a boundary for property running back from Goodramgate (p.389). In the 16th century Building 35 may be interpreted as a brewhouse (p.527). In 1403–4 the college plumber, Robert Plumer, was apparently employed to do some work on the malt heaters, and 3s 11d was paid to him for one lead gutter *in t' le mawtischawves* (YMA, VC 6/2/42). Between 1419 and 1421, £1 3s 9d was spent on repairs to the brewhouse which required 18 loads of tiles, sand, clay, kerbstones, lead, plaster, two vats and a barrel (YMA, VC 1/1; Harrison 1952, 161). The brewhouse also had a garden with a wall repaired in 1460 and 1470, possibly the later yard.

The counting house

By the 15th century a counting house, or treasury, had been constructed, and possibly a library and evidence room, although these may have been the same building. An evidence house was plundered during the Commonwealth, when the college was temporarily dissolved, and fitted out for meetings in 1725 (RCHMY 5, 57). Records in the Statute Book for 1419–22 (YMA, VC 1/1) suggest that repairs to the counting house were a major project during this period. Twenty shillings was received from Robert Lassell for *le selouring* (ceiling or panelling) of the *countynghous*. Of this, 16d went to Richard Plasterer for plaster and labour; 5d for 500 small nails for *le selouring*; 5s 6d to a sawer for *8 draght in les wanscott with 1 sole pete*; and 8s 8d for new glass and for mending old. Finally, Will Wright and Adam Brame were paid 13s for *le soling* and *remoying le Wall* and *seling .... le countynghous* for 2 weeks and one day.

It is not possible to identify this building with certainty, but it is suggested that it may have been Building 27. This is the only structure within the excavated area, apart from the hall and chapel, which was built from stone from the outset. Furthermore, it was constructed in the late 14th or early 15th century in a central location adjacent to the new communal hall and service wing. The nature of the fittings excavated within Building 27 suggests that it had a sustained use of a particular kind over a long period of time. It also appears to have been a two-storey building. The surprising and disproportionate thickness of the walls, the single and somewhat awkward access, the shelving or benches around the sides of the room, and the presumed use of braziers, all suggest that Building 27 was used for some secure storage purpose. This may have included storage of the college records and valuable books for use in the hall, as well as the college treasury. It is perhaps unlikely that the vicars would have split their valuables between two locations, although the possibility remains that either the library or treasury was outside the excavation, or is simply unidentified.

The latrines and longhouse

During the 13th century there appear to have been a number of open wattle-lined pits within the college precinct. Some were open latrine pits, although some may have been provided with wooden superstructures.

From at least the early 14th century the main latrine of the college appears to have been sited at the south-west edge of the college precinct. There are references in 1310 and 1319 to a fence between Bedern and the land of the priory of Newburgh (see Fig.188, p.387), and further references in 1328–9 to the fence behind the latrine (YMA, VC 6/2/1, 2, 4 and 10). The latrine is therefore identifiable as lying beyond the 23m long fence line, represented by post-holes, constructed in Period 5 on the south-west side of the precinct which defines an area of unknown extent, but included a line of four cess pits. It was probably of relatively solid construction. Materials purchased in 1304 suggest it was made of boards nailed to upright posts, the whole being daubed with clay or 'lute', a composition of clay or cement used as a waterproof sealant (YMA, VC 6/2/1).

In 1310 expenditure is recorded on mending the fence (*palitium*) between Bedern and land of the prior of Newburgh, including boards for covering the fence around the curtilage and buying 50 withies of clay for this fence and the small fence next to the latrine (YMA, VC 6/2/2). In 1319, 22s 11½d was spent on the fence in the garden behind the latrine (YMA, VC 6/2/4). Finally, in 1328–9, work was done on the 'fence behind the latrine, and at the entrance of the same and between us and the priory of Newburgh'. *Thakbords* were purchased, and men employed in daubing the fence towards the land of the prior of Newburgh and the hall, and for placing piles under the fence next to the entrance to the orchard, for daubing the fence behind the latrine, and for carrying away dung from the fence towards Aldwark (YMA, VC 6/2/10).

The archaeological evidence suggests that the fence line ceased to exist in Period 6 and the early part of Period 7 before being re-established in Period 7 Phase 2b during the first half of the 15th century. During the second half of the 14th century a latrine block in the college appears to have become known as the longhouse. This was probably a building which mid 15th century sources suggest was set back from the close on its north-east side. The north-east end of the longhouse, four yards long, was leased from 1723 and the whole building was leased from 1744, and soon afterwards pulled down. Repairs are mentioned intermittently from 1470 to 1744 (e.g. YMA, VC 6/6/3). A building labelled 'Long House', c.16m (north-west/south-east) × 4m, aligned north-west/south-east, is marked on a plan of 1851 (see Fig.349, p.636), set back from the line of Bedern by c.20m. As such it would have been outside the exca-

vated area, to the north-east of Area 14.IV, north-east of Buildings 16 and 21, but possibly reached by the passageway running north-east from Building 16 in Period 7.

This longhouse building probably served as the common latrine of the college, as the frequent need to cleanse it suggests; the Long Room at New College, Oxford, which still stands, was built in the late 14th century for this purpose. In 1360 two carpenters were paid 4d for mending *le Langhus* (YMA, VC 6/2/19). In 1362, 2d was paid for cleaning the longhouse (YMA, VC 6/2/21), and in 1362–3, 4d was spent on mending the lock (YMA, VC 6/2/22). In 1389–90 the janitor was employed on 'work on the langhows and other necessary things' (YMA, VC 6/2/33). At some stage in the 1390s one tiler and a boy were paid for work 'around' the longhouse. This involved five loads of daub and six loads of lute for the gutter (YMA, VC 6/2/35). In 1395 the padlock needed mending again and Will Porter was paid 1d for one night's work in the longhouse (YMA, VC 6/2/36), presumably because the dung was cleaned out by night.

It appears, however, that this was not the sole latrine used by the college. A number of individual stone- and brick-lined latrine pits were constructed from the late 14th century, during Period 7. The hall and kitchen, in particular, still needed their own facilities.

The close

The main college buildings were originally built around a central courtyard, Bedern Close, into which the entry from Goodramgate opened. If the medieval length of the close was the same as that preserved until Bedern was knocked through in 1852 then it would have been some 50m in length. It is likely that this layout was defined at least as early as Period 4 or Period 5, in the late 13th or early 14th century. In Period 5 Building 5 was shortened at its south-east end and would now have corresponded in length to the north-east side of the close. On the south-west side Building 14 was built back from the later street frontage, suggesting that the close was then at least 12m wide at the south-east end (see Fig.210, p.435). That width was preserved until the later 14th century when, in Period 7.2b, Building 24 encroached upon the close, narrowing it to 7·5m (Fig.248, p.487). The diagonal passageway which, from Period 4, ran along the side of Building 11 to Building 10, and later (Period 7.2b) ran between Buildings 17 and 24, would have provided access to those buildings to the south from the south-east corner of the close. The dimensions of Bedern Close may be compared with the surviving close at Wells, where there were 42 houses, which today comprises a roadway 141m (462ft) long by 17–19·8m (56–65ft) wide.

It appears that the close was grassed, with a pavement and gutter around the outside. In 1312 the Chamberlains' rolls record that two men were paid for making a pavement for seven days, including the purchase of gravel. They also made a 'bed' of rushes before the postern gate and made a gutter, for which clay was bought (YMA, VC 6/2/7). In 1312–13 two small planks were bought for the Bedern gutter and a capping? (*capit*) was made for the same. Gravel was brought for raising the road within the close before the door of Geoffrey Poncyn and J. de Wirethorp (YMA, VC 6/2/8). The state of the courtyard was of regular concern to the vicars throughout the 14th century, and needed frequent attention. In 1328–9, for example, it needed to be cleaned of dung and other '*inhonestis*' (YMA, VC 6/2/10). In 1343 there was a complaint that tree-trunks had been deposited on the pavement of Bedern which bordered the long plot of grass occupying the whole of the central space of the close, 'to the dishonouring of the place and the imminent risk to those who might move about the courtyard at night-time' (Harrison 1952, 49). Orders were given that the trees should be removed and that any vicar who should leave a brazier on the path should also remove it within eight days. The vicars were certainly assiduous in their concern for the appearance of the close. In 1421 John Hickling (vicar 1393–1432, and sub-chanter 1414–19 and 1422–32) was cited to answer a charge that he dug and carried away, from Clifton, near York, earth to the value of £20. Harrison (1952, 41) suggests that the earth was needed for renewing the middle of the close following building operations so that the soil could be sown with fresh grass-seed.

The south-western courtyard, gardens and orchard

When the vicars first acquired the site of their college in Bedern in the mid 13th century it included a substantial amount of open undeveloped land. St Andrewgate was described as a toft in the late 12th century and 9A and B Goodramgate included gardens and an orchard as well as houses and other buildings by the mid 13th century.

Although at least some of the original vicars' houses had their own gardens, the vicars created a common garden, which was subdivided through the centuries to provide gardens for houses without them, or for plots attached to newly built houses. From mentions in the leases this garden apparently formed an L-shaped area to the north-east and south-east of the backs of the Bedern buildings, some 30m wide, and with arms 40m and 60m long. If this is so then the main garden would have been largely outside the excavated area, to the north-east of Building 5, and subsequently largely below the continuation of Bedern cut through to St Andrewgate, although part of the south-eastern arm may have been excavated to the south-east of the Period 7 garden wall (p.477; see Fig.235, p.478). From the late 14th century there was also an open courtyard area south-west of the new hall. Excavation has shown that this was extensively pitted and was much used for the dumping of domestic refuse, although a gravelled path ran across it from north-west to south-east. The fence, which was constantly being repaired (p.577), would have marked the south-west perimeter of the precinct (see Fig.210, p.435).

Payments for work done in the garden recorded in the Chamberlains' rolls suggest a fairly ornamental garden, with raised beds and walkways. However, the garden also performed a practical function and the vicars planted various vegetables and herbs, and also cultivated a small vineyard (p.620). The vicars also bought in seedlings as well as growing vegetables from seed. There are references to a number of ditches which may have served to divide areas of the garden as well as being used for drainage. At any rate the gardens must have been enclosed as the various references to fencing and to locks bought for the garden and orchard doors suggest.

In 1328–9 two workmen were paid 2s 4d for 4½ days' work in the garden, including making an arbour (*herbarium*) and elevating the garden. There were further payments for making two ditches, for cleaning ditches of earth and dung, and for digging and planting seed in the garden (YMA, VC 6/2/10). It was also necessary to purchase a spade and a shovel, turf for the arbour, and drinks for the workers (Harrison 1952, 37). In 1403–4 there is a further payment for making a *herbarium* in the common garden (YMA, VC 6/2/42).

From at least the early 14th century there was an orchard walled off within the garden. In 1312, 27s 11d was spent on the fence around the orchard of Bedern, including the purchase of 250 boards, 500 stotnails, 500 chaknails, spireings and thaknails (YMA, VC 6/2/7). In 1395 there is a reference to a house in the corner of the apple orchard (YMA, VC 6/2/36).

Within the college gardens there were at least two wells, from which the vicars derived their water supply. The first is recorded as being to the north (RCHMY 5, 57). It is probably that for which a cord was bought in 1312–13 (YMA, VC 6/2/8), and replaced in 1352 (YMA, VC 6/2/15) and 1380 (YMA, VC 6/2/30). In 1363, 12d was spent on its repair (Harrison 1952, 118). Sometime between 1381 and 1391 a bucket was bought for the well and ligatures for the bucket (YMA, VC 6/2/32). A barrel-lined well was observed in Bedern north-east (Area 14.II) but, as it appears to have gone out of use in Period 1, truncated by a ditch, it must be assumed that this was not associated with the college, and that the Bedern well was outside the excavated area, in the gardens to the north-east of Building 5.

The second well was constructed in the garden south-west of the hall in 1401, presumably as a more convenient supply of water for the Period 7 kitchen block. This was a major project, incurring a total cost of £1 16s 11d for materials and £2 5s 5d for labour. The materials included 4 tonnes (barrels), garthes, mosse, doublespiking, middlespiking, making one *wymbilbite*, wainscots, *plat hupes et gugeons* of iron bought for the wheel/winding gear (*rot*), cobills for pavement, *ways* (?), thaktiles, stavebroddes, 2 bushells of plaster, ligatures, crokes and joints (all ironwork). The work extended over a period from the week including the feast of St Michael to the week of the feast of All Saints, that is, throughout October (YMA, VC 6/2/41). No trace of the barrel-lined phase of this well was found, but in Period 8 a brick-lined structure was sunk in the courtyard south-west of the hall, later referred to as the well near the dung hill in Back Bedern. This presumably removed all trace of its barrel-lined predecessor. A barrel-lined well was examined in detail during the excavation of the neighbouring Foundry site (p.169, Fig.72, *AY* 10/3).

The vicars' houses

The early date of the foundation of the college and the continued use of the term *cubiculi* for the vicars' residences may suggest that the first Bedern was designed according to monastic principles with the vicars sleeping in a dorter divided into cubicles by partitions of wood or later, perhaps, stone. The chamberlains' accounts of 1319 and 1328–9 refer to two halls within the college — the common hall, which is presumed to have been the main dining hall (see below), and the *magna aula*, which may correspond with Building 5 to the north-east of Bedern Close. If this is so then the payment of 8s in 1328–9 for the stopping up of the wall of the great hall with stone (see p.539) may refer to alterations to Building 5 represented by its subdivision or shortening in Period 5 (p.434). Just possibly, the *magna aula* may represent the original dorter and the reference of 1328–9 may record part of the process by which it was gradually replaced by a row of individual houses or rooms.

During the 14th century, therefore, the vicars may have occupied individual rooms as at Lincoln and elsewhere. It is clear that by the post-medieval period the vicars had small individual houses, probably two-storeyed with two rooms on each floor. The houses were occupied rent-free, and Harrison suggests that the community was responsible for repairs to the houses, although there is little evidence in the college's financial accounts of such work being carried out. In fact the evidence cited by Harrison suggests that the college took responsibility for repairing and upgrading vicars' houses only when they were vacant. When the houses were occupied, the vicars themselves were expected to maintain them in a satisfactory condition (Harrison 1952, 39).

As well as taking responsibility for minor repairs, it is evident that vicars living in Bedern furnished their own houses. Larger items, such as writing desks and windows, were the responsibility of the college (ibid.), but the surviving wills of vicars choral before 1500 show that most had furnishings to bequeath as well as clothes, books and other personal items. Virtually all had beds and bed linen, and several mention table linen and equipment. Usually these items were bequeathed to personal household servants or to other friends and relatives. Occasionally they were bequeathed to the common hall, as in the case of dominus John Crome (d.1414) who left to Bedern Hall his best table cloth, towel and lavatrum with bowl (YMA, L2/4 fo.173v). Others left similar gifts to the hall. Dominus John Tanfield (d.1492) left 40s for painting the cloth hangings in Bedern Hall (YMA, L2/4 fo.377v), and a few vicars refer to similar hangings in their houses. Many vicars' wills give the impression of men living in some comfort and, perhaps not surprisingly, a number owned quite elaborate ecclesiastical objects. Both objects and money were often bequeathed to Bedern Chapel. Dominus Robert Gillesland (d.1471), for example, left 3s 4d for repair of the Chapel of Holy Trinity in Bedern (YMA, L2/4 fo.325).

By the 15th century it is also apparent that vicars living in Bedern might rent small pieces of garden from the college. The first such garden rental is recorded in 1415 (YMA, VC 6/2/44), and by the 1470s at least three vicars are recorded as renting additional plots within Bedern (YMA, VC 6/2/62, 63). Of course by this date the college no longer supported 36 vicars and some of the rents paid might represent vicars renting extra living space. Yet it is perhaps unlikely that there was ever room for 36 houses within Bedern proper. When the college was at its largest some vicars may well have lived outside the main Bedern Close. In 1378 two vicars are listed as tenants in Little Bedern in Goodramgate to the north of the main college site, and in subsequent years it is also possible to find one or two vicars living in other properties owned by the college within the Minster Close or in a property known as Cambhallgarth opposite Bedern in Goodramgate (YMA, VC 6/2/28 et seq.). Such non-residence was perhaps only ever a problem for a minority of the college members but it does vividly illustrate the difficulties which the college faced in maintaining a common life as expected standards of privacy and housing for the vicars rose in the 14th century, culminating in the spiritual and physical reformation of the college in the 1390s (see p.582).

It is impossible to connect the properties traceable back by leases from the present day with the medieval vicars' houses. The houses are identified in the records by the current occupant, not by their position in the close, and it was customary, certainly later, for vicars to move to a more convenient or attractive house when it was vacated by the death or resignation of its tenant. Although it seems probable that the properties recorded on the 1852 Ordnance Survey map (Fig.263, facing p.505), each about 4·6m (15ft) wide, fronting onto the street, represent the position of vicars' houses, and some leases can be traced back to occupation by vicars before the Civil War, continuity from before the Reformation cannot be established with certainty.

One document which throws light on the late medieval arrangements is an agreement of 23 August 1408 whereby one vicar, Robert of Skelton, granted to another, Richard of Sutton, a piece of land at the east end of Bedern. This was 7 ells long from Skelton's house to the common garden, and 4 ells wide from Nicholas Wych's house on the south to the common entry to the garden on the north. At the same time Sutton was granted a further plot on which to build a study, 3 ells long from the common garden to Skelton's garden and 2 ells wide from Sutton's house to Wych's house. If the study was not built Sutton was to erect a fence 4 ells high between the gardens and this plot. This agreement suggests that at the east end of the close there were at least three houses side by side with gardens behind, the common garden beyond and an entry to it on the north, an arrangement still preserved in part in the 19th century when one house had an extension to the south-west around which an entry ran, perhaps representing Sutton's study (YMA, VC 1/1).

The common hall of the vicars choral (Figs.321–33, 388s, 390s)

The common hall was probably the most important of all the college buildings in promoting the collegiate identity of the vicars. All the administrative and disciplinary meetings of the college's governing body took place in the hall, and it was there that the vicars entertained all important guests, and even traders and workmen. It was also in the hall that the vicars assembled daily for their shared meals, and it was the place where they might meet each other for conversation over a few drinks in the evening. The practice of taking meals in common was enormously important in maintaining the common life of the college. It was, in a sense, one of the original reasons for establishing the college, so that every vicar might have accommodation and regular, sober meals away from the temptations of the secular city. Improving works were read at supper, and unexplained absences from the table were punishable by fines. To this extent the continuity of assembly within the common hall was used as a measure of the maintenance of the college spirit.

Prior to the mid 14th century the use of the term *aula*, or hall, alone was ambivalent. It was used as often to describe a whole residence, as it was to describe the open hall which was the focus of most households. Thus many of the early student communities of Oxford and Cambridge were known as halls, and the hall of the vicars choral of St Paul's, London, mentioned in 1273, may also refer to a complete residence (*VCH* 1909). From the early 14th century, however, the use of the term common hall (*aula communis*) is used to describe the central dining and meeting chamber alone. In London, in 1353, the minor canons of St Paul's acquired a plot of land for the construction of a 'common hall' in order that 'they might dine together for their mutual honour' (Dugdale 1818, 341–2). The hall was to form a nucleus for a new collegiate-style residence for the minor canons. For, although previously they had lived dispersed around the cathedral close, by 1353 five minor canons had already moved to houses adjoining the site of the new common hall (Brooke 1957, 74; Stow 1603, 327).

Among the communities of vicars choral the common hall was also often the first college building to be completed. In Lincoln, the common hall was completed by 1309, and in Wells by 1348 (Maddison 1878, 8; Rodwell 1982, 212). In Chichester, as in some university colleges, the vicars may have been housed temporarily in the old Guilden Hall in South Street in 1394–6, before construction work started on their close houses and the Guilden Hall itself was rebuilt to provide their common hall (Hannah 1914, 99; Tatton-Brown 1994). In Salisbury the vicars choral had no common buildings until 1409 when they were granted a former canonry house, which they adapted to form a common hall and a small courtyard surrounded by chambers on two floors (RCHME 1993, 88–96).

In York, a common hall would also have been one of the first requirements of the new college. In most of the colleges of vicars choral the hall occupied a prominent position. In Wells it is over the gatehouse and in Exeter it was directly opposite the entrance.

In York the surviving hall stands in the centre of the building complex and dominated the quadrangle to the south-west developed in the late14th century. However, this building probably stands on a different site from any 13th or early 14th century predecessor.

The common hall of the vicars in York is first mentioned in 1319 in a reference in the Chamberlains' accounts to the common cellar, and again in 1328–9 when extensive repairs were carried out, including the replacement of the iron and lead fittings of the door and windows and the repair of the main entrance door with *estrichboards*, a type of broad planking. A number of these planks and long boards were also purchased for the benches of the hall and 26 *stauntions* (the largest timbers, often using whole tree trunks and serving as the major supports of timber-framed buildings and roofs) were brought in for the repair of the ceiling. William Birchford, carpenter, worked there for three weeks making the step of the door (*gradu ostio*) and doing other jobs. Tiles were also bought from Beverley for this and a mason employed (YMA, VC 6/2/4 and 10).

It is clear from the Chamberlains' rolls that the common hall incorporated a cellar, probably at ground level or partially below ground level. In 1328–9 six iron crokes were bought for the entrance to the common cellar, and a mason was employed to mend the foundations of the cellar wall. The hall and cellar were cleaned when the work was completed. In 1331–2 the vicars were again mending the common cellar, using boards, iron bands, one lock and estrichebord (YMA, VC 6/2/11). In 1352 crokes, hasps and staples were bought for the door of the cellar (YMA, VC 6/2/15).

The location of a first hall of the 13th or early 14th century is perhaps suggested by the earliest reference to the Bedern kitchen, in 1360, which describes it as lying next to the chapel (YMA, VC 6/2/19). Since the chapel lay inside the gateway on the south-west side of the close (Fig.292, p.540) the original hall cannot have lain far away for it was the universal common domestic arrangement of the period that the hall should be separated from the kitchens by only a small yard or short passage (Willis and Clark 1886, 373–4). This might suggest that the first hall lay on the south-west side of the close, on or near the site of the present chapel. However, the extant hall is dated by dendrochronology to c.1370 (see p.602). It is known that this building was built up against an earlier structure identified as a buttery (Building 25, Period 7.1) which was presumably constructed to service an earlier hall on the site of the present one. This earlier hall has left no trace, but may have been wholly timber-framed. Unless it had an extremely short life the reference to the kitchen in 1360 cannot, therefore, be taken to indicated the location of the hall at that time.

The new hall

The dendrochronological date for the rafters in the roof of the standing hall (c.1370) is supported by the style-critical analysis of the architectural details of the vault and of the window tracery (see p.595). Archaeology indicates that a new kitchen was constructed a little earlier, being attached to the south-east side of the buttery building.

There is scant evidence for the date of the new hall and kitchen in the Chamberlains' accounts, which only record regular repairs to college property. For any major new work the vicars would have opened a separate fund and kept special accounts for it, as they did when they redeveloped major sites outside Bedern. Unfortunately, no such accounts for buildings in Bedern have survived. The reference to clearance of rubble from the door of the common hall in 1399, and payment for over two weeks' work tiling the roof of the hall in undated fragmentary accounts of the 1390s, must indicate repair work (YMA, VC 6/2/34, 38, 40).

The *compotus* roll of the Repairer, Elias de Walk-ington, survives for the year 1383, and this indicates major building activity in the college. The vicars were buying large quantities of timber from Snayth (presumably Snaith near Goole, East Riding of Yorkshire) which they paid to have shipped up the Ouse and then carried to the college. Though the hall is not mentioned, the vicars were evidentially building, and probably roofing, something quite substantial at that time. On the other hand, we know that the vicars kept lots of building materials in Bedern which were not necessarily used in the college itself.

Evidence for the date of new building in the college is the application made by the vicars in 1394 for the appropriation of the church of St Sampson in York in order that they might resume 'living together and keeping common house in the hall' (*Cal.Pat. 1391–6*, 386). At this date the vicars could not claim absolute poverty, as they had on earlier occasions in 1331 and 1349, for by 1390 they had enjoyed 30 years of unprecedented prosperity which marked the height of their economic fortunes. Harrison assumed that the grant of 1394 meant that the vicars had abandoned life in Bedern altogether (Harrison 1952, 32). This seems unlikely as there are frequent references to life in Bedern in the 1370s and 1380s. Indeed, as mentioned above, the new stone-built hall was constructed c.1370. Nevertheless, there was always a tendency for vicars to establish independent households and to fail to attend regularly in the common hall. The construction of the new hall in York slightly preceded the attempt to reform the communal life of the college, represented by a new set of statutes governing the domestic life of the college, which were issued in c.1390–1430 (ibid., 52–8), and also preceded attempts elsewhere in England in the 1380s and 1390s to reform and establish colleges of secular clergy in the cathedrals (see p.384).

Even at the height of the vicars' prosperity such reforms, outwardly expressed in the construction of a new courtyard, would have been an expensive undertaking, and it does seem at least possible that the application for St Sampson's church was made to help finance this project, which would indeed have succeeded in promoting the quality of life at the common table of the college. The application was successful, and the church was confirmed to the vicars by letter patent on 1 March 1393/4. The settlement of subsequent disputes among the vicars further emphasises the link between this church and the maintenance of the common hall, for it was settled that the revenues from the church were not to be used for absentee vicars, but were to be applied first for the use of vicars dining together in the hall, and that only the residue was to be used for other purposes such as the repair of the vicars' estates (*Cal.Pat. 1391–6*, 712; *Cal.Pat. 1399–1401*, 172). The vicars of York were not the only community to find the cost of maintaining a common table prohibitive. The vicars of Exeter, although provided with a hall and kitchens in 1388 for the purpose of dining in common, never in fact did so because of a lack of resources (Orme 1981, 87).

Architectural description

By D.A. Stocker

The building known as Bedern Hall (Fig.321) is a major domestic hall built on a near rectangular plan, c.13·9 × 9·2m (45 × 30ft), of stone and timber with a large, decorative, timber roof covered, latterly, in modern tile. The north-east and (originally) the south-west walls are of fine Magnesian Limestone ashlar. The north-west wall is also mostly of stone (though the gable is brick) but the south-east wall is of a half-timber construction (recased in brick in the 19th century).

The north-west wall was originally of limestone ashlar, but by 1978 many localised areas of repair were visible and the gable had been completely re-built in brickwork. This gable was evidently rebuilt in the later 18th or 19th century, perhaps when the first floor was inserted. The lower parts of the north-west wall were featureless in 1979, except for a large garage-sized door at the south-western end. Unlike the stonework of the north-east and south-west walls, however, the stonework at the north-western end contained at least six re-used fragments of moulding and many other less distinctive re-used items (pp.285–6, AY 10/4).

The lower part of the western corner of the hall had been almost completely replaced in brick. The original simple chamfered plinth survived below the modern ground level, however, as it did around most of the north-western part of the building (see pp.480–1; Fig.233, facing p.473). There were originally three windows in the south-west wall, which had also been punctured at a number of other points, and had two additional windows and a double door inserted in its upper parts. The additional window towards the north-western end had destroyed the head of a large, original window in this position, although a short length of the lower part of its south-eastern jamb survived intact in the lower part of the wall. The doorway destroyed the upper parts of the original window located in the centre of the south-west wall, though parts of its south-east jamb survived buried in later masonry (Figs.322–4).

On the ground floor a crude doorway had been pushed through the sill of the north-westernmost of the original windows in the south-west wall. At the north-west end, in the lower zone of the wall, a mod-ern doorway communicating with the 19th century factory building to the south-west had been driven through at a point of some structural complexity. Originally, we now know, there was a projecting bay in this location (Fig.321). The clearest evidence for this projecting bay is still contained within the wall. There is a tall narrow opening in the interior skin of the wall spanned by a cusped segmental arch-head composed originally of three very large stones (Fig.333, p.593). Still trapped within the thickness of the wall are the stub-ends of five stones from an elaborately decorated vault (described in greater detail below). This projecting bay was cut off and the opening into the hall blocked with brick at a relatively early stage in the post-medieval history of the hall.

The post-medieval sequence here is quite complex and would seem to be as follows. First, the projecting bay was demolished and replaced, perhaps in the mid 17th century. At this stage the medieval vault would have been dismantled. The opening between the hall and the bay was walled up leaving only a small doorway which gave access into a new brick-built structure on the site of the medieval bay which re-used parts of its foundations (see Fig.241, p.481). The north-west wall of this brick structure was itself re-used in the north-west wall of the 19th century factory building and the doorway was subsequently widened, but it is unclear at what stage the other two walls of the post-medieval brick structure were demolished.

From what survives it is clear that the medieval projecting bay was originally quite tall and narrow (see Fig.331, p.592). We know how wide it was (1·5m internally; 2·4m externally) from the location of the internal archway and from observations made in 1979–80, but we have no excavated evidence for the location of its south-western wall. However, the location of this wall can be pinpointed exactly because we are able accurately to reconstruct the vaulted ceiling over the bay. The bay was vaulted with a highly decorated stone ceiling (of which elements survive in situ) and which, although carved to look like a structural vault with ribs and webs, was probably composed of nineteen interlocking stones (Fig.332, p.592). The stub-ends of five of these stones remain embedded in the wall, where they were recorded in 1980. A further two stones which are undoubtedly from the same vault are now in the Yorkshire Museum, whilst two more were discovered in a garden at No.23 Stonegate by Dr C. Wilson and the author

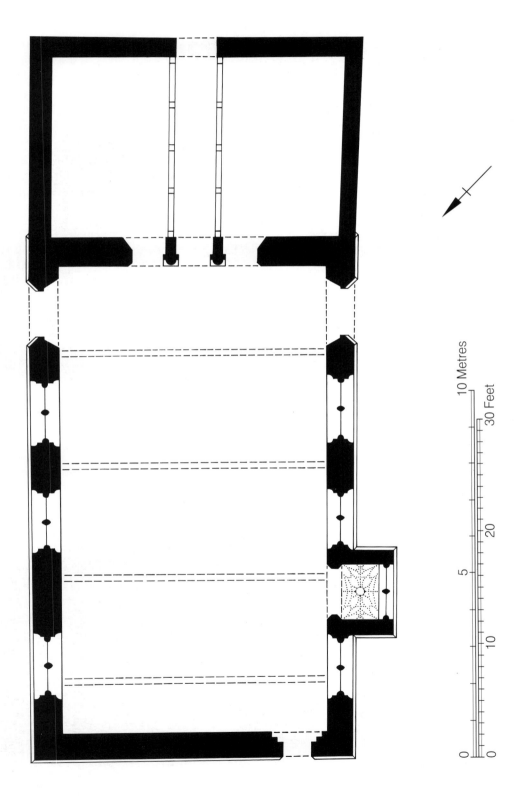

10 Metres

30 Feet

0   5   10   20

0

Fig.321   Reconstruction of the medieval plan of Bedern Hall and its service range (Building 25, at right). Scale 1:100

Fig.322 (above) Bedern Hall from
the south-west before restoration

Fig.323 (right) Bedern Hall from
the south-west after restoration

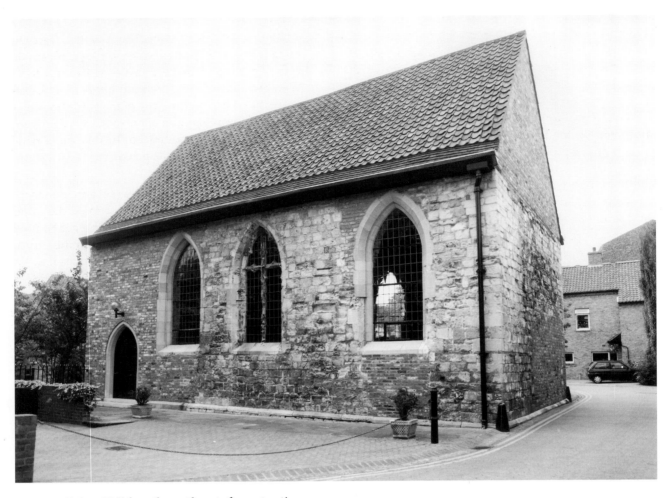

Fig.324 Bedern Hall from the north-east after restoration

in 1979 (Fig.330, p.591). These nine stones can be drawn out and the exact dimensions of the missing vault calculated (Fig.332, p.592). From these calculations it is clear that the projection was of rectangular plan and (presuming a uniform wall thickness — a narrow 0·37m) extended 2·15m beyond the south-west wall. The buried remains of the south-east and north-west walls of the projection were noted in 1979, along with a stone-flagged floor, which may have been the original floor of the bay. None of this evidence, however, was recorded in detail. The projecting bay did not extend to the full height of the hall as there is the trace of a weathering mark against the south-west wall, above the level of the vault stubs which indicates a pitched roof, probably originally covered with tiles (Fig.391s).

In architectural-historical terms the vault is an important discovery. It is not quite a true 'fan' vault, as its springers are not based on a truly semicircular

plan, but the miniature panel at the base of each springing does give rise to two equally sized ones above, as a true fan vault would (Leedy 1981, chapter 4). It is, instead, a miniature lierne vault into which cusped panels (as often found in true fan vaults) have been introduced. The central boss is, unfortunately, missing but would no doubt have formed an extravagant centrepiece to the ornate design. In the four springing panels at the bases of each conoid, the cusped panel is occupied by a small delicately carved lion's head mask surrounded by his mane and with a distinctive forked topknot.

There are several indications that this narrow, projecting bay (and its vault) was an original feature of the hall design. First, the plinth of the projection, which survived along its south-east and north-west walls, was continuous with the main plinth around the remainder of the hall. Secondly, both at foundation level and higher up, the surviving toothing of the north-west wall of the projection appears to be coursed in with the remainder of the south-west wall fabric. Thirdly, one in situ stone was noted in 1980 which incorporated both the jamb moulding for the north-westernmost window of the main fenestration and the return for the north-west wall of the projection. Finally, the layout of the hall itself must indicate that the projecting bay was planned from the start. The distance between the northwestern and central windows in both the north-east and south-west walls is almost double that between the central and south-eastern windows. It is most unlikely that this sort of planning eccentricity would have been introduced into a building of this quality unless some intervening feature requiring more space at this point was planned from the start.

At the south-eastern end of the south-west wall a broad modern doorway was noted in 1980, fashioned in the rebuilt brickwork. The whole of the south-eastern end of the hall had been partly recased, partly reconstructed, probably in the later years of the 19th century (to judge from the shape of the windows), perhaps when the adjacent buildings were demolished in 1879 (RCHMY 5, 60). It seems that the whole original height of the ashlar of the south-west wall was taken down, from the southern corner north-westwards for nearly 5m, and replaced in brick. This demolition removed the south-eastern jamb of the south-easternmost of the three large original windows, though its north-western jamb and part of its head have survived. Rather than tinker with the roof structure, the builders at this date retained the medieval wall fabric including the in situ framing of the upper part of the hall south-east wall.

The medieval south-east wall, trapped within its modern casing, was found to be in three parts when investigated in 1978 (Fig.234, p.474). The timber-framed gable, which is contemporary with the remainder of the hall roof structure, sits on a thin tie-beam and has a crown-post supporting a ridge purlin trapped below a thin collar. There is a socket for a longitudinal brace to the north-west for this purlin, though the brace itself was presumably removed in the last century. Other than the crown-post, the design simulates that of the other main roof trusses but with significant differences — made necessary, it would seem, by its location in the gable (Fig.234). The giant arch braces which form, in effect, principal rafters in the open trusses spring from the tie-beam here, not from

corbels below the wall-plate. These elements are tennoned into curved braces which spring from the tie-beam. Neither arch brace survived to be recorded in 1978; their location was indicated only by mortises. Above the collar the structure of the gable framing is the same as the remainder of the roof, in that the common rafters are scissor-braced. In this gable panel there is no record of ashlar pieces.

This timber-framed gable was set above a second panel of timber framing which occupied the upper half of the south-east wall. Unlike the gable, however, this panel cannot have belonged to the surviving phase of the hall; it must have related to an earlier building (i.e. Building 25, p.473). It consists of a series of studs rising from one rail and supporting a second. Alternate studs are supported by simple arched braces which are tennoned into the lower rail and into the stud about 0·3m below the upper rail. Passing through the centre of the panel are a series of horizontal pieces of minor scantling which are simply pegged into the upright components to give the impression of a single continuous horizontal member. This panel is separated from the tie supporting the gable framing by a gap of about 0·2m and it originally supported the gable panel by means of two chocks, one of which had fallen out by 1978. This is one clear indication that the two framing elements are not contemporary, the lower frame being the earlier. A second clear indication is that the bay division of the lower frame does not match the width of the present hall, whilst a third indication is provided by the observation made in 1978 that the 'chocks' were, in fact, sawn-off rafter-ends of a roof which had once risen to the south-east. These latter timbers were dovetailed into the upper rail, which must therefore be regarded as the wall-plate of an earlier building to the east of the present hall (Daniells 1979).

The timber framing in the upper part of the south-east wall was supported on a single-storeyed wall of limestone ashlar which was, until 1980, essentially of medieval fabric. This wall had been partly rebuilt (in the central third) and the remainder had been recased with modern brick both inside and out. Offset to the north there was a single large opening of post-medieval date. Investigation of the wall in 1978 and 1980 showed that the north-eastern jamb of a north-eastern doorway and the south-western jamb of a south-western doorway had survived the recasing and reconstruction (see Fig.234, p.474). These doorways were simple openings with two-centred arched heads, chamfered jambs and splayed rebates to the south-east. During the course of works in 1980 it was possible to observe the base of a central pillar which would have divided the south-westernmost door from a third, centrally placed one (Fig.325). The monolithic sub-base was rectangular in plan, with rebates for the door leaves to the south-east, but the remains of a chamfered semi-circular base sitting above it were also recorded.

The north-east wall had survived conversion into domestic and factory premises in better condition than the other three. It retained much of its original ashlar walling in its north-western parts, although a modern doorway had been forced through the sill of the north-westernmost of the three original windows here and the head of the window had also been destroyed in a brick repair. The south-easternmost of the three windows was only represented by its north-western jamb, because, exactly as on the south-west side, the south-easternmost 5m of the north-east wall had been completely rebuilt in brick and a modern door had been constructed through the brickwork at the south-eastern end. Of the medieval doorway, with a simple two-centred arched head, in this approximate

location and shown on a sketch elevation done for James Raine in 1874 (YCA, Acc.28: 38), there was no sign.

The north-east wall retained the only complete medieval window in the building and its tracery survived intact. It is placed centrally in the wall and, though very simple, the tracery is most unusual (Figs.326–7). The broad window is set under a two-centred head and has two main lights separated by a mullion rising uninterrupted from the sill to the apex of the arch-head. Two trefoiled tracery panels are created by a single transom set at the springing point of the arch-head. All four lights are decorated with cusps which, because of the rectangular arrangement of mullion and transom, are almost all at right-angles to the glazing. There is no sign that this window has been tampered with — this odd design appears to be original.

The medieval oak roof of the hall had survived the depredations of the post-medieval period with remarkably little damage (Fig.328). It is an important survival with a number of unusual features and is of four bays, plus a half bay at the north-western end. Of the three original main trusses only the north-westernmost survived intact to be recorded by the

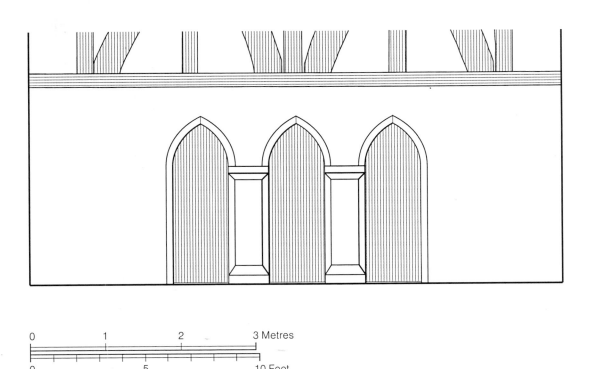

0   1   2   3 Metres

0   5   10 Feet

Fig.325   Bedern Hall: reconstruction of service doors, interior south-east wall. Scale 1:50

Fig.326 (above) *Bedern Hall: north-east wall, looking south-west, showing the only complete original window with its transom temporarily removed. Scale unit 0·5m*

Fig.327 (right) *Bedern Hall: original window in the north-east wall with the transom in place. Scale unit 0·1m*

Fig.328 (above) Bedern Hall: the roof, following reconstruction

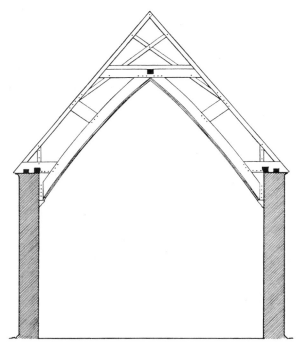

Fig.329 (left) Bedern Hall: cross-section showing main roof truss (© Crown copyright. National Monuments Record)

Fig.330 Fan vault components, originally from the Bedern Hall projecting bay. Top, from the Yorkshire Museum; bottom, from No.23 Stonegate. All four pieces are now in the Yorkshire Museum (accession codes: top, HB577 and HB578; bottom, YORYM 2001.622 and YORYM 2001.623). Reproduced by kind permission of Dr C. Wilson and the Yorkshire Museum

Royal Commission (Fig.329). That the next two trusses to the south-east were of the same form originally, however, was clear from surviving mortises in the appropriate locations.

Each truss was supported on a timber arch or giant arch brace, moulded below, which sprang from small, undecorated, stone corbels set below the cornice in the upper parts of the wall. These corbels also supported a wall-post which was tennoned into the underside of a substantial sole-plate, which was itself tennoned into the extrados of the main arch members. These sole-plates sat over the wall-plate and framed a decorative moulded cornice which ran from bay to bay. Above the cornice itself each common rafter was supported by a small ashlar piece and the Royal Commission recorded evidence that the spaces in between the ashlars were filled with plaster panels. The arch braces supported the common rafters by means of short thick struts in the middle part of the roof and by means of a heavy collar in the upper third. The arch braces were tennoned into the underside of this collar. The collar supported a chamfered collar-purlin in a rebate in its upper side and was lapped by scissor braces which connected every pair of common rafters near the ridge. The common rafters were spaced at close intervals, lapped together

at the ridge, and had all the same elements as the main trusses except for their main arches and struts.

The arrangement between the fourth bay and the half bay to the north-west was somewhat different. Here the moulding along the cornice originally turned to decorate the underside of a tie-beam crossing the roof space. The tie itself was sawn off, presumably when the floor was inserted, and any details of framing above it present in the underside of the appropriate rafters were not recorded.

In the central bay the common rafters were cut off above the collars, and the scissor braces were absent. This is clear evidence for the location of a large wooden louver in this position. All of the timbers of the roof were smoke-blackened to some extent, a feature which confirms that an open fire was provided in the hall below. Records were not made of the remains of the louver, however, and its appearance cannot be reconstructed. No records were made of the jointing techniques used or of the methods or materials originally used for covering the roof.

Reconstruction and function

As reconstructed from the information laid out above the building known as Bedern Hall was a high-

591

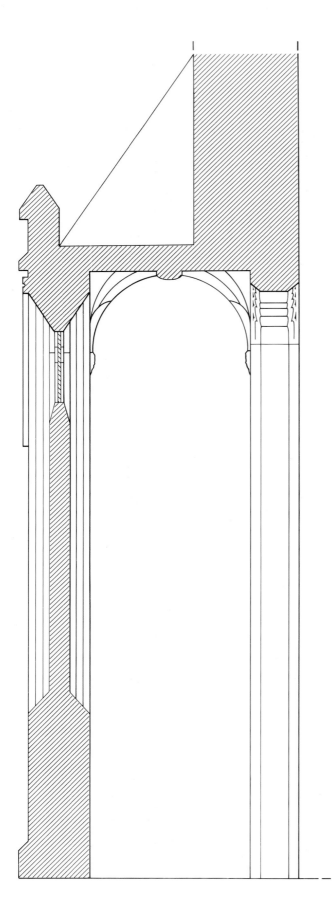

Fig.331 (left) Bedern Hall: reconstructed cross-section through the bay in the south-west wall. Scale 1:25

quality, though small, institutional hall of a well-known late medieval type. Rectangular in plan it had, as was usual, a low table end and a high table end. At the low table end (at the south-east) three quite simple doorways (Fig.325, p.588) led through to three service rooms, two of which, probably the buttery and the pantry, were contained in a rectangular cross-range. This cross-range comprised Building 25, up against the side wall of which the present hall was built (Fig.321, p.584).

In the north-east and south-west walls, at the south-eastern end of the hall, it is likely, again following the usual layout in such buildings, that there would have been doorways communicating with the outside world — one such doorway was recorded in 1874 (see p.588) — though all traces of them have now gone. In many late medieval halls a 'screens' arrangement is provided between these two doorways which divides the service doors from the body of the hall. The evidence that such a screen ever existed is now confined to a couple of crude, secondary mortises in the lower rail of the timber framing panel in the east wall. These may be evidence that a screen was in-

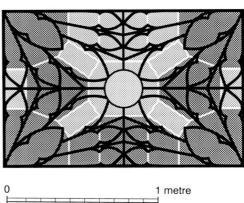

| 0 | | | | | | | | 1 metre |
| 0 | | | | | | | | 3 feet |

Fig.332 Reconstruction of the plan of the vault. The dark toned areas represent surviving pieces; the lighter areas are conjectured. Scale 1:25

Fig.333 *Bedern Hall: reconstruction of the bay and its vault, looking up into the projecting bay from inside the hall*

serted at a later date supported by braces located in these mortices, but they are not purposeful enough to suggest that it was intended from the start. In fact the traditional arrangement of screens to form a passage at the service end of the hall is thought to be a 15th century development (Wood 1965, chapter 9) and it may be that Bedern Hall was built before such arrangements had become the norm.

The hall was lit by a fine group of six two-light windows, three in each of the north-east and south-west walls (Figs.389s, 391s). Fragments remain of all six and it is clear that they were of the same type as the intact surviving example in the north-east wall (Figs.326–7), although we cannot know whether they all contained such unusual tracery.

It is likely that the projecting bay towards the north-western end of the south-west wall housed a bay window. The alternative explanation as a porch should be ruled out for several reasons. Firstly, this would be an unconventional position for a hall doorway. Secondly, the opening into the hall is 3·2m high by approximately 1·5m wide, with a segmental cusped archhead; these are unlikely details and proportions for a doorway. Finally, this archway carries no rebate or any other accommodation for a door leaf. There are, however, numbers of parallel examples of small vaulted projections from late medieval halls which are bay windows, even though they are mostly of later date (see below). In such an explanation we might expect the south-west wall of the projection to be pierced with a two-light window (perhaps with a traceried head) whilst there may have been room in the south-east and north-west walls for a tall single-light window.

This putative bay window is placed in an interesting position. Such windows are always placed in such a way that they light the high table. At Bedern the bay is placed in between the north-westernmost window and the central one, so, if we presume that its function here was to light the high table, we should conclude that the high table, probably on a dais, extended well into the centre of the hall. This is valuable information, though perhaps not unexpected. The college had 36 members in the 14th century and such a number could not be easily accommodated at a single high table set transversely across the north-west end. The location of the bay window suggests that there were two tables placed in ranks. Such deep daises which carry more than one high table are also found, for example, at Trinity College, Cambridge, and Christchurch, Oxford, and in these two cases the bay window is also separated from the high table end gable of the hall by a normal window. The vicars' rules required the vicars' warden and the other officials of the college to sit in the centre of the top table, but the others were allowed to sit anywhere (Harrison 1952, 56).

The vicars themselves, then, all dined at the high table end, presumably placing themselves above others dining in the lower parts of the hall. This represents a marked difference between the college and contemporary monastic houses, where, although the senior officers would dine at a table transversely across the 'high' end of the hall, the body of the convent would sit at tables along the two side walls set on raised 'foot-paces', with the central 'well' of the hall being left unused (Coppack 1990, 74–5). This contrast with monastic practice gives the vicars' ceremonial dining a secular feeling. Although they were living according to a 'rule', it did not, apparently, impose itself unduly on the dining arrangements.

Following monastic custom, however, it was required that one of the vicars read to the company assembled whilst dining, and for this purpose a *pulpitum* was provided (Harrison 1952, 58). The projecting bay in the south-west wall may well relate to this *pulpitum*. It is hard to see how the bay itself could have a structural pulpit built within it, like, for example, that at St Werbergh's Chester, as it is too cramped and tall relative to its width, but a wooden reading desk, placed here where the light was best, would be a very practical arrangement. Nor was it purely a practical consideration; the symbolism of the reading emerging into the hall with the light itself, enlightening the audience both literally and metaphorically, would not have been lost on contemporaries. Early bay windows were also sometimes used as serveries and so, in the light of the suggestion that the bay window housed the reading desk, it is worth noting that the rules required that not one but two vicars wait upon the rest at meals; one was to read, whilst the other served the food (Harrison 1952, 58).

Despite the reading, the 'secular' impression given by the layout of the high table would also have been reinforced by the central hearth, the presence of which, though not its exact location, is indicated by the louver in the roof. This hearth may have been the one onto which John of Middleton was thrown by his assailant Robert of Ripon during a dispute in 1419 (Harrison 1952, 61). At that time it had a *brand-reth* over it — a large iron structure to hold kettles etc. (YMA, VC 1/1, p.17, ink pagination).

The moulded tie-beam in the roof, which crossed the roof space towards the north-western end of the hall, has been interpreted as a frame for a canopy over the dais (RCHMY **5**, 60). This may well have been one of the functions of such a beam, but it is unlikely to have been solely for this purpose. As has been said, no records were made in this area to ascertain whether or not there was an internal division in the roof space at this point. One possible reconstruction, however, would be that the missing tie-beam supported a studded wall and the floor for a small chamber over the high table end of the hall. If this were the case, because the tie-beam is an original component of the roof, the chamber would have existed from the start. Such a chamber cannot have been accessed from anywhere but a staircase rising in a room to the north-west of the hall which probably lay in the building recognised during excavation as Building 26 (see p.482). It is, perhaps, quite likely that there was at least one door in the north-western wall of the hall communicating with the buildings beyond, but there is no trace of such features now. Had there been two-storey buildings to the north-west, then there would not have been room for windows here.

Dating evidence and architectural context

The surviving hall retains a number of features for which a close dating can be suggested. In addition, the design of the vault in the bay window (which we have seen is contemporary with the hall) can be dated style-critically to the 1360s and 1370s — the years when the eastern arm of the present Minster was being constructed. It shares many details with the eastern parts of the new eastern arm, which was begun in 1361 and was substantially complete by 1373 (Harvey 1977). Some of the decorative niches flanking the great east window of the Minster have pedestals of a form exactly similar to the vault springers and the same niches have vaulted canopies with small decorated sculptures in the springer panel, as at Bedern, though they are confined to representa-

tions of foliage. The Bedern lion masks themselves were once exactly paralleled, however, on the heads of some of the niches on the east front of the Minster. The niche heads were renewed in simplified form in 1824–7, but two original examples survive in the Yorkshire Museum with the same forked topknot as the Bedern lions (Dr C. Wilson, pers. comm.). Parallels could be multiplied but the correspondence in detail is so precise that it is likely that the Bedern vault, and perhaps the whole hall, was designed by the same master as the detailing at the east end of the Minster (either William Hoton, master mason between 1361 and 1368, or perhaps more likely, Robert de Patryngton, who occupied the post between 1369 and 1385; Harvey 1977; 1984).

The peculiar tracery in the surviving window is also of approximately this date. Although the design appears to be unique (surprisingly for one so simple), it does incorporate cusps standing at right-angles to the mullions and transoms which seem to be quite a feature of windows of the last few decades of the 14th century (Harvey 1978, 139). In York they are seen in the east window of St Denys Walmgate (which need not necessarily be the same date as the mid 15th century glass within it) and in the west window of All Saints Pavement. Of particular relevance here is the occurrence of windows with such cusping in the tracery in the aisle windows of the eastern parts of the Minster choir (1361–c.1373). The detail is also found more widely in Yorkshire, for example, in the window tracery at the chapter house at Howden Minster (built between 1380 and 1405), where there is a miniature version of the Bedern tracery arrangement at the top of each light.

The roof design is also of this later 14th century date, as are the mouldings with which the main timbers are decorated. The Royal Commission noted that this roof was one of a small group of examples using scissor bracing which were developed from the design of roof over the chapter house vestibule at the Minster, erected in the early 14th century (RCHMY **5**, lxvii). Ignoring the scissor bracing for a moment, the framing design used in the south-east gable panel at Bedern Hall also finds parallels in York buildings of the 14th and 15th centuries (from Nos.12–15 Newgate, dated to 1337, to Nos.41–3 Petergate, of the early 16th century; RCHMY **5**, lxviii ff). It is the arched braces springing from below the wall-plate which are perhaps the most unusual component of the Bedern Hall roof. However, this type of bracing cannot be dated any more closely than other features of the roof. The roof of the Old Deanery at Salisbury (dating from 1258–74) is an example of this feature (RCHME 1993), whilst in York itself the same feature was originally to be seen in the roof of the Merchant Adventurers' Hall which is close in date to Bedern Hall: 1357–61 (RCHMY 5, 82–8). Although not very closely datable, then, the design of the Bedern Hall roof is very comfortably accommodated in the second half of the 14th century.

The style-critical dating evidence for the hall, therefore, points to a date in the second half of the 14th century. To refine it further we would have to make the assumption that details such as those which occur in the vault were retained in the decorative repertoire for only a short time, once they had first appeared on the Minster. These Minster details are perhaps more likely to have been created towards the end of the building campaign than the start but, even so, these details suggest a date in the 1360s or 1370s. A construction date in the fourth quarter of the century rather than in the third, however, is implied by the one surviving potential documentary reference to building work at the hall. In an undated fragmentary account from the 1390s over two weeks' work is paid for, tiling the roof of the hall (YMA, VC 6/2/34, 38, 40). Even if this tiling is dated as early as 1390, it would still suggest that decorative details used on the Minster in the 1370s remained current twenty years later. This may not be impossible, however, especially if we presume that the details were designed by Robert of Patryngton, who was still active in York as late as 1385 (Harvey 1984, 229). Furthermore, the hall could have been a long time in building, perhaps taking a decade from design to completion. However, by deploying such arguments we are pushing the dating of the decorative details so late in the career of Robert of Patryngton merely to accommodate a single documentary reference. This would not be necessary if we interpret the tiling work done in the 1390s as a routine repair rather than the completion of work on a new hall. If we are prepared to accept that the tiling reference does not indicate the completion of building work, but rather the replacement and repair of tiles on a building which is already in use, then we can revert to the more straightforward style-critical arguments which suggest a date for the construction of the hall in the period between 1360 and 1380.

The plan of the hall is not at odds with a date within this bracket. Rectangular aisleless plans with service and high table ends are the norm for such halls throughout the medieval period, but bay windows at this date are much more unusual. Although in modern parlance the term oriel is confined to projections for windows which are set above ground floor, the medieval use of the term was not so closely defined and it was applied to most ground-level projections from larger buildings (Turner and Parker 1853, 82; Wood 1965, chapter 7). The earliest reference to such a structure is the *oriolum* recorded in the Pipe Roll for 1186 (Brown, Colvin and Taylor 1963, 122, 178; Wood 1965, 99ff.), but it is not clear that this was a structure intended to house windows. On the contrary, it seems likely that the many projecting buildings off the dais ends of early halls were more like small private chambers with a variety of functions. There are, however, documentary references to 13th century projections from halls whose primary purpose was to contain windows, although the surviving example at Nassington Prebendal Manor House, Northamptonshire (reported in Wood 1950, 48–51), has now been redated to the 15th century (RCHME 1984, 123–4). In the 14th century such bay windows are met with more frequently. A possible example may have existed at the archbishop's palace at Mayfield, Sussex, whilst there is a more certain one at Stanton's Farm, Black Notley, Essex. However, they could not be described as common until the end of the century, when the great new hall built by John of Gaunt at Kenilworth Castle between 1389 and 1394 was equipped with one (Wood 1965, 102–4). By the 15th century, however, such bay windows were becoming usual, often being added at that date to earlier halls which did not already have them. Such later windows often carry miniature stone vaults of the type now known from Bedern, though research has not revealed any examples earlier in date than that we propose was made for the vicars choral c.1370.

As has already been indicated, the vault in the bay window projection has details which suggest that it was designed by the Minster master mason. Given that, it is perhaps not quite so surprising that the hall appears to be innovative in its structural as well as its design details. The projecting bay window at Bedern is a remarkably early example of such a feature, even though such features were to become the norm within a generation. It is the case, however, that of the surviving halls of vicars choral at other cathedrals, two, Chichester and Wells, also have projecting bays at the high table end — indeed Wells has two, even if they were later additions of c.1500 (Colchester 1987, 167). The Chichester example was provided when the hall was comprehensively rebuilt between 1397 and 1403 (Tatton-Brown 1994, 236–9). Furthermore, before the Exeter hall was destroyed by bombing in 1943, the eastern end of the south wall had an apparently functionless transverse gable over it and, below, a panel of rebuilt masonry containing a late 14th century window, which looked reset (shown in Chanter 1933, pl.VII). These features might indicate that there had been a bay window at the Exeter hall also. It may be, then, that this still rare structural form was introduced in these vicars' halls for a reason connected with their function, and the one which springs to mind is the use of the bay to house the reading desk used by the vicar whose duty it was to read to the other diners. At Wells, however, the new bay windows of c.1500 were not used for this purpose, as the hall was also equipped with a purpose-built pulpit adjacent to the fireplace donated at approximately the same time, perhaps by Treasurer Sugar or his wife (Colchester 1987, 167). It would be fascinating to discover whether or not the Lincoln hall had such a window, and if so whether it was present from its first construction, but without this information it seems that the tradition of providing bay windows to light the high tables in vicars' halls starts at Bedern. Furthermore, it may be that the vicars' halls were influential early examples of this design detail, which became so common during the subsequent century.

Finally, it is worth comparing Bedern Hall more generally with what is known of the halls of the other colleges of vicars choral. The second York hall is almost exactly the same size as that at Lincoln according to the most recent study, which places the hall at the eastern end of the south range of the court, opposite the gatehouse (Jones, Major and Varley 1987). Unfortunately we know nothing about the internal layout of the hall here and the published documentation at Lincoln does not refer to readings during meals (Maddison 1878). All of the other known halls are smaller than this; Salisbury is as small as 28 × 22ft (RCHME 1993). In date, however, Lincoln (of the early 14th century) and Wells (begun c.1348) are significantly earlier than Bedern and, of the others, Ex-

eter, Chichester and Hereford (first hall) all date from c.1400, i.e. not long afterwards. As a group the halls are not homogeneous. Some, like Hereford (first hall) and Salisbury, were small ground-floor halls which were indistinguishable from those in other houses in the close (RCHME 1931; 1993). That at Chichester was not unlike the halls in the commercial premises alongside which it was built; that is, it was a long, narrow first-floor hall with an elaborate undercroft which opened onto the street (VCH 1935; Tatton-Brown 1994). Little or nothing is known of the halls at Lichfield and London, but Exeter, Wells and York seem to stand out as being relatively elaborate buildings. All three are detailed with architectural motifs taken from the most fashionable buildings of their time and no doubt both Wells and Exeter (and maybe others) made use of the skills available within the cathedral workshops just as we suggest that the vicars did at York.

The vicars' hall at Wells is now the only example where the hall can be clearly appreciated in relation to the buildings around it. It is a small hall and placed, uniquely, over a gateway (Fig.190, p.393); even so it retains the traditional layout with the high table (originally on a dais, perhaps) to the east, later lit by bay windows as we have seen (Fig.192, p.394). As at Bedern, the chapel is quite some way away, at the other end of the college, but the hall is connected to a variety of distinctive structures at the 'low table' end. In both its original layout and in its greatly altered state after c.1500 it seems to have been separated from the kitchen to the east only by the gable wall and arrangements of wooden screens, as there were no masonry dividing walls. However, the fenestration and access suggest a variety of uses at the low table end, so whole chambers may have been created with such screens. Such screens were required both when the hall was entered via the spiral stair to the north and later when passages were built connecting the hall both to the chapter house and the cathedral, and to the close houses (both via enclosed staircases). In the later phases at Wells there was access from the hall directly to a counting house and a muniment room above the staircase to the north, and also to a strong room used by the vicars as a treasury. These buildings were added to the hall in the 15th century and the latter, in particular, provides an excellent parallel for the proposed strong room (Building 27) to the south-east of the service block at Bedern.

The new Bedern Hall, then, was clearly a major building in its time, incorporating the most up-to-date features and details. It emphasises, perhaps better than anything else, that in the College of the Vicars Choral at York we are dealing with one of the more self-confident institutions of medieval York even though its wealth and influence must have been dwarfed by its 'parent' body — the Minster itself.

Other evidence for the dating of Bedern Hall came from dendrochronological study of the timbers. **Jennifer Hillam** provides the following report.

Twelve oak timbers (Table 14) were examined in 1981. Timbers 102, 106, 108, 112, 113 and 114 were samples from rafters, 109 and 116 were from rafter supports, 110 and 111 from gable wall-plates, 107 from a scissor-brace timber and 115 from a wall-plate tie. The samples were cleaned using an electric drill with sander attachment. Various grades of sanding disc from coarse to fine were used to give a high polish. The final finish was added by hand polishing with very fine wet-and-dry paper. The annual growth rings could be seen clearly after this preparation, each ring being distinct from the next.

The ring widths were measured on the Sheffield tree-ring measuring apparatus which consists of a travelling stage connected by a linear transducer to a display panel. The wood sample is placed on the stage and observed through a 10× binocular microscope. As each ring is traversed by moving the stage, the width in 0·1mm is shown on the display unit and is recorded manually. (This operation is now fully computerised.)

The Bedern Hall timbers had between 22 and 139 annual rings. Since sequences of less than 50 rings rarely give reliable dating, some samples (108, 109, 112) were rejected at this stage. In addition, sample 107 had a large knot which distorted its tree-ring record, and this too was discarded. The ring widths from the remaining samples were plotted against time in years on transparent semilogarithmic recorder paper. The use of transparent paper allows the ring patterns to be compared by superimposing one graph over another and searching for similarities between them. Computer programs (Baillie and Pilcher 1973; Munro 1984) are also available for crossdating purposes. They calculate the correlation value, Student's t, for each position of overlap between two ring sequences. A value greater than t = 3·5 indicates a tree-ring match if it is accompanied by an acceptable visual match — the quality of the latter is the important factor in crossdating (Baillie

1982, 82–5). The computer program is used to save time by indicating the possibility of a match, or to give a statistical evaluation of the degree of correlation between two tree-ring curves.

Four of the rafter sequences (102, 106, 113, 114) and one of the rafter support sequences (116) cross-matched to give a total sequence of 142 years (Fig.334). The agreement values vary between 1·20 and 7·45 (Table 15). The highest value results from a comparison between 102 and 106 which have an overlap of only 20 years. This contrasts with the comparison between 102 and 114 where an overlap of 25 years gives a value of 1·20. When the matches were examined visually, that between 102 and 114 was poor whilst the one between 102 and 106 was almost perfect, indicating that timbers 102 and 106 probably originated in the same tree (Fig.335) whereas 114 came from a different tree.

The ring patterns from the two gable wall-plates (110, 111) cross-matched with each other (t = 7·87, overlay 53 years) forming a total sequence of 77 years. Neither this nor the remaining timber (115) cross-matched with the sequences described above.

A Bedern master chronology (Table 16) was constructed by averaging the ring widths of the matching samples. This was also tested against 110, 111 and 115 but still no cross-matching was found. The master curve was then compared by computer with dated medieval tree-ring chronologies from the British Isles. (These are too numerous to list but see, for example, Baillie 1982; Fletcher 1977; Hillam 1981.) An acceptable match was found between Bedern and an unpublished sequence, 1214–1462, constructed from timbers in the central tower at York Minster. (The original measurement on these timbers was carried out by V. Siebenlist-Kerner; the data were processed and a chronology produced by R. Morgan. The data were reworked by J. Hillam in 1990 and a new chronology produced; this is available on request.) The match gave a t-value of 5·8 and dated the Bedern sequence to 1228–1369 (Fig.336). A second match (t = 4·3) with a chronology from the East Midlands (Laxton and Litton 1988) confirmed the dating. Timbers 110, 111 and 115 were also compared with the reference chronologies but no reliable crossdating was found.

The Bedern Hall tree-ring sequence dates to 1228–1369 but in order to relate this to the felling date of the timbers, and hence to the date of construction, it is necessary to examine the amount of sapwood, if any, remaining on the

Table 14 Details of Bedern Hall tree-ring samples. Sketches are not to scale; asterisks indicate unmeasured samples

No.	function	no. of rings	sapwood rings	average width (mm)	dimensions (cm)	sketch
102	roof rafter	77	–	2.05	10 x 14	
106	rafter	81	19	1.75	10–11 x 16	
*107	scissor	?	–	?	11 x 16	
*108	rafter	31	–	–	12 x 14–16	
*109	rafter support	22	–	–	13 x 13	
110	gable wall-plate	72	21	2.13	18–19 x 24	
111	gable wall-plate	58	–	1.96	20 x 19–22	
*112	rafter	29	–	–	12 x 12–13	
113	rafter	98	1	1.52	12 x 15	
114	rafter	88	22	1.77	11 x 15	
115	wall-plate tie	100	–	1.40	14 x 15	
116	rafter support	139	28 bark edge?	1.23	13 x 15	

	106	113	114	116
102	7.45 (20)	3.37 (61)	1.20 (25)	3.06 (74)
106		3.13 (57)	3.74 (88)	5.54 (81)
113			5.28 (62)	4.36 (98)
114				4.42 (88)

Table 15 Summary of *t*-values. Figures in brackets indicate the length of overlap (in years) between each pair of ring sequences

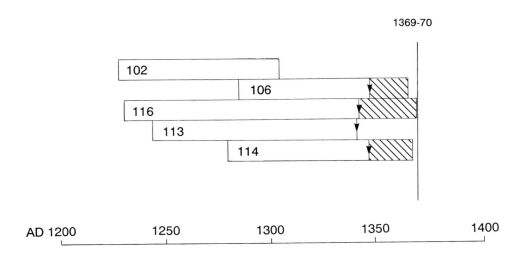

Fig.334 Bedern Hall tree-ring dating. Bar diagram illustrating the relative positions of the ring sequences. Sapwood rings are represented by hatching and the heartwood/sapwood transitions by arrows

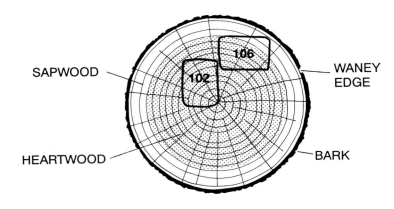

Fig.335 Bedern Hall tree-ring dating. Sketch of tree trunk showing the possible positions of samples 102 and 106. One or both timbers could, of course, have been taken from the opposite half of the trunk

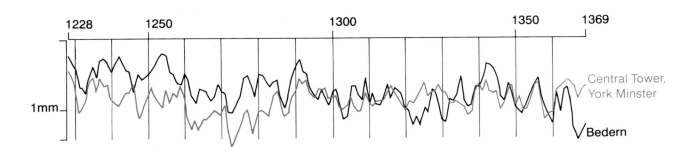

Fig.336 Bedern Hall tree-ring dating. Matching tree-ring curves: a section of the match between the Bedern and York Minster chronologies

Table 16 Bedern Hall master curve, 1228–1369. 'n' denotes the number of trees per decade

Year	Ring width (0.1 mm)										n
	0	1	2	3	4	5	6	7	8	9	
1228									34.0	27.0	1
1230	24.0	16.5	16.0	14.5	21.0	26.5	21.0	30.5	32.0	29.0	2
1240	23.5	28.0	33.5	28.0	24.3	23.3	15.0	22.7	19.7	20.7	3
1250	22.0	24.0	27.0	32.0	34.7	33.3	23.0	22.0	17.7	17.7	3
1260	22.0	18.3	13.3	11.3	15.7	15.3	14.70	12.0	13.3	17.3	3
1270	15.0	14.0	9.3	9.3	11.0	13.3	20.0	21.3	16.3	13.3	3
1280	21.8	21.3	18.5	16.5	18.5	17.8	12.3	10.0	12.5	21.5	4
1290	26.3	29.5	22.3	21.3	16.0	13.8	11.8	15.0	12.5	11.8	4
1300	15.0	16.0	11.5	8.3	8.0	16.5	16.7	13.7	12.2	20.2	4
1310	11.2	14.2	11.2	11.0	12.7	17.2	13.0	16.0	15.0	13.5	4
1320	10.5	9.2	7.0	8.5	7.0	10.2	9.2	15.5	14.7	10.7	4
1330	8.0	7.5	12.5	12.0	13.7	20.2	12.0	10.5	11.0	16.2	4
1340	16.5	20.0	27.7	27.0	24.3	20.0	13.3	12.0	17.7	14.0	3
1350	10.7	10.0	9.0	11.0	14.3	17.3	20.0	13.3	10.3	8.7	3
1360	7.3	14.3	9.3	15.3	16.3	13.0	6.5	5.0	6.0	7.0	3

timbers. Sapwood is the outer part of the tree which in oak is distinguishable by colour and structure from the inner heartwood (Fig.335). The number of sapwood rings in oak is relatively constant at 10–55 rings so if the heartwood-sapwood transition is present on a timber a fairly accurate felling date can be estimated (for further discussion, see Hillam et al. 1987). Of course, if the sapwood is preserved up to the bark or waney edge, a felling date exact to the year can be quoted. Of the matching samples, 106, 113, 114 and 116 had 19, 1, 22 and 28 sapwood rings respectively (Fig.334). Samples 106, 114 and 116 ended within five years of each other, and 116 appeared to have its full complement of sapwood rings. The waney edge,

the line separating the outermost sapwood ring from the bark, seemed to be present along one edge of the timber, but the outer ring was too worn to be absolutely certain. The outer ring on 116 was fully formed indicating that, if the presence of the waney edge is accepted, the tree was felled in the winter or early spring of 1369–70. It can be postulated therefore that the timber for the rafters and rafter supports was felled in 1369–70 or, allowing for the slight uncertainty about the waney edge, just after. The seasoning of timber for building purposes is a recent introduction. Unless it was to be used for furniture or panelling, timber was usually felled as required and used almost immediately (Harvey 1975, 115; Rackham 1976, 76), so that *felling dates and construction dates are often one and the same. The Bedern Hall roof therefore was constructed in 1369–70 or just after.*

Building construction techniques and materials

The majority of the structures erected within the college precinct were timber-framed, this tradition continuing from the 13th to the 16th centuries. Most of the buildings were represented by successive foundation sill walls, and some had additional post-pads indicating internal partition walls. Internal divisions within a timber-framed construction need not be load-bearing and therefore do not always help with interpretation of building form, although, in Building 8 (Period 3) the central line of post-pads may be seen as providing support for an upper storey (J. Grenville, pers. comm.).

The sills were rarely substantial, varying between 0·2 and 0·3m in width, and up to 0·5m in height; sometimes they were placed in construction trenches, but just as often they were run directly across the contemporary ground surface. Larger stones were placed at the corner junctions, and at regular points where they would have supported the main vertical timbers. The interval between such padstones seems generally to have been c.2m. Both continuous and interrupted sill beams were present, although the timbers themselves were rarely preserved. Traces of both an upright timber and a sill beam survived in Building 7 (Period 3), whilst a socket for a timber post was identified in the south-east wall of Building 20 (Period 6, Phase 2). Major freestanding post-pads, such as those supporting the aisle posts in Building 5 (Period 2), were generally set above stone-packed foundation pits. Some of the padstones were set over timber piles, as in Building 9 (Period 3), but this technique does not appear to have been used as extensively as on the neighbouring foundry site (pp.166–7, *AY* 10/3).

Construction of some of the timber elements of the buildings on site is suggested by a range of woodworking tools found in rubbish deposits on site, mainly from Period 7 levels south-west of Bedern Hall. These included a chisel, an auger bit, a saw blade, and six iron wedges. A hammer head and a builder's trowel were also found (*AY* 17/15 in prep.).

It is difficult to reconstruct the original appearance of the timber-framed buildings on the basis of the excavated evidence especially when, in most cases, their plans are incomplete. There was, however, good evidence for the character of Building 5, constructed in the second half of the 13th century (Period 2) on the north-east side of the Close (Fig.372s). Its full original length cannot be determined, but it must have been at least 45m. The width of the main part of the building was c.10·5m, although much of the south-west part of the building lay under the modern street and the foundations of the south-west wall only occurred in a small area in Area 14.IV. The south-eastern part of the building presumably existed as a cross-wing. Internally there is some evidence for regularity in the plan. For example, the spacing of the internal posts corresponds, up to a point, to the spacing of the post-pads in the north-east wall. Towards the south-east end the five posts dividing the central aisle from the north-east aisle between 1704 (north-west) and 1707 (south-east) were each c.2·2m apart, measured centre to centre, as were 4488 and 4487, the last two posts at the south-east end. In addition, the distance from three of the five posts referred to above (1605, 1703 and 1663) to the corresponding post-pads in the north-east wall was also c.2·2m. Further to the north-west three posts (1581, 1684 and 1705) were c.3m apart. In the line of posts dividing the central from the south-west aisle there were four posts (1733, 1732, 1727, 1731) each c.2·40m apart. Having noted this regularity in certain areas, it is, none the less, difficult to tell what the original form of the building was because the aisle posts in the main part do not run parallel to the north-east outer walls and the north-east aisle becomes progressively wider towards the north-west end of the building. It is possible that the building had a central aisle wider than the two side aisles, but, alternatively, it may have had two roughly equal sized aisles c.4m wide in the centre and on the south-west side and a third, narrower aisle on the north-east side c.2·5–3·0m wide. In the former case there was probably a single-gabled roof covering all three aisles. In the latter there may have been a double-gabled roof over the central and south-western aisles while the north-eastern aisle had a simple pitched roof. Building 5 appears to have been rebuilt, at least in part, in stone in Period 7.2b when the width of the wall footings on its north-east side was doubled. It may now have had a roof based on substantial tie-beams spanning its whole width.

During the late 14th century the vicars began to construct all their major buildings in stone; until this date the chapel had been the only stone structure within the precinct. Building 25, the service wing of the new hall, was built at the beginning of Period 7, with substantial stone footings, a stone-walled ground floor and a timber-framed upper storey. The first hall on the site was probably timber-framed, but was subsequently rebuilt entirely in stone. Building 27 was also completely stone-built; its walls consisted generally of facing stones of either rubble or ashlar, with interior and exterior plinth courses, and a concrete core. Buildings 26 and 30, constructed against the hall, may have been stone-built. Building 28, a minor outbuilding constructed against the south-east side of Building 27, was apparently built in brick.

Many of the foundation sills contained pieces of previously used stone, either moulded or ashlar blocks. Most of the identifiable forms seem to have originated from demolition of parts of the Minster. From 1291 until sometime after 1333 a quantity of late 12th century stone from both the west towers and the Chapel of St Sepulchre was made available for re-use (p.240, AY 10/4). It is suggested above that some of this was re-used in the fabric of Bedern Chapel in the early 1340s (see p.555). Secondly, the late 12th century choir of Roger of Pont l'Evêque was demolished during the late 14th century. It is suggested that in the period between 1361 and 1373 the east wall, the two eastern bays of the aisle walls and the vaults between would have been available for re-use. Between c.1390 and 1394 the remainder of the choir was demolished, releasing an enormous quantity of stone for re-use. Some of it was re-used in the Minster buildings south of the new choir, and more was used in the reconstruction of the east part of the crypt (p.239, AY 10/4). However, it is suggested that much remained for re-use at Bedern, as part of the major Period 7 building work in the late 14th and early 15th century. Apparently little stone was cut specifically for the sill walls of the college's timber-framed buildings, which mostly used fairly low-grade, rough Magnesian Limestone. There are no quarries near York and limestone not re-used from older medieval and Roman buildings would have been quarried from the Tadcaster area or from Huddleston near Sherburn-in-Elmet (RCHMY 5, xcv).

During the second half of the 14th century brick, hitherto used largely for hearths, was also introduced

for sill walls, such as the south-east wall of Building 16 (4311) and the rebuild of Building 17 both in Period 6. In the 15th century the vicars choral manufactured bricks and tiles on a large scale from which they derived a substantial income (see p.384). They presumably produced all the brick and tile required for their own use. The bricks recorded during the excavation were mostly of the usual medieval sizes and can be dated to the 14th or 15th century. The measurements tend to be around 260 × 133 × 35mm (long, broad and thin compared with modern examples). A few examples did not conform to these measurements, and have consequently been dated to the 16th to mid 18th century, using Betts' (1985) measurements.

Little evidence of the above-ground construction of the college buildings was apparent from the excavation. In most surviving timber-framed buildings in York the infilling between the framing is of thin bricks or wall tiles. The only material found on Bedern which could have been used for infilling seems to have been brick; no evidence of wattle and daub was found. At Lady Row, 60–72 Goodramgate, a row of timber-framed houses was constructed in 1316, possibly with the vicars as landlords. This is the earliest timber-framed building surviving in York which can be securely dated from documentary sources. At Lady Row, the infilling was of stone rubble, set in mortar and plastered (RCHMY 5, lxii–lxiii). This technique may also have been employed on the college buildings. There is evidence for plaster rendering on the interior of some buildings, such as Buildings 8 and 27. However, few fragments of wall plaster were recovered from medieval levels, and none earlier than Period 6. A concentration was found in deposits associated with the demolition of Building 14, and around Buildings 24, 25 and 27. Most fragments of wall plaster were plain white or cream, although there were a few with a pinkish wash or red patches over a buff background, and one piece with red and black lines. The only building which was definitely decorated was the chapel. Painted plaster was recovered from Period 8 and 9 deposits within the chapel, resulting from the construction of internal fittings. There appear to be red designs surrounded by black outlines and in places a red background with black details painted on it. Occasionally there are patches of yellow (pp.604–5). At some stage this plaster had been over-painted with plain white and so the designs are not recoverable. Nevertheless it is likely that these represent fragments of religious scenes painted on the medieval chapel walls which had later been whitewashed over, possibly during the Reformation.

The medieval painted wall plaster was examined by **L. Wong** who provides the following report.

Considerable quantities of medieval plaster were excavated from Bedern. Although much was undecorated, there was also a significant amount of painted material, notably from contexts in the chapel. Although the designs are difficult to interpret, these fragments are of great interest technically, and include possibly the earliest example of lead-tin yellow in surviving English wall painting. There were also significant finds of masonry pattern from the college buildings, and fragments with vermilion and ultramarine from the foundry. Remains of Roman painted plaster discovered in the excavation are not discussed in the present report.

Following excavation many of the fragments were cleaned and consolidated with a synthetic resin by the York Archaeological Trust conservation department. They were subsequently examined by the Conservation of Wall Painting Department of the Courtauld Institute, and a representative selection subjected to scientific examination.

Examination of the plaster proved particularly helpful for understanding the relationship of the various fragments. It included examination of the topography of the reverse of the fragments (which often preserves the impression of the original support), the colour of the plaster, the lime to aggregate ratio, the aggregate itself, the number and thickness of the individual layers, and the presence of any ground for the painting. Further examination of the layers and their constituents was undertaken by polishing the sides of some of the fragments, and by viewing mounted cross-sections of the paint and plaster.

The paint layers were examined with a binocular microscope, and minute samples were then taken to elucidate the nature of the pigments and their application. The samples were mounted as cross-sections (in polyester embedding resin) and as dispersions. Polished cross-sections were examined and photographed with an optical microscope at 100–400× magnification. Energy-dispersive X-ray (EDX) analysis was used with a scanning electron microscope (SEM) to provide elemental analysis in specific cases to confirm identifications made using polarised light microscopy and microchemical tests. Fourier transform infra-red microspectroscopy (FTIR) was employed

in an attempt to identify organic binding media, but this proved unsuccessful.

Bedern Chapel

Fragments of painted plaster were excavated from five Period 9 contexts: 9015, 9024, 9037, 9040 and 9053. All of these are 18th century pits or spreads associated with substantial alterations to the chapel (p.647). Most fragments retain at least two layers of limewash, presumably dating from the Reformation or later, and it appears that the plaster may have been stripped from the walls in the 17th or 18th century (p.647).

The most significant fragments were from contexts 9015 and 9040, and a representative selection were subjected to scientific examination. The fragments vary in size and bear painting in white, black, red, green and yellow. Although none of the designs can be deciphered, the varied palette suggests that the fragments may derive from a figural scheme (Fig.337).

All these fragments are composed of the same type of plaster, applied in two to three layers which are almost indistinguishable from one another. The lime content is high, with an approximate lime to aggregate ratio of 1:2, and the plaster is consequently very white. The aggregate consists mostly of fine non-calcareous material such as quartz and charcoal, with the largest particles measuring approximately 1 × 2 × 1mm. The irregular surface of the backs of some of the fragments suggests that the original support was a rubble wall, or at least a wall of very rough texture. The first layers of plaster appear to be levelling coats employed to smooth the surface of the wall, and therefore vary considerably in thickness. The final plaster layer is 2–3mm thick and was finished with a limewash ground to which the painting was applied.

The palette is quite varied, comprising red earth, yellow earth, carbon black, lime white, red lead, green earth, and lead-tin yellow. The first four of these pigments were inexpensive and very common in medieval wall painting. Red lead, identified on one fragment from context 9015, also occurs frequently, despite its tendency to darken (for examples from the 12th to the 16th century, see Hluvko 1991). Surprisingly, green earth is less common, but has been identified, for instance, in late 12th century paintings at Winchester Cathedral and at Glasgow Cathedral (Howard 1995, 96; Park and Howard forthcoming).

By far the most interesting pigment is lead-tin yellow, identified on the basis of its optical properties and by el-

Fig.337 *Painted wall plaster fragments from the chapel (context 9015) with painting in lead-tin yellow (fragment at lower right), red lead (top centre), red earth, carbon black and lime white. Although the designs cannot be deciphered, the varied palette may indicate a figural scheme*

emental analysis with SEM-EDX on a fragment from context 9015, where it is mixed with charcoal black, lime white and a small amount of green earth to provide a lime-green colour. Although first used in panel painting c.1300, this pigment was uncommon until the 15th century and went out of use during the 17th century (Eastaugh 1989; Kühn 1993).

Only a few other examples of lead-tin yellow have been identified in English medieval wall painting: in early 15th century paintings at Farleigh Hungerford Castle (Somerset) and Lichfield Cathedral (Howard et al. 1998, 62); in 15th century painting in the presbytery of St Albans Cathedral (Perry 1998, 6); in the major scheme of c.1479–87 in Eton College Chapel (Plummer 1986, 36); and in paintings of c.1510 in St Mark's Hospital, Bristol (Gill and Howard 1997, 101). Minute traces (possibly of 14th century date) have also been identified on sculpture on the west front of Exeter Cathedral (Sinclair 1991, 123–4), on late 15th century effigies at Arundel (Brodrick and Darrah 1986) and in a medieval shell palette from St Augustine's Abbey, Canterbury (Sherlock and Woods 1988, 200). The latter may have been used for manuscript illumination rather than for large-scale painting, but it is noteworthy that, as on the Bedern fragment, the lead-tin yellow was combined with other pigments to form a green — in this case, white lead, and an unidentified component, probably a copper green. The lead-tin yellow at Bedern may be the earliest surviving example in English wall painting, and is particularly useful in showing that these fragments are most unlikely to date from before the 14th century. If from the chapel, these fragments could have formed part of the original decoration of the 1340s, or be associated with the extension of the building undertaken probably in the late 14th century (p.555).

The overall ground suggests that a number of the pigments would have been applied to the fresh limewash, but neither red lead nor lead-tin yellow is compatible with lime, and therefore both would have been applied in an organic binding medium such as oil or glue. Unfortunately, however, as is typical with contaminated excavated fragments of wall painting, medium analysis proved unsuccessful.

In addition to these painted fragments, a substantial quantity of unpainted earthen render was excavated from the chapel (context 9040), which may have come from another building. Impressions on the backs of these fragments suggest a wood lath support of some type. The render is some 25mm thick in places, and appears to be a mixture of earth, some organic material and fairly large pieces of re-used lime plaster. The earthen render was finished with two 5mm layers of plaster, both of high lime content and with very fine aggregate. The fragments have quite a rough surface finish, and show no evidence of having been painted. They may well derive from one of the domestic buildings in Bedern, and in this context it is worth noting the large quantities of daub purchased by the vicars choral in the 14th century for building activities elsewhere in York (Fraser 1994).

Bedern South-West and North-East

Small fragments of plaster excavated from Bedern South-West and Bedern North-East have painted decoration. Masonry pattern can be identified on several fragments (e.g. sf529), while other fragments have painting in dark red which may represent drapery (another fragment of sf529). A third group has painting in red and black (e.g. sf2737), though the motif is not identifiable. The plaster of these fragments is different from that of the chapel, though the backs again have irregular surfaces. The plaster appears to consist of a single 10mm layer, with an approximate lime to aggregate ratio of 1:3. The aggregate, containing charcoal and fragments of brick, is very fine with particles measuring approximately 1mm³. All the fragments have a limewash ground for the painting. Incised guidelines occur on the fragments painted with possible drapery, their smooth edges suggesting that the incisions were made into fresh plaster.

The masonry pattern is of a common type, in which a red line is paired with a pale blue line, though the Bedern fragments do not provide sufficient evidence to determine whether this pairing is for vertical or horizontal lines, or both. The red is red earth and the blue is 'false blue'. The latter was produced by combining charcoal black and lime white, and the blue effect depends on the phenomenon known as Rayleigh scattering. 'False blue' is very common in medieval wall painting, where it provided an expedient alternative to expensive mineral blue pigments such as ultramarine (Howard 1990). At York, it has been identified in some of the fragments from St Andrew's Priory, Fishergate, perhaps dating from c.1200 (AY 11/2, 306–7), and even in the richly painted coffin lid of Archbishop Walter de Gray in York Minster, of c.1255 (Ramm et al. 1971, 24).

Masonry pattern is the most common type of decoration in medieval wall painting until about the middle of the 14th century. The Bedern fragments are of a more advanced type than early Romanesque masonry pattern which is characterised by thick single red lines, as at York Minster in the late 11th century (Phillips 1985, 99–101, pls.71–3). Later the lines become thinner and are often doubled, as in painting excavated from St Andrew's Priory, probably dating from c.1200 (AY 11/2, 302–5, fig.146b). Double-line masonry pattern was often executed in red and false blue, as in the mid 13th century scheme at Horsham St Faith Priory, Norfolk. Masonry pattern was rarely used after c.1350, and the Bedern examples would certainly conform to a 13th century date. They are therefore likely to be associated with one of the 13th century pre-chapel phases of the site.

Despite its unusually dark and rich appearance, the red on the possible drapery fragments is red earth, as is the red pigment on the third group of fragments.

Bedern Foundry

Various interesting but puzzling remains of painted plaster were excavated in the foundry. Two fragments (context 2380) from layers dumped in Period 3, Phase 4, in the mid to late 14th century (AY 10/3, Microfiche 1:C8) have remains of painting in vermilion on a white ground, the design on at least one of the fragments appearing to be scrollwork (Fig.338). The rather crude incised lines which roughly follow the decoration appear to have been added subsequently. Vermilion was an expensive pigment, but was used in wall painting throughout the medieval period (Hluvko 1991), and these fragments are not closely dateable on the basis either of the pigment or the design.

Another fragment (context 63) has a solid blue paint layer, with several layers of thin plaster and limewash (3mm thick) below over an initial layer of plaster 4–5mm thick. The blue pigment, applied in two layers, was identified by polarised light microscopy and microchemical tests as ultramarine. By far the most expensive of all pig-

Fig.338 Painted wall plaster fragments from the foundry (context 2380) with scrollwork in vermilion and later incisions. Actual maximum length of fragment at top, 40mm

ments in the medieval period, ultramarine was employed from at least the beginning of the 12th century in English wall painting, though its use seems to have declined from the 13th century onwards (Howard 1988). Its occurrence on this foundry fragment is puzzling since ultramarine would have been used in only the most luxurious schemes; moreover, the stratigraphy of the fragment suggests that the scheme to which it belonged was preceded by at least two or three earlier phases of decoration. As with the fragments from context 2380, neither the pigment nor the archaeological context provides any further evidence for dating.

A wide variety of ceramic roof furniture was recovered during the excavations. This is hardly surprising, given that brick and tile factories were owned by the vicars at Layerthorpe (see p.384). The following information on ceramic building material has been compiled with reference to S. Garside Neville's previous work on these materials in York.

The earliest medieval forms encountered were two examples of curved roof tile, dating to the 12th or early 13th century, one associated with Period 3 con-struction levels for Building 9. It is often difficult to distinguish curved tiles from later ridge tiles but the presence of a nail hole at the end of the tile normally indicates a curved tile. Curved tiles were used with flanged tiles, in much the same way as Roman tegulae and imbrices were used together (Garside-Neville 1995, 31–4).

For the most part, the buildings at Bedern were plain tiled. Plain tiles can be either nibbed or have peg holes; occasionally both features are present. They date from the early 13th century onwards, replacing the curved and flanged system. One example of a peg tile was recovered from Bedern. Several examples of glazed plain tiles were recovered. Glazing is not particularly common in York, with the majority of plain tiles being left unglazed.

Ridge tiles would have been used alongside the plain tiles. A variety of crested ridge tiles were recovered, with the crests varying in height, but all were of the fan-shaped form typical of York. A few examples were glazed. Some plain ridge tile was also present. A fragment of tile from Period 8 (5221) appears to be

607

part of a ridge tile, but has unusually smoothed and cut edges. It is possible that this may be the footing for a louver, chimney or finial to be fixed to the roof.

Two examples of hip tiles were found. Hip tiles, or bonnet hip tiles, provide a covering for the angle created by the obtuse exterior junctions of two adjacent roof pitches (Armstrong and Armstrong 1987, 238). They are used with plain tiles.

There would have been a smoke vent, chimney pot or louver in the ridge of those buildings where fumes needed to be cleared from the open hearths. Medieval chimney pots are normally dated to the 13th and 14th centuries. There are four examples from Bedern. Two fragments are slightly tapered and have thumbed strips running across the belly. A third piece with a green glaze has stab marks piercing right through the clay, an aperture cut out, and is sooted on the inner surface. The fourth is rounder in cross-section than the others, rather bell-shaped, and has thumbed strips running vertically. These examples have features comparable to those illustrated in Dunning (1961).

Ceramic louvers tend to be much larger and more ornate than chimney pots. The Chamberlains' accounts for c.1390 record that 1s 6d was spent on one

louver for the common kitchen, and a further 16d on mending two other louvers there (YMA, VC 6/2/34), though this may be a reference to wooden louvers. One definite ceramic louver was found among the Bedern material, plus two other possible examples. A group of fragments were recovered from Period 7 deposits (Area 14.II: 1225, 1418, 1427, 1450) to the north-east of Building 5, in construction levels for Buildings 22 and 23. A further piece was found in a spread within Room 5H, and another was in the upper fill (1505) of one of the Period 6 cess pits north-east of Building 5. All may ultimately have been derived from a louver on the roof of Building 5. Three pieces joined together to form about one-eighth of a louver, at least 0·4m high, with a dark green-brown glaze, a hooded aperture, thumbed strips running vertically, and with the top ending in a relatively narrow opening (Fig.339). There are kiln scar marks on the louver which suggest the piece was propped up in the kiln, perhaps with fragments of pottery used as spacers (B. Hurman, pers. comm.). The fabric is very similar to Humber ware pottery dated to the 15th century (A. Mainman, pers. comm.). A fragment of a second louver may have been found in a Period 8 deposit (1156) in the area of Building 22. Although of a similar fabric to the above pieces, it had a flaring rim and a light green glaze. A piece from another Period 7 deposit (1174) from Room 5H was unglazed, had a cut edge and was curved. It may not be from a louver, however, as no comparable forms were found.

One example of a decorative roof finial, probably of 13th or 14th century date, has been noted in the Bedern sample, recovered from a rubbish deposit (6213) associated with the reorganisation of the kitchen in Phase 2 of Period 7. It was thrown like a pot, and was possibly a pot base, but it had been decorated by the addition of two clay spurs. In the centre there was a raised shaft that was broken before firing, as evidenced by the glaze over the break.

Finally, there were two stone roofing tiles from the site, suggesting that some buildings may have been stone-tiled. A limestone tile with a circular nail hole was found in a demolition deposit (7006) for Building 18 in Period 8. One other roofing tile was published in *AY* 10/4 (*336*), a small tile (185 × 100mm and 8–13mm thick) of Magnesian Limestone with a small circular hole 6mm diameter towards one corner. This was found incorporated into the north-east wall of the kitchen (Period 7.1; p.475).

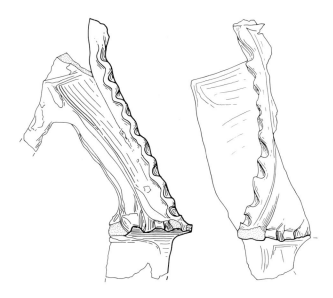

Fig.339 *Adjoining fragments from a ceramic roof louver excavated at Bedern. Scale 1:4*

Stone walls were used for the precinct boundaries, such as the garden wall to the south-east and the wall dividing the vicars from their neighbours on the foundry site to the south-west. Nevertheless, there was clearly access between these tenements, and a traffic of levelling materials from the foundry (p.203, *AY* 10/3). Burnt clay mould fragments appear to have been used to provide firm surfaces; broken pottery was also used (see also Armstrong et al. 1991, 38). External areas subject to continuous wear, such as the area north-east of Building 5 in Period 3, that to the north-west of Building 11, and that to the south-east of the garden wall, were often cobbled, and maintained. Gravel was used to provide firm pathways through the garden areas. We know from the Chamberlains' rolls that it was also used to repair the pavement in the close (YMA, VC 6/2/7). In 1403–4 the rolls record that 3s 8½d was spent on paving in Bedern (YMA, VC 6/2/42), although the excavation provided no evidence of stone flags.

From the 13th to the early 14th century, during Periods 1–5, it appears that the precinct was drained by a number of open gullies. Most of these had been backfilled by Period 6, and were replaced by capped drains, such as the one which ran perpendicular to the garden wall (p.497). In 1331–2 the Chamberlains' rolls record the use of clay, stones and mortar to mend the gutter in Bedern (YMA, VC 6/2/11). In 1378–9, 4d was spent on cement (*serramento*) for the common gutter (YMA, VC 6/2/28). The first major stone-lined drain was constructed in Building 5 during Period 4; by Period 7 substantial tile-lined drains appear to have become the norm. It has already been noted that c.1381–9, 100 'walltiles' were bought for a gutter in Bedern, possibly the kitchen drain (p.576).

Internal layers sometimes appear undifferentiated from external surfaces, making it difficult to distinguish the inside and outside of buildings. The evidence from almost all the college buildings is that they had only earth or mortar floors which often exhibit a minutely layered accumulation of occupation debris. If plank or other floor coverings did exist in some buildings, few remains of them have been found. The chapel was one exception, at least in the late medieval period, where a scattered distribution of small objects (see p.471) resting on a dark loam may be interpreted as items which had fallen through gaps in the floorboards beneath the side pews. The altar, central aisle and antechapel may have been tiled

(see below), or covered with rushes (Harrison 1952, 34); there are frequent references to straw being bought for the chapel from 1352 onwards (S. Rees Jones, pers. comm.). Building 28, and the area of the kitchen adjacent to the oven, were provided with brick floors; presumably these were areas subject to heavy use, and where planks or rushes would have been a fire hazard.

Considerable numbers of medieval floor tiles were recovered from Bedern, although since none of them was found in situ it is uncertain which, if any, of the buildings had a tiled floor. Parts of the chapel and hall are both likely to have been tiled. Thirteenth and 14th century decorated tiles were re-used in the later flooring at the altar end of the chapel, and may have been derived from earlier floors in that building (p.650). A group of plain tiles with green and yellow glazes were also recovered from the chapel in contexts dating from the mid 15th century. Much of the material had been re-used, with large amounts of mortar present on all surfaces, including broken ones.

A green and yellow glazed tile (sf2867) was recovered from the hall and two fragments of decorated tile were also recovered from Period 8 rubbish dumps (5114, 5237) in the yard south-west of the hall. It has not yet been possible to date the design on the two-colour inlaid tile from 5114, but it may be 14th century. The tile from 5237 is very worn, though it is obviously a two-colour inlaid tile. An unglazed fragment from the levelling deposit (6280) for Building 25 is an oddity, for which a parallel has yet to be found. It has a design in counter-relief, which may show the head of a figure.

Several types of plain glazed tiles have also been recovered. The largest group is primarily distinguished by a white slip under a green glaze ranging from light green with speckles to dark green. Nail holes in the corners and the centre of the tile are sometimes visible. The earliest contexts containing these tiles are dated to the mid 13th century. They are found from Period 3 onwards in and around Building 5 and in Period 6–7 in Area 13.X, being particularly concentrated in the rubbish dumps south-west of the hall. A single example of a green plain glazed tile with keying cut into the bottom surface was recovered from Period 6 levels in Building 17 (7353). According to Betts (1985, 432) keying is a 13th century feature.

Stopford (*AY* 11/2) dates plain glazed tiles to between the late 14th and early 16th century. This means that several of the Bedern examples are very early. It has been stated that tiles with nail holes, where the tiles have been pinned and trimmed before firing, are Flemish (Betts 1985, 44), though Stopford doubts this, because of the large numbers of such tiles found on English sites.

A single mosaic tile (sf1000) came from Area 14.IV. It is a long leaf shape and is quite worn. Eames (1985, 16–19) states that this type of tile floor was used from the early 13th century, but had passed out of fashion by the mid 14th century.

The floor tiles from excavations on the Bedern Chapel site were examined by **J. Stopford**, who comments as follows.

None of the ceramic floor tiles found during the excavation in Bedern chapel were found in situ. However, plain glazed tiles were found in sufficient numbers to suggest that they may have been part of a floor. Square tiles of 115–40mm across and 15–20mm deep with five nail holes in the upper surface (corners and centre) were from contexts dating between the late 14th and early 16th century. This agrees with the 15th century date which would be ascribed to these tiles on typological grounds. A single fragment from context 1504, Area 14.II, Period 2, dated as mid–late 13th century, suggests contamination of this context. The only unusual feature of this material is that the tiles are slipped, glazed and fired to either light or dark green. Slip is usually used to produce yellow tiles which were often laid alternately with green examples to give a chequered floor.

Two other sizes of plain glazed floor tile were found on the site. These were slipped and glazed in the usual way to produce either yellow or green tiles and nail holes were apparent on a few examples. The larger tiles measured about 260mm across and 39–48mm deep, and came from contexts dating from the mid 15th century. The mortar found on all faces suggests that they had been re-used as builders' rubble or make-up. The smaller tiles measured about 115mm across and 25–40mm deep. Many were worn and some burned. They were found in contexts dating from the late 14th to the early 16th century.

Seven decorated tiles were also found on the site of Bedern chapel. None was in situ or thought to have been used in a medieval floor here. Most were in post-medieval contexts. They are, however, of interest in terms of the regional study of the medieval tile industry. Three tiles are of series identified from sites elsewhere in the region. These comprise, firstly, a worn and abraded example (sf10) of the Inlaid series, design number (DN) 145 (regional design number series), dated on typological grounds to the mid 13th century. A plain tile of this series was also found. Secondly, there was one tile (sf11) and one fragment (sf117) of DN356, Nottingham series. These tiles were probably made in the Nottingham region in the mid 14th century.

Unknown from elsewhere in the region are a tile (sf14) and a fragment (sf13) of two different designs (DN401 and 402) but of similar manufacture. The decoration is inlaid to a maximum depth of 2mm using good-quality white clay and a fine, well-prepared body clay but poorly applied glaze. The fabric is largely reduced. Dimensions are 97mm across and 21mm deep. A further decorated tile fragment is of unidentifiable type (sf15) and the final example was not seen (sf12).

Often the presence of a hearth is the best indication that we are dealing with the interior of a building. A wide variety of hearths were excavated within the college precinct. The majority were of pitched tiles, usually set in a shallow construction cut, and sometimes with bricks on edge set around the perimeter (as in Building 11 in Period 5), sometimes with flat-laid brick edging (as in Building 6, Period 2), and sometimes with limestone and cobble kerbing. In Room 16F pitched tiles and broken edge-set pottery were used to form the body of the hearth; in Period 1 the hearth in Building 4 was constructed from limestone cobbles set in clay. The kitchen hearths were initially just burnt clay edged with bricks; these were replaced by brick hearths at the end of Period 7. All hearths were generally square or rectangular, although in Building 5 during Period 6 there is one semi-circular example, with pitched tiles radiating from half a millstone set at the centre. Most hearths were freestanding in the middle of a room, but some were provided with firebacks and set against external walls. During a later stage of kitchen usage all the hearths were set against the walls and provided with smoke hoods. In some cases it appears that portable braziers were used for additional heating, and would have been placed on brick standings.

We do not know the extent to which the Bedern buildings had glazed windows, aside from the hall, chapel and counting house (probably to be identified as Building 27). A relatively small number of lead window cames were recovered, compared to other medieval excavations in York (*AY* 17/15 in prep.). Fragments of medieval window glass were excavated (pp.572–3), although their distribution does not help in identifying the position of any glazed windows as, on the whole, they were found in secondary post-medieval contexts scattered widely across the site. There was certainly a concentration of window glass fragments and lead cames within the chapel, which we know from documentary sources (pp.562–5) and excavated fragments (pp.568–70) had stained glass in the windows. The Statute Book records the repair of glass windows in the counting house, chapel and common hall during 1419/22. In most buildings internal lighting would have been provided by oil lamps. During the 14th century oil for the chapel lamps is a regular purchase recorded in the Chamberlains' rolls. Three stone cresset lamps were recovered during the excavation (sfs135, 1444 and 1967). A number of fragments of glass hanging lamps were also excavated (sfs329, 338, 853 and 2537; *AY* 17/15 in prep.). These tend to be found on relatively wealthy sites. They are commonly shown in manuscript illustrations hanging above altars, and are also found on many monastic and ecclesiastical sites (R. Tyson, pers. comm.). In 1360 the vicars spent a comparatively large sum, 3s 5d, on a case for an oil lamp for the chapel (YMA, VC 6/2/19).

Various items of structural ironwork were recovered from Bedern (*AY* 17/15 in prep.) including a window bar (14.II, sf198), twelve hinge pivots and eleven hinge straps of various forms from doors or cupboards, as well as numerous nails and staples. There are references in the Chamberlains' rolls to the purchase of a variety of structural ironwork, often associated with the construction and maintenance of the garden fences (p.578), including *stotnails, chaknails, spireings and thaknails* (YMA, VC 6/2/7). A variety of hooks, which may have been used to hang items inside the buildings, were excavated along with eleven candleholders which would have assisted in the provision of lighting. A number of iron keys, hasps, locks and padlocks were also recovered from medieval deposits. Some of the keys may have been for use with lockable wooden chests, such as that repaired in the chapel in 1369–70 (YMA, VC 6/1/1). Others, however, were door keys, indicating that some, at least, of the Bedern buildings were lockable. In 1403–4 one lock was bought for the garden door (YMA, VC 6/2/42).

Refuse disposal and the local environment

It appears that there was little organisation in the disposal of rubbish within Bedern. Domestic waste was dumped over a wide area within the college precinct, although pits in the gardens were particularly favoured. Floor and occupation deposits within buildings, however, have been hard to detect, suggesting that the rooms were kept fairly clean. Distributions of a number of categories of finds were plotted in case these might provide clues to the localisation of activities within Bedern. Unfortunately all categories showed generalised distributions which merely serve to indicate the areas of rubbish disposal, rather than primary usage.

External surfaces, however, may have required periodic cleansing, despite the increasing attention to proper drainage and paving from the 14th century (see above). The Chamberlains' rolls record that in 1398–9 6d was spent on the carriage of dung and cleaning of roads within Bedern (YMA, VC 6/2/37); in 1401 again they record the carriage of dung from the close and from the door of Bedern (YMA, VC 6/2/41).

The plant remains suggest that for much of its history there were areas in Bedern which were wasteland, with weeds growing between the buildings. Apart from stinging nettle, other waste ground taxa included fat-hen, buttercup, greater celandine and deadly nightshade. Other probable weeds included hogweed and self-heal. Some other weeds, like corncockle, were clearly grain contaminants; this group also included corn marigold and shepherd's needle.

There was evidence of other vegetation typical of marginal wetland, peatland or water meadow communities, including *Sphagnum* moss leaves, cottongrass, water-plantain, toad-rush, bracken and heather. Some of these may have been growing locally on Bedern, beside drainage ditches. Water-plantain is characteristic of muddy substrata beside slow-flowing rivers, ponds, ditches and canals (Clapham et al. 1962, 934). Aquatic plants such as duckweed and pondweed may have been growing in pools of standing water on the site. The recovery of amphibian bones confirms the presence of nearby water. On the other hand, saw-sedge, which is normally found in cut wetland vegetation, may have been brought to the site in material for floor coverings.

Finally, there were a number of plants probably derived from hay-like material, including sedge, marsh marigold, yellow-rattle, ragged robin, red clover, cow parsley and buttercup. Many of these may have been derived from material imported into the college stables.

The animal bones may also throw some light on the micro-palaeoecology of the college precinct. **J.F. Hamshaw-Thomas** comments:

The remains of a number of rats, attributed to black rat (Rattus rattus), *attest to the widespread distribution of this species across York during the medieval period (AY 15/4, 258; AY 15/5, 365–6). The presence of isolated rodent bones and gnawing marks made by rodents indicates considerable infestation of Bedern (Fig.340). A more representative sample of the small mammal population is provided by the sieved contents of context 1505 (Area 14.II, Period 6, p.452; Scott 1985). The cess pit appears to have functioned as a trap for a number of unsuspecting small animals, thus giving some idea of the micro-palaeoecology of the area. The relatively high number of black rat bones is a better indication of this animal's prevalence on the site. The remains of bank vole, house and wood mouse indicate the presence of nearby overgrown vegetation. Bank vole in particular is a species which avoids open terrain. Interestingly the presence of amphibian (mainly frog but some toad) bones accords well with the botanical data illustrating the dank, and no doubt fetid, nature of parts of the site (see Table 17, p.617).*

From the sample of bird bones, species from the crow family (raven, magpie, rook, crow and jackdaw) indicate the presence of scavengers — a fairly common feature of

Fig.340 Rodent gnawing marks on a chicken tarsometatarsus indicating the presence of vermin in Bedern

urban archaeological samples (O'Connor 1993). Raptors were also recorded (goshawk, sparrow hawk, red kite and buzzard) which may have been either scavengers or sporting birds. A number of small birds, best described as commensals (blackbird, redwing, fieldfare, house sparrow, greenfinch and pigeon), were recorded.

Daily Life in the College

Further study of the documentary records of the college may yet, at some future date, reveal more about the daily life of a vicar choral. The following account draws upon Harrison (1952) supplemented, where possible, by archaeological evidence recovered from the Bedern excavations.

The most valuable guide to daily life in the medieval college is provided by the sets of rules (ibid., 43–73). Between c.1390 and c.1430 a number of rules were set down which are thought to reflect established practice within the college (ibid., 56–8). Many of the rules relate to dining, which was at the heart of communal college life.

The daily life of the vicars revolved around the seven canonical hours, with the precise timing of the services varying according to the number of hours of daylight available. The first service of the day, that of Matins (i.e. Lauds), was not to begin until break of day, except on Sundays and on certain feast days when it began at 4am, or on Christmas Day when it was at 2am. Depending upon the time of year, therefore, the vicars' day would have started between 2am and 5am, with breakfast normally being taken in the hall at the end of the service. Breakfast would have been followed by the morning offices of Prime and Terce which were regarded as preparation for the daily masses in the Minster. The chief of these was the capitular mass, so called because it was part of the obligation of the members of the chapter to be present, the mass being sung by a vicar and attended by all the vicars, who received the oblations offered at this mass. After the end of the capitular mass, at c.11am, the vicars would have had some time to attend to their own affairs.

In the afternoon the vicars were required to assemble in their hall for dinner, with the sub-chanter and officials at the high table. The vicars also had to attend to the hour-offices of Sext, None, Vespers and Compline. Supper was taken in the early evening, c.5–6pm. During the winter months the vicars were permitted one alcoholic drink after dinner and, after the washing of hands, one round the fire. After supper they were allowed three more drinks up to 8 o'clock, but the second and third occasions only with the consent of the sub-chanter. During the summer the vicars were also allowed an alcoholic drink in the morning, after Prime, as well as one drink after supper, and up to three drinks between 7pm and 9pm. The gate of Bedern was closed at dusk, and no vicar was supposed to be abroad in the city after dark.

From the 15th century any vicar was also allowed to entertain friends in his own house and have meals served from the kitchen. Should he order bread and ale from the common stock, however, he was expected to pay for them. A vicar who was suffering from illness was also allowed to dine in his own house, and to have one quart of ale from the kitchen at 5pm each day. Should a vicar give notice that he was to dine with a friend in the city, or with a canon as an ordinary guest, he was allowed a 1d rebate on his kitchen account.

Every vicar took a turn to read during dinner and to serve the food from the kitchen. The vicar who served during one week was expected to read the next week. Any vicar who, through his disorderly conduct in the hall or elsewhere, or by his 'vain questions pressed to the point of argument', caused discord in spite of his having been warned to desist, was liable to a fine of 12d. Nevertheless, there were occasional transgressions of this rule. Indeed, on 26 December 1419, an altercation arose between Robert Ripon and John of Middleton before supper. Middleton raised a poker against Ripon, who seized him and threw him on the fire grate (Harrison 1952, 61). There is no record of the cause of the dispute, but games of chess and draughts, betting and gambling and throwing dice, within the limits of the hall, were forbidden under a penalty of 3s 4d.

By the later 15th century it appears that a strict monastic rule was not always followed. On several occasions vicars were able to wander about the streets of York late at night. In 1472 the Dean and Chapter investigated a complaint that the gates of Bedern were often not closed until 10pm, on one occasion being left open all night, so that women of loose character were able to enter Bedern unobserved (ibid., 32). In spite of an order of the Dean and Chapter that a lamp be hung from the archway and lighted every night at dusk, John Fell (vicar 1469–1506) was able

to form the habit of leaving Bedern and not returning until 10pm.

It is clear, too, that some vicars had taken women
into their houses in Bedern. In 1462, for example,
William Holbeck, vicar choral, was accused of fornication with a woman called Agnes Smith, formerly a
domestic servant, of having kept her in his house in
Bedern, and of being the father of several children
whom she bore (ibid., 70). The worst offender, however, was William Burdcleuer (vicar 1459–1506). In
1461, only two years after entering the college, he
was charged with harbouring a woman named
Margaret Shilton, by whom he was the father of two
children, and whom he had kept in his house for two
months. In February and April 1466 he appeared
before the court again, each time charged with fornication with Joan Taylor of Bishophill, York, the offences having taken place within his house in Bedern.
In October 1466 he was charged with having, on three
separate occasions, women with him in his house.
Four years later he was accused of fornication with
Margaret Middleton, of St Andrewgate; two years
after this he was accused of a similar offence with
Joan, wife of Thomas Wilson, although on this last
occasion he was cleared of the charge (ibid., 70–1).
One might imagine that his days in the clergy were
numbered. Far from it — he even held the office of
succentor for six years (1483–9).

The vicars also fell prey to other vices. John
Hunter (vicar 1439–73), on being charged with ha-
bitual drunkenness, pleaded that his mouth felt so
dry that he must drink. Owing to his age and infir-
mity he was merely ordered to avoid taverns on pain
of being deprived of his choir habit (ibid., 71).

It also appears to have been difficult to maintain
reasonable behaviour amongst some vicars even
when in the choir itself; serious absenteeism, discord-
ant singing, incessant chattering and the unauthor-
ised shortening of divine services figure prominently
in visitation *comperta* of the 15th century. In 1472, for
example, it was reported that 'at matins it is difficult
to find four [vicars] on each side [of the choir]', and
that 'those processing into the choir sang discord-
antly' (Burton 1976). Such unseemly behaviour also
extended to the common meal times. John Fell and
his companions were found in 1472 to be inattentive
during the nightly bible readings in the common hall
'but sitting by the fire they chatter throughout the
time of reading' (ibid.).

Archaeological evidence for such irreligious behaviour comprises the various dice and gaming
pieces recovered from the college precinct. Of particular interest are the large number of coins, tokens
and gaming pieces lost beneath the floorboards of
the college chapel (see pp.648, 650).

On entering the college a prospective vicar was
examined as to both his musical ability and his moral
fibre, to ascertain that both were fitting for the office
he wished to assume. The musical talents of the vicars were guided by the precentor of the Minster, and
a weekly practice was held at which instruction and
correction took place. Attendance at services was
compulsory, and exceptions were made only when
reasonable cause could be shown. From 1291 onwards a system of fines was laid down for punish-
ment of absences.

Archaeology provides evidence for the vicars'
musical interests. For example, a number of bone
pegs have been found from adjoining sites at Bedern
and Aldwark. Two were found on the foundry site
(sf687 and *7984, AY* 17/12); eight on Bedern south-
west (*8063–4, 8066–71*); one from Bedern north-east
(*8065*) and one at 2 Aldwark (*8124*). Another two are
known from York from the medieval hospital site at
Union Terrace (*AY* 11/1). These objects have been
identified as harp tuning pegs (Wolfe 1993). In each
case the shaft of the peg is tapered to fit snugly in a
hole in the arm of the harp; the large end has a square
head which is turned by a key, and the small end has
a hole or slot to hold the end of the string. The harp
was probably played as entertainment during dinner or as an accompaniment for church music. Variations in the size of the Bedern pegs show that they
are derived from several different instruments. The
vicars also appear to have made, or at least repaired,
their own pegs within the college precinct. At least
one of the Bedern pegs had snapped at the hole and
had been redrilled; another had been left unfinished
as it was made of spongy bone and was probably too
poor to complete.

The preparation of manuscripts and psalm books
also probably took place within the precinct, although
the college was not a major centre of manuscript production. Nevertheless, a number of lead alloy and
bone points, or parchment prickers, were recovered
from the excavations, principally from the south-west
of Bedern Close. These have been interpreted as tools

used in the laying out of a manuscript page. Other examples are known from York from the medieval hospital of St Mary's in Union Terrace (*AY* 11/1, 27) and the Gilbertine Priory at Fishergate (*AY* 17/15 in prep.). At Bedern their distribution across the college precinct suggests that the vicars were involved in this task within their own residences. The college books, which would have been of considerable value, are likely to have been stored within the relative security of the library (Building 27), from where they would have been easily accessible for daily readings in the hall. A slate tablet (Area 13: sf1992), bevelled on three edges, indicating that it once had a wooden frame, was found in Period 8 deposits of the 16th century. The tablet was gridded on one side and lined on the other, where it was inscribed with the letters 'Adam' and 'H'.

The documentary sources suggest that many of the vicars enjoyed considerable personal wealth. From some 30 wills made by the vicars choral before 1500 it is clear that most had furnishings to bequeath as well as clothes, books and other personal items. Virtually all had beds and bed linen; many others mention table linen and equipment; some had painted wall hangings. Many of the vicars' wills give the impression of some wealth as they often owned quite elaborate ecclesiastical objects. See pp.579–80 for full details and references.

In addition to the written evidence, some of the finds from Bedern also suggest prosperity (*AY* 17/15 in prep.). A gold ring with a sapphire setting (sf390) was found associated with Building 5 and a gold brooch (sf2847) was recovered from a deposit outside Building 9. A jet counter or pendant carved with a crucifixion scene with the Virgin and St John (sf2601) was found south-west of the close. Two seal stamps (sfs2264, 2327) were found in residual contexts. A Spanish coin of James II of Aragon (*AY* 18/1, 207), probably deposited late in the 14th century, may be explained as a souvenir of a pilgrimage to Compostella. The large number of foreign coins and tokens from Bedern is indicative of high status and a cosmopolitan range of contacts.

The textiles from Bedern represent a full range of fabric-types, from coarse sackcloth, through wool clothing and household linen, to more prestigious textiles, such as silks and half-silks. The better-quality fabrics were found in the college precinct rather than

the foundry (P. Walton Rogers in *AY* 17/15 in prep.). Most textiles were recovered from the college gardens in Areas 13.III, IV and X, with two finds from the chapel and two from Area 14.II. Several come from pits, in at least one instance a cess pit. These are likely to be worn fabrics, torn up and re-used as latrine wipes.

The pottery from Bedern (pp.401–2) is largely indistinguishable from any medieval urban deposit in York, and does not appear to be diagnostic of the type of site. There is a range of tableware forms in the 13th century but the quality of the pottery declines in the 14th and 15th centuries, by which time it had probably been replaced by pewter or glass on the dining table. At Westminster Abbey in the late 14th century each monk used a plate, dish and saucer made out of pewter (Harvey 1993, 45).

Several styles of the most prestigious glass tableware were used at Bedern, including some which may have been individually commissioned. This compares more closely with the glass from castles and palaces of the period than with the more abstinent monastic sites. **Rachel Tyson** has commented as follows on the medieval glass vessels. A full report will be published in *AY* 17/15.

An impressive quantity and range of decorative tablewares was excavated, including a high-lead glass goblet (Area 14: sf513) and jug or pouring flask (Area 13: sfs2214, 2615, 2617, 2619, 2632, 2657), two enamelled beakers (Area 14: sf323; Area 13: sf757), a blue-painted bowl (Area 14: sf227), and one or two colourless bowls with blue-trailed decoration (Area 13: sfs2274, 2765). These all date to the late 13th and 14th centuries, when medieval tableware was at its most decorative. Manuscript illustrations of contemporary feasts suggest that it was used in a communal capacity, which allowed the host to make the most of his 'conspicuous consumption' as his vessels were passed around the guests. High social status could be maintained, and social differentiations perpetuated, by restricting the use of particular vessels to a specific group, for example, those dining at the high table. By the late 15th century, although there were still individual decorated vessels on the table, manuscript illustrations imply a more individual use of some vessels, particularly drinking vessels. Most illustrations of this date show each guest drinking from his own beaker. A deep red/purple fragment may come from a table vessel of the 15th century (Area 13: sf2404).

A number of potash glass flasks, urinals and possible items of distilling equipment were also excavated at Bedern. A wide variety of flasks with wide and narrow necks, kicked and convex rounded bases were made in medieval England, with diverse uses. These included the preparation of herbal, alcoholic and medicinal recipes, and colouring pigments. Distilling equipment was used in alchemy. Large deposits of distilling vessels have been found on monastic sites, such as Pontefract Priory (Moorhouse 1972), and alchemy, regarded as a philosophical discipline, is known to have been practised in monasteries. A single piece of tubing was found at Bedern (Area 14: sf836), which may have come from an alembic, or the neck of a flask. The convex fragments found (Area 14: sfs527, 850, 893; Area 13: sfs2555, 2561) may have come from either uroscopy vessels or the domes of alembics. There was also one vessel with an inverted rim (Area 14: sf206), possibly used in industrial or distilling contexts. Glass uroscopy vessels, with wide necks and rounded bases, were used to examine the colour of urine, an extremely widespread practice which was the principal method of medical diagnosis from the 13th to the 17th century. However, this form of vessel was also used in recipe preparations, and a similar shape is shown used as a consecration vessel (Fowler 1893). In addition, flasks with narrow necks, some with wrythen ribbed decoration, are likely to have been used as table vessels. The main concentration of kicked bases from flasks was found in Area 13.X, perhaps supporting a culinary or tableware function.

Apart from those objects related to the vicars' daily tasks within the Minster other finds indicate a variety of minor craft activities within the college precinct. On the whole, however, it appears that the college buildings were kept very clean. There are very few finds from internal floor levels and most medieval objects have been recovered from secondary rubbish deposits, including external spreads, rubbish pits and garden levels.

Quantities of mould fragments from the casting of copper alloy objects were recovered from floor levels, particularly towards the south-west end of the precinct (pp.422, 428, 497), but it appears that these had been redeposited from the adjacent foundry site (*AY* 10/3) as convenient hard-core. A chalk mould for casting pewter counters (sf778) was recovered from the long trench, and a second with bead-like impressions (sf2628) was found near Building 10. These are also likely to have originated outside the college, although probably not from the foundry, whose output appears to have been confined to cauldrons and small bells (ibid.). A considerable number of schist and sandstone hones were recovered from both sides of Bedern Close (Area 14: sfs268, 391, 437, 471, 486, 525; Area 13: sfs1865, 1955, 1981, 2207, 2390, 2394, 2447, 2574, 2713, 2779, 2785). These were probably carried by individual vicars for use in sharpening personal knives rather than providing evidence for industrial activity.

The practice of spinning at Bedern is attested by twelve spindle whorls (Area 14: sfs148, 224; Area 13: sfs207, 608, 618, 1501, 1576, 1743, 1911, 1964, 2406, 2859) and by a bundle of spinner's waste yarn-ends. This evidence is scattered through late medieval levels and is also represented by residual finds from post-medieval levels. Weaving, however, is only represented by a fragment of loom weight (Area 13: sf190) and a pin beater (Area 13: sf1903), both of which are almost certainly pre-12th century artefacts redeposited (P. Walton Rogers in *AY* 17/15 in prep.). It is clear that spinning was being practised, if intermittently, between the 11th/12th and 15th centuries. During the medieval period, spinning was done mostly by women outworkers, spinning in their own homes in order to supply yarn to the weaver or clothier (Swanson 1989, 30–2). The evidence from Bedern therefore supports the documentary evidence that some women may have been resident within the college precinct during the late medieval period.

The evidence for bone and antler working has been assessed by **J.F. Hamshaw-Thomas**, who has provided the following report.

While a small collection of horncores was recovered from the 1985 sample (Scott 1985) they were, together with sheep horncores, under-represented across the site as a whole. This is not unusual and may be attributed to the export of the horns to specialist horn workers in other parts of York (AY 15/5, 385–7).

One of the more interesting collections of bones relates to a most unusual craft activity. Of the sieved component of context 1505 (Area 14.II, Period 6, p.452) the mammal bone was dominated by the bones of red squirrel (Table 17), specifically distal limb elements. Metapodials and phalanges made up over 97% of the 267 squirrel bones. Such a specific range of skeletal elements is best interpreted as the waste from the later stages of the preparation of squirrel pelts, the distal extremities (feet) being brought

Fig.341 Cut marks on a cat mandible resulting from skinning

on to the site as 'riders' on semi-prepared pelts (Scott 1985). The presence of a knife cut on the lateral surface of a cuboid bone adds weight to this interpretation. It would not be unreasonable to speculate that these pelts were employed in the adornment of the vicars' clothing, possibly as the fur-edging used to trim their clerical gowns.

A second example of the use of animal skins is provided by the contents of another cess pit (4047, Period 8, Phase 3). This produced a small, mixed sample, dominated by the bones of several cats. The vast majority of the bones were from the fore limb. Of special note is the presence of a complete adult cat mandible, with a series of parallel knife cuts on the mesial/labial aspect (Fig.341). A large fragment of cat cranial vault from the same context also bore a series of fine cut marks on the frontal/nasal bone (Fig.342). Cut marks in this position are logically the result of skinning. A similar pattern of cut marks has previously been recorded on cat skulls from medieval deposits at Coppergate (O'Connor 1986a).

Three contexts, one from Period 8 (5268), one from Period 9 (5027) and another from the foundry Period 6 (2021), showed a marked over-representation of sheep metapodials, suggestive of some specialised deposit. This is fully discussed in AY 15/5, 367–8.

Finally, a number of worked bone and antler fragments were recorded. However, the limited nature of the sample simply indicates that some preparatory bone working was

Table 17 Number of bone fragments recovered from context 1505 by hand collection and sieving, excluding fish (from Scott 1985, table 12)

	No.	%
Cow	105	14.1
Sheep	80	10.7
Pig	30	4.0
Horse	2	0.3
Roe deer	1	0.1
Red deer	2	0.3
Squirrel	267	35.7
Mouse/Vole	1	0.1
Rabbit	10	1.3
Black rat	18	2.4
Bank vole	1	0.1
Wood mouse	1	0.1
House mouse	3	0.4
Dog	1	0.1
Domestic fowl	134	17.9
Domestic goose	24	3.2
Blackbird	2	0.3
Partridge	3	0.4
Small passerine	12	1.6
Wild duck	4	0.5
Woodcock	1	0.1
Large wader	1	0.1
Red grouse	4	0.5
Frog	38	5.1
Toad	2	0.3
Total	747	

617

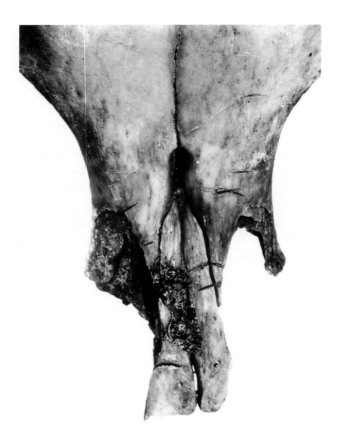

Fig.342 *Cut marks across the frontal and nasal areas of a cat skull, consistent with removal of the skin*

taking place on the site; it does not appear to have constituted a major economic activity.

The vicars' diet

From the study of the plant remains and animal bones from Bedern it is possible to make some preliminary observations about the daily diet of the vicars. It is to be hoped that at some stage the transcription and study of the college Kitchen Books will allow detailed comparison with the archaeological evidence. For the present such comparisons are limited to feasts when special purchases were sometimes recorded in other college accounts.

In 1419–22, for example, the Statute Book records the expenses incurred for a feast ordered for Robert Lassell and others coming with him. These included 7d on two chickens, 10d for twelve 'fieldfare' and 1d for pounding ginger (S. Rees-Jones, pers. comm.). In

1423–4, the Chamber-lain's rolls record money spent on entertaining the dean (William Gray), including 10s 8d for capons, pullets and cockerels; 14d for various delicacies bought for the same occasion; 4d for cheese; and 8d for a bottle of wine called 'treblane', 'on account of the dean' (Harrison 1952, 118). In 1489–90 the Suc-centors' rolls record 3s 8d spent on wine for the monks of St Mary's Abbey, York, when they dined in the hall. There are two later records of feasts, for 1589 (Harrison 1952, 129). For the first, on 11 September, the vicars were given half a venison and consumed a barrel of beer. There was further expenditure on salt, flour, butter, oil and one gallon of clear wine. They dined on venison again on 17 November, with three shoulders of mutton, butter, salt, flour, plus one firkin of beer and two gallons of clear wine. They also paid 8d to the waytes for playing in the hall. The chantry commissioners were entertained by the vicars to a dinner of venison and swan (YMA, VC 6/1/26).

The more usual college diet is represented by the Kitchen Books, the study of which is still awaited. In one week in 1562 they record that the menu included chicken, beef, venison and mutton. Bread was also no doubt a staple part of the diet and was probably baked in the college kitchens, the vicars having been provided with a mill in the 13th century (*VCHY*, 507).

In her study of the Benedictine house at Westminster Abbey, Harvey (1993) has looked at the monastic diet for the period c.1495–c.1525. In the absence of detailed work on the college Kitchen Books this provides a useful benchmark with which to compare Bedern. On most days of the year at Westminster Abbey dinner was probably served at 11.00 or 11.30am. By that time most of the monks had been up for about four to five hours, and some may have breakfasted on bread and ale, but they had not tasted cooked food since supper, a meal served in the late afternoon, on the previous day. Dinner was the main meal of day, consisting of several courses; supper was a light meal, at which the monks probably made do with a single cooked dish.

The monks at Westminster Abbey achieved a genteel standard of living, with an annual outlay of around £11 per monk, that is, 7d per day. In total, 37% of the net income of the Abbey was spent on foodstuffs. Of this nearly 50% was spent on meat, meat products and fish; 18% on ale; 13% on bread;

9% on wine, 5% on eggs and thereafter 3% or less on each of flour, dairy produce, fruit and vegetables, spices and salt (ibid., 37).

Fish constituted an important part of the medieval diet. At Westminster Abbey a monk normally ate fish on approximately 215 days in the year, although it was considered a dish for dinner rather than supper (ibid., 46). Approximately half of these meals consisted of preserved fish that had been salted, smoked, dried or pickled, and half comprised fresh fish. This pattern of consumption is typical of great households towards the end of the medieval period (Dyer 1988). At Westminster Abbey, by the late 15th century, the cod family made up half the fish served in the course of the year (Harvey 1993, 45). Herring, however, was a natural favourite of all kitcheners, both for its cheapness and for the ease with which it could be stored, salted in barrels, and in earlier times probably formed a higher proportion of fish consumed.

The monks at Westminster Abbey ate flesh-meat on about 75 days per year, but could expect to have it at supper as well as dinner. Mutton accounted for 46% of the total weight of flesh-meat served each year, beef 24%, pork 14% and veal 11.5% (ibid., 53). However, this may be a reflection of the aristocratic status of the monks and lower down the social scale beef is likely to have exceeded mutton in importance.

The monks also received an allowance of a gallon of ale per day, and a daily loaf of bread, probably weighing 2·5lbs. Fresh fruit and leafy vegetables were probably a rare item in the diet. Dairy products, on the other hand, probably played an important part, including milk, eggs and cheese (ibid., 60–1).

Plant foods

(The text in this section is based largely on reports written by Dr A.R. Hall.) Some of the pit fills gave good assemblages of foodplants, notably fruits and flavourings. It appears that both food waste and faecal material were preserved. However, the limited nature of the on-site sampling and subsequent analysis means that it is invalid to make detailed quantitative comparisons between samples, or to examine changes in food-plants through time. The relative abundance of fig and elderberry, for instance, probably owes as much to their capacity to resist decay

as their importance in diet; figs, of course, yield huge numbers of seeds from each fruit. Nevertheless it is possible to make some general statements about the role of plant foods in the diet of the vicars.

Cereal 'bran' was common in several samples, and was probably overlooked in many more, although the abundance of seed fragments of corncockle points to the presence of flour-based foods. It is not possible to determine in what form the cereals were consumed, although bread and gruel are the most likely. Corncockle was formerly a widespread and troublesome weed of cereals. Fragments of its seeds were also common in contemporary samples from Beverley (Armstrong et al. 1991, 215). Flour milled from contaminated grain is discoloured, and bread made with it is unpalatable and poisonous. Small doses may produce mild intoxication, but larger amounts can lead to delirium, convulsions, damage to the circulatory system, and even death (Hall 1981). It is unlikely that the residents of Bedern consumed it in such damaging quantities, although ironically it may have helped to reduce their worm burdens. Charred cereal grains were also identified in several samples, with oats being the most common, wheat and barley slightly less so. All were presumably from cultivated crops. Fragments of quernstone recovered from the college precinct may indicate that the vicars were grinding some flour on site, although they had been granted a separate mill during the 13th century. The quernstones may also have been used for grinding herbs and spices. In 1471–2, 6d was paid to Thomas Halton (a vicar) 'pro fundatione de Mustard stonys in coquina', that is, for making a foundation for the mustard stones (presumably some kind of grinding stones) in the kitchen (YMA, VC 6/6/3).

The presence of huge numbers of fig seeds, and of considerable quantities of grape pips and strawberry seeds, contrasts with the evidence from Anglian and Anglo-Scandinavian deposits from York where these plants are, to all intents and purposes, absent. Fig seeds were recovered from most samples. Both fig seeds and grape pips are particularly common in Roman and medieval cess pit deposits throughout the British Isles (Tomlinson 1993, 239–43). The grape pips could have been derived from raisins, which Allison (1969, 65) refers to as being imported into Hull from the Continent in the 14th century. However, from references in the Chamberlains' rolls it appears that for a short period at least the vicars cultivated vines, although they could have been grown for ornament as much as for their fruit. At some stage during 1381–9, Richard Pert and other labourers were working on the close of vines (*clausurum vinearum*) for a total of ten and a half days over three weeks between the feast of the annunciation of the Blessed Virgin Mary and Easter (YMA, VC 6/2/32). In 1403–4 the janitor spent three days pruning the vines in the Bedern garden. It is well documented that there were many English monastic vineyards in the medieval period (Darby 1977, 362–3). It is interesting that their cultivation at Bedern coincides with the 'reformation' of common life.

The strawberries may have been consumed fresh or as some kind of conserve. Blackberry and raspberry were also recognised, but these were not as common. The berries of all three may have been gathered wild in woodland around York, or the vicars may have grown the bushes in their garden. The abundance of strawberries may suggest that they, at least, were cultivated. Elderberry seeds were also very common, although the seeds are very robust. Some of the seeds might be interpreted as part of the disturbed ground assemblage, although their presence in faeces suggests that the vicars may have been gathering elderberries for food.

Remains of apples and plums were also recovered, although they were not as abundant as one might expect in food remains, given that the vicars had their own orchard (p.579). Both cherry and sloe fruitstones were also represented. Blackthorn, from which sloes were collected, is a native plant found in scrub, woods and hedges throughout England (Clapham et al. 1962, 44). It used to be commonly planted as a hedge, but rarely for its fruit. The medieval sloes were probably gathered from wild plants or hedges. The cherries are also likely to have been wild. Hazelnuts were relatively common, and there was one instance of walnut shell.

Other food plants recovered in small quantities comprised field bean, pea, leek and perhaps turnip. Peas and beans are probably under-represented in the archaeological record as they do not survive well in anoxic waterlogged conditions (Tomlinson 1993, 249). Leek has also been identified in deposits from Anglo-Scandinavian York and medieval Chester (ibid., 243). Linseed may have been eaten in a cereal and linseed gruel or in bread. Each of these may have been cultivated locally, possibly in the vicars' garden (pp.578–9). From the 1330s until the turn of the century the Chamberlains' rolls record that the vicars were buying seeds and vegetable plants for their garden, generally on an annual basis. Unfortunately, the varieties grown are often not mentioned but in 1352 cabbage seeds and plants were purchased (YMA, VC 6/2/15). In 1380, leeks were bought for the garden at a cost of 4d, and one woman was paid 4d for working there for a day (YMA, VC 6/2/30). In both 1399 and 1401 kale was planted (YMA, VC 6/2/38 and 41).

Archaeobotanical evidence was also recovered for a range of herbs, spices and flavourings, comprising coriander, fennel, opium poppy, dill, summer savory, and possibly celery seed and mustard. There are some differences in the range and quantity of remains of plants used as flavourings between medieval deposits at Bedern and Anglo-Scandinavian deposits of similar type at 16–22 Coppergate. Thus, fennel seed is often present in the faecal deposits at Bedern, sometimes in large numbers, but it is almost certainly absent from Coppergate. Coriander is recorded at both sites, whilst dill is common at Coppergate and rare at Bedern. The abundance of fennel parallels contemporary deposits from Beverley, where it was by far the most common herb represented (Armstrong et al. 1991, 215). Although fennel is native to southern England it is only rarely found in the north (Clapham et al. 1962, 525). It is therefore likely that the vicars cultivated the plants in their garden, although it was only the fruits (mericarps) which were recovered and these may have been traded dry as a flavouring. From references in the Chamberlains' rolls for the 14th century we know that the vicars were regularly buying parsley seeds for the garden.

Finally, hempseed was recovered from two deposits; it is probable that it was cultivated as a cash crop rather than for consumption. Godwin (1975) suggests that the cultivation of hemp was probably introduced during the Anglo-Saxon period, although there are records of the species from Roman deposits in York (Tomlinson 1993, 86). There is documentary evidence for the cultivation of hemp in the medieval period (Bradshaw et al. 1981), as well as archaeobotanical evidence from a number of urban sites, including Beverley and Hull (Tomlinson 1993, 88).

The animal bones

By J.F. Hamshaw-Thomas

The interpretation of the changing proportions of domestic animals over time is a matter of considerable complexity. Simple variation in the number of recorded fragments for each species may relate as much to taphonomic and methodological problems as to any change in dietary choice (pp.402–4). Notwithstanding these caveats, there are a number of general trends in the data which seem to reflect genuine changes in the form of the deposited assemblage. Periods 1 to 7 show remarkable similarity in terms of the relative proportion of the different taxa, but it is notable that there is a gradual increase in the proportion of poultry (here defined as chickens and geese), and a relatively high abundance of pig in Periods 6 and 7. Period 8 is marked by the apparent increase in the number of cattle bone fragments, a trend clearly reversed in Period 9 (Tables 18 and 19).

The bulk of the meat diet in all periods was provided by the common farmyard domesticates (cattle, sheep and pig). Whether cattle or sheep were eaten as veal/beef or lamb/mutton appears to have been determined by the prevailing husbandry strategies, rather than consumer choice. There is no indication that any other domestic mammals

formed a regular component in the meat diet. Poultry clearly formed an increasingly significant role in the diet.

The range of wild taxa which has been recovered and interpreted as food residue points to a diet of considerable diversity. Rabbit is first recorded in Period 5, but by Period 8 is well represented. This adds weight to the assertion that the rabbit was not widely marketed in the urban context prior to the 15th century. The fact that hare was consumed in all periods of occupation in Bedern, suggests that the time lag between the introduction of rabbits to Britain, and their incorporation into the diet, is cultural rather than simply biogeographical (O'Connor 2000, 46). The role of both rabbit and hare in the diet appears to have been as variety rather than bulk.

The remains of deer represent a small fraction of the recorded sample, which by any measure is a minor component. Fallow deer appears slightly more common than red deer, roe deer being the least common. There is an interesting disparity in the representation of the different body parts of fallow deer — the hind limb appears to be over-represented. That this was detected independently in both the 1985 sample (52% hind limb elements) and the 1994 sample (70% hind limb elements) seems to point to the selective import of prime quality meat. The documen-

Table 18 Species fragment counts by period, 1994 data (L.M. = large mammal, M.M. = medium mammal)

Period	Cattle	Sheep	Pig	L.M.	M.M.	Poultry	Goat	Horse	Cat	Dog	Red deer	Roe deer	Fallow deer	Hare	Rabbit	Rat
1	31	39	22	136	146	7	1	0	1	4	2	0	1	0	0	0
2–5	310	424	262	1099	1565	155	2	3	11	13	9	7	8	6	0	1
6	130	169	145	594	588	63	0	1	8	8	2	2	6	5	0	1
7	175	262	185	961	1009	99	3	1	10	6	5	3	4	1	0	4
8	109	72	51	321	326	64	0	1	25	1	0	0	0	1	0	0
9	15	37	21	74	125	40	0	0	1	0	0	0	1	1	1	0

Table 19 Species fragment counts by period, 1985 data

Period	Cattle	Sheep	Pig	Wild pig	Poultry	Goat	Horse	Cat	Dog	Red deer	Roe deer	Fallow deer	Hare	Rabbit
1	570	471	172	1	131	4	11	2	3	4	0	5	5	0
2–5	1366	1166	561	1	333	11	15	14	6	6	4	6	1	4
6	441	397	208	0	123	4	5	18	7	2	3	6	1	1
7	2495	1808	679	2	697	4	9	154	11	7	2	4	8	2
8	3518	2679	706	4	929	4	10	142	11	10	8	26	15	19
9	680	950	134	0	232	2	2	10	4	1	0	15	3	6

tary sources (p.618) point to the consumption of venison, which on one occasion was given to the vicars for feasts. The limited archaeological evidence seems to support this, implying that venison was eaten only very occasionally, and possibly only as the result of the gift of a 'side' — possibly more accurately described as a haunch — of venison. Interestingly, a similar pattern in the range of fallow deer bones was noted at Lurk Lane in Beverley (Scott 1991).

Wild boar, identified in small numbers, appears to represent another hunted component in the diet.

The one remaining mammal bone that appears to represent food debris is a butchered grey seal (Halichoerus grypus) mandible fragment (Scott 1985, 11). This is a most unusual addition to the diet, although grey seal has also been recorded from medieval deposits at Mount Grace Priory, N. Yorkshire (Bailey et al. 1994).

Of the wild bird species, most of the recorded taxa could be and probably were eaten. Duck, variously identified as domestic/mallard, teal, tufted, shelduck, small and medium, is the most numerous taxon. A number of other species indicate the occasional exploitation of wetland resources (swan, coot, heron, woodcock, lapwing, curlew, plover, godwit and, unusually in later medieval contexts, the crane). A number of game birds (grey partridge, pheasant and red and black grouse) demonstrate that wild birds were also taken from inland areas. The interpretation of such a small sample is difficult. The only possible example of a status-related species is the swan, which is frequently referred to as a 'banqueting bird' (Scott 1985). The range of species may, however, be related to preferential access to resources and the elevated social status of the vicars (AY 15/5, 395–8).

The role of fish in the diet of the occupants of Bedern is difficult to assess, principally because of the biased recovery of the sample (pp.402–3). Suffice it to say, the remains of fish are grossly under-represented. In general terms the sample is dominated by the bones of the larger gadids (notably cod, haddock and ling, but also whiting and saithe), with a surprisingly low occurrence of freshwater species. Of some interest is the greater numbers of ling in Period 8 at the college of vicars choral and Period 6, Phase 5, at the foundry. This accords well with the general pattern of the exploitation of progressively deeper, and more northerly waters during the medieval and post-medieval periods (AY 15/5, 398–401). The sieved sample from context 1505 demonstrates the significance of small-boned fish such as herring and eel which clearly formed a substantial part of the

diet. This sample confirms the bias in favour of marine species (Scott 1985). A number of other species were recorded in small numbers, but are of little interpretive value.

The fragmentary remains of two additional marine species, the oyster (Ostra edulis) and edible crab (Cancer pagurus) were recovered. These finds can only be taken as an indication that these animals were exploited; the extent of their contribution to the vicars' diet remains unquantified.

Animal husbandry

It is apparent from the analysis of carcass components that cattle, sheep and pigs were brought into Bedern on the hoof and slaughtered within the college buildings, or in close proximity to them. The butchery of these species appeared to follow the same basic pattern, the principal difference being that mutton appears to have been more often eaten on the bone, rather than as fillets. The principal division of the carcass was into sides, achieved by splitting the carcass along the sagittal plane, following the removal of the head and neck, which was cleaved off transversely. A certain regularity in this butchery pattern seems to point to the presence of either a standard method of butchery or, more likely, resident butchers. Of particular note in the butchery of cattle is the high incidence of the heavy reduction of the tarsal bones and the longitudinal splitting of the long bones. This would seem to point to the intensive exploitation of the hard skeleton, and specifically the production of broth/soup or glue and marrow extraction, a feature shared with the medieval assemblage from Coppergate (O'Connor 1986a).

A haddock cleithrum displaying an interesting cut mark was recorded (Fig.343). The position of this mark would seem to indicate that, contrary to the situation for the mammals, fish were butchered on a domestic rather than professional scale (B. Irving, pers. comm.).

As noted above, however, the majority of the meat intake was provided by cattle, sheep and pigs which were, in the main, brought in from outside. The age at death profile of these animals may be used to establish the nature of the prevailing animal husbandry systems (Table 20).

The age at death profile for cattle showed a clear selection of juvenile and adult/old individuals, with little exploitation of other age groups. The upper end of the age range is marked by the presence of a number of elderly individuals. At the other end of the scale, there is evidence for the selective cull of very young calves, aged between

Fig.343   Haddock cleithrum with large cut mark possibly indicating domestic/household butchery

two and four months old. This is based on the light wear on deciduous fourth premolars, which, given the fact that this tooth erupts shortly after birth, is difficult to age in absolute terms. Such a concentration on young calves implies considerable emphasis on the consumption of veal and/or the production of calf skin. A pattern such as this would normally be interpreted as indicating the presence of a dairy-based management system, the high incidence of veal being a direct result of a more organised and developed dairy economy, producing a surplus of young males (AY 15/5, 364, 415–16).

From the small sample available for metrical analysis, the size of the Bedern cattle appears to be relatively small compared to contemporaneous samples. This can be interpreted as the result of a predominantly adult female population of retired dairy cattle. The likelihood of cattle being utilised for traction is indicated by a number of pathological abnormalities, such as eburnation of the acetabulum (hip joint of the pelvis), and the degenerative condition of many phalangeal joints. Such arthropathies are normally

interpreted as responses to excessive physical stress or advancing age (Baker and Brothwell 1980).

The age at which sheep were culled is, however, rather different, with the representation of a greater range of age groups. The number of juveniles is very small, which, even taking into account the potential loss of small and fragile bones, indicates that very little lamb was eaten. At the other end of the age range, the majority of the 'old' animals were recorded as old on the basis of being dentally mature. The absolute age of these individuals is difficult to assess (Moran and O'Connor 1994) but they probably represent animals aged between four and five years old (T.P. O'Connor, pers. comm.). This pattern, showing the deliberate selection of adult animals (aged three to five years) is best interpreted as a compromise between the demands for live and dead carcass products (wool, milk and manure versus mutton). A similar interpretation has been made from post-medieval assemblages in York (T.P. O'Connor, pers. comm.).

The size of the Bedern sheep shows considerable variation, although the majority of the animals were of a size typical for sheep of this period. However the bones from the two contexts dating from Periods 8 and 9 (5268 and 5027) containing a total of 53 metacarpals were clearly from larger animals. Such a size difference may relate to improvements in post-medieval animal husbandry (O'Connor 1995). From the small collection of pathological bones there is some indication of a lapse in the quality of sheep husbandry, as depressions recorded on a number of horncores may relate to malnutrition (AY 15/4, 286). The relatively high incidence of damaged ribs may also have implications for the general management of sheep.

Table 20   Age assessment based on mandibular wear

	Juvenile	Immature	Sub-adult	Adult	Old
Cattle	12	0	0	2	18
Sheep	8	4	6	98	50
Pig	0	12	20	17	0

The pattern in the exploitation of pigs differs from that of both cattle and sheep. The pattern of infant and/or adult deaths is replaced by a more even spread in the middle of the age range, sub-adult being the best represented age class; juveniles are poorly represented. On the basis of the distribution of different wear stages on the first and second molar teeth, and the fusion of the elbow joint, a series of well-defined clusters of mortalities was detected. This indicated the selective cull of animals aged 12–18 months and 24–30 months old. The general pattern of the exploitation of immature to sub-adult animals represents a very different management strategy, whereby pigs were killed once a good meat weight was achieved, and offspring assured, but before they became expensive, in terms of diminishing returns of food for fodder. This is rather more ad hoc than the strategy proposed for the management of the bovids. The evidence for the selective cull of certain age groups does reflect a certain degree of organisation and possibly resource scheduling, which one would not expect to see if pigs were reared on a small household scale within Bedern. This is a rather different approach to the management of pigs than is recorded elsewhere in the medieval and post-medieval periods in York (O'Connor 1986a; 1986b).

Fig.344 *Pig mandibles showing abnormal wear on the first molar*

A number of pig mandibles showed abnormal wear on the first molar (Fig.344). The consistency and severity of this wear pattern may be interpreted as a result of penned pigs habitually chewing on something, such as the bars confining them. A similar pattern of abnormal wear was also noted on several pig mandibles from St Nicholas Hospital, Lawrence Street, a small sample of medieval date (Carrott et al. 1994).

The remaining domestic animals that were exploited for food were probably kept in and around Bedern. Of the domestic fowl bones, an appreciable number were recorded as immature. This is a biased representation of the age distribution, as difficulties with the recovery and identification of young fowl militate against their presence in the recorded assemblage. The apparent predominance of adults suggests an emphasis on egg production. To some extent this is borne out in the distribution of different sized animals, such that within the considerable size range there is a clear distinction between the more numerous, smaller female animals and the larger male animals. It is noteworthy that from the medieval Gilbertine Priory site in Fishergate, York, where sieving was undertaken, a large sample of juvenile fowl and eggshell was recovered (Carrott et al. 1994). If the geese (which could not be identified beyond Anser sp.) are indeed of domestic stock (AY 15/5, 355), we may expect a pattern of exploitation along similar lines to that of domestic fowl.

Tables 18 and 19 show clearly that goats were of minimal significance in their contribution to the meat diet. They may, however, have been kept on a modest scale primarily for their milk and manure. The presence of a mandibular fragment from a young kid may indicate the keeping of goats within the college precinct.

Apart from those domestic animals which were exploited for food, cats and dogs are both present in all periods (Tables 18 and 19). All the dog bones, and the bulk of the cat bones, were haphazardly mixed with other bone refuse, with the exception of the 'garden soil' contexts and the collection referred to on pp.617–18. Of the cat bones, both adult and immature individuals are represented, and all appear to be domestic. The bulk of the dog bones were from adults, although a radius from a very young animal was also recorded. The most interesting feature of the dog bones is the considerable variation in size and type of dog, best illustrated in the cranial material. The mandible of an elderly individual is clearly from an animal at the upper end of the size range with a foreshortened snout. A small maxillary fragment from a young and small dog also shows

a somewhat shortened snout. The reconstructed shoulder height could only be established from two bones, a humerus and a radius. This demonstrated the presence of terrier-sized animals between 0·3 and 0·4m tall at the shoulder (Harcourt 1974). It seems reasonable to suggest that dogs may have been kept both as pets and for vermin control. Evidence for dogs has been found on other ecclesiactical sites, such as Battle Abbey (Hare 1985) and the Augustinian Friary, Leicester (Mellor and Pearce 1981).

The faunal assemblage in a local and regional context

There are a number of difficulties in comparing Bedern with other local and regional sites, principally because there are a limited number of samples of directly comparable date.

In making general inter-site comparisons it is important to compare meaningful and useful variables which will have a wider archaeological relevance. In the context of medieval and post-medieval York a comparison of species abundance is of little value, given the taphonomic problems and diversity of site type. Suffice it to say that Bedern seems to compare well with the general pattern outlined by O'Connor (1986b, 3). Of greater significance is the variation in the age at death profiles of the domestic mammals, as this details chronological variation in the animal husbandry regimes, and indicates the nature of the economic system in operation.

In the environs of York in the 12th and 13th centuries cattle seem to have been used pragmatically, a balance being struck between their value as meat against their value for haulage, and the value of their meat and dung (O'Connor 1986a, 86; 1986b, 8; AY 15/2). The late medieval sample from Bedern clearly marks a change, with the introduction of the consumption of an appreciable amount of veal, quite possibly as a direct result of the development of an organised dairy 'industry'. Such an interpretation is supported by the biometric data, indicating that the majority of the adult cattle consumed within Bedern were female. This change in management strategy is supported by the small data set from the Gilbertine Priory, Fishergate (AY 15/4). The Bedern sample also shows a marked change in the exploitation of sheep, from the medieval emphasis on dairying, to a compromise involving greater emphasis on wool and meat production, typical of the post-medieval period (AY 15/5, 364, 387–8).

The pattern of exploitation of pigs is typified by the heavy cull of animals under three years old, often with the presence of perinatal individuals taken as evidence for some 'back yard' type rearing (O'Connor 1986b; 1989). In general terms the age at death profile for Bedern is similar to elsewhere in York, with the emphasis on young adults as a ready meat supply. The presence of small numbers of juvenile and neonatal individuals points to the possibility of some rearing on site. However, the detection of two quite distinct clusters in the age profile indicates a selective cull of some of the herd. The timing of this cull could be interpreted as a direct result of the problems of resource scheduling, with pigs being culled towards the end of the summer when meat was not immediately available from cattle or sheep. If this interpretation is accepted it indicates the organised husbandry of pigs in a way not previously seen in York.

On a regional scale some comparison with the material excavated from Lurk Lane, Beverley, is useful (Scott 1991). While the bulk of the faunal sample at Beverley is dated to deposits slightly earlier than those from Bedern, both sites were occupied by ecclesiastical communities (Armstrong et al. 1991). The general exploitation of cattle and sheep for secondary products is recorded at both sites, although the high incidence of calves at Bedern may reflect the change in level of organisation within the dairy industry through the medieval period. The pattern of exploitation of pigs is not dissimilar, in that meat is the primary concern. The evidence for specific culls in the Bedern sample may again be a reflection of a more organised system in operation. The range and proportions of wild taxa at the two sites show a number of similarities which may be a reflection of the range of resources available to the vicars, from land given as endowments to the college, and to the Canons of Beverley Minster.

In summary, the faunal material excavated from Bedern is of considerable significance owing to the ecclesiastical nature and chronology of the site. Despite the difficulty in translating fragment counts into numbers of animals and diet, it is possible to discern some general change in the proportion of animal bone material examined which may relate to dietary changes, most notably the gradual increase in poultry and the decline in the numbers of cattle in the post-college samples (Period 9). Cattle clearly constituted a substantial part of the meat diet, in the form of both veal, provided by animals surplus to the requirements of a developing dairy industry, and beef provided from older, retired work and dairy animals. Sheep were exploited within a system having a number of objectives, principally balancing the demands for wool and meat. As a result, animals were slaughtered in adulthood, having contributed to the maintenance of the flock and provided a number of wool clips. Pigs appear to have been managed in a rather different way. It is suggested that they were no longer being reared and marketed on a small scale but as a part of an integrated and organised system.

The diet of the vicars was clearly supplemented by both the eggs and meat of domestic fowl and geese. Wild mammals formed a small but important part of the diet, which in the case of venison possibly resulted only from direct gifts. This was supplemented by a wide range of wild birds and fish. Obviously the role of fish is especially difficult to establish in the absence of sieving, but clearly some emphasis was placed on the larger gadids as well as smaller fish such as herring and eel (Scott 1985). Although their diet was not radically different from the resident population of contemporary York, the range of species present is possibly some indication of distinct social status. Animals which are traditionally considered as indicators of high status, for example, hunted game like cervids and wild boar, 'banqueting birds' like swans, and salmonids, are present, but in very small numbers. The range of other activities present, and the interpretation offered for the age at death profiles, point to the integration of the college into the wider economic system.

The Post-Medieval Period

Documentary evidence

edited by J.D. Richards

Work on the documentary sources relevant to the post-medieval development of Bedern was originally undertaken by R.M. Butler. Subsequently, historical studies by Beechey (1976) and Finnegan (1979) have thrown particular light on 19th century York. A summary of information relevant to Bedern has been incorporated here.

A note on the documentary sources
By R.M. Butler

By the post-medieval period much of the college precinct was rented out to secular tenants. From the later years of the college the Kitchen Book, originally intended for recording the provision of common meals in the hall, was used for various notes on leases and regulations affecting the vicars and their tenants. Six lease books give details of the leases of college property made between 1628 and 1865; these can be supplemented with separate rentals of Bedern, with rent books and with surrendered leases. In 1866 the college property was handed over to the Church Commissioners who, during the next 30 years, sold much of it to tenants. Old title deeds and surrendered leases retained by the Commission are now held in the Borthwick Institute for Historical Research.

During the 20th century much of the vicars' former property in Bedern and Aldwark was acquired by two firms, G.E. Barton Ltd, confectioners and caterers, and William Wright and Sons Ltd, butchers and later manufacturers of meat products. Wrights sold all their holdings in this area to the City of York in 1971. The title deeds to this block of property are in the City Records Office. They usually go back to about 1850 but in some cases include a series of leases back to the 17th century. Some other documents, including a note of purchases of vicarial property in 1650, are also in the City Archives.

In addition to the title deeds, a few of which have plans of the properties leased or sold, there are some plans of the college property made in the early 19th century, of which only five relate to Bedern. The 1852 Ordnance Survey map of York at a scale of 60 inches to a mile shows the area in detail, but before that date only a plan of 1822 published by Baines shows more than a rough outline. In the collection of old views of York made by Dr Evelyn and now in the City Art Gallery there are several of Bedern before widespread demolition and rebuilding in the late 19th century (Fig.345). Only a few photographs exist, mostly in the Central Library, showing details of the chapel, hall and some houses. In contrast to many areas of York, however, few schedules and photographs of the tenements are available because most of the properties were cleared before the beginnings of the municipal slum clearance schemes (Beechey 1976, 143).

For the late 19th and 20th century it is possible to give details of most of the buildings, since surveys of Barton's properties were made for fire insurance in 1897 and 1927, the architect's plan of the National School is preserved, and there is a long description of Ebor Buildings, then regarded as an example of advanced and enlightened planning, with its sound-proofed floors. Reminiscences are also recorded of a mission to the poor in the area, run from a nearby room during the early part of the 20th century.

The later history of Bedern

The medieval history of the college, up to the end of the 16th century, has been discussed on pp.380–5; the post-medieval story is taken up here.

From 1640 the hall was leased to laymen and subdivided into three tenements, becoming a mineral water factory in the 19th century and, until recently, part of a meat-pie works. The former gatehouse was leased from 1690 on condition that the house was rebuilt within two years (RCHMY 5, 136). A house in Bartle Garth is recorded as being in use as a hospital in 1690. Several of the vicars' houses or 'cubicles' were let to lay tenants even before the Reformation and by 1700 only five were occupied by vicars. During the 18th century, 'vicarial mansion houses' replaced many of the old cubicles. By 1720 there were twenty such houses within the former precinct, three with stylish curved Dutch gables (Fig.346). New houses were built in the former garden or on the site

Fig.345 View of the south-west side of Bedern Close, looking south, after Nicholson, 1827. From the Evelyn Collection; reproduced by kind permission of the Yorkshire Architectural and York Archaeological Society

Fig.346 Three Dutch-gabled houses, formerly vicarial mansions, and (right) Turf House/White House, on the north-east side of Bedern Close (from Benson 1911, fig.44)

of the orchard; all other college buildings, except the chapel, were let out on lease. The college also still owned a substantial amount of property within York. The latest surviving rent roll is for 1719, when rent was being paid on 137 houses, derived from 33 other streets in York as well as from Bedern (Harrison 1952, 120–1).

Petitions to establish a university in York, submitted to Parliament in 1641 and 1647, suggested the suitability for this purpose of Bedern, 'with a large hall for the readers, and good convenient lodgings for the students, also divers other fair houses, of late the dean and prebends', which, though now in lease, may in time expire, and remain unto some pious uses (Johnson 1848, 2, 276). St Peter's School moved to Bedern when its buildings in The Horsefair were damaged in the siege of 1644 and remained there until c.1730, when it was transferred to the nearby former church of St Andrew in St Andrewgate (*AY* 11/1). It was perhaps during the siege of York that one of the occupants of Bedern buried his wealth in the former college garden. Whellan records that: 'During the progress of the improvements here in 1852, a number of coins were found concealed in an old flower-pot and coffee-pot. They were principally of the reigns of Elizabeth, James I and Charles I' (Whellan 1857, 486).

The position of Bedern as an extra-parochial area in St Peter's Liberty with apparently little supervision made it attractive for those at odds with the State over religion. Catholic recusants are said by Aveling to have been numerous there, though there may be some confusion with the Minster Close, and the highest number given is ten in 1735. In 1743–4, in the run up to the 1745 Jacobite Rebellion, a warrant was issued to enable the homes of papists in St Peter's Liberty and Bedern to be searched for arms (Aveling 1970, 273). A few years later, in 1747, the first Methodists in York met in Mr Thomas Stodhart's house at 'the bottom of the street', presumed to be at the end of the close (Lyth 1885, 61). Unfortunately Stodhart does not appear in the college records as either a tenant or an occupier. John Wesley preached here on three or four occasions but in 1751 the congregation transferred to Lady Huntington's Chapel in College Street, as a result of 'the opposition and annoyance to which the congregations were subjected' (Camidge 1906, 4). On one occasion when Wesley himself was preaching in Bedern (presumably in Stodhart's house) a mob gathered outside to throw stones. They

broke the windows, damaged the furniture, and nearly injured Wesley himself (Lyth 1885, 62). The Methodists later met more regularly in Newgate from 1753 to 1755 and then in a permanent chapel in Aldwark from 1759 to 1806. In 1827 the York Institute of Art, Science and Literature was founded in a small room in Bedern.

The attack on the Methodists is one of the first indications that the Bedern precinct was becoming rather unruly, the college effectively operating as an absentee landlord. It is unclear how many vicars were now resident in Bedern, but it appears that those who elected not to live in the houses which they had been allotted could let them out to other tenants. The college's lack of control over the estate resulted in a lack of proper maintenance and tidiness by the tenants. Many of the leaseholders moved out and sublet their property to others, resulting in even less control over the property. From 1757–85 the books of leases list the following occupations of tenants of the college: joiner, linen-draper, cabinet-maker, barber-surgeon, brass-caster, licenser of hawkers and pedlars, yeoman, goldsmith, apothecary, wine-merchant, brewer, ale-draper, saddler, inn-holder, grocer, whitesmith, carpenter, stay-maker, merchant, blacksmith (Harrison 1952, 264).

During the 19th century Bedern became a slum, increasingly notorious for poor sanitary conditions and the dilapidated state of its buildings (Digby 1981). The former mansions and their outbuildings were subdivided into a vast number of dwellings. As early as 1818 Hargrove (2, 145) described Bedern as 'the sad receptacle of poverty and wretchedness' and in 1844 Laycock reported:

Of 98 families living there, 67 have only one room for all purposes, 18 have two rooms, and 13 have three rooms or more. One entire building is let off in single rooms. The staircase windows are so made that they cannot open, the rooms are low and confined, the light of day almost excluded, and the walls and ground damp and undrained. The building is occupied by 16 families, two abominably filthy privies being appropriated to all, and situate, with their accompanying 'ash-hole', or 'bog-hole', in a little back court. As might be expected, the smell in rooms of this kind is most disgusting and oppressive. Against the back wall of a cottage there is sometimes a dung-hill, the fluid from which soaks into the house (Laycock 1844, 8–9).

In addition, adjoining the dilapidated dwellings in Back Bedern there were piggeries, stables and dung-heaps.

Nevertheless, despite chronic overcrowding and appalling sanitary conditions, Bedern was a flourishing centre of prostitution, discussed in detail by Finnegan (1979). From 1837–47 almost one-quarter of all offences associated with prostitution in York took place in Bedern. In 1843 the Chief Constable listed the addresses of 118 prostitutes resident in York in the previous year; he reported that 33 (28%) inhabited Bedern (ibid., 51). In November 1839 thirteen brothel-keepers were charged, in one court session, with keeping bawdy houses in Bedern (ibid., 49). The prosecutions apparently had little effect. A petition to the Church Commissioners, dated July 1844, testifies to the continuing problem:

The place called Bedern was the College of the Vicars Choral, and more or less their residence; and by the ancient Statutes, they ought to reside there, and close the gates every evening at 8 o'clock to keep women out — that they have since leased the property out to various individuals and that in consequence of houses having been erected in the suburbs of the city ... nearly all the respectable part of the inhabitants, have left their residences and gone there.

That their late residences have all been let off in single rooms, many of them filled with whores, thieves, street-walkers, etc., thereby bringing great incumbrances upon the Liberty, besides great disgrace and scandal upon the Church of England by the Lessors continuing still to lease the said property after knowing the condition of the place, and that there is no remedy for the evil except by a complete renovation of the place ...

Your petitioners three years ago, in order to get the whores out of it, prosecuted one at great expense to the said Liberty, and with difficulty got evidence and a conviction for one month's imprisonment in the House of Correction — at the expiration of which time she went back in a Cab or Fly, preceded by a band of music and her associates flocked back double in number. The place is in that state that, if crime be committed, the inmates of it dare not give evidence for fear of their lives or property being injured by it (Petition to the Ecclesiastical Commissioners for England and Wales, July 1844).

Though the tenements in Bedern were largely let off into single rooms there is some evidence to suggest that certain brothels in the close were larger than this, and could accommodate several whores. In November 1840, for instance, two prostitutes were charged with robbing a 'Jew Hawker' of jewellery. Apparently he had been invited to step inside one of the houses of ill repute and exhibit his wares, whereupon he was set upon by four or five women who rifled his jewellery box (Finnegan 1979, 50).

As a result of the Great Famine of 1845–9 there was a tremendous influx of Irish refugees into York which has been the subject of a study by Beechey (1976). Immigration may originally have started because of the opportunities for employment provided by the new railways after 1839, but increased later because those seeking refuge and work after the Great Famine settled where their compatriots were already concentrated. Bedern, Walmgate and the Water Lanes, being less fashionable areas of the city with older houses, low rents and opportunities for subdivision, were favoured by immigrants from Ireland.

In the 1841 census there were 430 Irish recorded as living in York. Only 23 were recorded as living in Minster Yard with Bedern, representing 2·6% of its total population. By 1851 the total number of Irish in York had increased to 1,928. Minster Yard with Bedern now housed 374, representing 33·8% of its total population of 1,130, and 14·3% of the total Irish in York (Beechey 1976, 118). Bedern had the highest proportion of Irish residents in York. Merrington's, Pulleyn's, and Snarr's Buildings had been almost wholly taken over by 329 Irish. Moreover, individual houses were further subdivided into colonies from particular Irish counties. The Boynes, Merlerkeys and Colphens who were tenants at No.1 Snarr's Buildings were from Sligo; those in Nos.10–13 were solidly from Mayo (VCHY, 282).

Many Irish people were drawn to York by the hope of employment. They may have sought work in villages around York but were prevented from living there because of the hostile attitudes of the rural landowners (Beechey 1976, 141).

These poor Irish people ... were probably attracted to York by the prospect of obtaining work in connection with the cultivation of chicory, for which the district was then noted (Rowntree 1903, 10).

In 1851, 89·2% of all employed Irish in Bedern were agricultural labourers and, on the basis of this sample, Armstrong (1974) reached the conclusion that most of the Irish in York were agricultural labourers. This is misleading, however, as Bedern is unrepresentative of the Irish population as a whole. This was because the highly homogeneous group in Bedern originated almost entirely from three Irish counties.

There were various efforts to relieve the abject conditions of the Irish population. In 1847 a Wesleyan Ragged Sunday School had been set up in two rooms in Bedern. Initially attendance was irregular, especially in the mornings. The committee therefore started giving the children breakfast, the bill partly being met by George Hudson, the railway entrepreneur (Royle 1981, 222), and attendance increased to 40. Early in 1848 the school transferred to larger premises in St William's College, where a joint committee of various city churches had established a ragged industrial school. Eighteen of the 'most destitute' of Bedern children were enrolled in this full-time school, where the aim was:

to reclaim the most neglected and degraded children resident in the city of York by providing them with a sound Christian education combined with training in such branches of industry and household employment as are suitable to their condition in life (1st Annual Report of the Ragged Schools Committee 1849).

The Ragged Schools Committee also believed that the prospect of agricultural employment was the main factor in drawing the Irish to York. They stated that:

Your Committee believe that the majority of Irish in these schools is larger than in the generality of Ragged Schools, which is attributable, they think, to the extensive cultivation of chicory in the neighbourhood.

However, by their 3rd Annual Report the Committee believed that the School was itself attracting the Irish to York, and limited admission to those who had been resident in the city for at least a year (Beechey 1976, 62).

Overcrowding and increasingly desperate sanitary conditions led to serious outbreaks of disease. In 1847 there was a major epidemic of typhus. Richard Thomas, the Union Surgeon, reported an increase in October due to:

its gradual extension from the destitute Irish to our own inhabitants in the various localities of Walmgate, Water Lanes, Long Close Lane, Bedern etc ... attributed not alone to their dirty, ill drained and worse ventilated residences, but in a greater measure to the fact that no step having been taken when sickness already exists ... entirely to eradicate the disease (quoted in Beechey 1976, 75).

In 1849, following an outbreak of cholera in York, the editor of the *Gazette* wrote:

The respectable classes in this city can have no conception of the condition of certain localities. Take Bedern for instance and what do you find — filth, misery, drunkenness, disease and crime. Let those who doubt the proof of this assertion examine (if they have the courage) for themselves and they will find that no language can describe the feelings excited by observing the swarms of human beings hording together, without the slightest regard to the decencies of life. Let them for a short time inhale the close and pestilential atmosphere of these abodes of filth, and contemplate if they can without horror man in his lowest state displaying a brutal unconsciousness of his degradation (Gazette, 27 October 1849).

Snarr's Buildings were among of the worst offenders. In his Report to the General Board of Health, Richard Thomas wrote in 1850:

fever is constantly prevalent there, and in two years, I have never been one day out of the place, and sometimes I have had 20 persons affected with diseases of that nature. ... There are many houses which are totally unfit for human habitations; they are occupied by the poor Irish, and they are not fit even for pigsties. No doubt you would see in Bedern low cellars underground, with a few shavings, where the people live upon a little Indian meal. They get the money upon which they live as well as they can. They beg, or they commence the trade of chopping wood, and send their children with it into the streets to sell (quoted in Beechey 1976, 77).

A report to the City Council from the Inspector of Nuisances in January 1852 described the condition of the yards and outhouses in Back Bedern as follows:

The wide passage leading into Back Bedern is in a filthy and unwholesome condition, a privy situate in Back

Bedern belonging to Mrs Jane Jackson, is in a foul and offensive state, two privies situate in Back Bedern are in a foul and offensive condition. The average number of persons using the above places is nearly 300 of both sexes, and I am of the opinion that the present privies are insufficient for their accommodation (York Council Minute Books, 27 January 1852, quoted in Beechey 1976, 143).

Occasional references in the Council Minute Books and newspapers indicate that pigs added to the squalor of Back Bedern; Irishman Miles Barnical, for example, was the subject of a complaint in this respect in 1851 (Beechey 1976, 143).

For the Watch Committee, the Irish presented a problem for the maintenance of law and order. In 1848 and again in 1851 the committee complained of the 'disturbances continually occurring' in Walmgate and Bedern and of the 'violent and lawless conduct of the Irish' (VCHY, 282). Under the headline of 'Another Bedern Riot', the *Herald* for 21 September 1850 reported that a John Callaghan was charged with rescuing a prisoner from police officer Reynolds. At about one o'clock on Sunday morning:

one of those scenes which so often occur in Bedern took place. There were not less than 150 Irish people collected together and he was very roughly handled by them (quoted in Beechey 1976, 308).

Trouble arose again in Bedern in 1853, apparently over a very minor matter. The parish constable, Matthew Cowton, had taken an Irish boy into custody for playing ball on Sunday, 'a common practice in this locality on the Sabbath'. They were followed to the Station House by a crowd of about 100 Irishmen, two of whom rescued the boy from the constable (Beechey 1976, 309). Cowton, who himself lived in Bedern with his wife and six children, does not appear to have endeared himself to the local inhabitants. In the following year, during a Bedern 'uproar', he was threatened with a knife. Eight months later he was attacked and kicked in a dark passage off the street. In 1857 Cowton and a fellow officer, P.C. Holmes, tried to arrest one Thomas Lyons for drunkenness. According to Holmes' testimony Lyons seized a pan and struck Holmes three times on the head, whilst his wife threw a pan of hot water at them. Cowton and Holmes retreated but returned with reinforcements, overpowering Lyons and his wife. Both

were taken into custody but soon discharged as the female prisoner was badly injured. The incident resulted in charges of assault and wilful damage being preferred against nine police officers, including Cowton. The latter, apparently aware that this time he had exceeded his duties, chose to do away with himself, rather than face the consequences; Holmes was fined £2 (ibid., 312–15).

Nevertheless, although Bedern became even more insanitary and overcrowded, and continued to be one of the most lawless and disreputable places in the city, the Irish merely aggravated already appalling conditions. Finnegan has shown that its association with prostitution was almost completely destroyed (1979, 53–4); the Irish community, though poor, contributed few women to prostitution. In the 28-year period following Irish colonisation, there are no further references to problems of prostitution in Bedern. Indeed, only one brothel was reported as being situated there after 1846. This was kept by Henry Ashbrook, in Milner's Buildings. Henry and his first wife Ann, 'two notorious characters who have figured frequently before the magistrates', were charged in March 1855 with being involved in a disturbance in Bedern. By the following year Henry appears to have a new wife, Mary, listed as being only 23 years old in 1861 and of Irish birth. In February 1856 she was charged with theft from a man who accompanied her to a brothel, and in July of the same year she and another prostitute were involved in the garrotte robbery of a youth they had taken to a brothel in St Andrewgate.

During the second half of the 19th century Irish immigration stabilised, although the Irish remained a significant proportion of the inhabitants of Minster Yard with Bedern. By the 1861 census the number of Irish was 371, representing 11·5% of the Irish population in York, but 39·4% of the Bedern population; by 1871 the population was down to 250, which although still 36% of the parish's residents, was only 8·3% of the total number of Irish in York.

Housing conditions also improved. By 1864 an inspection stated that Wide Yard, Back Bedern, now contained four privies used by only 100 persons. Houses along the north-east side of the street, including the large vicarial mansion, were gradually demolished and replaced, and there were various initiatives to improve the area. In 1852 a connection was opened up between Bedern Close and St Andrewgate, presumably to destroy the 'den of crime' atmosphere. Around 1855 the sub-chanter of the vicars choral removed the stone-shattered glass from the lane-side of the chapel, and blocked up the window openings. He laid a new brick floor, inserted a stove, and soon attracted a small but 'greatly edified' Friday congregation (Camidge 1906).

In 1866 the Church Commissioners took over the ownership of the property of the vicars, with the exception of the chapel, which was transferred to the Dean and Chapter. Henceforth the rest of the property was administered by the Church Commissioners and the vicars received an annual sum, initially set at £1400, out of which their stipends were to be paid. Their number was apparently set at five. The extra-parochial area of Minster Yard with Bedern was annexed to the church of Holy Trinity, Goodramgate, in 1869 (*VCHY*, 372).

The 'repossession' of the properties of the vicars choral in Bedern by the Church led to the next major change in the character of the neighbourhood. The Elementary Education Act of 1870 stated that a school should be within reach of every child. A Roman Catholic school known as St Patrick's was held in a large room in Bedern in 1870, but this appears to have been a temporary arrangement prior to completion of its new building in Monkgate (*VCHY*, 455). In 1872–3 the Bedern National School 'for the children and adults of the labouring, manufacturing, and other poorer classes in the township of Bedern' was built on the south-west side, occupying about half the street frontage (Fig.347). In 1879 its north-west wing was extended across the former kitchen block of the hall, notorious as Snarr's Buildings for overcrowding, its lease now having expired. A map of 1891 shows the school as an E-shaped building, extending from Bedern Hall to St Andrewgate, with the long range adjoining Bedern Close, and the three short ranges running back. The boys occupied the end of the building nearest the hall, the infants were in the middle, and the girls were in the St Andrewgate end of the school. At the rear were two playgrounds, a large one for the boys, and a smaller one for the

Fig.347   Bedern National School, looking north-west, photographed by Joseph Duncan c.1883

633

girls and infants. The toilet blocks were at the end of the playgrounds.

Vehicular access to Bedern was, by this stage, controlled by a simple wooden barrier across the opening into Goodramgate. It was not removed until c.1940 when the outbreak of the Second World War made ease of access for firefighters a requirement (Peter Hanstock, pers. comm.).

In 1883 there was some demolition of old mansion houses in Bedern, including the three Dutch-gabled houses. A 'model lodging house' of five storeys, named Ebor Buildings (Fig.348), was erected by Charles Ernest opposite the boys' end of the school, and behind it (to the north-east) a similar one called Hawarden Buildings, themselves demolished in 1947. These were 'huge unattractive' buildings according to John Lyth in 1885, although he thought the school was 'neat' and that Bedern was 'much improved' by the recent alterations (1885, 61). The 1891 map also shows a timber yard on the north-east side of the street. On the south-west side was first the chapel, then Barton's bakery, with beyond it, and concealing the hall, the Manor Rooms, built in 1898 for 'public entertainments' but also used as a kindergarten for the children of the well-to-do, and finally the National School.

When the Church Commissioners began to sell freehold plots in Bedern, the purchasers mainly used the properties for trade rather than as dwelling houses. The lodging houses came under strict scrutiny by the corporation, which armed itself with extra by-laws for the purpose. Gradually the lodging houses closed down and were taken over for industrial and trading premises. The rise of the chocolate industry was creating prosperity in the city, and the Bedern residents were dispersed to the many housing estates that were going up in the suburbs, many of them going to Bell Farm Estate, off Huntington Road (Peter Hanstock, pers. comm.).

In May 1936 the College of the Vicars Choral was dissolved, following the Cathedrals Measure of 1931. The hall was incorporated into a factory, and the abandoned chapel fell further into decay. By August 1941 the school had been closed because of 'a shortage of scholars' and in 1950 the Dean and Chapter sold the freehold to Barton's bakery for use as a store. In the second half of the 20th century the corpora-

Fig.348 Ebor Buildings on the north-east side of Bedern, looking north-west, photographed by Florence Hanstock, 1947. Reproduced by kind permission of Peter Hanstock

tion began to encourage factories and warehouses to move to industrial zones on the perimeter of the city, and to acquire abandoned sites for redevelopment of the city centre. It invited the architects Brett and Pollen to plan an outline development of an area to include Aldwark and Bedern. The firm's senior partners, Lord Esher and Francis Pollen, advised that the old shops fronting Goodramgate should be retained, but that the corporation should acquire the remainder of the private land in Bedern, demolish all the industrial buildings, and build a mixed stock of houses, maisonettes, flats and bed-sits. These were to have varying roof heights, and be interspersed with paved garage-mews, green courts planted with trees, and small back gardens within brick walls (Esher and Pollen 1971; Rae 1976; Cornford and Branch 1992).

By 1976 all the old buildings in the former close except the chapel, hall and remains of the gatehouse had been demolished. The ruined chapel and hall have now been restored. In 1984 the hall was extended with modern facilities to become a meeting place for three city guilds. It is now a Grade II listed building and scheduled ancient monument. The chapel has been restored by the Dean and Chapter, but at the expense of lowering the original height of the building.

The topography of Bedern (Figs.349–50)

Although views and plans of the buildings fronting Bedern are not known to survive for the period before 1800, the appearance of the close as it must have looked for much of the 18th century can be described with reasonable confidence. It is clear from the earliest views that most of the houses then standing were of 17th century or earlier date, and that some were probably medieval. The small houses or cubicles occupied by individual vicars, and all their common holdings except the chapel, were mostly leased out to tenants from the 16th century. Refronting, subdivision and the erection of new houses in gardens makes it difficult to sort out the appearance and even the precise relationships of the 28 separate properties in Bedern, intermingled as they became with others in Goodramgate, Aldwark and St Andrewgate, which also belonged to the college. However, the distinction made in the documents between properties in Bedern and others goes back to the 17th century and probably retains a medieval arrangement.

The close runs north-west/south-east with the chapel and hall parallel to its south-west side. In the 18th century there were, on the north-east side, six timber-framed houses, each with a front to the street about 15ft wide. Of these the north-westernmost retained its gable end and jetty into the 19th century; the next two had been combined in an 18th century façade with a roof parallel to the street, and the other three had brick fronts and 'Dutch' gables. Beyond these and set back some 20ft was a large house of brick with stone dressings, known as the Turf House. It had three storeys with tall cross-mullioned windows above a basement and a front door with a curved pedimental head reached by a flight of steps. Since this house was not demolished until 1883, there are photographs and drawings of it, when it was known as 'The White House' (Fig.346, p.628, at right). Camidge's pamphlet of 1906, *Bedern and its Chapel*, describes its interior and fine staircase. From the leases it appears to have been built by Dr Halley c.1690 on the site of a turf house or peat store. The appearance of the house next to it on the north-east, also set back, is not recorded, apart from a distant view in the *Bird's Eye View of York* where it appears to have been similar to the White House. The house, later probably divided into two, which closed the end of Bedern only appears distantly in a view by Nichol-son, where the right-hand half is shown with a Dutch gable (Fig.345, p.628).

The longhouse, a medieval building formerly used in common by the college, was set back from the street on its north-east side and was reached by a passage (Fig.349). Its north end, four yards long, was leased from 1723 and the whole building was leased from 1744, and then pulled down and rebuilt in 1762 and its site incorporated in Timothy Mortimer's new house. Repairs are mentioned intermittently from 1470 to 1744. During the period covered by the Repairer's Book of 1709–69 it was cleaned about every five years and frequently needed a new door and locks. Several keys were made, presumably so that it could be used by a number of tenants. Also incorporated in Mortimer's leasehold was a former bowling alley, described as next to the dead (blank) wall adjoining St Andrewgate and measuring 35 yards along it by 7 yards wide (*Charters*, 12). It is mentioned in 1737 and was presumably laid out in the 17th century, when bowls was a popular pastime. There was a bowling green in the deanery garden in 1647, another at the King's Manor, and a third at Sir Arthur Ingram's house, north of the Minster, newly made in 1634.

The south-west side of the street is only recorded in a view by Henry Cave of 1804 (Fig.351, p.638) and two by George Nicholson, one dated 24 May 1827 (Fig.308, p.545). The six or seven houses south-east of the chapel were apparently timber-framed, of two storeys and an attic, with the gable end on the street. The building second along from the chapel was in use as a poor house in 1776. The exception at the south-east end had a rectangular façade with a cornice. From the lease books it was described in 1742 as newly built by Robert Mawe, carpenter, and from a plan of 1853 it measured 20ft 6in. to the street by 30ft 3in. along the passage to the hall with a staircase between two ground-floor rooms. The other houses, with their mullioned and shuttered windows, look 16th–17th century, but may have had medieval cores. The identity of the tenants is confirmed by two signs in Nicholson's sketch: 'Streeton, Ales and Porter' and 'Robert Walker, Dealer in Tea' (Fig.345, p.628). Thomas Streeton leased the former vicarial mansion from year to year as a public house, 'The Barleycorn'; Robert Walker was a shoemaker, tenant of a 'little house of 15ft 8in. frontage'.

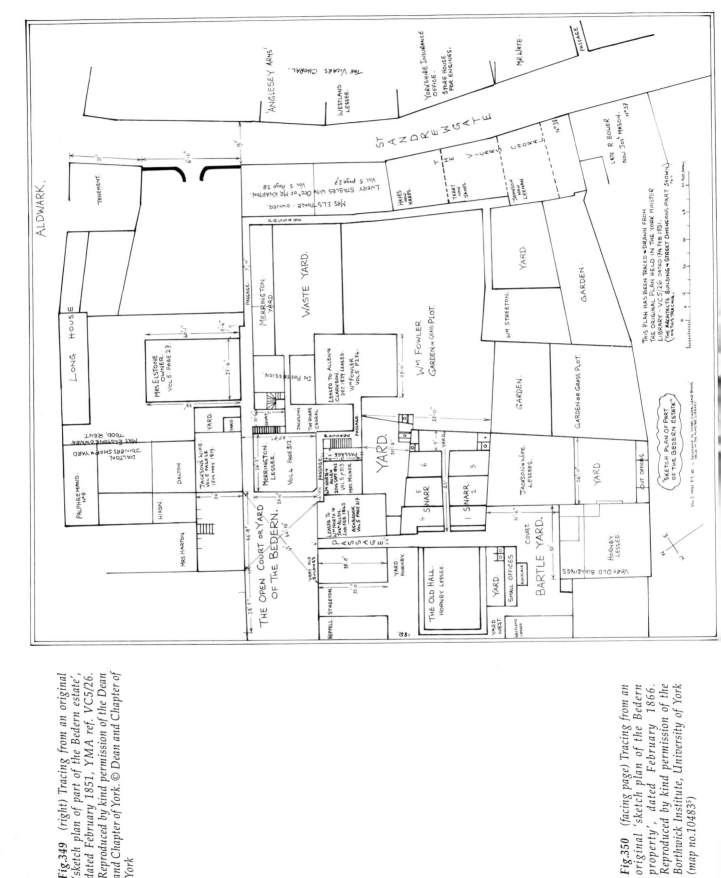

Fig.349 (right) Tracing from an original 'sketch plan of part of the Bedern estate', dated February 1851, YMA ref. VC5/26. Reproduced by kind permission of the Dean and Chapter of York. © Dean and Chapter of York

Fig.350 (facing page) Tracing from an original 'sketch plan of the Bedern property', dated February 1866. Reproduced by kind permission of the Borthwick Institute, University of York (map no.10483⁵)

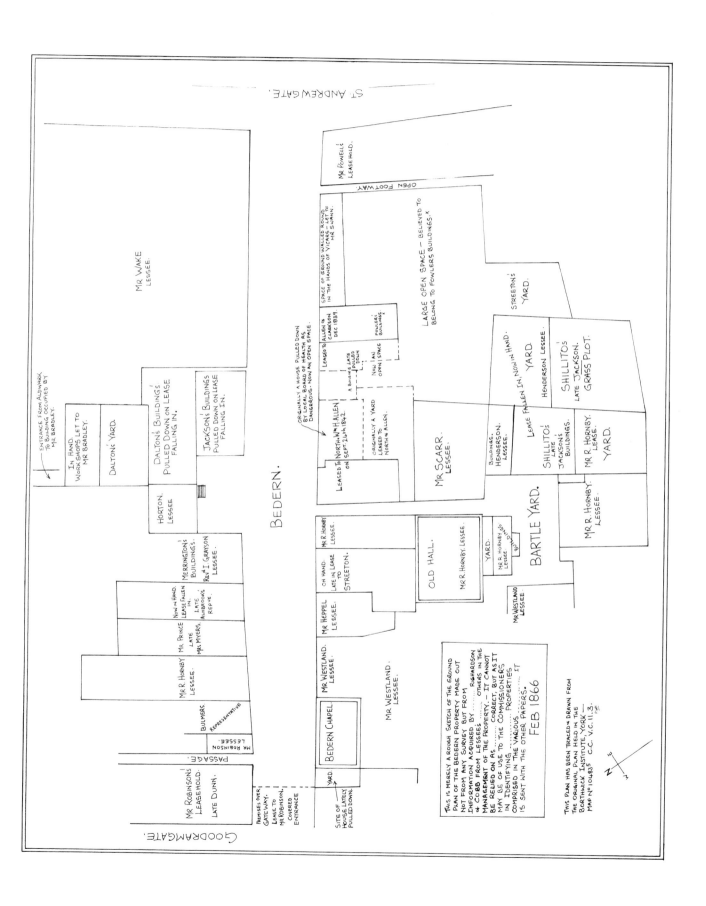

GOODRAMGATE.

ST. ANDREWGATE.

BEDERN.

Mr Robinsons Lease Hold. Late Dunn.

Mr Robinson Lessee.

PASSAGE.

BULMERS. Representative

Mr R Hornby. Lessee.

Mr Prince Late Mrs Myers, Representative.

Now in Hand. Lease Fallen in. Late Ambrooks Reeve.

Merrington's Buildings. Rev.d I Grayson Lessee.

Premises over Gateway. Lease to Mr Robinson, Covered Entrance

Site of House lately Pulled down.

YARD.

Bedern Chapel.

Mr Westland. Lessee.

Mr Westland. Lessee.

Mr Heppel Lessee.

on Hand. Late in Lease to Streeton.

Mr R. Hornby. Lessee.

OLD HALL. Mr R. Hornby. Lessee.

YARD. Mr R. Hornby. Lessee.

Mr R Hornby Lessee

Mr Westland Lessee

BARTLE YARD.

Buildings. Henderson. Lessee.

Lease fallen in now in Hand.

Henderson Lessee YARD.

Shillito's Late Jacksons Buildings.

Mr R. Hornby. Lease YARD.

Shillito's Late Jackson. GRASS PLOT.

Streeton's YARD.

Mr Scarr. Lessee.

Leased to Wm H Allen on Sept. 24th 1842.

Originally a Yard Leased to North Allen.

Leased to Allen & Clarkson Dec. 1839.

A Building Late Pulled Down.

Now in an Open Space.

Fowlers Buildings.

Originally a house pulled down by Local Board of Health as dangerous. Now an open space.

Space of ground walled round in the hands of Vicars — Let to Mr Swann.

Large Open Space — believed to belong to Fowlers Buildings. ×

OPEN FOOTWAY.

Mr Powells Lease Hold.

Entrance from Aldwark to Building occupied by Mr Bradley.

In Hand. Workshops Let to Mr Bradley.

Daltons Yard.

Horton. Lessee.

Daltons Buildings. Pulled Down on lease falling in.

Jacksons Buildings Pulled Down on lease falling in.

Mr Wake. Lessee.

This is merely a rough sketch of the Ground Plan of the Bedern Property made out not from any survey but from Information acquired by .... Richardson & Cobb from Lessees .... others in the Management of the Property. — It cannot be relied on as .... correct, but as it may be of use to the Commissioners in identifying .... Properties comprised in the various .... It is sent with the other Papers.
FEB 1866

This plan has been traced & drawn from the Original Plan held in the Borthwick Institute, York. Map Nᵒ 104835 C.C. V.C. 11.3. plan

Fig.351 *Bedern Chapel and adjacent buildings, by Henry Cave, 1804. Reproduced by kind permission of York City Art Gallery*

Further to the south-east was the entrance to a long passage, 4–5ft wide (Figs.350 and 351, at far left). From Bedern this ran for 54ft through the screens passage of the former hall (which had been sub-divided into three tenements since 1790) into a court-yard described on the Ordnance Survey map of 1852 as Back Bedern but known since as early as 1650 as Bartle Garth or Bartle Yard, perhaps from Robert Bartill, apparently a college servant or tenant in the late 16th century. Around this yard, later to be en-tirely occupied by a mineral water works, were sev-eral houses, probably built by Charles Mace c.1660, and a common well, presumably that made in 1401 at a cost of £4 3s 4d. It ceased to be public from 1721, when it was leased, together with the well house over it, to the tenant of a nearby property. A passage lead-ing out of the yard to the south-east was described as 'the entry to the Dunghill'. A small old house on the west side was known as The Helm from 1650 to 1836, perhaps from the shape of its roof, or after the helmet in the coat of arms of George Gayle, who may

have been its first owner (Peter Hanstock, pers. comm.). It was in use as stables by the second half of the 18th century, but was not demolished until 1897.

Although at least some of the original vicars' houses had their own gardens, there was a common garden, first mentioned in 1328–9, which was sub-divided through the centuries to provide gardens for houses without them or for plots attached to newly built houses. From the mention in the leases it ap-parently formed an L-shaped area to the north-east and south-east of the backs of the Bedern houses, some 100ft wide with arms 130ft and 200ft long (see p.578). Walled off within it was the common orchard, subdivided into four by 1650. The parts of it which can be located were behind the houses at the far end of the close, now largely beneath the continuation cut through to St Andrewgate. It must have been at least 80ft square. In 1630 it was decided that as all the neighbours and tenants of the vicars had had free access to the orchard, in future there should be only one key to the door, kept by the repairer. This key should only be lent to the vicars and to the women who kept the orchard tidy, and no one should be permitted to lay clothes on the grass to be dried (Harrison 1952, 42). In 1650 Richard Sykes was sold the freehold of 'a close of pasture ground with appurtenances called the Common Garden lying in the Bedderne', along with the kitchen and buttery.

For the period before 1800 both plans and views are lacking but the evidence of leases and other documents suggests that the houses had occupied the same positions since at least 1660 with some re-fronting, probably in brick, and the building of new houses in the gardens. The tenants were respectable members of the professional and skilled artisan classes. Amongst the most prominent to occupy houses in Bedern were Timothy Mortimer and his son, an attorney of the same name, who from 1737 until 1802 had a large house at the end of Bedern Close, with an extensive garden fronting onto St Andrewgate. This building, later called Hawarden House, but locally simply known as 'The Mansion', was not demolished until 1947, although it was reduced in length when Bedern Close was extended into St Andrewgate in 1852. In the first part of the 20th century it is described as having heavy mahogany doors and a stone paved entrance hall with stone columns and a large curving balustraded stone staircase (Peter Hanstock, pers. comm.).

Also resident in Bedern in the 18th century was James Barnard, mercer and alderman, lord mayor in 1735 and 1752, whose block of property, leased by him from 1721 to 1757, lay south-west of the chapel. Since the leasehold property of the vicars, which passed to relatives on the death of tenants, was sold (or rather leases were assigned for payment) and mortgaged, the main tenant whose name appears in the college lease books was often non-resident. The tenements are further identified by the sub-tenants who actually occupied them. In the later records not only are the recent tenants and sub-tenants named, but, for additional certainty in identifying a property, the tenants or occupiers of the adjoining holdings and the dimensions are noted.

In addition to tenants and sub-tenants there must have been other residents who do not appear in the college records, since the registers of the parish church of Holy Trinity, Goodramgate, for this period mention many other people with addresses given as Bedern. For the century 1700–1800 the approximate figures are 105 tenants, about 150 sub-tenants, and 94 others recorded in the registers. Since there were only 28 properties, which each changed hands about five times a century, this would still only give a few adults in each house at a time. However, many of those in the registers may have been temporary lodgers in a few houses used as guest-houses, even though they cannot be identified as such from the leases. Others may have been servants. Certainly the impression given by the 17th century leases, when there were only 15 tenants in Bedern and up to five other houses were occupied by the sub-chanter and vicars, is that the tenants actually lived in this leasehold property. This impression is confirmed by documents drawn up in Bedern and witnessed by people otherwise known as tenants.

It is possible to trace the descent of most of the plots within Bedern (R.M. Butler, pers. comm.). For example, the area of Buildings 26 and 30 (see Fig.353, p.642), comprising a kitchen, one other low room and two chambers, was leased to a John Richmond, a singing man and parish clerk, in 1641. In 1696 Benjamin Maxwell, carpenter, 'took over a house in the Bedern consisting of three low rooms, three chambers and a garret ... with a yard on the backside'. In 1736 ownership passed to Dorothy Kirby, spinster; in 1753 to Robert Kirby, and then in 1768 to James Hebden. In 1782 the tenement was leased by a Richard Matterson of Bishopthorpe, comprising a 'house in the Beddern consisting of three low rooms, three chambers and a garret ... Also a yard behind the premises and now divided into two'. There follows a succession of occupiers: 1796, Thomas Godson, yeoman; 1811, Preston Hornby, druggist; 1827, Emmanuel Siddall, common brewer; 1843, William North, jeweller; and Joseph Allen, flaxdraper, until 1872, when the Dean and Chapter received 1200 square yards, including this tenement, from the Church Commissioners for Bedern National School.

Bedern Hall (Fig.352)

Although the vicars took the decision to discontinue the rule of dining in common in 1574 (Harrison 1952, 139), the hall continued in use for official meetings and feasts until the early 17th century; the latest meeting recorded by Harrison as having taken place in the hall was in 1628 (ibid., 241).

The hall was leased from 1 June 1640, initially to Thomas Yorke, gent., and then to a succession of other private tenants (R.M. Butler, pers. comm.). In 1650 Richard Sykes was sold the freehold by the Commonwealth Committee of 'all that messuage or tenement now or late in the tenure of William Smith, situate lying or being in Bedderne, and knowne by the name of the hall, haveing two chambers above it, together with a garden'. Presumably the freehold was returned to the vicars at the Restoration as they were once more leasing it from the late 17th century. In 1769 James Hebden of York agreed to lease the hall from the vicars for a term of 40 years, at the rent of 10s each half-year. It was presumably sold to the lessee shortly afterwards as in 1771, with the agreement of the vicars, Hebden sold the building to Thomas Waud for the sum of £150 (Harrison 1952, 38). In 1800 Hannah Buck was assigned the lease of the hall and yard adjoining, the hall now being converted into three dwelling houses.

We have little information about the appearance of the hall by this time. Since the 18th century, if not much earlier, it had been concealed by other buildings, and so did not attract the attention of artists. Writing in 1857, Thomas Whellan recorded that:

> *The old Collegiate Hall ... is now converted into dwellings, and parts of the ancient outer walls of the edifice, with the evident remains of Gothic windows, and other vestiges of former days, may yet be traced on the south side of the buildings behind the houses that abut on the street a little beyond the Chapel* (Whellan 1857, 485).

The only records of the hall's appearance in the 19th century are schematic drawings made for James Raine in 1872 and photographs of 1893 (Fig.352) and 1897, when the north-east side was exposed by demolition.

Fig.352 *Bedern Hall: north-east wall, in the snow in 1893. Reproduced by kind permission of North Yorkshire County Library Service (York Library, Local Studies Collection Y9 BED. ACC No.407)*

In 1893 George Edward Barton was sold the freehold by the Church Commissioners, together with the former Bartle Yard and the area between the hall and the street, for £294 10s. In 1919 these assets were transferred to G.E. Barton Ltd. In 1927 the hall was described in an insurance policy as a coach house with a joiner's workshop and store above. Then, in 1953, it was bought from Bartons' by William Wright Ltd.

These changes in use of the hall entailed great damage to the original fabric, and by 1970 most of the building's distinctive features had been either obscured or removed. In particular, a floor had been inserted, dividing the hall space horizontally, and a number of doors and windows had been opened through the original walls. The fine roof, however, was more or less intact and what remained of the building was extensively repaired and refurbished between 1979 and 1984. From 1982 it was used as a Guild Hall by a company representing the York Guild of Building, the Guild of Freemen and the Company of Cordwainers. An extension was added to provide essential services and the committee room was completed in December 1984. It is now a Grade II listed building and scheduled ancient monument.

The Excavation

Within the college precinct the most recent foundations of the late 19th century school and 20th century bakery had removed evidence for post-medieval development across much of the site. Given the additional factor that post-medieval deposits were not excavated and recorded to a consistent level during the project, in many cases being machined off, it has proved impossible to describe a coherent post-medieval sequence on a site-wide basis.

Period 9: mid 17th century onwards
(Fig.353)

By the mid 17th century many of the medieval buildings had been demolished, having been replaced by mansion houses which were increasingly sublet. By 1700 we know that only five vicars remained within the college precinct (p.627). North-east of the close, no structures survived from the medieval period, the hall (Building 5) having been demolished by the mid 16th century. The post-medieval cellars recorded here may represent all that remains of the vicarial mansion houses that replaced it.

On the south-west side of the close the college chapel and hall were still standing. At the end of the close Building 24 may have been extant, with beyond it Building 17, but no levels later than the 16th century are recorded, and Building 18 had clearly been demolished in the 16th–17th century. The post-medieval sequence is unclear along the street frontage here because of later disturbance caused by the construction of the National School in the 19th century. Attached to the hall, the former service wing, represented by Building 25 and Building 27 and its annexe, was also still standing. The kitchen block and brewhouse (Building 35) had been demolished, although the garden wall still provided a major property boundary running north-east/south-west across the site, defining an open area to the south-east into which the two latrines attached to Building 27 intruded. South-west of the hall, Bartle Yard survived as an open area until the early 19th century, with Buildings 26 and 30, attached to the hall on the north-west side, and Buildings 32 and 33 to the south-west.

Bedern North-East

Phase 1: mid 17th–mid 19th century
(Figs.354–7, 388s)

To the north-east of Bedern a series of 17th–19th century cellars had been cut into the earlier levels. In Area 14.II the three cellars to the north-west may have belonged to the Dutch-gabled buildings on the street frontage in this area; the fourth, and largest, appears to have belonged to the Turf House, or White House, which is known to have been set back from the street (see Fig.346, p.628).

The earliest post-medieval structure was represented by a small cellar (1071*) set well back from the street frontage. This may have been at the rear of one of the Dutch-gabled houses. It was set in a construction trench, c.1·8m

641

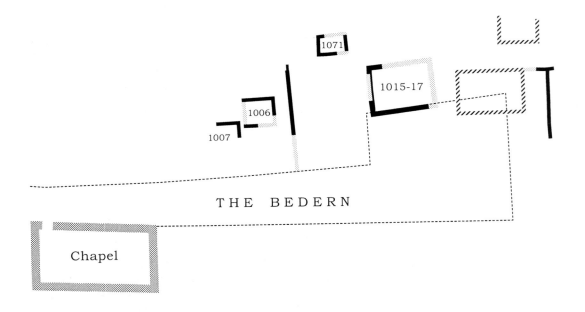

THE BEDERN

Chapel

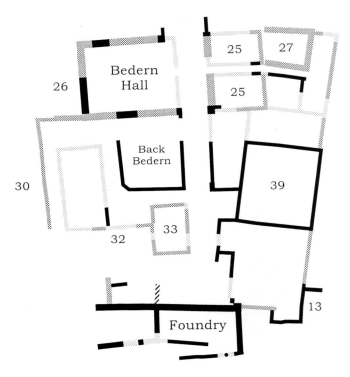

Fig.353 *Period 9: interpretative summary phase plan, showing building development. For the key, see Fig.195, p.409. Scale 1:400*

× 2·6m, backfilled with rubble, including a number of worked stones (Fig.354). These comprised two fragments of detached shafts in Purbeck marble (165–6), a fragment from a poorly cut detached shaft (164), a fragment of attached shaft (252), a section of moulding (281) possibly from the same fireplace fender as a fragment (282) found in Period 8 deposits, and a fragment of roll moulding (241, AY 10/4). The cellar had two phases of flooring (1004–5) with 17th and 18th century pottery in it. A small brick structure (1069) was possibly a support for a small barrel. One metre south-west of the cellar, and cutting the remains of the outer wall of Building 5, was a brick-lined cess pit (1055*) containing a thin cess fill covered by various rubble and ash deposits (Fig.355). A stone cresset lamp (sf135) and three handled jugs were also found in the backfill. Nearby there was a brick-lined sump (1023) set in a construction trench (1019), a pit (1039) containing a 15th century French copper alloy jetton (AY 18/1, 241) and 17th century pottery, and a demolition spread (1092).

An 18th century brick wall (1076*), running perpendicular to the street frontage, may represent the division between the building described above and that to its north-west. In the same area there was also a shallow pit (1056) and, against the street frontage, a brick-lined pit (1051*, 1052*), in which was found a Richard II penny (AY 18/1, 136), originally deposited in the early 15th century. A section of a large string course (195, AY 10/4) was found in these levels.

To the south-east, three of the original walls of a second cellar, at least 6 × 5·6m, could be traced (Fig.356), comprising the south-west wall (1015*), the north-west wall (1016*) and the north-east wall (1017*). These walls mark the position of a building set back from the street frontage at the south-east end of Area 14.II, probably to be identified as the Turf House, or White House (p.635). Each wall was built of mortar-bonded re-used limestone blocks, with some brickwork. Within the cellar there were traces of a fragmentary floor (1010*) of re-used brick, laid on mortar (1011–12). The drainage system (1013*) for the cellar had been cut from the top of this mortar levelling in the 18th–19th century. There were traces of a circular brick-lined sump (1033*) replaced in the 19th century by a second sump (1014*). The drains and sumps contained various modern fills (1020, 1032).

To the north-west of wall 1076* there were at least two further cellars. The first was a brick-floored cellar (1006*) with stone steps, divided into two by a single brick wall (Fig.357). The cellar builders had re-used at least one fragment of worked stone (316, a fragment of late medieval parapet; AY 10/4). The smaller, north-western end, was thought to have been used as a coal cellar. A well-built brick drain (1046*) set in a construction trench (1044*) ran from the cellar in the direction of Bedern Close. A mortar-filled pit (1059) cut this trench. The second cellar (1007*) was also brick-built with a roughly constructed partition wall (1037*) which separated two floor levels (1040–1). The

Fig.354 Area 14.II, Period 9: cellar 1071, looking south-east. Scale unit 0·1m

Fig.355 Area 14.II, Period 9: cess pit 1055, looking south-east, showing three handled jugs. Scale unit 0·1m

Fig.356 (left) Area 14.II, Period 9: cellar 1015–17, looking north-east, showing internal drainage system 1013. Scale unit 0·5m

Fig.357 (below) Area 14.II, Period 9: cellar 1006, looking south-east, showing the internal brick partition wall. Scale unit 0·1m

cellar floor was reached by a flight of brick and stone steps at the north-western end.

To the rear of these cellars was another limestone-lined cess pit (1095*) containing a fill of sand (1091) and a lens of mortar. A sample contained moderate amounts of faecal concretions, mineralised fly puparia and mortar. Only fig seeds were recorded as identifiable plant remains (Hall et al. 1993b). To the north-west, another cess pit (1042*; Figs.283–4, p.528), originally constructed in Period 8 Phase 2 and used within Building 5, is thought to have been re-used in this period, as suggested by the dates of the pottery within the surviving fills. The lower fill consisted of a clay loam (1030) containing a high proportion of small mortar pieces, as well as mammal, bird and fish bone, insect remains, snails, shellfish, grape pips, nutshell (probably hazel), 18th century pottery, metal, glass, wood, charcoal and slag (Hall et al. 1993b). This was sealed by a deposit of large limestone rubble (1028) set into fine sand. In the north corner of the site there was a 19th century drainage sump (1022*) which had cut the Period 8 pits (1146, 1149). It contained a keeled shaft (*162, AY 10/4*) which had been roughly squared off, probably for use at Bedern.

To the south-east, in Area 14.IV, the position of another post-medieval structure was indicated by a cellar (4029*) with an associated drain (4030–1*) on the north-east edge of the excavation. There was also a brick-built 18th century drain (4015*) and drain trench (4003*).

In the north-east central part of Area 14.IV there was a brick-lined pit (4125*), with fill (4114), cut in two by a modern intrusion. In the eastern corner of the site there was a brick wall (4124*) on sound footings of mortar and bonded limestone and cobbles, and a cobble feature (4127*).

Phase 2: late 19th–20th century

During the late 19th century the cellared buildings to the north-east of Bedern were demolished and their cellars backfilled. From documentary sources it is known that the White House and three Dutch-gabled buildings were demolished in 1883 (pp.634, 635). Directly beneath the modern clearance, a series of features was revealed in the north-western half of the site, including pipe trenches and brick walls, as well as various clay dumps, unidentifiable brick features and demolition pits. These are presumed to be associated with the Ebor Buildings which replaced earlier structures to the north-east of Bedern, and were themselves demolished in 1947 (p.634).

At the south-east end of Area 14.II the earlier cellar defined by walls 1015–17 was overlain by a modern demolition level (1481), and then cut by a modern pit (1603). In cellar 1007 the floor levels were covered by 19th century backfill (1003, 1008), and cellar 1006 was also backfilled

with rubble (1001). The floor of cellar 1071 was cut by a large irregular feature (1002). There were also several pits (1009, 1027) and a number of demolition spreads (1025, 1592).

In Area 14.IV wall trenches 4006*, 4013* and 4026* probably indicate the location of another cellar. Otherwise the features recorded here do not form a coherent plan or phase of development. They include several brick walls (4012*, 4017*, 4018*, 4023–4*) and a 19th–20th century pipe trench (4022*). In the northern corner of the site a number of features were assigned to this phase, including a burnt clay dump (4041*), a clay and tile spread (4072*), and a rubble-filled pit (4036*). In the western corner of the site there was a linear feature (4064*), cut by wall trench (4013*), a pit with a fill of mortar and clay (4068*), a linear scoop with a fill of limestone chippings (4054*), cut by a shallow pit with a fill of clay and limestone chippings (4053*), and a shallow pit with a dark clay loam fill (4115*). In the south-western central part of the trench there were spreads of clay (4248*) and mortar (4249), a brick feature (4025*), and a rectangular pit with a sandy silt and tile fill (4065*). Four plant taxa were observed in a sample of the fill, three of them probably from more or less wetland habitats (Hall et al. 1993c). On the south-western trench edge, there were the fragmentary remains of a double row of half and re-used bricks (4078*). In the southern corner there was a shallow pit with a fill of lime mortar, cobbles and limestone rubble (4132*), probably representing demolition of some kind. Other features belonging to this phase were masonry (4128), a brick wall (4052) robbed by a linear cut (4050) with a fill of rubble and clay, a brick feature (4066–7) and a patchy clay spread (4111). The Period 5 drain (4016) also silted up during Period 9, with a number of sandy silty clay fills (4340–2). Samples from these fills provided evidence of a number of plants, including further evidence for greater celandine; the other components included amphibian bone, shellfish, fish bone and scale, eggshell and metallic slag. There were also single examples of two species of beetle, both probably originating in a building (Hall et al. 1993c).

The modern clearance levels (1000/4000) contained a number of architectural fragments, derived from earlier buildings, including four sections of shafts (*7–9, 16*), a section of chevron-moulded jamb (*23*), two rib sections (*47–8*), a capital fragment (*153*), a damaged voussoir section (*292*), a section of moulded vault rib (*50*), a section of chamfer moulding (*173*), a section from a string course with a projecting roll moulding (*192*), a fragment of small roll moulding (*269*), a double chamfered section (*295*) and an undiagnostic fragment (*227*). Most of these re-used worked stones were probably ultimately derived from the Minster choir demolished in 1394 (*AY 10/4*).

A number of coins were also recovered from these clearance levels. These comprised a German jetton (*AY 18/1,*

301), a William III farthing dated 1697 (*308*), a George II halfpenny of c.1750 (*318*), and two George III halfpennies, the first dated 1775 (*322*), the second dated 1799 (*327*). A copper alloy disc of halfpenny size (*409*) and a second German jetton of Conrad Laufer (*304*), dated c.1660, probably used as a gaming counter, were also found.

The post-medieval chapel (Period 9)
by J.D. Richards and D.A. Stocker

Phases 1 and 2: mid–late 17th century
(Fig.358)

There is good reason to think that the Period 7 chapel retained its medieval form until the mid 17th century. The chapel was kept in repair and a bequest for 'sylling' (i.e. making weatherproof) the chapel was made by Robert Gillow in 1505 (*Test. Ebor.* 1865, 281a). There is no reason to doubt that similar alterations to those described in such

detail in the 18th century were also being undertaken in the 16th and 17th centuries but they have simply not been documented. However, there is evidence in the fabric of the south-east and north-west walls for alterations following a change in the function of the chapel prior to the 18th century (Phase 1). It seems likely that the two doorways in the centres of the south-east and north-west walls were knocked through during this early post-medieval period. They were covered by the early 18th century wainscotting so they had gone out of use before then, but both doorways take the form of simple rectangular openings, and must have needed a wooden frame in which to hang any door leaf. Consequently both are likely to be post-medieval, perhaps 17th century, in date, even if this means that they were not in use for a long period of time.

Whilst it is true that the north-west doorway, crude though it must have been, could be used whilst the building was in use as a chapel, the south-east door, emerging right behind the altar, is unlikely to have been used whilst the building was laid out for ecclesiastical purposes. In

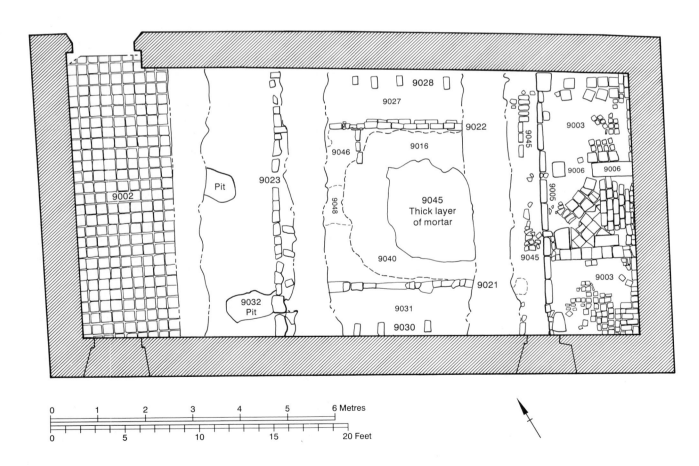

Fig.358   Bedern Chapel: plan of excavated features in Period 9. Scale 1:80

fact both doors look like communicating doorways between the chapel and the domestic buildings which we know were up against either end of the chapel at this date. Furthermore the account of the 1757 repairs (p.648) suggests that there may have been a third doorway opening from another domestic property into the chapel from the south, which had also been crudely covered over in the recent past. The doorways seem to be clear evidence, then, for a period when the chapel was appropriated by the tenants of adjoining properties, who knocked crude doorways through its walls to gain access to its interior.

There is only one likely context for this apparent attempt to appropriate the chapel space and connect it to the adjoining properties — the period following the temporary dissolution of the college during the Civil War and Interregnum. In effect nothing is known of the fate of the vicars during the Interregnum beyond the fact that their income ceased to be accounted (Harrison 1952, 253–4). However the chapel bell was repaired in 1642–3 (YMA, VC 6/6/25) which would indicate, presumably, that an ecclesiastical use was still intended at that date. However in 1663 the Dean and Chapter inquiry into the status of the vicars choral obtained the following declaration, 'As for our Chappel — we make use of it for the performance of God's service upon occasion, it being according to order newly put in sufficient repere' (YMA, VC 1/5/2). This would seem to confirm that the chapel had been recently restored to ecclesiastical use, probably shortly after the Restoration when the members of the college re-assembled (Harrison 1952, 253–4). The two blocked doors in the south-east and north-west walls of the chapel, however, may be the best evidence we have for an unofficial seizure of deserted vicars' property by their neighbours during the Interregnum.

The unusual lancet window in the north-eastern end of the south-east wall must also have been blocked up at some date in the early post-medieval period. The Nicholson drawing of 1827 (Fig.308, p.545) shows quite clearly why it was blocked — there is a jettied timber-framed building obscuring the south-east wall. This building is hard to date from the surviving drawings but it appears to have had rectangular windows with heavy stone mullions. Although it is quite likely that it was the occupants of this house who knocked the doorway through south-east wall of the chapel, there is no reason to think that the building of the house itself and the consequent blocking of the lancet window belong to the Interregnum period.

These depredations were evidently reversed by a phase of reconstruction (Phase 2) following the Restoration. Almost the only information we have comes in the few words of the vicar's declaration in 1663 (above) that they have recently repaired the chapel and put it back into use. Clearly this would have involved blocking the intercon-

necting doorways between the chapel and adjacent properties and it may have been at this time that the two doorways in the south-west wall were finally blocked up. At any rate they were blocked by the time the wainscotting was installed in the following century.

When the houses in Bedern were let, the vicars became responsible for the spiritual welfare of their tenants. The chapel was probably never licensed for weddings, but funerals and baptisms were held there, one of the earliest entries in the register of baptisms being the infant son of George Halley in 1683 (Harrison 1952, 35). In the 1690s Torre reported the chapel as being 'in good repairs for the use of divine service'.

Archaeological support for this brief phase of secular use followed by restoration is provided by the demolition of the Period 8 small, brick side wall for the south-west pews which was covered by clay (9049, Fig.232b, facing p.472) on the south-west side. This clay also butted against the Period 8 north-east/south-west wall (9023), without covering it. At the same time spreads of sand (9034, 9041, Fig.232a) were put down at the north-west end, also butting against wall 9023.

A pit (9053) was dug at the north-west end of the chapel, and filled with crushed wall plaster. This exhibited traces of painting with what appear to be red designs surrounded by black outlines and in places a red background with black details painted on it. Occasionally there are patches of yellow. This has been over-painted with plain white and so the designs are not recoverable. Nevertheless, it is likely that these represent fragments of religious scenes painted on the medieval chapel walls which had been whitewashed over (see pp.604–6).

A new floor was then deposited in the central passage, comprising a thin spread of mortar (9050) covered by sandy silt (9048). At the south-east end a north-east/south-west line of bricks was placed in a linear cut, and bonded with a thick layer of mortar (9045*, Fig.232b–c). These bricks formed the edge to a passageway running from the door at the south-east end of the south-west wall. The altar area was to the south-east of this passage. There were no bricks in the centre of the passageway in front of the altar, suggesting that the altar was usually approached along the central axis of the chapel. A thick clay layer (9046*) was laid down in the north-eastern part of the centre of the chapel, followed by a layer of sand (9047, Fig.232b).

These layers represent the foundations and preparations for interior alterations which involved a new tile floor and new brick foundation walls for pew stalls. At the north-west end of the chapel a tile floor (9007, Fig.232a) consisting of large cream-glazed quarry tiles, set onto a mortar bedding, was laid over the earlier sand (9041,

Fig.232a). The side walls (9021*, 9022*, Fig.232b) for the pew stalls were then built, set on clay bedding layers (9027, 9031, both on Fig.232b–c) which had been laid over the earlier sand (9047, Fig.232b). Within the bedding layers two copper alloy strap-ends (sfs129–30) and a lead alloy weight (sf38) were found (*AY* 17/15 in prep.). The walls consisted of mortar-bonded bricks, laid two deep. At the south-east these walls had originally butted up against the north-east/south-west passageway (9045) and a thin mortar spread (9012, Fig.232c) was laid between them, possibly to strengthen the approach to the altar. Sand packing (9042, Fig.232b) was placed against the south-western wall (9021, Fig.232b) and may have spread across part of the chapel interior. A layer of sand (9029) was also placed inside the base to the south-west pew stall, also butting against the wall (9021). A sand spread (9010, Fig.232c) was placed above the mortar (9012) at the altar end. On top of this a dump of clay (9026) may have been added to strengthen wall 9021.

At the same time more bricks (9028*, 9030*) were placed against the north-east and south-west walls, presumably to support a wooden floor to the pew stalls. Beneath both pew stalls layers of mortar were dumped (9011, 9018, both on Fig.232b). Both deposits contained a number of small objects which may have dropped through gaps in the boards onto the bedding layers. These included a lace tag (sf70) and lead shot (sf68) as well as a number of coins of the early 16th and 17th centuries, comprising a Netherlands brass coin weight of the *Gouden Reaal* of Philip II of Spain, struck for his territories in the Spanish Netherlands, 1556–98 (*AY* 18/1, *246*) and two German jettons (*262–3*). A mortar floor deposit (9009, Fig.232c) at the altar end appears to be of similar date.

Phase 3: 18th century

In the early 18th century, we know that there was a continuous effort to keep the chapel in good condition and it seems likely that this effort began following the Restoration. This information comes from the surviving repairers' rolls (YMA, VC 6/6) which detail many repairs made to the chapel between 1709 and 1769. From this we can see that small sums were spent at intervals of five or ten years on minor repairs and, occasionally, larger works were sponsored. In 1720–1 work (costing a total of £17 1s 3d) was done to the floor, and plastering and painting took place inside. In 1730 the chapel was reported to be in much the same condition as in Torre's time (Gent 1730, 190). More painting, whitewashing and 'mending' was needed in 1733 and 1734, when the altar and the formes (the stalls and screens) are specifically mentioned. The work in 1733–4 was also quite expensive (a total cost of £11 2s) and this may indicate that the reredos and its accompanying woodwork was reconstructed at this date. In 1750 and 1754 more work was done to the floor (presumably parts of the tiling

recorded in 1922), and by 1755–6 bricklayers were being employed.

In 1757 an interesting entry in the Repairer's Office Book describes the work undertaken that year (Appendix). The description documents a complete reconstruction of the building and starts:

In the summer of the year 1757 a grand piece of work was perform'd at the Bedern Chapel: the whole expense of which is contain'd in the following account, audited May 11th 1758. Our great aims therein were effectually to strengthen the Roof and Walls, make them durable: to render ye chapel independent of ye neighbouring Houses, in case of their being hereafter taken down, or burnt; (which latter accident we had particular Consideration of in what we built at each End of the Chapel:) & as far as we could go, to make things Neat and Decent.

The account then goes on to describe the works undertaken in detail, giving the cost for each activity. The total cost of the works was £86 16s 6d. At the south-west end of the south-east wall they found a 'rent' in the fabric which they interpreted as an old doorway cut through the south-east wall giving access into a domestic building to the south of the chapel (and apparently not the doorway for which we have survey evidence in the centre of the south-east wall). Repairing this area involved taking down the whole corner and rebuilding from the ground up. The new brickwork here is clearly visible in the 1980 survey (Fig.306, facing p.545). Although it is not mentioned, it must have been at this time that the south-easternmost window in the south-western wall was reduced from the three lights clearly recorded by Torre to the two lights which survived until 1961. It is likely, perhaps, that the similar, though more crude, alteration to the south-easternmost window in the north-east wall (whereby the south-easternmost light was simply built up in brickwork) also belongs to this phase of alterations and was undertaken to strengthen the east corner below the new gable (see below). In addition to this major area of rebuilding, other unspecified areas of repair to the fabric and a complete repointing were undertaken.

The account is apologetic for not having taken down the north-east wall and rebuilt it; it was clearly supported by a raking shore into the street at that time but the workmen assured the vicars that it was stable in this condition. The south-east gable was raised in brick so that the roof tiles would no longer oversail the south-east wall and so that an encroachment onto their roof by the domestic building to the south could be removed. It was presumably at this date that the rectangular window high up in the gable, recorded as blocked in the 1922 survey, was provided. It would have gathered light above the roofs of the neighbouring building to the south-east. The north-west wall 'had time out of mind, reached no higher than about three yards from ye Floor, the Top of it forming a sort of bench from one side of ye chapel to the other: at ye Back of which Bench ye wall of ye adjoining House'. In other words there was no north-western gable at all in 1757, the roof being built up against the wall of an adjoining building to the north-west. This situation was rectified by building a new gable in brick on top of the reduced chapel north-west wall 'so as to answer the Height of the Chancel End'. The extent of this brickwork is clearly visible in the 1980 survey (Fig.307, facing p.545) and it is likely that the north quoin and perhaps the area over the north doorway was rebuilt in 1757 also. The roof was then completely reconstructed, but using, in the main, the original timbers. It was in 1757 that the 'windbraces' recorded in 1922 were added and the frames against the gable walls recorded at that time must have been put together. Several of the tie beams recorded in 1922 also seem to have been inserted or replaced in 1757. The bell frame was moved from a position at the extreme north-western end of the roof 'toward ye midlength of ye chapel' and the roof was retiled. Although there was a ceiling in the chapel already, a new plaster one was constructed.

There is archaeological evidence for considerable building work within the chapel during the 18th century. A pit (9024) was dug into the tiled floor to the north-west of the screen, and filled with broken pieces of wall plaster, some painted. The pit was then partially covered by a sand spread (9025, Fig.232a, facing p.472) containing pottery of the late 17th or early 18th century and a small fragment of blue and white tin-glazed Delftware wall tile dating to the 18th century. A second very large trench was then dug in the centre of the chapel, avoiding the pews, in an L-shape. This was also filled with plaster. At the same time a third pit (9015, Fig.232a) was dug near the first, and filled with painted plaster. Immediately north-east of the screen a fourth, rectangular, pit was cut (9040, Fig.232b). It appeared to be filled with a mixture of peat and sand, perhaps representing the remains of a decayed wooden post, and contained pottery of the first half of the 18th century. This was capped with a sand and mortar spread (9035, Fig.232b) and the whole centre of the chapel was then levelled with a dark sandy loam (9036, Fig.232b).

A layer of sand (9038, Fig.232b) was then dumped in the centre of the chapel, and covered by a patch of broken plaster (9037, Fig.232b). At the same time sand (9033, Fig.232b–c) was dumped against the inside face of the Period 8 wall (9022) and spread across to meet the plaster. More sand (9020, Fig.232b) was dumped over the Period 8 clay (9026). This contained two sherds of 17th or 18th century date.

The majority of the plaster recovered from these pits and spreads was white, although contexts 9015, 9037 and 9040 produced fragments with traces of painting (p.604). There appear to be red designs surrounded by black outlines and in places a red ground with black details painted on it. Occasionally there are patches of yellow. This has been over-painted with plain white and so the designs are not recoverable. Nevertheless it is likely that these represent fragments of religious scenes painted on the medieval chapel walls which at some stage, possibly during the Reformation, had been whitewashed over. This plaster may have been hacked from the walls in the 17th or 18th century as part of some internal refitting, possibly as part of the construction of wooden panelling.

Another large pit (9016*, Fig.232b) was dug at this stage, and filled with mortar, quarry tiles and some glazed tiles. A sandy dump (9013) capped the earlier pit (9015). A black soil (9014, Fig.232b) built up beneath the south-western pew stall, containing 17th century pottery and two 17th century jettons (AY 18/1, 293, 302), one of which had probably been used as a gaming counter. This layer also contained a fragment of silk tabby (sf75). This is a fine lightweight textile with silver strip spun round a silk core for the warp and flat silver strip inserted into the weft (AY 17/15 in prep.). Within the north-eastern pew stall there was a charcoal loam (9008, Fig.232b) which contained a penny of Edward III (AY 18/1, 133), probably originally deposited in the late 14th or early 15th century, a 15th century French jetton (228), and a number of 16th and 17th century German jettons (281, 291–2, 299). Both layers (9008 and 9014) probably contained objects which had fallen through gaps in the wooden stall floors. As well as the coins there were also an amber bead (sf19), a copper alloy buckle (sf21), an ivory handle (sf77), an ivory mount (sf46), a comb (sf76), various pins (sfs32–3, 80–81, 111), two lace tags (sfs60, 112) and two lead musket balls (sfs23, 95).

Phase 4: 19th century

Although more minor payments were made subsequently, the repairs of 1757 represent the last major refurbishment of the chapel. Little repair work was undertaken at the chapel in the 19th century, which was now little used and increasingly dilapidated. In 1817–18 Clark, a whitesmith, was paid £7 2s 6d for work done on removing the fine medieval stained glass from the windows and replacing it with plain glass (Hargrove 1818, 150). Although the chapel had been inspected in March 1646 for any superstitious images which it might contain, this glass had survived until the 19th century when it was intended to transfer it to some newly erected church. However, Dean Markham having heard of this prevented it from leaving York and is reported to have kept the glass in the Minster, although it has not been traced. (See pp.559–72 for a full discussion of the window glass from Bedern Chapel.) Writing in 1818, Hargrove reports that:

About sixteen years ago divine service was performed here at nine o'clock on the morning of each Wednesday and Friday in Lent; the bell which was then rung for the service, and occasionally tolled in cases of death, yet remains; but it is never used now, the clerical duties there, being at present confined to the christening of children, and the churching of women (Hargrove 1818, 150).

A Sunday School for Girls was held in the chapel from 1801 to 1825, when it was moved to a larger room in Ogleforth (Camidge 1906, 9). Hargrove (1818, 152) recorded that the old font was still near the door, but the altar table was merely a slab of freestone on a wooden frame, replacing the earlier marble one referred to by Drake (1736; repeating James Torre in 1690–1, published in Harrison 1924, and quoted fully on p.563).

Considerable repairs were carried out in 1831 which were aimed at strengthening the north-east wall which was still leaning, as it still did in 1980 (RCHMY 5). The windows on the north side of the chapel, which 'were a favourite target for the wastrels of the square' (Camidge 1906, 6), were blocked up with brick and plastered over in imitation of stonework. In the mid 19th century, James Richardson, sub-chanter, instituted a weekly service, but not necessarily for the vicars: 'Each Friday morning he had prayers, and a small congregation gathered, who were greatly edified, especially when he added to the prayers one of his inspirational addresses' (ibid., 9). Writing in 1857, Whellan records that the chapel was 'now no longer used for the general services of the Church, but is confined to the baptism of children and the churching of women; though up to about eight years ago Divine Service was performed in it every Wednesday' (Whellan 1857, 485). However, by the late 1850s the chapel was said to be in great disrepair (Raine 1858, 98). When in 1866 the property of the vicars was granted to the Church Commissioners, the vicars were left with the responsibility of maintaining a chapel for which there was no use and the inhabitants of Bedern became parishioners of a neighbouring parish (Harrison 1952, 36).

Nevertheless the vicars continued to use the chapel for the election of their members until the election of Canon Harrison in 1919 when it was judged to be too dirty and unsafe for the usual ceremony to be observed (Harrison 1924, 209). In 1925 restoration work was carried out to stabilise the leaning north-east wall and two concrete beams were set in the floor to support iron girders, first recorded on a photograph by W. Watson (Fig.309, p.548). By this stage the quarry tile floor had been taken up and many of the wooden fittings, shown on an earlier photograph by Weston (Fig.310, p.548), had also been removed, probably as part of the stabilisation work. In 1941, the 15th century font and 18th century font cover (Morrell 1949, 172, fig.202) were placed in the Minster crypt for use in baptisms (*VCHY*, 356).

The excavation showed that during the 19th century, new altar step stones (9005*) were laid down, set into a large dump of bedding mortar (9004, Fig.232c, facing p.472) at the altar end. A spread of sand (9019) containing 17th and early 18th century pottery was laid over the central part of the chapel, perhaps to level up for the concrete floor. The altar tiles (9003*) were also laid. Many of the tiles were badly frost-damaged but the extant tiles include eight of 13th century inlaid type with one scooped key. The others were a mixture of fairly poor-quality tiles, possibly of 14th century date. It has been suggested that these represent unskilled local tile manufacture to make up numbers of second-hand tiles (J. Stopford, pers. comm.). All these tiles must have been lifted from an earlier floor and re-used in this later reconstruction. Several altar stones (9006*) must have supported a standing structure (Fig.311, p.549).

Finally a levelling layer (9001) containing mainly 18th century pottery was laid down for the concrete floor (9000). The levelling dump contained a number of earlier coins, comprising one French jetton (*AY* 18/1, 242) and two German ones (*290, 294*). A quarry tile floor (9002*) was laid over the concrete at the north-west end, possibly re-using earlier tiles (Fig.312, p.549). Camidge, writing in 1906, records that the 'floor is laid with plain red tiles of modern character' (1906, 7), and suggests that the floor was probably laid in the mid-19th century, when James Richardson, sub-chanter, re-instituted a weekly service in the chapel. The plan of 1922 shows large 9in. square tiles in the main body of building, with smaller tiles at the south-east end (see Fig.297, p.544). These were taken up at the time that the concrete beams were inserted, in 1925 (see above). In the trench outside the south-west wall, a general clearance layer of modern rubble and concrete (Fig.214, p.441) produced mainly 19th and 20th century pottery.

Bedern South-West

Building 39 (Figs.359–62, 390s)

A large brick house, Building 39, 9·4 × 8·4m, was constructed on the south-east side of the courtyard. It made use of part of the south-west wall of the college kitchen, but the remaining stretch was demolished and rebuilt. It appears from the 1852 OS map that the house may also have encompassed the area of the college kitchen, although this could not be demonstrated archaeologically. At the same time as this house was built the south-west end of the garden wall was demolished. Pottery and coin dating evidence allows us to date the construction of Building 39 to the mid 17th century or later.

Phase 1

The little structural evidence remaining suggests that Building 39 originally had a central passageway and four rooms on the ground floor, and a cellar, 5·3 × 2·7m, located in the north corner (Figs.360–1). The passageway ran from a doorway in the centre of the south-east wall.

This doorway was represented by the footings for a pair of light internal walls. A brick platform (unnumbered) against the interior of the mid-point of the south-east wall indicated the position of the door. The passage gave access to the rooms on either side and to the stair.

The reason for the scarcity of archaeological evidence in the form of floor deposits within Building 39 is that it probably had a wooden joist floor inserted at a level high enough to allow sufficient headroom in the cellar. The 1852 Ordnance Survey map shows the building having an entrance on the north-west side with five steps leading to a raised ground floor (Fig.263, facing p.505).

The interior of the cellar, however, does provide evidence for fittings. The layout of wooden beams is interpreted as the base of a stair, with the brick surface as the floor of an understair area. The remaining cellar area was also covered by a brick floor cut by a brick drain with associated runnels, and a sump. The quantity of undecorated cream or white plaster recovered from later dumps associated with this building makes it likely that its walls were plastered.

The interior of the remainder of the building consisted mainly of mixed underfloor deposits of sand, clay and mortar with numerous tile and rubble inclusions. Some of these deposits showed evidence of burning.

Outside there were a number of outbuildings, a brick drain and sump, and a cobbled surface. To the south-east was an extensive garden area. The area to the north-west, showing extensive garden deposits and rubbish dumps, is identifiable as Back Bedern Court, shown on the 1852

Fig.359 *Area 13.X, Period 9: general view looking north-west, showing Building 39. Scale unit 0·5m*

Fig.360 *Area 13.X, Period 9: south-west end of the cellar of Building 39, looking north-west, showing internal brick features. Scale unit 0·1m*

Fig.361 *Area 13.X, Period 9: cellar of Building 39, looking south-west, after the removal of brick features. Scale unit 0·5m*

Fig.362 Area 13.X, Period 9: south-west cellar wall 5014 of Building 39, showing re-used medieval stones in the foundations. Scale unit 0·1m

Ordnance Survey map of the area. Fronting onto Back Bedern Court, and just to the south-west of it, the medieval structures, Buildings 32 and 33, remained in use until the early 19th century, when they were demolished and rubble spreads accumulated. A brick-lined well was used in association with these buildings.

Construction of the house was preceded by the deposition of mixed layers of clay loam, tiles, mortar, charcoal and brick fragments (5058, 5060*, 5061*, 5067*) cut by a pit (5282). The construction also called for the demolition of the south-west portion of the garden wall (5300) down to its foundations, although the north-east section remained standing and in use.

Construction trenches were dug to take the footings of each of the walls. In most cases the walls occupied their full width; where this was not the case, the trenches were backfilled with mortar. The footings of the exterior and cellar walls contained some re-used medieval stones. A peculiarity of the bonding material was the inclusion of large quantities of broken window glass.

Building 39 used the surviving (Period 7, Phase 1) south-west wall of the kitchen block (5016*, Fig.366s) as its north-east wall, but all other walls were new. It appears that not all the new walls were constructed at the same time. One of the first to be built was the north-east portion (5101*) of the south-east wall, surviving as foundations of limestone and cobbles packed with clay. This was of a simi-

lar construction to 5016 but of a different build to its own south-west continuation (5015*) which contained some re-used medieval blocks (15, 108, AY 10/4). Both 5101 and 5015 overlay the foundations for the demolished garden wall 5300.

It appears that the rest of the house was then built, preceded by the deposition of more construction levels of mortar, sandy clay and charcoal (5054–6*). These were then cut by the construction trench (5094*, 5103) for wall 5015. The south-west portion of this wall consisted of brick on limestone footings, the north-east portion of stone rubble. The construction trench was backfilled with mortar and some limestone blocks. The construction trench (5070*, Fig.366s) for the south-west wall (5014*, Fig.366s) was cut through loam (5046, Fig.367s) containing mortar, brick rubble and charcoal. This wall was built of coursed stone rubble patched with brick and topped with up to three brick courses. It contained a large number of re-used medieval blocks (12–13, 22, 36, 42–4, 109, AY 10/4; Fig.362). The construction trench was backfilled with mortar and limestone fragments (5087*, Fig.366s). The north-west wall (5099*) was set within a construction trench (5071*) which continued along the external north-west wall of the cellar (5009*), although the cellar had been inserted within a construction pit.

The cellar walls (5009*, 5012–13*, 5017*) were built in small foundation trenches (5072*, 5096–8) set within a large pit (5031*) measuring c.6·5 × 3·9m. The cellar walls were built on a plinth of medieval stone, at this point only one course high, containing a number of worked blocks (14, 18, 55, 59, 65, AY 10/4). The bricks used in the walling measured on average 260 × 120 × 60mm, and they were laid in an irregular stretcher bond with occasional header ties, set in the same type of mortar as had been used for the foundation work. The exterior cellar walls were composed of solid brick work with an average thickness of 0·4m, whilst the south-east and south-west walls were thinner, about 0·25m thick, but also of solid construction. The construction pit for the cellar was then backfilled with mortar and brick rubble against the inserted walls. Wall 5017* removed the north-west continuation of the old kitchen range wall.

Within Building 39 there was also an internal division (5095*) set into a construction trench (5078*) filled with mortar, tile and brick chips, cutting a deposit of mixed sand (5079). This wall continued the line of the cellar wall 5013* towards wall 5014*. Several other slight structural remains were also identified relating to the passageway noted on p.650: 4m from the north-east end of wall 5101 was the brick platform (unnumbered) which had been set into the construction trench before it was backfilled. This platform measured 1·4 × 0·5m with its long axis running north-east/south-west. From its north corner a fragmentary wall (unnumbered) ran north-west for a surviving distance of c.2·1m. A similar, but rather more damaged, wall-line was recorded as running parallel to it, 1m to the south-west, forming the footings for the central passageway.

Within the cellar, or north bay, irregularities in the base of the construction cut (5031) were levelled up with a deposit of silty sand and rubble (5090). The stair base comprised a pair of timber beams (of which one is shown on Fig.390s: 5089*), placed in shallow slots running parallel to each other across the cellar, in a north-west/south-east direction. These beams were 0·9m apart, and the space between them was filled with a silty clay (5093), a sand spread (5092) and a deposit of wood ash (5091). The beams were sealed with mortar and capped with tile, and then overlain by a single course of mortared brick laid on edge. Capping this sequence of spreads was a layer of sand on to which a brick floor (5040*) was set. The remaining area of the cellar was then sealed under a deposit of sand (5038) capped by another brick floor (5069), the remains of which could be seen in the north corner. Half bricks and mortar had been used to fill the resulting gap between the floor and those bricks placed above the south-west beam.

Cutting through the brick floor was a drain (5039*), later filled with silt (5085), and a sump (5043*), later filled with sandy silt loam (5088). The sump was situated in the west corner of the cellar and was fed by two runnels, one along the south-west wall, and another longer one which followed the line of the north-west wall for a short dis-

tance before diverging from it. At a distance of c.0·7m from the north-east wall this drain was crossed at right-angles by a third runnel. All the drains and the sump were of unmortared brick set into construction trenches, the drains possessing brick capping (Fig.360, p.652).

Within the west bay of Building 39 there was a sequence of largely burnt deposits, consisting mainly of sand, clay and mortar spreads, containing tile and brick inclusions (5026, 5073–6, 5080–2). The latest of these was cut by a feature (5007) with a fill of dark grey clay with much mortar, plaster, brick and tile inclusions. Within the south bay there were several mortar and rubble spreads with inclusions of charcoal, bricks and cobbles (5041–2, 5047–50, 5068).

A brown silty clay (5064) with inclusions of coal and brick chips, and larger lumps of plaster and mortar, was located in the central passageway of the house. Set into this was a collection of limestone and sandstone blocks (5065*) with broken bricks set in a brown rubbly soil.

Located in the east bay of the house were several clay loam and rubble deposits (5066*, Fig.366s, 5057, 5059*, 5063) with charcoal and brick inclusions. These deposits contained a 17th century copper alloy token farthing issued by William Wilson of Thirsk (AY 18/1, 384). A small circular rubble layer (5062*) inside a larger circular feature was situated within this bay. All these spreads were overlain by a dark sandy silt with charcoal flecks, cobbles, brick rubble, limestone and mortar flecks (5044).

Outside the west corner there were a series of rubble and tile-filled deposits (5033, 5141, 5151–2), as well as a cobble surface with sand packing (5148*). The rubble deposits contained a French jetton (AY 18/1, 224) of the late 14th/early 15th century. An outbuilding was added to the west corner, over these deposits. A north-west/south-east mortar-bonded rubble wall (5150*), surviving for a length of c.2m, continued the line of the south-west wall which it abutted. A return wall, running south-west to the edge of the excavation, was represented by a robbed construction trench (5166*, Fig.367s) containing clay loam, tile rubble and mortar. There were related spreads of clay loam with inclusions of tile, mortar, charcoal and shell (5167, 5184) to the south-west.

A short section of walling (5350*, Fig.367s) was also built from the south corner, continuing the line of the south-east wall, and running to the edge of the excavation. A brick-built sump (5308*, Fig.367s) cut this wall; it was eventually backfilled with clay loam and rubble.

To the south-west, parallel with the south-west wall of Building 39, there was a brick drain (5083*) with a silty fill. In this same area a shallow depression (5086) was filled with mortar, bricks and limestone chips in sand. To the north-east, and abutting the building, was a clay loam (5100) with patches of charcoal and clay, and a pit (5164) with a fill of clay loam, charcoal, peat, mortar and limestone rubble. To the south-east there was a typical 'garden' soil (5102, Fig.367s), whilst to its north-west was a deposit of broken tiles and mortar (5120) covered in turn by a spread of sandy clay (5124) containing rubble, limestone chips, mortar and charcoal flecks. In the north-east central part of the site was a layer of cobbling with a sand bedding (5084), from which was recovered part of a 13th century seal stamp (sf2264).

Initially, a new floor level (6063*, 6070, Fig.366s, 6125) was laid down in the kitchen area, consisting of an extensive deposit of laminated fine ash and charcoal with kitchen and domestic debris, deposited in a piecemeal fashion.

Phase 2

During the later 18th century the floor of the cellar was raised, perhaps in an attempt to deal with drainage problems, the earlier brick floor being covered in rubble and levelled to form the base for the next brick floor. It is likely that this new floor re-used the brick from the earlier floor which had been extensively robbed out. A new brick stairway was also constructed at this time, as was a brick sump cutting through the new brick floor.

Within the cellar c.0·2m of rubble and mortar (5011*) was dumped to form the basis for the second floor (5010*). This rubble and mortar also formed the basis for the new brick stairway constructed of quarter-round moulded bricks and built in the same position as the earlier one. The new brick sump (5045*) was inserted against the north-west cellar wall cutting through the floor (5010), which was repaired and packed with half bricks after completion of the work.

To the south-east the garden soil 5102 (Fig.367s) was subsequently overlain by a clay spread (5028, Fig.367s) containing brick, mortar, cobbles and shell, covered by an extensive dark grey silt (5027*, Fig.367s) with mortar chips, brick fragments and tile which spread over almost the entire south-east end of the site. Within this spread was an Edward II penny (AY 18/1, 118) initially deposited in the late 14th century, and a dump of clay tobacco pipes (sfs1693, 1704, 1708, 1723–4, 2883–97). The animal bone assemblage from spread 5027 mainly comprised cattle and sheep, with some pig, and a little cat, dog, hare and rabbit. The cattle bones included part of the skull of a young calf. The assemblage also included parts of at least two goat horncores, one of them sawn across at the base. Goose, duck, heron and lapwing were also represented, as was halibut.

A poorly made cement-bonded brick wall (5025*) was set into this deposit, running north-west/south-east, and

surviving for c.6m. There were traces of a second parallel wall c.9m to the north-east. Partly overlying 5027 was a spread of demolition rubble and mortar (5029).

Building 32

Only one fragment of wall 5024* survived of a room added to the north-east of Building 32, consisting of four courses of cement-bonded bricks capped with broken sandstone coping, resting upon a cement foundation raft, c.0·03m thick. At its north-east end there was a fired brick projecting beyond the wall-line which must be all that survived of the north-west/south-east return to the wall, running to the north-west edge of the excavation.

Buildings 25 and 27 (Figs.287, 363, 390s)

The service block (Buildings 25 and 27) south-east of the hall was leased from before 1650, when it was described as 'consisting of two rooms below — a kitchinge and a butterie called the Colledge Kitchinge and Butterie — and another lowe room, with three chambers over the same'. With the addition of another structure south-west of Building 27, the block remained standing until 1879 and in the 1850s was occupied by 300 people with only two privies between them (pp.631–2). As Snarr's Buildings this was one of the most notorious slums in York. Plans of 1835 and 1851 have calculations of the volume of each room, allowing only 110 cubic feet per person. Nevertheless another house nearby was then described as 'the worst place in Bedern and might be termed a modern Black Hole of Calcutta ... 30 persons are frequently accommodated in one room about 12 foot square'. In 1880 the Dean and Chapter as trustees received the site from the Church Commissioners; the area of 144 square yards to be used for an extension to the Bedern National School. In 1950 G.E. Barton Ltd bought the freehold from the Church Commissioners together with the rest of the school site.

Phase 1: early 19th century

By the beginning of the 19th century, the north-east and south-west parts of Bedern south-west of the close were largely cleared of buildings, although they remained in the central area. From documentary evidence we know that Bedern became a slum during the first part of the 19th century. In the north-east of Area 13.X, the demolished buildings were replaced by a sequence of levelling materials cut by rubbish pits and brick-lined drains, and overlain by brick surfaces.

In the central area a passageway was built through Building 25, dividing it into two approximately equal parts. On the north-east side of the passageway a short stretch of limestone wall (6011*) was found running from the north-east jamb of the entrance into Building 25. It was set on a thin mortar spread (6016), was one course deep and survived to only one course high. A parallel wall on the south-west side of the passageway is shown on Fig.390s, a continuation of wall 6023* described below. At this time therefore the south-east side of Building 25 at least (the remainder was not available for excavation) was divided into two rooms of approximately equal area, separated by a lobby 0·9m in width. A fairly substantial laminated deposit of daub material (6132), consisting largely of ash and charcoal, was found in the building. Near the bottom was a lens of limestone set in mortar, which may represent a floor level.

South-east of Building 25 and south-west of Building 27 a structure was added measuring 4 × 3·5m. The north-east wall (6023*, Fig.368s) made a butt joint with the south-west jamb of the doorway in the south-east wall of Building 25. The construction was unusual in that it had been built almost as a 'cavity' wall, with the south-west 'skin' being formed by a single row of irregular limestone blocks giving way at the south-east end to pitched half-bricks, and the north-east 'skin' being entirely composed of pitched half-bricks. It contained a worked medieval stone (*141, AY 10/4*). Although some of the bricks and limestones showed traces of mortar, the wall was not mortar-bonded, and the entire structure was set into a shallow construction trench with a fill of loose lime mortar.

At the south-east end of wall 6023 a stone return wall (6024*) was built on top of a mixed spread of hard mortar (6114, Fig.366s) which overlay a clay loam (6139*) with brick rubble and mortar. All that remained of this south-east wall of the structure was a single course of individual limestones, with no evidence for the bonding material. The south-west wall was probably formed in part by the north-east wall of the former college kitchen, although no trace survived of this. A plan of c.1890 suggests that access to this new structure was through its south-west wall. Cut into 6114 was a small pit (6124) with a fill of mortar, charcoal, bone and small tile rubble.

Between the structure just described and Building 27 there was a continuation of the passageway in Building 25; this is shown on the Ordnance Survey map of 1852 as covered. From this it may be inferred that Buildings 25 and 27, and the new structure, possessed upper floors at that date. The passageway led out into an open yard, as shown on the 1852 map. This map also clearly indicates that the area to the south-east of Building 27 was incorporated into this yard. Hence by this date the demolition of the annexe to Building 27 and its rebuilt (Period 8, Phase 1) south-west wall (6062) must have taken place. Within Building 27 the brick pit in the south-east corner continued to function, and the fill (6027) of rubble and dark silty clay produced 19th century pottery.

In the yard a brick-lined well or cess pit (6005*, Fig.366s) was sunk, set in a circular construction pit (6086)

c.0·2m greater in diameter than the well itself, and backfilled with a silty clay loam and rubble. The exceedingly poor standard of construction — the walls were built up with very friable bricks, laid in stretcher bond with brown clay as the bonding material — rendered excavation difficult below 1·6m. At this depth a cess fill (6201, 6002, Fig.366s) of 19th century date was encountered. The insect fauna recovered from samples of this fill included a mite, a flea, a cockroach and a number of bed bugs, although the latter may have been associated with pigeons rather than humans. The plants included moderate quantities of leaf fragments, probably from broad-leaved trees. The list of plants offered little useful information, being a mixture of plants representing a variety of habitats or sources. Fig, linseed and blackberry may have been foodplants, but only blackberry was present in moderate amounts. The samples also contained nutshell, small mammal and fish bone, shellfish and eggshell. There was no trace of parasite eggs (Hall et al. 1993a).

The Period 8, Phase 1, brick-lined pits (6012–13) were still in use in this period and a structure enclosing them appears to be shown on the 1852 OS map. The upper fills (6014) were of brick rubble, interpreted as collapsed materials from the upper levels. They incorporated a range of post-medieval domestic refuse and residual medieval finds, including a bone apple corer (sf2129), a bone tuning peg (*8071, AY 17/12*), two bone handles (sf2127, sf2172), a bone button (sf2128), a bone disc (sf2147), a stone gaming piece (sf2146), a fired clay wig curler (sf2138) and a pestle (sf2908). The animal bone assemblage from fill 6014 consisted mainly of cattle and sheep, with some pig, plus domestic fowl and geese, and duck and woodcock. Cod and ling were also represented. This fill also produced an interesting chicken tarsometatarsal with the spur sawn off (Scott 1985, 32). This is taken as evidence of cock-fighting as the bony spur was often replaced with a metal equivalent, in order to improve the bird's performance (West 1982). Below this a thick ashy layer yielding a substantial quantity of 19th century pottery was excavated; in the earlier pit this in turn sealed a dark grey sandy clay with a good deal of brick and tile rubble which also produced 19th century pottery. The garden wall in this area had by now been demolished down to its foundations. Another layer of garden soil (6007) was laid down in this area, and contained a coin of Charles I, 1625–49 (*AY 18/1, 188*). The area was crossed by a number of modern brick drains which had cut through the earlier garden soils.

In the north-east area of the site a dark loam (7040, Fig.368s) and a mixed clay loam (7036, Figs.366s, 368s, 370s) were deposited during the 19th century, although the latter contained a mid 14th century French jetton (*AY 18/1, 212*), as well as a bone tuning peg (*8070, AY 17/12*). The remains of a possible wall-line (7033, Fig.368s) of mixed brick and limestone rested on this layer. It is possible that this wall-line related to an irregular north-east/

south-west line of bricks (7021) resting on a layer of mixed clay loam (7038, Fig.368s). In this area were two small circular pits (7017, 7041) with a fill of dark loam and modern brick, similar to another pit (7014, Fig.370s) filled with tile and charcoal-flecked loam. The top layers of pit 7041 appear to have been broken brick and tile bedding for the broken brick surface (7012, Fig.370s) which partially overlay it. A brick on-edge feature (7009) was cut into the Period 8 clay (7011), possibly a north-east/south-west drain.

In the south-west part of the site a construction pit (5160, Fig.367s) for a brick floor removed part of wall 5023 and its foundation trench 5161. The fill (5108, Fig.367s) of this construction pit consisted of a loam with inclusions of broken brick, tile, stone rubble and mortar. A brick feature (5111, Fig.367s) was then constructed, comprising a clay-bonded brick floor with walls on its north-west and south-east sides composed of limestone and brick capped with clay. A German jetton of Hans Schultes (*AY* 18/1, *275*) was recovered from this feature, dated c.1550–74. After the construction of 5111, more of the fill 5108 was deposited as infilling within the foundation trench.

In the centre of the south-west area of the site were a sequence of sandy demolition spreads (5030, 5032) and a feature (5052) with a sandy soil fill containing charcoal, mortar and tile inclusions. A modern feature (5077) cut the earlier deposit 5026. Also in this area was an extensive ash layer containing coal, charcoal and lumps of wall plaster and mortar chunks (5105–6) forming a refuse dump which incorporated oyster shells. This was covered by a sequence of clay and rubble layers containing charcoal, shells and bones (5051, 5035, Fig.367s). A shallow depression was located in 5035 filled with mortar and occasional flecks of charcoal (5110).

Backfill was then placed within the Period 8 well (5008), its lower fill (5037) consisting of a sandy deposit with very little rubble, covered by a layer of fine rubble, mortar and a quantity of building materials (5036), the whole being topped by an upper fill (5034) of rubble, mortar and moulded plaster. A brick and limestone rubble-filled pit (5137) cut the well cut 5125, and may possibly have been some kind of foundation packing.

At this time a dark silty loam (5005) was deposited in the north corner of the south-west arm of the trench and was cut by a brick wall (5004*), forming three sides of a new rectangular building to the north-east. Forming a structural division within this building was a regular slot-like feature (5002*), possibly a shallow or truncated foundation trench which cut 5005*. It contained a glass bottle (sf1728) inscribed 'Bedern'. This feature was later filled with demolition material (5000). Contemporary with both 5004 and 5002 was an ash and loam layer (5001*) confined within the limits of 5004 and perhaps related to its demolition. It overlay the footings of 5004, as did another demo-

lition loam (5003*) south-east of the building with a high proportion of rubble, tile and stone. Within the building defined by wall 5004* was a small brick-lined sump (5109*) cutting 5001. At a similar time, another wall (5019*) was constructed to the south-east of wall 5004, consisting of a shallow, cement-bonded brick footing aligned north-east/south-west. Abutting the north-east end of 5019 was a brick wall (5006*) set in a construction trench running to the north-east edge of the excavation. A brick wall with two offsets (5018*) ran in a south-easterly direction from the south-west end of 5019 and butted up to Building 39.

In the east and west trial trenches south-west of the hall a modern brick wall was cut through wall 5397/5426, covered by an even later wall (5398, Fig.262, facing p.504) built directly over its line. In the remainder of this area at this time was a dark sandy clay (5333, Figs.262, 371s) covering wall 5351, and on top of which were some re-used limestone blocks (5384, *258*, *AY* 10/4; Fig.371s). A plain floor tile, glazed yellow with brown streaks and cut into a triangle, was found in the clay.

Phase 2: late 19th century

Towards the end of the 19th century brick drains, pits and other features were cut in the north-east part of Bedern south-west of the close (Area 13.X). The garden wall was by now completely demolished, and it is possible that the kitchen range had also fallen into disuse. In the kitchen, in the region of the large hearth, and responsible for the destruction of approximately half of it, were two pits — one very large one to the north-west, and another smaller one to the south-east. Clearly each of these could only have been dug after the demolition of the stack which is known to have been in use at the end of the 19th century. The construction of a north-east/south-west brick drain showing two distinct phases of early modern construction marks the demolition of Building 25, as it ran over the foundations of its north-east wall.

It was at this time also that Building 39 was demolished, with the resulting accumulation of rubble deposits over its foundations. A series of almost circular shallow scoops were sited in this area to take large Yorkstone slabs, the biggest of which measured 0·80 × 0·64m. These features formed no identifiable pattern but are interpreted as bases for posts or stanchions, although no floor levels for the associated structure were identified. The building of which they formed part was finally removed for the construction of the late 19th and 20th century factory which occupied the site until its demolition prior to the excavation.

Across the north-east part of the site a drain trench (7004) was cut by two modern drain pits (7001), and cut into the general mixed layers in this area was a brick drain or sump (7023), a sandstone and brick drain (7016), a shal-

Fig.363 *Area 13.X, Period 9: brick drain 6003, looking north-west. Scale unit 0·1m*

Also of a late date was a general loamy soil (6001) in the centre of the trench with rubble and clay containing two Victorian halfpennies (*AY* 18/1, *358, 370*), a modern cellar set into a construction trench (6006), a linear feature (6034) with a fill very similar to garden soil, a 19th century sump (6206) overlying a clay loam and mortar (6216), and a rubble- and mortar-filled pit (6039, Fig.366s) cutting an irregular pit (6096) filled with tile. The sump produced a halfpenny dated to 1865 (*AY* 18/1, *355*) and the bone handle from a toothbrush (sf2258). There was a construction/repointing trench (6026*) appearing as a small linear feature on the south-west side of the north-east stone wall of Building 27. A limestone and brick feature (6057*), possibly the stub of a wall foundation, ran east from the concrete apron at the end of the hall. It was of an irregular build with a face of moulded stone, and an apparently disturbed 'kerb' of on-edge bricks. Also dug at this time was a pit (6108) with a tiled lining and a small pit (6056, Fig.366s) with a fill of rubble and sandy loam.

The side walls of brick drain (6003*) were composed of thin, vertically set bricks, with no remaining capping, whilst at the south-west end the base was constructed with bricks laid across the long axis (Fig.363). The walls had been built up in half bricks with some stretchers and survived to a maximum height of four courses. A fragment of lava quern stone (sf2216) had been incorporated into the drain construction. Traces of a slight construction cut were visible from the highest remaining level of the drain. The fill (6004), which was thinly spread over the whole excavated length of the drain, and reached a maximum depth of 0·03m, was of olive green rather coarse sand. Both this and a light grey sandy clay (6051), with a high proportion of mortar and charcoal flecks which appeared to overlie drain 6003, were under modern clearance (6000) and contained much earlier material, and nine coins (*AY* 18/1, *103, 167, 190, 276–7, 298, 335, 352, 403*), of which the earliest dates to c.1300 and the latest to 1862.

Bedern long trench (Fig.390s)

A limestone wall (1006*) was constructed part way across the trench, approximately 8m to the north-west of the garden wall (1500) and parallel to it. It was set in a construction trench packed with rubble (1024/1032), and a band of clay (1025) was laid against it. The alignment of 1006 suggests it represented the continuation of wall 5166 in Area 13.X (see p.654).

A circular brick oven was constructed at the south-west end of wall 1006 over a foundation pit filled with clay, brick rubble and sand (1044/1054, Fig.364s). In its initial phase this had a brick floor (1046, Fig.364s) covered by a layer of burnt mortar (1045). At some stage the oven had been refloored with a layer of bricks set on edge (1023, Fig.364s) which were covered by an ash use-deposit (1022), and a layer of burnt orange sand (1004). At this point, the

low cut containing charcoal (7002), a loamy soil (7018), and a cobble and brick feature (7024). There was a spread of dark loamy soil (7045) also located here. 7291 was a small modern intrusion. Everything was sealed by a layer of modern clearance (7000) containing five coins (*AY* 18/1, *176, 220, 261, 300, 356*), of which the latest dates to 1865.

oven had also been given a curving brick wall (1005*, Fig.364s) set on burnt orange sand (1042, Fig.364s) over a clay bedding (1043, Fig.364s). This oven was probably associated with the post-medieval bakery on the foundry site (p.666).

A layer of garden loam (1034, Fig.364s) was deposited between the garden wall (1500) and wall 1006. Pottery from this layer is of 17th century date. A number of walls, of which fragments remained, were built on this layer. They include a very short stretch of limestone wall (1030) and a short brick wall (1029*) abutting the north-west side of wall 1500*. At its north-west end 1029 returned to the north-east and it may have formed the south-west end of the drainage sump (5308*) encountered in Area 13.X. A more substantial wall (1008*, Fig.364s) ran north-east/south-west across the trench; at its north-east end it turned a right-angle and as 1007* continued north-westwards to join wall 1006. Both 1007 and 1008 had footings of bricks set on edge; in wall 1008 there were the remains of bricks laid flat over these foundations, while in wall 1007 a few re-used limestone blocks survived in situ.

Another wall (1031), comprising a single fragmentary line of bricks and limestone blocks, also joined wall 1006. It had apparently been set into a clay-filled construction trench (1056). Pottery associated with the wall showed it to have been built sometime after the late 17th century. There were traces of an adjacent cobble surface (1039) cut by a small pit (1047).

At the north-west end of the trench a sand and rubble layer (1018, Fig.364s) extended over the wall footings of Building 13. It was overlain by a tile spread (1017) and closely packed brick rubble (1019/1020). At some stage this was covered by a layer of plaster rubble (1002).

To the south-east of wall 1500 there was a garden loam (1505/1513, Fig.364s) similar to 1034, overlain by a number of late 17th and 18th century features. These included two linear limestone and rubble spreads running north-east/south-west (1507, Fig.364s, 1508), the first cut by a post-hole (1515) and overlain by a layer of mortar (1518, Fig.364s). There were also several rubble-filled pits (1506, 1517, 1521), a loam spread (1512), a square of clay (1524) and a brick-packed post-hole (1540). During the 19th century a further layer of garden loam (1014, 1504, both on Fig.364s) was dumped across the trench, south-east of wall 1006.

Finally, the garden loam was cut by a number of modern features, including seven rubble- and mortar-filled pits (1011, 1012, Fig.364s, 1021, Fig.364s, 1503, 1509–11), a concrete base (1501) set in clay (1526), and a slate bed (1502). There was also a modern drain (1009; fills 1015–16), set in a construction trench backfilled with brick and limestone rubble (1010) with a modern drain-pipe (1519 in clay bedding 1520) and a similar drain (1563) in Area IV.

The post-medieval college: discussion

Whilst the precinct of the College of the Vicars Choral remained in the nominal ownership of the college until the late 19th century, it no longer functioned as a collegiate community from at least the late 16th century. Nonetheless, a small number of vicars, probably no more than half-a-dozen at a time, continued to reside in the precinct in their vicarial mansions. Excavations have revealed three cellars to the north-east of the former close that may have belonged to the Dutch-gabled buildings (p.641). A fourth cellar (made up of walls 1015–17, see p.643 and Fig.353, p.642) appears to have belonged to the building later known as the Turf House, or White House, which is known to have been set back from the street. A map of 1851 (Fig.349, p.636) indicates that the former longhouse of the college was still standing in the north-east part of the precinct (pp.577, 635).

On the south-west side of the close the college chapel and hall were still standing, and the former was still used by the vicars. Nonetheless, it was much reduced in splendour, the medieval painted walls having been whitewashed, probably during the Reformation, and the roof hidden behind a flat ceiling. By the early 19th century the stained glass had been removed. The congregation had also changed, and objects, including a number of gaming tokens, which had slipped through the floorboards, attest to their more worldly nature. Attached to the hall, the former service wing, represented by Building 25 and Building 27 and its annexe, was also still standing, although now converted into private accommodation. A passageway ran directly south-west from the close, through the former screens passage, and into Bartle Yard, and was still in use in the 19th century.

To the south-west excavation revealed the foundations of Building 39 on the south-east side of Bartle Yard. This was probably a two-storey structure, with at least four rooms on each floor, and a cellar. It may be regarded as typical of a post-medieval bourgeois residence and may itself have been a vicarial mansion. Certainly there is little to distinguish the post-medieval residences of the vicars from secular accommodation of the period, but this is not surprising as the vicars no longer followed any 'monastic-type' rule. New buildings were now invariably brick-built rather than timber-framed, although medieval stonework continued to be re-used in their foundations. Cellars were floored with brick, whilst other rooms had raised timber floors. Walls appear to have been plastered. Arrangements for rubbish disposal continued to be fairly primitive during this period. Latrine pits continued to be the norm, although they were now generally brick-lined. Better attention was paid to drainage, however, with a number of brick-lined drains and sumps being installed in connection with new post-medieval buildings.

The medieval layout of the college certainly continued to determine the post-medieval development of the area. Apart from the obvious survival of medieval buildings, the college courtyard or close became an open yard and from 1852, a thoroughfare. The second courtyard, Back Bedern or Bartle Garth, was also still an open yard on the 1852 Ordnance Survey map (Fig.263, facing p.505). The main garden wall, established in the late 14th century, which ran north-east/south-west to the south-east of the hall, continued to function as a major property boundary.

The 19th century slum

Whilst the documentary records provide a graphic insight into the appalling conditions endured by the 19th century inhabitants of Bedern, there is little archaeological evidence for this. The excavation records do support the dilapidation of the chapel and the continued decay of the medieval hall. However, they tell us little about the nature of the slum buildings. From documentary sources we know that Buildings 25 and 27, and another building south-west of Building 27, remained standing until 1879 and in the 1850s were occupied by 300 people with only two privies between them. The archaeological record simply indicates the subdivision of a medieval building into smaller rooms (pp.655–6).

The privies referred to were presumably the pair of brick-lined pits which had been constructed adjacent to Building 27 in the 15th century, to the south-east of the main garden wall (Period 8, see p.521). One glimpse into the lives of the post-medieval inhabitants of Bedern who used these pits is provided by the recovery of the leg of a bird which had been used in cock-fighting (p.656). An adjacent cess pit (6005) yielded an insect fauna suggestive of crowded and insanitary conditions, including a mite, a flea, a cockroach and a number of bed bugs. Unlike the me-

dieval cess fills, however, there was no trace of the parasitic worms that had plagued the medieval inhabitants of Bedern.

Two 19th century bone assemblages from Bedern South-West provide some evidence for light industrial activity. The assemblages complement each other in that context 5027 was dominated by sheep metapodials, whereas 6014 was markedly depleted in those elements. This is unlikely to have resulted from butchery; it appears that the metapodials must have been gathered for a purpose. Sheep metapodials provide small, straight tubes of bone, well suited to modification into artefacts such as knife handles or bobbins. It is not possible to point to finished examples from the same deposits, but it is a useful working hypothesis to suggest that the metapodial accumulations were collections of raw material for artefact manufacture, material which was abandoned for some reason before being used. This assemblage is similar to those recovered from the foundry site in 15th century levels (p.157, *AY* 10/3); a pair of bone handles and a large number of bone offcuts were recovered from post-medieval contexts on the foundry site.

There are few large post-medieval bone groups, and the picture is further complicated by the degree of residuality to be expected in the post-medieval deposits. Nevertheless the samples do confirm the reduction in the variety of the diet of the post-medieval population, with none of the unusual species represented in the medieval groups. There is also a return to the dominance of sheep, pig and poultry. The late medieval period was marked by the apparent increase in the number of cattle bone fragments, a trend clearly reversed in the post-medieval period.

Finally, although the post-medieval finds have not yet been fully studied, they do not appear to provide any unusual characteristics that might allow one to label the group a slum assemblage. A number of stone pencils and marbles from both Areas 13 and 14 may be derived from the use of various buildings in Bedern as school premises. During restoration, the sole of a child's shoe (sf2865) was found in a niche in the north-west wall of Bedern Hall and amongst the more unusual post-medieval finds were two ceramic wig curlers (Area 14: sf586; Area 13: sf2138). In addition, broken pottery, clay tobacco pipes and glass vessels were found, typical of most 19th century deposits in York.

Conclusion

The Bedern project demonstrates the potential of urban archaeology for providing new information about even relatively well-documented groups within medieval society, and about the subsequent use of the area they occupied. Colleges of vicars choral were significant institutions within England's medieval cathedral towns and this is the first time that one has been subjected to intensive archaeological scrutiny. Large-scale open-area excavation has made it possible to trace the evolution and development of the college buildings, and to chart the changing role of the college itself. It has allowed us to gain insights into the daily life of the vicars choral, as well as into their relative status within the ecclesiastical hierarchy.

As in the case of many of the major rescue excavations of the 1970s the longevity and unfocused nature of the Bedern project has posed some substantial logistical problems of post-excavation and publication, compounded by the fragility of the original evidence. The slight nature of the foundations of many of the college's timber-framed buildings, coupled with later disturbance, means that many of them are still poorly understood. The same disturbance, principally pit-digging and the consequent recycling of earlier deposits, means that residuality has been a significant constraint on interpretation of the finds evidence, and has denied us the use of intra-site spatial analysis. Nevertheless, the Bedern excavations have contributed much to our knowledge of medieval York, and have indicated the prospects for further research. Environmental archaeology, in particular, has been shown to have great potential for increasing our understanding. Far from being the conclusion of the project, this volume is the first stage in making the evidence available to a wider audience and will be followed by contributions on other aspects of the site.

Acknowledgements

York Archaeological Trust is most grateful to the original owner of the site, York City Council, and the subsequent owner, Simons of York, and also to the Dean and Chapter of York Minster who own the Chapel, for making the land available for excavation, and for giving every assistance during the work. The excavations were supported by grants from the Department of the Environment, now English Heritage. Many of the excavation assistants were employed on a STEP scheme administered by the Manpower Services Commission, whilst the supervisory staff were financed directly by the Department of the Environment. From 1976–8 the excavation was staffed with DOE-funded excavation assistants and supervisors who were supplemented by Manpower Services Commission Job Creation Programme staff from 1978–9. Later all employees were replaced with MSC Special Temporary Employment Programme personnel although the DOE continued to provide funding for supervision. Until 1979 additional summer help was provided by many hard-working volunteers, students from the University of Pennsylvania and the College of Ripon and York St John, and inmates from HM Open Prison at Askham Bryan.

The Bedern excavations were initially directed for York Archaeological Trust by B. Whitwell, then by M.J. Daniells, and finally by M. Stockwell. The foundry site was supervised in 1973 by P. Mills (Trench I) and I. Reed (Trench II), in 1974 by P. Mills, and from 1975–6 by R. Bartkowiak. The latter also conducted some post-excavation ordering of the foundry site archive. For Bedern South-West and Bedern North-East, initial post-excavation analysis and production of the archive report was undertaken by A. Clarke and M. Stockwell.

In addition to contributing the architectural sections on the Hall and Chapel to this report, D. Stocker also contributed to the discussions of the phasing and layout of the York Bedern and to the sections on other colleges of vicars choral in England. His earlier report on the worked stones from Bedern (AY 10/4) formed one strand of evidence for the understanding of the later medieval sequences. His assistance in the final pre-publication stages of this report is gratefully acknowledged. Photographic records and notes on Bedern Hall were made by the Royal Commission in the 1960s; the east gable wall was recorded in 1978 by a team led by C. Briden. Mr Stocker's report makes use of the 1978 work by YAT and RCHME information, supplemented by notes made by the author during the reconstruction of the building between 1979 and 1981. Mr Stocker also gratefully acknowledges the help of C. Wilson in providing information and analytical commentary on Bedern Hall and P. Everson for his help in producing the plan of the Vicars' Hall at Wells. Rectified photography of Bedern Chapel was overseen by R. Dallas, then of the IAAS Survey Unit in York.

Pottery from Bedern was initially examined by C.M. Brooks, and further studied by S. Jennings. A preliminary inspection of a sample of the roofing material was undertaken by S. Garside-Neville, who is grateful to B. Hurman for advice on the ceramic louver and for access to the G. Dunning archive. The decorated floor tile was examined by J. Stopford. The medieval painted wall plaster was examined by L. Wong, who gratefully acknowledges the help of S. Cather, H. Howard, D. Park and A. Smith. The window glass from Bedern Chapel and elsewhere within the college precinct was examined by D. O'Connor, who expresses gratitude to his friend H. Murray FSA for his invaluable heraldic advice.

The copper alloy objects were examined by A. Goodall and the iron objects by I.H. Goodall and P. Ottaway. The medieval glass vessels were examined by R. Tyson. The stone objects were examined by G.D. Gaunt. The textile remains were examined by P. Walton Rogers, with identification of the animal coat fibres by H.M. Appleyard. The other finds identifications were provided by D. Tweddle, H. Cool and N. Rogers. Thanks are also due to C. McDonnell and the Trust finds staff who provided ready access to the finds, and to the Trust conservators for their work on the painted wall plaster.

General advice on the environmental evidence and animal bones has been provided by the staff of the Environmental Archaeology Unit at York University. The investigation of the animal bones was supervised by K. Dobney and T.P. O'Connor; processing was carried out by S. Scott and J. Hamshaw-Thomas, with help from other EAU staff, particularly J. Carrott and B. Irving. T.P. O'Connor provided a report on the post-medieval animal bones. The investigation of plant and invertebrate remains was supervised by A.R. Hall, H.K. Kenward and A. Robertson. Sorting and processing of samples was also carried out by C. Fisher, R. Nicholson, A. Sutherland, S. Pearsall and A. Ruddock. Most of the analysis of intestinal parasitic worms was undertaken by B. Douglas, under the supervision of A.K.G. Jones. In addition to the main series of analyses, student projects were carried out by A. Cameron and H. Topsey, then undergraduates at the University of Bradford. Their results have been incorporated into the text.

Samples were taken for archaeomagnetic dating by M. Noel, then of the University of Newcastle-upon-Tyne. The interpretation of the results has subsequently been modified as a result of discussion with C. Batt, of the University of Bradford. Several timber samples were examined in order to provide tree-ring dating for Bedern Hall by J. Hillam at the Dendrochronology Laboratory of the University of Sheffield. Ms Hillam is grateful to R. Morgan for making available her data from the Central Tower, York Minster. The work was financed by the Department of the Environment, now English Heritage. YAT is grateful to C. Groves for her help with the text and illustrations for the dendrochronology section in the prepublication stage.

Work on the documentary sources for Bedern was originally carried out by R.M. Butler, and the author is grateful for permission to make use of his notes on the site. Research on a possible bridge to facilitate access to the Minster Close was carried out by M.J. Jones, with P. Chitwood, C. Fraser, M. Prescott, J. Smith and R.L. Smith (report in the YAT archive). Further research on the early history of the College has been conducted by S. Rees Jones, who has also taken responsibility for joint authorship of the historical sections. In addition, the authors are grateful to N. Tringham for providing access to his edition of the vicars' charters, in advance of publication, and also for commenting on the text for this fascicule. P. Hanstock kindly permitted us to make use of his collection of 19th century views of Bedern.

All line illustrations were produced by T. Finnemore, except Figs.336 and 339 by C. Bentley; Figs.302–7 by K. Biggs; Figs.192 and 317–20 by G. Boyles; Figs.334–5 by P. Chew; and Figs.232, 331–3 and 365–71 by S. Chew. Some of the figures were based on drafts prepared by J. Kestle, J. McComish, R. Marwood and D. Stocker. Fig.189 is reproduced with the permission of J. Atherton Bowen, Figs.190–1 with the permission of W. Rodwell, Fig.349 with the permission of the Dean and Chapter of York, and Fig.350 with the permission of the Borthwick Institute of Historical Research. The excavation photographs were taken by R. Bartkowiak and M. Duffy. Further photography has been undertaken by S.I. Hill, FRPS (Scirebröc). Other photographs are reproduced by kind permission of the following: Figs.294 and 332, the National Monuments Record; Figs.296–300 and 345, the Yorkshire Architectural and York Archaeological Society; Figs.308 and 351, York City Art Gallery; Figs.309–10 and 352, York Library (309–10 from the Yorkshire Philosophical Society Collection); Fig.316, the Bodleian Library, University of Oxford, and York Minster Archive; Fig.330, Dr Christopher Wilson; Figs.337–8, Courtauld Institute of Art; Figs.346–8, Peter Hanstock.

The summary was translated into French by C. Sheil-Small and into German by K. Aberg. The academic editor was P. Ottaway; the final publication was supervised and paged by F.P. Mee. This fascicule is published with the aid of a generous grant from English Heritage.

Summary

The College of the Vicars Choral in York was established in 1252 in an area south-east of Goodramgate, later known as Bedern, where the common hall, chapel and gatehouse still stand. The office of vicar choral derived from the obligation upon absentee canons to appoint personal deputies to take their place in the choir of York Minster. Throughout the 14th century the college housed 36 vicars, but it began to decline from the end of the 15th century. In 1574 the vicars ceased to dine in common, although the college was not formally dissolved until 1936.

Excavations between 1973 and 1980 revealed an extensive complex of college buildings. In total, an area of c.2,500m² was investigated, representing about 30% of the estimated college precinct at its maximum extent. During the first half of the 13th century Bedern was subject to agricultural usage, with a series of drainage gullies and ditches representing property boundaries running back from Goodramgate, and some structures of which the remains were slight (Period 1). In the mid 13th century this land was acquired by the college, which erected its first buildings on either side of an open courtyard, running back from Goodramgate, which was to become Bedern Close. On the north-east side of the close a large building — the great hall — was constructed; on the south-west side a stone building (on the site of the later chapel) and a smaller timber-framed structure were built (Period 2). As the college expanded the vicars required more accommodation. An aisled hall was constructed along the south-west side of the close although this appears to have been short-lived, and a smaller structure was built behind it (Period 3). By the late 13th century (Period 4) buildings were constructed in the south-west part of the site. In the early 14th century the chapel was constructed and there were major changes to the buildings on the south-west side of the close (Period 5). In the middle of the 14th century the college reached the peak of its prosperity. An early timber-framed common hall was constructed, the great hall was rebuilt, apparently to provide separate houses, and new individual residences were also built on the south-west side of the close (Period 6). There was major building activity throughout the precinct from the mid 14th century to the early 15th century (Period 7), creating a second courtyard to the south-west. The great hall was now rebuilt in stone, and a new stone-built common hall was constructed south-west of the close, with adjacent service accommodation, kitchen block, archive room and college gardens. The chapel was enlarged and a number of new houses were built. Many of these developments coincided with attempts to revive the corporate life of the college through a new set of statutes issued in c.1390–1430. A stone wall now marked a division in the precinct between the courtyard south-west of the hall and a garden to the south-east, whilst any further expansion of the college to the south-west was constrained by the presence of a medieval foundry. From the mid 15th century to the early 17th century (Period 8) there was less new building work, although existing structures continued to be modified as the vicars increasingly lived away and sublet their houses to lay tenants.

The post-medieval period (Period 9) saw further changes. The excavations provided archaeological evidence for some of this later development; most deposits, however, had been disturbed by modern features and so documentary records have provided invaluable supplementary evidence. North-east of the close post-medieval cellars may represent all that remains of the vicarial mansion houses that replaced the medieval hall. Many of these houses were sublet, and by 1700 there were only five vicars resident in Bedern. On the south-west side of the street the college chapel and hall survive as standing buildings. The chapel was used sporadically for religious services until the 20th century, and excavation within the building revealed evidence for several phases of refitting. From 1640 the hall was leased to laymen and swas ubdivided into three tenements. The former service wing of the hall and the college kitchens were converted into residential accomodation. In the areas adjacent to the hall, excavation revealed a number of buildings around an open yard named Bartle Garth, or Back Bedern, which formed a second courtyard within the college precinct. These included a substantial mansion erected at the end of the 17th century.

During the first half of the 19th century Bedern became a notorious slum; it was home to a large number of Irish immigrants and subsequently a high proportion of York's prostitutes operated from rooms in Bedern. From the middle of the century attempts were made to improve Bedern. The street was opened up to St Andrewgate in 1852; the Bedern National School was built in 1872–3; the Ebor and Hawarden Buildings provided model lodging houses from 1883. Thereafter Bedern was taken over for light industrial premises, the hall becoming a mineral water factory in the 19th century and later part of a meat-pie works, until the area was returned to residential housing in the 1980s.

To the south-west the medieval foundry was replaced by a bakery in the mid 16th century. Excavations here revealed a series of bread ovens, in use until the mid 17th century. It is suggested that the bakery may still have had a connection with York Minster, possibly baking communion bread for use in the Minster services. This bakery will be published in a future fascicule in *AY* 13.

The development of the college buildings mirrors the growth and decline of the college, and the trend away from communal life to individual houses. The excavation has provided a valuable insight into life in a medieval urban religious house. This is complemented by reports on the finds, pottery, animal bones and plant remains. The fascicule also presents the documentary evidence for the development of the college, and gives details of the architectural history of the chapel and hall, as well as reporting on the techniques and materials used to construct and embellish the college buildings.

Résumé

Le College of the Vicars Choral d'York a été construit en 1252, dans la partie au sud-est de Goodramgate, ultérieurement connue sous le nom de Bedern, où la salle commune, la chapelle et la loge sont encore visibles. L'office de 'vicar choral' provenait de l'obligation dans laquelle étaient les chanoines absents de désigner des suppléants particuliers pour les remplacer dans le chœur de York Minster. Pendant tout le 14ème siècle, le collège abrita 36 vicaires, mais il commença à subir un déclin à partir de la fin du 15ème siècle. En 1574, les vicaires s'arrêtèrent de dîner ensemble, bien que le collège ne fut pas formellement dissout avant 1936.

Des fouilles menées entre 1973 et 1980 révélèrent un complexe étendu de bâtiments collégiaux. En tout, une superficie d'environ 2,500m² fut explorée, représentant environ 30% de l'enceinte estimée du collège avec une approximation maximale de sa superficie. Pendant la première moitié du 13ème siècle, Bedern fut utilisé à des fins agricoles, avec une série de caniveaux de drainage et de fossés représentant les limites de la propriété à partir de Goodramgate, et certaines structures dont il ne restait pas grand chose (Période 1). Au milieu du 13ème siècle, cette terre fut acquise par le collège, qui érigea ses premiers bâtiments de chaque côté d'une cour ouverte, à partir de Goodramgate, qui allait devenir Bedern Close. Sur le côté nord-est de Bedern Close, un grand bâtiment — la grande salle — fut construit; sur le côté sud-ouest, un bâtiment de pierre (sur le site à venir de la chapelle) et une plus petite structure en pans de bois furent construits (Période 2). Au fur et à mesure de l'expansion du collège, les vicaires eurent besoin d'un supplément de place. Une salle à bas-côtés fut construite le long du côté sud-ouest de Bedern Close bien qu'elle ne semble pas avoir duré longtemps, et une plus petite structure fut construite derrière cette salle (Période 3). A la fin du 13ème siècle (Période 4), des bâtiments furent construits dans la partie sud-ouest du site. Au début du 14ème siècle, la chapelle fut construite, et de grands changements furent effectués sur le côté sud-ouest de Bedern Close (Période 5). Le milieu du 14ème siècle connut l'apogée du collège. Une salle commune en pans de bois fut construite, la grande salle fut reconstruite, apparemment pour fournir des maisons séparées, et de nouvelles maisons individuelles furent aussi con-struites sur le côté sud-ouest de Bedern Close (Période 6). Il y eut une importante activité de construction dans toute l'enceinte, du milieu du 14ème siècle au début du 15ème siècle (Période 7), créant une seconde cour au sud-ouest. La grande salle fut alors reconstruite en pierre et une nouvelle salle commune en pierre fut construite au sud-ouest de Bedern Close communs adjacents, un bâtiment cuisine, une salle des archives et les jardins collégiaux. La chapelle fut agrandie et plusieurs nouvelles maisons furent construites. Nombre de ces développements coincidèrent avec des tentatives de reprise de la vie commune du collège par le biais d'une nouvelle série de statuts émis entre environ 1390 et 1430. Un mur de pierre marqua dorénavant une séparation dans l'enceinte entre la cour au sud-ouest de la salle et un jardin au sud-est, bien que toute autre expansion du collège au sud-ouest fusse limitée par la présence d'une fonderie médiévale. Entre le milieu du 15ème siècle et le début du 17ème siècle (Période 8), il y eut moins de travaux de nouvelle construction, bien que les structures existant déjà continuèrent à être modifiées car, de plus en plus, les vicaires vivaient ailleurs et sous-louaient leurs maisons à des locataires laïcs.

La période post-médiévale (Période 9) fut le témoin d'autres changements. Les fouilles fournirent des indices archéologiques de certains développements de cette Période; la plupart des dépôts avaient toutefois été perturbés par des structures modernes et les archives documentaires ont donc fourni de précieux indices supplémentaires. Au nord-est de Bedern Close, des caves post-médiévales représentent peut-être tout ce qui reste des demeures des vicaires qui remplacèrent la salle médiévale. Nombre de ces maisons furent sous-louées et, en 1700, il n'y avait plus que cinq vicaires résidant à Bedern. Sur le côté sud-ouest de la rue, la salle et chapelle du collège survivent encore en tant que bâtiments. Des offices religieux eurent lieu sporadiquement dans la chapelle jusqu'au 20ème siècle, et les fouilles à l'intérieur du bâtiment révélèrent des indices de plusieurs phases de remise en état. A partir de 1640, la salle fut louée sur bail à des laïcs et fut subdivisée en trois logements. L'ancienne aile des communs de la salle et les cuisines du collège furent converties en logements. A proximité de la salle, les fouilles révélèrent plusieurs bâtiments autour d'une cour ouverte appelée Bartle Garth ou Back Bedern, qui formait une seconde cour au sein de l'enceinte du collège. Parmi ces bâtiments se trouvait un grand hôtel particulier érigé à la fin du 17ème siècle.

Pendant la première moitié du 19ème siècle, Bedern devint un taudis notoire; un grand nombre d'émigrants irlandais y vivaient et, par la suite, une grande partie des prostituées d'York exercèrent leur métier dans des chambres de Bedern. A partir du milieu du siècle, il y eut quelques tentatives de rénovation de Bedern. La rue fut ouverte jusqu'à St Andrewgate en 1852; la Bedern National School fut construite en 1872–3; les Ebor et Hawarden Buildings offrirent des pensions modèles à partir de 1883. Par la suite, Bedern fut repris pour des locaux consacrés à l'industrie légère, la salle devenant une usine d'eau minérale au 19ème siècle et, plus tard, fit partie d'une manufacture de pâtés en croûte, jusqu'au retour aux habitations pendant les années 1980.

Au sud-ouest, la fonderie médiévale fut remplacée par une boulangerie au milieu du 16ème siècle. Ici, les fouilles révélèrent une série de fours à pain, utilisés jusqu'au milieu du 17ème siècle. On pense que la boulangerie aurait encore pu avoir un lien avec York Minster, peut-être fabriquant des hosties pour les offices du Minster. Cette boulangerie sera publiée dans un futur fascicule dans *AY* 13.

Le développement des bâtiments du collège reflète la croissance et le déclin du collège et la tendance à s'éloigner de la vie commune en faveur de maisons individuelles. Les fouilles ont donné un précieux aperçu de la vie d'une maison religieuse urbaine médiévale. S'y ajoutent des rapports sur les découvertes, la céramique, les ossements d'animaux et les vestiges de plantes. Le fascicule présente aussi les indices documentaires sur le développement du collège et donne des détails sur l'histoire architecturale de la chapelle et de la grande salle, ainsi qu'un rapport sur les techniques et matériaux utilisés pour construire et embellir les bâtiments du collège.

Zusammenfassung

Das Kollegiat Vicars Choral in York war 1252 auf einem Areal südöstlich der Goodramgate gegründet worden. Auf dieser Lokalität, die später unter dem Namen Bedern erscheint, sind heute noch das Refektorium, die Kapelle und das Tor erhalten. Das Amt des 'vicar choral', des Chorvikars, entstand aus der Verpflichtung, daß abwesende Kanoniker Stellvertreter zu ernennen hatten, welche dann den Platz des Kanonikers im Münsterchor einzunehmen hatten. Durch das 14. Jahrhundert hindurch beherbergte das Kollegiat 36 Vikare, vom 15. Jahrhundert an begann jedoch ein Rückgang und 1574 hörten die Vikare auf die Mahlzeiten gemeinsam einzunehmen. Das Kollegiat selbst wurde jedoch erst 1936 formell aufgelöst.

Ausgrabungen in der Zeit zwischen 1973 und 1980 legten einen ausgedehnten Bereich der Kollegiatsgebäude frei. Im ganzen wurde ein Areal von circa 2500m² untersucht, dies stellt ungefähr 30% des angenommen Kollegiatsbereiches zur Zeit seiner größten Ausdehnung dar. In der ersten Hälfte des 13. Jahrhunderts wurde das Areal Bedern landwirtschaftlich genutzt mit einer Reihe von Drainagerinnen, mit Gräben, die die Besitzgrenzen kennzeichneten und von der Goodramgate her verliefen und einigen Bauten, deren Reste jedoch gering waren (Periode 1). In der Mitte des 13. Jahrhundert wurde dieses Areal von dem Kollegiat erworben, das dann begann die ersten Bauten auf den beiden Seiten eines offenen Hofes zu errichten, der von der Goodramgate aus verlief und später zum Bedern Close wurde. Auf der Nordostseite des Hofes entstand ein großer Bau — the great hall — das Dormitorium. Auf der Südwestseite errichtete man einen Steinbau (auf dem Areal der späteren Kapelle) sowie einen kleinen Fachwerkbau (Periode 2). Mit dem Anwachsen des Kollegiats wurden mehr Unterkünfte für die Vikare benötigt. Eine mehrschiffige Halle wurde entlang der Südostseite des Hofes angelegt, doch scheint diese nur kurze Zeit in Gebrauch gewesen zu sein und ein kleinerer Bau wurde hinter ihr errichtet (Periode 3). Gegen Ende des 13. Jahrhunderts (Periode 4) wurde dann auf dem Südwesten des Areals gebaut. Zu Beginn des 14. Jahrhunderts entstand die Kapelle und weitgreifende Änderungen wurden an den Gebäuden auf der Südwestseite des Hofes durchgeführt (Periode 5). In der Mitte des 14. Jahrhunderts erreichte das Kollegiat den Höhepunkt seines Wohlstandes.

Ein erstes Refektorium in Fachwerk wurde errichtet und die große Halle (Dormitorium) umgebaut, anscheinend um einzelne Häuser zu schaffen und weitere individuelle Unterkunfte wurden auf der Südwestseite des Hofes gebaut (Periode 6). Ausgedehnte Bautätigkeit fand dann auf dem gesamten Kollegiatsbereich von der Mitte des 14. Jahrhunderts bis in das frühe 15. Jahrhundert statt (Periode 7). Hierbei wurde ein zweiter Hof südwestlich davon angelegt. Die große Halle wurde jetzt als Steinbau neuerrichtet und ein neues Refektorium (common hall) in Stein im Südwesten erbaut, mit anschließenden Dienstgebäuden, einem Küchentrakt, Archiväumen und einem Kollegiatsgarten. Die Kapelle wurde erweitert und eine Reihe von neuen Häusern wurde gebaut. Viele dieser Bauprojekte erscheinen zur selben Zeit wie Versuche das kommunale Leben in dem Kollegiat durch neue Statute, die zwischen 1390–1430 erlassen wurden, neu zu beleben. Eine Steinmauer markiert jetzt eine Unterteilung des Bezirkes zwischen dem Hof südwestlich der großen Halle und dem Garten in Südosten. Eine weitere Ausdehnung des Kollegiats nach Südwesten wurde durch die Existenz einer mittelalterlichen Eisengießerei eingeschränkt. Von der Mitte des 15. Jahrhunderts bis zum frühen 17. Jahrhundert (Periode 8) gab es wenig Neubauten, obwohl die bestehende Bausubstanz weiterhin modifiziert wurde, da die Vikare in zunehmendem Maße auswärts wohnten und ihre Häuser an Laien weiter vermieteten.

Die Neuzeit (Periode 9) sah weitere Änderungen. Die Ausgrabungen erbrachten den archäologischen Befund für einige dieser späteren Entwicklungen. Der größte Teil der Ablagerungen war jedoch durch moderne Anlagen gestört und aus diesem Grund haben dokumentarische Quellen wertvolle zusätzliche Informationen geliefert. Nordöstlich des Hofes mögen neuzeitliche Keller die Reste sein, die von den Vikarhäusern, die die mittelalterliche Halle ersetzten, übriggeblieben sind. Viele dieser Häuser waren weitervermietet worden und gegen 1700 lebten nur noch fünf Vikare in Bedern. Auf der Südwestseite der Straße haben die Kollegiatskapelle und die Halle als aufgehende Gebäude überlebt. Die Kapelle wurde gelegendlich bis in das 20. Jahrhundert für Gottesdienste benutzt, und Ausgrabungen innerhalb des Gebäudes haben Beweise für mehrere Phasen der

Neuausstattung erbracht. Von 1640 an wurde die Halle an Laien verpachtet und in drei Mietswohnungen unterteilt. Der frühere Dienstflügel der Halle und die Küchen des Kollegiats wurden zu Wohnbauten umgebaut. Auf dem Areal neben der Halle haben Ausgrabungen eine Anzahl von Bauten um einen offenen Hof, der den zweiten Hof innerhalb des Kollegiatsbezirkes gebildet hatte, freigelegt. Dieses Hofareal ist unter dem Namen Bartle Garth oder Back Bedern bekannt. Zu diesen Bauten gehört ein großes Wohnhaus, das gegen Ende des 17.Jahrhunderts erbaut wurde.

In der ersten Hälfte des 19.Jahrhunderts verfiel Bedern zu einem berüchtigten Armenviertel; eine große Zahl der irischen Einwanderer lebte dort und danach war eine große Anzahl der in York tätigen Dirnen in Räumen in Bedern ansässig. Von der Mitte des 19.Jahrhunderts an wurden Versuche unternommen, die Situation in Bedern zu verbessern. 1852 wurde eine Straße auf die St Andrewsgate hin geöffnet; 1872–3 wurde die Bedern Nationalschule gebaut; 1883 entstanden mit den Ebor und Hawarden Bauten Modellmietshäuser. Danach zogen Werkstätten für Leichtindustrie in Bedern ein, die Halle wurde im 19.Jahrhundert zu einer Mineralwasserfabrik und später zum Teil einer Fabrik für die Herstellung von Schweinepasteten, das Areal wurde dann um 1980 wieder zu einem Wohngebiet umgewandelt.

Südwestlich der mittelalterlichen Eisengießerei bestand seit der Mitte des 16.Jahrhunderts eine Bäckerei. Ausgrabungen haben hier eine Reihe von Backöfen freigelegt, die bis in das 17.Jahrhundert in Gebrauch waren. Es wird vermutet, daß die Bäckerei noch mit dem Münster in Verbindung gestanden haben könnte, möglicherweise als Bäckerei der Oblaten für die Abendmahlsgottesdienste des Münsters. Diese Bäckerei wird in einem zukünftigen Faszikel *AY* 13 veröffentlicht werden.

In der Entwicklung der Kollegiatsgebäude spiegeln sich das Wachstum und der Verfall des Kollegiats wieder, zusammen mit der Tendenz fort vom gemeinschaftlichen Leben und hin zu individuellen Häusern. Die Ausgrabung erlaubt einem wertvollen Einblick in das Leben eines mittelalterlichen religiösen Hauses innerhalb des städtischen Bereiches. Dies wird vervollständigt durch Berichte über Funde, Keramik, Tierknochen und Pflanzenreste. Das Faszikel legt weiterhin die dokumentarischen Quellen mit Bezug auf die Entwicklung des Kollegiats vor und gibt weitere Informationen zur architektonischen Geschichte der Kapelle und der Halle. Weiterhin wird über die Techniken und Materialien, die für den Bau und die Ausschmückung der Kollegiats benutzt wurden, berichtet.

Abbreviations

Most abbreviations are those recommended by the Council for British Archaeology but the following are used in addition. Bibliographical brief references used in the text are explained in the bibliography.

AML	Ancient Monuments Laboratory
BIHR	Borthwick Institute for Historical Research
EAU	Environmental Archaeology Unit
ME	Middle English
OE	Old English
OS	Ordnance Survey
RCHME	Royal Commission on the Historical Monuments of England
sf	small find
SS	Surtees Society
YASRS	*Yorkshire Archaeological Society Record Series*
YAT	York Archaeological Trust for Excavation and Research
YCA	York City Archives
YMA	York Minster Archives

Bibliography

Manuscripts consulted

BIHR, B8, 1336/1977, Vicars' Red Scrapbook

—— Reg. Rotherham, Register of Archbishop Rotherham, i, fo.100

YCA, Acc.28: 38

—— C 82.4

YMA, E 3 Fabric rolls

—— L2/1 Dean and Chapter register: 'Liber Albus'

—— L2/2a Dean and Chapter register: 'Liber Domesday'

—— L2/4 Dean and Chapter, register of wills, 1321–1493

—— VC 1/1 The Vicars Choral Statute Book

—— VC 1/5/2 The Vicars' answers to the Dean and Chapter inquiry of 1663

—— VC 3/1/1 Vicars Choral cartulary

—— VC 3/3 Vicars Choral foundation deeds for obits and chantries

—— VC 3/Vi Vicars Choral property deeds

—— VC 4/1 Vicars Choral rent rolls and lease books

—— VC 6/1 Vicars Choral sub-chanters' rolls

—— VC 6/2 Vicars Choral chamberlains' rolls and rent rolls

—— VC 6/4 Vicars Choral bursars' rolls

—— VC 6/6 Vicars Choral repairers' rolls

—— VC 6/7 Vicars Choral tileworks accounts

—— VC 6/9 Vicars Choral building accounts

Printed works

Alexander, J. and Binski, P. (eds), 1987. *Age of Chivalry: Art in Plantagenet England 1200–1400*, Royal Academy of Arts (London)

Allison, K.J. (ed.), 1969. *Victoria County History, Yorkshire, East Riding* 1

Armstrong, P. and Armstrong, S.J., 1987. 'The clay roof tile' in Armstrong and Ayers 1987, 234–40

Armstrong, P. and Ayers, B., 1987. *Excavations in High Street and Blackfriargate*, E. Riding Archaeol. 8

Armstrong, P., Tomlinson, D. and Evans, D.H., 1991. *Excavations at Lurk Lane Beverley, 1979–82*, Sheffield Excavation Reports 1

Armstrong, W.A., 1974. *Stability and Change in an English County Town: A Social Study of York, 1801–1851* (Cambridge)

Aston, P., 1977. 'Music since the Reformation' in Aylmer and Cant 1977, 395–429

Aveling, J.C.H., 1970. *Catholic Recusancy in the City of York 1558–1791*

AY. Addyman, P.V. (ed.). *The Archaeology of York* (London)

3 *The Legionary Fortress:*

  3 P. Ottaway, 1996. *The Fortress Defences and Adjacent Sites 1971–90*

6 *Roman Extra-mural Settlement and Roads*:

  1 D. Brinklow, R.A. Hall, J.R. Magilton and S. Donaghey, 1986. *Coney Street, Aldwark and Clementhorpe, Minor Sites, and Roman Roads*

7   *Anglian York (AD 410–876):*

   2   D. Tweddle, J. Moulden and E. Logan, 1999. *Anglian York: A Survey of the Evidence*

10   *The Medieval Walled City north-east of the Ouse:*

   2   R.A. Hall, H. MacGregor and M. Stockwell, 1988. *Medieval Tenements in Aldwark, and Other Sites*

   3   J.D. Richards, 1993. *The Bedern Foundry*

   4   D.A. Stocker, 1999. *The College of the Vicars Choral of York Minster at Bedern: Architectural Fragments*

11   *The Medieval Defences and Suburbs:*

   1   J.D. Richards, C. Heighway and S. Donaghey, 1989. *Union Terrace: Excavations in the Horsefair*

   2   R.L. Kemp with C.P. Graves, 1996. *The Church and Gilbertine Priory of St Andrew, Fishergate*

14   *The Past Environment of York:*

   5   H.K. Kenward, A.R. Hall and A.K.G. Jones, 1986. *Environmental Evidence from a Roman Well and Anglian Pits in the Legionary Fortress*

   6   A.R. Hall and H.K. Kenward, 1990. *Environmental Evidence from the Colonia: General Accident and Rougier Street*

   7   H.K. Kenward and A.R. Hall, 1995. *Biological Evidence from Anglo-Scandinavian Deposits at 16–22 Coppergate*

15   *The Animal Bones:*

   1   T.P. O'Connor, 1984. *Selected Groups of Bones from Skeldergate and Walmgate*

   2   T.P. O'Connor, 1988. *Bones from the General Accident Site, Tanner Row*

   4   T.P. O'Connor, 1991. *Bones from 46–54 Fishergate*

   5   J.M. Bond and T.P. O'Connor, 1999. *Bones from Medieval Deposits at 16–22 Coppergate and Other Sites in York*

16   *The Pottery:*

   1   J. Holdsworth, 1978. *Selected Pottery Groups AD 650–1780*

   3   C.M. Brooks, 1987. *Medieval and Later Pottery from Aldwark and Other Sites*

   5   A.J. Mainman, 1990. *Anglo-Scandinavian Pottery from 16–22 Coppergate*

   9   A.J. Mainman, in prep. *Medieval Pottery from York*

17   *The Small Finds:*

   12   A. MacGregor, A.J. Mainman and N.S.H. Rogers, 1999. *Craft, Industry and Everyday Life: Bone, Antler, Ivory and Horn from Anglo-Scandinavian and Medieval York*

   13   C.A. Morris, 2000. *Craft, Industry and Everyday Life: Wood and Woodworking in Anglo-Scandinavian and Medieval York*

   15   P. Ottaway and N.S.H. Rogers, in prep. *Craft, Industry and Everyday Life: Medieval Finds from York*

18   *The Coins:*

   1   E.J.E. Pirie, 1986. *Post-Roman Coins from York Excavations, 1971–81*

Aylmer, G.E. and Cant, R. (eds.), 1977. *A History of York Minster* (Oxford)

Bailey, S., Carrott, J., Dobney, K., Hall, A., Jaques, D., Jones, A., Milles, A. and Turner, E., 1994. *Assessment of the Biological Remains from Excavations at Mount Grace Priory, N. Yorkshire (MG89–92)*, EAU Report 94/10

Baillie, M.G.L., 1982. *Tree-Ring Dating and Archaeology* (London)

Baillie, M.G.L. and Pilcher, J.R., 1973. 'A simple crossdating program for tree-ring research', *Tree Ring Bulletin* **33**, 7–14

Baker, J.R. and Brothwell, D.R., 1980. *Animal Diseases in Archaeology* (London)

Barrett, P., 1980. *The College of Vicars Choral at Hereford Cathedral* (Hereford)

Batt, C.M., 1997. 'The British Archaeomagnetic Calibration Curve: an Objective Treatment', *Archaeometry* **39**/1, 153–68

Beechey, F.E., 1976. (unpublished) *The Irish in York 1840–1875*, D.Phil. thesis, University of York

Benson, G., 1911. *York from its Origin to the End of the 11th Century* (York)

Berry, W., c.1830. *An Encyclopoedia Heraldica*, 3 vols

Betts, I.M., 1985. (unpublished) *A Scientific Investigation of the Brick and Tile Industry of York to the Mid 18th Century*, Ph.D. thesis, University of Bradford

Bradshaw, R.H.W., Coxon, P., Greig, J.R.A. and Hall, A.R., 1981. 'New fossil evidence for the past cultivation and processing of hemp (*Cannabis sativa* L.) in eastern England', *New Phytol.* **89**, 503–10

Brain, C., 1981. *The Hunters or the Hunted?* (Chicago)

Brodrick, A. and Darrah, J., 1986. 'The fifteenth century polychromed limestone effigies of William Fitzalan, 9th Earl of Arundel, and his wife, Joan Nevill, in the Fitzalan Chapel, Arundel', *Church Monuments* **1**, 65–94

Brooke, C.N.L., 1957. 'The Earliest Times to 1485' in W.R. Matthews and W.M. Atkins (eds.), *A History of St Paul's Cathedral and the Men associated with it* (London), xxx–xx

Brown, S., 1980. (unpublished) *The Peculiar Jurisdiction of York Minster during the Middle Ages*, D.Phil. thesis, University of York

——— 1984. *The Medieval Courts of the York Minster Peculiar*, Borthwick Papers **66**

Brown, A., Colvin, H. and Taylor, A.J., 1963. *The History of the Kings Works, Volume 1: The Middle Ages* (London)

Burton, J., 1976. 'The Vicars Choral of York and the Bedern', *Interim: Archaeology in York*, Bull. York Archaeol. Trust **4**/2, 27–32

Cal.Pat. Calendar of Patent Rolls 1391–6, 1399–1401 (HMSO, London, 1911)

Camidge, W., 1906. *The Bedern or Bederne and its Chapel*

Carrott, J., Dobney, K., Hall, A., Irving, B., Issitt, M., Jaques, D., Kenward, H., Large, F. and Milles, A., 1994. *Assess-*

ment of the Biological Remains from Excavations at 148 Lawrence Street, York, EAU Report 94/25

Cartulary of Chichester. Peckham, W.D. (ed.), 1946. The Cartulary of the High Church of Chichester, Sussex Record Soc. 46

Catalogue of the Muniments. Cox, J.C. (ed.) 1886. Catalogue of the Muniments and MSS Books Pertaining to the Dean and Chapter of Lichfield, William Salt Archaeological Society Collections, 6(ii) (London)

Cert. Chantries. Page, W. (ed.), 1892. Certificate of Chantries, Guilds, Hospitals etc. for the County of York 1546, SS 91

Chanter, J.F., 1933. 'The Custos and College of the Vicars Choral of the Choir of the Cathedral Church of St Peter, Exeter', Trans. Exeter Diocesan Archit. and Archaeol. Soc. (Exeter)

Charters. Tringham, N. (ed.), 1993. Charters of the Vicars Choral of York Minster: City of York and its Suburbs to 1546, YASRS 148 (Leeds)

Clapham, A.R., Tutin, T.G. and Warburg, E.F., 1962. Flora of the British Isles (Cambridge)

Clark, A.J., Tarling, D.H. and Noel, M., 1988. 'Developments in archaeomagnetic dating in Britain', J. Archaeol. Science 15, 645–67

Colchester, L.S., 1987. Wells Cathedral (London)

Cook, G.H., 1959. English Collegiate Churches of the Middle Ages (London)

Coppack, G., 1990. Abbeys and Priories (London)

Cornford, W. and Branch, J., 1992. The Bedern, unpublished typescript in York City Library produced by The Architecture Workshop, Cobalt (UK) Ltd

Cross, C.M., 1977. 'From the Reformation to the Restoration' in Aylmer and Cant 1977, 193–232

—— (ed.), 1984. York Clergy Wills, 1: The Minster Clergy, Borthwick Texts and Calendars

Crossley, F.H., 1962. The English Abbey (London)

Dainton, M., 1992. 'A quick, semi-quantitative method for recording nematode gut parasite eggs from archaeological deposits', Circaea 9, 58–63

Daniells, M., 1979, 'Bedern', Interim: Archaeology in York, Bull. York Archaeol. Trust 6/1, 14–21

Darby, H.C., 1977. Domesday England (Cambridge)

Digby, A., 1981. 'The Relief of Poverty in Victorian York: Attitudes and Policies' in C. Feinstein (ed.), York 1831–1981 (York), 160–87

Dobney, K., Hall, A.R., Kenward, H. and Milles, A., 1992. 'A working classification of sample types for environmental archaeology', Circaea 9, 24–6

Dobson, R.B., 1967. 'The Foundation of Perpetual Chantries by the Citizens of Medieval York', Studies in Church History 7, 22–38

—— 1977. 'The Later Middle Ages, 1215–1500' in Aylmer and Cant 1977, 44–109

Drake, F., 1736. Eboracum, or the History and Antiquities of the City of York, with the History of the Cathedral Church (London)

Dugdale, Sir W., 1658. History of St Paul's Cathedral (London) Another edition with additions, by Henry Ellis (London, 1818)

Dunning, G.C., 1961. 'Medieval chimney pots' in E.M. Jope (ed.), Studies in Building History (London), 78–93

Dyer, C., 1988. 'The consumption of fresh-water fish in medieval England' in M. Aston (ed.), Medieval Fish, Fisheries and Fishponds in England, Brit. Archaeol. Rep. Brit. Ser. 182, i (Oxford), 27–35

Eames, E., 1985. English Medieval Tile (London)

Early Yorkshire Charters. Farrer, W. (ed.), 1914–16. Early Yorkshire Charters, being a Collection of Documents Anterior to the Thirteenth Century, 3 vols, YASRS, Extra Series (Edinburgh)

Eastaugh, N.J., 1989. (unpublished) Lead Tin Yellow: Its History, Manufacture, Colour and Structure, Ph.D. thesis, London University

Edwards, K., 1967. The English Secular Cathedrals in the Middle Ages (Manchester)

Esher, Lord and Pollen, F., 1971. Aldwark: Renewal Project for the City of York (London)

Finnegan, F., 1979. Poverty and Prostitution: a Study of Victorian Prostitutes in York (Cambridge)

Fletcher, J.M., 1977. 'Tree-ring chronologies for the 6th to 16th centuries for oaks of southern and eastern England', J. Archaeol. Science 4, 335–52

Fowler, J.T., 1893. 'Mural paintings in Pittington Church', Yorks. Archaeol. J. 12, 38–41

—— (ed.), 1903. The Rites of Durham, SS 107

Fraser, C.J., 1994. (unpublished) The Building Accounts of the Vicars Choral: the Development of Benetplace and Cambhall Garth, 1360–64, M.A. thesis, University of York

French, T.W., 1971. 'Observations on some Medieval Glass in York Minster', Antiq. J. 51, 86–93

—— 1995. York Minster: The Great East Window, Corpus Vitrearum Medii Aevi Great Britain, Summary Catalogue 2 (Oxford)

French, T.W. and O'Connor, D., 1987. York Minster, A Catalogue of Medieval Stained Glass: The West Windows of the Nave, Corpus Vitrearum Medii Aevi Great Britain, III/1 (Oxford)

Garside-Neville, S., 1995. 'Tile File — Curved and Flanged Medieval Roof Tile', Interim: Archaeology in York 20/2, 31–4

Gayre, G.R., 1956. The Heraldry of the Knights of S. John (Allahabad)

Gee, E.A., 1969. 'The Painted Glass of All Saints' Church, North Street, York', Archaeologia 102, 151–202

—— 1977. 'Architectural History until 1290' in Aylmer and Cant 1977, 111–48

Gent, T., 1730. The Ancient and Modern History of the Famous City of York (York)

Gill, M. and Howard, H., 1997. 'Glimpses of Glory: Paintings from St Mark's Hospital, Bristol' in L. Keen (ed.), 'Almost the Richest City': Bristol in the Middle Ages, Brit.

Archaeol. Assoc. Conference Transactions **19** (London), 97–106

Gilyard-Beer, R., 1958. *Abbeys: an Introduction to the Religious Houses of England and Wales* (HMSO, London)

Godwin, H., 1975. *The History of the British Flora: a Factual Basis for Phytogeography* (Cambridge)

Hall, A.R., 1981. 'The Cockle of rebellion, insolence, sedition', *Interim: Archaeology in York*, Bull. York Archaeol. Trust **8**/1, 5–8

Hall, A.R., Kenward, H. and Robertson, A., 1993a. *Medieval and Post-Medieval Plant and Invertebrate Remains from Area X, The Bedern (south-west), York*, AML Rep. 56/93

—— 1993b. *Medieval and Post-Medieval Plant and Invertebrate Remains from Area II, The Bedern (north-east), York*, AML Rep. 58/93

—— 1993c. *Medieval and Post-Medieval Plant and Invertebrate Remains from Area IV, The Bedern (north-east), York*, AML Rep. 57/93

Hamshaw-Thomas, J., 1994. The 1994 Analysis of the Animal Bones from Excavations in the Area of the College of the Vicars Choral, Bedern, York, between 1978–1980. Unpublished archive report, YAT

Hannah, I.C., 1914. 'The Vicars' Close and adjacent buildings, Chichester', *Sussex Archaeol. Coll.* **56**, 92–109

Harcourt, R., 1974. 'The dog in prehistoric and early historic Britain', *J. Archaeol. Science* **1**, 151–75

Hare, J.N., 1985. *Battle Abbey: The Eastern Range and the Excavations 1978–80* (London)

Hargrove, W., 1816. *History and Description of the Ancient City of York*, 2 vols (York)

—— 1818. *History and Antiquities of York*, 2 vols (York)

Harrison, F., 1922. 'The West Choir Clerestory Windows in York Minster', *Yorks. Archaeol. J.* **26**, 353–71

—— 1924. 'The Bedern Chapel, York', *Yorks. Archaeol. J.* **27**, 197–209

—— 1927. 'The Sub-Chanter and the Vicars-Choral', *York Minster Historical Tracts*

—— 1936. 'The Bedern College and Chapel', *Yorks. Archit. and York Archaeol. Soc. Proc.* **2**, 19–43

—— 1952. *Life in a Medieval College. The Story of the Vicars Choral of York Minster* (London)

Harvey, B., 1993. *Living and Dying in England 1100–1540: The Monastic Experience* (Oxford)

Harvey, J.H., 1975. *Medieval Craftsmen* (London)

—— 1977. 'Architectural History from 1291 to 1558' in Aylmer and Cant 1977, 149–92

—— 1978. *The Perpendicular Style* (London)

—— 1984. *English Medieval Architects* (London)

Hill, R.M.T. and Brooke, C.N.L., 1977. 'From 627 until the Early Thirteenth Century' in Aylmer and Cant 1977, 1–43

Hillam, J., 1981. 'An English tree-ring chronology, A.D. 404–1216', *Medieval Archaeol.* **25**, 31–44

Hillam, J., Morgan, R. and Tyers, I., 1987. 'Sapwood estimates and the dating of short ring sequences' in R.G.W. Ward (ed.), *Applications of Tree-Ring Studies: Current Research in Dendrochronology and Related Areas*, Brit. Archaeol. Rep. Int. Ser. 333 (Oxford), 165–85

Hluvko, S., 1991. (unpublished) *Red Pigments in English Medieval Wall Painting*, Courtauld Institute of Art, London University

Howard, H., 1990. '"Blue" in the Lewes Group' in S. Cather, D. Park and P. Williamson (eds.), *Early Medieval Wall Painting and Painted Sculpture in England*, Brit. Archaeol. Rep. Brit. Ser. **216** (Oxford), 195–9

—— 1995. 'Techniques of the Romanesque and Gothic wall paintings in the Holy Sepulchre Chapel, Winchester Cathedral' in A. Wallert, E. Hermens and M. Peek (eds), *Historical Painting Techniques, Materials and Studio Practice* (Preprints of a symposium at the University of Leiden, June 1995) (Los Angeles), 91–104

Howard, H. et al., 1998. 'Late medieval wall painting techniques at Farleigh Hungerford Castle and their context' in A. Roy and P. Smith (eds.), *Painting Techniques: History, Materials and Studio Practice* (Preprints of the IIC 17th International Congress, Dublin 1998) (London), 59–64

Jennings, S., 1991. 'Just Part of the Story'. *Interim: Archaeology in York*, Bull. York Archaeol. Trust **16**/2, 30–4

—— 1992. *Medieval Pottery in the Yorkshire Museum* (York)

Johnson, G.W. (ed.), 1848. *The Fairfax Correspondence: Memoirs of the Reign of Charles the First*, 2 vols (London)

Jones, S., Major, K. and Varley, J., 1987. *The Survey of Ancient Houses in Lincoln, II: Houses to the South and West of the Minster* (Lincoln)

Kenward, H.K., Hall, A.R. and Jones, A.K.G., 1980. 'A tested set of techniques for the extraction of plant and animal macrofossils from waterlogged archaeological deposits', *Sci. Archaeol.* **22**, 3–15

Kenward, H.K., Engleman, C., Robertson, A. and Large, F., 1986. 'Rapid scanning of urban archaeological deposits for insect remains', *Circaea* **3**, 163–72

Kettle, A.J. and Johnson, D.A., 1970. 'The Cathedral of Lichfield' in *The Victoria History of the County of Staffordshire* **3**, 140–98

Knowles, D., 1948. *The Religious Orders in England* (Cambridge)

Knowles, J.W., 1956. 'Notes on some Windows in the Choir and Lady Chapel of York Minster', *Yorks. Archaeol. J.* **38**, 91–118

—— 1962: 'The East Window of St Michael-le-Belfrey Church, York', *Yorks. Archaeol. J.* **40**, 145–59

Kühn, H., 1993. 'Lead-tin yellow' in A. Roy (ed.), *Artists' Pigments: A Handbook of their History and Characteristics* 2 (Washington), 83–112

Laxton, R.R. and Litton, C.D., 1988. *An East Midlands Master Tree-Ring Chronology and its Use for Dating Vernacular Buildings*, University of Nottingham, Dept of Classical and Archaeol. Studies, Monogr. Series **3**

Laycock, T., 1844. *Report on the State of the City of York. First Report of the Royal Commission for Enquiring into the State of Large and Populous Districts*, Parliamentary Papers **17**

Leach, A.F. (ed.), 1897. *Memorials of Beverley Minster: the Chapter Act Book of the Collegiate Church of St John of Beverley, 1286–1347*, SS **98**

Leak, A., 1990. *The Liberty of St Peter of York, 1800–1838*, Borthwick Papers **77**

Leedy, W.C., 1981. *Fan Vaulting: A Study of Form, Technology, and Meaning* (London)

Levitan, B., 1982. *The Sieving and Sampling Program. Excavations at West Hill Uley. 1979*, Western Archaeol. Trust occas. papers **10** (Bristol)

Lyth, J., 1885. *Glimpses of Early Methodism in York* (York)

Maddison, A.R., 1878. *A Short Account of the Vicars Choral, Poor Clerks, Organists and Choristers of Lincoln Cathedral, from the 12th Century to the Accession of Edward VI* (Lincoln)

Mellor, J.E. and Pearce, T., 1981. *The Austin Friars, Leicester*, Counc. Brit. Archaeol. Res. Rep. **35** (London)

Mills, P. and Oliver, J., 1962. *Survey of Building Sites in the City of London after the Great Fire of 1666*, reproduced in facsimile from Guildhall Library, MS 84. London Topographical Society (London)

Milner-White, E., 1959. *York Minster: An Index and Guide to the Ancient Windows of the Nave*

Moorhouse, S.A. et al., 1972. 'Medieval distilling apparatus of glass and pottery', *Medieval Archaeol.* **16**, 88–104

Moran, N. and O'Connor, T.P., 1994. 'Age attribution in domestic sheep by skeletal and dental maturation: a pilot study of available sources', *Int. J. Osteoarchaeology* **41**, 267–85

Morrell, J.B., 1949. *Woodwork in York*

Munro, M.A.R., 1984. 'An improved algorithm for cross-dating tree-ring series', *Tree Ring Bulletin* **44**, 17–27

Newton, R. and Davison, H., 1988. *The Conservation of Glass*

Noel, M., 1978. 'Archaeomagnetism or archaeomagic?' *Interim: Archaeology in York*, Bull. York Archaeol. Trust **5/4**, 11–15

O'Connor, D., 1989. 'The Medieval Stained Glass of Beverley Minster' in C. Wilson (ed.), *Medieval Art and Architecture in the East Riding of Yorkshire*, Brit. Archaeol. Assoc. Conference Transactions 9 (Leeds), 62–90

O'Connor, D. and Harris, H., 1995. 'The East Window of Selby Abbey, Yorkshire', in L. Hoey (ed.), *Yorkshire Monasticism: Archaeology, Art and Architecture from the 7th to 16th Centuries*, Brit. Archaeol. Assoc. Conference Transactions 16 (Leeds)

O'Connor, D. and Haselock, J., 1977. 'The Stained and Painted Glass' in Aylmer and Cant 1977, 313–93

O'Connor, T.P., 1986a. *Hand-Collected Bones from the Medieval Deposits at 16–22 Coppergate, York (YAT code 1976–81.7)*, AML Rep. 20/86

—— 1986b. *Bones from Archaeological Deposits in York: An Overview of Results to 1986*, AML Rep. 47/86

—— 1989. 'Deciding priorities with urban bones: York as a case study' in D. Serjeantson and T. Waldron (eds.), *Diet and Crafts in Towns*, Brit. Archaeol. Rep. Brit. Ser. **199** (Oxford), 189–201

—— 1993. 'Birds and the scavenger niche', *Archaeofauna* **2**, 158–62

—— 1995. 'Size increase in post-medieval English sheep: the osteological evidence', *Archaeofauna* **4**, 81–91

—— 2000. 'Bones as evidence of meat production and distribution in York' in E. White (ed.), *Feeding a City: York*, Leeds Prospect Books, 42–59

Orme, N., 1981. 'The Medieval Clergy of Exeter Cathedral. I. The Vicars and Annuellars', *Rep. Trans. Devonshire Assoc. Advmnt Sci.* **113**, 79–102

Palliser, D.M., 1978. 'The medieval street-names of York', *York Historian* **2**, 2–16

Pantin, W.A., 1959. 'Chantry Priests' Houses and other medieval lodgings', *Medieval Archaeol.* **3**, 216–58

—— 1962–3. 'Medieval English Town House Plans', *Medieval Archaeol.* **6–7**, 202–39

Papworth, J. and Morant, A. (eds), 1874. *Ordinary of British Armorials* (London)

Park, D. and Howard, H., forthcoming. 'Late twelfth-century architectural polychromy' in S.T. Driscoll, *Excavations at Glasgow Cathedral 1988-1997*

Perry, M., 1998. (unpublished) 'St Albans Cathedral: The Upper West Wall of the Presbytery' (conservation report)

Pevsner, N., 1963. *The Buildings of England: Herefordshire* (Harmondsworth)

Phillips, D., 1985. *Excavations at York Minster 2: The Cathedral of Archbishop Thomas of Bayeux* (London)

Plummer, P., 1986. 'The wallpaintings in Eton College Chapel' in P. Burman (ed.), *Conservation of Wall Paintings* (London), 36–40

Rackham, O., 1976. *Trees and Woodland in the British Landscape* (London)

Rae, P., 1976. 'The Property Game: renewal in Aldwark', *Yorkshire Life* **30/10**, 3–5

Raine, A., 1955. *Medieval York* (London)

Raine, J. (ed.), 1858. *The Fabric Rolls of York Minster*, SS **35**

—— 1886. *The Historians of the Church of York and Its Archbishops* 2 *The Chronicles and Memorials of Great Britain and Ireland During the Middle Ages*, Rolls Series (HMSO, London)

Ramm, H.G. et al., 1971. 'The tombs of Archbishops Walter de Gray (1216–55) and Godfrey de Lindham (1258–65) in York Minster, and their contents', *Archaeologia* **103**, 101–47

RCHME, 1931. *Royal Commission on Historical Monuments of England. An Inventory of the Historical Monuments of Herefordshire Vol.1, South-West* (HMSO, London)

—— 1939. *The City of Oxford* (HMSO, London)

—— 1959. *The City of Cambridge* (HMSO, London)

—— 1984. *An Inventory of the Historical Monuments in the County of Northampton. 6: Architectural Monuments in North Northamptonshire* (HMSO, London)

—— 1993. *Royal Commission on Historical Monuments of England. Salisbury. The Houses of the Close* (HMSO, London)

RCHMY. Royal Commission on Historical Monuments (England). *An Inventory of the Historical Monuments in the City of York.* **3**: *South-West of the Ouse* (1972); **5**: *The Central Area* (1981) (HMSO, London)

Rees Jones, S.R., 1987. (unpublished) *Property, Tenure and Rents: Some Aspects of the Topography and Economy of Medieval York*, D.Phil. thesis, University of York

Rodwell, W., 1982. 'The Buildings of Vicars' Close' in L.S. Colchester (ed.), *Wells Cathedral: A History* (Shepton Mallet), 212–26

Rowntree, B.S., 1903. *Poverty: A Study of Town Life* (London)

Royle, E., 1981. 'Religion in York 1831–1981' in C. Feinstein (ed.), *York 1831–1981* (York), 205–33

Scott, S., 1985. *The Animal Bones from the Bedern*, AML Rep.4821

—— 1991. 'The animal bones' in Armstrong et al. 1991, 216–33

Sherlock, D. and Woods, H., 1988. *St Augustine's Abbey: Report on Excavations, 1960–78*, Kent Archaeol. Soc. Monogr. Series 4 (Maidstone)

Sinclair, E., 1991. 'The west front: 2. The west front polychromy' in F. Kelly (ed.), *Medieval Art and Architecture at Exeter Cathedral*, Brit. Archaeol. Assoc. Conference Transactions 11 (London), 116–33

Smith, J.T., 1955. 'Medieval aisled halls and their derivatives', *Archaeol. J.* **112**, 76–94

Stallibrass, S., 1984. 'The distinction between the effects of small carnivore and humans on post-glacial faunal assemblages' in J. Clutton-Brock and C. Grigson (eds), *Animals and Archaeology 4*, Brit. Archaeol. Rep. Int. Ser. **227**, 259–69

Statutes. 1900. *York Minster. Dean and Chapter, The Statutes, etc., of the Cathedral Church of York* (Leeds)

Stocker, D.A., 1986. 'The Shrine of Little St Hugh' in *Art, Architecture and Archaeology at Lincoln Minster*, Proc. Brit. Archaeol. Assoc. 1982 (London), 109–17

Stocker, D.A. and Wilson, C., 1980a. 'Bedern Hall, part 1', *Interim: Archaeology in York*, Bull. York Archaeol. Trust **7**/1, 21–6

—— 1980b. 'Bedern Hall, part 2', *Interim: Archaeology in York*, Bull. York Archaeol. Trust **7**/2, 30–8

Stockwell, M., 1984. 'Foundation Preparation and the Archaeologist' in P.V. Addyman and V.E. Black (eds), *Archaeological Papers from York Presented to M.W. Barley* (York), 158–62

Stow, J., 1603. *A Survey of the Cities of London and Westminster and the Borough of Southwark. Reprinted from the edition of 1603 with introduction by C. L. Kingsford*, Vol.1, 1908

Swanson, H., 1989. *Medieval Artisans* (Oxford)

Tatton-Brown, T., 1990. 'Archaeology at Chichester Cathedral' in *The Archaeology of Chichester and District* (Chichester), 41–6

—— 1994. 'The buildings of the Bishop's Palace and the Close' in M. Hobbs (ed.), *Chichester Cathedral, an Historical Survey* (Chichester), 225–46

Test. Ebor. Raine, J. (ed.),1865. *Testamenta Eboracensia* 3 SS

Tomlinson, P.R.B., 1993. (unpublished) *Development and Analysis of an Archaeobotanical Computer Database for the British Isles*, D.Phil. thesis, University of York

Tringham, N., 1978. (unpublished) *An Edition of the Cartulary of the Vicars Choral of York Minster*, Ph.D. thesis, University of Aberdeen

—— 1990. 'The Cathedral and Close' in *The Victoria History of the County of Staffordshire*, xiv

Turner, T. and Parker, J.H., 1853. *Some Account of Domestic Architecture in England, vol.2* (Oxford)

Valor Ecclesiasticus. Caley, J. (ed.), 1810–34. *Valor Ecclesiasticus temp. Hen. VIII Auctoritate Regia Institutus* (London)

VCH. Page, W. (ed.), 1909. *The Victoria County History of the Counties of England: London* 1 (London)

VCH. Salzman, L.F. (ed.), 1935. *The Victoria History of the County of Sussex* 3 (Oxford)

VCHY. Tillott, P.M. (ed.), 1961. *The Victoria County History of Yorkshire: The City of York* (London)

Watkins, G., 1987. 'The Pottery' in Armstrong and Ayers 1987, 53–182

West, B., 1982. 'Spur development: recognising caponised fowl in archaeological material' in B. Wilson, C. Grigson and S. Payne (eds), *Ageing and Sexing Animal Bones from Archaeological Sites*, Brit. Arcaehol. Rep. **109**, 255–61 (Oxford)

Whellan, T., 1857. *History and Topography of the City of York and The North Riding of Yorkshire* (Beverley)

Willis, R. and Clark, J., 1886. *The Architectural History of the University of Cambridge* (Cambridge)

Wolfe, M., 1993. 'Music in The Bedern', *Interim: Archaeology in York*, Bull. York Archaeol. Trust 17/3, 34–40

Wood, M.E., 1950. 'Thirteenth-century domestic architecture in England', *Archaeol. J.* **150**, supplement

—— 1965. *The English Medieval House* (London)

Woodcock, T., Grant, J. and Graham, I. (eds), 1996. *Dictionary of British Arms: Medieval Ordinary* **2**, 4 vols (London)

York Minster Fasti, **1**. Clay, C.T. (ed.), 1958. *York Minster Fasti*, YASRS **123**

York Minster Fasti, 2. Clay, C.T. (ed.), 1959. *York Minster Fasti*, YASRS **124**

Index

By Susan Vaughan

Illustrations are denoted by page numbers in *italics* or by (*illus*) where figures are scattered throughout the text. The letter n following a page number denotes that the reference will be found in a note. Places are in York unless indicated otherwise. The following abbreviations have been used in this index: Berks – Berkshire; C – century; Cambs – Cambridgeshire; Ches – Cheshire; E Riding – East Riding of Yorkshire; *f* – facing; Glos – Gloucestershire; Heref – Herefordshire; Lincs – Lincolnshire; m. – married; N Yorks – North Yorkshire; Northants – Northamptonshire; Notts – Nottinghamshire; Oxon – Oxfordshire; Som – Somerset; Staffs – Staffordshire; Warks – Warwickshire; Wilts – Wiltshire; Worcs – Worcestershire.

Gent, Thomas, 560, 565, 568
Gerald, son of Serlo, 382
Gillesland, Robert, 580
Gillow, Robert, 646
glass vessels, 402, 615–16
    Period 2, 419
    Period 3, 429
    Period 4, 433
    Period 5, 437, 444
    Period 6, 457, 458, 464
    Period 7, 469, 470, 482, 484, 494, 505
    Period 8, 528
    Period 9, 657, 660
    see also beads; glassmaking debris; lamps; window glass
glassmaking debris, 408, 433, 445, 502
Glover, Robert, 560
goat hair, 499
Godson, Thomas, 639
Golding, Thomas, 385
Goodramgate
    Bedern access, 377, *540*, 634
    bridge over, 384, 467, 540
    Cambhallgarth, 580
    Hugate (Hugaterent), 390
    Lady Row, 603
    land acquired by vicars choral, 386, *387*, 388–91, 578
Gower, John, 390
granary, 540
grapes, 619–20; *see also* vineyard
gravel, 578, 609
Gray, Walter de, archbishop of York, 383, 386, 389, 411, 606
Gray, Dean William, 618
Great Bedern (*Bederna Magna*), 377
Greystock arms, 563, 565, 568
Guild of Building, 641
Guild of Freemen, 641
Guild Hall, 641
Guisborough priory (Redcar and Cleveland), York properties, *387*, 390
gutter, Bedern Close, 576, 578, 609
Gyles, Henry, 573

Hagent, Sir William, 388, 390
Haget, Robert, 390
Hailes (Glos), lancet windows, 554
Hall
    architectural description, 583, *584–6*, 587, *588–90*, 591
    dating evidence, 595–602
    discussion, 580–2
    documentary evidence
        medieval period, 384, 385, 580, 611
        post-medieval period, 397, 639, *640*, 641
    excavation evidence, *378*, *379*, 397
        foundation elevations, *f473*
        Period 7: Phase 1, *466*, 467–8, *474*; Phase 2, 477, *478*, *480–2*; Phase 4, 503, 506, *507*, 508
        Period 8, 509, *510*, 511, 518
        Period 9, 641
    floor, 609
    location, *396*
    reconstruction and function, 591, *592–3*, 594–5
    vaulted ceiling, 583, 586, *591–3*
    see also communa aula
Halley, George, 635, 647
Halton, Thomas, 619
hammer head, 602

handles
    bone, 656, 658, 660
    ivory, 472, 649
    jet, 457
Hargrove, William, 407, 560, 629, 649
harness equipment, 408
harps, 614; *see also* tuning pegs
Harrison, Canon Frederick, 380, 650
hasps, iron, 611
Hawarden Buildings, 634
Hawarden House, 639
Haxey, Thomas, 384
hazelnuts, 620
hearths
    construction techniques, 610
    dating, 400
    excavation evidence
        Building 4, 410, 412
        Building 5: Period 3, 421, 422, 423; Period 4, 429–30, 432; Period 5, 434, 439; Period 6, 449, *451*, 452, 459, *461*; Period 7, 486, 488, 489, *490–1*, 504; Period 8, 509, 513, *514*, 527
        Building 6, 415, 420
        Building 9, 422, 427
        Building 10: Period 3, 422–3, 428; Period 4, 433; Period 5, 437, 445; Period 6, 450, 456
        Building 11: Period 4, 432; Period 5, 436, 442
        Building 14: Period 5, 436, 444; Period 6, 450, 460, *463*
        Building 15, 437, 445
        Building 16: Period 6, 454; Period 7, 467, 468, 469, 477, *479*
        Building 17, 449, 455
        Building 23, 486, 492, 500, 501
        Building 24: Period 7, 488, 494, *495*; Period 8, 517
        Building 27, 511, 527, 530
        Building 28, 488, 496
        Building 29, 500, 501
        Building 31: Period 7, 503, 505; Period 8, 511, *519*
        Building 34, 526, 529
        Building 35, *532*
        Building 36, 535, 537
        Hall, 477, 594–5
        kitchen: Period 7, 476, 477, 482, 500, 501, 503, 505–6; Period 8, 511, 519, *520*
        not assigned: Period 1, 410, 412, 413; Period 7, 467
    interpretation, 575
    see also fireplace; ovens
Hebden, James, 639, 640
The Helm, 638
hemp, 456, 620
herbs and spices, 620
Hereford (Heref), Vicars Choral
    college buildings, 391, 395, 558, 597
    reform, 384
Hickling, John, 578
hinge pivots, 611
hinge straps, 611
hoard *see under* coins
Holbeck, William, 614
holdfast, iron, 514
Holgate, R., archbishop of York, 385
hones, 457, 472, 616
hooks, iron, 611
Hornby, Preston, 639
horncores, 616, 655
horse hair, 501